WHS £·   1/87

CW00347620

THE **GUINNESS** BOOK OF
OLYMPICS
FACTS AND FEATS

STAN GREENBERG

GUINNESS SUPERLATIVES LIMITED
2 CECIL COURT, LONDON ROAD, ENFIELD, MIDDLESEX

ACKNOWLEDGEMENTS

Any book about the Olympic Games must rely very heavily on the original research previously done by a dedicated few. Of these Erich Kamper (AUT) whose *Enzyklopädie der Olympischen Spiele* (1972), *Lexicon der Olympischen Winter Spiele* (1964) and *Lexicon der 14,000 Olympioniken* (1983) are recognised as the basic texts on the Games. Also particular mention must be made of *Die Olympischen Spiele von 1896 bis 1980* by Volker Kluge (GDR) who has taken up where Kamper left off, as well as adding some new material to the earlier research. Other main sources are, in alphabetical order:

The Associated Press and Grolier – *Pursuit of Excellence, The Olympic Story* (1979)
Pat Besford (GBR) – *Encyclopaedia of Swimming* (1976)
Sándor Barcs (HUN) – *The Modern Olympics Story* (1964)
John Durant (USA) – *Highlights of the Olympics* (1961)
Lord Killanin (IRE) and John Rodda (GBR) – *The Olympic Games* (1976)
Peter Matthews (GBR) – *The Guinness Book of Athletics Facts and Feats* (1982)
Norris and Ross McWhirter (GBR) – *The Guinness Book of Olympic Records* (1980)
Melvyn Watman (GBR) – *The Encyclopaedia of Track and Field Athletics* (1981)

Other experts and organisations whose publications and personal help have been invaluable include:
Richard Ayling, Howard Bass, Ian Buchanan, Harry Carpenter, Jim Coote, Peter Diamond (USA), Maurice Golesworthy, John Goodbody, Marc Heller, Richard Hymans, Peter Johnson, Bill Mallon (USA), Ferenc Mézo (HUN), Ron Pickering, Jack Rollin, Colin Shields, Bob Sparks, Stuart Storey, Dave Terry, Lance Tingay, Ernest Trory, Martin Tyler, David Vine, Alan Weeks, Dorian Williams, Don Wood. The Association of Track and Field Statisticians (ATFS) and its members, British Olympic Association, International Amateur Athletic Federation (IAAF), International Olympic Committee publications, International Weightlifting Federation, National Ski Federation of Great Britain, National Union of Track Statisticians (NUTS) and its members, *New York Times* publications, *Sports Illustrated*, *The Times*, *Track and Field News* publications, and many national and international governing bodies and individuals.

Where contradictions have been found in different sources I have invariably used Kamper and Kluge as the final arbiters.

Acknowledgement is made to the following for the reproduction of illustrations on the following pages:

All Sport **33–40**, 67, 70, 71, 91, 122, 170 (right), **185–192**, 198 (right)
Associated Press 59, 61, 62, 66, 73, 97 (right), 104, 116, 131, 134, 142, 226 (right), 233 (top)
BBC Hulton Picture Library 29, 53, 89 (bottom), 121 (top), 153 (top right), 168 (right), 226 (left), 233 (bottom right), 243
Canoeing Magazine 97 (left)
Gerry Cranham 51
Mary Evans Picture Library 49 (bottom)
Stan Greenberg **40** (bottom)
George Herringshaw 79
Keystone Press 108
Ed Lacey 74
National Film Archives 42
Popperfoto 64 (right), 69, 77, 81, 114, 223 (bottom left and right)
Colin Shields 244
Dave Terry 13 (right), 19, 20, 21, 26 (top), 27, 43, 45, 46, 89 (top), 103 (top), 109, 110, 129, 135, 136, 143, 145 (right), 150, 151, 152 (centre and left), 153 (bottom), 154 (right), 167 (above and right), 169 (right), 198 (left), 203, 211, 246, 247
John Topham 199
UPI 154 (left), 170 (centre)
Don Wood 55, 57, 58, 68, 226 (above)
World Sports 64 (left)

Figures in bold type refer to colour illustrations.

Editor: Alex E Reid
Design and Layout: David Jones

© **Stan Greenberg and Guinness Superlatives Ltd 1983**

Published by
Guinness Superlatives Ltd
2 Cecil Court, London Road,
Enfield, Middlesex EN2 6DJ

'Guinness' is a registered trade mark of
Guinness Superlatives Ltd

British Library Cataloguing in Publication Data
Greenberg, Stan
    The Guinness book of olympics facts and feats.
    1. Olympic Games – Records
    I. Title
    796.4'809   GV 721.8
    ISBN 0–85112–273–6
    ISBN 0–85112–293–0 Pk.

Colour separation by Newsele Litho, Milan
Photoset, printed and bound in Great Britain by
Redwood Burn Limited, Trowbridge, Wiltshire.

CONTENTS

This book is dedicated partly to the thousands of sportsmen and woman who have entertained us and shown us the incredible speed, grace and power that human beings are capable of producing without the stimulus of fear, greed or war. In particular I wish to dedicate it to the memory of the late Jesse Owens who was an inspiration to many, and not least to the author. Finally it is dedicated to my wife who has had to put up with much, and undoubtedly will have to put up with more, in the pursuit of my sporting interests.

Stan Greenberg

PREFACE

I hope and trust that this book will provide the correct factual answers to most of the queries about the Olympic Games, which have become such an important focus of attention for peoples all over the world. Indeed they have ascended to an importance seemingly way beyond mere sporting endeavour.

There are many, often serious, errors which have crept into Olympic histories and which have been perpetuated over time by chroniclers who have not done their homework. I have found that various data and stories which have long been cherished have no basis in fact. Certainly the official reports issued after each Games are not the fully correct sources that they should be, particularly so in the case of the early celebrations.

OFFICIAL OLYMPIC ABBREVIATIONS FOR MEMBER COUNTRIES

AFG	Afghanistan	GHA	Ghana	NZL	New Zealand
AHO	Netherlands Antilles	GRE	Greece	OMA	Oman
ALB	Albania	GUA	Guatemala	PAK	Pakistan
ALG	Algeria	GUI	Guinea	PAN	Panama
AND	Andorra	GUY	Guyana	PAR	Paraguay
ANG	Angola	HAI	Haiti	PER	Peru
ANT	Antigua	HKG	Hong Kong	PHI	Philippines
ARG	Argentina	HOL	Netherlands	POL	Poland
AUS	Australia	HON	Honduras	POR	Portugal
AUT	Austria	HUN	Hungary	PRK	Democratic People's Republic of Korea
BAH	Bahamas	INA	Indonesia	PUR	Puerto Rico
BAN	Bangladesh	IND	India	QAT	Qatar
BAR	Barbados	IRL	Ireland	ROM	Romania
BEL	Belgium	IRN	Iran	SAL	El Salvador
BEN	Benin	IRQ	Iraq	SAF	South Africa
BER	Bermuda	ISL	Iceland	SAU	Saudi Arabia
BIR	Burma	ISR	Israel	SEN	Senegal
BIZ	Belize	ISV	Virgin Islands	SEY	Seychelles
BOH	Bohemia (prior to 1920)	ITA	Italy	SIN	Singapore
BOL	Bolivia	IVB	British Virgin Islands	SLE	Sierra Leone
BOT	Botswana	JAM	Jamaica	SMR	San Marino
BRA	Brazil	JOR	Jordan	SOM	Somalia
BRN	Bahrain	JPN	Japan	SRI	Sri Lanka (formerly Ceylon)
BUL	Bulgaria	KEN	Kenya	SUD	Sudan
CAF	Central African Republic	KOR	Korea	SUI	Switzerland
CAN	Canada	KUW	Kuwait	SUR	Surinam
CAY	Cayman Islands	LAO	Laos	SWE	Sweden
CGO	Congo	LAT	Latvia (prior to 1948)	SWZ	Swaziland
CHA	Chad	LBA	Libya	SYR	Syria
CHI	Chile	LBR	Liberia	TAI	Taiwan
CHN	China	LES	Lesotho	TAN	Tanzania
CIV	Ivory Coast	LIB	Lebanon	TCH	Czechoslovakia
CMR	Cameroun	LIE	Liechtenstein	THA	Thailand
COL	Colombia	LIT	Lithuania (prior to 1948)	TOG	Togo
CRC	Costa Rica	LUX	Luxembourg	TPE	Taipei (formerly Formosa)
CUB	Cuba	MAD	Madagascar	TRI	Trinidad & Tobago
CYP	Cyprus	MAL	Malaysia	TUN	Tunisia
DEN	Denmark	MAR	Morocco	TUR	Turkey
DOM	Dominican Republic	MAW	Malawi	UAE	United Arab Emirates
ECU	Ecuador	MEX	Mexico	UGA	Uganda
EGY	Egypt	MGL	Mongolia	URS	USSR (Soviet Union)
ESP	Spain	MLI	Mali	URU	Uruguay
EST	Estonia (prior to 1948)	MLT	Malta	USA	United States
ETH	Ethiopia	MON	Monaco	VEN	Venezuela
FIJ	Fiji	MOZ	Mozambique	VIE	Vietnam
FIN	Finland	MRI	Mauritius	VOL	Upper Volta
FRA	France	MTN	Mauretania	YAR	Yemen Arab Republic
FRG	Federal Republic of Germany	NCA	Nicaragua	YMD	Yemen Democratic Republic
GAB	Gabon	NEP	Nepal	YUG	Yugoslavia
GAM	Gambia	NGR	Nigeria	ZAI	Zaire
GBR	Great Britain	NGU	Papua-New Guinea	ZAM	Zambia
GDR	German Democratic Republic	NIG	Niger	ZIM	Zimbabwe
GER	Germany (prior to 1968)	NOR	Norway		

TRACK AND FIELD CONVERSION TABLES

1·55 metres=	5 ft 1 in
1·60	5 ft 3 in
1·65	5 ft 5 in
1·70	5 ft 7 in
1·75	5 ft 8¾ in
1·80	5 ft 10¾ in
1·85	6 ft 0¾ in
1·90	6 ft 2¾ in
1·95	6 ft 4¾ in
2·00	6 ft 6¾ in
2·05	6 ft 8¾ in
2·10	6 ft 10¾ in
2·15	7 ft 0½ in
2·20	7 ft 2½ in
2·25	7 ft 4½ in
2·30	7 ft 6½ in
2·35	7 ft 8½ in
5·50 metres =	18 ft 0½ in
5·75	18 ft 10½ in
6·00	19 ft 8¼ in
6·25	20 ft 6¼ in
6·50	21 ft 4 in
6·75	22 ft 1¾ in
7·00	22 ft 11¾ in
7·25	23 ft 9½ in
7·50	24 ft 7¼ in
7·75	25 ft 5¼ in
8·00	26 ft 3 in
8·25	27 ft 0¾ in
8·50	27 ft 10¾ in
8·75	28 ft 8½ in
9·00	29 ft 6½ in
3·00 metres =	9 ft 10 in
3·20	10 ft 6 in
3·40	11 ft 1¾ in
3·60	11 ft 9¾ in
3·80	12 ft 5½ in
4·00	13 ft 1½ in
4·20	13 ft 9¼ in
4·40	14 ft 5¼ in
4·60	15 ft 1 in
4·80	15 ft 9 in
5·00	16 ft 4¾ in
5·20	17 ft 0¾ in
5·40	17 ft 8½ in
5·60	18 ft 4½ in
5·80	19 ft 0¼ in
12·50 metres =	41 ft 0¼ in
13·00	42 ft 8 in
13·50	44 ft 3½ in
14·00	45 ft 11¼ in
14·50	47 ft 7 in
15·00	49 ft 2½ in
15·50	50 ft 10¼ in
16·00	52 ft 6 in
16·50	54 ft 1¾ in
17·00	55 ft 9¼ in
17·50	57 ft 5 in
18·00	59 ft 0¾ in
18·50	60 ft 8½ in
19·00	62 ft 4 in
19·50	63 ft 11¾ in
20·00	65 ft 7½ in
20·50	67 ft 3¼ in
21·00	68 ft 10¾ in
21·50	70 ft 6½ in
22·00	72 ft 2¼ in
40·00 metres =	131 ft 3 in
42·00	137 ft 9 in
44·00	144 ft 4 in
46·00	150 ft 11 in
48·00	157 ft 6 in
50·00	164 ft 0 in
52·00	170 ft 7 in
54·00	177 ft 2 in
56·00	183 ft 9 in
58·00	190 ft 3 in
60·00	196 ft 10 in
62·00	203 ft 5 in
64·00	210 ft 0 in
66·00	216 ft 6 in
68·00	223 ft 1 in
70·00	229 ft 8 in
72·00	236 ft 3 in
74·00	242 ft 9 in
76·00	249 ft 4 in
78·00	255 ft 11 in
80·00	262 ft 5 in
82·00	269 ft 0 in
84·00	275 ft 7 in
86·00	282 ft 2 in
88·00	288 ft 8 in
90·00	295 ft 3 in
92·00	301 ft 10 in
94·00	308 ft 5 in
96·00	314 ft 11 in
98·00	321 ft 6 in
100·00	328 ft 1 in

WEIGHTLIFTING CONVERSION TABLE

kg	lb
100	220¼
125	275½
150	330½
175	385¾
200	440¾
225	496
250	551
275	606¼
300	661¼
325	716½
350	771½
375	826½
400	881¾
425	936¾
450	992
475	1047
500	1102¼
525	1157¼
550	1212¼
575	1267½
600	1322¾

PARTICIPATING COUNTRIES

Only four countries have never failed to be represented at all celebrations of the Summer Games since 1896 (including those of 1906): Australia, Greece, Great Britain and Switzerland. Of those only Great Britain has been present at all Winter Games as well, including the skating and ice hockey events of 1908 and 1920.

A total of 68 973 have competed in the Summer Games and 10 952 in the Winter Games. The top ten countries by numbers of entries are:

	Summer	Winter	Total
UNITED STATES	5134	1027	6161
GREAT BRITAIN	4331	462	4793
FRANCE	4212	464	4676
GERMANY[1]	3164	717	3881
USSR[2]	2947	532	3479
ITALY	2799	546	3345
SWEDEN	2620	630	3250
HUNGARY	2356	130	2486
CANADA	1809	590	2399
POLAND	1786	417	2203
	31 158	5515	36 673

[1] Including only FRG competitors from 1952.   [2] Including competitors from Russia in 1908–12.

That total of 36 673 represents 46·1 per cent of all the competitors to appear in the Games. Four countries have only had one competitor; Central African Republic, Gabon, Swaziland and Upper Volta.

The most successful countries based on the ratio of their medallists to their total competitors are:

Gold medals		All medals	
USSR	0·115	USSR	0·294
UNITED STATES	0·107	GDR (since 1968)	0·272
GDR (since 1968)	0·101	UNITED STATES	0·262

WINTER GAMES: PARTICIPATING COUNTRIES

Country	Debut at Games	Games attended
Andorra	1976	2
Argentina	1908	9
Australia	1936	9
Austria[1]	1924	13
Belgium	1920	12
Bolivia	1956	2
Bulgaria	1936	10
Canada	1920	14
Chile	1948	7
China	1980	1
Cyprus	1980	1
Czechoslovakia	1920	14
Denmark	1948	5
Estonia[2]	1928	2
Finland	1920	14
France	1920	14
Germany[3]	1908	12
German Democratic Republic[4]	1968	4
Great Britain	1908	15
Greece	1936	9
Hungary[5]	1924	13
Iceland	1948	8
India	1964	2
Iran	1956	5
Italy	1924	13
Japan[6]	1928	11
Korea[7]	1928	8
Latvia[2]	1924	3
Lebanon	1948	9
Liechtenstein	1936	9
Lithuania[2]	1928	1
Luxembourg	1928	2
Mexico	1928	1
Mongolia	1964	4
Morocco	1968	1
Netherlands	1928	11
New Zealand	1952	6
North Korea[7]	1964	3
Norway	1920	14
Philippines	1972	1
Poland	1924	13
Portugal	1952	1
Romania	1928	11
Russia[8]	1908	1
San Marino	1976	1
South Africa[9]	1960	1
Spain	1936	10
Sweden	1908	15
Switzerland	1920	14
Taiwan	1972	2
Turkey	1936	7
United States	1908	15
USSR[8]	1956	7
Yugoslavia	1924	11

[1] Not invited in 1920.

[2] Annexed by the USSR in 1940.

[3] Not invited in 1920, 1924 and 1948; German Federal Republic from 1968.

[4] Separate team from 1968.

[5] Not invited in 1920.

[6] Not invited in 1948.

[7] Country divided in 1945, separate regimes established in 1948; prior to 1964 only South Korean team.

[8] Initial entry by Czarist Russia in 1908.

[9] Not invited in 1964 and 1968; expelled from IOC in 1970.

SUMMER GAMES: PARTICIPATING COUNTRIES

Country	Debut at Games	Games attended
Afghanistan	1936	8
Albania	1972	1
Algeria	1964	4

Country	Year	No.	Country	Year	No.	Country	Year	No.
Andorra	1976	2	India	1900	15	Somalia	1972	1
Angola	1980	1	Indonesia	1952	6	South Africa[15]	1904	13
Antigua	1976	1	Iran	1948	8	Spain	1900	14
Argentina	1920	13	Iraq	1948	5	Sri Lanka (formerly		
Australia[1]	1896	20	Ireland[8]	1924	12	Ceylon)	1948	8
Austria[2]	1896	19	Israel	1952	7	Sudan	1960	3
Bahamas	1952	7	Italy	1900	18	Surinam	1968	3
Barbados	1968	3	Ivory Coast	1964	4	Swaziland	1972	1
Belgium	1900	18	Jamaica[9]	1948	9	Sweden	1896	19
Benin	1980	1	Japan	1912	13	Switzerland	1896	20
Bermuda	1936	9	Jordan	1980	1	Syria	1948	4
Bolivia	1936	5	Kenya	1956	5	Taiwan	1956	5
Botswana	1980	1	Korea[10]	1948	8	Tanzania (formerly		
Brazil	1920	13	Kuwait	1968	4	Tanganyika)	1964	4
British Honduras			Laos	1980	1	Thailand	1952	7
(now Belize)	1968	3	Latvia[5]	1924	4	Togo	1972	1
Bulgaria	1896	12	Lebanon	1948	8	Trinidad and		
Burma	1948	8	Lesotho	1972	2	Tobago[9]	1948	9
Cambodia	1956	3	Liberia	1956	5	Tunisia	1960	5
Cameroun	1964	5	Libya	1968	3	Turkey	1908	13
Canada	1900	18	Liechtenstein	1936	8	Uganda	1956	6
Cayman Islands	1976	1	Lithuania[5]	1924	2	United States	1896	19
Central African			Luxembourg	1912	14	Upper Volta	1972	1
Republic	1968	1	Madagascar	1964	4	Uruguay	1924	12
Chad	1964	3	Malawi	1972	1	USSR[13]	1952	8
Chile	1896	14	Malaysia[11]	1956	6	Venezuela	1948	9
China	1932	4	Mali	1964	4	Vietnam[12]	1952	7
Colombia	1932	10	Malta	1928	7	Virgin Islands	1968	3
Congo	1964	3	Mexico	1924	13	Yugoslavia	1912	15
Costa Rica	1936	6	Monaco	1920	11	Zaire	1968	1
Cuba	1900	13	Mongolia	1964	5	Zambia (formerly		
Cyprus	1980	1	Morocco	1960	5	Northern		
Czechoslovakia[3]	1900	18	Mozambique	1980	1	Rhodesia)	1964	4
Dahomey	1972	1	Nepal	1964	4	Zimbabwe		
Denmark	1896	19	Netherlands	1900	18	(formerly		
Dominican			Netherlands			Rhodesia)	1928	4
Republic	1964	5	Antilles	1952	6			
Ecuador	1924	5	New Zealand[1]	1908	16			
Egypt[4]	1906	14	Nicaragua	1968	4			
El Salvador	1968	2	Niger	1964	3			
Estonia[5]	1920	5	Nigeria	1952	7			
Ethiopia	1956	6	North Korea[10]	1972	3			
Fiji	1956	5	Norway	1900	18			
Finland	1906	17	Pakistan	1948	8			
France	1896	19	Panama	1928	8			
Gabon	1972	1	Paraguay	1968	3			
Germany[6]	1896	16	Papua-New					
German Demo-			Guinea	1976	1			
cratic Republic[7]	1968	4	Peru	1936	9			
Ghana (formerly			Philippines	1924	12			
Gold Coast)	1952	5	Poland	1924	13			
Great Britain	1896	20	Portugal	1912	15			
Greece	1896	20	Puerto Rico	1948	9			
Guatemala	1952	5	Romania	1924	11			
Guinea	1968	2	Russia[13]	1900	4			
Guyana (formerly			Saar[14]	1952	1			
British Guiana)	1948	8	San Marino	1960	5			
Haiti	1900	7	Saudi Arabia	1976	1			
Honduras	1968	2	Senegal	1964	5			
Hong Kong	1952	7	Seychelles	1980	1			
Hungary[2]	1896	19	Sierra Leone	1968	2			
Iceland	1908	12	Singapore[11]	1948	8			

[1] Australia and New Zealand combined as Australasia 1908–1912.

[2] Not invited in 1920.

[3] Represented by Bohemia up to 1912.

[4] As United Arab Republic 1960–1972.

[5] Annexed by the USSR in 1940.

[6] Not invited in 1920, 1924 and 1948.

[7] Separate team from 1968.

[8] Part of Great Britain team till 1924.

[9] Jamaica and Trinidad combined as Antilles in 1960.

[10] Country divided in 1945, separate regimes established in 1948.

[11] Prior to 1964 consisted of Malaya and North Borneo; in 1964 also included Singapore.

[12] From 1952 to 1972 only a South Vietnamese team competed.

[13] As Czarist Russia 1900–1912.

[14] Independent 1947–1957 then incorporated in Germany.

[15] Not invited since 1960.

THE GAMES

ANCIENT GAMES

The Olympic Games evolved from legendary conflicts among the Greek gods, and the religious ceremonies that they gave rise to. Historical evidence dates the Games from about 900 BC but there is good reason to believe that a similar festival had been celebrated for at least four centuries previously. Indeed the modern word 'athlete' is derived from Aethlius the King of Elis, the area in which Olympia lies. One of his successors, Iphitus, was instrumental in reviving the then faltering concept in the late 9th century BC. He also arranged for the truce between the continually warring states of the region which recognized the neutrality and sanctity of Olympia, and which lasted for the period of the Games.

The first firm record dates from 776 BC, and the Ancient Games were numbered at four-yearly intervals from then by later Greek historians. At that time the Games consisted of only one event, the *stade* race of approximately 192 metres, and the winner, the first recorded Olympic champion, was Coroibos of Elis. After thirteen Olympiads, in 724 BC, a race of two stade, the *diaulus* was also contested, and in the following celebration the 24-stadia *dolichus*, about 4·5 kilometres in length, was instituted. Twelve years later came the *pentathlon*, consisting of running, jumping (with the aid of hand-held weights), throwing the discus and javelin, and wrestling. Eventually chariot racing, running in armour and boxing were included, and in 648 BC, the *pankration*, a rather brutal mixture of boxing and wrestling. Numerous variants of these sports appeared over the years, as did also activities of a less sporting nature, such as contests for trumpeters.

Initially competitors wore simple shorts-like garments, but from about the Fifteenth Games (720 BC) they competed in the nude. Until 692 BC the Games lasted for only a single day. This was later increased to 2 days, and in 632 BC to a total of 5 days, of which the middle three were for actual competitions.

For the next six centuries the fame of Olympia spread throughout the known world and many famous people visited the Games. Victors, in those early days, won a crown of wild olive leaves, but they were greatly rewarded by their home states and often became very wealthy. Crowd figures were not published but archaeologists have estimated that the Stadium at Olympia could have accommodated over 20 000 spectators.

Among the most famous champions of those days was the runner Leonidas of Rhodes who won the three 'track' events on four consecutive occasions 164–152 BC, making a total of 12 victories which has not been surpassed since. The first recorded triple gold medallist at one Games was Phanas of Pellene in 512 BC, while Chionis of Sparta, from 664–656 BC won the stade in three successive Games. Other excellent champions included Theagenes of Thassos who won eight titles at boxing, wrestling and the pankration from 468–456 BC, and Milon of Croton the winner of six wrestling titles 536–516 BC. However, the very fame of the Olympic Games was the basis of its downfall. Eventually the importance of winning at Olympia, and the reflected glory it bestowed on the winner's birthplace, led to cities hiring professionals and bribing judges. With the dawn of the Christian Era the religious and physical background to the Games were attacked. An irreversible decline set in with the spread of Roman influence, reaching its nadir in AD 67 when a drunken Emperor Nero entered the chariot race, and was crowned victor even though there were no other entrants (who could blame them) and he did not even finish the course.

In AD 393 the Roman Emperor Theodosius I issued a decree in Milan which prohibited the celebration of the Olympic Games. Within two

10

centuries the ravages of foreign invaders, earth-quakes and flooding had virtually obliterated the site of Olympia and the world forgot the glory that once had been.

MALE CHAUVINISTS

For reasons not fully understood today women, and slaves, were strictly forbidden, under pain of death, to attend the Games. An exception does seem to have been made for high ranking priestesses of the most important gods. However, it was possible for a woman to gain an Olympic prize. This was because in the chariot racing the chaplet of olive leaves was awarded to the owner of the horses and not the drivers. One of the first women to win an Olympic title in this way was Belistike from Macedonia in 268 BC as owner of the champion 2-horse chariot. It is recorded that some women did defy the rules and disguised themselves, but were thrown to their deaths on discovery. There is a story, perhaps

The IOC in 1896, seated—Baron de Coubertin (FRA), Demetrius Vikelas (GRE), A de Boutovsky (URS), standing—Dr W Gebhardt (GER), Jiri Guth-Jarkovsky (CZE), Francois Kémény (HUN) and General Victor Balck (SWE).

apocryphal, that Pherenice of Rhodes acted as a second to watch her son, Pisidores, win his event. In her excitement she gave herself away, but when it was discovered that not only her son, but also her father and brothers had all been Olympic champions, she was pardoned.

CELEBRATIONS OF THE MODERN OLYMPIC GAMES

	Year	Venue	Date	Countries	Total Competitors
I	1896	Athens, Greece	6–15 April	13	311
II	1900	Paris, France	20 May–28 October	22	1330
III	1904	St Louis, USA	1 July–23 November	13[2]	625
*	1906	Athens, Greece	22 April–2 May	20	884
IV	1908	London, England	27 April–31 October	22	2056
V	1912	Stockholm, Sweden	5 May–22 July	28	2546
VI	1916	Berlin, Germany	Not held due to war	—	—
VII	1920	Antwerp, Belgium	20 April–12 September	29	2692
VIII	1924	Paris, France	4 May–27 July	44	3092
IX	1928	Amsterdam, Netherlands	17 May–12 August	46	3014
X	1932	Los Angeles, USA	30 July–14 August	37	1408
XI	1936	Berlin, Germany	1–16 August	49	4066
XII	1940	Tokyo, then Helsinki	Not held due to war	—	—
XIII	1944	London, England	Not held due to war	—	—
XIV	1948	London, England	29 July–14 August	59	4099
XV	1952	Helsinki, Finland	19 July–3 August	69	4925
XVI	1956[1]	Melbourne, Australia	22 November–8 December	67	3184
XVII	1960	Rome, Italy	25 August–11 September	83	5346
XVIII	1964	Tokyo, Japan	10–24 October	93	5140
XIX	1968	Mexico City, Mexico	12–27 October	112	5530
XX	1972	Munich, FRG	26 August–10 September	122	7156
XXI	1976	Montreal, Canada	17 July–1 August	92	6085
XXII	1980	Moscow, USSR	19 July–3 August	81	5326
XXIII	1984	Los Angeles, USA	28 July–12 August	—	—
XXIV	1988	Seoul, South Korea	17–20 September–5 October	—	—

* This celebration (to mark the tenth anniversary of the Modern Games) was officially intercalated but is not numbered.

[1] The equestrian events were held in Stockholm, Sweden, 10–17 June with 158 competitors from 29 countries.

[2] Including newly discovered French national.

WINTER GAMES

	Year	Venue	Date	Countries	Total Competitors
I	1924	Chamonix, France ....25 January–4 February		16	294
II	1928	St Moritz, Switzerland ....11–19 February		25	495
III	1932	Lake Placid, USA ....4–15 February		17	306
IV	1936	Garmisch-Partenkirchen, Germany................................6–16 February		28	755
V	1948	St Moritz, Switzerland ....30 January–8 February		28	713
VI	1952	Oslo, Norway ....14–25 February		22	732
VII	1956	Cortina d'Ampezzo, Italy............26 January–5 February		32	819
VIII	1960	Squaw Valley, USA ....18–28 February		30	665
IX	1964	Innsbruck, Austria....................29 January–9 February		36	1093
X	1968	Grenoble, France......................6–18 February		37	1293
XI	1972	Sapporo, Japan ....3–13 February		35	1232
XII	1976	Innsbruck, Austria....................4–15 February		37	1128
XIII	1980	Lake Placid, USA ....13–24 February		37	1067
XIV	1984	Sarajevo, Yugoslavia.................8–19 February		—	—
XV	1988	Calgary, Canada ....*13-28* .23 February 6 March		—	—

TABLE OF OLYMPIC MEDAL WINNERS BY NATION 1896-1980

These totals include all first, second and third places, including those events no longer on the current (1984) schedule. The 1906 Games which were officially staged by the International Olympic Committee (IOC) have also been included. However, the medals won in the Art Competitions 1912–48 have *not* been included, but are listed elsewhere.

Note: Medals won in 1896, 1900 and 1904 by mixed teams from two countries have been counted for both countries.

Figures in brackets denote positions in medal tables for both Summer and Winter Games.

		SUMMER					WINTER					Combined Total
		Gold	Silver	Bronze	Total		Gold	Silver	Bronze	Total		
1	United States*	627	468	417	1512	(1)	36	42	31	109	(3)	1621
2	USSR	340	292	253	885	(2)	62	38	41	141	2 (3)	1026
3	Great Britain ..	163	201	176	540	(3)	6	4	10	20	(14)	560
4	Germany[1]	129	174	169	472	(4)	22	21	20	63	(7)	535
5	Sweden	129	125	156	410	(6)	28	23	27	78	(6)	488
6	France	142	156	155	453	(5)	12	9	13	34	(12)	487
7	Italy.............	127	111	108	346	(8)	10	9	7	26	(13)	372
8	GDR[2]	116	94	97	307	(9)	21	17	23	61	(8)	368
9	Finland	92	72	102	266	(10)	25	39	26	90	(4)	356
10	Hungary	113	106	130	349	(7)	—	2	4	6	(=16)	355
11	Norway	40	29	31	100	(22)	51	55	48	154	(1)	254
12	Switzerland	40	59	52	151	(14)	16	18	19	53	(9)	204
13	Japan............	73	64	61	198	(11)	1	3	1	5	(18)	203
14	Australia........	64	53	70	187	(12)	—	—	—	—		187
15	Poland	38	51	86	175	(13)	1	1	2	4	(=19)	179
16	Netherlands ...	36	43	52	131	(17)	10	15	10	35	(=10)	166
17	Austria..........	17	26	32	75	(24)	25	33	29	87	(5)	162
18	Canada..........	26	42	52	120	(19)	12	9	14	35	(=10)	155
19	Czechoslovakia	42	45	47	134	(=15)	2	5	7	14	(15)	148
20	Denmark	31	54	49	134	(=15)	—	—	—	—		134
21	Romania.......	28	37	59	124	(18)	0	0	1	1	(=21)	125
22	Belgium........	34	47	38	119	(20)	1	1	2	4	(=19)	123
23	Bulgaria........	27	50	39	116	(21)	0	0	1	1	(=21)	117
24	Greece..........	22	38	37	97	(23)	—	—	—	—		97
25	Cuba............	23	21	15	59	(25)	—	—	—	—		59

		SUMMER					WINTER				Combined Total
		Gold	Silver	Bronze	Total		Gold	Silver	Bronze	Total	
26	Yugoslavia	16	21	16	53	(26)	—	—	—	—	53
27	South Africa³	16	15	21	52	(27)	—	—	—	—	52
28	Argentina.......	13	18	13	44	(28)	—	—	—	—	44
29	Turkey..........	23	12	7	42	(29)	—	—	—	—	42
= 30	New Zealand ..	15	3	13	31	(= 30)	—	—	—	—	31
= 30	Mexico..........	7	9	15	31	(= 30)	—	—	—	—	31
32	Iran	4	10	15	29	(32)	—	—	—	—	29
33	Brazil...........	5	2	15	22	(33)	—	—	—	—	22
34	Estonia⁴	6	6	9	21	(34)	—	—	—	—	21
35	Kenya...........	5	7	7	19	(35)	—	—	—	—	19
36	South Korea...	1	6	11	18	(36)	—	—	—	—	18
= 37	Egypt...........	6	5	6	17	(= 37)	—	—	—	—	17
= 37	Spain	2	9	5	16	(39)	1	0	0	1	(= 21)	17
= 37	Jamaica.........	4	7	6	17	(= 37)	—	—	—	—	17
40	India.............	8	3	3	14	(40)	—	—	—	—	14
41	North Korea⁵ .	2	5	5	12	(= 41)	0	1	0	1	(= 21)	13
42	Ireland	4	3	5	12	(= 41)	—	—	—	—	12
= 43	Ethiopia	5	1	4	10	(= 43)	—	—	—	—	10
= 43	Mongolia.......	0	5	5	10	(= 43)	—	—	—	—	10
= 45	Uruguay	2	1	6	9	(= 45)	—	—	—	—	9
= 45	Portugal	0	4	5	9	(= 45)	—	—	—	—	9
= 47	Pakistan	2	3	2	7	(= 47)	—	—	—	—	7
= 47	Trinidad........	1	2	4	7	(= 47)	—	—	—	—	7
= 47	Chile.............	0	5	2	7	(= 47)	—	—	—	—	7
= 50	Liechtenstein	—	—	—	—		2	2	2	6	(= 16)	6
= 50	Philippines.....	0	1	5	6	(50)	—	—	—	—	6
= 52	Uganda	1	3	1	5	(= 51)	—	—	—	—	5
= 52	Venezuela......	1	2	2	5	(= 51)	—	—	—	—	5
= 52	Tunisia	1	2	2	5	(= 51)	—	—	—	—	5
55	Lebanon........	0	2	2	4	(54)	—	—	—	—	4
= 56	Latvia⁴	0	2	1	3	(= 55)	—	—	—	—	3
= 56	Colombia.......	0	1	2	3	(= 55)	—	—	—	—	3
= 56	Ghana..........	0	1	2	3	(= 55)	—	—	—	—	3
= 59	Luxembourg...	1	1	0	2	(= 58)	—	—	—	—	2
= 59	Bahamas........	1	0	1	2	(= 58)	—	—	—	—	2
= 59	Tanzania	0	2	0	2	(= 58)	—	—	—	—	2
= 59	Taiwan..........	0	1	1	2	(= 58)	—	—	—	—	2
= 59	Haiti.............	0	1	1	2	(= 58)	—	—	—	—	2
= 59	Puerto Rico	0	0	2	2	(= 58)	—	—	—	—	2
= 59	Nigeria..........	0	0	2	2	(= 58)	—	—	—	—	2
= 59	Panama	0	0	2	2	(= 58)	—	—	—	—	2
= 67	Peru	1	0	0	1	(= 66)	—	—	—	—	1
= 67	Zimbabwe......	1	0	0	1	(= 66)	—	—	—	—	1
= 67	Sri Lanka.......	0	1	0	1	(= 66)	—	—	—	—	1
= 67	Iceland..........	0	1	0	1	(= 66)	—	—	—	—	1
= 67	Morocco	0	1	0	1	(= 66)	—	—	—	—	1
= 67	Singapore	0	1	0	1	(= 66)	—	—	—	—	1
= 67	Cameroun......	0	1	0	1	(= 66)	—	—	—	—	1
= 67	Iraq	0	0	1	1	(= 66)	—	—	—	—	1
= 67	Niger	0	0	1	1	(= 66)	—	—	—	—	1
= 67	Bermuda........	0	0	1	1	(= 66)	—	—	—	—	1
= 67	Thailand........	0	0	1	1	(= 66)	—	—	—	—	1
= 67	Guyana	0	0	1	1	(= 66)	—	—	—	—	1

[1] Germany 1896–1964, West Germany, from 1968.   [2] GDR, East Germany, from 1968.   [3] South Africa, up to 1960.   [4] Estonia and Latvia, up to 1936.
[5] From 1964.
* Adjusted by the reinstatement in 1982 of Jim Thorpe (USA), the 1912 decathlon/pentathlon champion.

1896 *Summer*

THE Ist OLYMPIC GAMES

ATHENS, GREECE
6–15 APRIL 1896

(25 March – 3 April by the Julian Calendar).
Attended by representatives of 13 countries, comprising 311 competitors.

There had been a resurgence of interest in Ancient Greece in the 17th and 18th centuries and references to the Olympic Games in the poems of Pindar and other Greek poets were noted. In Britain the Cotswold Olympic Games were inaugurated in 1636 and in 1850 the Much Wenlock Olympic Society was founded by Dr Penny Brooke. At the end of the 18th century, in Germany, the famed founder of modern gymnastics, Johann Guts Muth had suggested a revival of the Olympic ideal. Some 50 years later

The man who saved the honour of a nation, Spyridon Louis, Greece's only winner of an athletics event in the first Modern Games, and right **the first Olympic champion of modern times, James Connolly (USA) the winner of the triple jump.**

a fellow countryman, Ernst Curtius, who had done some archaeological work at Olympia (started by the French in 1829), reiterated the idea in a lecture he gave in Berlin in 1852. In Greece itself Major Evangelis Zappas organized a Pan-Hellenic sports festival in 1859 which attracted a great deal of public support, and which was revived at intervals over the next 30 years.

The true founder of the modern Olympic movement is commonly acknowledged to be Pierre de Fredi, Baron de Coubertin of France. In 1889 the French government had commissioned him to make a study of modern physical culture methods. On his many foreign trips, and in Britain in particular where he met Dr Brooke, he formed his concept of a modern revival of the Olympic Games. He first propounded these ideas publicly at a lecture in the Sorbonne, Paris, on 25 November 1892. Their enthusiastic reception gave him an impetus as did his meeting with representatives of the top American universities in the following year. In June 1894 he convened an international conference, again in the Sorbonne, at which 12 countries were represented and another 21 sent messages of support. The outcome was a resolution, on 23 June, calling for sports competitions along the lines of the Ancient Games to be held every fourth year. The International Olympic Committee (IOC) was also inaugurated under the presidency of Demetrius Vikelas of Greece, with de Coubertin as secretary-general. The Frenchman had expected the inaugural celebration to herald the new century and be held in Paris in 1900. The delegates were impetuous and did not want to wait so long. Budapest in Hungary was strongly mooted at first, but, at the instigation of Vikelas, Athens was finally selected and the date set as 1896.

Unfortunately the Greek government appears not to have been consulted, and confronted by numerous political and financial problems they were lukewarm in their attitude. Luckily the Greek populace were very enthusiastic, but it was not until Crown Prince Constantine set up a committee and began organizing and collecting funds that the project became feasible, and the prospect of Budapest getting the honour by default faded.

The turning point came with the generosity of an extremely wealthy Greek businessman, Georgios

Averoff (formerly Avykeris) who actually lived in Alexandria, Egypt. He offered to pay for the reconstruction of the Panathenean Stadium, in Athens, at a cost of 920 000 drachma. The Stadium had first been built in 330 BC by the orator Lycurgus, a disciple of Plato. It was rebuilt 500 years later by Herodes Atticus, but had gradually disintegrated and was covered up until 1870 when King George of Greece had arranged its excavation by the German, Ziller. The new track measured 333·33 metres and had very sharp turns, with competitors obliged to run in a clockwise direction.

The opening of the Games coincided with the 75th anniversary of the declaration of Greek independence. Over 40 000 spectators in the stadium, plus thousands more on the surrounding hills saw King George I formally open the proceedings. The first competition was heat one of the 100 metres, and it was won by Francis Lane (USA) who thus became the first winner, in 12·5 sec, of an Olympic event in modern times. However, the first modern gold medallist was James Brendan Connolly (USA) who won the hop, step and jump. In fact the American team dominated events in the stadium, despite arriving only the day before the start of the competitions, having travelled by ship to France and then by train to Greece. The victors actually received a silver medal and a crown of olive leaves, runners-up were awarded bronze medals and a crown of laurel. There were no awards made for third place.

Of the 311 competitors, the great bulk, 230, were from the host country. An Italian, his country's only representative, apparently walked all the way from Milan only to be ruled out as a professional on arrival. Many athletes entered privately, and the British contingent included two employees of the Embassy in Athens. Yet another member of the British team was an Irishman, John Boland, who happened to be on holiday in Greece at the time and entered for the tennis events. He won the singles and partnering a German also the pairs. Another nice touch of the period was provided by the French sprinter who insisted on wearing his gloves as he was running before royalty.

Setting a pattern for future Games the greatest number of medals was won by a gymnast, Hermann Weingärtner (GER), with three wins, two second places and a third place. A Frenchman, Paul Masson, won three cycling events, thus setting a record which though equalled has not been bettered by any other cyclist. Perhaps the most remarkable achievement was that of Carl Schuhmann of Germany who not only won three gymnastic events but also won the wrestling title. Another athlete to gain medals in two sports was gymnast Fritz Hofmann of Germany, whose total of five placings included a second in the 100 metres.

In shooting John and Sumner Paine (USA) became the first brothers to win Olympic gold medals in military pistol and free pistol respectively. Two new events held at these Games were the discus throw and the marathon race. Both were based on Greek antiquity and the Greeks were eager to win them. However, the former was won by Robert Garrett (USA) who had inadvertently practised with an implement much larger and heavier than the one actually used at Athens. He also won the shot and was placed in the high and long jumps.

The marathon race had been proposed by a Frenchman, Michel Bréal, to commemorate the legendary run of a Greek courier, possibly Pheidippides, with the news of a Greek victory over

The start of the 100 m final in 1896. Note the modern starting position of Burke, the winner, in lane four. Other finallists (left to right), Chalkokondylis (GRE), Hofmann (GER), Szokolyi (HUN) and Lane (USA).

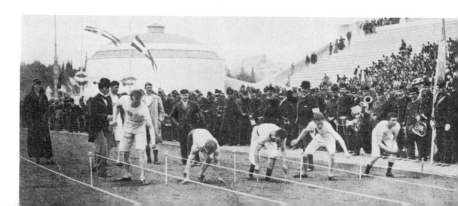

the Persians in 490 BC. He is supposed to have run from the site of the battle at Marathon to Athens, and after crying out 'Rejoice! We have won' he collapsed and died. The concept quickly caught the public imagination and it was a matter of national pride that the race be won by a Greek. Sixteen runners took part in the 40 km race and only four were not representatives of the host country. These included the Australian Edwin Flack, winner of the 800 m and 1500 m, Albin Lermusiaux of France, Arthur Blake (USA) and Hungary's Gyula Kellner. To the great delight of the thousands who waited at the stadium, the winner was Spiridon 'Spyros' Louis, a shepherd from Amaroussi who had only been placed fifth in the second of the two trial races. He was escorted into the stadium by Crown Prince Constantine and his brother Prince George. To seal the national triumph the second and third runners were also Greek, although the latter was eventually disqualified and his place taken by Kellner.

The oldest gold medallist at the Games was the winner of the free rifle contest Georgios Orphanidis (GRE) aged 37 yr. The youngest was Alfred Hajos (HUN) aged 18 yr 70 days when he won the 100 m and 1200 m freestyle events.

In view of the modern saturation coverage by the media it is noteworthy to record that the British press gave little space to reports from Athens, despite an earlier complaint in *The Times* about the lack of knowledge of the Games in the country and Britain's inadequate representation. Nevertheless the Games had been a tremendous success and certainly Greece looked forward to the forthcoming celebrations which they also expected to host.

FINAL MEDAL STANDINGS

Nation	Gold	Silver	Bronze
UNITED STATES	11	7	1
GREECE	10	19	17
GERMANY	7	5	2
FRANCE	5	4	2
GREAT BRITAIN	3	3	1
HUNGARY	2	1	2
AUSTRIA	2	—	3
AUSTRALIA	2	—	—
DENMARK	1	2	4
SWITZERLAND	1	2	—

1900 *Summer*

THE IInd OLYMPIC GAMES

PARIS, FRANCE
20 MAY – 28 OCTOBER 1900

Attended by representatives of 22 countries, comprising 1330 competitors, of which 12 were women.

After the success of the Athens Games, the Greeks called for the exclusive right to organize the Games in future. Baron de Coubertin was able to overcome this enthusiasm and finally got agreement on Paris. However, he made a serious mistake in making the Games a part of the Universal Exposition which was also held in Paris. Instead of being the grand spectacle of 4 years previously, the Olympic Games ended up as merely a sideshow to the international fair. Numerous internal rivalries within French sport left many of the sports without experienced officials or venues. The track and field events were held on uneven turf at Croix-Catelan, in the Bois de Boulogne, where it is reported that the jumpers had to dig their own pits. Generally there were very few spectators, and these were nearly reduced in number when the 1896 discus champion despatched the implement into the crowd on all three of his throws.

There was much confusion with a multiplicity of events spread over a 5 month period, and many of them hardly Olympian in character. Thus cricket, croquet and golf produced Olympic champions, but motorboating and fishing in the Seine were denied official recognition. Interspersed with all these were other events specifically for professional sportsmen. It was not surprising that many competitors, even medal winners, did not realize until much later that they had been competing at the Olympic Games. It should be noted that the Americans were still not part of an official national team, but representatives of individual colleges and clubs.

Well over half of all competitors were from the host country, France having 880 male and 4 female competitors, the largest national team ever to be entered in the Olympic Games.

The track and field competitions began on Saturday 14 July, Bastille Day, and the French organizers, expecting few spectators would turn up on a National holiday, moved a number of finals to the next day. Many of the American athletes were prevented from competing on a Sunday by the rules of their colleges and this led to recriminations that the French decision had been a deliberate attempt to restrict the number of transatlantic victories. If this was the case it had little effect as the US contingent from the clubs easily filled the gaps. A strange decision was that marks gained in the field event qualifying rounds on the Saturday counted in the final, so that Myer Prinstein, a Jew but under the aegis of the strongly Methodist University of Syracuse, gained a silver medal without competing in the final. It seems likely that Prinstein, the world record holder, would have defeated the eventual winner Alvin Kraenzlein in that final and thus prevented the latter from gaining four individual victories, (he also won the 60 m, 110 m hurdles and 200 m hurdles) a feat never surpassed in track and field competition at one Olympic Games.

The start of another unique Olympic record began at Paris with the triple gold medal wins in the standing jumps by Ray Ewry (USA), all on the same day. Ewry incidentally, who suffered from polio as a child, went on to amass a record ten individual gold medals in subsequent Games, a performance unlikely ever to be matched.

It is unlikely that any Olympian will ever match the ten gold medals won by Ray Ewry (USA) in the standing jumps in four Games.

The first female competitor ever to win an Olympic gold medal, Charlotte Cooper (GBR) won five Wimbledon titles, and was also a county class hockey player.

Behind him in the standing jumps at Paris was a countryman Irving Baxter, who had already won the regular high jump and the pole vault, to become the first athlete of American Indian ancestry to win at the Olympic Games. In a similar vein, Norman Pritchard of India, later to become an actor in Hollywood silent films, won the first medals by an Asian sportsman with two silvers in the 200 m flat and hurdles races.

Another unique record was set up in the rowing events although the exact details have never been ascertained. In the final of the coxed pairs a small French boy was drafted in at the last moment (then allowed by the rules) to cox the Dutch crew of Francois Brandt and Roelof Klein. He was no more than 10 years old and may have been as young as 7, in either case certainly the youngest ever Olympic gold medallist. His name, however, was never recorded and he has never been traced. The oldest Olympic champion at these Games was Eugène Mougin (FRA) in archery aged 47 yr 193 days.

Also these Games saw the first women competitors in Olympic history, but only in the golf and tennis events. The honour of being the first female gold medallist in the Olympic Games went to Britain's Charlotte Cooper, a Wimbledon champion, who won the tennis singles on 9 July.

Press coverage was barely apparent with many of the events not mentioned at all, and for years afterwards there was much confusion as to the names and nationalities of the medallists. The first Olympic medals won by Canada, with the gold and bronze gained by George Orton, were not 'discovered' for some years, as Orton had been entered by his American university and was billed as an American.

FINAL MEDAL STANDINGS

Nation	Gold	Silver	Bronze
FRANCE	27	35	34
UNITED STATES	19	15	16
GREAT BRITAIN	17	8	12
BELGIUM	5	6	3
SWITZERLAND	5	3	1
GERMANY	4	2	2
AUSTRALIA	2	—	4
DENMARK	2	3	2
ITALY	2	2	—
NETHERLANDS	1	2	3
HUNGARY	1	2	2
CUBA	1	1	—
CANADA	1	—	1
SWEDEN	1	—	1
AUSTRIA	—	3	3
NORWAY	—	2	3
CZECHOSLOVAKIA	—	1	2
INDIA	—	2	—

1904 *Summer*

THE IIIrd OLYMPIC GAMES

ST LOUIS, USA
*1 JULY –
23 NOVEMBER
1904*

Attended by representatives of 13 countries, comprising 625 competitors, of which 8 were women.

The third celebration had for a time been mooted for Britain, and then Philadelphia, but de Coubertin had wanted New York. The IOC finally agreed on Chicago, but at the request of the US President Theodore Roosevelt, also honorary president of the US Olympic Committee, the venue was changed to St Louis to coincide with the World's Fair being held there on the centenary of the Louisiana Purchase. For the second time in succession the Olympic Games became merely a sideshow. Held in the centre of the North American continent the problems of distance and cost of travel meant that very few overseas entries were present. Of the 625 total competitors, 533 were from the host country, and eventually 238 of the 282 medals available were won by the USA. The Games became virtually a tournament between various American clubs and universities, and indeed in the track and field events a points table was published noting that the New York AC had beaten the Chicago Athletic Association and the Milwaukee AC for the team title. In swimming it was also noted that New York beat Germany and Hungary overall.

In such circumstances the Olympic Games degenerated into such a farce that the cycling events, which had no foreign entries and apparently accepted a number of professional riders, were refused official status. (The unique achievement of Marcus Hurley in winning four cycling events therefore has no relevance in Olympic annals.)

Under the rather loose controls imposed on most of the sports some rather strange things occurred. In the 400 m track race no heats were held and all 13 entrants ran in the final, which was won in Olympic record time of 49·2 sec by Harry Hillman (USA), who also won two other events.

The rowing events were over a 1½ mile course which entailed making a turn. The swimming events were held over Imperial distances, while the athletics track measured one-third of a mile in circumference and had a 220 yard straight-away which was quite an innovation for the visiting Europeans.

In the track and field programme, held on a three laps to the mile track in the grounds of Washington University, St Louis, only two events went to non-Americans. The French Canadian policeman Etienne Desmarteau won the 56 lb *25·4 kg* weight throw. He died the following year of typhoid and later a park was named after him in his home city of Montreal. The 10-event All-round competition, a forerunner of the decathlon, was won by one of the only two British entries, Thomas Kiely, who incidentally like the silver medallist in the 2500 m steeple-chase, John Daly, was an Irishman. Another very busy athlete was Myer Prinstein (USA) who redressed what he felt was the wrong done to him four years before by winning the long jump with a new Games record. In addition to winning the hop, step and jump yet again, he was also placed fifth in the 60 m and 400 m finals, competing in the colours of the Greater New York Irish AA. Archie Hahn (USA) won a unique Olympic 200 m race: unique in that it was held on a straightaway, i.e. no turn. All three of his final opponents were given a one yard 0·99 m handicap under the rules of the day governing false starts.

Also running in the 400 m was George Poage, who went on to place third in both the 200 m hurdles and the 400 m hurdles races. He and Joseph Stadler, silver medallist in the standing high jump, became the first black men to win medals in the Olympic Games.

Despite the absence of overseas athletes the standard in many sports was high and the multiple victories of Archie Hahn (USA), 60 m/100 m/200 m, Harry Hillman (see above), James Lightbody (USA), 800 m/1500 m/2500 m steeplechase, Ray Ewry yet again and Charles Daniels (USA) in swimming, were outstanding. Daniels in winning the 220 yd, 440 yd and mile freestyle events as well as taking a silver in the 100 yd was the prototype of the Americans who were to dominate Olympic freestyle swimming. However, the greatest medal winner, in number terms at least, was gymnast Anton Heida (USA) with five golds and one silver.

As was to happen so often, much attention was focused on the marathon race, this time owing to a scandal. The first man out of the stadium, Fred Lorz (USA) was also the first man back, looking remarkably fresh. It was some time before it was discovered that he had had a lift in a car for about half the distance, having dropped out with cramp. When the car itself broke down about 4 miles from the stadium he resumed running and entered to receive the crowd's plaudits. When the true winner, Thomas Hicks arrived, dirty and exhausted, the ruse was discovered, and initially Lorz was banned for life even though he insisted he only did it as a joke and would not have kept up the charade. Bearing in mind present day attitudes it is interesting that Hicks finished in a daze due to the administering of strychnine by his handlers as a stimulant, a common practice then. In ninth place was Lentauw (SAF) the first black African distance runner to compete in the Games.

The oldest winner of a gold medal at these Games was Reverend Galen Spencer (USA) as a member of the winning team in archery aged 64 yr 2 days. The youngest was the winner of the heavyweight boxing title, Samuel Berger (USA) at 19 yr 274 days.

A final insult to the Games were the Anthropology Days during which competitions were held which parodied the regular Olympic competitions with events for aboriginal peoples, such as American Indians, African pygmies, Patagonians, Ainus from Japan, and the like. Finally in November, with the Association Football competition won by a Canadian college over two American teams, the IIIrd Olympic Games came to an end, and many in Europe wondered if the fledgling movement would recover.

One of the few Europeans to win gold medals in 1904 was Emil Rausch (GER) in the 880 yards and 1 mile freestyle swimming events.

FINAL MEDAL STANDINGS

Nation	Gold	Silver	Bronze
UNITED STATES	70	74	67
CUBA	5	2	3
GERMANY	4	4	5
CANADA	4	1	—
HUNGARY	2	1	1
AUSTRIA	2	1	1
GREAT BRITAIN	1	1	
SWITZERLAND	1	—	1
GREECE	1	—	1
FRANCE	—	1	—

1906 *Summer*

THE INTERIM or INTERCALATED GAMES

ATHENS,
GREECE
22 APRIL –
2 MAY 1906

Paul Pilgrim (USA) wins the 400 m title in 1906 from Halswelle (GBR), on the right, and Barker (AUS). Two years later the Briton figured in a unique Olympic incident.

Attended by representatives of 20 countries, comprising 884 competitors, of which 7 were women.

The Greeks had not forgotten their desire to have the Olympic Games held permanently in their country, but political and financial problems had prevented them from pressing too hard in 1900 and 1904. Though de Coubertin was opposed to the concept he realized that something was required to revive the Olympic spirit after the last two débâcles. He therefore agreed to a series of 4-yearly meetings interspersed with the main Games, the first of which would be held as a tenth anniversary celebration of the 1896 occasion. It was decided that although they would have the blessing of the IOC these Interim Games would not be numbered in sequence.

For the first time for 10 years large crowds attended Olympic events. The marble stadium in Athens was full to capacity and the enthusiasm of the spectators helped overcome some of the organizational mishaps. The record number of countries included Finland for the first time, with the father of the famous Järvinen family, Werner, winning his country's first gold medal in the Greek-style discus throw. The American team was an 'official' one selected and sent by the US Olympic Committee, so ending the previous practice of colleges, clubs and private individuals entering themselves.

The programme of track and field events had been altered with a reduction in the number of sprint and hurdle races, but with the addition of a pentathlon and the javelin throw. Despite the undoubted efforts made by the hosts, the Games never really made the impact that had been made in 1896.

Of course there were some outstanding performers and performances, not least the two victories of the perennial Ray Ewry. Another American, who had only been added to their team at the very last moment after he had privately raised the money for his fare, was Paul Pilgrim. He had won a gold medal in 1904 as a member of the winning 4 mile team from New York AC. This time he created a surprise by winning both the 400 m and the 800 m races, a feat not equalled until 1976. The New York policeman Martin Sheridan won another two gold and three silver medals to add to his 1904 discus title. He further increased this total at the next Games. The new pentathlon event, consisting of a 192 m run, the standing long jump, discus and javelin throws and Greco-Roman wrestling, was won by Hjalmar Mellander of Sweden. A real surprise winner came in the 1500 m walk event, which was the scene of a number of chauvinistic decisions by the various national judges. The American distance runner George Bonhag had disappointed in the 5 mile and 1500 m runs, and entered the walk, an entirely new event to him, in a last effort to win a medal. Owing mainly to the excessive number of disqualifications he won his gold medal. With all three previous Olympic marathons having been won by the host country, the Greeks were hopeful of continuing the tradition. Despite half of the entrants coming from Greece it was won by the Canadian William Sherring by a margin of nearly 7 minutes.

The oldest gold medallist was Maurice Lecoq (FRA) aged 52 yr 15 days when he won the rapid fire pistol event. The youngest at these Games was Giorgio Cesana (ITA) who was the coxswain of the winning coxed fours crew aged 14 yr 10 days.

Despite the soft cinder track in the stadium, the

Gymnastics on the opening day of the 1906 Games in the Panathenean stadium, originally built for the 1896 celebration.

poor facilities for the swimmers in the sea at Phaleron, and complaints about the food, these Interim Games put the whole Olympic concept back on a path towards de Coubertin's ideal. It was intended that another such Interim meeting be held in 1910 but political upheavals in Greece made it impossible and the subject was not raised again.

FINAL MEDAL STANDINGS

Nation	Gold	Silver	Bronze
FRANCE	15	9	16
UNITED STATES	12	6	5
GREECE	8	13	13
GREAT BRITAIN	8	11	6
ITALY	7	6	3
SWITZERLAND	5	4	2
GERMANY	4	6	4
NORWAY	4	1	—
AUSTRIA	3	3	2
SWEDEN	2	5	7
HUNGARY	2	5	3
BELGIUM	2	2	3
DENMARK	2	2	1
FINLAND	2	—	1
CANADA	1	1	—
NETHERLANDS	—	1	2
AUSTRALIA	—	—	3
CZECHOSLOVAKIA	—	—	2
SOUTH AFRICA	—	—	1

1908 *Summer*

THE IVth OLYMPIC GAMES

LONDON, GREAT BRITAIN *27 APRIL – 31 OCTOBER 1908*

Attended by representatives of 22 countries, comprising 2056 competitors, of which 36 were women.

The Games scheduled for 1908 had originally been awarded to Rome but during the Interim Games the Italian authorities informed the IOC that they would have to withdraw. London was proposed and on 19 November 1906 formally accepted the honour. Drawing on the expertise of many British sporting governing bodies—the Amateur Swimming Association, founded in 1869, and the Amateur Athletic Association in 1880—the organizing committee under Lord Desborough went to work. A stadium capable of accommodating 68 000 spectators was built, for

£40 000, in West London. (It is reported that this 'capacity' figure was well exceeded on a number of occasions.) It contained an athletics track measuring three laps to a mile lying inside a 660 yd banked concrete cycle track. On the grass infield stood a giant swimming pool 330 ft *100 m* long and 50 ft *15·24 m* wide. Rowing events were held on the Thames at Henley, tennis was at the All-England Club, Worple Road, Wimbledon, yachting at Ryde, Isle of Wight and on the Clyde, and the new sport of motorboating on Southampton Water.

Although the period of the Games extended over a record 6 months, starting with rackets in April and ending with rugby, soccer (association football) and hockey in October, the main competitions took place in July. The formal opening by King Edward VII took place at the White City Stadium on 13 July. In all there were 21 different sports catered for. For the first time entries were made entirely by nations and not by individuals and clubs. This emphasis on nationalism undoubtedly caused some of the disputes and accusations which marred this first truly international sporting event.

The Americans particularly were incensed by the inadvertent omission of their flag from those flying around the stadium. Sweden was missed as well. Then in the march past they refused to dip the Stars and Stripes to King Edward. The Finnish team would not march behind the flag of Czarist Russia, so they entered the stadium without any banner. From those beginnings things got worse as complaints from all sides, but especially from the US officials, came thick and fast. One complaint was highlighted in quite a remarkable way when Forrest Smithson, an American student of theology, won the 110 m hurdles in a new world record time of 15·0 sec, carrying a bible in his left hand, as a protest against Sunday competition. British judges and officials were accused of 'fixing' heats, coaching their competitors illegally and otherwise breaking rules to aid their competitors. The British weather did its bit by producing some of its foulest conditions for many a summer, and thus badly affected the cycling and tennis in particular.

All the rancour came to a head in the 400 m run. Three of the four men in the final were from the United States, with the other Lieut Wyndham Halswelle representing Great Britain. The British judges accused the Americans of impeding the Briton, disqualified the 'offender', Carpenter, who had won the race, and ordered a re-run for the next day. The other US runners refused to appear and Halswelle gained the gold medal with the only walk-over in Olympic history. Finally the bitterness reached such a level that it was thought necessary to produce a booklet entitled 'Replies to Criticism of the Olympic Games', which, owing to its rather pompous tone, did little to alleviate the situation. One result of all this was the decision that future control of competitions should be in the hands of the various international governing bodies of the sports and not left solely to the host country. One of the American runners involved in that 400 m final was John Taylor who, as a member of the winning medley relay team, became the first black man to win an Olympic gold medal.

Nevertheless there were many excellent performances throughout the Games. The ubiquitous Ray Ewry, now 33 years old, won his record breaking ninth and tenth gold medals in the standing jumps. Martin Sheridan, who had been the American flag bearer in the opening ceremony incident, added two more discus titles to his haul, while the 40 year old John Flanagan won his third hammer gold medal. Incidentally, at its meeting at The Hague in 1907 the IOC had decided that gold medals should be awarded, with silver for second and bronze for third. Mel Sheppard (USA) was one of two triple gold

One of the five occasions when Dorando collapsed during the last lap of the White City track at the end of the 1908 marathon. He was finally assisted through the tape.

The official winner of the 1908 marathon, Johnny Hayes (USA), running through Willesden on his way to the stadium.

medallists as he won the 800 m, 1500 m and was part of the winning relay team. The other was British swimmer Henry Taylor, who won the 400 m and 1500 m freestyle events and was part of the 4 × 200 m relay team. Charles Daniels (USA) won the 100 m freestyle to add to his three titles in the last two Games, and set a record of four individual swimming golds which still stands. Another swimmer, Zoltan von Halmay (HUN) increased his total medal haul to nine since 1900, a total unsurpassed at the sport until 1972.

An Olympic 'first' occurred in the Running Deer team shooting event, won by Sweden, when a father and son, Oscar and Alfred Swahn, won gold medals. Though already 60 years of age Oscar was to set even more records, not least by qualifying for the Swedish team in 1924. Another 'first' was occasioned by the introduction of the first Winter sports into the Olympic Games attracting 14 male and 7 female competitors, with four skating events held at the Prince's Club Rink. The titles were won by representatives of Sweden, Germany, Great Britain and Russia. This latter was the first Olympic title gained by that country, and was won by Nikolai Panin (actually Kolomenkin) who 4 years later was a member of the Russian fourth-placed revolver shooting team.

Undoubtedly the most famous incident from these Games came in the marathon race. Originally the distance was to be about 25 miles, but the suggestion that a start should be made at Windsor Castle extended that to an exact 26 miles. The final distance of 26 miles and 385 yards *42 195 m* was due to a request by Princess Mary that the start at Windsor be made from under the windows of the Royal nursery. This arbitrarily arrived at distance was 16 years later accepted worldwide as the standard marathon length.

The race itself, watched by a crowd estimated at over 250 000 people, was run in intensely hot and humid conditions, quite the opposite of most of the preceding weather, which took its toll of the runners. The little Italian Dorando Pietri reached the stadium first in a state of near collapse, and fell five times on the last part-lap of the track. Over-zealous officials rushed to his aid and helped lift him over the finish line. On behalf of the second finisher, Johnny Hayes, the Americans lodged a protest which was upheld and the Italian was disqualified. The wave of public sympathy found expression in the gift of Queen Alexandra to Pietri of a special gold cup.

Great Britain won the greatest number of medals throughout the competitions, but the United States, as always, came out well in front in the centrepiece of the Games, the track and field events.

Two sportsmen, Ivan Osiier (DEN) a fencer, and Magnus Konow (NOR) a yachtsman, though unplaced in their events, began Olympic careers which continued until the XIVth Games in London in 1948, setting a record breaking span for Olympic competition of 40 years.

The oldest gold medallist at these Games was Sir Thomas Glen-Coats (GBR) in the 12 m class yacht *Hera* aged 62 yr 175 days, while the youngest was William Foster, a member of the winning British 4 × 200 m freestyle swimming team aged 18 yr 6 days.

Six days after his valiant but disqualified run Queen Alexandra presented Dorando with a special gold cup, which now has a place of honour in the offices of his club in Carpi, Italy.

FINAL MEDAL STANDINGS

Nation	Gold	Silver	Bronze
GREAT BRITAIN	56	48	37
UNITED STATES	23	12	11
SWEDEN	7	5	10
FRANCE	5	5	9
CANADA	3	3	8
HUNGARY	3	4	2
GERMANY	2	4	4
NORWAY	2	3	3
ITALY	2	2	—
BELGIUM	1	5	2
AUSTRALIA*	1	2	1
FINLAND	1	1	3
SOUTH AFRICA	1	1	—
DENMARK	—	2	3
GREECE	—	3	1
RUSSIA	—	2	—
CZECHOSLOVAKIA	—	—	2
AUSTRIA	—	—	1
NETHERLANDS	—	—	1
NEW ZEALAND*	—	—	1

* Australia and New Zealand combined as Australasia.

SKATING MEDALS

Nation	Gold	Silver	Bronze
GREAT BRITAIN	1	2	3
SWEDEN	1	1	1
GERMANY	1	1	—
RUSSIA	1	—	—

1912 *Summer*

THE Vth
OLYMPIC
GAMES

STOCKHOLM,
SWEDEN
*5 MAY –
22 JULY 1912*

Attended by representatives of 28 countries, comprising 2546 competitors, of which 55 were women.

Sweden had wanted to host the Olympic Games from the very first. After the rows and recriminations of London they received the honour at a critical time for the Olympic movement. A 32 000 capacity stadium was designed and built

One of the greatest athletes of all time, Jim Thorpe. The IOC has finally restored him to the roster of champions after his original disqualification for alleged professionalism.

The official timekeepers in 1912 were certainly more colourful than the early electrical timing apparatus which was also in evidence (box in foreground) at Stockholm.

by Torben Grut, with the 383 m track laid out under the direction of Charles Perry, an Englishman who had been responsible for the 1896 and 1908 tracks. The Games were opened officially by King Gustav V. At Baron de Coubertin's insistence the number of sports was cut to a more manageable 14, most of them consisting of the 'purer' Olympic events. The competitions were marked by extremely high standards of sportsmanship as well as performance, with virtually no arguments or protests. About the only com-

24

The Games 1912

plaint was from the Finns who still objected to competing under the Russian flag, causing the great runner Kolehmainen to state that he almost wished he had not won rather than see the Russian flag raised for his victories. Incidentally these Games were to see the last appearance of a Russian team for 40 years.

There were a number of innovations including the first use in the Games of electrical timing and photo-finish equipment for the running events, albeit rather primitive mechanisms. Also a number of new events were added, and a whole new era opened up with the addition of artistic competitions (see p 247) comprising architecture, painting, sculpture, music and literature.

Among those new events was the modern pentathlon (see p 134) consisting of five disciplines in different sports. This had been included at the request of de Coubertin and aroused great interest. Dominated by the Swedes, it is noteworthy that in fifth place was Lieut George S Patton, later a famous and controversial American general of the Second World War.

As previously, the American team lived on the boat which had transported them across the Atlantic, and in this case it was, perhaps ironically, a liner named *Finland*. For it was in Stockholm that the first of the 'Flying Finns' made his appearance on the track and began a domination which lasted till the 1940s. Hannes Kolehmainen was one of three brothers, one a professional runner and the other a teammate at Stockholm, and he captivated the spectators with his wins over 5000 m, 10 000 m and the 12 000 m cross-country race. He also set a world record in a heat of the 3000 m team race, but his team failed to qualify for the final. His race with the Frenchman Jean Bouin over 5000 m was one of the most enthralling races ever seen to that time with the Finn winning by a stride in 14 min 36·6 sec which improved the world record by a margin of 24·6 sec. Others to receive the adulation of the crowds included the young American Ted Meredith who won the 800 m in a new world record of 1 min 51·9 sec, and Ralph Craig (USA) the winner of the 100 m and 200 m sprints. This latter was to reappear as a yachtsman, in the Dragon class, 36 years later. In swimming the imagination was caught by the first of the great Hawaiian competitors, Duke Kahanamoku, who

won the 100 m freestyle for the United States. The son of Hawaiian royalty he received his first name as a mark of respect for the Duke of Edinburgh, Queen Victoria's second son, who was visiting the islands at the time. He competed in three more Games and then became a film star.

There was only one cycling event but it was unique in that it was the longest road race ever to be held in the Games. Over a distance of 320 km it was won by Rudolph Lewis of South Africa in a time of 10 hr 42 min 39 sec, with Sweden taking the team title. A great impetus was given to the game of soccer by these Games which saw Britain defeat Denmark in the final match by 4 goals to 2 in front of some 25 000 spectators. Gymnastics, which like the wrestling, was held outdoors, also gained a new status. The wrestling itself caused some problems owing to the length of some of the bouts. In the light-heavyweight final the judges called a halt after the bout had gone on for 9 hours and gave both wrestlers a silver medal, with no gold awarded. Even this was surpassed in the middleweight category, where the tussle for the silver medal was between Alfred Asikáinen (FIN) and Martin Klein, an Estonian representing Russia. The latter finally triumphed after 11 hr 40 min, the longest bout ever recorded in the sport. The first known twins to win Olympic gold medals were the Swedish Carlberg brothers, Vilhelm (who won three) and Eric (with two) in the shooting programme. An even rarer sibling combination occurred in the 6 m class yachting which was won by the French boat *Mac Miche*, crewed by the three Thubé brothers, Amédée, Gaston and Jacques.

However, the name on everybody's lips at Stockholm was that of Jim Thorpe. Of Irish, French, but mainly American Indian ancestry, Thorpe, whose tribal name meant 'Bright Path', won both of the newly constituted athletic pentathlon and decathlon events. The pentathlon, comprising long jump, javelin, discus, 200 m and 1500 m runs, was scored according to the positions achieved in each discipline. Thorpe won the first four and placed third in the last. The 10-event decathlon, held then over 3 days, is scored according to a predetermined table of points allocated to each performance. In this he finished 688 points ahead of the runner-up. In addition he placed fifth in the individual high jump competition and seventh in the long jump. Presenting him with his medals King Gustav V called him 'the greatest athlete in the world'. Thorpe reportedly replied, 'Thanks King'. Six months later, in January 1913, a sportswriter for the *Worcester Telegram* in Massachusetts, Roy Johnson, reported that Thorpe had played minor baseball for money prior to the Games and therefore was not an amateur. Owing to the violent amateur/ professional dichotomy of the time, perhaps reinforced by anti-Indian prejudice, Thorpe's medals were taken back and his performances stricken from Olympic annals. It seems fairly certain that Thorpe had not played the baseball concerned for the money primarily. In any event it was not much, and he was certainly ignorant of the implications to his amateur career. Various moves were made over the years to have his medals restored. To their credit the runners-up to Thorpe, Hugo Wieslander (SWE) and Ferdinand Bie (NOR) initially refused to accept the gold medals when they were sent to them although their names were inscribed in Olympic annals as the winners of the events.

It was not until 1973 that he was reinstated as an amateur by the American Athletic Union (AAU), by which time he had been dead for 20 years. The IOC stubbornly refused all entreaties to place him back on the honour rolls, and it has been suggested that his cause was not helped by the fact that the President of the IOC from 1952 to 1972 was Avery Brundage, a team-mate in 1912 who had placed 5th (or 6th according to your view) in the pentathlon. Finally, in October 1982, the man who had been voted in 1950 as the greatest athlete of the first half-century was 'pardoned' by the IOC, and the medals were ordered to be presented to his family.

Oscar Swahn (SWE) became the oldest ever Olympic gold medallist as part of the running deer shooting team at the age of 64 yr 258 days. The youngest at these Games was Greta Johansson (SWE) who won the platform diving aged 17 yr 186 days. Only 40 days older was Isabella Moore (GBR) in the winning freestyle swimming relay team, to become Britain's youngest ever female gold medallist.

The Games of Stockholm marked the point where the Olympic movement finally 'came of age' and the tremendous efforts of the organizing committee under Sigfrid Edström, later Presi-

dent of the IOC, must get much of the credit. The only unfortunate incident had been the death of Francisco Lazzaro (POR) who had collapsed and died during the marathon. Ironically it was the first Games that Portugal had attended. Another newcomer had been Japan, and the Games were beginning to achieve the world-wide support originally envisaged for them.

FINAL MEDAL STANDINGS

Nation	Gold	Silver	Bronze
UNITED STATES[1]	27	19	19
SWEDEN	24	24	17
GREAT BRITAIN	10	15	16
FINLAND............................	9	8	9
FRANCE.............................	7	4	3
GERMANY..........................	5	13	7
SOUTH AFRICA	4	2	—
NORWAY	4	1	5
HUNGARY..........................	3	2	3
CANADA	3	2	3
ITALY................................	3	1	2
AUSTRALIA[2]	2	2	2
BELGIUM	2	1	3
DENMARK	1	6	5
GREECE	1	—	1
NEW ZEALAND[2]	1	—	1
SWITZERLAND	1	—	—
RUSSIA	—	2	3
AUSTRIA............................	—	2	2
NETHERLANDS	—	—	3

[1] Adjusted by the reinstatement in 1982 of Jim Thorpe (USA).

[2] Australia and New Zealand combined as Australasia.

1920 *Summer*

THE VIIth OLYMPIC GAMES

ANTWERP, BELGIUM
*20 APRIL –
12 SEPTEMBER
1920*

Attended by representatives of 29 countries, comprising 2692 competitors, of which 64 were women.

When the venue of the VIth Games, due in 1916,

came to be discussed at Stockholm three cities were put forward as candidates – Budapest, Alexandria and Berlin. It is said that the latter was chosen in an attempt to avert the war that was then threatening Europe. With the outbreak of hostilities in 1914 hopes of holding the Games failed although the Germans still made preparations for them, believing the war would not last very long.

Six years previously Antwerp had been suggested as the venue for 1920, and though the city was sorely affected by the human tragedy and economic ruin of the war the organizing committee under Count Henri de Baillet-Latour, later IOC President, overcame all difficulties.

The Games were opened by King Albert and there was a record number of competitors from a record number of countries, including New Zealand as a separate entity (previously it had been part of an Australasian team). The recent enemies, Germany, Austria, Hungary and Turkey were not invited.

The concept of the Olympic oath was introduced at Antwerp, and the first sportsman to take the oath was Victor Boin, an excellent choice, who had competed in the two previous Games, winning medals at water polo, and here he was to gain another in the fencing competitions.

Another newcomer at these Games was the newly devised Olympic flag. It had been designed by Baron de Coubertin in 1913, based on a design depicted on an ancient Greek artefact, and consisted of five interlaced rings coloured blue, yellow, black, green, red, from left to right. The rings were meant to symbolize the friendship of mankind, and the colours represented all nations, as every national flag in the world contains at least one of these colours.

A new 30 000 seat stadium had been built, but Charles Perry (see p 23) had not been able to do much with the 400 m running track surface which was very poor and badly affected by the consistent rain which fell. Owing to the weather and the economic aftermath of the recent conflict crowds generally were small. The athletes were housed in school buildings, which caused something of a revolt among the US team—though they were much more incensed by the intolerable conditions experienced on the old freighter which had brought them to the Games.

Ludowika and Walter Jakobsson of Finland were 36 and 38 respectively when they won their skating pairs title in 1920. Eight years later they placed fifth.

Britain's Jack Beresford won his three gold medals in three different rowing events at three different Games, a unique achievement in the sport.

The star of the 1912 Games, Hannes Kolehmainen, made a surprise return to win the marathon, but his mantle had been taken over by another young Finn, Paavo Nurmi. Although he lost his very first Olympic final, over 5000 m to the gassed French war veteran Joseph Guillemot, he was at the start of an outstanding career in which he won 12 Olympic medals, 9 of them gold, and set 29 world records of one type or another. Here he led Finland to victories in the 10 000 m and the 8000 m cross-country race, also gaining a gold in the latter team race. This time the Finns were competing under their own flag, having gained independence in 1917, and they celebrated the occasion by halting the American track and field juggernaut by gaining as many gold medals as the American athletes. Charlie Paddock, however, retained the 100 m sprint title for the United States, delighting onlookers with his spectacular jump finish. A Second World War Marine Corps hero, he posthumously had a ship named after him. But not all glory on the track went to either the Finns or the Americans. Albert Hill, a 31 year old Briton who had fought throughout the war, won both the 800 m and the 1500 m, a double not repeated for 44 years. Hill even went one better by gaining a silver in the 3000 m team race. Second to him in the 1500 m was Philip Baker, who later in life as Philip Noel-Baker MP, was the recipient of the 1959 Nobel Peace Prize—the only Nobel Prize winner to also excel at the Olympic Games. The greatest number of medals was won at these Games by two American marksmen, Willis Lee, with five golds, one silver and one bronze, and Lloyd Spooner, with four golds, one silver and two bronzes. The shooting events also produced the first gold medal won by a South American country when Guilherme Paraense of Brazil took the rapid-fire pistol title. The remarkable Oscar Swahn (SWE) became the oldest ever Olympic medallist, in any sport, when he gained a silver medal aged 72 yr 280 days in the running deer team event. Equally outstanding in the fencing events was Nedo Nadi (ITA) who added two more individual wins to his 1912 victory to equal the record of the Cuban, Ramon Fonst, in 1900 and 1904. In addition he won another three team golds for a then record-equalling five at one Games. His younger brother Aldo increased the family total with three more.

Returning to Olympic competition for the first time since 1906 Hubert van Innis of the host country won four golds and two silvers to add to his previous haul of two golds and a silver, and was Antwerp's oldest champion aged 54 yr 187 days. High diving for women was won by Aileen Riggin (USA) aged only 14 yr 119 days, the youngest individual event Olympic champion to that date. She almost lost the honour to Sweden's Nils Skoglund who placed second in the men's plain high diving aged 3 months younger.

Swimming was dominated by two swimmers, both Americans, who captured three gold medals each. Ethelda Bleibtrey won all events open to

Eventual winner of a record eleven shooting medals, Carl Osburn was a Commander in the US Navy when he won four golds in 1920.

her, the 100 m, 300 m and relay, even though she had suffered from polio as a child. Norman Ross won the 400 m, 1500 m and was part of the victorious men's relay team. He also figured in an unusual incident when he was disqualified in the 100 m final for impeding an Australian swimmer. The race had been won by Duke Kahanamoku in world record time. The re-swim was also won by the Hawaiian but in slower time. Another incident, of a more serious kind, occurred in the soccer final in which Czechoslovakia were disqualified for leaving the field after 40 min play in protest at the decisions of the British referee. Belgium was leading 2–0 at that point. Daniel Carroll completed a unique double in the rugby final when he won a second gold medal as part of the US team. He had played in the victorious Australian team of 1908, but had emigrated in the meantime. The tennis events saw the victory of one of the greatest players in the game, Suzanne Lenglen (FRA), eventually six times winner of the Wimbledon singles. Winner of the single sculls, and, teamed with a cousin, the double sculls was John Kelly. Earlier in the year the American had been refused entry to the Henley Regatta on the grounds that as a bricklayer he had an unfair advantage over 'gentlemen'. Ironically, his son John Jr won at Henley in the 1940s and his daughter Grace, the film actress, became Princess of Monaco. Coincidentally, these were the first Games at which Monaco had participated.

Two winter sports were also held, ice hockey and figure skating, attracting 73 men and 12 women from 10 countries. The latter witnessed the first gold medals won by a husband and wife, in the pairs champions, Ludowika (born in Germany) and Walter Jakobsson of Finland. On this subject it may be that the first marriage resulting from an Olympic Games was that of the American diver Alice Lord, and Olympic high jump champion, Dick Landon, soon after they returned home.

FINAL MEDAL STANDINGS

Nation	Gold	Silver	Bronze
UNITED STATES	41	26	27
SWEDEN	17	19	26
GREAT BRITAIN	15	15	12
BELGIUM	14	11	10
FINLAND	14	10	9
NORWAY	13	7	8
ITALY	13	5	5
FRANCE	9	19	13
NETHERLANDS	4	2	5
DENMARK	3	9	1
SOUTH AFRICA	3	4	3
CANADA	2	3	3
SWITZERLAND	2	2	7
ESTONIA	1	2	—
BRAZIL	1	1	1
AUSTRALIA	—	2	1
JAPAN	—	2	—
SPAIN	—	2	—
GREECE	—	1	—
LUXEMBOURG	—	1	—
CZECHOSLOVAKIA	—	—	1
NEW ZEALAND	—	—	1

SKATING & ICE HOCKEY MEDALS

Nation	Gold	Silver	Bronze
SWEDEN	2	1	0
FINLAND	1	—	—
CANADA	1	—	—
NORWAY	—	2	1
UNITED STATES	—	1	1
GREAT BRITAIN	—	—	1
CZECHOSLOVAKIA	—	—	1

1924 *Winter*

THE 1st WINTER GAMES

CHAMONIX/ MONT BLANC, FRANCE *25 JANUARY – 4 FEBRUARY 1924*

Attended by representatives of 16 countries, comprising 294 competitors of which 13 were women.

After the skating and ice hockey events held in 1908 and 1920 as part of the Summer Games celebrations it was finally decided to hold a separate Winter festival. This had been initially opposed by the Scandinavian countries who felt it would detract from their own Nordic Games. At first the Chamonix gathering was entitled the 'International Winter Sports Week' but later, in 1926, they were retrospectively accorded the official title of Winter Games. The French Under-Secretary for Physical Education, Gaston Vidal, officially opened the proceedings, and the oath was taken by all the flag bearers, that of France being by a skier Camille Mandrillon. Seventeen countries marched in the opening ceremony but Estonia did not have any competitors in the actual competitions.

The first ever official Olympic Winter gold medallist was Charles Jewtraw (USA) when he won the 500m speed skating event on 26 January, which made it the earliest gold medal ever won in an Olympic year (see p 11). It was the only medal won by a speed skater from other than Finland or Norway. Clas Thunberg (FIN) won three golds, one silver and one bronze (tied) to dominate the sport. In skiing, only the Nordic variety was held as Alpine Skiing was still in its infancy: Norway's Thorleif Haug won three gold medals. He was also originally awarded the bronze in the special jumping event, but 50 years later it was discovered that the points had been incorrectly added together and that the fourth placed jumper, Anders Haugen, a Norwegian-born American had beaten him. In place of her deceased father, Haug's daughter presented the

Clas Thunberg (FIN) added five world titles to his record seven Olympic speed skating medals between 1923 and 1931.

1924 *Summer*

THE VIIIth OLYMPIC GAMES

PARIS,
FRANCE
*4 MAY –
27 JULY 1924*

bronze medal to the 86 year old Haugen in 1974.

Canada retained its title from 1920 in ice hockey, scoring 110 goals to 3 against in five matches. At figure skating Gillis Gråfström (SWE) gained the second of his three gold medals. He was later to gain even more fame as coach of Sonja Henie (NOR) who was an 11 year old competitor at Chamonix placed eighth and last in the women's event. Aside from her Olympic successes she was to earn an estimated $47·5 million from her film and ice show activities, making her the richest ever female Olympian. The inaugural 4-man bobsleigh title was won by the Swiss, the first of a record four titles they have won in this discipline. Curling and a military patrol were held as demonstration events.

The oldest gold medallist at Chamonix was the previously mentioned 36 year old Anders Haugen (USA), while the youngest was a member of Switzerland's 4-man bob team, Heinrich Schläppi, aged 18 yr 279 days.

One result of these Winter Games was the founding, two days before the closing ceremony, of the International Ski Federation (FIS).

FINAL MEDAL STANDINGS

Nation	Gold	Silver	Bronze
NORWAY	4	7	6
FINLAND	4	3	3
AUSTRIA	2	1	—
UNITED STATES	1	2	1
SWITZERLAND	1	—	1
CANADA	1	—	—
SWEDEN	1	—	—
GREAT BRITAIN	—	1	2
BELGIUM	—	—	1
FRANCE	—	—	1

Attended by representatives of 44 countries, comprising 3092 competitors, of which 136 were women.

Originally scheduled to be held in Amsterdam, the Games were transferred to Paris at the request of de Coubertin, because it was the thirtieth anniversary of the concept of the Modern Games and also because he wanted to eradicate the bad image that Paris had acquired after the 1900 débâcle. In this connection the IOC had taken steps to impose its authority on the staging of the Olympic Games so that never again could a host country add events as it wished. The stadium at Colombes, with a 500 m track built in 1909, was enlarged for the occasion to accommodate 60 000 spectators. An Olympic village had been proposed but the idea was not carried through, although the athletes were housed in a collection of huts scattered around the main stadium. Four of the five 'enemy' countries in the war were included in the record number of nations accepting invitations, but Germany was not present. Franco-German relations were particularly frosty at this time. Among the newcomers were Ireland, competing separately from Britain for the first time, Romania and Poland. Polish sportsmen had competed before but always in the teams of other countries. The Games were formally opened by the President of France, Gaston Doumergue, and were attended by well over 600 000 spectators in total. The weather was too good at times, reported as over 40°C for the cross-country race.

Despite, for the first time, all sports being organized by their international governing bodies, and the instigation of International Juries of Appeal, there were a number of complaints about unfair decisions. In particular this was so at the boxing where Britain's Harry Mallin retained his middleweight title under unusual circumstances (see p 90).

The newly instituted Olympic motto, *Cirius, Altius, Fortius* (faster, higher, stronger) originally composed by Father Henri Didon in 1895, was taken to heart. Numerous records were set, sometimes unexpectedly. The long jump was won by William DeHart Hubbard (USA), with 7·44 m. Another American, Robert LeGendre, had been left out of that event but entered in the athletic pentathlon in which he broke the world long jump record with 7·76 m on the way to winning a bronze medal. Two British runners caused upsets, when Harold Abrahams became the first European to win an Olympic sprint title, and Eric Liddell, who had withdrawn from the 100 m because it was run on a Sunday, won the 400 m in a new world record time of 47·6 sec. Abrahams later recollected that there were no victory ceremonies and that he had received his gold medal by post some weeks later. A unique double was achieved by Harold Osborn (USA) by taking the decathlon title and the individual high jump. In the latter event, Osborn's habit of pressing the bar back against the uprights with his hand as he jumped using the Western Roll style led to a change in the event's rules.

The rules in another event resulted in a strange set of circumstances when the third finisher in the 400 m hurdles was credited with a new Olympic record (also bettering the world mark). This happened because the winner, Frank Morgan Taylor (USA) had knocked down a hurdle, while the second finisher Charles Brookins (USA) had been disqualified for leaving his lane. The eventual silver medallist, third finisher Erik Vilen (FIN) claimed the record. In fourth place was Georges André (FRA) who had taken the oath at the opening ceremony and who had placed second in the 1908 high jump.

The track events were dominated by the Finns with their outstanding stars Paavo Nurmi and Ville Ritola. Nurmi won five gold medals, then a record, and the American-based Ritola won four golds and two silvers for a record six medals in all. Nurmi's victories consisted of the 1500 m

Harold Abrahams wins the 1924 Olympic 100 m. (Left to right) Porritt (NZL) third, Abrahams (GBR), Bowman

and 5000 m titles, won within 100 minutes on the same day, the 3000 m team race, and the 10 000 m cross-country team and individual titles. In this latter event, run in record high temperatures, only 15 of the 38 starters finished, as Nurmi beat Ritola by well over a minute. The statue of Nurmi which stands outside the stadium in Helsinki was sculpted in 1925 to commemorate his Paris achievements.

Swimming saw the debut of Johnny Weissmuller, who not only won three gold medals in freestyle events but also gained a bronze as a member of the US water polo team. After more gold medals 4 years later, he turned to films and became the most famous 'Tarzan' of all time. His teammate Gertrude Ederle, who had become the youngest person ever to set a world record in 1919 at the age of 12 yr 298 days, here won a gold in the relay, and 2 years later was the first woman to swim the English Channel. The swimming pool at Paris saw the introduction into the Olympics of lane dividers. In rowing, another American later to gain fame in a different field was Benjamin Spock, number 7 in the victorious Yale crew representing the United States. He was to gain world-wide renown as a best-selling writer and paediatrician.

France came into her own in the fencing and cycling events. In the former Roger Ducret won three golds and one silver, while in the latter, Armand Blanchonnet won the 188 km road race by a near-record margin of over 9 min. A pointer to the future came in the soccer final which was won by Uruguay, the first South American country to enter the Olympic football competition.

(USA) fourth, Scholz (USA) second, Murchison (USA) sixth, Paddock (USA) fifth.

FINAL MEDAL STANDINGS

Nation	Gold	Silver	Bronze
UNITED STATES	45	27	27
FINLAND	14	13	10
FRANCE	13	15	10
GREAT BRITAIN	9	13	12
ITALY	8	3	5
SWITZERLAND	7	8	10
NORWAY	5	2	3
SWEDEN	4	13	12
NETHERLANDS	4	1	5
BELGIUM	3	7	3
AUSTRALIA	3	1	2
DENMARK	2	5	2
HUNGARY	2	3	4
YUGOSLAVIA	2	—	—
CZECHOSLOVAKIA	1	4	5
ARGENTINA	1	3	2
ESTONIA	1	1	4
SOUTH AFRICA	1	1	1
LUXEMBOURG	1	1	—
GREECE	1	—	—
URUGUAY	1	—	—
AUSTRIA	—	3	1
CANADA	—	3	1
IRELAND	—	1	1
POLAND	—	1	1
HAITI	—	—	1
JAPAN	—	—	1
NEW ZEALAND	—	—	1
PORTUGAL	—	—	1
ROMANIA	—	—	1

Now aged 45 yr Alfred Swahn, the son of the incredible Oscar, who had qualified for the team but was too ill to travel to Paris, won his ninth medal in four Games. With those won by his father the family total was six golds, four silvers, five bronzes. Carl Osburn (USA) by gaining a silver in shooting brought his individual total since 1912 to eleven medals, consisting of five gold, four silver and two bronze.

Tennis made its last appearance but had an all-star cast, with all titles won by Wimbledon champions, including Norris Williams, who partnered Hazel Wightman in the mixed doubles, and who had been one of the survivors of the *Titanic* disaster in 1912. Rugby also disappeared leaving the United States as reigning Olympic champions.

The oldest gold medallist at these Games was Allen Whitty a member of the British team in the running deer shooting event. A major in the Worcestershire regiment awarded the DSO in 1916 Whitty was aged 58 yr 82 days, and became Britain's oldest ever Olympic gold medal winner. The youngest winner at Paris was featherweight boxing champion Jackie Fields (USA) aged 16 yr 162 days. The youngest female winner was 400 m freestyle champion Martha Norelius (USA) at 16 yr 177 days, while the oldest female gold medallist was Ellen Osiier (DEN), wife of the redoubtable Ivan (see p 22), aged 33 yr 326 days when winning the inaugural women's fencing title.

The United States won the major share of the medals at Paris but a record number of 30 countries shared in the total.

1928 *Winter*

THE IInd WINTER GAMES

ST MORITZ, SWITZERLAND
11–19 FEBRUARY 1928

Attended by representatives of 25 countries, comprising 495 competitors, of which 27 were women.

The decision that the same country should host both Summer and Winter editions of the Games had to be abandoned in 1928, although the principle was thought to be a sound one. The Games were officially declared open by the President of

Switzerland, Edmund Schulthess and the oath was taken by Hans Eidenbenz, a Swiss skier. Newcomers at Winter Games were teams from Japan, Holland, Romania and Mexico. Unseasonal weather threatened the programme and led to the cancellation of one speed skating event, and the curtailment of the bobsleigh from four runs to two. On one day the temperature varied by over 20°C from morning to afternoon.

The cancellation of the 10 000 m skating by the Norwegian referee particularly caused bad feeling among the American team as at that point Irving Jaffee (USA) was surprisingly leading (see p 237). Despite vigorous protests by all nationalities no medals were awarded. In the other events Clas Thunberg (FIN) added two more golds to his 1924 haul to amass a total of five golds, one silver and one bronze, a record for the sport. There was a unique occurrence in the 500 m in which two men tied for first place and three men for third, with no silver medals awarded.

Another uncommon happening was in the skeleton toboggan conducted on the famous Cresta Run, where brothers Jennison and John Heaton (USA) gained the gold and silver medals respectively. The bobsleigh, for the first and only time composed of 5-man teams, also went to the United States. The driver of their team, William Fiske, aged only 16 yr 260 days, was the youngest ever male gold medallist at a Winter Games. At the other end of the scale, pair skating witnessed the last appearance of the 1920 champions Ludowika and Walter Jakobsson (FIN) who were placed fifth, their ages totalling 89 years.

The men's skating event gave Gillis Gräfström (SWE) his third consecutive gold medal, but the name on everybody's lips was that of the winner of the women's title, Sonja Henie (NOR). Her interpretation of the 'Dying Swan' from Tchaikowsky's *Swan Lake* ballet began a whole new era for the sport.

In the Nordic skiing, Johan Grottumsbraaten (NOR) won the 18 km race and the Nordic Combination, racing and jumping, title to match Thunberg's two wins. The individual jump event went to Alf Andersen (NOR) after the defending champion Jacob Tullin-Thams (NOR) nearly killed himself crashing at the end

Johan Gröttumsbraaten (NOR) won the 18 km and combination events in 1928, and then retained the combination title in 1932.

of a phenomenal jump of some 73 m on a hill only designed for jumps of 8 m less. A true Olympian he returned in 1936 to win a silver medal at yachting.

As was becoming a habit the Canadians easily won the ice hockey tournament scoring a total of 38 goals to none against. The only demonstration event was a military patrol contest.

The oldest gold medallist at St Moritz was Clifford Gray (USA) in the 5-man bob aged 36 yr 21 days, while the youngest was Sonja Henie at 15 yr 316 days.

FINAL MEDAL STANDINGS

Nation	Gold	Silver	Bronze
NORWAY	6	4	5
UNITED STATES	2	2	2
SWEDEN	2	2	1
FINLAND	2	1	1
CANADA	1	—	—
FRANCE	1	—	—
AUSTRIA	—	3	1
BELGIUM	—	—	1
CZECHOSLOVAKIA	—	—	1
GERMANY	—	—	1
SWITZERLAND	—	—	1
GREAT BRITAIN	—	—	1

Double gold-medallist Miruts Yifter of Ethiopia
circles the track in the shadow of the Olympic
flame at Moscow. He had missed the previous
Games because of the 'African' boycott.

The Zimbabwe ladies hockey team on the rostrum after their surprise victory in the 1980 tournament. On the right is the then President of the IOC, Lord Killanin. Below: Hanni Wenzel of Liechtenstein in the 1980 giant slalom, the first of her two title winning events. Only five countries won more gold medals than she did at Lake Placid.

In addition to his Olympic triumphs at Munich and Montreal Vasiliy Alexeyev set up an unmatched total of 80 world records during his career.

Below: **Irena Szewinska (née Kirszenstein) of Poland after winning the 400 m title in 1976.**

Vera Caslavska (CZE) on the beam in 1964, one of the events she won that year. Her total of seven gold medals, won in 1964 and 1968, is the most ever gained by a woman in individual events.

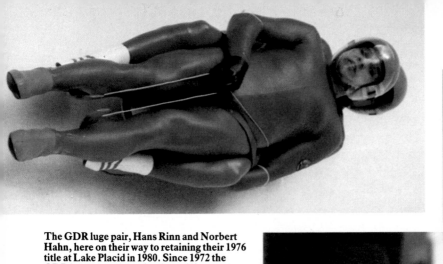

The GDR luge pair, Hans Rinn and Norbert Hahn, here on their way to retaining their 1976 title at Lake Placid in 1980. Since 1972 the GDR luge teams have dominated the sport winning eight of the nine titles available.

Eric Heiden, America's yellow flash in 1980 when he won an unprecedented five gold medals at Lake Placid in speed skating. After the Games he turned his talents to cycling.

Britain's middle distance triumvirate, Steve Ovett, Steve Cram and Sebastian Coe in the 1980 1500 m final. They have made the event a British preserve since 1978, winning all the major titles and setting numerous world records.

Left: **In the gymnastics events at Moscow it was a man, Aleksandr Ditiatin, who won the attention that had been reserved for the female stars in the previous four Games. He won a medal in each discipline open to him, winning a record total of eight medals at a single Games.**

Right: **Rosi Mittermaier (FRG) was the star of the skiing at Innsbruck in 1976, narrowly failing to emulate Sailer and Killy as the winner of all three Alpine events at one Games.**

Below: **Lasse Viren completes the 'double' by adding the 5000 m to his 10 000 m title at Munich in 1972. Seen here beating Mohamed Gammoudi (TUN) and Ian Stewart (GBR), the latest of the Flying Finns repeated his triumphs in 1976 for a unique double 'double'.**

Above: **The only diver to win an Olympic title on three consecutive occasions, Klaus Dibiasi of Italy won the highboard event from 1968 to 1976 after having placed second in 1964. Right: Aleksandr Tikhonov (URS) won a gold medal on the biathlon relay for the fourth consecutive time in 1980.**

The Munich Olympic complex, showing the massive steel and acrylic roofing which accounted for a sizeable portion of the £300 million plus outlay on the 1972 Games.

1928 *Summer*

THE IXth OLYMPIC GAMES

AMSTERDAM, NETHERLANDS
17 MAY – 12 AUGUST 1928

Attended by representatives of 46 countries, comprising 3014 competitors, of which 290 were women.

The Dutch finally hosted the Games after unsuccessfully applying for those of 1916, 1920 and 1924. A new stadium holding 40 000 spectators was built on reclaimed land. It contained a 400 m running track (this size was then standardized for future Games) encircled by a cycle track. The design of the stadium won the architect, Jan Wils, an Olympic prize in the architecture competition. An innovation was the building of a large results board. Other new ideas, at the opening ceremony, were the release of hundreds of pigeons – a symbol of peace derived from the Ancient Games – and the burning of an Olympic flame throughout the period of the competitions. The formal opening was by HRH Prince Hendrik, the consort of Queen Wilhelmina who was on a State visit to Norway, although the Queen herself handed out medals at the end of the Games. The record number of countries included Rhodesia and Panama for the first time, and the return of Germany in great strength.

Ville Ritola (FIN) leading Paavo Nurmi (FIN) and Edvin Wide (SWE) in the 10 000 m at Amsterdam. The three won a total of 25 medals between 1920 and 1928.

After much argument in world sporting circles, women were allowed to compete in track and field for the first time. They were only allowed five events, but world records were set in all five, including the 800 m which witnessed such harrowing scenes of distress that 'distance' events were omitted from the women's programme until 1964. In winning the 800 m Lina Radke won the first ever Olympic track and field gold medal for Germany. Her teammate, Anni Holdmann, became the first girl to win an Olympic track race by finishing first in heat 1 of the 100 m on 30 July. Another first in the sport was a gold medal for Japan by Mikio Oda in the triple jump.

The Finns again dominated the athletics events, although Nurmi only won one gold (the 10 000 m) and two silvers. Looking far older than his 31 years, due to his increasing baldness, the dour Finn offered some light relief when he fell at the water jump in the steeplechase and consistently had problems with the other barriers. Nevertheless he gained one of his silver medals in the event, although he had damaged his ever-present stopwatch in his fall. The unheralded Canadian youngster, Percy Williams, won both sprints. Lord Burghley became the first member of the British House of Lords to win an Olympic athletic title with an Olympic record in the 400 m hurdles, and his team-mate Douglas Lowe successfully defended his 800 m title. The Americans were virtually shut out of the track races, gaining only the 400 m and relays. The marathon was taken by Mohamed El Ouafi, an Algerian representing France, who was the pathfinder for the great African distance runners to come.

The US team was under the control of the President of the US Olympic Committee, Major-General Douglas MacArthur, later in charge of the victorious US forces in the Pacific theatre of the Second World War. Though predominant in the swimming pool they also had shocks there too. In Amsterdam the Japanese won their first swimming medals, an indication of things to come. Honour was saved by Johnny Weissmuller in the 100 m and 4 × 200 m freestyle events. Dorothy Poynton (USA) won a silver medal in springboard diving when only 23 days past her 13th birthday, one of the youngest medallists ever. She won gold medals at the next two Games. There was an unfortunate mix-up in the result of the men's high diving when Farid Simaika of Egypt was initially awarded the gold medal on the basis of his greater total points score. The result was later reversed and the medal given to Pete Desjardins (USA) as more first place decisions had been made in his favour by the judges.

The Egyptian, Ibrahim Moustafa, won the light-heavyweight wrestling title to become the first non-European to take a Greco-Roman event in the Games. In yachting, Crown Prince Olav, later King Olav V of Norway, gained the first Olympic victory by a member of a Royal house when he was a crew member of *Norna* in the 6 m class.

In front of 50 000 spectators India won the hockey title for the first time. They were to retain the title until 1960. Their goalkeeper, Richard Allen, did not concede a single goal in the tournament, and only a total of three in the next two Games, while India scored a total of 102

goals. In the soccer tournament Uruguay retained its title, beating another South American country, Argentina, in the final.

One of the outstanding performances at the Games came in the show jumping where Frantisek Ventura of Czechoslovakia won the title on *Eliot* collecting no faults, an achievement unmatched until 1976.

The oldest gold medallist at these Games was Johann Anker, a team-mate of Crown Prince Olav in the Norwegian 6 m class yachting aged 57 yr 44 days. The youngest, also water-borne, was the cox of the Swiss pairs crew Hans Boúrquin aged only 14 yr. The youngest female champion was Elizabeth Robinson (USA) who gained the 100 m title aged 16 yr 343 days, while the oldest woman to win a gold medal was Virginie Hériot (FRA) in the 8 m yachting class aged 38 yr 15 days.

YOU OUGHT TO BE IN PICTURES

The 1928 Olympic Games turned out to be a goldmine for Hollywood talent scouts. In swimming, besides Johnny Weissmuller, there was also Buster Crabbe, bronze in the 1500 m freestyle and later to achieve fame as Buck Rogers. Though unplaced in 1928 Eleanor Holm (USA) won gold in 1932 and later became a glamorous leading lady, often playing opposite her two teammates. Silver medallist in the shot put was Herman Brix, who, as a much slimmed-down actor, under the name of Bruce Bennett, also started his film career as Tarzan but graduated to more serious roles. Sonja Henie (NOR) became one of the highest paid, and most popular, stars on the screen.

Olympic silver medallist in the 1928 shot put Herman Brix was one of the many sportsmen to play Tarzan in the movies. Under his screen name of Bruce Bennett, he later developed into a fine dramatic actor.

FINAL MEDAL STANDINGS

Nation	Gold	Silver	Bronze
UNITED STATES	22	18	16
GERMANY	10	7	14
FINLAND	8	8	9
SWEDEN	7	6	12
ITALY	7	5	7
SWITZERLAND	7	4	4
FRANCE	6	10	5
NETHERLANDS	6	9	4
HUNGARY	4	5	—
CANADA	4	4	7
GREAT BRITAIN	3	10	7
ARGENTINA	3	3	1
DENMARK	3	1	2
CZECHOSLOVAKIA	2	5	2
JAPAN	2	2	1
ESTONIA	2	1	2
EGYPT	2	1	1
AUSTRIA	2	—	1
AUSTRALIA	1	2	1
NORWAY	1	2	1
POLAND	1	1	3
YUGOSLAVIA	1	1	3
SOUTH AFRICA	1	—	2
INDIA	1	—	—
IRELAND	1	—	—
NEW ZEALAND	1	—	—
SPAIN	1	—	—
URUGUAY	1	—	—
BELGIUM	—	1	2
CHILE	—	1	—
HAITI	—	1	—
PORTUGAL	—	—	1
PHILIPPINES	—	—	1

1932 *Winter*

THE IIIrd WINTER GAMES

LAKE PLACID,
NEW YORK
STATE, USA
*4–15
FEBRUARY 1932*

Attended by representatives of 17 countries, comprising 306 competitors, of which 32 were women.

Using the North American mass-start system, Irving Jaffee (USA) wins the 5000 m speed skating title in 1932.

The Games were opened by the Governor of New York State, Franklin D Roosevelt, later to be President of the United States. His wife Eleanor took a ride down the bobsled course. The oath on behalf of all the competitors was taken by the American speed skater Jack Shea. An Olympic first was set in the opening ceremony by the British contingent when their flag was carried by a woman, skater Mollie Phillips.

Variable weather conditions necessitated that snow had to be brought in from Canada by lorries to make good some parts of the cross-country skiing runs. Indeed a thaw caused the 4-man bob event to be postponed until after the official closing ceremony on 13 February.

The figure skating events, held indoors for the first time, drew capacity crowds, and as many as 14 000 spectators watched the bobsledding events—a 2-man event having been inaugurated here.

Not surprisingly the Scandinavians swept the Nordic skiing, but an upset occurred in the speed skating where the Americans and Canadians dominated. It is arguable whether this was as much to do with the abilities of the North Americans as with the change of rules that the organizing committee had invoked. Instead of the more usual European system of competition taking place in pairs with the fastest times deciding the medal placings, American rules were in force, under which mass start races were held, similar to track running, with heats and finals. Lack of familiarity with the tactics employed, often quite physical, put the Europeans at a distinct disadvantage. Indeed Finland's four time gold medallist Clas Thunberg did not even bother to appear at Lake Placid.

The figure skating competitions saw the peerless Sonja Henie (NOR) easily retain her title, but triple champion Gillis Gräfström (SWE) was the victim of an unfortunate accident. During the compulsory figures he collided with a movie camera which had been allowed too near and fell heavily suffering a mild concussion, which may well have cost him an unprecedented fourth title. The women's event also saw the debut of the youngest ever Winter Olympics competitor, Cecilia Colledge, who at 11 yr and 24 days of age, was also Britain's youngest ever Olympic contestant at any sport. At the other end of the scale was the oldest ever Winter Games representative, Joseph Savage (USA) who took part in the pairs skating aged 53 yr. By successfully defending the pairs title Pierre and Andrée (née Joly) Brunet (FRA) became the only pair to win both as an unmarried and a married couple.

In ice hockey the Canadians won the gold medal for the fourth consecutive time, but only on goal average after three periods of overtime against the United States in the final game.

Making history of a different kind in the USA 4-man bob was Eddie Eagan, who as a late and virtually untried draftee to the team, driven by William Fiske, won a gold medal, and thus became the only man ever to win events in the Summer and Winter celebrations of the Olympic Games.

There were demonstrations given of curling, dog sled racing (won by Emile St Goddard of Canada), and three speed skating events for women. Women's speed skating, 28 years later, became an established Olympic event.

The oldest gold medallist at Lake Placid was Jay O'Brien (USA) in the 4-man bob aged 48 yr 359 days. The youngest was Sonja Henie (NOR) winning her second skating title aged 19 yr 308 days.

FINAL MEDAL STANDINGS

Nation	Gold	Silver	Bronze
UNITED STATES	6	4	2
NORWAY	3	4	3
CANADA	1	1	5
SWEDEN	1	2	—
FINLAND	1	1	1
AUSTRIA	1	1	—
FRANCE	1	—	—
SWITZERLAND	—	1	—
GERMANY	—	—	2
HUNGARY	—	—	1

1932 *Summer*

THE Xth OLYMPIC GAMES

LOS ANGELES, USA
30 JULY –
14 AUGUST 1932

Attended by representatives of 37 countries, comprising 1408 competitors, of which 127 were women.

As early as 1920 the US delegation led by William May Garland had applied for either the 1924 or 1928 Games to be held in Los Angeles. However, both of these celebrations had already been allocated and the American proposal was amended to refer to 1932. At the IOC meeting in Rome in 1923 the invitation was accepted. Some trepidation was evident as the only other occasion on which the Games were held outside Europe, in 1904 at St Louis, they had been somewhat of a farce. Also worrying were the great distances, and therefore cost, involved for most countries to get to the west coast of the United States. On the favourable side was the undoubted excellent weather conditions that would prevail, and the announcement by the organizing committee that they would subsidize the transportation, housing and feeding costs of all contingents greatly offset the critics. Another major problem which eventually arose was the spread of the Great Depression which was felt to be an inappropriate period in which to hold such a sports festival.

These considerations gave birth to the Olympic 'Village', a concept previously considered but never realized. Consisting of 550 specially designed small houses, it was located in the Baldwin Hills, but was only for male contestants. It was strictly guarded by cowboys who 'rode the fences' around the perimeter. Female competitors were housed separately in the Chapman Park Hotel, and the rule barring women from the village was so strict that the Finnish team's lady cook was not allowed entry.

Although many of the European teams undertook journeys lasting 2 weeks to reach Los Angeles, they found, as promised, excellent weather and first class facilities awaiting them. The main stadium was the Los Angeles Coliseum, which had been begun in 1921 and opened the year the Games were awarded to the city.

In 1930 it had been enlarged to hold 101 000 spectators, all seated, and it had a new crushed peat running surface. In addition there was the 10 000 seat Swimming Stadium, the State Armory where the fencing was conducted, the Olympic Auditorium, seating 10 000 to watch the boxing, wrestling and weightlifting events, and the Los Angeles Museum of History, Science and Art which was home for the fine art competitions. Long Beach Harbour was the venue for the yachting, and the Long Beach Marine Stadium hosted the rowing. A specially built wooden track was erected in the world-famous Pasadena Rose Bowl for the cycling events.

The Games were formally opened by the Vice President of the United States, Charles Curtis, on behalf of President Hoover who was in the middle of an electioneering tour. The oath on behalf of all the competitors was taken by an American fencer Lieut George Calnan of the US Navy, who died the following April when the dirigible *Akron* crashed into the Pacific Ocean. Although the number of teams, and total competitors, were lower than at Amsterdam, there were two countries which had never before attended, Columbia and China, both with sole representatives, neither of whom achieved any success. However, another small team, Ireland with only eight men, finished well up the medal table with two gold medals.

Los Angeles saw the introduction of a number of new ideas. Included in these was the use of photo-finish equipment—the Kirby Two-Eyed Camera—for the track and field races. Although it could accurately give times to one-hundredth of a second it was only used to decide close finishes, and only a few of the timings have ever come to light. Another innovation was the use of a three-tiered victory stand, with medal awarding ceremonies involving the raising of national flags taking place at the end of each day's events. In boxing, the system of having the referee in the ring with the boxers was introduced into the Games for the first time, although it did not settle all arguments in that sport. Remarkably there was only one knockout, and that was a technical knockout (TKO) in the preliminaries of the heavyweight division, throughout the whole boxing programme.

As with all such international gatherings there were some unfortunate incidents, but in the main they were of minor importance. Prior to the arrival of teams there was a major 'scandal' with the banning of the great Finnish runner Paavo Nurmi under charges of professionalism—he was accused of accepting unduly large expenses on a German tour. Despite rigorous protests on his behalf the Finnish Federation finally accepted the ruling although they had already picked him for the marathon race and indeed he arrived with the team in Los Angeles. The Finns were also involved in another incident once the Games were underway when the runners in the 3000 m steeplechase ran an extra lap due to a miscalculation by the lap counter. Luckily the error did not appear to have altered the final medal placings. Another minor irritation was the American habit of announcing all the field event results only in Imperial units of measurements, much to the annoyance, and bafflement, of the foreign competitors and spectators. But there were two more serious occurrences, one on the track and one in the swimming pool. The first was when the eventual winner of the 5000 m, Lauri Lehtinen (FIN) deliberately blocked the American, Ralph Hill, twice in the final stages of the race, a not uncommon practice in Europe, but one which drew loud booing from the basically partisan crowd. They were quickly quietened by the announcer, Bill Henry, whose words 'Remember please, these people are our guests' have entered Olympic lore.

The second incident was of a much more serious nature when the Brazilian water polo team, after losing 7–3 to Germany, lost their tempers and insulted the referee. They were disqualified from the tournament.

Over 100 000 people packed into the Coliseum in Los Angeles for the opening ceremony of the 1932 Games. The stadium will also host the 1984 ceremony.

The Austrian team arriving at the Olympic village in the hills outside Los Angeles in 1932

men's jumping events.

The oldest gold medallist at Los Angeles was Xavier Lesage (FRA) who won the dressage event aged 46 yr 290 days. The youngest was Kusuo Kitamura (JAP) who won the 1500 m freestyle swimming event aged 14 yr 309 days. The youngest female champion was Claire Dennis (AUS) winner of the 200 m breaststroke aged 16 yr 117 days. The oldest female winner was Lillian Copeland (USA) who won the discus aged 27 yr 251 days.

As in previous Games the host country was allowed to put on demonstration sports and here they were American Football and Lacrosse. During the closing ceremony the President of the IOC, Count de Baillet-Latour, presented Olympic Merit Awards for Alpinism to Franz and Toni Schmid (GER) for the first climb of the north face of the Matterhorn.

Despite all the economic and organizational misgivings the Xth Games were a great success, attended by a total of 1¼ million spectators, and at the end there was a profit of about $1 million.

On the brighter side there were the inevitable stars of the Games, and perhaps the outstanding individual was a woman, Mildred Ella 'Babe' Didrikson, an American born of Norwegian parents. Much to her annoyance she was only allowed to enter for three events. She set world and Olympic records in each of them, winning the javelin and the 80 m hurdles, and gaining the silver medal in the high jump. A strange judgement was made in this event, for though she cleared the same height as her teammate Jean Shiley, and then tied in a jump-off, the judges decided that her 'Western Roll' style of jump had been performed illegally, with her head preceding her body over the bar, and illogically they placed her second.

Another unusual event occurred in the 400 m hurdles reminiscent of 1924 (see p 30), in which the Irishman, Bob Tisdall, who is reported to have spent most of the preceding days in bed recuperating from a long and tiring journey, won the gold medal with a clocking of 51·7 sec. However, the world record went to the silver medallist Glenn Hardin (USA), with 52·0 sec. This was due to the fact that Tisdall had knocked down the tenth and last hurdle.

Other crowd favourites were the Indian hockey team, who while not quite so invincible as previously, nevertheless set a record winning score by beating the United States by 24–1, with Roop Singh scoring 12 of them. Similarly in the water polo competition, Hungary beat Japan by 18–0, for a record score.

Particularly noteworthy was the rise of Japan as a force in the men's swimming, highlighted by their remarkable improvement of the 4 × 200 m relay world record by 37·8 sec, and also in the

FINAL MEDAL STANDINGS

Nation	Gold	Silver	Bronze
UNITED STATES	41	32	30
ITALY	12	12	12
FRANCE	10	5	4
SWEDEN	9	5	9
JAPAN	7	7	4
HUNGARY	6	4	5
FINLAND	5	8	12
GERMANY	4	12	5
GREAT BRITAIN	4	7	5
AUSTRALIA	3	1	1
ARGENTINA	3	1	—
CANADA	2	5	8
NETHERLANDS	2	5	—
POLAND	2	1	4
SOUTH AFRICA	2	—	3
IRELAND	2	—	—
CZECHOSLOVAKIA	1	2	1
AUSTRIA	1	1	3
INDIA	1	—	—
DENMARK	—	3	3
MEXICO	—	2	—
LATVIA	—	1	—
NEW ZEALAND	—	1	—
SWITZERLAND	—	1	—
PHILIPPINES	—	—	3
SPAIN	—	—	1
URUGUAY	—	—	1

1936 *Winter*

THE IVth WINTER GAMES

GARMISCH-PARTENKIRCHEN, GERMANY
6–16 FEBRUARY 1936

Attended by representatives of 28 countries, comprising 755 competitors, of which 80 were women.

The Games were seen by many as a test case of how the German Olympic Committee would react to the demands of the National Socialist government of Germany. There had been much heated discussion around the world as to the advisability of attending these, or the later Summer Games, due to the racialist policies of that government. A record entry included teams from Bulgaria, Turkey, Australia, Spain and Liechtenstein for the first time. The Games were declared open by Chancellor Adolf Hitler, and Wilhelm Bogner, a skier, took the oath on behalf of the competitors. By the end of the competitions, over 500 000 paying spectators had watched the six different sports. These now included Alpine skiing, although the only event was a combination one, for both men and women.

Sonja Henie (NOR) in 1936 climaxed a unique Olympic skating career, having competed first in 1924 when only 11 years old.

Birger Ruud (NOR) successfully defended his jumping title, the only ski jumper ever to do so, and then caused a surprise by winning the downhill segment of the men's Alpine combination. By dint of a 5·9 sec margin of victory in the slalom segment the title went to Germany's Franz Pfnur and Ruud fell back to fourth place. In the women's event there was a similar situation when the downhill race was won by 16 year old Laila Schou Nilsen (NOR), who held five world speed skating records but had entered the skiing in the absence of such events for women. In the slalom segment Christel Cranz (GER), who was eventually to win a record 12 world skiing championships, won by the quite remarkable margin of 11·3 sec and took the overall gold medal, Nilsen gaining the bronze.

The top medal winner was Ivar Ballangrud of Norway who won three golds and one silver in the speed skating. Contrary to the Lake Placid conditions the racers competed under European-style rules with pairs of skaters racing against the clock. Sonja Henie bade the sport farewell with a third consecutive gold medal, to add to her ten world championships, and headed for Hollywood, followed some time later by the 12th placed British girl, Gladys Jepson-Turner, who gained cinematic fame as Belita. The British caused a major upset in ice hockey when their team, composed mainly of Anglo-Canadians, won the title from the previously all-conquering Canadians. In the ice hockey competition appeared Rudi Ball, one of only two athletes of Jewish origin to be selected by Germany in 1936, the other was in the Summer Games. Ball, a bronze medallist from 1932, was specially requested to return from his exile in France to compete. Much was made of this by the host country to offset criticism of its attitude to Jewish sportsmen and women.

A most unusual double was sought by Ernst Baier (GER) who won the pairs skating with Maxi Herber, but only came second in the men's individual skating event. It was still the highest such double placing ever. Sister and brother Ilse and Erik Pausin (AUT) the pairs silver medallists, were the youngest ever couple to gain a medal in the event, their ages totalling 32 yr 307 days. Demonstrations of German curling and the military patrol were held.

The youngest gold medallist at Garmisch was Maxi Herber (see above) aged 15 yr 128 days, while the oldest was Alan Washbond (USA) in the 2-man bob aged 36 yr 124 days.

FINAL MEDAL STANDINGS

Nation	Gold	Silver	Bronze
NORWAY	7	5	3
GERMANY	3	3	—
SWEDEN	2	2	3
FINLAND	1	2	3
AUSTRIA	1	1	2
SWITZERLAND	1	2	—
GREAT BRITAIN	1	1	1
UNITED STATES	1	—	3
CANADA	—	1	—
FRANCE	—	—	1
HUNGARY	—	—	1

1936 *Summer*

THE XIth OLYMPIC GAMES

BERLIN, GERMANY
1–16 AUGUST 1936

Attended by representatives of 49 countries, comprising 4066 competitors, of which 328 were women.

The Games had been awarded to Germany just prior to the rise to power of Adolf Hitler and the National Socialist (Nazi) Party. Abhorrence of Germany's policies under this government and revulsion at its racialist attitudes led many countries, not least the United States, to seriously consider boycotting the Games. The President of the US Olympic Committee, Avery Brundage, was strongly in favour of going and eventually won the day. In Germany itself the notorious Heinrich Himmler was opposed to the Games being held, but Josef Goebbels convinced Hitler that they would present tremendous propaganda opportunities. The Games were held under very heavy political overtones, an example

being the last minute withdrawal of the Spanish team owing to the outbreak of civil war in their country.

It had been intended to enlarge the stadium which had been built for the aborted 1916 Games, but when Hitler took over he decreed that a new giant stadium be constructed. The architect of the 100 000 capacity structure was Werner March, whose father had designed the 1916 stadium. In addition other fine stadia and halls were built, as well as an Olympic village of 150 buildings far superior to anything seen before. The yachting events were catered for at Kiel on the north-west coast. At the instigation of Carl Diem, the main organizer, a torch relay was inaugurated to bring the sacred Olympic flame from the Temple of Zeus at Olympia to the stadium in Berlin. Over 3000 runners crossed seven countries taking 10 days to cover the distance.

The Games were formally opened by Chancellor Hitler, as a specially commissioned $16\frac{1}{2}$ ton bell was rung and thousands of pigeons set free. As the massive German contingent, 406 strong, entered, the giant airship *Hindenburg* flew over the stadium. With full government backing the team was undoubtedly the best prepared team ever to compete in the Games.

As a sop to foreign criticism it contained one athlete of Jewish origin, the 1928 gold medal fencer Helène Mayer, who had been persuaded to return from America for the Games, with the promise of full 'Aryan' classification. Ironically she placed second to an Hungarian Jewess Ilona Elek in the foil event. At the opening, the 1896 marathon victor, Spiridon Louis, attired in national dress, presented Hitler with an olive branch—signifying peace—from Olympia. In the march-past of teams a number of them gave the Nazi salute, but the United States and Great Britain merely made the traditional 'eyes right'. The music for the opening ceremony was conducted by the famous composer Richard Strauss. An indication of the future came with the first ever use of television to cover the Games, with a closed circuit system to special halls, operated by the Reich Rundfunkgesellschaft, and watched by 150 000 people at 28 venues.

Very high standards were reached at the Games, and in the forefront of the record breaking were

Aerial view of the 1936 Olympic complex showing some of the immense crowds which packed the stadium and swimming pool every day.

the ten black members of the American track and field team. Anathema to the German propaganda machine, which dubbed them 'Black Auxiliaries' they won seven gold, three silver and three bronze medals between them, more than any other national team, including their own white teammates. Outstanding among them was sprinter-jumper Jesse Owens who won the 100 m, 200 m and long jump and was a member of the world record breaking relay team. The runner-up to Owens in the 200 m was Mack Robinson, whose brother Jackie was the first black major league baseball player.

Much has been written about Hitler refusing to meet and congratulate Owens and other black gold medallists. In fairness it should be realized that after he had made a point of personally greeting the German victors on the first day he was rebuked for the practice by the President of the IOC, Henri Baillet-Latour, who told him that only IOC designated people performed such duties in an Olympic stadium. After that he refrained from further congratulatory meetings, although it is reported that he met all German medallists in private.

Other track highlights included the superb sprinting of Helen Stephens (USA), the decathlon victory by teammate Glenn Morris, later to be yet another screen Tarzan, and the 1500 m world record by Jack Lovelock (NZ). This last event was considered by many as the highlight of the Games. The Finns took all three places in the 10 000 m, as well as first two places in the

5000 m and steeplechase, Volmari Iso-Hollo successfully defending his title in the latter.

Equally outstanding in the swimming pool were the Dutch women led by Hendrika Mastenbroek who personally won three golds and a silver. The winner of the women's springboard diving title, Marjorie Gestring (USA) became the youngest ever female gold medallist, and the youngest ever Olympic individual event winner, at the age of 13 yr 268 days. Robert Charpentier (FRA) won three gold medals in the cycling, where Toni Merkens (GER) won the 1000 m sprint event

One of the greatest athletes the world has known, Jesse Owens (USA) joined the Olympic immortals with his four gold medals at Berlin.

despite being fined, but not disqualified, for obstruction in the first race. In the wrestling, Kristian Palusalu of Estonia matched the achievement of Ivar Johansson (SWE) in 1932 winning titles in both the free and Greco-Roman styles of the sport. Johansson equalled the all-time record by winning his third wrestling gold medal.

In the list of gold medallists at Berlin can be found the name *Nurmi*, but in this case it is the name of the horse ridden by Ludwig Stubbendorf (GER) to his easy victory in the tough three-day event. Of the fourteen teams which started, only four finished with sufficient scorers. These included Britain, whose final placer, Capt Richard Fanshawe gained his team the bronze medal despite numerous penalty points incurred resulting from an arm broken during the competition.

Canoeing and basketball made their official Olympic debut, both having been demonstration sports at previous Games. The inventor of the latter, Dr James Naismith, was present in Berlin to see the US team begin its remarkable winning streak (see p 87).

At the end of the Games a magnificent film *Olympiad* was produced by Leni Riefenstahl, which though criticized by some as propaganda, is considered the best documentary record of an Olympics ever made.

The oldest gold medallist at these Games was Friedrich Gerhard (GER) in the dressage team aged 52 yr 20 days. The youngest was the above mentioned Marjorie Gestring. The youngest male champion was Adolph Kiefer (USA) who won the 100 m backstroke aged 18 yr 48 days. The oldest female winner was fencer Ilona Elek (HUN) at 29 yr 79 days.

THE OLYMPIC CONCEPT

One of the innovations at Berlin was the use of two sentences attributed to Baron de Coubertin, but actually based by him on words uttered by the Bishop of Pennsylvania at a service in St Paul's Cathedral prior to the opening of the 1908 Games in London. These words are now displayed on scoreboards at every opening ceremony.

The airship *Hindenburg*, named after the President of Germany, flying over the stadium on the day of the opening ceremony of the 1936 Games.

'The most important thing in the Olympic Games is not to win but to take part, just as the most important thing in life is not the triumph but the struggle. The essential thing is not to have conquered but to have fought well.'

FINAL MEDAL STANDINGS

Nation	Gold	Silver	Bronze
GERMANY	33	26	30
UNITED STATES	24	20	12
HUNGARY	10	1	5
ITALY	8	9	5
FINLAND	7	6	6
FRANCE	7	6	6
SWEDEN	6	5	9
JAPAN	6	4	8
NETHERLANDS	6	4	7
GREAT BRITAIN	4	7	3
AUSTRIA	4	6	3
CZECHOSLOVAKIA	3	5	—
ARGENTINA	2	2	3
ESTONIA	2	2	3
EGYPT	2	1	2
SWITZERLAND	1	9	5
CANADA	1	3	5
NORWAY	1	3	2
TURKEY	1	—	1
INDIA	1	—	—
NEW ZEALAND	1	—	—
POLAND	—	3	3
DENMARK	—	2	3
LATVIA	—	1	1
ROMANIA	—	1	—
SOUTH AFRICA	—	1	—
YUGOSLAVIA	—	1	—
MEXICO	—	—	3
BELGIUM	—	—	2
AUSTRALIA	—	—	1
PHILIPPINES	—	—	1
PORTUGAL	—	—	1

1948 *Winter*

**THE Vth
WINTER
GAMES**

**ST MORITZ,
SWITZERLAND
*30 JANUARY – 8
FEBRUARY 1948***

Attended by representatives of 28 countries, comprising 713 competitors, of which 77 were women.

In 1936 the Winter Games of 1940 had been awarded to Sapporo, Japan, but with the onset of the Sino-Japanese conflict they were re-awarded to St Moritz. Disagreements with the Swiss led the IOC to transfer the Games yet again, in June 1939, to Garmisch-Partenkirchen. At the same time they decided that the 1944 Games should go to Cortina d'Ampezzo in Italy. The Second World War put paid to all those plans and in 1946 a postal vote of IOC members gave the Vth Games to St Moritz. Untouched by the war St Moritz in neutral Switzerland was an obvious choice. As a winter sports resort there were plenty of hotels in which to put the competitors, as well as foreign visitors. However, poor weather conditions affected some of the competitions, and there were a number of disputes. Chile, Denmark, Iceland, Korea and Lebanon competed for the first time in the Winter Games. The oath was taken by ice hockey player Richard Torriani (SWI) on behalf of all the competitors, which did not include any from uninvited Germany or Japan, and President Enrico Celio of Switzerland formally declared the Games open. There were now six Alpine events and they attracted larger fields than the Nordic runs.

The most medals were won by Henri Oreiller (FRA) with gold in the downhill (by a record margin of 4·1 sec) and combination events and a bronze in the slalom. Gretchen Fraser (USA), unusually old for a female skier (see below), gained the first skiing title ever won by a non-European. In Nordic skiing the Swedes broke the Norwegian monopoly. They had the three medals and fifth place in the 18 km, first two and

fifth in the 50 km and won the 4 × 10 km relay by a margin of nearly 9 minutes. They also won their first ever speed skating gold medal when Ake Seyffarth won the 10 km event.

The athletic American figure skaters brought a new concept to the sport as Dick Button gained an easy victory. The ice hockey competition was the cause of a major row. Two American teams appeared at St Moritz. One represented the Amateur Hockey Association of the United States (AHA) and the other was one picked by the US Olympic Committee. The AHA, while not affiliated to the USOC, was a member of the International Hockey Federation (IHF). This last was the governing body of most of the other teams at the Games and threatened to withdraw all the hockey teams if the AHA team were not allowed to play. The USOC in turn threatened to withdraw its whole team if it did. Initially the IOC decided to bar both teams, but then agreed with the Swiss organizers and the IHF to allow the AHA team to compete. Strangely the USOC team members marched in the opening ceremony. The AHA team eventually finished fourth, but a year later the AHA was disqualified for non-affiliation to the Olympic movement. The Canadians won the title once more, but only just. The title was decided on goal average, with the team from Czechoslovakia taking the silver medal. The Swiss team in third place contained the man who had taken the oath Richard 'Bibi' Torriani, thus adding another bronze medal to the one he had won 20 years earlier when he was just past his sixteenth birthday.

The US bobsleds were sabotaged prior to the competitions, but it did not prevent them from gaining a gold and two bronze medals. In the skeleton toboggan, which is only held when the Games are at St Moritz, on the Cresta Run, John Heaton (USA) won his second silver medal, 20 years after his first. The gold medal was won by

Twenty five years after his Olympic triumph in 1948 Nino Bibbia (ITA) was still winning races on the Cresta Run.

Nino Bibbia of Italy, a country perhaps surprisingly not refused an invitation like its wartime ally, Germany. Bibbia was a master of the Cresta Run and won many titles and championships over the next quarter of a century.

The great Norwegian ski jumper, Birger Ruud, nearly 37 years old and a survivor of a wartime concentration camp, ended his Olympic career with a silver medal to add to his golds in 1932 and 1936. He and his brother Sigmund had made the event a family preserve since 1928. A third brother, Asbjörn was also in the 1948 team.

A record thirteen countries shared out the medals, and Italy (Bibbia) and Belgium (Micheline Lannoy and Pierre Baugniet in pair skating) gained their first ever Winter Games gold medals.

There were two demonstration events held in 1948: a military ski patrol, and a winter pentathlon. The latter consisted of 10 km cross-country skiing, pistol shooting, downhill skiing, fencing and horse riding over 3·5 km. No medals were awarded, but the second place winner was Captain Willie Grut (SWE) of whom much more was to be heard 6 months later, in London.

The oldest gold medallist at St Moritz was Francis Tyler (USA) in the 4-man bob aged 43 yr 58 days. The youngest was Dick Button (see above) aged 18 yr 202 days. The winner of the women's figure skating, Barbara-Ann Scott (CAN) was the youngest female champion aged 19 yr 273 days while the oldest female gold medallist was Gretchen Fraser (USA) in the slalom aged 28 yr 360 days.

FINAL MEDAL STANDINGS

Nation	Gold	Silver	Bronze
NORWAY	4	3	3
SWEDEN	4	3	3
SWITZERLAND	3	4	3
UNITED STATES	3	4	2
FRANCE	2	1	2
CANADA	2	—	1
AUSTRIA	1	3	4
FINLAND	1	3	2
BELGIUM	1	1	—
ITALY	1	—	—
CZECHOSLOVAKIA	—	1	—
HUNGARY	—	1	—
GREAT BRITAIN	—	—	1

1948 *Summer*

THE XIVth OLYMPIC GAMES

LONDON, GREAT BRITAIN
29 JULY – 14 AUGUST 1948

Attended by representatives of 59 countries, comprising 4099 competitors, of which 385 were women.

In 1936 the XIIth Games were awarded to Tokyo, to take place from 24 August – 8 September 1940. When the Sino-Japanese war began in 1938 the Games were then transferred to Helsinki, but the Soviet invasion of Finland cancelled all these plans. In June 1939, a very optimistic IOC awarded the XIIIth games, for 1944, to London, over competing claims of Detroit, Lausanne and Rome. A postal vote of IOC members called by the President, Sigfrid Edström of Sweden, in 1946 awarded the XIVth Games to London. In the meantime, Baron de Coubertin had died, in 1936, and his heart was buried at Olympia.

Organized by the British Olympic Association, under the Presidency of Lord Burghley, the 1948 Olympics were an austerity Games. Coming out of 6 years of war Britain still continued the rationing of food and clothing. Housing, particularly in London, was very short owing to the wartime bombing. Olympic competitors were housed in RAF and Army camps (for men) and college buildings (for women). A temporary running track was laid at the 83 000 capacity Wembley Stadium, the home of British football. Other existing buildings were adapted. Rowing events were held at Henley on the River Thames and the yachting was at Torbay, Devon. The total expenditure amounted to no more than £600 000, and final accounts suggested that a profit of over £10 000 was made. The Games were opened by King George VI. Not surprisingly Germany and Japan were not invited, but newcomers were Burma, Ceylon (now Sri

Lanka), British Guiana (now Guyana), Iraq, Iran, Jamaica, Korea, Lebanon, Pakistan, Puerto Rico, Singapore, Syria, Trinidad and Venezuela. Photo-finish equipment was used in the track and field events to decide places. Some of the hottest weather for years occurred on the opening days, but then it rained. The star of the Games was Francina 'Fanny' Blankers-Koen (HOL) who won four gold medals, a record for a woman, in the 100 m, 200 m, 80 m hurdles and sprint relay. The 30 year old Dutchwoman, a mother of two children, had finished equal sixth in the 1936 high jump. In 1948 she held seven world records including those in the high jump and long jump, neither of which she contested in London. In the high jump Dorothy Tyler (née Odam) (GBR) placed second again, 12 years after her other silver medal—both times she had cleared the same height as the winner. Bob Mathias (USA) became the youngest ever male Olympic champion in track and field events when he won the decathlon aged 17 yr 263 days. He was to retain the title 4 years later, have a film made of his life, and be elected to the US Congress. Another athlete to catch the attention was Emil Zatopek (TCH), not so much by his easy win in the 10 000 m, but by his remarkable

last 300 m sprint to narrowly lose the 5000 m. An American, Harrison Dillard, was acknowledged as the world's greatest high hurdler, but he had fallen in the US trials and failed to make their team in that event. In London he won his 'second string' event, the 100 m, and also won a gold medal in the sprint relay. Two of the new countries made their mark early in the Games. Duncan White of Ceylon gained the only medal his country has ever won by placing second in the 400 m hurdles. Jamaica made an even bigger impact by gaining one gold, two silvers and two other finallists in the 200 m, 400 m and 800 m. The marathon provided its usual drama when the first man to enter the stadium at the end of the race, Etienne Gailly, a Belgian paratrooper, was passed by two others before he finished completely exhausted.

One of the greatest sportsmen of this or any other Olympics must be the winner of the modern pentathlon event at London, Willie Grut (SWE). In this five-sport event he won three of the disciplines (riding, fencing, swimming) and placed fifth and eighth in the others, to win by a large margin. The son of the designer of the 1912 Olympic stadium he had already performed ex-

The first of Fanny Blankers-Koen's four gold medals—the 100 m in 1948. (Left to right) **Manley (GBR)** second, **Jones (CAN)** fifth, **Strickland (AUS)** third, **Thompson (JAM)** sixth, **Myers (CAN)** fourth.

tremely well at the Winter Games (see p 52). Another exceptional champion was the South African boxer George Hunter, who not only won the light-heavyweight title but also the Val Barker Trophy for the best stylist in the whole competition. However, lack of experienced referees and judges in the boxing resulted in much criticism. There were problems too at Herne Hill stadium where some of the cycling events finished in very bad light due to the lack of floodlighting.

There was an unfortunate turn of events in the equestrian competition where the team contest in the dressage was won by the Swedish team. However, the following year they were disqualified, and their medals taken away, when it was learned that one of their number, Gehnäll Persson was not a commissioned officer as the rules of the competition then required.

In the fencing Ilona Elek (HUN) retained her 1936 title even though she was now over 41 years old. Her sister Margit was in sixth position. The 1932 champion, Ellen Müller-Preis (AUT) gained the bronze medal. An even more outstanding veteran was Heikki Savolainen the famed Finnish gymnast, who in his fourth Olympics won his first gold medal, in the pommel horse, in his 41st year.

Sweden, the winners of the soccer tournament, were involved in one of the strangest goals in sports history in their semi-final against Denmark. The Swedish centre-forward Gunnar Nordahl, one of three brothers in the gold medal team, leaped into the Danish net at one point to avoid being offside during a Swedish attack. At the end of the move his inside-left Henry Carlsson headed into the goal, where in the absence of the Danish goalkeeper it was caught in the back of the net by Nordahl.

Yachting witnessed the end of one long Olympic career when the 1912 double sprint champion Ralph Craig reappeared in the unplaced American Dragon class boat. It also saw the start of another with the appearance of Durward Knowles for Britain, who then represented the Bahamas in the next six Games (see p 212). At the Empire Pool, site of the swimming competitions, Vickie Draves (USA) gained both women's diving titles. In freestyle swimming two other Americans, Ann Curtis and Jim McLane, both

won two golds and a silver. In all US swimmers and divers took 12 of the 15 events in the pool, excluding water polo which was won by Italy, its first medal in the sport. The winner of the women's 100 m was Greta Andersen (DEN) who in 1964 set a female record for swimming the English Channel.

The oldest gold medallist at these Games was Paul Smart (USA) in the Star class yachting aged 56 yr 212 days. The youngest was Thelma Kalama (USA) in the 4×100 m freestyle swimming relay aged 17 yr 135 days. Bob Mathias (see above) was the youngest male champion, while the oldest female gold medallist was the Hungarian fencer Ilona Elek aged 41 yr 77 days.

FINAL MEDAL STANDINGS

Nation	Gold	Silver	Bronze
UNITED STATES	38	27	19
SWEDEN	16	11	17
FRANCE	10	6	13
HUNGARY	10	5	12
ITALY	8	12	9
FINLAND	8	7	5
TURKEY	6	4	2
CZECHOSLOVAKIA	6	2	3
SWITZERLAND	5	10	5
DENMARK	5	7	8
NETHERLANDS	5	2	9
GREAT BRITAIN	3	14	6
ARGENTINA	3	3	1
AUSTRALIA	2	6	5
BELGIUM	2	2	3
EGYPT	2	2	1
MEXICO	2	1	2
SOUTH AFRICA	2	1	1
NORWAY	1	3	3
JAMAICA	1	2	—
AUSTRIA	1	1	3
INDIA	1	—	—
PERU	1	—	—
CANADA	—	1	2
YUGOSLAVIA	—	2	—
PORTUGAL	—	1	1
URUGUAY	—	1	1
CEYLON (now Sri Lanka)	—	1	—
CUBA	—	1	—
SPAIN	—	1	—
TRINIDAD AND TOBAGO	—	1	—
KOREA	—	—	2
PANAMA	—	—	2
BRAZIL	—	—	1
IRAN	—	—	1
PUERTO RICO	—	—	1
POLAND	—	—	1

1952 *Winter*

THE VIth WINTER GAMES

OSLO, NORWAY 14–25 FEBRUARY 1952

Attended by representatives of 22 countries, comprising 732 competitors, of which 109 were women.

This had been the only Winter Games to be held in a Nordic country even though Norway, Sweden and Finland between them have won over 222 medals, of which 104 were gold. A feature of these Games was the enormous crowds at all venues, including a record for any Olympic event, at the ski jumping at Holmenkollen, estimated at 150 000. An innovation was the Olympic flame coming, not from Olympia, but from Morgedal in southern Norway, the home of Sondre Nordheim, the father of modern skiing. The last relay 'runner' who brought the flame into the Bislet Stadium was Eigil Nansen, the grandson of the renowned Polar explorer Fridtjof Nansen. The oath was taken by ski jumper Torbjörn Falkanger. All entrants from Commonwealth countries wore black armbands as the opening day coincided with the funeral of Britain's King George VI. As King Haakon and the Crown Prince were in London for this, the Games were opened by HRH Princess Ragnhild. Back in the Olympic fold were Germany and Japan, and for the first time in Winter Games entries included Portugal and New Zealand. Bad weather conditions necessitated the start of some competitions, the women's giant slalom and the 2-man bob, prior to the opening ceremony on 15 February. Of the three Alpine events, the giant slalom and downhill races were held some 120 km from Oslo, at Norefjell.

In the men's giant slalom Stein Eriksen (NOR) became the first ever Nordic winner of an Alpine event. Skiers from the Nordic countries were not to gain another gold medal in these events until 1980.

The star of the Games was Hjalmar Andersen of the host country who won three speed skating gold medals. In winning the ladies figure skating title Jeanette Altwegg won Britain's first skating gold medal since Madge Syers in 1908. Instead of turning professional, as did most of her contem-

Part of the record breaking Olympic crowd at the Holmenkollen ski jump outside Oslo during the 1952 winter Games.

56

for orphan children, Pestalozzi in Switzerland.
The men's title went to defending champion
Dick Button (USA) with some of the most
remarkable jumps ever seen in competition. Finishing seventh in this contest was Alain Giletti
(FRA), at 12 yr 5 months the youngest ever male
athlete in Olympic Winter Games. Just ahead of
him, in sixth, was Carlo Fassi (ITA) later coach
of Britain's John Curry and Robin Cousins.

The basic running abilities required by cross-
country skiers were highlighted by the Nordic
skiing, when the 18 km title was won by Hallgeir
Brenden (NOR), who during the following years
won two Norwegian steeplechase titles. In sixth
place was his countryman Martin Stokken who
had placed fourth in the 1948 10 000 m track
run, and by competing again in Helsinki became
one of the few men to compete in a Winter and
Summer Games in the same year. For the first
time there was a Nordic ski race for women,
which was dominated by Finland with four of the
first five places.

Bandy, a distant relative of ice hockey, was
played as a demonstration sport and won by
Sweden.

The oldest gold medallist at Oslo was Franz
Kemser (GER) in the 4-man bob aged 41 yr 103
days. The youngest was Andrea Mead-Lawrence
(USA) in the slalom aged 19 yr 301 days. The
youngest male winner was Robert Dickson
(CAN) in ice hockey aged 20 yr 308 days, while
the oldest female champion was Lydia Wideman
(FIN) in the 10 km cross-country race aged 31 yr
282 days.

FINAL MEDAL STANDINGS

Nation	Gold	Silver	Bronze
NORWAY	7	3	6
UNITED STATES	4	6	1
FINLAND	3	4	2
GERMANY	3	2	2
AUSTRIA	2	4	2
ITALY	1	—	1
CANADA	1	—	1
GREAT BRITAIN	1	—	—
NETHERLANDS	—	3	—
SWEDEN	—	—	4
SWITZERLAND	—	—	2
FRANCE	—	—	1
HUNGARY	—	—	1

The parade of the record number of countries
witnessed the return, after 40 years, of the
Russians now in the guise of the Soviet Union.
Attending the Games for the first time were
teams from the Bahamas, Gold Coast (now
Ghana), Guatemala, Dutch Antilles, Hong
Kong, Indonesia, Israel, Nigeria, Thailand,
Vietnam, and, for the only time ever, the Saar.
Because Mainland China had been invited, the
Nationalist Chinese (Taiwan) had withdrawn.
Although they all marched together, there were
two Olympic villages; surprisingly the IOC had
allowed the Soviet bloc to set up their own at
Otaneimi, while everybody else was at Käpylä.

The athlete of the Games was the Czech runner
Emil Zatopek who won an unprecedented triple,
of the 5000 m, 10 000 m and marathon. To

Emil Zatopek (CZE) passing some British sailors from HMS *Swiftsure* on his way to winning the 1952 marathon and a unique distance triple.

crown his achievements his wife Dana, born on exactly the same day as himself, also won a gold medal in the javelin, within an hour of her husband's 5000 m victory; another unique occasion. The star of the women's track events was Marjorie Jackson (AUS) who easily won the 100 m and 200 m, and seemed certain to gain a third gold in the relay until the baton was dropped as she set off on the last leg. Though retrieving it the Australian team finished in fifth place, leaving the gold medal to the American team which narrowly defeated the Germans. In that American team was Barbara Jones who became the youngest ever track and field gold medallist at the age of 15 yr 123 days. She was not the youngest gold medallist at the Games however as the cox of the winning French pair rowing crew was Bernard Malivoire aged 14 yr 94 days. The Jamaicans again scored some outstanding results with Herb McKenley placing second in both the 100 m and 400 m before putting his team in a winning position in the 4 × 400 m relay. The 1948 sprint champion Harrison Dillard, here back to his first love, won the 110 m hurdles title and won his fourth gold medal, in the 4 × 100 m relay. A problem was set for the band as they took some time finding the anthem of Luxembourg when Josy Barthel scored an upset win in the 1500 m to gain his

country's first and only gold medal. America's first win in a distance run since 1908 came in the steeplechase when Horace Ashenfelter set an inaugural world record for the event. The Press had great fun with the fact that Ashenfelter was an FBI agent and was here followed home by a Russian. The Soviet Union's first ever gold medal (see p 22) was won by Nina Romashkova in the women's discus. Highly questionable disqualifications by blatantly biased judges marred the 10 000 m walk but did not stop the Swiss and Russian second and third place medallists literally running to the line. However, the event was dropped from future Games. The winner of the high jump, Walt Davis (USA) was the tallest, at 2·04 m, ever to win an individual Olympic gold medal.

In the swimming pool the Hungarians won four of the five events for women. Almost matching the Zatopeks were Éva Székely, who won the 200 m breaststroke, and her husband Dezsö Gyarmati, a member of the victorious Hungarian water polo team four days later. Possibly more attention was gained by the men's 400 m freestyle final, when the father of the winner, Jean Boiteux (FRA) jumped fully clothed into the pool to congratulate his son. In diving, tiny (1·56 m tall) Sammy Lee, an American of

Jean Boiteux (FRA) helps his father out of the pool after 'Papa' had leapt in to congratulate his son on winning the 400 m freestyle at Helsinki.

Korean origin, won the highboard to become the first man to successfully defend a diving title.

The gymnastics competitions were dominated by the Soviet teams, led by Maria Gorokhovskaya, winning a Helsinki Games record of seven medals (two gold, five silver), and Viktor Chukarin, with four gold and two silver. The Finnish veteran, Dr Heikki Savolainen, who had taken the oath at the opening ceremony, gained a team bronze, the fifth consecutive Games at which he had won a medal and just two months short of his 45th birthday. Other veterans did well in 1952. Ilona Elek (HUN) added a silver to her two fencing golds at the age of 45 yr 41 days. In the dressage André Jousseaume (FRA) won an individual bronze medal two days after his 58th birthday, and 20 years after his gold medal at Los Angeles. In all he placed in the first five positions in five Olympic Games. Another great sportsman won the rapid fire pistol for the second time. Károly Takács had won the European title before the war as a right-handed shot. In 1938 he lost his right hand when a grenade exploded while he was holding it. But he taught himself to shoot with his left.

On a less uplifting note there was the disqualification of Ingemar Johansson (SWE) in the heavyweight boxing final for 'not trying'. His silver medal was withheld for 14 years. In 1959 he won the world professional title from the 1952 Olympic middleweight champion Floyd Patterson (USA).

The oldest gold medallist at these Games was

Everard Endt (USA) in the 6 m yachting class aged 59 yr 112 days. The youngest male and female champions were Bernard Malivoire and Barbara Jones (see above). The oldest female winner was Sylvi Saimo (FIN) in the 500 m kayak event aged 37 yr 260 days.

The Games ended with a then record 43 countries winning medals of some sort. It was also announced that Avery Brundage had taken over the Presidency of the IOC from the retiring Sigfrid Edström.

FINAL MEDAL STANDINGS

Nation	Gold	Silver	Bronze
UNITED STATES	40	19	17
USSR	22	30	19
HUNGARY	16	10	16
SWEDEN	12	12	10
ITALY	8	9	4
CZECHOSLOVAKIA	7	3	3
FRANCE	6	6	6
FINLAND	6	3	13
AUSTRALIA	6	2	3
NORWAY	3	2	—
SWITZERLAND	2	6	6
SOUTH AFRICA	2	4	4
JAMAICA	2	3	—
BELGIUM	2	2	—
DENMARK	2	1	3
TURKEY	2	—	1
JAPAN	1	6	2
GREAT BRITAIN	1	2	8
ARGENTINA	1	2	2
POLAND	1	2	1
CANADA	1	2	—
YUGOSLAVIA	1	2	—
ROMANIA	1	1	2
BRAZIL	1	—	2
NEW ZEALAND	1	—	2
INDIA	1	—	1
LUXEMBOURG	1	—	—
GERMANY	—	7	17
NETHERLANDS	—	5	—
IRAN	—	3	4
CHILE	—	2	—
AUSTRIA	—	1	1
LEBANON	—	1	1
IRELAND	—	1	—
MEXICO	—	1	—
SPAIN	—	1	—
KOREA	—	—	2
TRINIDAD AND TOBAGO	—	—	2
URUGUAY	—	—	2
BULGARIA	—	—	1
EGYPT	—	—	1
PORTUGAL	—	—	1
VENEZUELA	—	—	1

1956 *Winter*

THE VIIth WINTER GAMES

CORTINA D'AMPEZZO, ITALY
26 JANUARY – 5 FEBRUARY 1956

The star of the 1956 winter Games was Toni Sailer (AUT) who swept all before him to win all three Alpine skiing events.

Attended by representatives of 32 countries, comprising 819 competitors, of which 132 were women.

Some £2·5 million were spent on these Games, most of it coming from the Italian Soccer Pools, but despite excellent facilities there were still problems with the weather. Once again the snow had to be 'imported' for some of the events. The President of Italy, Giovanni Gronchi, formally opened the Games. Guiliana Chenal-Minuzzo, who won the 1952 bronze medal in downhill skiing, became the first woman in Olympic history to pronounce the oath on behalf of all competitors. The last runner in the torch relay, Guido Caroli an Italian speed skater, fell as he completed a circuit of the arena but happily the flame did not go out. The entry of the Soviet Union provided the first Russian competitors in Winter Games events since 1908 (see p 22). These were the first Winter Games to be televised and this undoubtedly resulted in smaller numbers of spectators than previously.

The star performer was Toni Sailer, a young Austrian plumber, who gained a grand slam of all three Alpine races, downhill, slalom and giant slalom, winning in treacherous conditions by remarkable margins of 3·5 sec, 4·0 sec and 6·2 sec respectively. Second in the slalom was Asia's first Winter medallist, Chiharu Igaya (JAP), an American college student, who had to wait while the jury investigated an unsubstantiated claim from Sweden and the United States that he had missed a gate. Madeleine Berthoud (SUI) won the women's downhill race by a still record margin of 4·7 sec.

The most medals won at Cortina were by Nordic skier Sixten Jernberg (SWE) who gained one gold, two silver and one bronze. Hallgeir Brenden (NOR) successfully defended his 1952 title, now reduced from 18 km to 15 km, the only man ever to do so at cross-country skiing. Despite having won 15 of the 18 medals available in ski-jumping since 1924, the Norwegians failed to place in the first six at Cortina, with the Finns, using a new style taking the gold and silver medals. Though Germany competed as one team the bronze, won by Harry Glass, is claimed by the GDR as its first Olympic medal.

The speed skating surface, on Lake Misurina at an altitude of 1755 m, prepared by the Swedish expert Gösta Nilsson, was considered to be the fastest ever, and witnessed a wholesale attack on the record book. The winner of the 500 m title, Yevgeniy Grishin (URS) had been a member of the Soviet cycling team in Helsinki. Both figure skating singles were won by the United States, and Hayes (gold) and David (bronze) Jenkins were the first brothers to win medals in the same skating event. The lady champion, Tenley Albright, had been a victim of polio as a child.

A member of the winning Italian 2-man bob was Giacomo Conti at 47 yr 216 days, the oldest ever Winter Olympics gold medallist. The youngest champion at these Games was Elisabeth Schwartz (AUT) in the pair skating aged 19 yr 199 days. The youngest male winner was Toni Sailer (AUT) in the giant slalom aged 20 yr 73 days. The oldest female champion was Siiri Rantanen (FIN), a member of the cross-country relay team aged 31 yr 49 days.

FINAL MEDAL STANDINGS

Nation	Gold	Silver	Bronze
USSR	7	3	6
AUSTRIA	4	3	4
FINLAND	3	3	1
SWITZERLAND	3	2	1
SWEDEN	2	4	4
UNITED STATES	2	3	2
NORWAY	2	1	1
ITALY	1	2	—
GERMANY	1	—	1
CANADA	—	1	2
JAPAN	—	1	—
HUNGARY	—	—	1
POLAND	—	—	1

1956 *Summer*

THE XVIth OLYMPIC GAMES

(a) STOCKHOLM, SWEDEN
10–17 JUNE 1956
(b) MELBOURNE, AUSTRALIA
22 NOVEMBER – 8 DECEMBER 1956

Attended by (a) representatives of 29 countries, comprising 158 competitors, of which 13 were women; (b) representatives of 67 countries, comprising 3184 competitors, of which 371 were women.

In 1949 the IOC had decided on Melbourne by only one vote, and they were disquieted, to say the least, by first the apparent tardiness in finishing facilities, and second the inability of the Australians to hold the equestrian events, due to their stringent quarantine laws. Thus for the first and only time, contrary to the Olympic Charter, a sport was detached from the main Games and held elsewhere, in Stockholm. Except for the cross-country section of the three-day event the venue was the 1912 Olympic Stadium. The host country won three of the six titles, but there was strong criticism and accusations of chauvinism by the judges in the dressage competition. Also

the above-mentioned cross-country was thought to be far too dangerous in the existing wet conditions.

The Games proper, the first in the Southern Hemisphere, opened under a cloud of international ill will, occasioned by the Soviet invasion of Hungary, and British and French intervention in the Suez Canal dispute between Israel and Egypt. The Netherlands, Switzerland and Spain withdrew because of the former, and Egypt and Lebanon because of the latter. This time Mainland China withdrew because of the presence of Taiwan. Perhaps surprisingly the Hungarian team did compete, and with effect. In addition to Taiwan, Olympic Games debuts were made by teams from Ethiopia, Fiji, Kenya, Liberia, Uganda, Malaya and North Borneo (the two latter now combined as Malaysia). Cambodia's appearance in the Stockholm equestrian events was its first Olympic participation. HRH The Duke of Edinburgh opened the Games in the Melbourne Cricket Ground, the main venue. The final torch bearer was a 19 year old Australian miler, Ron Clarke, who was to become one of the world's greatest distance runners.

The distance runs in Melbourne were dominated by the Soviet sailor, Vladimir Kuts, with record breaking victories at 5000 m and 10 000 m. Ireland won its first gold medal since 1932 when Ronnie Delaney, running an exceptionally fast last 200 m took the 1500 m event. In the sprints, both Bobby-Joe Morrow (USA) and Betty Cuthbert (AUS) gained three gold medals, including the 4 × 100 m relays. Teamed with Cuthbert in the women's relay was Shirley de la Hunty (née Strickland) who ended her three Games career with an unbeaten total of seven medals (three gold, one silver, three bronze). A recently discovered photo-finish picture indicates that she also was placed third, not fourth, in the 200 m final in 1948, but no official change to the result is anticipated. After placing second to Emil Zatopek in three Olympic races since 1948, Alain Mimoun (FRA) finally beat him, into sixth place, and became the oldest winner of an Olympic marathon at 35 yr 335 days. The 50 km walk was won by Norman Read, representing his adopted country, New Zealand. As a former English junior mile walk champion Read had watched the 1952 Games as a spectator (sitting

Later multi-record holder Ron Clarke (AUS), then world junior mile record breaker, carries the torch into the stadium in Melbourne in 1956.

next to the author).

Another English-born competitor, Murray Rose (AUS) was the first male swimmer to win two individual freestyle events since 1924. He also won a third in the relay. Pat McCormick (USA) achieved a unique double 'double' by retaining the springboard and highboard titles she had won at Helsinki. Boxing too had its record breaker when László Papp (HUN) gained an unprecedented third gold medal, retaining his light-middleweight title of 1952 to add to the middleweight gold of 1948.

John Kelly Jr, the son of the 1920 gold medallist, won a bronze in the single sculls as Vyacheslav Ivanov (URS) gained the first of his record three consecutive titles. At the shooting range Gerard Ouellette (CAN) won the prone small bore rifle event with a world record 'maximum' of 600, only to have the record, but not the gold medal, disallowed because the range was found to be $1\frac{1}{2}$ metres short of the stipulated 50 m.

By beating Yugoslavia by 1–0 in the soccer final on the last day of the Games, 8 December, the Soviet Union went into history as winners of the latest gold medal ever won in an Olympic year.

Not surprisingly bad feelings erupted in the water polo semi-final between Hungary and the Soviet Union. By a nice touch of irony the referee was from that perennially neutral country Sweden. With Hungary leading 4–0 he brought the game to an end as it had degenerated into a 'boxing-match under water'.

At the closing ceremony for the first time the athletes entered not in teams but *en masse*, signifying the friendship of the Games. The idea for this had come from an Australian-born Chinese boy, John Wing, in a letter to the chairman of the organizing committee, the Hon W S Kent-Hughes.

The oldest gold medallist at these Games was Henri Saint Cyr (SWE) in the dressage competition aged 54 yr 93 days. The youngest was Sandra Morgan (USA) a member of the 4 × 100 m freestyle swimming relay aged 14 yr 183 days. The youngest male champion was Murray Rose, the Australian swimmer (see above) in the men's freestyle relay aged 17 yr 332 days. The oldest female winner was Hungarian gymnast Agnes Keleti aged 35 yr 171 days.

A happy postscript to the Games occurred in March 1957, in Prague, Czechoslovakia, when the winner of the hammer Harold Connolly (USA) married Olga Fikotova, the women's discus champion. The best man at this 'Olympic' wedding was, appropriately, Emil Zatopek.

FINAL MEDAL STANDINGS

Nation	Gold	Silver	Bronze
USSR	37	29	32
UNITED STATES	32	25	17
AUSTRALIA	13	8	14
HUNGARY	9	10	7
ITALY	8	8	9
SWEDEN	8	5	6
GERMANY	6	13	7
GREAT BRITAIN	6	7	11
ROMANIA	5	3	5
JAPAN	4	10	5
FRANCE	4	4	6
TURKEY	3	2	2
FINLAND	3	1	11
IRAN	2	2	1
CANADA	2	1	3
NEW ZEALAND	2	—	—
POLAND	1	4	4
CZECHOSLOVAKIA	1	4	1
BULGARIA	1	3	1
DENMARK	1	2	1
IRELAND	1	1	3
NORWAY	1	—	2
MEXICO	1	—	1
BRAZIL	1	—	—
INDIA	1	—	—
YUGOSLAVIA	—	3	—
CHILE	—	2	2
BELGIUM	—	2	—
ARGENTINA	—	1	1
KOREA	—	1	1
ICELAND	—	1	—
PAKISTAN	—	1	—
SOUTH AFRICA	—	—	4
AUSTRIA	—	—	2
BAHAMAS	—	—	1
GREECE	—	—	1
SWITZERLAND	—	—	1
URUGUAY	—	—	1

1960 *Winter*

**THE VIIIth
WINTER
GAMES**

SQUAW
VALLEY, USA
*18–28
FEBRUARY 1960*

Attended by representatives of 30 countries, comprising 665 competitors, of which 144 were women.

At the time the IOC took its decision, with a close vote of 32–30 over Innsbruck, to give the Games to Squaw Valley, virtually nothing existed at the site. Owing to the efforts of Alexander Cushing, who owned most of the area, it became the first purpose-built Winter Games centre. Despite delays everything was ready on time for the official opening by the Vice-President of the United States, Richard Nixon. The opening ceremony was under the direction of Walt Disney. The last relay runner was Ken Henry, the 500 m speed skating champion of 1952, and the oath taken by figure skater Carol Heiss, who went on to win the ladies title. There were a number of protests and problems. Bobsledding had been dropped as the American organizers considered the cost of erecting a run not acceptable due to the small number of entries expected. Artificial obstacles were built into the downhill ski runs to make them more difficult, and the Nordic skiing authorities expressed concern about the excessive altitude (over 1900 m) at which their events would be held. The problem of East and West Germany competing as one entity was partly solved by agreement to play the popular theme from Beethoven's Ninth Symphony for any victory ceremonies instead of their respective national anthems. South Africa entered a team for the first and only time in the Winter Games, as they were banned thereafter. A Winter biathlon and four speed skating events for women made their début in

Roger Staub won Switzerland's only gold medal in the men's events at the 1960 winter Games.

the programme. The biathlon was a successor to the military patrol event which had been a demonstration event on four previous occasions.

Speed skating times were excellent with Knut Johannesen (NOR) beating the 10 000 m world mark by 46·0 sec, the greatest margin achieved in this century, to take the gold medal. Yevgeniy Grishin (URS) equalled his own world record to become the first man to successfully defend a 500 m title. Helga Haase (GER) was the first ever women's Olympic champion in speed skating when she won the 500 m event. In figure skating all gold medals were won by non-Europeans for the first time. By winning the men's gold medal David Jenkins kept the title in the family as his brother Hayes was the holder. The family became even more Olympian two months after the Games ended when the ladies champion, Carol Heiss, married the latter brother.

Another first came in the Nordic combination when Georg Thoma, a German postman from the Black Forest who was often forced to deliver the mail on skis, achieved the first victory by a non-Scandinavian in the event. The winner of the inaugural biathlon, Klas Lestander (SWE), was only 15th in the cross-country segment of the contest but scored a maximum possible 20 in the shooting. The Soviet Union's women dominated their 10 000 m race taking the first four places, but they lost the relay when their first girl fell and broke a ski. A protest was made against the first Swedish girl skier who was accused of deliberate fouling, but it was not upheld.

Alpine skiing witnessed the first use in the Games of metallic skis. Unlike 4 years before no skier won more than one event, five countries sharing the six gold medals, and only Penny Pitou (USA) won more than one medal, with two silvers. The outstanding competitor was Anne Heggtveit (CAN) who won the women's slalom by a margin of 3·3 sec, only ever bettered by the 1936 combination winner Christel Cranz.

The oldest gold medallist at Squaw Valley was Veikko Hakulinen (FIN) in the cross-country relay aged 35 yr 52 days. The youngest was Heidi Biebl (GER) who won the women's downhill race 3 days past her 19th birthday. The youngest male champion was American ice hockey player Thomas Williams aged 19 yr 317 days. The oldest female gold medallist was Sonja

Ruthström (SWE) a member of the cross-country relay team aged 29 yr 94 days.

FINAL MEDAL STANDINGS

Nation	Gold	Silver	Bronze
USSR	7	5	9
GERMANY	4	3	1
UNITED STATES	3	4	3
NORWAY	3	3	—
SWEDEN	3	2	2
FINLAND	2	3	3
CANADA	2	1	1
SWITZERLAND	2	—	—
AUSTRIA	1	2	3
FRANCE	1	—	2
NETHERLANDS	—	1	1
POLAND	—	1	1
CZECHOSLOVAKIA	—	1	—
ITALY	—	—	1

1960 *Summer*

THE XVIIth OLYMPIC GAMES

ROME, ITALY
*25 AUGUST –
11 SEPTEMBER
1960*

Attended by representatives of 83 countries, comprising 5346 competitors, of which 610 were women.

After just missing out in 1908 the Games finally were held in the home city of the Emperor Theodosius who had ended the Ancient Games some 1567 years before. Along with a brand-new stadium and other specially built facilities, some of the old Roman sites were utilized. The Baths of Caracalla housed the gymnastics and the Basilica di Massenzio had the wrestling competitions. The marathon began at the Capitol Hill and finished on the Appian Way, near the Arch of Constantine. It was the first time that an Olympic marathon had not started or finished in the main Olympic stadium. Yachting was held in the Bay of Naples under the shadow of Mt Vesuvius. The Games were opened by the President of Italy, Giovanni Gronchi, before 100 000

64

spectators. Morocco, Tunisia, Sudan and San Marino made their Olympic débuts, while Jamaica and Trinidad combined under the heading of Antilles. Nationalist China protested, but competed, when they were told by the IOC to appear under the name of Taiwan and not China. These Games were the first to have world-wide television coverage.

An unknown runner Abebe Bikila won the marathon barefoot setting a world's best time for the event, and his victory signalled the entry of a new force, Ethiopia, onto the world distance running scene. Australasians swept the middle distance events. Peter Snell (NZ) won the 800 m, beating the world record holder, Roger Moens; Herb Elliott (AUS) won the 1500 m by a record margin of 2·8 sec in world record time; and Murray Halberg (NZ), handicapped by a withered arm, won the 5000 m. The team from Taiwan was cheered somewhat when their decathlete Chuan-Kwang Yang had a tremendous fight with Rafer Johnson (USA), a teammate at the University of California, and only lost the gold medal by a narrow margin. Wilma Rudolph (USA) was an easy winner of the women's sprints. One of 19 children and a polio victim as a child she won a third gold in the relay. Sisters Irina and Tamara Press (URS) won the 80 m hurdles and shot put respectively while a countrywoman, Ludmila Shevtsova won the first 800 m event for women since 1928.

Swimming, yet again, was virtually a straight fight between Australia and the United States. The only one of the 15 events not won by one of their representatives was the 200 m breaststroke for women in which the gold medal went to Britain's Anita Lonsbrough.

The star of the pool was America's Christine von Saltza, a descendant of Prussian/Swedish nobility, who won three golds and one silver. The standard in swimming was very high with Olympic records broken in every event. An unfortunate incident occurred in the men's 100 m freestyle, when Lance Larson (USA) was timed at one-tenth of a second faster than John Devitt (AUS) but was placed second to the Australian, despite slow-motion film indicating that the American was first. In future Games full electronic timing was used. Only the second Royal gold medal in Olympic history was won by

Left, **Boris Shakhlin (URS) retains his pommel horse title in 1960. From 1956 to 1964 he won 13 medals.**
Right, **Edoardo Mangiarotti (ITA) won his first gold medal in 1936 and his last in 1960.**

Crown Prince Constantine (later King Constantine II of Greece) in the Dragon class yachting in the Bay of Naples. In the Flying Dutchman class Peder Lunde Jr (NOR) became the third generation of his family to win a medal, equalling his grandfather's feat of 1924, but going one better than his mother and father in 1952. Paul Elvström (DEN) won his fourth consecutive individual gold medal in dinghy sailing, the first sportsman to achieve this feat in any sport.

The most medals won at these Games were the seven (four golds, two silvers and one bronze) gained by Boris Shakhlin (URS) in Gymnastics. Aladar Gerevich (HUN) aged 50 yr 178 days won his sixth sabre fencing gold medal in as many Olympic Games, a record unsurpassed by any other Olympic competitor. In the foil and épée events Edoardo Mangiarotti (ITA) brought his total of fencing medals to a record 13 for the sport in five Olympic Games 1936–60. They comprise six golds, five silvers and two bronze. The light-heavyweight gold medal in boxing went to Cassius Clay, who as Muhammad Ali, amassed the greatest amount ever earned by a sportsman, $68 million in a career which started when he turned professional immediately after the Games. In soccer Yugoslavia won the gold medal after three consecutive runner-up placings. The first loss by India in Olympic hockey, since they entered the competition in 1928, occurred when Pakistan beat them 1–0 in the final.

One sad note was struck in the cycling when Knut Jensen (DEN) collapsed and died in the 100 km team event. Originally diagnosed as due to the excessive heat which affected Rome during the period of the Games, it was later revealed that his death was due to a drug overdose.

The oldest gold medallist at the Games was the Hungarian fencer Aladar Gerevich (see above), while the youngest was a member of the US women's 4 × 100 m freestyle relay team, Carolyn Wood, aged 14 yr 260 days. The oldest female winner was discus champion Nina Ponomareva (URS) at 31 yr 131 days, and the youngest male gold medallist was Michael Obst aged 16 yr 73 days when he coxed the German fours crew to victory.

At the end of the Games a then record 44 countries had shared in the medals.

FINAL MEDAL STANDINGS

Nation	Gold	Silver	Bronze
USSR	43	29	31
UNITED STATES	34	21	16
ITALY	13	10	13
GERMANY	12	19	11
AUSTRALIA	8	8	6
TURKEY	7	2	—
HUNGARY	6	8	7
JAPAN	4	7	7
POLAND	4	6	11
CZECHOSLOVAKIA	3	2	3
ROMANIA	3	1	6
GREAT BRITAIN	2	6	12
DENMARK	2	3	1
NEW ZEALAND	2	—	1
BULGARIA	1	3	3
SWEDEN	1	2	3
FINLAND	1	1	3
AUSTRIA	1	1	—
YUGOSLAVIA	1	1	—
PAKISTAN	1	—	1
ETHIOPIA	1	—	—
GREECE	1	—	—
NORWAY	1	—	—
SWITZERLAND	—	3	3
FRANCE	—	2	3
BELGIUM	—	2	2
IRAN	—	1	3
SOUTH AFRICA	—	1	2
NETHERLANDS	—	1	2
ARGENTINA	—	1	1
EGYPT (United Arab Republic)	—	1	1
CANADA	—	1	—
GHANA	—	1	—
INDIA	—	1	—
MOROCCO	—	1	—
PORTUGAL	—	1	—
SINGAPORE	—	1	—
TAIWAN	—	1	—
BRAZIL	—	—	2
JAMAICA*	—	—	2
IRAQ	—	—	1
MEXICO	—	—	1
SPAIN	—	—	1
VENEZUELA	—	—	1

* Part of an Antilles team

1964 *Winter*

THE IXth WINTER GAMES

INNSBRUCK, AUSTRIA
29 JANUARY – 9 FEBRUARY 1964

Attended by representatives of 36 countries, comprising 1093 competitors, of which 200 were women.

Awarded to Innsbruck in 1959 these Games were the most successful yet with over one million spectators attending the various events, which were now increased to a record 34 in total. Among them were lugeing and a second ski jump competition. Once again the weather caused problems and snow had to be manhandled to the worst affected venues by the Austrian Army. During practice before the Games began there were two tragic deaths of a Briton and an Austrian. The official opening by the Austrian President, Dr Adolf Schärf took place at the Bergisel ski jump, the last relay runner who lit the flame was a skier Joseph Rieder, and the oath was taken by Paul Aste, a bobsledder. Mongolia and India competed in the Winter Games for the first time while Korea was split into North and South teams. South Africa had now been banned from the Games. An innovation was the use of computers officially to aid the judges as well as provide electronic timing.

Lydia Skoblikova (URS), a teacher from Siberia, won all four women's speed skating events to give her a total of six gold medals in two Games, a record for the sport. In figure skating the Soviet husband and wife pair, Ludmila Belousova and Oleg Protopopov, brought a new concept, that of classical ballet, to the sport. The silver medal went for the second consecutive occasion to Marika Kilius and Hansjürgen Bäumler (GER), but two years later they were disqualified owing to professional activities which had then come to light. The individual women's title was won by Sjoukje Dijkstra, Holland's first ever Winter Games gold medal. The youngest medallist at these Games was Scott Allen (USA) who won the bronze medal in the men's skating event just two days short of his 15th birthday.

Klaudia Boyarskikh (URS) won three gold medals in Nordic skiing, while Sixten Jernberg (SWE) brought his total to a record nine medals in three Games, by winning his fourth gold in the 4 × 10 000 m relay. Marielle and Christine Goitschel (FRA) became the first sisters to win golds at the same Games when they swapped first and second places in the two Alpine slalom events.

The re-introduced bobsledding events were won for the first time by countries which did not possess bob runs of their own. Additionally, Britain's 2-man victory (Tony Nash and Robin Dixon) was the first by a 'lowland' country. Some credit for their feat must go to the great Italian bobsledder Eugenio Monti, who lent them a bolt from his sled after the one on the British sled had broken. He was later awarded the Pierre de Coubertin Fair Play Trophy for his action.

A demonstration of German curling was held. The Games ended with the shock realization that Switzerland had not won a single medal, the first and last time that was to happen at the Winter Games.

FINAL MEDAL STANDINGS

Nation	Gold	Silver	Bronze
USSR	11	8	6
AUSTRIA	4	5	3
NORWAY	3	6	6
FINLAND	3	4	3
FRANCE	3	4	—
SWEDEN	3	3	1
GERMANY	3	2	3
UNITED STATES	1	2	4
CANADA	1	1	1
NETHERLANDS	1	1	—
GREAT BRITAIN	1	—	—
ITALY	—	1	3
NORTH KOREA	—	1	—
CZECHOSLOVAKIA	—	—	1

The oldest gold medallist at Innsbruck was Sixten Jernberg (SWE) who won his fourth gold medal in two Games in the cross-country relay race aged 35 yr 2 days. The youngest champion was Manfred Stengl (AUT) in the 2-man luge

This 500 m title was the first of the four gold medals won by Lydia Skoblikova (URS) in four days at Innsbruck in 1964.

aged 17 yr 310 days. The youngest female gold medallist was Marielle Goitschel (FRA) in the giant slalom aged 18 yr 128 days, and the oldest female champion was Alevtina Koltschina (URS) in the cross-country relay aged 33 yr 88 days.

1964 *Summer*

THE XVIIIth OLYMPIC GAMES

TOKYO, JAPAN
10–24 OCTOBER 1964

Attended by representatives of 93 countries, comprising 5140 competitors, of which 683 were women.

The first Games held in Asia witnessed enormous crowds at all venues, and a tremendous assault on the record books of most of the sports. Vast sums, estimated to be as much as $3 billion had been spent not only on stadia but also on transport facilities, which, of course remained part of the civil framework of the city after the Games. Teams from 14 countries made their first appearance in the Olympic Games, but South Africa was no longer among the entries. Also missing were Indonesia and North Korea whose athletes who had competed at the previous year's unsanctioned GANEFO (Games of the New Emergent Forces) meeting had been banned. Emperor Hirohito performed the formal opening, and the flame was brought into the stadium by a young runner who had been born near Hiroshima on the day that the atom bomb had been dropped there in 1945. The Olympic flag was raised to the top of a flagpole which measured 15·21 m *49 ft 10¾ ins*, the distance reached in the triple jump by Mikio Oda in 1928 when he became Japan's first Olympic gold medallist. The growth of the Games can best be emphasized by quoting the remark made by the great Australian runner Ron Clarke, who himself had lit the flame in 1956. After failing to win the expected gold medal in the 10 000 m he said that after having dropped all the best known runners in the event he looked over his shoulder and saw 'an Ethiopian, a North African Arab, and an American Indian'. This latter, Billy Mills, a part-Sioux Indian Marine officer, won the event for the first ever US victory over the distance.

The track and field events generally were outstanding. Bikila of Ethiopia, this time wearing shoes, became the first man to defend successfully the marathon title, while Peter Snell (NZ) not only retained his 800 m crown but added the 1500 m, the first time that double had been achieved since 1920. The winner of the 100 m, Bob Hayes, ran a phenomenal last leg in the relay to regain the title which the United States had only lost once in 44 years. One of the beaten teams decried the US team to the effect that all they had was Hayes. This was met by the now famous rejoinder, 'Man, that's all we needed.' Britain won its first ever gold medal in the women's events when Mary Rand broke the world record in the long jump. Her room-mate, Ann Packer, added the 800 m title for good measure.

At the much admired swimming pool the United States and Australia won all the titles bar one. That was the women's 200 m breaststroke, the event which had also prevented a clean sweep by the two superpowers in 1960, gained by Galina

Dawn Fraser, (AUS) the three-time Olympic 100 m freestyle champion was also the first girl to break the 60 sec barrier for the event.

Prozumenshchikova, the Soviet Union's first ever swimming gold medallist, Don Schollander (USA) became the first swimmer to win four gold medals in a single Games. Close behind him was Sharon Stouder (USA) who won three golds and one silver in the women's events. Australia's Dawn Fraser, just past her 27th birthday, won her third consecutive 100 m title, a unique achievement in swimming, and also added a silver medal in the relay to amass a record total for a female swimmer of eight medals. Another competitor to complete a unique triple was the Soviet rower Vyacheslav Ivanov in winning the single sculls yet again. An unusual event occurred in the eights event where the cox of the winning American crew, Robert Zimonyi, aged 46, had been cox of the third placed Hungarian pair in 1948. In water polo the Hungarian veteran Deszö Gyarmati won his third gold medal, and his fifth medal in as many Games.

The greatest haul of medals at the Games was by Larissa Latynina (URS) with two golds, two silvers and two bronze in gymnastics. Her teammate Boris Shakhlin brought his total of gold medals since 1956 to seven, of which a record six were individual events. In weightlifting Norbert Schemansky (USA) won a bronze to add to his previously won gold, silver and bronze medals since 1948, giving him a record total for his sport of four medals. Having won an unprecedented three consecutive silver medals in Greco-Roman featherweight wrestling Imre Polyak (HUN) finally won the gold medal in his fourth Olympics. Of the two new sports included in 1964, the other was volleyball, judo had been added at the express wish of the host country.

The medal ceremony that brought pain to a nation—Anton Geesink (HOL) having won the Open judo title at the Tokyo Games in 1964.

The sport was considered a Japanese monopoly, and the whole country suffered a terrible shock when the open title was won by the giant Dutchman, 1·98 m *6 ft 6 in* tall Anton Geesink. Leading the US basketball team to its sixth consecutive victory was its captain Bill Bradley, later a top class professional player and then a US Senator.

The oldest gold medallist at the Games was William Northam (AUS) when he skippered the 5·5 m yacht *Barrenjoey* to victory aged 59 yr 23 days. The youngest was Debbie 'Pokey' Watson (USA) a member of America's winning freestyle swimming relay team aged 14 yr 96 days. The oldest female winner was Katalin Juhász-Nagy (HUN), a member of the winning foil team at 31 yr 328 days. The youngest male gold medallist was American swimmer, Richard Roth who won the 400 m medley 18 days past his 17th birthday.

FINAL MEDAL STANDINGS

Nation	Gold	Silver	Bronze
UNITED STATES	36	26	28
USSR	30	31	35
JAPAN	16	5	8
GERMANY	10	22	18
ITALY	10	10	7
HUNGARY	10	7	5
POLAND	7	6	10
AUSTRALIA	6	2	10
CZECHOSLOVAKIA	5	6	3
GREAT BRITAIN	4	12	2
BULGARIA	3	5	2
FINLAND	3	—	2
NEW ZEALAND	3	—	2
ROMANIA	2	4	6
NETHERLANDS	2	4	4
TURKEY	2	3	1
SWEDEN	2	2	4
DENMARK	2	1	3
YUGOSLAVIA	2	1	2
BELGIUM	2	—	1
FRANCE	1	8	6
CANADA	1	2	1
SWITZERLAND	1	2	1
BAHAMAS	1	—	—
ETHIOPIA	1	—	—
INDIA	1	—	—
SOUTH KOREA	—	2	1
TRINIDAD AND TOBAGO	—	1	2
TUNISIA	—	1	1
ARGENTINA	—	1	—
CUBA	—	1	—
PAKISTAN	—	1	—
PHILIPPINES	—	1	—
IRAN	—	—	2
BRAZIL	—	—	1
GHANA	—	—	1
IRELAND	—	—	1
KENYA	—	—	1
MEXICO	—	—	1
NIGERIA	—	—	1
URUGUAY	—	—	1

1968 *Winter*

THE Xth WINTER GAMES

GRENOBLE, FRANCE
6–18 FEBRUARY 1968

Attended by representatives of 37 countries, comprising 1293 competitors, of which 228 were women.

A budget of $200 million was allocated, and among facilities built was a 12 000 seat indoor ice stadium. The opening ceremony was held in a specially constructed stadium which was later demolished. Complaints were made about the fact that venues were very widespread with some sites as much as 40 km distant from Grenoble. Sex tests for female competitors were held for the first time. The political split between East and West Germany was finally acknowledged by the Olympic authorities and two separate teams were entered. Morocco made its début in the Winter

Games. The official opening was performed by the President of France, Charles de Gaulle. The last relay runner was Alain Calmat, the 1964 figure skating silver medallist, while the oath was taken by Leo Lacroix, the skier, also a 1964 silver medal winner. The IOC attempted to control the exploitation of the Games by commercial interests by banning the use of trade names on competitors' equipment. Following the threat of a withdrawal by some leading skiers, who relied very heavily on ski company sponsorship, it was finally decided that they need only remove the equipment before appearing in photographs or on television.

The star of the Games was Jean-Claude Killy (FRA) who matched Toni Sailer's 1956 record by winning all three Alpine races. However, in the last event of the three, the slalom, Karl Schranz (AUT) claimed that in his second round run he had been distracted by a policeman cutting across the course ahead of him. He was allowed another run, which he accomplished in faster time to become overall winner. Then it was decided that on his first attempt he had already missed a gate before the policeman incident and his rerun was disqualified. The best of the women Alpinists was Canada's Nancy Greene with a gold in the giant slalom and a silver in the slalom. The latter was won by Marielle Goitschel (FRA) to keep the title not only in France but also in the family, as her sister had won it in 1964.

The most successful Nordic skier was Toini Gustafsson (SWE) who won two golds and one silver in the women's events. A big upset was the victory of Franco Nones (ITA) in the 30 km cross-country race, making him the first winner of a Nordic skiing event in the Olympics to come from a country outside Scandinavia. Another shock to the Scandinavians occurred in the two jumps and the combination event when their only medal of the nine available was a bronze.

Another upset came in the women's luge where the three East German girls, with runs putting them in first, second and fourth places, were disqualified for illegally heating their sled runners. The bob run at Alpe d'Huez, which was badly sited and considered to be very dangerous, was the scene of total triumph for Eugenio Monti (ITA). After two silvers and two bronzes since

Jean-Claude Killy (FRA) winning the downhill race at Grenoble, the first of his record equalling three gold medals in the Alpine skiing events.

FINAL MEDAL STANDINGS

Nation	Gold	Silver	Bronze
NORWAY	6	6	2
USSR	5	5	3
FRANCE	4	3	2
ITALY	4	—	—
AUSTRIA	3	4	4
NETHERLANDS	3	3	3
SWEDEN	3	2	3
WEST GERMANY (FRG)	2	2	3
UNITED STATES	1	5	1
FINLAND	1	2	2
EAST GERMANY (GDR)	1	2	2
CZECHOSLOVAKIA	1	2	1
CANADA	1	1	1
SWITZERLAND	—	2	4
ROMANIA	—	—	1

1956, and holder of nine world championships, he finally achieved his ambition and won gold medals in both the 2-man and 4-man events.

In the 2-man event the total times after four runs for both Monti's bob and that of the German bob were equal. The tie was decided in the Italian's favour as he had clocked the fastest single run time, a track record of 1 min 10·05 sec. Aged 40 yr 24 days Monti was the oldest gold medallist at Grenoble.

Ludmila and Oleg Protopopov (URS) retained their pairs skating title, with Ludmila becoming the oldest female champion at these Games aged 32 yr 84 days. The winner of the women's singles, Peggy Fleming (USA), was the youngest winner in Grenoble aged 19 yr 198 days. The youngest male champion was Wolfgang Schwarz, at 20 yr 155 days, in gaining Austria's first individual skating victory since 1936.

For the only time to date no speed skater gained more than one event. The women's 500 m was reminiscent of the results of the men's event in 1948 and 1964, as three girls tied for the silver medal. Making this occasion unique was the fact that all three of them were from the same country, the United States.

1968 *Summer*

THE XIXth OLYMPIC GAMES

MEXICO CITY, MEXICO
12–27 OCTOBER 1968

Attended by representatives of 112 countries, comprising 5530 competitors, of which 781 were women.

From the moment that the IOC awarded the Games to Mexico City in 1963 there was a gradually increasing furore about the effects of its altitude, 2240 m, on competitors in events which required endurance. Some medical authorities even forecast possible deaths. While this extreme view was, thankfully, unduly pessimistic, certainly many cases of severe exhaustion occurred. Also it should be noted that when Australian distance runner Ron Clarke developed serious heart trouble in 1981 there was much speculation as to how much his condition had been aggravated by his efforts in Mexico City in 1968. As well as the danger to the athletes, it was claimed that the standard of performance would be low in many events, those in which there was over three minutes of continuous effort. This claim was correct, but the same conditions contributed to other quite startling performances.

The thin air was not the only complaint raised about these Games. Some felt that the traditional 'mañana' attitude attributed to the Mexicans would result in incomplete facilities. In fact all was ready in good time. There was the threat of a boycott by many Black African nations when the IOC readmitted South Africa to the Olympic

The extreme altitude of Mexico City presented major problems, if not acute danger, to distance runners, who needed oxygen badly at the end of their exertions.

fold early in the year. After 40 countries had threatened to withhold their teams from the Games the IOC reversed its decision and South Africa was barred again. In August Czechoslovakia was invaded by the Soviet Union and its allies. A few weeks before the Games began serious student riots erupted at the University of Mexico which were ruthlessly dealt with by the police and army. Dozens were killed and hundreds injured. In America there was a move to get black athletes to boycott the US team to protest against the alleged bad treatment of Blacks in general in the United States. When this appeared to get little support, the organizers implied that some type of demonstration would be held at the Games. Despite all the troubles President Gustavo Diaz Ordaz of Mexico declared the Games open to a record breaking number of teams and athletes. Enriqueta Basilio, a hurdler, became the first woman in Olympic history to light the flame in the stadium.

Two things were immediately clear in the track and field events in the stadium. Firstly, that the distance races were going to be dominated by athletes who lived and trained at high altitude, such as the Kenyans and Ethiopians. Secondly, that the short distance and explosive events would produce remarkable results. Outstanding among the latter was the 8·90 m long jump by Bob Beamon (USA)—a performance considered by many experts to be of 21st-Century quality. The jump was beyond the limits of the measuring device in use at the pit and a steel tape had to be used. At the time of writing, some 14 years later, the world records set in the 100 m, 400 m, 4 × 400 m relay and the long jump still stand. In the triple jump seven men beat the existing Olympic record, and the world record was improved on five occasions. The winner of the high jump, Dick Fosbury (USA), used the 'flop' style which he had pioneered and which was to revolutionize standards in the event. Al Oerter (USA) made history with his fourth consecutive win in the discus, and Wyomia Tyus (USA) became the only sprinter to successfully defend an Olympic 100 m title, other than Archie Hahn (USA) at the Intercalated Games of 1906. The men's 100 m final was unique in that all eight finalists were black. A more heralded expression of black power was the demonstration by the Black Power supporters, Tommie Smith and John Carlos in the 200 m victory ceremony. The Americans, who had come first and third respectively, raised black-gloved, clenched fists, during the playing of the American anthem. For this action they were suspended and expelled from the Olympic village.

The greatest number of medals were won, as usual, by gymnasts. Although Mikhail Woronin (URS) won a total of seven (two golds, four silvers and one bronze), the star of the sport was Vera Cáslavská (TCH) who won four golds (one shared) and two silvers. Her floor exercises routine, to the music of the 'Mexican Hat Dance' was immensely popular. Soon after her events were over, but still during the Games, she married her countryman, Josef Odlozil, the 1964 1500 m silver medallist. Incidentally, Woronin's wife, Sinaida, won a gold, a silver and two bronze medals in the Soviet women's team.

The outstanding swimmers were Charles Hickcox (USA), with three golds and a silver, and Debbie Meyer (USA), who, uniquely to that date, won three individual events. Six other swimmers won two gold medals, including an eighteen year old American named Mark Spitz (see p 152). Mexico's first ever swimming gold medal was won by Felipe Munoz in the 200 m breaststroke.

Janice Romary (USA) set a record although eliminated in the early rounds of the women's foil fencing. She was competing in her sixth consecutive Games, a record for a woman in any sport. The 5·5 m class yachting, held at the resort city of Acapulco, produced the unique result of triple gold medal siblings. The Swedish brothers, Ulf, Peter and Jörgen Sundelin crewed *Wasa IV* to an easy victory. Behind them, skippering the

second placed Swiss boat *Toucan* was Louis Noverraz, at 66 yr 154 days, the oldest medallist at these Games.

For the first time since they entered the hockey competition in 1928 India failed to reach the final. In soccer, won for a record third time by Hungary, the surprise bronze medallist was Japan. They were the first, and to date only, Asian team to win a soccer medal, and the first non-European team to do so since 1928.

The oldest gold medallist at the Games was Josef Neckarmann, a member of the German dressage team aged 56 yr 141 days, while the youngest was Günther Tiersch (GDR) who coxed the winning eight crew aged 14 yr 172 days. The oldest female champion was Liselott Linsenhoff, in the same dressage team as Neckermann at 41 yr 58 days. A member of the American 4 × 100 m medley swimming team, Susan Pedersen, one day past her 15th birthday, was the youngest female gold medallist.

The oldest competitor at Mexico City was Roberto Soundy, a trapshooter from El Salvador aged 68 yr 229 days. The same country was represented by the youngest male competitor, Ruben Guerrero in the medley swimming relay aged 13 yr 351 days. The youngest competitor of

One man to whom the altitude 'problem' of the 1968 Games presented a chance in a lifetime—and Bob Beamon (USA) took it to set a phenomenal long jump record.

all was Liana Vicens of Puerto Rico, only 11 yr 328 days in the 100 m breaststroke for women, while the oldest female competitor was Britain's Lorna Johnstone who was 13th in the dressage event aged 66 yr 51 days.

The tallest competitor at these Games was the Soviet basketball player Sergey Kovalenko at 2·17 m *7 ft 1½ in.*

A record 30 countries won at least one gold medal, a feat unsurpassed in Olympic history.

FINAL MEDAL STANDINGS

Nation	Gold	Silver	Bronze
UNITED STATES	45	28	34
USSR	29	32	30
JAPAN	11	7	7
HUNGARY	10	10	12
EAST GERMANY (GDR)	9	9	7
FRANCE	7	3	5
CZECHOSLOVAKIA	7	2	4
WEST GERMANY (FRG)	5	11	10
AUSTRALIA	5	7	5
GREAT BRITAIN	5	5	3
POLAND	5	2	11
ROMANIA	4	6	5
ITALY	3	4	9
KENYA	3	4	2
MEXICO	3	3	3
YUGOSLAVIA	3	3	2
NETHERLANDS	3	3	1
BULGARIA	2	4	3
IRAN	2	1	2
SWEDEN	2	1	1
TURKEY	2	—	—
DENMARK	1	4	3
CANADA	1	3	1
FINLAND	1	2	1
ETHIOPIA	1	1	—
NORWAY	1	1	—
NEW ZEALAND	1	—	2
TUNISIA	1	—	1
PAKISTAN	1	—	—
VENEZUELA	1	—	—
CUBA	—	4	—
AUSTRIA	—	2	2
SWITZERLAND	—	1	4
MONGOLIA	—	1	3
BRAZIL	—	1	2
BELGIUM	—	1	1
SOUTH KOREA	—	1	1
UGANDA	—	1	1
CAMEROUN	—	1	—
JAMAICA	—	1	—
ARGENTINA	—	—	2
GREECE	—	—	1
INDIA	—	—	1
TAIWAN	—	—	1

1972 *Winter*

THE XIth WINTER GAMES

SAPPORO, JAPAN
3–13 FEBRUARY 1972

Attended by representatives of 35 countries, comprising 1232 competitors, of which 217 were women.

The Games finally came to Sapporo, 32 years after they were first awarded to the city but cancelled due to the Second World War. It was the most populous city, with one million inhabitants, ever to host the Winter Games. Over a 5 year period some $555 million was spent preparing facilities for the Games, not least for the enormous number of media personnel who outnumbered the competitors by over two to one. The arguments between the IOC and the sponsored skiers, which had caused problems in 1968, came to a head and resulted in Austria's star skier, Karl Schranz, being expelled before the Games even started. Although there was a list of 40 competitors apparently under threat of suspension, only he was banned. This led initially to a threat of an Austrian withdrawal, but at Schranz's urging this was averted. Another aspect of the amateur/professional debate was highlighted by Canada's refusal to compete in the ice hockey competition because of the State-sponsored players from Eastern Europe. Their call for Olympic ice hockey to be 'open' was ignored. The games were formally opened by Emperor Hirohito. The flame was delivered by Hideki Takada, a speed skater, and another, Keichi Suzuki, took the oath. Teams from Taiwan and the Philippines competed in the Winter Games for the first time. First ever Winter gold medals were won by Poland (ski jumping), Spain (slalom), and the host country (ski jumping). In this latter event, on the 70 m hill, Japan had a grand slam taking all three medals for a unique Olympic jumping achievement. To win only the second ever gold medal by a Spanish sportsman, Francisco Fernández-Ochoa beat the Italian brothers Gustavo and Rolando Thoeni. The women's slalom was won by Barbara Cochran (USA) by the smallest margin, 0·02 sec, ever in an Olympic Alpine event. Her sister Marilyn and a brother Bob were also in the US team.

Three gold medals each were won by Galina Kulakova (URS) in Nordic skiing, and Ard Schenk (HOL) in speed skating. Schenk might have had more but he fell in the 500 m event and finished 34th out of 37 competitors. East Germany returned to total domination of the luge competitions. The women's event was won by Anna-Maria Müller, one of the three girls who had been disqualified for heating their runners at the previous Games.

In figure skating Trixi Schuba (AUT) took the women's title although she only placed seventh in the free skating segment. Her compulsory figures were excellent and at that time the two segments were scored on a 50–50 basis. Soon after the Games this method of scoring was changed. An 'affaire de coeur' involving Alexey Ulanov (URS) who with Irina Rodnina won the pairs, and Ludmila Smirnova, his team-mate who placed second with Andrei Surakin, titillated the skating world in Sapporo. Later they married and competed internationally as partners but never with the success they had attained with their former partners.

The youngest gold medallist at the Games was Anne Henning (USA) who won the women's

500 m speed skating title aged 16 yr 157 days. The oldest was Jean Wicki in the Swiss 4-man bob aged 38 yr 239 days. The oldest female winner was Christina Baas-Kaiser (HOL) with her 3000 m speed skating victory at 33 yr 268 days, and the youngest male champion was Wojciech Fortuna (POL) who won the 90 m ski jump aged 19 yr 189 days.

Medals were won by a record 17 countries, of which 14 gained the gold variety, another record for the Winter Games.

FINAL MEDAL STANDINGS

Nation	Gold	Silver	Bronze
USSR	8	5	3
EAST GERMANY (GDR)	4	3	7
SWITZERLAND	4	3	3
NETHERLANDS	4	3	2
UNITED STATES	3	2	3
WEST GERMANY (FRG)	3	1	1
NORWAY	2	5	5
ITALY	2	2	1
AUSTRIA	1	2	2
SWEDEN	1	1	2
JAPAN	1	1	1
CZECHOSLOVAKIA	1	—	2
POLAND	1	—	—
SPAIN	1	—	—
FINLAND	—	4	1
FRANCE	—	1	2
CANADA	—	1	—

1972 *Summer*

THE XXth OLYMPIC GAMES

MUNICH, FEDERAL REPUBLIC OF GERMANY
26 AUGUST – 10 SEPTEMBER 1972

Attended by representatives of 122 countries, comprising 7156 competitors, of which 1070 were women.

Awarded the Games in May 1966, Munich built a magnificent complex on the rubble from the Second World War bombing. It was reported that total costs amounted to $650 million. A

The powerful Dutch speed skater Ard Schenk winning his third gold medal, in the 10 000 m, at the 1972 Games in Sapporo.

week before the Games began the IOC expelled the team from Rhodesia under intense pressure from Black African nations. A number of new electronic devices were used in the conduct of the Games including a triangulation device to measure distances in the athletics throwing events. Archery and men's handball returned to the Olympic programme, and there were additions to other sports, making a total of 195 gold medals available. They became the most widely covered Games in history with over 4000 representatives of the world's media on hand. When the German President Gustave Heinemann opened the Games in a colourful ceremony there was a television audience estimated at an all-time live viewing record of 1000 million. The oath was taken by athlete Heidi Schüller, the first woman ever to do so. The record number of countries taking part included first timers, Albania, Dahomey, Lesotho, Malawi, Upper Volta, Somalia, Swaziland, Togo and North Korea (South Korea sent a separate team).

The first week of the Games was dominated by the American swimmer Mark Spitz who smashed all records for a single Olympics by winning seven gold medals, four individual and three in relays, with world records broken in each event. Added to his medals from Mexico City his overall total was nine golds, one silver and one bronze. Only athlete Ray Ewry (USA) had gained more Olympic victories. Spitz's female equivalent in the pool was Shane Gould (AUS) who won three golds, one silver, and one bronze. She swam in a total of 12 races, itself a record for a woman swimmer in the Games. The men's 400 m medley final resulted in the closest ever win in Olympic history when Gunnar Larsson (SWE) was declared the victor over Tim McKee (USA) by two-thousandths of a second. This decision led to a change in international swimming rules so that in future times and places should be decided in hundredths. On the running track Valery Borzov (URS) was the first European to win a sprint double. A pre-Games dispute led to the banning of the poles used by the American pole vaulters, a decision which helped to cause their run of 16 consecutive victories in the event (excluding the 1906 Interim Games) to come to an end. When Ulrike Meyfarth (FRG) won the women's high jump, equalling the world record of 1·92 m, aged 16 yr

Outstanding backstroke swimmer Roland Matthes (GDR) became one of the few Olympians to win a double 'double' in 1968 and 1972.

123 days, she became the youngest ever individual track and field event gold medallist. In hockey, for the first time since 1920 a team, Germany, from outside the Indian sub-continent won the title. The oustanding attraction of the first few days of the Games was Olga Korbut (URS) a gymnast whose gamin qualities stole the limelight from her more illustrious colleague, Ludmila Tourischeva (who later married sprint champion Borzov). Virtually overnight, with blanket media coverage, she became a 'superstar'.

On the morning of 5 September all the euphoria of the Games evaporated when a band of eight Arab terrorists broke into the quarters of the Israeli team at 31 Connollystrasse in the Olympic village. Two of the Israeli team were killed immediately and nine others held hostage, as German police and the world's press surrounded the area. After protracted negotiations the terrorists and their hostages were allowed to go to the airport, where an abortive rescue attempt resulted in the murder of all nine Israelis and the death of some of their captors. The following morning the Games were suspended for a memorial ceremony in a packed stadium, but with the agreement of most parties involved, including the Israeli officials, competitions were resumed later in the day. The overall feeling seemed to be that the Games should go on, although a number of individuals, notably from Norway, Holland and the Philippines decided to withdraw. The Israeli team returned home immediately.

The track and field events resumed next day with Kipchoge Keino (KEN) adding the 3000 m steeplechase title to that at 1500 m he had won four years previously. This made him the first runner since James Lightbody (USA) in 1904 to win Olympic titles at 1500 m and at the steeplechase. Lasse Viren (FIN) won the 5000 m/10 000 m double, setting a world record in the latter despite falling over, and Frank Shorter (USA) won the marathon in the town of his birth. In the women's discus Lia Manoliu competed in her record sixth Games. In the women's pentathlon Heide Rosendahl (FRG) theoretically held the Olympic and world records for the event for 1·12 sec, the difference between her winning time in the last discipline, 200 m, and that of the eventual overall champion, Mary Peters (GBR).

By winning the five-sport modern pentathlon individual title Hungary's András Balczó brought his total medal haul since 1960 to an event record of three golds and two silvers. For the second consecutive Games the three medallists in skeet shooting all achieved the same score, the tie being broken by shooting another 25-bird round. Aleksandr Medved (URS) won his third wrestling title in a row (and his tenth world championship), after a disputed decision over the giant American Chris Taylor. Taylor, report-

Wilfried Dietrich (FRG) wrestling the gigantic Chris Taylor (USA) in the 1972 Games super-heavyweight division. The 'little' man won.

edly weighing 182 kg or more, was the heaviest known man to have competed in the Olympic Games. Another record three-time winner was Daniel Morelon (FRA) in the cycling events.

The United States suffered an unusual number of misfortunes and reverses at these Games. Two prospective 100 m medallists, Eddie Hart and Rey Robinson, failed to take part in the second round heats due to a misreading of the starting time by their coach. Then there was the previously mentioned pole vault fracas. Jim Ryun, then world record holder at 1500 m, fell in the heats and was eliminated. During the victory ceremony for the 400 m gold and silver medallists, Vince Matthews and Wayne Collett made an allegedly 'Black Power' protest for which they were banned from further Olympic competition. This meant that the United States could not field a 4 × 400 m relay team, thus failing to win a medal for the first time since 1920. Another incident, with a happier conclusion, occurred when the 800 m champion, Dave Wottle, in his excitement forgot to remove his lucky cap during the American national anthem. He was very embarrassed and proffered apologies to everyone who would listen. An unhappier incident resulted in the American basketball team refusing to collect their silver medals. A highly controversial decision by an international official, R W Jones of Great Britain, gave the Soviet team an extra few seconds at the end of the final game during which they scored the winning points to take the title by 51–50. They thus ended America's remarkable run of 63 consecutive victories in Olympic basketball since its introduction in 1936.

Another unfortunate occurrence was the disqualification of swimmer Rick DeMont after the American had won a close victory in the 400 m freestyle swimming final. A dope test proved positive, due apparently to the inclusion of a prohibited substance in a drug that DeMont took to alleviate asthma. If the US team officials had notified the IOC beforehand he would have been the youngest champion at these Games, as he was only 16 yr 133 days old. More serious disqualifications due to doping included that of Bakhaavaa Buidaa, who had won the wrestling silver medal for Mongolia, Jaime Huelamo (ESP) who had won a bronze in the cycling road race, and the Dutch four who had gained third place in the cycling team race.

The oldest gold medallist at the Games was Hans Günter Winkler (FRG) when a member of the winning equestrian show jumping team aged 46 yr 49 days. His countrywoman, Liselott Linsenhoff, was the oldest female winner at 45 yr 13 days, and as gold medallist in the dressage was

FINAL MEDAL STANDINGS

Nation	Gold	Silver	Bronze
USSR	50	27	22
UNITED STATES	33	31	30
EAST GERMANY (GDR)	20	23	23
WEST GERMANY (FRG)	13	11	16
JAPAN	13	8	8
AUSTRALIA	8	7	2
POLAND	7	5	9
HUNGARY	6	13	16
BULGARIA	6	10	5
ITALY	5	3	10
SWEDEN	4	6	6
GREAT BRITAIN	4	5	9
ROMANIA	3	6	7
CUBA	3	1	4
FINLAND	3	1	4
NETHERLANDS	3	1	1
FRANCE	2	4	7
CZECHOSLOVAKIA	2	4	2
KENYA	2	3	4
YUGOSLAVIA	2	1	2
NORWAY	2	1	1
NORTH KOREA	1	1	3
NEW ZEALAND	1	1	1
UGANDA	1	1	—
DENMARK	1	—	—
SWITZERLAND	—	3	—
CANADA	—	2	3
IRAN	—	2	1
BELGIUM	—	2	—
GREECE	—	2	—
AUSTRIA	—	1	2
COLOMBIA	—	1	2
ARGENTINA	—	1	—
LEBANON	—	1	—
MEXICO	—	1	—
MONGOLIA	—	1	—
PAKISTAN	—	1	—
SOUTH KOREA	—	1	—
TUNISIA	—	1	—
TURKEY	—	1	—
BRAZIL	—	—	2
ETHIOPIA	—	—	2
SPAIN	—	—	1
GHANA	—	—	1
INDIA	—	—	1
JAMAICA	—	—	1
NIGER	—	—	1
NIGERIA	—	—	1

also the first woman to win an individual equestrian event. The youngest gold medallist at Munich was Deana Deardurff (USA) in the 4 × 100 m medley swimming relay aged 15 yr 118 days. The youngest male champion was Uwe Benter (FRG) who coxed the winning fours crew when 16 yr 276 days old. Another record-breaker at these Games was Lorna Johnstone (GBR) who reached the final 12 in the dressage event at the remarkable age of 70 yr 5 days, making her the oldest woman known to compete in the Olympic Games.

The tallest competitor at the Games, and the tallest medallist in Olympic history was Tom Burleson (USA) the 2·23 m *7 ft 4 in* basketball player. One of the runners in the torch relay bringing the Olympic flame to Munich was Edgar Fried, a former general-secretary of the Austrian Olympic Committee, who had been in the original torch relay in 1936 and was the only one to repeat in that of 1972, in his 78th year.

At the end of the XXth Games a record 48 countries had won at least one medal.

1976 *Winter*

THE XIIth WINTER GAMES

INNSBRUCK, AUSTRIA
4–15 FEBRUARY 1976

Attended by representatives of 37 countries, comprising 1128 competitors, of which 228 were women.

In 1970 the Games were awarded to Denver, Colorado, USA, but at the end of 1972 a Colorado State referendum decided against providing the necessary finance. So in February 1973 Innsbruck became the first centre to be awarded the Winter Games twice. Most of the facilities needed were still available from 1964 and 'only' $44 million was required to refurbish and update. The Games were opened by the President of Austria, Dr Rudolf Kirchschläger, and uniquely two Olympic flames were lit, by Christl Haas, 1964 gold medal skier, and Josef Feistmantl, 1964 gold medal lugeist. The oath was taken by Werner Delle-Karth, a bobsledder. A total of 1½ million spectators watched the 37 event schedule, as well as another 600 million television viewers around the world. Unfortunately an influenza outbreak affected a number of competitors. Two of the smallest States in the world, Andorra and San Marino, made their Winter Games débuts.

The outstanding performer was Rosi Mittermaier (FRG) who by winning the downhill and slalom races, and taking second place in the giant slalom, set up the best series of performances ever by a female Alpine skier. She failed by 0·13 sec, in the giant slalom, to match the male record of three golds held by Sailer and Killy. In winning the men's downhill on the Patscherkofel course Franz Klammer of the host country averaged a speed of 102·828 km/h, the fastest ever in Olympic competition. Raisa Smetanina (URS) won two golds and a silver to be the most successful Nordic skier, but her team-mate Galina Kulakova lost a bronze in the 5000 m cross-country race when she was disqualified after a banned drug was found to be present in a nasal spray she was using to combat the effects of influenza. However, she was allowed to compete in other events and won a gold medal as well as another bronze.

The most medals won at the Games was two gold and two bronze by Tatyana Averina (URS) in speed skating. Preventing a clean sweep of those titles by the Soviet women was Sheila Young (USA) who took the 500 m gold medal, and later in the year won her second world cycling championship. In figure skating Irina Rodnina appeared with a new partner, her husband Aleksandr Zaitsev, and successfully defended her title. The men's champion, Britain's John Curry, brought balletic art to the singles just as the Protopopovs had to the pairs in 1964 and 1968. His Italian/American coach, Carlo Fassi, became the first to have trained both individual champions at a single Games when Dorothy Hamill (USA) won the ladies title. In the new ice dancing event Soviets were placed first, second and fourth. All five luge and bobsled events were won by competitors from the GDR. The Games

No female Alpine skiier has come nearer than Rosi Mittermaier (FRG) to winning all three gold medals, when she lost the 1976 giant slalom event by only $^{12}/_{100}$ sec.

ended as they had begun with an Austrian victory, by Karl Schnabl in the 90 m ski jump.

The oldest gold medallist was Meinhard Nehmer (GDR) in the 2-man bob aged 35 yr 25 days. The youngest was Kathy Kreiner (CAN) who won the giant slalom for women aged 18 yr 285 days. The youngest male gold medallist was Sergey Babinov (URS) in the champion ice hockey team aged 20 yr 218 days. The oldest female champion was Galina Kulakova (URS) in the $4 \times 7\cdot5$ km relay aged 33 yr 289 days. The oldest competitor was 46 year old Carl Erik Eriksson (SWE) in the bob events while the youngest was Yelena Vodorezova (URS) who was aged 12 yr 265 days at the start of the figure skating competition.

FINAL MEDAL STANDINGS

Nation	Gold	Silver	Bronze
USSR	13	6	8
EAST GERMANY (GDR)	7	5	7
UNITED STATES	3	3	4
NORWAY	3	3	1
WEST GERMANY (FRG)	2	5	3
FINLAND	2	4	1
AUSTRIA	2	2	2
SWITZERLAND	1	3	1
NETHERLANDS	1	2	3
ITALY	1	2	1
CANADA	1	1	1
GREAT BRITAIN	1	—	—
CZECHOSLOVAKIA	—	1	—
LIECHTENSTEIN	—	—	2
SWEDEN	—	—	2
FRANCE	—	—	1

1976 *Summer*

THE XXIst OLYMPIC GAMES

MONTREAL, CANADA
*17 JULY –
1 AUGUST 1976*

Attended by representatives of 92 countries, comprising 6085 competitors, of which 1251 were women.

The Games were awarded to Montreal primarily due to the efforts of the city's Mayor Jean Drapeau. It was initially estimated that the staging of the Olympics would cost $310 million. Because of planning errors, labour strikes and slowdowns, and, it has been suggested, widespread corruption, the final bill amounted to a massive $1400 million. The stadium alone cost $485 million, and the projected 160 m high tower and the roof which was to be suspended from it was never completed. Security arrangements involving 16 000 police and soldiers accounted for $100 million. Six months before the opening it seemed that the main facilities would not be finished in time, but by the official opening pronounced by Queen Elizabeth II all that was necessary was ready. The expected number of entries was well down owing to a last minute boycott by 20 Third World, mainly African, countries. They were protesting against the inclusion of New Zealand, a country whose rugby union team had visited South Africa. Taiwan withdrew because Canada refused to recognize them under the title of Republic of China, a situation which owed much, it was generally thought, to Canada's grain-trading relations with Mainland China. The withdrawals, mostly only 2 days prior to the start of competitions caused some problems with seeding arrangements, and particularly affected boxing and running events.

Attempts had been made to prune the number of events on the programme, and to this end the 50 km walk, tandem cycling, slalom canoeing, the free rifle and three swimming events had been eliminated. However, with the inclusion of women's basketball and handball, four canoeing races and seven rowing events, of which six were for women, the total number of gold medals available was now 198. This was three more than at Munich. The torch was brought into the stadium by two 15 year olds, a boy and a girl: one was of English descent the other of French stock, each with a hand on the torch, signifying Canada's joint heritage (see p 244). In true storybook fashion the pair were married some years later. The star of Munich, Olga Korbut, was at Montreal but she was overshadowed by a 14 year old Romanian girl, Nadia Comaneci, who scored the first ever maximum 10·00 marks achieved in the Olympics on the first day of the gymnastics. By the end of the competitions she had scored another six maximums (Nelli Kim of the Soviet Union also scored two) and drawn a world record gymnastics crowd of 18 000 to the finals of the women's events. The men's individual champion, Nikolai Andrianov (URS) won the most medals at Montreal with four golds, two silvers and a bronze. Two swimmers also won four golds, and a silver each; Kornelia Ender (GDR) and John Naber (USA). Ender brought her total of Olympic medals in two Games to four golds and four silvers. She later married her team-mate, backstroke specialist Roland Matthes, who had gained four golds, two silver and two bronze in three Games. The GDR women only failed to win two of their 13 events on the Montreal swimming programme. The American men only lost one of their thirteen, and that went to David Wilkie who won Britain's first male swimming gold medal since 1908 by winning the 200 m breaststroke in a world record time of 2 min 15·11 sec. In highboard diving the Austrian-born Italian, Klaus Dibiasi, competing in his fourth Games, became the first diver to gain three consecutive gold medals. In the Hungarian water polo team, which won their country's record sixth victory in the sport, was István Szivós, whose father had been in the winning 1952 and 1956 teams.

Events in the main stadium were highlighted by the exploits of the latest 'Flying Finn', Lasse Viren, who completed an outstanding 'double double' by successfully defending his 5000 m and 10 000 m titles. Attempting to emulate Zatopek's 1952 feat he finished fifth in the marathon as well. Alberto Juantorena (CUB),

Nadia Comaneci (ROM) on the beam in 1976. She scored a total of seven perfect scores (10·00) in front of capacity crowds in the Montreal Forum.

the winner but an error was discovered which gave her a tie with her team-mate Lanny Bassham. A closer examination of the targets then relegated her to second place. Although Raimondo d'Inzeo (ITA) only placed 12th in the show jumping Grand Prix he set an unprecedented record as he was competing in his eighth Olympic Games, 1948–1976. Alwin Schockemöhle (FRG) became only the third rider in Olympic history to win the jumping title without any faults.

The new Olympic sport of women's basketball produced the tallest known woman ever to compete in the Games. She was Iuliana Semenova (URS) who was unofficially reported to be 2·18 m *7 ft 1¾ in* tall and weighed 127 kg *280 lb*. Her team won the title, and she is one of the tallest, including men, to win an Olympic gold medal. In weightlifting two Bulgarians and a Pole who had won medals were later disqualified for failing the dope test. A far greater scandal occurred in the modern pentathlon when one of the favourites, Boris Onischenko (URS), was discovered to have tampered with his épée in the fencing segment of the competition. It came to light when he was fighting Britain's Jim Fox and the latter's indicator light flashed even though he had not been touched by the Soviet's weapon. Onischenko's disqualification eliminated the Soviet team and the gold medal in the team contest went to Great Britain.

The revenge match which the American basketball team were eagerly waiting for never materialized as the Soviet team were beaten by Yugoslavia in the semifinals. Thus the United States regained the title making their Olympic match record—played 70, won 69.

The oldest gold medallist at these Games was Harry Boldt (FRG) a member of the winning dressage team aged 46 yr 157 days. The youngest was Maria Filatova (URS) who won a gold medal in the gymnastics team championship on her 15th birthday. The youngest male champion was Brian Goodell (USA) aged 17 yr 109 days when he won the 1500 m freestyle title. The oldest female to win a gold medal was Sinaida Turchina (URS) a member of the winning handball team aged 30 yr 72 days. One of the youngest competitors ever was Antonia Real (ESP) who competed in the women's 400 m freestyle aged 12 yr 310 days.

known as 'The Horse', won the 400 m/800 m double for the first time in Olympic history, if one excludes the performances of America's Paul Pilgrim in the 1906 Interim Games. Irena Szewinska (POL), aged 30, won the 400 m in her fourth Games to bring her total of medals to a record-equalling seven, comprising three gold, two silver and two bronze. The winner of the men's javelin, Miklos Nemeth (HUN), was the son of Imre Nemeth who had won the hammer title in 1948. They are the only father and son in track and field to win gold medals.

Three sets of brothers did very well in the Montreal rowing competitions. Frank and Alf Hansen (NOR) won the double sculls, while the Landvoigt twins from GDR, Jörg and Bernd, took the coxless pairs title. Another set of GDR twins, Walter and Ullrich Diessner, were in the silver medal coxed four crew. In women's fencing Elena Novikova-Belova (URS) won her record fourth gold medal in the team contest, while Hungary's Ildikó Sagi-Retjö set an all-medal record of seven, comprising two gold, three silver and two bronze collected in five Games. The first woman to win a shooting medal was Margaret Murdock (USA) in the small-bore rifle (three positions) event. She was unlucky not to have won the gold as initially she was declared

FINAL MEDAL STANDINGS

Nation	Gold	Silver	Bronze
USSR	49	41	35
EAST GERMANY (GDR)	40	25	25
UNITED STATES	34	35	25
WEST GERMANY (FRG)	10	12	17
JAPAN	9	6	10
POLAND	7	6	13
BULGARIA	6	9	7
CUBA	6	4	3
ROMANIA	4	9	14
HUNGARY	4	5	13
FINLAND	4	2	—
SWEDEN	4	1	—
GREAT BRITAIN	3	5	5
ITALY	2	7	4
FRANCE	2	3	4
YUGOSLAVIA	2	3	3
CZECHOSLOVAKIA	2	2	4
NEW ZEALAND	2	1	1
SOUTH KOREA	1	1	4
SWITZERLAND	1	1	2
JAMAICA	1	1	—
NORTH KOREA	1	1	—
NORWAY	1	1	—
DENMARK	1	—	2
MEXICO	1	—	1
TRINIDAD AND TOBAGO	1	—	—
CANADA	—	5	6
BELGIUM	—	3	3
NETHERLANDS	—	2	3
PORTUGAL	—	2	—
SPAIN	—	2	—
AUSTRALIA	—	1	4
IRAN	—	1	1
MONGOLIA	—	1	—
VENEZUELA	—	1	—
BRAZIL	—	—	2
AUSTRIA	—	—	1
BERMUDA	—	—	1
PAKISTAN	—	—	1
PUERTO RICO	—	—	1
THAILAND	—	—	1

1980 *Winter*

THE XIIIth WINTER GAMES

LAKE PLACID, NEW YORK STATE, USA

13–24 FEBRUARY 1980

Attended by representatives of 37 countries, comprising 1067 competitors, of which 234 were women.

Lake Placid had been applying for the Games unsuccessfully since 1962 when they were finally rewarded in 1974. Most of the facilities from 1932 had to be rebuilt and new ones constructed. The budget for the 1980 Games was nearly 80 times the $1·1 million spent on the 1932 celebration. A number of complaints were made before the sport began, particularly about the 'village' for competitors which was a building later to be converted into a penal institution. As a report noted 'at least security will not be a problem'. Once the Games were under way it was found that the accommodation was quite suitable and acceptable. The official opening was made by Walter Mondale, the Vice-President of the United States. The last relay runner was Dr Charles Kerr, a psychiatrist, and with outstanding foresight speed skater Eric Heiden was selected to take the oath. The People's Republic of China and Cyprus made their Winter Games débuts. One pre-Games worry which did materialize into a major problem was the transport facilities for spectators and the press. At times it was virtually impossible to reach venues and/or return from them.

Eric Heiden (USA) won the most medals at these Games with an unprecedented sweep of all five speed skating gold medals, all in Olympic record times. His sister, Beth, also won a bronze in the women's events. Leah Poulos-Mueller (USA) won two silver medals but could not match her husband Peter's gold performance of 1976.

Slalom specialist Ingemar Stenmark (SWE) won both of his races to be the most successful male Alpine skier, but Hanni Wenzel from tiny Liechtenstein won both women's slaloms and the silver medal in the downhill. Her brother Andreas added a silver medal to put their country in sixth place on the unofficial medal table. (Another sister Petra was also in the team of seven competitors.)

In Nordic skiing Nikolai Simyatov (URS) won three golds, a unique achievement in the sport at a single Games. Ulrich Wehling (GDR) won his third consecutive gold medal in the Nordic combination event, while Aleksandr Tikhonov

The Games 1980

(URS) won a fourth consecutive gold medal in the biathlon relay, another record. His teammate Galina Kulakova continued the record breaking by winning a silver in the Nordic relay to bring her total to a women's Winter Games record of eight medals (four golds, two silvers and two bronze) in the four Games since 1968.

In winning the 90 m ski jump Jouko Törmänen (FIN) made the longest jump ever attained in Olympic competition when he cleared 117 m. In the 70 m jump there was an unfortunate incident when after nine competitors had already taken their jumps the judges decided that conditions were too dangerous due to the high wind causing the jumpers to descend the hill too fast. The start was moved lower down, to reduce take-off speed, and the competition begun again.

The closest ever result in Olympic skiing occurred in the 15 km cross-country event when Thomas Wassberg (SWE) won the gold medal from Juha Mieto (FIN) by one-hundredth of a second with a time of 41 min 57·63 sec. The unlucky Finn had lost a bronze medal in 1972 by only six-hundredths, but had won a gold medal in the 1976 relay.

The bobsledding was virtually a replay of the 1976 rivalry between the Swiss and GDR teams. A member of the American 12th placed 4-man bob was Willie Davenport, who had competed in the Summer Games from 1964 to 1976 and had won the 110 m hurdles title in 1968.

Irina Rodnina (URS) equalled the record of three gold medals by a figure skater when she retained the pairs title with her husband Aleksandr Zaitsev. By successfully defending the men's singles for Great Britain Robin Cousins won his country's only gold medal of the Games. In all a record 19 countries won at least one medal at Lake Placid.

The oldest gold medallist was Meinhard Nehmer (GDR) in the 4-man bob aged 39 yr 42 days, while the youngest was Karin Enke (GDR) who won the 500 m speed skating for women aged 18 yr 240 days. The youngest male gold medallist was Mike Ramsey of the victorious United States ice hockey team aged 19 yr 83 days. The oldest female champion was Irina Rodnina (URS) winning her third pairs title aged 30 yr 159 days. A special mention must be made of

At Lake Placid Nikolai Simyatov (URS) won a unique three gold medals in Nordic skiing. He also placed fourth in another event having raced a total of 105 000 m within 7 days.

Marina Tcherkasova (USA) who won a silver medal in the pair skating 93 days past her 15th birthday.

By far the most popular win was that of the US ice hockey team over the Soviet Union (their first defeat since 1964) on the way to the final against Finland which they also won. The following celebrations were described on American television as the biggest since the end of the Second World War.

At the end of the Games only Great Britain, Sweden and the United States could claim to have been represented in all winter events of the Modern Olympics, including those of 1908 and 1920.

FINAL MEDAL STANDINGS

Nation	Gold	Silver	Bronze
USSR	10	6	6
EAST GERMANY (GDR)	9	7	7
UNITED STATES	6	4	2
AUSTRIA	3	2	2
SWEDEN	3	—	1
LEICHTENSTEIN	2	2	—
FINLAND	1	5	3
NORWAY	1	3	6
NETHERLANDS	1	2	1
SWITZERLAND	1	1	3
GREAT BRITAIN	1	—	—
WEST GERMANY (FRG)	—	2	3
ITALY	—	2	—
CANADA	—	1	1
HUNGARY	—	1	—
JAPAN	—	1	—
BULGARIA	—	—	1
CZECHOSLOVAKIA	—	—	1
FRANCE	—	—	1

1980 *Summer*

THE XXIInd OLYMPIC GAMES

MOSCOW, USSR
19 JULY –
1 AUGUST 1980

Attended by representatives of 81 countries, comprising 5326 competitors, of which 1088 were women.

There had been only a little dissent in 1974 when the IOC voted by a substantial majority to award the 1980 Games to Moscow. Tsarist Russia had competed in 1900 and from 1906 to 1912. Athletes from Estonia and Latvia, which had been provinces of Russia prior to 1918 and were taken over by the Soviet Union in 1940, had competed independently from 1920 to 1936. The Soviet Union had entered the Games in force in 1952 and was now the second highest medal scorer of all time. In December 1979 the Soviet Union invaded Afghanistan, and much of the non-Communist world, led by the United States, tried to impose a boycott on the Games—but not, it should be noted, on trade and other economic activity. Not all countries supported the boycott, although sports within those countries sometimes did. It is difficult to complete a list of those who did not go to Moscow in support of the boycott, as a number of those previously included were unlikely to attend anyway for other, usually financial, reasons. The most reliable estimate is 45–50, of which the most important in sporting terms were the United States, the Federal Republic of Germany and Japan. When the Games were officially opened by Leonid Brezhnev, President of the USSR, there were eight first time entries to the Games, not including Zimbabwe which had previously been at the Olympics as Rhodesia.

Facilities, including the 103 000 capacity Lenin Stadium, were excellent and large crowds attended most sports. New competitions such as women's hockey, two extra judo classes, one extra weightlifting class, and reintroduced

events brought the total of gold medals available to a record 203 (barring ties).

The heroine of Montreal, Nadia Comaneci (ROM) returned but was not the force she had been, and the star of the gymnastics was a male, Aleksandr Ditiatin (URS). By winning three golds, four silvers and one bronze he set a record for the most medals ever won by a competitor, of any sport, in a single Games. He also was awarded a maximum 10·00 in the horse vault, the first such score ever to a man in the Olympics. His team-mate Nikolai Andrianov brought his total of medals to a record 15, comprising seven golds, five silvers and three bronze, in three Games. This total has only ever been exceeded in Olympic history by Larissa Latynina (URS) also a gymnast (see p 121).

In the Lenin stadium East African athletes dominated the distance runs, led by Miruts Yifter (ETH) who completed the 5000 m/10 000 m double. The 100 m result was the closest for 28 years with Allan Wells (GBR) given the verdict over Silvio Leonard (CUB), both clocking 10·25 sec. Two other Britons, Steve Ovett and Sebastian Coe, each won their 'wrong' event, in taking the 800 m and 1500 m titles respectively. Waldemar Cierpinski (GDR) became only the second man ever to successfully defend the marathon title although he was 1 min 8 sec slower than in 1976. In the triple jump Viktor Saneyev (URS) ended his remarkable career with a silver to add to the three gold medals he had won since 1968 in the event. By repeating her Montreal gold medals in the 200 m and 4 × 100 m relay Barbel Wöckel (GDR) equalled the female Olympic track and field record of four gold medals. In the relay Ludmila Maslakova of the silver medal Soviet team was running in her fourth consecutive relay final since 1968. Although only winning the silver medal in the pentathlon, Olga Rukavishnikova (URS) theoretically held the world record, albeit for only 0·4 sec, as she finished first by that margin in the last discipline, 800 m, of the five-event competition. That gave her the shortest reign of any world record holder ever.

As four years earlier the GDR girls won 11 of the 13 swimming events. Caren Metschuck won three golds and a silver for them, but Ines Diers was their highest medal scorer with two golds, two silvers and a bronze. More unusually her team-mate Rica Reinisch won three gold medals all in world record times. Overall the GDR women won 26 of the 35 possible medals.

In canoeing Vladimir Parfenovich (URS) became the first in the sport to win three gold medals at the same Games. The Landvoigt twins (GDR), Jörg and Bernd, retained their 1976 coxless pairs rowing title, beating the Soviet Pimenov twins, Yuri and Nikolai, into second place. The other GDR rowing twins, Ullrich and Walter Diessner, won gold medals in the coxed fours event. The wrestling competitions produced yet another pair of victories for twins when Anatoly and Sergey Beloglasov (URS) won the 52 kg and 57 kg freestyle events respectively. The Cuban heavyweight boxer, Teofilo Stevenson, became the only boxer to win the same event in three Games: the Hungarian Laszlo Papp had won his three golds at two different weights.

The inaugural women's hockey competition resulted in Zimbabwe gaining a gold medal on its début in the Olympic Games, while India was back to its former winning ways by taking its record eighth title in the men's final. In the yachting events held at Tallinn, the former capital of Estonia, the Finn class dinghy event was won by a Finn, Esko Rechardt.

The oldest gold medallist at the Games was Valentin Mankin (URS) in the Star class yachting aged 41 yr 346 days. The youngest was swimmer Rica Reinisch (GDR) who was only 15 yr 105 days when she was a member of the winning 4 × 100 m medley relay team. The oldest female winner was Vera Misevich (URS) at 36 yr 112 days in the dressage team event, while the youngest male gold medallist was the Hungarian winner of the 200 m backstroke title, Sandor Wladar, at 17 yr 7 days. The youngest competitor of all was Anita Jokiel (POL) aged only 13 yr 232 days when the gymnastics competitions began. Also in those competitions was the smallest competitor, Myong Hui Choe of North Korea, standing 1·35 m *4 ft 5 in* with a weight of 25 kg *55 lb*. The tallest was the Soviet basketball player Vladimir Tkachenko at 2·20 m *7 ft 2½ in* tall, and the heaviest was Roman Codrean (ROM), a 170 kg *375 lb* Greco-Roman wrestler whose size did not prevent him from being eliminated in the second round.

FINAL MEDAL STANDINGS

Nation	Gold	Silver	Bronze
USSR	80	69	46
EAST GERMANY (GDR)	47	37	42
BULGARIA	8	16	17
CUBA	8	7	5
ITALY	8	3	4
HUNGARY	7	10	15
ROMANIA	6	6	13
FRANCE	6	5	3
GREAT BRITAIN	5	7	9
POLAND	3	14	15
SWEDEN	3	3	6
FINLAND	3	1	4
CZECHOSLOVAKIA	2	3	9
YUGOSLAVIA	2	3	4
AUSTRALIA	2	2	5
DENMARK	2	1	2
BRAZIL	2	—	2
ETHIOPIA	2	—	2
SWITZERLAND	2	—	—
SPAIN	1	3	2
AUSTRIA	1	2	1
GREECE	1	—	2
BELGIUM	1	—	—
INDIA	1	—	—
ZIMBABWE	1	—	—
NORTH KOREA	—	3	2
MONGOLIA	—	2	2
TANZANIA	—	2	—
MEXICO	—	1	3
NETHERLANDS	—	1	2
IRELAND	—	1	1
UGANDA	—	1	—
VENEZUELA	—	1	—
JAMAICA	—	—	3
GUYANA	—	—	1
LEBANON	—	—	1

1984 *Winter*

THE XIVth WINTER GAMES

SARAJEVO, YUGOSLAVIA
8–19 FEBRUARY 1984

Sarajevo, with a population of about 500 000, is the second largest city to host the Winter Games. (Only Sapporo was larger.) Construction of facilities is ahead of schedule and plans for ensuring adequate transportation for the expected 2300 competitors, over 4000 media representatives and thousands of visitors are well advanced. An unusual feature will be the accommodation of most of those visitors in private homes instead of hotels. All competition sites are within 27 km of the city. The IOC has sanctioned one new event, a 20 km Nordic race for women, and is considering the inclusion of an Alpine Combination event, which has not been contested since 1948.

1984 *Summer*

THE XXIIIrd OLYMPIC GAMES

LOS ANGELES, USA
28 JULY –
12 AUGUST 1984

The IOC awarded the Games of 1984 to Los Angeles only after involved negotiations about the financial guarantees usually required from the city hosting the Olympics. Various innovations to protect Los Angeles from a Montreal-like deficit have been implemented, not least the widespread sponsorship by private corporations.

The Los Angeles Memorial Coliseum, the site of the 1932 Games, will again be the main venue, but many new facilities are being built, including a velodrome for cycling and a swimming and diving stadium. Halls and stadia at the many universities in the Los Angeles area will be used for most sports. Yachting will be at Long Beach, and rowing and canoeing on Lake Casitas. The Coliseum, which has not been used for track and field meetings since 1974, will be fully refurbished and a new synthetic surface will be laid on the track and jump areas. Seating capacity is currently 92 604. The show jumping section of the equestrian events will be held at the world-famous Santa Anita racetrack.

A number of new events have been added to the 1984 programme. Women's cycling will make its début with an individual road race, and there will

also be a men's individual points race. In boxing a super-heavyweight class has been added. Rhythmic gymnastics will be represented by a single event, while a K4 500 m race for women has been added to the canoeing events. In the swimming pool three events, comprising the 200 m medley for men and women and the men's 4 × 100 m freestyle, will be reinstated, and a synchronized swimming (duet) competition for women will be added. Four new shooting events will be held comprising a men's air rifle contest and three events for women (air rifle, small-bore rifle, and pistol). Board sailing (commonly but incorrectly called windsurfing) has been included in the yachting programme, while the women's 400 m hurdles, 3000 m and marathon races have been included in track and field. In total there will be a record 220 official events plus demonstrations of baseball and tennis. It has been estimated that there will be a television audience of 2500 million for these Games.

The Future

The XVth Winter Games have been awarded to Calgary, Canada, with provisional dates of 23 February–6 March 1988 as the most likely period. There is a possibility of freestyle skiing being included for the first time.

The XXIVth Olympic Games have been awarded to Seoul, South Korea with provisional dates of 20 September–5 October 1988 as the probable period. An IOC meeting in October 1981 decided that tennis and table tennis should be included in the list of sports acceptable for inclusion at Seoul.

A number of cities are considering making a bid for the Games of 1992, the site for which will be decided by the IOC in 1985. For the Winter Games they include Nice, Falun (Sweden), Garmisch-Partenkirchen, and Lillehammer (Norway), and for the Summer Games they include; Amsterdam, Barcelona, Brisbane or Sydney, Budapest, New Delhi, Nice or Paris, Stockholm and Vienna.

The site of the Games of 1996, the centenary year, seems most likely to be Athens, so setting the seal on the twentieth century's most beset and belittled, but no less remarkable, international movement—the Olympic Games.

THE SPORTS

ARCHERY

The sport made its first appearance in the Games at Paris in 1900 with six events on the programme. There is considerable disagreement among Olympic historians about whether another, live pigeon shooting, was an official Olympic event or not. The majority think not, and this book follows that opinion. The contests were held in Continental style, with each archer shooting a single arrow at a time in competition order, as opposed to the British method of shooting three arrows at each turn. Hubert van Innis (BEL) was the high scorer winning two gold medals and a silver.

The eligibility of the 1904 archery competitions is also disputed by some particularly as only American archers took part. However the majority of historians and the author accept them as Olympic Games events. The competitors in the women's archery contests were among the first women to compete in the Olympics, only the 1900 tennis players have a prior claim. The stars of St Louis were Miss M C Howell of the Cincinatti Archery Club who won three gold medals and Phillip Bryant of the Boston AA who won two golds and a silver in the individual and team events. One of the members of the winning team in 1904 was the Rev Galen Spencer who became the oldest ever archery gold medallist at 2 days past his 64th birthday. A team-mate of Bryant in the bronze medal team from Boston was Henry Richardson, at 15 yr 126 days the youngest ever archery medallist.

The competitions in 1908 were accorded a much higher status than previously although only three countries were involved. The only medallist other than from Britain or France was the afore-

Early female Olympic champions such as Queenie Newall (GBR) were able to be fashionable as well as functional.

mentioned Henry Richardson who again won a bronze medal for the United States. The men's York Round was won by William Dod (GBR) and his remarkable sister, Charlotte, took the silver medal behind Queenie Newall. Lottie Dod, then over 36 years old, was one of the greatest sportswomen of her, or any other, generation. She had won the Wimbledon tennis singles title five times, the British Ladies golf title in 1904, and had represented England at hockey. She also excelled at ice skating and tobogganing. Archery was not included in the 1912 Games but reflecting Belgium's great interest in the sport there were ten events at Antwerp in 1920, all in the Belgian style of shooting. Mainly because of the insistence on

Gold	Silver	Bronze
1900		
Au cordon doré—50 m Henri Herouin (FRA)	Hubert van Innis (BEL)	Emile Fisseux (FRA)
Au cordon doré—33 m Hubert van Innis (BEL)	Victor Thibaud (FRA)	Charles Petit (FRA)
Au chapelet—50 m Eugène Mougin (FRA)	Henri Helle (FRA)	Emile Mercier (FRA)
Au chapelet—33 m Hubert van Innis (BEL)	Victor Thibaud (FRA)	Charles Petit (FRA)
Sur la perche à la herse Emmanuel Foulon (FRA)	Serrurier (FRA)	—
	Druat Jr (FRA)	
Sur la perche à la pyramide Emile Grumiaux (FRA)	Louis Glineux (FRA)	—
1904		
Men		
Double York Round Phillip Bryant (USA)	Robert Williams (USA)	William Thompson (USA)
Double American Round Phillip Bryant (USA)	Robert Williams (USA)	William Thompson (USA)
Team Round Potomac Archers (USA)	Cincinatti Archery Club (USA)	Boston AA (USA)
Women		
Double National Round M C Howell (USA)	H C Pollock (USA)	E C Cooke (USA)
Double Columbia Round M C Howell (USA)	E C Cooke (USA)	H C Pollock (USA)
Team Round Cincinatti Archery Club (USA)	Potomac Archers (USA)	—
1908		
Men		
York Round William Dod (GBR)	R B Brooks-King (GBR)	Henry Richardson (USA)
Continental Style E G Grisot (FRA)	Louis Vernet (FRA)	Gustave Cabaret (FRA)
Women		
National Round Queenie Newall (GBR)	Charlotte Dod (GBR)	Hill-Lowe (GBR)
1920		
Fixed bird target—small birds—individual		
Edmond van Moer (BEL)	Louis van de Perck (BEL)	Joseph Hermans (BEL)
Fixed bird target—small birds—team		
Belgium	—	—
Fixed bird target—large birds—individual		
Edouard Cloetens (BEL)	Louis van de Perck (BEL)	Firmin Flamand (BEL)
Fixed bird target—large birds—team		
Belgium	—	—
Moving bird target—28 m—individual		
Hubert van Innis (BEL)	Léonce Quentin (FRA)	—
Moving bird target—28 m—team		
Netherlands	Belgium	France
Moving bird target—33 m—individual		
Hubert van Innis (BEL)	Julien Brulé (FRA)	—
Moving bird target—33 m—team		
Belgium	France	—
Moving bird target—50 m—individual		
Julien Brulé (FRA)	Hubert van Innis (BEL)	—
Moving bird target—50 m—team		
Belgium	France	—

DOUBLE FITA ROUND (maximum possible score 2880 points)

Men

1972 John Williams (USA) 2528 pts	Gunnar Jarvil (SWE) 2481 pts	Kyösti Laasonen (FIN) 2467 pts
1976 Darrell Pace (USA) 2571 pts	Hiroshi Michinaga (JPN) 2502 pts	Giancarlo Ferrari (ITA) 2495 pts
1980 Tomi Poikolainen (FIN) 2455 pts	Boris Isachenko (URS) 2452 pts	Aleksandr Gazov (URS) 2449 pts

Women

1972 Doreen Wilber (USA) 2424 pts	Irena Szydlowska (POL) 2407 pts	Emma Gapchenko (URS) 2403 pts
1976 Luann Ryon (USA) 2499 pts	Valentina Kovpan (URS) 2460 pts	Zebeniso Rustamova (URS) 2407 pts
1980 Keto Losaberidze (URS) 2491 pts	Natalya Butuzova (URS) 2477 pts	Päivi Meriluoto (FIN) 2449 pts

this style there were only three countries represented, Belgium, France and the Netherlands. Hubert van Innis (BEL), now 54 years old brought his total medals to a record six gold and three silver. Two other Belgians, Edmond van Moer and Edouard Cloetens gained three gold medals each. Archery was not included again until 1972 when the events were standardized into contests over Double FITA Rounds for men and women. A FITA (Fédération Internationale de Tir à l'Arc) Round consists of 144 arrows, comprising 36 each over distances of 90 m, 70 m, 50 m and 30 m for men, and 70 m, 60 m, 50 m and 30 m for women. The winner of the 1972 men's event, John Williams (USA) was the youngest archery gold medallist ever at 18 yr 355 days, and he set world records for the Single FITA (1268 points) and Double FITA (2528 points) Rounds. The women's event went to his team-mate Doreen Wilber, also in a Double FITA record of 2424 points, and at the age of 42 yr 246 days she was the oldest ever female champion.

OLYMPIC RECORDS—ARCHERY

Event	Points	Name & Country	Year
Men's Double FITA	2571	Darrell Pace (USA)	1976
Women's Double FITA	2499	Luann Ryon (USA)	1976

ARCHERY—MEDALS

	Men			Women			
	G	S	B	G	S	B	Total
UNITED STATES	5	3	4	5	3	2	22
FRANCE	6	9	6	—	—	—	21
BELGIUM	10	7	2	—	—	—	19
USSR	—	1	—	1	2	2	6
GREAT BRITAIN	1	1	—	1	1	1	5
FINLAND	1	—	1	—	—	1	3
ITALY	—	—	2	—	—	—	2
NETHERLANDS	1	—	—	—	—	—	1
JAPAN	—	1	—	—	—	—	1
POLAND	—	—	—	—	1	—	1
SWEDEN	—	1	—	—	—	—	1
	24[1]	23[2]	15[3]	7	7	6[4]	82

[1] Only a gold medal awarded in two 1920 team events. [2] Two silver medals awarded in a 1900 event. [3] No bronze medals in two events in 1900 and six in 1920. [4] No bronze medal in 1904 team event.

BASKETBALL

The game made its official Olympic début in 1936, although it had been a demonstration sport in 1904, and the analogous Dutch game Korfball was demonstrated in 1928.

The 1936 tournament was uniquely played outdoors and involved 21 teams. One of the referees was Avery Brundage (USA) who was later to become President of the IOC. The man who had devised the modern game of basketball in 1891, Dr James Naismith, was one of the dignitaries who presented the medals. The gold medal team was from the United States, thus beginning a winning streak comprising seven gold medals and 63 victories from a walkover against Spain in 1936 up to the 1972 final in which they were beaten by the Soviet Union 51–50. The 1972 final was much disputed with the Americans claiming that too much overtime was played during which the Soviet player Aleksandr Belov (who tragically died 6 years later) scored the winning basket. Three seconds from the end of the game Doug Collins (USA) was fouled when the Americans were behind 49–48. Scoring with both of his free throws he put his team into a 50–49 lead. With one second to go the Soviet team's inbounds pass was deflected and everyone thought the game was over, and spectators jumped onto the court. They were cleared off and the Soviet team was given another inbounds chance, but did not score. Again the game seemed to be over. But Dr William Jones (GBR) Secretary-General of FIBA (Fédération Internationale de Basketball Amateur) stated that play was incorrectly restarted at one second and that there should have been three seconds allowed. The clock was then reset to three seconds and the Soviet team scored. The United States team protested vigorously and eventually refused to accept the silver medals.

The greatest number of entries for the Olympic basketball tournament is 23 in 1948 and 1952. In 1952 the number of finalists was limited to 16 and qualifying conditions have changed from Games to Games. In 1976 the IOC allowed the participation of 18 teams in basketball, so allowing FIBA to allocate 12 places to the men's competition and six to an inaugural women's tournament.

The tallest player ever in Olympic basketball competition, probably the tallest ever Olympic competitor in any sport, and certainly the tallest medallist, is Tommy Burleson (USA) at 2·23 m *7 ft 4 in* in 1972. The tallest female player, the tallest female competitor in Olympic history and the tallest to win a gold medal is Iuliana Semenova (URS) at 2·18 m *7 ft 1¾ in* in 1976 and 1980. She was also the heaviest female gold medallist of all time at 129 kg *284 lb*.

The venue of the 1968 tournament, the Palacio de los Deportes, in Mexico City, provided the greatest number of spectators for an Olympic basketball game with a capacity of 22 370 seats. One of the most star-studded American teams was that of 1960 which had Oscar Robertson, Jerry West and John Havlicek on its strength, all players who later reached the highest ranks in the professional game. Another member of that team was the only player to win two gold medals, Burdette Haldorson (USA) in 1956 and 1960. Also in the 1956 US team was Bill Russell, another who made a major impact on the professional game. The only player to win medals in four Games is Sergey Belov (URS) with one gold and three bronzes between 1968 and 1980. At the latter Games he was given the honour of bringing the torch into the stadium at the opening ceremony and lighting the Olympic flame.

The highest aggregate scored in an Olympic basketball game is 221 points. This was achieved twice in 1980 when the Soviet Union beat Spain 119–102, and when Brazil beat India 137–64. The Brazilian score is the highest ever reached by a team in a single game in Olympic competition. The greatest margin of victory is 100 points achieved twice in 1948 when Korea beat Iraq 120–20 and when China beat Iraq 125–25. In women's basketball Japan beat Canada in 1976 by 121–89 for a record points aggregate of 210. The highest total by a team in a single game is 122 by the Soviet Union against Bulgaria (83) in 1980. The greatest margin of victory was 66 points when the Soviet Union beat Italy 119–53, also in 1980.

The youngest player to win a gold medal was Jerome Shipp (USA) aged 19 yr 26 days in the 1964 final. The oldest was Gennadiy Volnov (URS) aged 32 yr 286 days in 1972.

	Gold	Silver	Bronze
Men			
1936	United States	Canada	Mexico
1948	United States	France	Brazil
1952	United States	USSR	Uruguay
1956	United States	USSR	Uruguay
1960	United States	USSR	Brazil
1964	United States	USSR	Brazil
1968	United States	Yugoslavia	USSR
1972	USSR	United States	Cuba
1976	United States	Yugoslavia	USSR
1980	Yugoslavia	Italy	USSR

1896–1932 Event not held

	Gold	Silver	Bronze
Women			
1976	USSR	United States	Bulgaria
1980	USSR	Bulgaria	Yugoslavia

1896–1972 Event not held

Countries placing in first eight

	1936	1948	1952	1956	1960	1964	1968	1972	1976	1980
Argentina	–	–	4	–	–	–	–	–	–	–
Australia	–	–	–	–	–	–	–	–	8	8
Brazil	–	3	6	6	3	3	4	7	–	5
Bulgaria	–	–	7	5	–	–	–	–	–	–
Canada	2	–	–	–	–	–	–	–	4	–
Chile	–	6	5	8	–	–	–	–	–	–
Cuba	–	–	–	–	–	–	–	3	7	6
Czechoslovakia	–	7	–	–	5	–	–	8	6	–
France	–	2	8	4	–	–	–	–	–	–
Italy	7	–	–	–	4	5	8	4	5	2
Korea	–	8	–	–	–	–	–	–	–	–
Mexico	3	4	–	–	–	5	–	–	–	–
Peru	8	–	–	–	–	–	–	–	–	–
Philippines	5	–	–	7	–	–	–	–	–	–
Poland	4	–	–	–	7	6	6	–	–	7
Puerto Rico	–	–	–	–	–	4	–	6	–	–
Spain	–	–	–	–	–	–	7	–	–	4
United States	1	1	1	1	1	1	1	2	1	–
Uruguay	6	5	3	3	8	8	–	–	–	–
USSR	–	–	2	2	2	2	3	1	3	3
Yugoslavia	–	–	–	–	6	7	2	5	2	1

BASKETBALL—MEDALS

	Men			Women			
	G	S	B	G	S	B	Total
UNITED STATES	8	1	—	—	1	—	10
USSR	1	4	3	2	—	—	10
YUGOSLAVIA	1	2	—	—	—	1	4
BRAZIL	—	—	3	—	—	—	3
URUGUAY	—	—	2	—	—	—	2
BULGARIA	—	—	—	—	1	1	2
FRANCE	—	1	—	—	—	—	1
ITALY	—	1	—	—	—	—	1
CANADA	—	1	—	—	—	—	1
MEXICO	—	—	1	—	—	—	1
CUBA	—	—	1	—	—	—	1
	10	10	10	2	2	2	36

Boxing

The oldest man to win an Olympic boxing title, Richard Gunn lived to celebrate his ninetieth birthday.

BOXING

ANCIENT GAMES

Boxing existed in early Crete and well before the arrival of the Greeks in the Aegean area it was an established pastime. Contests were included in the ancient Games for the first time in 688 BC. Competitors wore leather straps on their hands, which, as the status of the Games deteriorated in Roman times, had metal studs added. Later still the boxers wore metal 'knuckledusters'. One of the earliest known champions was Onomastos of Smyrna. The last known champion before the Games were abolished was Varazdetes (or Varastades), the winner in AD 369, who achieved such fame that he became King of Armenia. Early boxing should not be confused with the *pankration* event, which was a brutal event combining boxing and wrestling in which virtually anything was permitted. To illustrate the lengths reached in this contest it is recorded that Arrachion of Phigalia was awarded the title in 564 BC, owing to his opponent 'giving up'—although he was by then lying dead in the arena.

Boxing was first included in the Games in 1904 when the USA won all the titles. A pattern was set by the first heavyweight champion, Samuel Berger, when he turned professional after his victory. Incidentally he was a member of the San Francisco Olympic Club which had also produced 'Gentleman Jim' Corbett who had won the world title in 1892. Over the years the weight limits for the various classes have changed and new classes added. Bronze medals for losing semi-finalists were not awarded until 1952.

Two men have won three gold medals at boxing. László Papp (HUN), a southpaw, won the middleweight division in 1948, and the light-middleweight division in 1952 and 1956. Teofilo Stevenson (CUB) uniquely won the same class, heavyweight, in 1972, 1976 and 1980. In 1904 Oliver Kirk (USA) became the only boxer to win two events at the same Games when he won gold medals in the bantamweight and featherweight classes.

On two occasions one country has won all titles available; the United States in 1904 (seven in all), and Great Britain in 1908 (five).

In the Ancient Games it is recorded that Tisamenos of Naxos won four Olympic crowns between 540 and 528 BC.

Of the four men who have won two titles only Boris Lagutin (USSR), light-middleweight in 1964 and 1968, gained another medal—a bronze in 1960. The others were Oliver Kirk (USA), see above, Harry Mallin (GBR) middleweight in 1920 and 1924 (thus becoming the first boxer to successfully defend an Olympic title), and Jerzy Kulej (POL) light-welterweight in 1964 and 1968.

Despite blatant chauvinistic judging in 1924, Harry Mallin (GBR) retained the title he had first won in Antwerp 4 years earlier.

DECISIONS AND DISQUALIFICATIONS

In the 1924 Games the French followed the then European custom of seating the referees outside the ring. Often it was impossible to hear their instructions, and the standard of refereeing was highly suspect to the British and Americans.

In the preliminary bouts of the middleweight division defending champion Harry Mallin (GBR) was continually fouled by his French opponent, and ended the fight with teeth marks on his chest. Despite this the outclassed French boxer was declared the winner. An immediate appeal, backed by the threatened withdrawal of all the English-speaking countries, was upheld.

The middleweight title in 1908 was also the scene of some controversy when John Douglas (GBR)—who was later to captain England at cricket—defeated Reg 'Snowy' Baker (AUS) for the gold medal. The Australian understandably complained that the referee had not been impartial—he was Douglas's father.

A unique occurrence in Olympic boxing annals was the disqualification of Ingemar Johansson (SWE) in the second round of the 1952 heavyweight final and the withholding of the silver medal due to his 'inactivity in the ring'. Thirty years later he was finally presented with his medal.

AMATEUR TO PROFESSIONAL

Many Olympic boxing medallists have gone on to further success in the professional ranks. Gold medallists who have won world professional titles include:

Other Olympic medallists, silver and bronze, who have won world professional titles include; Carmelo Bossi (ITA), Johnny Caldwell (IRL), Ingemar Johansson (SWE), Marvin Johnson (USA), Sandro Lopopolo (ITA), Alan Minter (GBR), Lou Salica (USA), John Tate (USA) and Jose Torres (USA).

MISCELLANEOUS

America's Norvel Lee went to Helsinki in 1952 as reserve for the heavyweight class, but at the last moment was entered in the light-heavyweight competition. He had to lose over 6 kg in a matter of days. Not only did he win the title, but he was awarded the Val Barker Cup for being the most proficient boxer in the Games. A team-mate, Charles Adkins, also travelled as a reserve but won a gold medal, in the light-welterweight class.

The first, and so far only, brothers to win gold medals in Olympic boxing are Leon and Michael Spinks in 1976. Both have since turned professional and won world titles.

When the 1932 heavyweight champion Santiago Lovell (ARG) returned home after the Games, instead of a welcoming party he was sent to jail. It transpired that he had 'breached the peace' on the ship which took the Argentinian team back to Buenos Aires.

	Olympic Gold		*World Professional*	
Nino Benvenuti (ITA)	1960	Welter	1965	Junior Middle; 1967 Middle
Cassius Clay (later Muhammad Ali) (USA)	1960	Light Heavy	1964	Heavy
Jackie Fields (USA)	1924	Feather	1929	Welter
George Foreman (USA)	1968	Heavy	1973	Heavy
Joe Frazier (USA)	1964	Heavy	1970	Heavy
Frankie Genaro (USA)	1920	Fly	1928	Fly
Fidel LaBarba (USA)	1924	Fly	1927	Fly
Ray Leonard (USA)	1976	Light Welter	1979	Welter; 1981 Light Middle
Mate Parlov (YUG)	1972	Light Heavy	1978	Light Heavy
Floyd Patterson (USA)	1952	Middle	1956	Heavy
Pascual Perez (ARG)	1948	Fly	1954	Fly
Leon Spinks (USA)	1976	Light Heavy	1978	Heavy
Michael Spinks (USA)	1976	Middle	1981	Light Heavy

Boxing

The Hungarian triple gold medallist, László Papp, prevented from becoming a professional until over 30 years of age by his government, never fought for the world title, but won the European middleweight crown in 1962.

Laszlo Papp (HUN) winning the first of his three titles by defeating Johnny Wright (GBR) in 1948.

OLDEST AND YOUNGEST

The oldest boxer to win an Olympic title was Richard Gunn (GBR) who took the featherweight gold medal in 1908 when aged 37 years and 254 days.

The youngest gold medallist was Jackie Fields (USA) who won the 1924 Featherweight title aged 16 years and 162 days. Floyd Patterson (USA) won the 1952 middleweight gold medal at 17 years and 211 days. Four years later Patterson became the youngest ever to win the world professional heavyweight crown.

BOXING—MEDALS

	Gold	Silver	Bronze	Total
UNITED STATES	33	16	25	74
USSR	13	18	15	46
GREAT BRITAIN	12	10	18	40
POLAND	8	9	21	38
ITALY	12	10	11	33
CUBA	12	8	5	25
ARGENTINA	7	7	9	23
GERMANY (FRG)	4	10	7	21
SOUTH AFRICA	6	4	9	19
ROMANIA	1	7	9	17
HUNGARY	9	2	3	14
FINLAND	2	1	9	12
FRANCE	3	3	5	11
DENMARK	1	5	5	11
GDR	3	1	6	10
MEXICO	2	2	5	9
BULGARIA	2	1	6	9
SWEDEN	—	4	5	9
CANADA	2	2	4	8
KOREA	—	3	4	7
IRELAND	—	2	5	7
CZECHOSLOVAKIA	3	1	2	6
YUGOSLAVIA	2	1	3	6
NORWAY	1	2	2	5
N. KOREA (PRK)	1	2	1	4
BELGIUM	1	1	2	4
UGANDA	—	3	1	4
AUSTRALIA	—	1	3	4
KENYA	—	1	3	4
VENEZUELA	1	2	—	3
JAPAN	1	—	2	3
CHILE	—	1	2	3
GHANA	—	1	2	3
NIGERIA	—	—	3	3
NETHERLANDS	1	—	1	2
PHILIPPINES	—	1	1	2
COLOMBIA	—	—	2	2
PUERTO RICO	—	—	2	2
NEW ZEALAND	1	—	—	1
CAMEROUN	—	1	—	1
ESTONIA	—	1	—	1
BERMUDA	—	—	1	1
BRAZIL	—	—	1	1
EGYPT	—	—	1	1
GUYANA	—	—	1	1
SPAIN	—	—	1	1
TRINIDAD	—	—	1	1
TUNISIA	—	—	1	1
URUGUAY	—	—	1	1
	144	144	223	511

From 1952 each losing semi-finalist was awarded a bronze medal.

LIGHT FLYWEIGHT
Weight up to 48 kg 105·8 lb.

	Gold	Silver	Bronze
1968	Francisco Rodriguez (VEN)	Yong-ju Jee (KOR)	Harlan Marbley (USA)
			Hubert Skrzypczak (POL)
1972	György Gedo (HUN)	U Gil Kim (PRK)	Ralph Evans (GBR)
			Enrique Rodriguez (ESP)
1976	Jorge Hernandez (CUB)	Byong Uk Li (PRK)	Payao Pooltarat (THA)
			Orlando Maldonado (PUR)
1980	Shamil Sabirov (URS)	Hipolito Ramos (CUB)	Byong Uk Li (PRK)
			Ismail Moustafov (BUL)

1896–1964 Event not held

FLYWEIGHT

From 1948 the weight limit has been *51 kg* 112½ lb. In 1904 it was 105 lb *47·6 kg*. From 1920 to 1936 it was 112 lb *50·8 kg*.

	Gold	Silver	Bronze
1904	George Finnegan (USA)	Miles Burke (USA)	—*
1920	Frank De Genaro (USA)	Anders Petersen (DEN)	William Cuthbertson (GBR)
1924	Fidel LaBarba (USA)	James McKenzie (GBR)	Raymond Fee (USA)
1928	Antal Kocsis (HUN)	Armand Appel (FRA)	Carlo Cavagnoli (ITA)
1932	István Énekes (HUN)	Francisco Cabanas (MEX)	Louis Salica (USA)
1936	Willi Kaiser (GER)	Gavino Matta (ITA)	Louis Laurie (USA)
1948	Pascual Perez (ARG)	Spartaco Bandinelli (ITA)	Soo-Ann Han (KOR)
1952	Nathan Brooks (USA)	Edgar Basel (GER)	Anatoliy Bulakov (URS)
			William Toweel (SAF)
1956	Terence Spinks (GBR)	Mircea Dobrescu (ROM)	John Caldwell (IRL)
			René Libeer (FRA)
1960	Gyula Török (HUN)	Sergey Sivko (URS)	Kiyoshi Tanabe (JPN)
			Abdelmoneim Elguindi (EGY)
1964	Fernando Atzori (ITA)	Artur Olech (POL)	Robert Carmody (USA)
			Stanislav Sorokin (URS)
1968	Ricardo Delgado (MEX)	Artur Olech (POL)	Servilio Oliveira (BRA)
			Leo Rwabwogo (UGA)
1972	Gheorghi Kostadinov (BUL)	Leo Rwabwogo (UGA)	Leszek Blazynski (POL)
			Douglas Rodriguez (CUB)
1976	Leo Randolph (USA)	Ramon Duvalon (CUB)	Leszek Blazynski (POL)
			David Torosyan (URS)
1980	Petar Lessov (BUL)	Viktor Miroshnichenko (URS)	Hugh Russell (IRL)
			Janos Varadi (HUN)

1896–1900, 1906–1912 Event not held   *No third place

BANTAMWEIGHT

From 1948 the weight limit has been *54 kg* 119 lb. In 1904 it was 115 lb *52·16 kg*. In 1908 it was 116 lb *52·62 kg*. From 1920 to 1936 118 lb *53·52 kg*.

	Gold	Silver	Bronze
1904	Oliver Kirk (USA)	George Finnegan (USA)	—*
1908	Henry Thomas (GBR)	John Condon (GBR)	W Webb (GBR)
1920	Clarence Walker (SAF)	Christopher Graham (CAN)	James McKenzie (GBR)
1924	William Smith (SAF)	Salvatore Tripoli (USA)	Jean Ces (FRA)
1928	Vittorio Tamagnini (ITA)	John Daley (USA)	Harry Isaacs (SAF)
1932	Horace Gwynne (CAN)	Hans Ziglarski (GER)	José Villanueva (PHI)
1936	Ulderico Sergo (ITA)	Jack Wilson (USA)	Fidel Ortiz (MEX)
1948	Tibor Csik (HUN)	Giovanni Zuddas (ITA)	Juan Venegas (PUR)
1952	Pentti Hämäläinen (FIN)	John McNally (IRL)	Gennadiy Garbuzov (URS)
			Joon-Ho Kang (KOR)
1956	Wolfgang Behrendt (GER)	Soon-Chun Song (KOR)	Frederick Gilroy (IRL)
			Claudio Barrientos (CHI)
1960	Oleg Grigoryev (URS)	Primo Zamparini (ITA)	Brunoh Bendig (POL)
			Oliver Taylor (AUS)
1964	Takao Sakurai (JPN)	Shin Cho Chung (KOR)	Juan Fabila Mendoza (MEX)
			Washington Rodriguez (URU)
1968	Valeriy Sokolov (URS)	Eridadi Mukwanga (UGA)	Eiji Morioka (JPN)
			Kyou-Chull Chang (KOR)
1972	Orlando Martinez (CUB)	Alfonso Zamora (MEX)	George Turpin (GBR)
			Ricardo Carreras (USA)
1976	Yong Jo Gu (PRK)	Charles Mooney (USA)	Patrick Cowdell (GBR)
			Chulsoon Hwang (KOR)
1980	Juan Hernandez (CUB)	Bernardo Pinango (VEN)	Dumitru Cipere (ROM)
			Michael Anthony (GUY)

* No third place.

1896–1900, 1906, 1912 Event not held

FEATHERWEIGHT

From 1952 the weight limit has been *57 kg* 126 lb. In 1904 it was 125 lb *56·70 kg*. From 1908 to 1936 it was 126 lb *57·15 kg*. In 1948 it was *58 kg* 127¾ lb.

	Gold	Silver	Bronze
1904	Oliver Kirk (USA)	Frank Haller (USA)	Fred Gilmore (USA)
1908	Richard Gunn (GBR)	C W Morris (GBR)	Hugh Roddin (GBR)
1920	Paul Fritsch (FRA)	Jean Gachet (FRA)	Edoardo Garzena (ITA)
1924	John Fields (USA)	Joseph Salas (USA)	Pedro Quartucci (ARG)
1928	Lambertus van Klaveren (HOL)	Victor Peralta (ARG)	Harold Devine (USA)
1932	Carmelo Robledo (ARG)	Josef Schleinkofer (GER)	Carl Carlsson (SWE)
1936	Oscar Casanovas (ARG)	Charles Catterall (SAF)	Josef Miner (GER)
1948	Ernesto Formenti (ITA)	Denis Shepherd (SAF)	Aleksey Antkiewicz (POL)
1952	Jan Zachara (TCH)	Sergio Caprari (ITA)	Joseph Ventaja (FRA)
			Leonard Leisching (SAF)
1956	Vladimir Safronov (URS)	Thomas Nicholls (GBR)	Henryk Niedzwiedzki (POL)
			Pentti Hämäläinen (FIN)
1960	Francesco Musso (ITA)	Jerzy Adamski (POL)	William Meyers (SAF)
			Jorma Limmonen (FIN)
1964	Stanislav Stepashkin (URS)	Antony Villaneuva (PHI)	Charles Brown (USA)
			Heinz Schultz (GER)
1968	Antonio Roldan (MEX)	Albert Robinson (USA)	Philip Waruinge (KEN)
			Ivan Michailov (BUL)
1972	Boris Kuznetsov (URS)	Philip Waruinge (KEN)	Clemente Rojas (COL)
			András Botos (HUN)
1976	Angel Herrera (CUB)	Richard Nowakowski (GDR)	Juan Paredes (MEX)
			Leszek Kosedowski (POL)
1980	Rudi Fink (GDR)	Adolfo Horta (CUB)	Viktor Rybakov (URS)
			Krzysztof Kosedowski (POL)

1896–1900, 1906, 1912 Event not held

LIGHTWEIGHT

From 1952 the weight has been *60 kg* 132 lb. In 1904 and from 1920 to 1936 it was 135 lb *61·24 kg*. In 1908 it was 140 lb *63·50 kg*. In 1948 it was *62 kg*. 136½ lb.

	Gold	Silver	Bronze
1904	Harry Spanger (USA)	James Eagan (USA)	Russell Van Horn (USA)
1908	Frederick Grace (GBR)	Frederick Spiller (GBR)	H H Johnson (GBR)
1920	Samuel Mosberg (USA)	Gotfred Johansen (DEN)	Clarence Newton (CAN)
1924	Hans Nielsen (DEN)	Alfredo Coppello (ARG)	Frederick Boylstein (USA)
1928	Carlo Orlandi (ITA)	Stephen Halaiko (USA)	Gunnar Berggren (SWE)
1932	Lawrence Stevens (SAF)	Thure Ahlqvist (SWE)	Nathan Bor (USA)
1936	Imre Harangi (HUN)	Nikolai Stepulov (EST)	Erik Agren (SWE)
1948	Gerald Dreyer (SAF)	Joseph Vissers (BEL)	Svend Wad (DEN)
1952	Aureliano Bolognesi (ITA)	Aleksey Antkiewicz (POL)	Gheorghe Fiat (ROM)
			Erkki Pakkanen (FIN)
1956	Richard McTaggart (GBR)	Harry Kurschat (GER)	Anthony Byrne (IRL)
			Anatoliy Lagetko (URS)
1960	Kazimierz Pazdzior (POL)	Sandro Lopopoli (ITA)	Richard McTaggart (GBR)
			Abel Laudonio (ARG)
1964	Józef Grudzien (POL)	Vellikton Barannikov (URS)	Ronald Harris (USA)
			James McCourt (IRL)
1968	Ronald Harris (USA)	Józef Grudzien (POL)	Calistrat Cutov (ROM)
			Zvonimir Vujin (YUG)
1972	Jan Szczepanski (POL)	László Orban (HUN)	Samuel Mbugua (KEN)
			Alfonso Perez (COL)
1976	Howard Davis (USA)	Simion Cutov (ROM)	Ace Rusevski (YUG)
			Vasiliy Solomin (URS)
1980	Angel Herrera (CUB)	Viktor Demianenko (URS)	Kazimierz Adach (POL)
			Richard Nowakowski (GDR)

1896–1900, 1906, 1912 Event not held

LIGHT-WELTERWEIGHT
Weight up to *63·5 kg* 140 lb.

	Gold	Silver	Bronze
1952	Charles Adkins (USA)	Viktor Mednov (URS)	Erkki Mallenius (FIN) Bruno Visintin (ITA)
1956	Vladimir Yengibaryan (URS)	Franco Nenci (ITA)	Henry Loubscher (SAF) Constantin Dumitrescu (ROM)
1960	Bohumil Nemecek (TCH)	Clement Quartey (GHA)	Quincy Daniels (USA) Marian Kasprzyk (POL)
1964	Jerzy Kulej (POL)	Yegeniy Frolov (URS)	Eddie Blay (GHA) Habib Galhia (TUN)
1968	Jerzy Kulej (POL)	Enrique Regueiferos (CUB)	Arto Nilsson (FIN) James Wallington (USA)
1972	Ray Seales (USA)	Anghel Anghelov (BUL)	Zvonimir Vujin (YUG) Issaka Daborg (NIG)
1976	Ray Leonard (USA)	Andres Aldama (CUB)	Vladimir Kolev·(BUL) Kazimierz Szczerba (POL)
1980	Patrizio Oliva (ITA)	Serik Konakbayev (URS)	Jose Aguilar (CUB) Anthony Willis (GBR)

1896–1948 Event not held

WELTERWEIGHT
From 1948 the weight limit has been *67 kg* 148 lb. In 1904 it was 143¾ lb *65·27 kg*. From 1920 to 1936 it was 147 lb *66·68 kg*.

	Gold	Silver	Bronze
1904	Albert Young (USA)	Harry Spanger (USA)	Joseph Lydon (USA) James Eagan (USA)
1920	Albert Schneider (CAN)	Alexander Ireland (GBR)	Frederick Colberg (USA)
1924	Jean Delarge (BEL)	Héctor Mendez (ARG)	Douglas Lewis (CAN)
1928	Edward Morgan (NZL)	Raul Landini (ARG)	Raymond Smillie (CAN)
1932	Edward Flynn (USA)	Erich Campe (GER)	Bruno Ahlberg (FIN)
1936	Sten Suvio (FIN)	Michael Murach (GER)	Gerhard Petersen (DEN)
1948	Julius Torma (TCH)	Horace Herring (USA)	Alessandro D'Ottavio (ITA)
1952	Zygmunt Chychla (POL)	Sergey Schtsherbakov (URS)	Victor Jörgensen (DEN) Günther Heidemann (GER)
1956	Nicholae Lince (ROM)	Frederick Tiedt (IRL)	Kevin Hogarth (AUS) Nicholas Gargano (GBR)
1960	Giovanni Benvenuti (ITA)	Yuriy Radonyak (URS)	Leszek Drogosz (POL) James Lloyd (GBR)
1964	Marian Kasprzyk (POL)	Ritschardas Tamulis (URS)	Pertti Purhonen (FIN) Silvano Bertini (ITA)
1968	Manfred Wolke (GDR)	Joseph Bessala (CMR)	Vladimir Musalinov (URS) Mario Guilloti (ARG)
1972	Emilio Correa (CUB)	Janos Kajdi (HUN)	Dick Murunga (KEN) Jesse Valdez (USA)
1976	Jochen Bachfeld (GDR)	Pedro Gamarro (VEN)	Reinhard Skricek (GER) Victor Zilberman (ROM)
1980	Andres Aldama (CUB)	John Mugabi (UGA)	Karl-Heinz Krüger (GDR) Kazimierz Szczerba (POL)

1896–1900, 1906–1912 Event not held

LIGHT-MIDDLEWEIGHT
Weight up to *71 kg* 157 lb

	Gold	Silver	Bronze
1952	László Papp (HUN)	Theunis van Schalkwyk (SAF)	Boris Tishin (URS) Eladio Herrera (ARG)
1956	László Papp (HUN)	José Torres (USA)	John McCormack (GBR) Zbigniew Pietrzkowski (POL)

1960	Wilbert McClure (USA)	Carmelo Bossi (ITA)	Boris Lagutin (URS)
			William Fisher (GBR)
1964	Boris Lagutin (URS)	Josef Gonzales (FRA)	Nojim Maiyegun (NGR)
			Jozef Grzesiak (POL)
1968	Boris Lagutin (URS)	Rolando Garbey (CUB)	John Baldwin (USA)
			Günther Meier (FRG)
1972	Dieter Kottysch (GER)	Wieslaw Rudkowski (POL)	Alan Minter (GBR)
			Peter Tiepold (GDR)
1976	Jerzy Rybicki (POL)	Tadija Kacar (YUG)	Rolando Garbey (CUB)
			Viktor Savchenko (URS)
1980	Armando Martinez (CUB)	Aleksandr Koshkin (URS)	Jan Franck (TCH)
			Detlef Kastner (GDR)

1896–1948 Event not held

MIDDLEWEIGHT

From 1952 the weight limit has been *75 kg* 165 lb. From 1904 to 1908 it was 158 lb *71·68 kg*. From 1920 to 1936 it was 160 lb *72·57 kg*. In 1948 it was *73 kg* 161 lb.

	Gold	*Silver*	*Bronze*
1904	Charles Mayer (USA)	Benjamin Spradley (USA)	—*
1908	John Douglas (GBR)	Reginald Baker (AUS/NZL)	W Philo (GBR)
1920	Harry Mallin (GBR)	Georges Prud'homme (CAN)	Moe Herscovitch (CAN)
1924	Harry Mallin (GBR)	John Elliott (GBR)	Joseph Beecken (BEL)
1928	Piero Toscani (ITA)	Jan Hermánek (TCH)	Léonard Steyaert (BEL)
1932	Carmen Barth (USA)	Amado Azar (ARG)	Ernest Pierce (SAF)
1936	Jean Despeaux (FRA)	Henry Tiller (NOR)	Raúl Villareal (ARG)
1948	László Papp (HUN)	John Wright (GBR)	Ivano Fontana (ITA)
1952	Floyd Patterson (USA)	Vasile Tita (ROM)	Boris Nikolov (BUL)
			Stig Sjolin (SWE)
1956	Gennadiy Schatkov (URS)	Ramón Tapia (CHI)	Gilbert Chapron (FRA)
			Victor Zalazar (ARG)
1960	Edward Crook (USA)	Tadeusz Walasek (POL)	Ion Monea (ROM)
			Evgeniy Feofanov (URS)
1964	Valeriy Popentschenko (URS)	Emil Schultz (GER)	Franco Valle (ITA)
			Tadeusz Walasek (POL)
1968	Christopher Finnegan (GBR)	Aleksey Kisselyov (URS)	Agustin Zaragoza (MEX)
			Alfred Jones (USA)
1972	Vyatcheslav Lemechev (URS)	Reima Virtanen (FIN)	Prince Amartey (GHA)
			Marvin Johnson (USA)
1976	Michael Spinks (USA)	Rufat Riskiev (URS)	Alec Nastac (ROM)
			Luis Martinez (CUB)
1980	Jose Gomez (CUB)	Viktor Savchenko (URS)	Jerzy Rybicki (POL)
			Valentin Silaghi (ROM)

* No third place.

1896–1900, 1906, 1912 Event not held

LIGHT HEAVYWEIGHT

From 1952 the weight limit has been *81 kg* 178½ lb. From 1920 to 1936 it was 175 lb *79·38 kg*. In 1948 it was *80 kg* 186¼ lb.

	Gold	*Silver*	*Bronze*
1920	Edward Eagan (USA)	Sverre Sörsdal (NOR)	H Franks (GBR)
1924	Harry Mitchell (GBR)	Thyge Petersen (DEN)	Sverre Sörsdal (NOR)
1928	Victor Avendano (ARG)	Ernst Pistulla (GER)	Karel Miljon (HOL)
1932	David Carstens (SAF)	Gino Rossi (ITA)	Peter Jörgensen (DEN)
1936	Roger Michelot (FRA)	Richard Vogt (GER)	Francisco Risiglione (ARG)
1948	George Hunter (SAF)	Donald Scott (GBR)	Maurio Cla (ARG)
1952	Norvel Lee (USA)	Antonio Pacenza (ARG)	Anotiliy Perov (URS)
			Harri Siljander (FIN)
1956	James Boyd (USA)	Gheorghe Negrea (ROM)	Carlos Lucas (CHI)
			Romualdas Murauskas (URS)
1960	Cassius Clay (USA)	Zbigniew Pietrzykowski (POL)	Anthony Madigan (AUS)
			Giulio Saraudi (ITA)
1964	Cosimo Pinto (ITA)	Aleksey Kisselyov (URS)	Aleksandr Nikolov (BUL)
			Zbigniew Pietrzykowski (POL)
1968	Dan Poznyak (URS)	Ion Monea (ROM)	Georgy Stankov (BUL)
			Stanislav Dragan (POL)

1972	Mate Parlov (YUG)	Gilberto Carrillo (CUB)	Isaac Ikhouria (NGR)
			Janusz Gortat (POL)
1976	Leon Spinks (USA)	Sixto Soria (CUB)	Costica Danifoiu (ROM)
			Janusz Gortat (POL)
1980	Slobodan Kacar (YUG)	Pavel Skrzecz (POL)	Herbert Bauch (GDR)
			Ricardo Rojas (CUB)

1896–1912 Event not held

HEAVYWEIGHT

From 1952 the class has been for those over *81 kg* 178½ lb. From 1904 to 1908 it was over 158 lb *71·67 kg*. From 1920 to 1936 it was over 175 lb *79·38 kg*. In 1948 it was over *80 kg* 176¼ lb.

	Gold	*Silver*	*Bronze*
1904	Samuel Berger (USA)	Charles Mayer (USA)	William Michaels (USA)
1908	A L Oldham (GBR)	S C H Evans (GBR)	Frederick Parks (GBR)
1920	Ronald Rawson (GBR)	Sören Petersen (DEN)	Xavier Eluère (FRA)
1924	Otto von Porat (NOR)	Sören Petersen (DEN)	Alfredo Porzio (ARG)
1928	Arturo Rodriguez Jurado (ARG)	Nils Ramm (SWE)	Jacob Michaelsen (DEN)
1932	Santiago Lovell (ARG)	Luigi Rovati (ITA)	Frederick Feary (USA)
1936	Herbert Runge (GER)	Guillermo Lovell (ARG)	Erling Nilsen (NOR)
1948	Rafael Iglesias (ARG)	Gunnar Nilsson (SWE)	John Arthur (SAF)
1952	Hayes Edward Sanders (USA)	Ingemar Johansson* (SWE)	Andries Nieman (SAF)
			Ilkka Koski (FIN)
1956	Peter Rademacher (USA)	Lev Mukhin (URS)	Daniel Bekker (SAF)
			Giacomo Bozzano (ITA)
1960	Franco de Piccoli (ITA)	Daniel Bekker (SAF)	Josef Nemec (TCH)
			Günter Siegmund (GER)
1964	Joe Frazier (USA)	Hans Huber (GER)	Guiseppe Ros (ITA)
			Vadim Yemelyanov (URS)
1968	George Foreman (USA)	Ionas Tschepulis (URS)	Giorgio Bambini (ITA)
			Joaquin Rocha (MEX)
1972	Teofilo Stevenson (CUB)	Ion Alexe (ROM)	Peter Hussing (GER)
			Hasse Thomsen (SWE)
1976	Teofilo Stevenson (CUB)	Mircea Simon (ROM)	Johnny Tate (USA)
			Clarence Hill (BER)
1980	Teofilo Stevenson (CUB)	Pyotr Zayev (URS)	Jurgen Fanghanel (GDR)
			Istvan Levai (HUN)

* Originally silver medal not awarded; Johansson disqualified but reinstated in 1982.

1896–1900, 1906, 1912 Event not held

VAL BARKER CUP

This cup is presented by the International Amateur Boxing Association (AIBA) to the competitor who shows the best style and is the most proficient boxer at the Olympic Games. First awarded in 1936, the winners have been:

1936	Louis Laurie (USA)	*Bronze—flyweight*
1948	George Hunter (SAF)	*Gold—light heavyweight*
1952	Norvel Lee (USA)	*Gold—light heavyweight*
1956	Dick McTaggart (GBR)	*Gold—lightweight*
1960	Giovanni Benvenuti (ITA)	*Gold—welterweight*
1964	Valeriy Popentschenko (URS)	*Gold—middleweight*
1968	Philip Waruinge (KEN)	*Bronze—featherweight*
1972	Teofilo Stevenson (CUB)	*Gold—heavyweight*
1976	Howard Davis (USA)	*Gold—lightweight*
1980	Patrizio Oliva (ITA)	*Gold—light welterweight*

CANOEING

Official canoeing competitions were first held in 1936, although there had been demonstrations of kayak and Canadian events in 1924. At Berlin Francis Amyot won the C1 1000 m race, the only Canadian ever to win a canoeing title at the Olympic Games.

The most successful competitor has been Gert Fredriksson (SWE) who won six golds, one silver, and one bronze between 1948 and 1960, all in kayaks. The best by a woman is three golds and a bronze by Ludmila Pinayeva (née Khvedosyuk) of the Soviet Union between 1964 and 1972. Only one man, Vladimir Parfenovich (URS) in 1980 has won three gold medals in one Games.

The most countries to compete in canoeing

Aleksandr Shaparenko (URS) won the 1972 K1 title after placing second in the event in 1968, when he had also won a gold medal in the kayak pairs.

After record breaking success in four Olympics Gert Fredriksson returned in 1964 as coach to the Swedish canoeing team.

events was 27 on the Canal de Cuemanco, Xochimilco in 1968, a venue experts consider to be the best ever Olympic site for the sport.

The highest speed achieved in the Games over the standard 1000 m course is 19·70 km/h when the Soviet K4 team clocked 3 min 02·70 sec in a heat in 1980. Over the first 250 m of the race they reached 21·15 km/h.

Uniquely in 1972, at Munich, four slalom events were held bringing the total canoeing titles available to a record 11 in one Games.

The oldest ever canoeing gold medallist was Gert Fredriksson (SWE) aged 40 yr 292 days when he gained his last title in the K2 over 1000 m in 1960. The youngest champion was Bent Peter Rasch (DEN) in the 1952 C2 at 1000 m aged 18 yr 58 days. The youngest female gold medallist was Birgit Fischer (GDR) aged 18 yr 158 days when she won the K1 in 1980. The oldest woman to win a title was Sylvi Saimo (FIN) in the K1 in 1952 aged 37 yr 259 days.

Men

500 METRES KAYAK SINGLES (K-1)

	Gold	Silver	Bronze
1976	Vasile Diba (ROM) 1:46·41	Zoltan Szytanity (HUN) 1:46·95	Rüdiger Helm (GDR) 1:48·30
1980	Vladimir Parfenovich (URS) 1:43·43	John Sumegi (AUS) 1:44·12	Vasile Diba (ROM) 1:44·90

1896–1972 Event not held

1000 METRES KAYAK SINGLES (K-1)

	Gold	Silver	Bronze
1936	Gregor Hradetzky (AUT) 4:22·9	Helmut Cämmerer (GER) 4:25·6	Jacob Kraaier (HOL) 4:35·1
1948	Gert Fredriksson (SWE) 4:33·2	Johan Kobberup (DEN) 4:39·9	Henri Eberhardt (FRA) 4:41·4
1952	Gert Fredriksson (SWE) 4:07·9	Thorvald Strömberg (FIN) 4:09·7	Louis Gantois (FRA) 4:20·1
1956	Gert Fredriksson (SWE) 4:12·8	Igor Pissaryev (URS) 4:15·3	Lajos Kiss (HUN) 4:16·2
1960	Erik Hansen (DEN) 3:53·00	Imre Szöllösi (HUN) 3:54·02	Gert Fredriksson (SWE) 3:55·89
1964	Rolf Peterson (SWE) 3:57·13	Mihály Hesz (HUN) 3:57·28	Aurel Vernescu (ROM) 4:00·77
1968	Mihály Hesz (HUN) 4:02·63	Aleksandr Shaparenko (URS) 4:03·58	Erik Hansen (DEN) 4:04·39
1972	Aleksandr Shaparenko (URS) 3:48·06	Rolf Peterson (SWE) 3:48·35	Geza Csapo (HUN) 3:49·38
1976	Rüdiger Helm (GDR) 3:48·20	Geza Csapo (HUN) 3:48·84	Vasile Diba (ROM) 3:49·65
1980	Rüdiger Helm (GDR) 3:48·77	Alain Lebas (FRA) 3:50·20	Ion Birladeanu (ROM) 3:50·49

1896–1932 Event not held

10 000 METRES KAYAK SINGLES (K-1)

Gold	*Silver*	*Bronze*
1936 Ernst Krebs (GER) 46:01·6	Fritz Landertinger (AUT) 46:14·7	Ernest Riedel (USA) 47:23·9
1948 Gert Fredriksson (SWE) 50:47·7	Kurt Wires (FIN) 51:18·2	Ejvind Skabo (NOR) 51:35·4
1952 Thorvald Strömberg (FIN) 47:22·8	Gert Fredriksson (SWE) 47:34·1	Michel Scheuer (GER) 47:54·5
1956 Gert Fredriksson (SWE) 47:43·4	Ferenc Hatlaczky (HUN) 47:53·3	Michel Scheuer (GER) 48:00·3

1896–1932, 1960–1980 Event not held

500 METRES KAYAK PAIRS (K-2)

Gold	*Silver*	*Bronze*
1976 GDR 1:35·87	USSR 1:36·81	ROMANIA 1:37·43
Joachim Mattern	Sergey Nagorny	Larion Serghei
Bernd Olbricht	Vladimir Romanovski	Policarp Malihin
1980 USSR 1:32·38	SPAIN 1:33·65	GDR 1:34·00
Vladimir Parfenovich	Herminio Menendez	Bernd Olbricht
Sergey Chukhrai	Guillermo Del Riego	Rüdiger Helm

1896–1972 Event not held

1000 METRES KAYAK PAIRS (K-2)

Gold	*Silver*	*Bronze*
1936 AUSTRIA 4:03·8	GERMANY 4:08·9	NETHERLANDS 4:12·2
Adolf Kainz	Ewald Tilker	Nicolaas Tates
Alfons Dorfner	Fritz Bondroit	Willem van der Kroft
1948 SWEDEN 4:07·3	DENMARK 4:07·5	FINLAND 4:08·7
Hans Berglund	Ejvind Hansen	Thor Axelsson
Lennart Klingström	Bernhard Jensen	Nils Björklöf
1952 FINLAND 3:51·1	SWEDEN 3:51·1	AUSTRIA 3:51·4
Kurt Wires	Lars Glassér	Max Raub
Yrjö Hietanen	Ingemar Hedberg	Herbert Wiedermann
1956 GERMANY 3:49·6	USSR 3:51·4	AUSTRIA 3:55·8
Michel Scheuer	Mikhail Kaaleste	Max Raub
Meinrad Miltenberger	Anatoliy Demitkov	Herbert Wiedermann
1960 SWEDEN 3:34·7	HUNGARY 3:34·91	POLAND 3:37·34
Gert Fredriksson	András Szente	Stefan Kaplaniak
Sven-Olov Sjödelius	György Mészáros	Wladyslaw Zielinski
1964 SWEDEN 3:38·4	NETHERLANDS 3:39·30	GERMANY 3:40·69
Sven-Olov Sjödelius	Antonius Geurts	Heinz Buker
Nils Utterberg	Paul Hoekstra	Holger Zander
1968 USSR 3:37·54	HUNGARY 3:38·44	AUSTRIA 3:40·71
Aleksandr Shaparenko	Csaba Giczi	Gerhard Seibold
Vladimir Morozov	István Timár	Gunther Pfaff
1972 USSR 3:31·23	HUNGARY 3:32·00	POLAND 3:33·83
Nikolai Gorbachev	Jozsef Deme	Wladyslaw Szuszkiewicz
Viktor Kratassyuk	Janos Ratkai	Rafal Piszez
1976 USSR 3:29·01	GDR 3:29·33	HUNGARY 3:30·56
Sergey Nagorny	Joachim Mattern	Zoltan Bako
Vladimir Romanovski	Bernd Olbricht	Istvan Szabo
1980 USSR 3:26·72	HUNGARY 3:28·49	SPAIN 3:28·66
Vladimir Parfenovich	István Szabó	Luis Ramos-Misione
Sergey Chukhrai	István Joós	Herminio Menendez

1896–1932 Event not held

10 000 METRES KAYAK PAIRS (K-2)

Gold	*Silver*	*Bronze*
1936 GERMANY 41:45·0	AUSTRIA 42:05·4	SWEDEN 43:06·1
Paul Weavers	Viktor Kalisch	Tage Fahlborg
Ludwig Landen	Karl Steinhuber	Helge Larsson

1948	SWEDEN 46:09·4	NORWAY 46:44·8	FINLAND 46:48·2
	Gunnar Akerlund	Ivar Mathisen	Thor Axelsson
	Hans Wetterström	Knut Östbye	Nils Björklöf
1952	FINLAND 44:21·3	SWEDEN 44:21·7	HUNGARY 44:26·6
	Kurt Wires	Gunnar Akerlund	Ferenc Varga
	Yrjö Hietanen	Hans Wetterström	Jozsef Gurovits
1956	HUNGARY 43:37·0	GERMANY 43:40·6	AUSTRALIA 43:43·2
	Janos Uranyi	Fritz Briel	Dennis Green
	Laszlo Fabian	Theo Kleine	Walter Brown

1896–1932, 1960–1980 Event not held

1000 METRES KAYAK FOURS (K-4)

	Gold	Silver	Bronze
1964	USSR 3:14·67	GERMANY 3:15·39	ROMANIA 3:15·51
1968	NORWAY 3:14·38	ROMANIA 3:14·81	HUNGARY 3:15·10
1972	USSR 3:14·02	ROMANIA 3:15·07	NORWAY 3:15·27
1976	USSR 3:08·69	SPAIN 3:08·95	GDR 3:10·76
1980	GDR 3:13·76	ROMANIA 3:15·35	BULGARIA 3:15·46

1896–1960 Event not held

500 METRES CANADIAN SINGLES (C-1)

	Gold	Silver	Bronze
1976	Aleksandr Rogov (URS) 1:59·23	John Wood (CAN) 1:59·58	Matija Ljubek (YUG) 1:59·60
1980	Sergey Postrekhin (URS) 1:53·37	Lubomir Lubenov (BUL) 1:53·49	Olaf Heukrodt (GDR) 1:54·38

1896–1972 Event not held

1000 METRES CANADIAN SINGLES (C-1)

	Gold	Silver	Bronze
1936	Francis Amyot (CAN) 5:32·1	Bohuslav Karlik (TCH) 5:36·9	Erich Koschik (GER) 5:39·0
1948	Josef Holeček (TCH) 5:42·0	Douglas Bennett (CAN) 5:53·3	Robert Boutigny (FRA) 5:55·9
1952	Josef Holeček (TCH) 4:56·3	János Parti (HUN) 5:03·6	Olavi Ojanperä (FIN) 5:08·5
1956	Leon Rotman (ROM) 5:05·3	István Hernek (HUN) 5:06·2	Gennadiy Bukharin (URS) 5:12·7
1960	János Parti (HUN) 4:33·93	Aleksandr Silayev (URS) 4:34·41	Leon Rotman (ROM) 4:35·87
1964	Jürgen Eschert (GER) 4:35·14	Andrei Igorov (ROM) 4:37·89	Yevgeny Penyayev (URS) 4:38·31
1968	Tibor Tatai (HUN) 4:36·14	Detlef Lewe (FRG) 4:38·31	Vitaly Galkov (URS) 4:40·42
1972	Ivan Patzaichin (ROM) 4:08·94	Tamas Wichmann (HUN) 4:12·42	Detlef Lewe (GER) 4:13·63
1976	Matija Ljubek (YUG) 4:09·51	Vasiliy Urchenko (URS) 4:12·57	Tamas Wichmann (HUN) 4:14·11
1980	Lubomir Lubenov (BUL) 4:12·38	Sergey Postrekhin (URS) 4:13·53	Eckhard Leue (GDR) 4:15·02

1896–1932 Event not held

10 000 METRES CANADIAN SINGLES (C-4)

	Gold	Silver	Bronze
1948	Frantisek Capek (TCH) 62:05·2	Frank Havens (USA) 62:40·4	Norman Lane (CAN) 64:35·3
1952	Frank Havens (USA) 57:41·1	Gabor Novak (HUN) 57:49·2	Alfred Jindra (TCH) 57:53·1
1956	Leon Rotman (ROM) 56:41·0	János Parti (HUN) 57:11·0	Gennadiy Bukharin (URS) 57:14·5

1896–1936, 1960–1980 Event not held

500 METRES CANADIAN PAIRS (C-2)

	Gold	Silver	Bronze
1976	USSR 1:45·81	POLAND 1:47·77	HUNGARY 1:48·35
	Sergey Petrenko	Jerzy Opara	Tamas Buday
	Aleksandr Vinogradov	Andrzej Gronowicz	Oszkar Frey
1980	HUNGARY 1:43·39	ROMANIA 1:44·12	BULGARIA 1:44·83
	László Foltán	Ivan Patzaichin	Borislaw Ananiev
	István Vaskuti	Istvan Capusta	Nikolai Ilkov

1896–1972 Event not held

1000 METRES CANADIAN PAIRS (C-2)

	Gold	*Silver*	*Bronze*
1936	CZECHOSLOVAKIA 4:50·1 Vladimir Syrovátka Jan-Felix Brzák	AUSTRIA 4:53·8 Rupert Weinstabl Karl Proisl	CANADA 4:56·7 Frank Saker Harvey Charters
1948	CZECHOSLOVAKIA 5:07·1 Jan-Felix Brzák Bohumil Kudrna	UNITED STATES 5:08·2 Stephen Lysak Stephan Macknowski	FRANCE 5:15·2 Georges Dransart Georges Gandil
1952	DENMARK 4:38·3 Bent Peder Rasch Finn Haunstoft	CZECHOSLOVAKIA 4:42·9 Jan-Felix Brzák Bohumil Kudrna	GERMANY 4:48·3 Egon Drews Wilfried Soltau
1956	ROMANIA 4:47·4 Alexe Dumitru Simion Ismailciuc	USSR 4:48·6 Pavel Kharin Gratsian Botev	HUNGARY 4:54·3 Károly Wieland Ferenc Mohácsi
1960	USSR 4:17·94 Leonid Geyshtor Sergey Makarenko	ITALY 4:20·77 Aldo Dezi Francesco La Macchia	HUNGARY 4:20·89 Imre Farkas András Törö
1964	USSR 4:04·64 Andrey Khimich Stepan Oschepkov	FRANCE 4:06·52 Jean Boudehen Michel Chapuis	DENMARK 4:07·48 Peer N. Nielsen John Sorenson
1968	ROMANIA 4:07·18 Ivan Patzaichin Serghei Covaliov	HUNGARY 4:08·77 Tamás Wichmann Gyula Petrikovics	USSR 4:11·30 Naum Prokupets Mikhail Zamotin
1972	USSR 3:52·60 Vlados Chessyunas Yuri Lobanov	ROMANIA 3:52·63 Ivan Patzaichin Serghei Covaliov	BULGARIA 3:58·10 Fedia Damianov Ivan Bourtchine
1976	USSR 3:52·76 Sergey Petrenko Aleksandr Vinogradov	ROMANIA 3:54·28 Gheorghe Danielov Gheorghe Simionov	HUNGARY 3:55·66 Tamas Buday Oszkar Frey
1980	ROMANIA 3:47·65 Ivan Patzaichin Toma Simionov	GDR 3:49·93 Olaf Heukrodt Uwe Madeja	USSR 3:51·28 Vasiliy Yurchenko Yuriy Lobanov

1896–1932 Event not held

10 000 METRES CANADIAN PAIRS (C-2)

	Gold	*Silver*	*Bronze*
1936	CZECHOSLOVAKIA 50:33·5 Vaclav Mottl Zdenek Skrdlant	CANADA 51:15·8 Frank Saker Harvey Charters	AUSTRIA 51:28·0 Rupert Weinstabl Karl Proisl
1948	UNITED STATES 55:55·4 Stephen Lysack Stephan Macknowski	CZECHOSLOVAKIA 57:38·5 Vaclav Havel Jiri Pecka	FRANCE 58:00·8 Georges Dransart Georges Gandil
1952	FRANCE 54:08·3 Georges Turlier Jean Laudet	CANADA 54:09·9 Kenneth Lane Donald Hawgood	GERMANY 54:28·1 Egon Drews Wilfried Soltau
1956	USSR 54:02·4 Pavel Kharin Gratsian Botev	FRANCE 54:48·3 Georges Dransart Marcel Renaud	HUNGARY 55:15·6 Imre Farkas Jozsef Hunics

1896–1932, 1960–1980 Event not held

4 × 500 METRES KAYAK SINGLES (K-1) RELAY

	Gold	*Silver*	*Bronze*
1960	GERMANY 7:39·43	HUNGARY 7:44·02	DENMARK 7:46·09

1896–1956, 1964–1980 Event not held

10 000 METRES FOLDING KAYAK SINGLES (K-1)

	Gold	*Silver*	*Bronze*
1936	Gregor Hradetzky (AUT) 50:01·2	Henri Eberhardt (FRA) 50:04·2	Xaver Hörmann (GER) 50:06·5

1896–1932, 1948–1980 Event not held

10 000 METRES FOLDING KAYAK PAIRS (K-2)

	Gold	*Silver*	*Bronze*
1936	SWEDEN 45:48·9 Sven Johansson Eric Bladström	GERMANY 45:49·2 Willi Horn Erich Hanisch	NETHERLANDS 46:12·4 Pieter Wijdekop Cornelis Wijdekop

1896–1932, 1948–1980 Event not held

SLALOM RACING
(Only held in 1972)

KAYAK SINGLES (K-1)

Gold	*Silver*	*Bronze*
Siegbert Horn (GDR) 268·56	Norbert Sattler (AUT) 270·76	Harald Gimpel (GDR) 277·95

CANADIAN SINGLES (C-1)

Gold	*Silver*	*Bronze*
Reinhard Eiben (GDR) 315·84	Reinhold Kauder (FRG) 327·89	Jamie McEwan (USA) 335·95

CANADIAN PAIRS (C-2)

Gold	*Silver*	*Bronze*
GDR 310·68 Walter Hofmann Rolf-Dieter Amend	FRG 311·90 Hans-Otto Schumacher Wilhelm Baues	FRANCE 315·10 Jean-Louis Olry Jean-Claude Olry

Women

500 METRES KAYAK SINGLES (K-1)

	Gold	*Silver*	*Bronze*
1948	Karen Hoff (DEN) 2:31·9	Alide Van de Anker-Doedans (HOL) 2:32·8	Fritzi Schwingl (AUT) 2:32·9
1952	Sylvi Saimo (FIN) 2:18·4	Gertrude Liebhart (AUT) 2:18·8	Nina Savina (URS) 2:21·6
1956	Elisaveta Dementyeva (URS) 2:18·9	Therese Zenz (GER) 2:19·6	Tove Söby (DEN) 2:22·3
1960	Antonina Seredina (URS) 2:08·08	Therese Zenz (GER) 2:08·22	Daniela Walkowiak (POL) 2:10·46
1964	Ludmila Khvedosyuk (URS) 2:12·87	Hilde Lauer (ROM) 2:15·35	Marcia Jones (USA) 2:15·68
1968	Ludmila Pinayeva (URS) 2:11·09	Renate Breuer (FRG) 2:12·71	Viorica Dumitru (ROM) 2:13·22
1972	Yulia Ryabchinskaya (URS) 2:03·17	Mieke Jaapies (HOL) 2:04·03	Anna Pfeffer (HUN) 2:05·50
1976	Carola Zirzow (GDR) 2:01·05	Tatyana Korshunova (URS) 2:03·07	Klara Rajnai (HUN) 2:05·01
1980	Birgit Fischer (GDR) 1:57·96	Vanya Ghecheva (BUL) 1:59·48	Antonina Melnikova (URS) 1:59·66

1896–1936 Event not held

500 METRES KAYAK PAIRS (K-2)

	Gold	*Silver*	*Bronze*
1960	USSR 1:54·76	GERMANY 1:56·66	HUNGARY 1:58·22
	Maria Zhubina	Therese Zenz	Vilma Egresi
	Antonina Seredina	Ingrid Hartmann	Klára Fried-Bánfalvi
1964	GERMANY 1:56·95	UNITED STATES 1:59·16	ROMANIA 2:00·25
	Roswitha Esser	Francine Fox	Hilde Lauer
	Annemarie Zimmermann	Gloriane Perrier	Cornelia Sideri
1968	FRG 1:56·44	HUNGARY 1:58·60	USSR 1:58·61
	Annemarie Zimmermann	Anna Pfeffer	Ludmila Pinayeva
	Roswitha Esser	Katalin Rosznyói	Antonina Seredina
1972	USSR 1:53·50	GDR 1:54·30	ROMANIA 1:55·01
	Ludmila Pinayeva	Ilse Kaschube	Maria Nichiforov
	Ekaterina Kuryshko	Petra Grabowsky	Viorica Dumitru
1976	USSR 1:51·15	HUNGARY 1:51·69	GDR 1:51·81
	Nina Gopova	Anna Pfeffer	Barbel Koster
	Galina Kreft	Klara Rajnai	Carola Zirzow
1980	GDR 1:43·88	USSR 1:46·91	HUNGARY 1:47·95
	Carsta Genäuss	Galina Alexeyeva	Éva Rakusz
	Martina Bischof	Nina Trofimova	Mária Zakariás

1896–1956 Event not held

SLALOM RACING
(Only held in 1972)

KAYAK SINGLES (K-1)

Gold	*Silver*	*Bronze*
Angelika Bahmann (GDR) 364·50	Gisela Grothaus (FRG) 398·15	Magdalena Wunderlich (FRG) 400·50

CANOEING—MEDALS

	MEN				WOMEN				TOTAL				Total Medals
	Gold	Silver	Bronze		Gold	Silver	Bronze		Gold	Silver	Bronze		
USSR	17	8	5	....	8	2	3	....	25	10	8	....	43
HUNGARY	4	12	9	....	—	2	4	....	4	14	13	....	31
ROMANIA	6	7	7	....	—	1	3	....	6	8	10	....	24
GDR	7	2	6	....	4	1	1	....	11	3	7	....	21
GERMANY	2	6	4	....	2	5	1	....	4	11	5	....	20
SWEDEN	7	2	1	....	—	—	—	....	7	2	1	....	10
AUSTRIA	2	2	3	....	—	1	1	....	2	3	4	....	9
DENMARK	2	2	2	....	1	—	1	....	3	2	3	....	8
FRANCE	—	2	5	....	—	—	—	....	—	2	5	....	7
CZECHOSLOVAKIA	4	2	—	....	—	—	—	....	4	2	—	....	6
BULGARIA	1	1	3	....	—	1	—	....	1	2	3	....	6
FINLAND	1	1	2	....	1	—	—	....	2	1	2	....	5
NETHERLANDS	—	1	2	....	—	2	—	....	—	3	2	....	5
CANADA	1	2	1	....	—	—	—	....	1	2	1	....	4
UNITED STATES	—	1	1	....	—	1	1	....	—	2	2	....	4
POLAND	—	1	2	....	—	—	1	....	—	1	3	....	4
SPAIN	—	2	1	....	—	—	—	....	—	2	1	....	3
NORWAY	1	—	1	....	—	—	—	....	1	—	1	....	2
YUGOSLAVIA	1	—	1	....	—	—	—	....	1	—	1	....	2
AUSTRALIA	—	1	—	....	—	—	—	....	—	1	—	....	1
ITALY	—	1	—	....	—	—	—	....	—	1	—	....	1
	56	56	56		16	16	16		72	72	72		216

Cycling

CYCLING

The first Olympic cycling champion was Léon Flameng (FRA) who won the 100 km race on 8 April 1896 in Athens. The event was held on a 333·33 m cement track and involved 300 circuits.

Four men have won a record three gold medals: Paul Masson (FRA) in 1896, Francisco Verri (ITA) in 1906, Robert Charpentier (FRA) in 1936, and Daniel Morelon (FRA) in 1968 (two) and 1972. Of these only Morelon won another medal, a bronze in 1964. He also won a record seven world amateur titles. The cycling events held at St Louis in 1904 were not accepted as official Olympic events but it should be noted that Marcus Hurley (USA) won four of them.

The first pair of brothers to win a medal was the Götze duo, Bruno and Max, of Germany who won the tandem silver in 1906. The greatest family performance in Olympic cycling is that by the Pettersson brothers of Sweden, Gösta, Sture, Erik and Tomas. The first three with Sven Hamrin won a bronze medal in the 1964 team road race. Then in 1968 they included their younger brother and all four won the silver, only 99·54 sec behind the gold medal team over the 102 km course.

Although it is known that a number of athletes, particularly distance runners, were taking stimulants in the early celebrations of the Games, one of the first cases in the post-Second-World-War era came to light in cycling. In the 1960 100 km race two Danish riders collapsed, and one, Knut Jensen, died from what was first diagnosed as sunstroke. Later it was reported that they had taken overdoses of a blood-circulation stimulant.

The sport also furnished two extremes in the field of sportsmanship. In 1936 Robert Charpentier (FRA) beat his team-mate Guy Lapébie by 0·2 sec at the end of the 100 km road race, the latter inexplicably slowing down just before the line. It was later discovered, in a photograph of the finish, that Charpentier had pulled Lapébie back by his shirt. More credit-worthy was the action of another Frenchman, Léon Flameng,

The winners of the pursuit race in 1908, (left to right) Leon Meredith, Ernie Payne, Charles Kingsbury and Ben Jones of Great Britain.

who was far ahead of the only other competitor, a Greek, left in the 1896 100 km track race, when this man's cycle broke down. Flameng stopped and waited until it was replaced, before continuing to win by six laps.

Excellent facilities have been built for many of the Olympic cycling programmes since the special track constructed around the athletics circuit at the White City, London in 1908. One of the most remarkable sites was the magnificent Hachioji velodrome, Tokyo for the 1964 events, built at a cost of $840 000, used for only 4 days during the Games, then within a year demolished as part of another building scheme. In 1968 the short distance events, as in other sports, benefited greatly from the altitude of Mexico City. In the tandem race Daniel Morelon and Pierre Trentin of France achieved the greatest speed ever in Olympic Games cycling when they clocked 9·83 sec for the last 200 m, an average speed of 73·24 km/h *45·51 mph*. The highest speed reached by an individual rider is 68·76 km/h *42·73 mph* by Sergey Kopylov (URS) at the Krylatskoye stadium in Moscow in 1980 when he was timed in 10·47 sec for the last 200 m in the 1000 m time-trial. The longest race ever in the Games was the 1912 road race which was held over a 320 km *198·8 miles* course.

The French tandem champions, Schilles and Auffray, at the London Games. The former also placed second in the 5000 m individual race.

Relatively few top professional cyclists competed at the Olympics as amateurs. Eddy Merckx (BEL), five times winner of the Tour de France and arguably one of the greatest road racers of all time, competed in the Games only once, in 1964. Unfortunately he was involved in an accident not far from the finish and came 12th, although only 0·11 sec behind the winner. Coincidentally, the man with whom he shares the record of five wins in the Tour de France, Jacques Anquetil (FRA), also finished in 12th place in the Olympic road race, in 1952. Patrick Sercu (BEL), gold medallist in the 1964 1000 m time-trial, holds the record for professional six-day racing events with 86 victories to the end of 1982.

The youngest rider to win a gold medal was Franco Giorgetti (ITA) in the 1920 team pursuit event aged 17 yr 304 days. The oldest gold

After a bronze medal in 1964 Pierre Trentin (FRA) won two golds and another bronze four years later in Mexico City. Here he is setting a world record in the 1000 m time-trial.

medallist was Maurice Peeters (HOL) who won the 1000 m sprint in 1920 aged 38 yr 99 days. Four years later he gained a bronze in the tandem event aged 42 yr 83 days to become the oldest ever medallist in Olympic cycling.

OLYMPIC RECORDS—CYCLING

Event	Min/Sec	Name & Country	Year
1000 metres time trial	1:02·955	Lothar Thoms (GDR)	1980
4000 metres individual pursuit	4:34·92	Robert Dill-Bundi (SUI)	1980
4000 metres team pursuit	4:14·64	USSR	1980

1000 METRES TIME-TRIAL

	Gold	Silver	Bronze
1896[1]	Paul Masson (FRA) 24·0	Stamatios Nikolopoulos (GRE) 25·4	Adolf Schmal (AUT) 26·6
1906[1]	Francesco Verri (ITA) 22·8	H Crowther (GBR) 22·8	Menjou (FRA) 23·2
1928	Willy Falck-Hansen (DEN) 1:14·4	Gerard Bosch van Drakestein (HOL) 1:15·2	Edgar Gray (AUS) 1:15·6
1932	Edgar Gray (AUS) 1:13·0	Jacobus van Egmond (HOL) 1:13·3	Charles Rampelberg (FRA) 1:13·4
1936	Arie van Vliet (HOL) 1:12·0	Pierre Georget (FRA) 1:12·8	Rudolf Karsch (GER) 1:13·2
1948	Jacques Dupont (FRA) 1:13·5	Pierre Nihant (BEL) 1:14·5	Thomas Godwin (GBR) 1:15·0
1952	Russell Mockridge (AUS) 1:11·1	Marino Morettini (ITA) 1:12·7	Raymond Robinson (SAF) 1:13·0
1956	Leandro Faggin (ITA) 1:09·8	Ladislav Foucek (TCH) 1:11·4	J Alfred Swift (SAF) 1:11·6
1960	Sante Gaiardoni (ITA) 1:07·27	Dieter Gieseler (GER) 1:08·75	Rotislav Vargashkin (URS) 1:08·86
1964	Patrick Sercu (BEL) 1:09·59	Giovanni Pettenella (ITA) 1:10·09	Pierre Trentin (FRA) 1:10·42
1968	Pierre Trentin (FRA) 1:03·91	Niels-Christian Fredborg (DEN) 1:04·61	Janusz Kierzkowski (POL) 1:04·63
1972	Niels-Christian Fredborg (DEN) 1:06·44	Daniel Clark (AUS) 1:06·87	Jürgen Schuetze (GDR) 1:07·02
1976	Klaus-Jürgen Grunke (GDR) 1:05·93	Michel Vaarten (BEL) 1:07·52	Niels-Christian Fredborg (DEN) 1:07·62
1980	Lothar Thoms (GDR) 1:02·955	Aleksandr Pantilov (URS) 1:04·845	David Weller (JAM) 1:05·241

[1] Held over 333·33 metres.   1908–1924 Event not held

1000 METRES SPRINT

	Gold	Silver	Bronze
1896[1]	Paul Masson (FRA) 4:56·0	Stamatios Nikolopoulas (GRE)	Léon Flemeng (FRA)
1900[1]	Georges Taillandier (FRA) 2:52·0	F Sanz (FRA)	Lake (USA)
1906	Francesco Verri (ITA) 1:42·2	H C Bouffler (GBR)	Eugène Debougnie (BEL)
1920	Maurice Peeters (HOL) 1:38·3	H Thomas Johnson (GBR)	Harry Ryan (GBR)
1924[3]	Lucien Michard (FRA) 12·8	Jacob Meijer (HOL)	Jean Cugnot (FRA)
1928	René Beaufrand (FRA) 13·2	Antoine Mazairac (HOL)	Willy Falck-Hansen (DEN)
1932	Jacobus van Egmond (HOL) 12·6	Louis Chaillot (FRA)	Bruno Pellizzari (ITA)
1936	Toni Merkens (GER) 11·8	Arie van Vliet (HOL)	Louis Chaillot (FRA)
1948	Mario Ghella (ITA) 12·0	Reginald Harris (GBR)	Axel Schandorff (DEN)

1952	Enzo Sacchi (ITA) 12·0	Lionel Cox (AUS)	Werner Potzernheim (GER)
1956	Michel Rousseau (FRA) 11·4	Guglielmo Pesenti (ITA)	Richard Ploog (AUS)
1960	Sante Gaiardoni (ITA) 11·1	Leo Sterckx (BEL)	Valentino Gasparella (ITA)
1964	Giovanni Pettenella (ITA) 13·69	Sergio Bianchetto (ITA)	Daniel Morelon (FRA)
1968	Daniel Morelon (FRA) 10·68	Giordano Turrini (ITA)	Pierre Trentin (FRA)
1972	Daniel Morelon (FRA) 11·25	John Nicholson (AUS)	Omari Phakadze (URS)
1976	Anton Tkac (TCH) 10·78	Daniel Morelon (FRA)	Hans-Jurgen Geschke (GDR)
1980	Lutz Hesslich (GDR) 11·40	Yave Cahard (FRA)	Sergey Kopylov (URS)

[1] Held over 2000 metres. In 1900 Taillander's last 200 was 13·0 sec.   [2] There was a 1000 metres sprint event in the 1908 Games, but it was declared void because 'the riders exceeded the time limit, in spite of repeated warnings.'   [3] Since 1924 only times over the last 200 metres of the event have been recorded.
1904, 1908[2]–1912 Event not held

4000 METRES INDIVIDUAL PURSUIT

Note: Bronze medal times are set in a third place race, so can be faster than those set in the race for first and second place.

	Gold	Silver	Bronze
1964	Jiři Daler (TCH) 5:04·75	Giorgio Ursi (ITA) 5:05·96	Preben Isaksson (DEN) 5:01·90
1968	Daniel Rebillard (FRA) 4:41·71	Mogens Frey Jensen (DEN) 4:42·43	Xaver Kurmann (SUI) 4:39·42
1972	Knut Knudsen (NOR) 4:45·74	Xaver Kurmann (SUI) 4:51·96	Hans Lutz (FRG) 4:50·80
1976	Gregor Braun (GDR) 4:47·61	Herman Ponsteen (HOL) 4:49·72	Thomas Huschke (GDR) 4:52·71
1980	Robert Dill-Bundi (SUI) 4:35·66	Alain Bondue (FRA) 4:42·96	Hans-Henrik Örsted (DEN) 4:36·54

1896–1960 Event not held

4000 METRES TEAM PURSUIT

Note: Bronze medal times are set in a third place race, so can be faster than those set in the race for first and second place.

	Gold	Silver	Bronze
1908[1]	GREAT BRITAIN 2:18·6	GERMANY 2:28·6	CANADA 2:29·6
1920	ITALY 5:20·0	GREAT BRITAIN n.t.a.	SOUTH AFRICA n.t.a.
1924	ITALY 5:15·0	POLAND n.t.a.	BELGIUM n.t.a.
1928	ITALY 5:01·8	NETHERLANDS 5:06·2	GREAT BRITAIN n.t.a.
1932	ITALY 4:53·0	FRANCE 4:55·7	GREAT BRITAIN 4:56·0
1936	FRANCE 4:45·0	ITALY 4:51·0	GREAT BRITAIN 4:52·6
1948	FRANCE 4:57·8	ITALY 4:36·7	GREAT BRITAIN 4:55·8
1952	ITALY 4:46·1	SOUTH AFRICA 4:53·6	GREAT BRITAIN 4:51·5
1956	ITALY 4:37·4	FRANCE 4:39·4	GREAT BRITAIN 4:42·2
1960	ITALY 4:30·90	GERMANY 4:35·78	USSR 4:34·05
1964	GERMANY 4:35·67	ITALY 4:35·74	NETHERLANDS 4:38·99
1968	DENMARK 4:22·44[2]	FRG 4:18·94	ITALY 4:18·35
1972	FRG 4:22·14	GDR 4:25·25	GREAT BRITAIN 4:23·78
1976	FRG 4:21·06	USSR 4:27·15	GREAT BRITAIN 4:22·41
1980	USSR 4:15·70	GDR 4:19·67	CZECHOSLOVAKIA[3]

[1] Held over 1810·5 metres.   [2] Federal Republic of Germany finished first but were disqualified for illegal assistance. After the Games ended the International Cycling Federation awarded them the silver medal.   [3] Italy disqualified in third place race.   1896–1906, 1912 Event not held

2000 METRES TANDEM

	Gold	Silver	Bronze
1906	GREAT BRITAIN 2:57·0	GERMANY 2:57·2	GERMANY n.t.a.
	J Matthews	Max Götze	Eduard Dannenberg
	Arthur Rushen	Bruno Götze	Otto Küpferling
1908	FRANCE 3:07·8	GREAT BRITAIN n.t.a.	GREAT BRITAIN n.t.a.
	Maurice Schilles	F G Hamlin	Colin Brooks
	André Auffray	H Thomas Johnson	Walter Isaacs
1920	GREAT BRITAIN 2:49·4	SOUTH AFRICA n.t.a.	NETHERLANDS n.t.a.
	Harry Ryan	James Walker	Frans de Vreng
	Thomas Lance	William Smith	Petrus Ikelaar
1924[1]	FRANCE 12·6	DENMARK	NETHERLANDS
	Lucien Choury	Willy Falck Hansen	Gerard Bosch van Drakestein
	Jean Cugnot	Edmund Hansen	Maurice Peeters
1928	NETHERLANDS 11·8	GREAT BRITAIN	GERMANY
	Bernhard Leene	John Sibbit	Karl Köther
	Daan van Dijk	Ernest Chambers	Hans Bernhardt

1932	FRANCE 12·0	GREAT BRITAIN	DENMARK
	Maurice Perrin	Ernest Chambers	Willy Gervin
	Louis Chaillot	Stanley Chambers	Harald Christensen
1936	GERMANY 11·8	NETHERLANDS	FRANCE
	Ernest Ihbe	Bernhard Leene	Pierre Georget
	Carl Lorenz	Hendrik Ooms	Georges Maton
1948	ITALY 11·3	GREAT BRITAIN	FRANCE
	Ferdinando Teruzzi	Reg Harris	René Faye
	Renato Perona	Alan Bannister	Georges Dron
1952	AUSTRALIA 11·0	SOUTH AFRICA	ITALY
	Lionel Cox	Raymond Robinson	Antonio Maspes
	Russell Mockridge	Thomas Shardelow	Cesare Pinarello
1956	AUSTRALIA 10·8	CZECHOSLOVAKIA	ITALY
	Ian Browne	Ladislav Foucek	Giuseppe Ogna
	Anthony Marchant	Vaclav Machek	Cesare Pinarello
1960	ITALY 10·7	GERMANY	USSR
	Giuseppe Beghetto	Jürgen Simon	Boris Vasilyev
	Sergio Blanchetto	Lothar Stäber	Vladimir Leonov
1964	ITALY 10·75	USSR	GERMANY
	Angelo Damiano	Imant Bodnieks	Willi Fuggerer
	Sergio Blanchetto	Viktor Logunov	Klaus Kobusch
1968	FRANCE 9·83	NETHERLANDS	BELGIUM
	Daniel Morelon	Jan Jansen	Daniel Goens
	Pierre Trentin	Leijn Loevesijn	Robert van Lancker
1972	USSR 10·52	GDR	POLAND
	Vladimir Semenez	Otto Werner	Andrzej Bek
	Igor Tselovalnikov	Jürgen Geschke	Benedykt Kocot

[1] Since 1924 only times over last 200 m have been recorded.   1896–1904, 1912, 1976–1980 Event not held

TEAM ROAD RACE
(Consisting of the combined times of the best three—four 1912-20—riders from each country in the individual race. In 1956 based on placings).

	Gold	*Silver*	*Bronze*
1912	SWEDEN 44 h 35:33·6	GREAT BRITAIN 44 h 44:39·2	UNITED STATES 44 h 47:55·5
1920	FRANCE 19 h 16:43·2	SWEDEN 19 h 23:10·0	BELGIUM 19 h 28:44·4
1924	FRANCE 19 h 30:14·0	BELGIUM 19 h 46:55·4	SWEDEN 19 h 59:41·6
1928	DENMARK 15 h 09:14·0	GREAT BRITAIN 15 h 14:49·0	SWEDEN 15 h 27:49·0
1932	ITALY 7 h 27:15·2	DENMARK 7 h 38:50·2	SWEDEN 7 h 39:12·6
1936	FRANCE 7 h 39:16·2	SWITZERLAND 7 h 39:20·4	BELGIUM 7 h 39:21·0
1948	BELGIUM 15 h 58:17·4	GREAT BRITAIN 16 h 03:31·6	FRANCE 16 h 08:19·4
1952	BELGIUM 15 h 20:46·6	ITALY 15 h 33:27·3	FRANCE 15 h 38:58·1
1956	FRANCE 22 points	GREAT BRITAIN 23 points	GERMANY 27 points

ROAD TEAM TIME-TRIAL
Over 100 km except in 1964 (109·89 km), 1968 (102 km), 1980 (101 km).

	Gold	*Silver*	*Bronze*
1960	ITALY 2 h 14:33·53	GERMANY 2 h 16:56·31	USSR 2 h 18:41·67
1964	NETHERLANDS 2 h 26:31·19	ITALY 2 h 26:55·39	SWEDEN 2 h 27:11·52
1968	NETHERLANDS 2 h 07:49·06	SWEDEN 2 h 09:26·60	ITALY 2 h 10:18·74
1972	USSR 2 h 11:17·8	POLAND 2 h 11:47·5	*
1976	USSR 2 h 08:53·0	POLAND 2 h 09:13·0	DENMARK 2 h 12:20·0
1980	USSR 2 h 01:21·7	GDR 2 h 02:53·2	CZECHOSLOVAKIA 2 h 02:53·9

* Netherlands finished in third place but their bronze medal was withdrawn following a dope test.   1896–1908 Event not held

INDIVIDUAL ROAD RACE

	Gold	Silver	Bronze
1896	Aristidis Konstantinidis (GRE) 3 h 22:31·0	August Goedrich (GER) 3 h 42:18·0	F Battel (GBR) d.n.a
1906	B Vast (FRA) 2 h 41:28·0	M Bardonneau (FRA) 2 h 41:28·4	Luget (FRA) 2 h 41:28·6
1912	Rudolph Lewis (SAF) 10 h 42:39·0	Frederick Grubb (GBR) 10 h 51:24·2	Carl Schutte (USA) 10 h 52:38·8
1920	Harry Stenqvist (SWE) 4 h 40:01·8	Henry Kaltenbrun (SAF) 4 h 41:26·6	Fernand Canteloube (FRA) 4 h 42:54·4
1924	Armand Blanchonnet (FRA) 6 h 20:48·0	Henry Hoevenaers (BEL) 6 h 30:27·0	René Hamel (FRA) 6 h 40:51·6
1928	Henry Hansen (DEN) 4 h 47:18·0	Frank Southall (GBR) 4 h 55:06·0	Gösta Carlsson (SWE) 5 h 00:17·0
1932	Attilio Pavesi (ITA) 2 h 28:05·6	Guglielmo Segato (ITA) 2 h 29:21·4	Bernhard Britz (SWE) 2 h 29:45·2
1936	Robert Charpentier (FRA) 2 h 33:05·0	Guy Lapébie (FRA) 2 h 33:05·2	Ernst Nievergelt (SUI) 2 h 33:05·8
1948	José Beyaert (FRA) 5 h 18:12·6	Gerardus Voorting (HOL) 5 h 18:16·2	Lode Wouters (BEL) 5 h 18:16·2
1952	André Noyelle (BEL) 5 h 06:03·4	Robert Grondelaers (BEL) 5 h 06:51·2	Edi Ziegler (GER) 5 h 07:47·5
1956	Ercole Baldini (ITA) 5 h 21:17·0	Arnaud Geyre (FRA) 5 h 23:16·0	Alan Jackson (GBR) 5 h 23:16·0
1960	Viktor Kapitonov (URS) 4 h 20:37·0	Livio Trapè (ITA) 4 h 20:37·0	Willy van den Berghen (BEL) 4 h 20:57·0
1964	Mario Zanin (ITA) 4 h 39:51·63	Kjell Rodian (DEN) 4 h 39:51·65	Walter Godefroot (BEL) 4 h 39:51·74
1968	Pierfranco Vianelli (ITA) 4 h 41:25·24	Leif Mortensen (DEN) 4 h 42:49·71	Gösta Pettersson (SWE) 4 h 43:15·24
1972	Hennie Kuiper (HOL) 4 h 14:37·0	Kevin Sefton (AUS) 4 h 15:04·0	Jaime Huelamo (ESP) 4 h 15:04·0
1976	Bernt Johansson (SWE) 4 h 46:52·0	Giuseppe Martinelli (ITA) 4 h 47:23·0	Mieczyslaw Nowicki (POL) 4 h 47:23·0
1980	Sergey Sukhoruchenkov (URS) 4 h 48:28·9	Czeslaw Lang (POL) 4 h 51:26·9	Yuriy Barinov (URS) 4 h 51:26·9

This event has been held over the following distances: 1896—87 km; 1906—84 km; 1912—320 km; 1920—175 km; 1924—188 km; 1928—168 km; 1932 and 1936—100 km; 1948—194·63 km; 1952—190·4 km; 1956—187·73 km; 1960—175·38 km; 1964—194·83 km; 1968—196·2 km; 1972—182·4 km; 1976—175 km; 1980—189 km. 1900–1904, 1908 Event not held

DISCONTINUED EVENTS
660 yards (603·5 metres) sprint

	Gold	Silver	Bronze
1908	Victor Johnson (GBR) 51·2	Emile Demangel (FRA) close	Karl Neumer (GER) 1 length

5000 METRES TRACK

	Gold	Silver	Bronze
1906	Francesco Verri (ITA) 8:35·0	H Crowther (GBR) 2 lengths	B Vast (FRA) 5 lengths
1908	Benjamin Jones (GBR) 8:36·2	Maurice Schilles (FRA) close	André Auffray (FRA)

10 000 METRES TRACK

	Gold	Silver	Bronze
1896	Paul Masson (FRA) 17:54·2	Léon Flameng (FRA)	Adolf Schmal (AUT)

20 000 METRES TRACK

	Gold	Silver	Bronze
1906	William Pett (GBR) 29:00·0	M Bardonneau (FRA) 29:30·0	B Vast (FRA) 29:32·0
1908	Charles Kingsbury (GBR) 34:13·6	Benjamin Jones (GBR) close	Joseph Werbrouck (BEL)

50 000 METRES TRACK

	Gold	Silver	Bronze
1920	Henry George (BEL) 1 h 16:43·2	Cyril Alden* (GBR) close	Petrus Ikelaar (HOL) close
1924	Jacobus Willems (HOL) 1 h 18:24·0	Cyril Alden (GBR) 1 length	Frederick Wyld (GBR) 1 length

* Most eyewitnesses considered Ikelaar (HOL) finished in second place

100 km TRACK

	Gold	Silver	Bronze
1896	Léon Flameng (FRA) 3 h 08:19·2	G Kolettis (GRE) 6 laps	★
1908	Charles Bartlett (GBR) 2 h 41:48·6	Charles Denny (GBR) 1 length	Octave Lapize (FRA)

★ Only two riders finished.

12 HOURS TRACK

	Gold	Silver	Bronze
1896	Adolf Schmal (AUT) 314·997 km	F Keeping (GBR) 314·664 km	Georgios Paraskevopoulos (GRE) 313·330 km

CYCLING—MEDALS

	Gold	Silver	Bronze	Total
FRANCE	27	15	19	61
ITALY	25	14	6	45
GREAT BRITAIN	8	21	14	43
NETHERLANDS	8	10	4	22
GERMANY (FRG)	5	8	9	22
BELGIUM	5	6	9	20
DENMARK	5	6	7	18
USSR	7	3	7	17
SWEDEN	3	2	7	12
GDR	4	4	3	11
AUSTRALIA	4	4	2	10
SOUTH AFRICA	1	4	3	8
POLAND	—	4	3	7
CZECHOSLOVAKIA	2	2	2	6
GREECE	1	3	1	5
SWITZERLAND	1	2	2	5
AUSTRIA	1	—	2	3
UNITED STATES	—	—	3	3
NORWAY	1	—	—	1
CANADA	—	—	1	1
JAMAICA	—	—	1	1
SPAIN	—	—	1	1
	108	108	106[1]	322

[1] No bronze medals in 1896 100 km event and 1972 road team time trial.

Russell Mockridge won two gold medals in the 1952 cycling events having been included in the Australian team only days before the Games began.

EQUESTRIANISM

In the Ancient Games the first known event using horses was a chariot race in 680 BC. Horses with riders were included in the Games from 648 BC.

The first equestrian gold medallist of the Modern Olympics was Aime Haegeman (BEL) on *Benton II* who won the show jumping on 29 May 1900.

The greatest number of entries, 158 from 29 countries, was in 1956, when the equestrian events were held separately, at Stockholm, from the main Games due to the strict Australian quarantine laws.

The record total of gold medals by a rider is five (one individual and four team events) by Hans-Günter Winkler (FRG) between 1956 and 1972. His total of seven medals, including a silver and a bronze, is also a record for the sport. The oldest equestrian gold medallist was Josef Neckermann

(FRG), a member of the winning dressage team in 1968, aged 56 yr 141 days. The oldest individual gold medallist was Ernst Lindner (SWE), later a General, in the dressage in 1924 aged 56 yr 91 days. The youngest champion was Mauro Checcoli (ITA) in the 1964 three-day event aged 21 yr 232 days.

Raimondo d'Inzeo (ITA) competed in a record eight Games from 1948 to 1976, during which he won one gold, two silver and three bronze medals. No other Olympic competitor in any sport has matched this number of appearances. His older brother Piero competed in four Games between 1956 and 1972 bringing the family total of medals to one gold, four silver and seven bronze. A Bulgarian, Kroum Lekarski, competed in the three-day event over a record period of 36 years between 1924 and 1960, but only appeared in four Games, those of 1924, 1928, 1956 and 1960. Gustav-Adolf Boltenstern Jr (SWE) won dressage medals over a record 24-year period 1932–56.

A few competitors have competed with distinction in two different equestrian disciplines. The most successful have been Åge Lundström (SWE) with a gold in the 1920 three-day event and another in the 1924 show jumping team; Earl Thomson (USA) with a gold in the three-day event and a silver in the dressage team in 1948; and Claes König (SWE) with a gold in show jumping in 1920 and a silver in the three-day event in 1924. The first female riders competed in the Games in 1952, and the first to win a medal was Lis Hartel (DEN) with a silver in the dressage, which she repeated in 1956. In 1944 she had suffered a disabling attack of polio.

The only horse to be ridden to medals in three celebrations of the Games was *Absent* in the Soviet dressage team, winning a gold and two bronze medals with Sergey Filatov in 1960 and 1964 and then a silver with Ivan Kalita in 1968.

In 1936 Germany completed the only six gold medal 'clean sweep' in Olympic equestrian history. In the 1912 and 1920 dressage competition for individual riders Sweden took the first three places both times, a unique occurrence in Olympic equestrianism. No country has competed in all Games equestrian programmes since they began in 1900, although France and the United States contested every occasion until 1980.

At Los Angeles in 1984 the sport will be the only one in which men and women compete on equal terms against each other in individual events.

SHOW JUMPING

This was the first equestrian event to be included in the Olympic Games, along with high and long jumping contests, in 1900. From 1924, when the team contest was instituted, until 1968 teams comprised three members, all counting for the final score. This led to many teams not finishing, as in 1932 when no team medals were awarded at all, and 1948 when only four of the 14 competing teams finished. Since 1972 teams have consisted of four riders with the best three scoring. The most gold medals have been won by Hans-Günter Winkler (FRG) (see above). Only Pierre Jonquères d'Oriola (FRA) has won the individual title twice, in 1952 and 1964. The first woman to win a medal was Pat Smythe (GBR) with a bronze in the 1956 team event. The first female individual medallist was Marion Coakes (GBR) with a silver in 1968.

The oldest gold medallist was Winkler in 1976 aged 46 yr 49 days, while the oldest individual champion was Jonquères d'Oriola aged 44 yr 266 days in 1964. Bill Steinkraus (USA) holds the record for winning medals over a twenty year

Capt Ludwig Stubbendorff on *Nurmi* on his way to an easy victory in the three-day event in 1936, when only four teams finished the very tough course.

period with a team bronze in 1952 and a team silver in 1972. This is matched by Winkler with individual and team golds in 1956 and a team silver in 1976. The youngest gold medallist was Jim Day (CAN) aged 22 yr 117 days when a member of the winning team in 1968.

The lowest score obtained by a winner is no faults by Frantisek Ventura (TCH) on *Eliot* in 1928, Pierre Jonquères d'Oriola (FRA) on *Ali Baba* in 1952, and Alwin Schockemöhle (FRG) on *Warwick Rex* in 1976. The most successful horse has been Hans-Günter Winkler's *Halla* which was ridden to three gold medals in 1956 and 1960.

DRESSAGE

Only Henri St Cyr (SWE) has won the individual title twice, in 1952 and 1956. In total he won a record four gold medals and this would have been even greater but his team was disqualified in 1948, after finishing in first place, because one of its members, Gehnäll Persson, was not a fully commissioned officer, as was required by the rules at that time. With the rules changed Persson was a member of both 1952 and 1956 winning teams. This Swedish team of St Cyr, Persson and Gustav-Adolf Boltenstern Jr created an unique Olympic feat by finishing in first place three times in a row with the same team members, and can claim to be the most successful combination in Olympic history.

The first medal won by a woman was that by Lis Hartel (see above). The first female gold medallist was Liselott Linsenhoff (FRG) in 1972, who had also been a member of the all-female team, Linsenhoff, Hannelore Weygand and Anneliese Küppers, which won the silver medal in 1956.

The oldest gold medallist was Josef Neckermann (see above) who was also the oldest medallist when he gained an individual bronze in 1972 aged 60 yr 96 days. The oldest competitor in Olympic equestrian history was General Arthur von Pongracz (AUT) who began his Olympic career in 1924 at the age of 60 and ended it in 1936, just missing a team bronze medal, at 72, making him one of the oldest Olympians ever. The oldest woman ever to compete in the Olympic Games, was Lorna Johnstone (GBR) who placed 12th at Munich in 1972 five days after celebrating her 70th birthday. The

Three gold medals and a silver were won by this team of Charles Pahud de Mortanges (HOL) and *Marcroix* in 1928 and 1932.

youngest rider to win a gold medal was Heinz Pollay, a member of Germany's winning team in 1936 aged 28 yr 181 days.

André Jousseaume (FRA) 1932–1952, Josef Neckermann (FRG) 1960–1972 and Gustav-Adolf Boltenstern Jr (SWE) 1932–1956 all won medals in four celebrations of the Games. The latter did not compete in 1936.

The most successful horse has been *Dux* ridden by Reiner Klimke (FRG) to two golds and a bronze in 1964 and 1968.

THREE-DAY EVENT

Competitions actually last 4 days as the dressage segment occupies 2 days.

Only Charles Pahud de Mortanges (HOL) has won the individual title twice, in 1928 and 1932. Later a member of the IOC, he also won a record total of four golds and one silver between 1924 and 1932. His Dutch team, including Gerard de Kruyff and Adolph van der Voort van Zijp, uniquely won two team titles with the same team members. He also uniquely won gold medals in three consecutive Games. The longest span of competition by a medal winner is 16 years by Earl Thomson (USA) who won a gold and a silver in 1932, a silver in 1936, and a gold in 1948.

The first woman to take part was Helena Dupont (USA) in 1964 when she finished in 33rd position as her teammates won the silver team medal. The first gold medals by female riders were by Mary Gordon-Watson and Bridget Parker (both GBR)

Equestrianism

in the 1972 team contest.

The oldest gold medallist was Derek Allhusen (GBR) aged 64 yr 286 days when a member of the winning team in 1968. The youngest gold medallist was Mauro Checcoli (see above).

The oldest medallist was William Roycroft (AUS) who won a bronze team medal in 1976 aged 61 yr 129 days.

In 1920 the three-day event did not include a dressage segment but comprised two cross-country runs, at 50 km and 20 km, as well as the jumping discipline. The 1936 cross-country course was so tough that only four teams finished of the 14 which had started. Captain Richard Fanshawe (GBR) finished next to last with 8754·2 penalties having chased and caught his horse which had bolted after a bad fall in which he broke his arm. This action enabled his team to take the bronze medals. The most successful horse has been *Marcroix* ridden by Charles Pahud de Mortanges (HOL) to three golds and one silver in 1928 and 1932. *Silver Piece* ridden by Voort van Zijp in the Dutch team of 1924 and 1928 also won three gold medals.

The only equestrian medal ever won by Japan went to Baron Takeichi Nishi and *Uranus*, winners of the 1932 show jumping title.

GRAND PRIX (JUMPING)

	Gold	Silver	Bronze
1900	Aimé Haegeman (BEL) *Benton II*	Georges van de Poele (BEL) *Windsor Squire*	M de Champsavin (FRA) *Terpsichore*
1912	Jean Cariou (FRA) 186 pts *Mignon*	Rabod von Kröcher (GER) 186 *Dohna*	Emanuel de Blomaert de Soye (BEL) 185 *Clonmore*
1920	Tommaso Lequio (ITA) 2 faults *Trebecco*	Alessandro Valerio (ITA) 3 *Cento*	Gustaf Lewenhaupt (SWE) 4 *Mon Coeur*
1924	Alphonse Gemuseus (SUI) 6 faults *Lucette*	Tommaso Lequio (ITA) *Trebecco*	Adam Krolikiewicz (POL) 10 *Picador*
1928	Frantisek Ventura (TCH) no faults *Eliot*	Pierre Bertrand de Balanda (FRA) 2 *Papillon*	Charles Kuhn (SUI) 4 *Pepita*
1932	Takeichi Nishi (JPN) 8 pts *Uranus*	Harry Chamberlin (USA) 12 *Show Girl*	Clarence von Rosen Jr (SWE) 16 *Empire*
1936	Kurt Hasse (GER) 4 faults *Tora*	Henri Rang (ROM) 4 *Delius*	József von Platthy (HUN) 8 *Sellö*
1948	Humberto Mariles Cortés (MEX) 6·25 faults *Arete*	Rubén Uriza (MEX) 8 *Harvey*	Jean d'Orgeix (FRA) 8 *Sucre de Pomme*
1952	Pierre Jonquères d'Oriola (FRA) no faults *Ali Baba*	Oscar Cristi (CHI) 4 *Bambi*	Fritz Thiedemann (GER) 8 *Meteor*
1956	Hans Günter Winkler (GER) 4 faults *Halla*	Raimondo d'Inzeo (ITA) 8 *Merano*	Piero d'Inzeo (ITA) 11 *Uruguay*
1960	Raimondo d'Inzeo (ITA) 12 faults *Posillippo*	Piero d'Inzeo (ITA) 16 *The Rock*	David Broome (GBR) 23 *Sunsalve*
1964	Pierre Jonquères d'Oriola (FRA) 9 faults *Lutteur*	Hermann Schridde (GER) 13·75 *Dozent*	Peter Robeson (GBR) 16 *Firecrest*
1968	William Steinkraus (USA) 4 faults *Snowbound*	Marian Coakes (GBR) 8 *Stroller*	David Broome (GBR) 12 *Mister Softee*
1972	Graziano Mancinelli (ITA) 8 faults *Ambassador*	Ann Moore (GBR) 8 *Psalm*	Neal Shapiro (USA) 8 *Sloopy*

| 1976 | Alwin Schockemöhle (FRG) no faults *Warwick Rex* | Michael Vaillancourt (CAN) 12 *Branch County* | Francois Mathy (BEL) 12 *Gai Luron* |
| 1980 | Jan Kowalczyk (POL) 8 faults *Artemor* | Nikolai Korolkov (URS) 9·50 *Espadron* | Joaquin Perez Heras (MEX) 12 *Alymony* |

1896, 1904–1908 Event not held

GRAND PRIX (JUMPING) TEAM

	Gold	*Silver*	*Bronze*
1912	SWEDEN 545 pts	FRANCE 538	GERMANY 530
1920	SWEDEN 14 faults	BELGIUM 16·25	ITALY 18·75
1924	SWEDEN 42·25 pts	SWITZERLAND 50	PORTUGAL 53
1928	SPAIN 4 faults	POLAND 8	SWEDEN 10
1932[1]	—	—	—
1936	GERMANY 44 faults	NETHERLANDS 51·5	PORTUGAL 56
1948	MEXICO 34·25 faults	SPAIN 56·50	GREAT BRITAIN 67
1952	GREAT BRITAIN 40·75 faults	CHILE 45·75	UNITED STATES 52·25
1956	GERMANY 40 faults	ITALY 66	GREAT BRITAIN 69
1960	GERMANY 46·50 faults	UNITED STATES 66	ITALY 80·50
1964	GERMANY 68·50 faults	FRANCE 77·75	ITALY 88·50
1968	CANADA 102·75 faults	FRANCE 110·50	FRG 117·25
1972	FRG 32 faults	UNITED STATES 32·25	ITALY 48
1976	FRANCE 40 faults	FRG 44	BELGIUM 63
1980	USSR 16 faults	POLAND 32	MEXICO 39·25

[1] There was a team competition but no nation had three riders complete the course.   1896–1908 Event not held

GRAND PRIX (DRESSAGE)

	Gold	*Silver*	*Bronze*
1912	Carl Bonde (SWE) 15 pts *Emperor*	Gustaf-Adolf Boltenstern Sr (SWE) 21 *Neptun*	Hans von Blixen-Finecke (SWE) 32 *Maggie*
1920	Janne Lundblad (SWE) 27 237 pts *Uno*	Bertil Sandström (SWE) 26 312 *Sabel*	Hans von Rosen (SWE) 25 125 *Running Sister*
1924	Ernst Linder (SWE) 276·4 pts *Piccolo-mini*	Bertil Sandström (SWE) 275·8 *Sabel*	Xavier Lesage (FRA) 265·8 *Plumard*
1928	Carl von Langen (GER) 237·42 pts *Draüfgänger*	Charles Marion (FRA) 231·00 *Linon*	Ragnar Olsson (SWE) 229·78 *Günstling*
1932	Xavier Lesage (FRA) 1031·25 pts *Taine*	Charles Marion (FRA) 916·25 *Linon*	Hiram Tuttle (USA) 901·50 *Olympic*
1936	Heinz Pollay (GER) 1760 pts *Kronos*	Friedrich Gerhard (GER) 1745·5 *Absinth*	Alois Podhajsky (AUT) 1721·5 *Nero*
1948	Hans Moser (SUI) 492·5 pts *Hummer*	André Jousseaume (FRA) 480·0 *Harpagon*	Gustaf-Adolf Boltenstern Jr (SWE) 477·5 *Trumpf*
1952	Henri St Cyr (SWE) 561 pts *Master Rufus*	Lis Hartel (DEN) 541·5 *Jubilee*	André Jousseaume (FRA) 541·0 *Harpagon*
1956	Henri St Cyr (SWE) 860 pts *Juli*	Lis Hartel (DEN) 850 *Jubilee*	Liselott Linsenhoff (GER) 832 *Adular*
1960	Sergey Filatov (URS) 2144 pts *Absent*	Gustav Fischer (SUI) 2087 *Wald*	Josef Neckermann (GER) 2082 *Asbach*
1964	Henri Chammartin (SUI) 1504 pts *Woermann*	Harry Boldt (GER) 1503 *Remus*	Sergey Filatov (URS) 1486 *Absent*
1968	Ivan Kizimov (URS) 1572 pts *Ikhov*	Josef Neckermann (FRG) 1546 *Mariano*	Reiner Klimke (FRG) 1537 *Dux*
1972	Liselott Linsenhoff (FRG) 1229 pts *Piaff*	Elena Petuchkova (URS) 1185 *Pepel*	Josef Neckermann (FRG) 1177 *Venetia*
1976	Christine Stückelberger (SUI) 1486 pts *Granat*	Harry Boldt (FRG) 1435 *Woycek*	Reiner Klimke (FRG) 1395 *Mehmed*
1980	Elisabeth Theurer (AUT) 1370 pts *Mon Cherie*	Yuriy Kovshov (URS) 1300 *Igrok*	Viktor Ugryumov (URS) 1234 *Shkval*

1896–1908 Event not held

GRAND PRIX (DRESSAGE) TEAM

	Gold	Silver	Bronze
1928	GERMANY 669·72 pts	SWEDEN 650·86	NETHERLANDS 642·96
1932	FRANCE 2818·75 pts	SWEDEN 2678	UNITED STATES 2576·75
1936	GERMANY 5074 pts	FRANCE 4846	SWEDEN 4660·5
1948[1]	FRANCE 1269 pts	UNITED STATES 1256	PORTUGAL 1182
1952	SWEDEN 1597·5 pts	SWITZERLAND 1759	GERMANY 1501
1956	SWEDEN 2475 pts	GERMANY 2346	SWITZERLAND 2346
1964	GERMANY 2558 pts	SWITZERLAND 2526	USSR 2311
1968	FRG 2699 pts	USSR 2657	SWITZERLAND 2547
1972	USSR 5095 pts	FRG 5083	SWEDEN 4849
1976	FRG 5155 pts	SWITZERLAND 4684	UNITED STATES 4670
1980	USSR 4383 pts	BULGARIA 3580	ROMANIA 3346

[1] Sweden were originally declared winners with 1366 pts but were subsequently disqualified one year later. 1896–1924, 1960 Event not held

THREE-DAY EVENT

	Gold	Silver	Bronze
1912	Axel Nordlander (SWE) 46·59 pts *Lady Artist*	Friedrich von Rochow (GER) 46·42 *Idealist*	Jean Cariou (FRA) 46·32 *Cocotte*
1920	Helmer Mörner (SWE) 1775 pts *Germania*	Age Lundström (SWE) 1738·75 *Yrsa*	Ettore Caffaratti (ITA) 1733·75 *Traditore*
1924	Adolph van der Voort van Zijp (HOL) 1976 pts *Silver Piece*	Fröde Kirkebjerg (DEN) 1853·5 *Meteor*	Sloan Doak (USA) 1845·5 *Pathfinder*
1928	Charles Pahud de Mortanges (HOL) 1969·82 pts *Marcroix*	Gerard de Kruyff (HOL) 1967·26 *Va-t-en*	Brúno Neumann (GER) 1944·42 *Ilja*
1932	Charles Pahud de Mortanges (HOL) 1813·83 pts *Marcroix*	Earl Thomson (USA) 1811 *Jenny Camp*	Clarence von Rosen Jr (SWE) 1809·42 *Sunnyside Maid*
1936	Ludwig Stubbendorff (GER) 37·7 faults *Nurmi*	Earl Thomson (USA) 99.9 *Jenny Camp*	Hans Mathiesen-Lunding (DEN) 102·2 *Jason*
1948	Bernard Chevallier (FRA) +4 pts *Aiglonne*	Frank Henry (USA) −21 *Swing Low*	Robert Selfelt (SWE) −25 *Claque*
1952	Hans von Blixen-Finecke (SWE) 28·33 faults *Jubal*	Guy Lefrant (FRA) 54.50 *Verdun*	Wilhelm Büsing (GER) 55·50 *Hubertus*
1956	Petrus Kastenman (SWE) 66·53 faults *Iluster*	August Lütke-Westhues (GER) 84·87 *Trux von Kamax*	Frank Weldon (GBR) 85·48 *Kilbarry*
1960	Lawrence Morgan (AUS) +7·15 pts *Salad Days*	Neale Lavis (AUS) −16·50 *Mirrabooka*	Anton Bühler (SUI) −51·21 *Gay Spark*
1964	Mauro Checcoli (ITA) 64·40 pts *Surbean*	Carlos Moratorio (ARG) 56·40 *Chalan*	Fritz Ligges (GER) 49·20 *Donkosak*
1968	Jean-Jacques Guyon (FRA) 38·86 pts *Pitou*	Derek Allhusen (GBR) 41·61 *Lochinvar*	Michael Page (USA) 52·31 *Faster*
1972	Richard Meade (GBR) 57·73 pts *Laurieston*	Alessa Argenton (ITA) 43·33 *Woodland*	Jan Jonsson (SWE) 39·67 *Sarajevo*
1976	Edmund Coffin (USA) 114·99 pts *Bally-Cor*	John Plumb (USA) 125·85 *Better & Better*	Karl Schultz (FRG) 129·45 *Madrigal*
1980	Federico Roman (ITA) 108·60 pts *Rossinan*	Aleksandr Blinov (URS) 120·80 *Galzun*	Yuriy Salnikov (URS) 151·60 *Pintset*

1896–1908 Event not held

THREE-DAY EVENT TEAM

	Gold	Silver	Bronze
1912	SWEDEN 139·06 pts	GERMANY 138·48	UNITED STATES 137·33
1920	SWEDEN 5057·5 pts	ITALY 4735	BELGIUM 4560
1924	NETHERLANDS 5297·5 pts	SWEDEN 4743·5	ITALY 4512·5
1928	NETHERLANDS 5865·68 pts	NORWAY 5395·68	POLAND 5067·92
1932	UNITED STATES 5038·08 pts	NETHERLANDS 4689·08	—[1]
1936	GERMANY 676·75 pts	POLAND 991·70	GREAT BRITAIN 9195·50
1948	UNITED STATES 161·50 faults	SWEDEN 165·00	MEXICO 305·25
1952	SWEDEN 221·49 pts	GERMANY 235·49	UNITED STATES 587·16

1956	GREAT BRITAIN 355·48 pts	GERMANY 475·61	CANADA 572·72
1960	AUSTRALIA 128·18 pts	SWITZERLAND 386·02	FRANCE 515·71
1964	ITALY 85·80 pts	UNITED STATES 65·86	GERMANY 56·73
1968	GREAT BRITAIN 175·93 pts	UNITED STATES 245·87	AUSTRALIA 331·26
1972	GREAT BRITAIN 95·53 pts	UNITED STATES 10·81	FRG − 18·00
1976	UNITED STATES 441·00 pts	FRG 584·60	AUSTRALIA 599·54
1980	USSR 457·00 pts	ITALY 656·20	MEXICO 1172·85

[1] No other teams finished.   1896–1908 Event not held

DISCONTINUED EVENTS

EQUESTRIAN HIGH JUMP

	Gold	*Silver*	*Bronze*
1900	Dominique Gardères (FRA) 1·85 m *Canela* — Gian Giorgio Trissino (ITA) 1·85 m *Oreste*		A Moreau (FRA) 1·70 *Ludlow*

EQUESTRIAN LONG JUMP

	Gold	*Silver*	*Bronze*
1900	Constant van Langhendonck (BEL) 6·10 m *Extra Dry*	Gian Giorgio Trissino (ITA) 5·70 *Oreste*	de Prunelle (FRA) 5·30 *Tolla*

FIGURE RIDING
(Only open to soldiers below the rank of NCO)

	Gold	*Silver*	*Bronze*
1920	Bouckaert (BEL) 30·5 pts	Fiel (FRA) 29·5	Finet (BEL) 29·0
	Teams BELGIUM	FRANCE	SWEDEN

EQUESTRIANISM—MEDALS

	Gold	Silver	Bronze	Total		Gold	Silver	Bronze	Total
GERMANY (FRG)	18	15	15	48	NORWAY	—	1	—	1
SWEDEN	17	8	13	38	HUNGARY	—	—	1	1
FRANCE	10	11	8	29					
UNITED STATES	5	11	9	25		91[1]	89[1]	89[2]	269
ITALY	7	9	7	23					
USSR	6	5	4	15					
GREAT BRITAIN	5	3	7	15					
SWITZERLAND	4	6	4	14					
BELGIUM	4	2	5	11					
NETHERLANDS	5	3	1	9					
MEXICO	2	1	4	7					
POLAND	1	3	2	6					
AUSTRALIA	2	1	2	5					
DENMARK	—	3	1	4					
CANADA	1	1	1	3					
PORTUGAL	—	—	3	3					
SPAIN	1	1	—	2					
AUSTRIA	1	—	1	2					
CHILE	—	2	—	2					
ROMANIA	—	1	1	2					
CZECHOSLOVAKIA	1	—	—	1					
JAPAN	1	—	—	1					
ARGENTINA	—	1	—	1					
BULGARIA	—	1	—	1					

[1] Two gold medals in 1900 high jump event—no silver.   [2] No bronze medal in 1932 3-Day team event.

Pierre Jonquières d'Oriola (FRA) on *Lutteur,* **winners of the 1964 show jumping gold medal. The Frenchman is the only rider to win the individual title twice.**

FENCING

Ellen Preis (GER) won the gold medal in 1932 and bronze medals in the next two Games. She also won three world championships.

One of the original sports held in the Games of 1896, when the first Olympic fencing gold medallist was Emile Gravelotte (FRA) who won the foil title. It is the only sport in which professionals have openly competed in the Games, as special events for fencing masters were held in 1896 and 1900. In 1900 there was even an event in which the fencing masters competed against the other competitors, so that Albert Ayat (FRA) beat his pupil Ramón Fonst (CUB) in an épée contest. When Léon Pyrgos won the foil event for fencing masters in 1896 he became the first Greek gold medallist of modern times. A foil contest for women was introduced in 1924 and a team competition for them in 1960. Electronic scoring equipment was introduced for the épée events in 1936, and for foil in 1956.

The most gold medals won is seven by Aladar Gerevich (HUN) in the sabre between 1932 and 1960. The record for most medals of all types is held by Edoardo Mangiarotti (ITA) with 13 in foil and épée between 1936 and 1960 comprising six gold, five silver and two bronze. His older brother Dario won a gold and two silver medals in 1948 and 1952. Nedo Nadi (ITA) won an unequalled five gold medals at one celebration in 1920, and his younger brother Aldo won three gold and a silver to make the family total a record for such a combination in one Games at any sport. The most individual gold medals won is three by Ramón Fonst (CUB) in 1900 and 1904 (two), and by Nedo Nadi (ITA) in 1912 and 1920 (two).

The only fencer, and also the only Olympic competitor at any sport, to win gold medals at six consecutive Games is Aladar Gerevich (HUN) (see above). His medal winning span of 28 years is also a record. Britain's Bill Hoskyns also competed in six Games, from 1956 to 1976, but he only won two silver medals. The equal longest span of competition by any Olympic competitor (see p 22) is 40 years by Ivan Osiier (DEN) who was in fencing events from 1908 to 1948. During this period he won a silver medal in 1912 and

became the oldest ever Olympic fencer in 1948 aged 59 yr 240 days. His wife Ellen won a gold medal in 1924.

Only two fencers have gained individual medals in all three disciplines at one Games. The outstanding one is Roger Ducret (FRA) with a foil gold and épée and sabre silvers in 1924. In the sparsely supported 1904 fencing events Albertson Van Zo Post, an American competing for Cuba, won a foil silver and bronzes in the other two disciplines.

The youngest Olympic fencing champion was Ramón Fonst (CUB) when he won the épée title in 1900 aged 16 yr 289 days. The oldest was Aladar Gerevich (HUN) aged 50 yr 178 days when he won his last gold medal in 1960. His family has a unique position in Olympic fencing, as he won seven gold, one silver and two bronze medals, his wife Erna Bogen won a bronze in 1932, his father-in-law Albert Bogen won a silver in 1912 competing for Austria, and Aladar and Erna's son Pal won bronze medals in 1972 and 1980. The only twins to win gold medals in fencing were Paul and Henri Anspach (BEL) in the winning 1912 épée team.

FOIL

The only men to win two individual titles are Nedo Nadi (ITA) in 1912 and 1920, and Christian d'Oriola (FRA) in 1952 and 1956. The latter also holds the record for most successful fencer in this discipline with four gold and two silver medals from 1948 to 1956.

The oldest gold medallist was Henri Jobier (FRA) who was over 44 years old as a member of the winning 1924 team, and the youngest was Nedo Nadi (see above) who won the 1912 individual title aged 18 yr 29 days.

ÉPÉE

Ramón Fonst (CUB) is the only double winner of the individual title in 1900 and 1904. The most successful fencer was Edoardo Mangiarotti (ITA) with five gold, one silver and two bronze medals in épée events between 1936 and 1960.

The oldest gold medallist was Fiorenzo Marini (ITA) aged 46 yr 179 days in the 1960 team event, and the youngest was Fonst (see above).

SABRE

Jean Georgiadis (GRE) in 1896 and 1906, Jenö Fuchs (HUN) in 1908 and 1912, Rudolf Karpati (HUN) 1956 and 1960, and Viktor Krovopouskov (URS) 1976 and 1980, all won two individual titles. Gerevich (see above) won a record seven gold medals (only one individual) and was also the oldest sabre gold medallist. The youngest was Mikhail Burtsev (URS) in the winning team in 1976 aged 20 yr 36 days.

The Hungarians have dominated this event to an unparalleled extent. In the individual event they have taken 11 gold, six silver and eight bronze medals. They have won the team event nine times, taken second once and third place on three occasions. The 1960 team included Aladar Gerevich, Rudolf Karpati and Pal Kovacs, who between them amassed a total of 19 gold, one silver and three bronze medals. Their winning 1948 and 1952 teams were composed of the same members.

Rylskiy (URS) congratulates Aladar Gerevich (HUN) on the Hungarian team's sixth consecutive gold medal in 1956. On the right is the Polish team.

WOMEN'S FOIL

Only Ilona Elek (HUN) has won two individual titles, in 1936 and 1948. Elena Novikova-Belova (URS) won a record four gold medals (one individual) between 1968 and 1976. The most medals of all types won is seven (two gold, three silver, two bronze) in a record five Games by Ildikó Sagi-Retjö (formerly Ujlaki-Retjö) of Hungary between 1960 and 1976. Ellen Müller-Preis (AUT) competed over a record span of 24 years from 1932 to 1956, and this is the longest competition span by any female Olympian.

The youngest gold medallist was Isabelle Boeri-Begard (FRA) in the winning 1980 team aged 20 yr 20 days. The oldest was Ilona Elek (HUN) aged 41 yr 77 days when she won the title in 1948, and she was also the oldest medallist winning the silver in 1952 aged 45 yr 71 days.

When Gillian Sheen (GBR) won her gold medal in 1956 there were hardly any members of the British Press on hand as they considered fencing a 'minor' sport and she had not been expected to achieve anything special.

FOIL (INDIVIDUAL)
Wins are assessed on both wins (2 pts) *and* draws (1 pt) so, as in 1928, the winner does not necessarily have most wins.

	Gold	Silver	Bronze
1896	Emile Gravelotte (FRA) 4 wins	Henri Callott (FRA) 3	Perikles Mavromichalis-Pierrakos (GRE) 2
1900	Emile Coste (FRA) 6 wins	Henri Masson (FRA) 5	Jacques Boulenger (FRA) 4
1904	Ramón Fonst (CUB) 3 wins	Albertson Van Zo Post[1] (CUB) 2	Charles Tatham[1] (CUB) 1
1906	Georges Dillon-Kavanagh (FRA) d.n.a.	Gustav Casmir (GER) d.n.a.	Pierre d'Hugues (FRA) d.n.a.
1912	Nedo Nadi (ITA) 7 wins	Pietro Speciale (ITA) 5	Richard Verderber (AUT) 4
1920	Nedo Nadi (ITA) 10 wins	Philippe Cattiau (FRA) 9	Roger Ducret (FRA) 9
1924	Roger Ducret (FRA) 6 wins	Philippe Cattiau (FRA) 5	Maurice van Damme (BEL) 4
1928	Lucien Gaudin (FRA) 9 wins	Erwin Casmir (GER) 9	Giulio Gaudini (ITA) 9
1932	Gustavo Marzi (ITA) 9 wins	Joseph Levis (USA) 6	Giulio Gaudini (ITA) 5
1936	Giulio Gaudini (ITA) 7 wins	Edouard Gardère (FRA) 6	Giorgio Bocchino (ITA) 4
1948	Jean Buhan (FRA) 7 wins	Christian d'Oriola (FRA) 5	Lajos Maszlay (HUN) 4
1952	Christian d'Oriola (FRA) 8 wins	Edoardo Mangiarotti (ITA) 6	Manlio di Rosa (ITA) 5
1956	Christian d'Oriola (FRA) 6 wins	Giancarlo Bergamini (ITA) 5	Antonio Spallino (ITA) 5

1960	Viktor Zhdanovich (URS) 7 wins	Yuriy Sissikin (URS) 4	Albert Axelrod (USA) 3
1964	Egon Franke (POL) 3 wins	Jean-Claude Magnan (FRA) 2	Daniel Revenu (FRA) 1
1968	Ion Drimba (ROM) 4 wins	Jenö Kamuti (HUN) 3	Daniel Revenu (FRA) 3
1972	Witold Woyda (POL) 5 wins	Jenö Kamuti (HUN) 4	Christian Nöel (FRA) 2
1976	Fabio Dal Zotto (ITA) 4 wins	Aleksandr Romankov (URS) 4	Bernard Talvard (FRA) 3
1980	Vladimir Smirnov (URS) 5 wins	Paskal Jolyot (FRA) 5	Aleksandr Romankov (URS) 5

[1] Van Zo Post and Tatham were American citizens but competed for Cuba.   1908 Event not held

FOIL (TEAM)

	Gold	Silver	Bronze
1904	CUBA	USA	CUBA[1]
1920	ITALY	FRANCE	UNITED STATES
1924	FRANCE	BELGIUM	HUNGARY
1928	ITALY	FRANCE	ARGENTINA
1932	FRANCE	ITALY	UNITED STATES
1936	ITALY	FRANCE	GERMANY
1948	FRANCE	ITALY	BELGIUM
1952	FRANCE	ITALY	HUNGARY
1956	ITALY	FRANCE	HUNGARY
1960	USSR	ITALY	GERMANY
1964	USSR	POLAND	FRANCE
1968	FRANCE	USSR	POLAND
1972	POLAND	USSR	FRANCE
1976	FRG	ITALY	FRANCE
1980	FRANCE	USSR	POLAND

[1] No other teams entered.   1896–1900, 1906–1912 Event not held

ÉPÉE (INDIVIDUAL)

	Gold	Silver	Bronze
1900	Ramón Fonst (CUB)	Louis Perree (FRA)	Léon Sée (FRA)
1904	Ramón Fonst (CUB) 3 wins	Charles Tatham (CUB) 2	Albertson Van Zo Post (CUB) 1
1906	Georges de la Falaise (FRA) d.n.a.	Georges Dillon-Kavanagh (FRA) d.n.a.	Alexander van Blijenburgh (HOL) d.n.a.
1908	Gaston Alibert (FRA) 5 wins	Alexandre Lippmann (FRA) 4	Eugène Olivier (FRA) 4
1912	Paul Anspach (BEL) 6 wins	Ivan Osiier (DEN) 5	Philippe Le Hardy de Beaulieu (BEL) 4
1920	Armand Massard (FRA) 9 wins	Alexandre Lippmann (FRA) 7	Gustave Buchard (FRA) 6
1924	Charles Delporte (BEL) 8 wins	Roger Ducret (FRA) 7	Nils Hellsten (SWE) 7
1928	Lucien Gaudin (FRA) 8 wins	Georges Buchard (FRA) 7	George Calnan (USA) 6
1932	Giancarlo Cornaggia-Medici (ITA) 8 wins	Georges Buchard (FRA) 7	Carlo Agostini (ITA) 7
1936	Franco Riccardi (ITA) 5 wins	Saverio Ragno (ITA) 6	Giancarlo Cornaggia-Medici (ITA) 6
1948	Luigi Cantone (ITA) 7 wins	Oswald Zappelli (SUI) 5	Edoardo Mangiarotti (ITA) 5
1952	Edoardo Mangiarotti (ITA) 7 wins	Dario Mangiarotti (ITA) 6	Oswald Zappelli (SUI) 6
1956	Carlo Pavesi (ITA) 5 wins	Giuseppe Delfino (ITA) 5	Edoardo Mangiarotti (ITA) 5
1960	Giuseppe Delfino (ITA) 5 wins	Allan Jay (GBR) 5	Bruno Khabarov (URS) 4
1964	Grigoriy Kriss (URS) 2 wins	William Hoskyns (GBR) 2	Guram Kostava (URS) 1
1968	Gyözö Kulcsár (HUN) 4 wins	Grigoriy Kriss (URS) 4	Gianluigi Saccaro (ITA) 4
1972	Csaba Fenyvesi (HUN) 4 wins	Jacques la Degaillerie (FRA) 3	Gyözö Kulcsár (HUN) 3
1976	Alexander Pusch (FRG) 3 wins	Jürgen Hehn (FRG) 3	Gyözö Kulcsár (HUN) 3
1980	Johan Harmenberg (SWE) 4 wins	Ernö Kolczonay (HUN) 3	Philippe Riboud (FRA) 3

1896 Event not held

ÉPÉE (TEAM)

	Gold	Silver	Bronze
1906	FRANCE	GREAT BRITAIN	BELGIUM
1908	FRANCE	GREAT BRITAIN	BELGIUM
1912	BELGIUM	GREAT BRITAIN	NETHERLANDS
1920	ITALY	BELGIUM	FRANCE
1924	FRANCE	BELGIUM	ITALY
1928	ITALY	FRANCE	PORTUGAL

1932	FRANCE	ITALY	UNITED STATES
1936	ITALY	SWEDEN	FRANCE
1948	FRANCE	ITALY	SWEDEN
1952	ITALY	SWEDEN	SWITZERLAND
1956	ITALY	HUNGARY	FRANCE
1960	ITALY	GREAT BRITAIN	USSR
1964	HUNGARY	ITALY	FRANCE
1968	HUNGARY	USSR	POLAND
1972	HUNGARY	SWITZERLAND	USSR
1976	SWEDEN	FRG	SWITZERLAND
1980	FRANCE	POLAND	USSR

1896–1904 Event not held

SABRE (INDIVIDUAL)

	Gold	*Silver*	*Bronze*
1896	Jean Georgiadis (GRE) 4 wins	Telemachos Karakalos (GRE) 3	Holger Nielsen (DEN) 2
1900	Georges de la Falaise (FRA) d.n.a.	Léon Thiébaut (FRA) d.n.a.	Siegfried Flesch (AUT) d.n.a.
1904	Manuel Diaz (CUB) 4 wins	William Grebe (USA) 3	Albertson Van Zo Post (CUB) 2
1906	Jean Georgiadis (GRE) d.n.a.	Gustav Casmir (GER) d.n.a.	Federico Cesarano (ITA) d.n.a.
1908	Jenö Fuchs (HUN) 6 wins	Béla Zulavsky (HUN) 6	Vilem Goppold von Lobsdorf (BOH) 4
1912	Jenö Fuchs (HUN) 6 wins	Béla Békéssy (HUN) 5	Ervin Mészáros (HUN) 5
1920	Nedo Nadi (ITA) 11 wins	Aldo Nadi (ITA) 9	Adrianus E W de Jong (HOL) 7
1924	Sándor Posta (HUN) 5 wins	Roger Ducret (FRA) 5	János Garai (HUN) 5
1928	Ödön Tersztyánszky (HUN) 9 wins	Attila Petschauer (HUN) 9	Bino Bini (ITA) 8
1932	György Piller (HUN) 8 wins	Giulio Gaudini (ITA) 7	Endre Kabos (HUN) 5
1936	Endre Kabos (HUN) 7 wins	Gustavo Marzi (ITA) 6	Aladár Gerevich (HUN) 6
1948	Aladár Gerevich (HUN) 7 wins	Vincenzo Pinton (ITA) 5	Pál Kovács (HUN) 5
1952	Pál Kovács (HUN) 8 wins	Aladár Gerevich (HUN) 7	Tibor Berczelly (HUN) 5
1956	Rudolf Kárpáti (HUN) 6 wins	Jerzy Pawlowski (POL) 5	Lev Kuznyetsov (URS) 4
1960	Rudolf Kárpáti (HUN) 5 wins	Zoltán Horvath (HUN) 4	Wladimiro Calarese (ITA) 4
1964	Tibor Pézsa (HUN) 2 wins	Claude Arabo (FRA) 2	Umar Mavlikhanov (URS) 1
1968	Jerzy Pawlowski (POL) 4 wins	Mark Rakita (URS) 4	Tibor Pézsa (HUN) 3
1972	Viktor Sidiak (URS) 4 wins	Peter Maroth (HUN) 3	Vladimir Nazlimov (URS) 3
1976	Victor Krovopouskov (URS) 5 wins	Vladimir Nazlimov (URS) 4	Viktor Sidiak (URS) 3
1980	Viktor Krovopouskov (URS) 5 wins	Mikhail Burtsev (URS) 4	Imre Gedovari (HUN) 3

SABRE (TEAM)

	Gold	*Silver*	*Bronze*
1906	GERMANY	GREECE	NETHERLANDS
1908	HUNGARY	ITALY	BOHEMIA
1912	HUNGARY	AUSTRIA	NETHERLANDS
1920	ITALY	FRANCE	NETHERLANDS
1924	ITALY	HUNGARY	NETHERLANDS
1928	HUNGARY	ITALY	POLAND
1932	HUNGARY	ITALY	POLAND
1936	HUNGARY	ITALY	GERMANY
1948	HUNGARY	ITALY	UNITED STATES
1952	HUNGARY	ITALY	FRANCE
1956	HUNGARY	POLAND	USSR
1960	HUNGARY	POLAND	ITALY
1964	USSR	ITALY	POLAND
1968	USSR	ITALY	HUNGARY
1972	ITALY	USSR	HUNGARY
1976	USSR	ITALY	ROMANIA
1980	USSR	ITALY	HUNGARY

1896–1904 Event not held

WOMEN'S FOIL (INDIVIDUAL)

	Gold	*Silver*	*Bronze*
1924	Ellen Osiier (DEN) 5 wins	Gladys Davis (GBR) 4	Grete Heckscher (DEN) 3
1928	Helène Mayer (GER) 7 wins	Muriel Freeman (GBR) 6	Olga Oelkers (GER) 4
1932	Ellen Preis (AUT) 9 wins	Heather Guinness (GBR) 8	Ena Bogen (HUN) 7
1936	Ilona Elek (HUN) 6 wins	Helène Mayer (GER) 5	Ellen Preis (AUT) 5
1948	Ilona Elek (HUN) 6 wins	Karen Lachmann (DEN) 5	Ellen Müller-Preis (AUT) 5
1952	Irene Camber (ITA) 5 wins	Ilona Elek (HUN) 5	Karen Lachmann (DEN) 4
1956	Gillian Sheen (GBR) 6 wins	Olga Orban (ROM) 6	Renée Garilhe (FRA) 5
1960	Heidi Schmid (GER) 6 wins	Valentina Rastvorova (URS) 5	Maria Vicol (ROM) 4
1964	Ildikó Ujlaki-Rejtö (HUN) 2 wins	Helga Mees (GER) 2	Antonella Ragno (ITA) 2
1968	Elena Novikova (URS) 4 wins	Pilar Roldan (MEX) 3	Ildiko Ujlaki-Rejtö (HUN) 3
1972	Antonella Ragno-Lonzi (ITA) 4 wins	Ildikó Bóbis (HUN) 3	Galina Gorokhova (URS) 3
1976	Ildikó Schwarczenberger (HUN) 4 wins	Maria Collino (ITA) 4	Elena Novikova-Belova (URS) 3
1980	Pascale Trinquet (FRA) 4 wins	Magda Maros (HUN) 3	Barbara Wysoczanska (POL) 3

1896–1920 Event not held

WOMEN'S FOIL (TEAM)

	Gold	*Silver*	*Bronze*
1960	USSR	HUNGARY	ITALY
1964	HUNGARY	USSR	GERMANY
1968	USSR	HUNGARY	ROMANIA
1972	USSR	HUNGARY	ROMANIA
1976	USSR	FRANCE	HUNGARY
1980	FRANCE	USSR	HUNGARY

1896–1956 Event not held

DISCONTINUED EVENTS

FOIL FOR FENCING MASTERS

	Gold	*Silver*	*Bronze*
1896	Léon Pyrgos (GRE)	M Perronnet (FRA)	K Miliotis-Komninos (GRE)
1900	Lucien Mérignac (FRA)	Alphonse Kirchhoffer (FRA)	Jean-Baptiste Mimiague (FRA)

ÉPÉE FOR FENCING MASTERS

	Gold	*Silver*	*Bronze*
1900	Albert Ayat (FRA)	Emile Bougnol (FRA)	Henri Laurent (FRA)
1906	Cyrille Verbrugge (BEL)	Mario Gubiani (ITA)	Ioannis Raissis (GRE)

ÉPÉE FOR AMATEURS AND FENCING MASTERS

	Gold	*Silver*	*Bronze*
1900	Albert Ayat (FRA)	Ramón Fonst (CUB)	Léon Sée (FRA)

SABRE FOR FENCING MASTERS

	Gold	*Silver*	*Bronze*
1900	Antonio Conte (ITA)	Italo Santelli (ITA)	Milan Neralic (AUT)
1906	Cyrille Verbrugge (BEL)	Ioannis Raissis (GRE)	—

THREE CORNERED SABRE

	Gold	Silver	Bronze
1906	Gustav Casmir (GER)	George van Rossem (HOL)	Péter Tóth (HUN)

SINGLE STICKS

	Gold	Silver	Bronze
1904	Albertson Van Zo Post[1] (CUB)	William Grebe (USA)	William O'Connor (USA)

[1] Van Zo Post was an American citizen competing for Cuba.

FENCING—MEDALS

	Gold	Silver	Bronze	Total		Gold	Silver	Bronze	Total
FRANCE	30	29	23	82	SWEDEN	2	2	2	6
ITALY	28	31	17	76	DENMARK	1	2	3	6
HUNGARY	30	17	22	69	ROMANIA	1	1	4	6
USSR	17	13	13	43	SWITZERLAND	—	2	3	5
GERMANY (FRG)	6	7	5	18	BOHEMIA				
POLAND	4	5	7	16	(CZECHOSLOVAKIA)	—	—	2	2
CUBA	6	4	3	13	MEXICO	—	1	—	1
BELGIUM	5	3	5	13	ARGENTINA	—	—	1	1
UNITED STATES	—	4	7	11	PORTUGAL	—	—	1	1
GREAT BRITAIN	1	9	—	10					
GREECE	3	3	3	9		135	135	133[1]	403
NETHERLANDS	—	1	7	8					
AUSTRIA	1	1	5	7					

[1] No bronze medals in one event in 1904 and another in 1906.

GYMNASTICS

In gymnastics there are eight interlinked events for men and six for women. A team competition comes first comprising one compulsory and one optional exercise for each separate discipline. For men these are: floor exercises, side horse, rings, horse vault, parallel bars and horizontal bar. For women they are: floor exercises, asymmetrical bars, horse vault and balance beam. Each competitor is marked out of 10·00 for both the compulsory and the optional exercise at each discipline. The best total of five gymnasts per country decides the team competition. The best 36 individuals then qualify for the individual all-round competition. They each complete a further optional exercise for each discipline and are awarded new marks. These are then added to the average of their previous total marks from the team competition. The best six in each discipline go forward to the individual final for that event. A new mark for a further optional exercise in that discipline is added to the average of their previous marks from the team competition. With the exception of 1948, when scores were marked out of 20·00, points since 1936 are of some comparative value.

The first gymnastic gold medals were won by the German team in the parallel bars event on 9 April 1896, and the first individual champion was Karl Schumann of Germany later on the same day, on

Having won three gold medals in gymnastics Carl Schuhmann (GER), left, shakes hands with Tsitas (GRE) prior to also winning the Olympic wrestling title in 1896.

Gymnastics

the vaulting horse.

Because of the number of separate disciplines in the sport, each with their own medals awarded, gymnasts are among the greatest collectors of medals in Olympic history. The most successful has been Larissa Latynina (URS) who amassed a record total of 18 medals from 1956 to 1964. This comprised nine gold (the most by any female Olympian), five silver and four bronze—unsurpassed in any sport. The most individual gold medals won is seven by Vera Caslavska (TCH) in 1964 and 1968. The male record for individual golds is six by Boris Shakhlin (URS) and Nikolai Andrianov (URS). The latter also holds the record for most medals by a man, both in gymnastics or any other sport, with a total of fifteen. In 1980 Aleksandr Ditiatin (URS) became the only male gymnast to gain a medal in all eight categories open to him in the same Games.

GYMNASTICS MOST PROLIFIC MEDAL WINNERS
(Ten or more)

The 1936 individual champion Alfred Schwartzmann (GER) performing a standing balance in the floor exercises.

Double gold medallist Istvan Pelle (HUN), here exhibiting the 'crucifix' position on the rings in 1932.

		G	S	B
Larissa Latynina (URS)	1956–64	9	5	4
Sawao Kato (JPN)	1968–76	8	3	1
Nikolai Andrianov (URS)	1972–80	7	5	3
Boris Shakhlin (URS)	1956–64	7	4	2
Vera Caslavska (TCH)	1960–68	7	4	0
Viktor Chukarin (URS)	1952–56	7	3	1
Akinori Nakayama (JPN)	1968–72	6	2	2
Takashi Ono (JPN)	1952–64	5	4	4
Agnes Keleti (HUN)	1952–56	5	3	2
Polina Astakhova (URS)	1956–64	5	2	3

In recent years the sport has captured the attention of the media and the public, especially via television, owing to a series of exceptional performers. In 1968 it was the attractive blonde Czech Vera Caslavska, who caught the imagination not only because of her excellence but also by her defeat of the Soviet girls only two months after the invasion of her country. Four years later Olga Korbut (URS) was the focus of all attention even though she was outshone, technically, by her team-mate Ludmila Tourischeva. In 1976 it was the unsmiling Nadia Comaneci of Romania who thoroughly deserved the adulation of the thousands who watched her in the competition arena and via television score the ultimate 10·00 on six occasions. Nelli Kim (URS) also scored that figure twice. Aleksandr Ditiatin (URS) stole the show from the girls in 1980 with the greatest number of medals ever won by a male at an Olympic Games, in any sport.

The maximum score of 10·00 first achieved by Comaneci, has now been scored in Olympic competition by seven women and five men. They are: Comaneci (ROM), Kim (URS), Natalya Shaposhnikova (URS), Elena Davydova (URS), Maxi Gnauck (GDR), Emilia Eberle (ROM), Melita Rühn (ROM), Ditiatin (URS), Aleksandr Tkachev (URS), Zoltan Magyar (HUN) Michael Nikolay (GDR), and Stoyan Deltchev (BUL).

The oldest gold medallist was Masao Takemoto (JPN) aged 40 yr 344 days as a member of the winning team in 1960. Only 24 days younger was Heikki Savolainen (FIN) in the 1948 team event, who in 1952 became the oldest ever medallist with a bronze at the age of 44 yr 297 days. He also competed in a record five Games over a record span of 24 years from 1928 to 1952. The youngest gold medallist was Nadia Comaneci (ROM) in 1976 aged 14 yr 313 days, while the oldest female champion was Agnes Keleti (HUN) aged 35 yr 171 days in 1956.

122

The closest margin of victory in the individual all-round competition has been 0·05 of a point, in 1956 when Viktor Chukarin (URS) beat Takashi Ono (JPN), four years later when Ono lost again to Boris Shakhlin (URS), and in 1968 when Sawao Kato (JPN) beat Mikhail Voronin (URS). The closest in the women's competition was 0·075 by Elena Davydova (URS) over Maxi Gnauck (GDR) and Nadia Comaneci (ROM) in 1980.

Two husband and wife teams have totalled 13 medals between them. The foremost is Valentin and Sofia Muratov (URS) with six gold, three silver and four bronze medals from 1952 to 1960, while the other is Mikhail and Zinaida Voronin (URS) with three gold, seven silver and three bronze medals in 1968 and 1972.

Alberto Braglia (ITA) won the individual gold medal in 1908. He then joined a circus as an acrobat and in 1912 competed again, presumably

The delightful Larissa Latynina (URS) whose total of 18 medals is unsurpassed in Olympic annals. Twenty years later she now coaches the Soviet national team.

as a 'professional', and successfully defended his title. The largest crowd to watch an Olympic gymnastic event was 18,000 at the Forum, Montreal for the final of the women's individual apparatus competitions in 1976.

TEAM (Men)

	Gold	Silver	Bronze
1904	UNITED STATES 374·43 pts	UNITED STATES 356·37	UNITED STATES 349·69
1906	NORWAY 19·00 pts	DENMARK 18·00	ITALY 16·71
1908	SWEDEN 438 pts	NORWAY 425	FINLAND 405
1912	ITALY 265·75 pts	HUNGARY 227·25	GREAT BRITAIN 184·50
1920	ITALY 359·855 pts	BELGIUM 346·745	FRANCE 340·100
1924	ITALY 839·058 pts	FRANCE 820·528	SWITZERLAND 816·661
1928	SWITZERLAND 1718·625 pts	CZECHOSLOVAKIA 1712·250	YUGOSLAVIA 1648·750
1932	ITALY 541·850 pts	UNITED STATES 522·275	FINLAND 509·995
1936	GERMANY 657·430 pts	SWITZERLAND 654·802	FINLAND 638·468
1948	FINLAND 1358·3 pts	SWITZERLAND 1356·7	HUNGARY 1330·35
1952	USSR 575·4 pts	SWITZERLAND 567·5	FINLAND 564·2
1956	USSR 568·25 pts	JAPAN 566·40	FINLAND 555·95
1960	JAPAN 575·20 pts	USSR 572·70	ITALY 559·05
1964	JAPAN 577·95 pts	USSR 575·45	GERMANY 565·10
1968	JAPAN 575·90 pts	USSR 571·10	GDR 557·15
1972	JAPAN 571·25 pts	USSR 564·05	GDR 559·70
1976	JAPAN 576·85 pts	USSR 576·45	GDR 564·65
1980	USSR 589·60 pts	GDR 581·15	HUNGARY 575·00

1896–1900 Event not held

INDIVIDUAL COMBINED EXERCISES (Men)

	Gold	Silver	Bronze
1900	Gustave Sandras (FRA) 302 pts	Noël Bas (FRA) 295	Lucien Démanet (FRA) 293
1904	Julius Lenhart[1] (AUT) 69·80 pts	Wilhelm Weber (GER) 69·10	Adolf Spinnler (SUI) 67·99
1906[2]	Pierre Payssé (FRA) 97 pts	Alberto Braglia (ITA) 95	Georges Charmoille (FRA) 94
1906	Pierre Payssé (FRA) 116 pts	Alberto Braglia (ITA) 115	Georges Charmoille (FRA) 113
1908	Alberto Braglia (ITA) 317·0 pts	S W Tysal (GBR) 312·0	Louis Ségura (FRA) 297·0
1912	Alberto Braglia (ITA) 135·0 pts	Louis Ségura (FRA) 132·5	Adolfo Tunesi (ITA) 131·5
1920	Giorgio Zampori (ITA) 88·35 pts	Marco Torrés (FRA) 87·62	Jean Gounot (FRA) 87·45
1924	Leon Stukelj (YUG) 110·340 pts	Robert Prazák (TCH) 110·323	Bedrich Supcik (TCH) 106·930
1928	Georges Miez (SUI) 247·500 pts	Hermann Hänggi (SUI) 246·625	Leon Stukelj (YUG) 244·875

1932	Romeo Neri (ITA) 140·625 pts	István Pelle (HUN) 134·925	Heikki Savolainen (FIN) 134·575
1936	Alfred Schwarzmann (GER) 113·100 pts	Eugen Mack (SUI) 112·334	Konrad Frey (GER) 111·532
1948	Veikko Huhtanen (FIN) 229·7 pts	Walter Lehmann (SUI) 229·0	Paavo Aaltonen (FIN) 228·8
1952	Viktor Chukarin (URS) 115·70 pts	Grant Shaginyan (URS) 114·95	Josef Stalder (SUI) 114·75
1956	Viktor Chukarin (URS) 114·25 pts	Takashi Ono (JPN) 114·20	Yuriy Titov (URS) 113·80
1960	Boris Shakhlin (URS) 115·95 pts	Takashi Ono (JPN) 115·90	Yuriy Titov (URS) 115·60
1964	Yukio Endo (JPN) 115·95 pts	Shuji Tsurumi (JPN) 115·40	—
		Viktor Lisitsky (URS) 115·40	
1968	Sawao Kato (JPN) 115·90 pts	Mikhail Voronin (URS) 115·85	Akinori Nakayama (JPN) 115·65
1972	Sawao Kato (JPN) 114·650 pts	Eizo Kenmotsu (JPN) 114·575	Akinori Nakayama (JPN) 114·325
1976	Nikolai Andrianov (URS) 116·650 pts	Sawao Kato (JPN) 115·650	Mitsuo Tsukahara (JPN) 115·575
1980	Aleksandr Ditiatin (URS) 118·650 pts	Nikolai Andrianov (URS) 118·225	Stoyan Deltchev (BUL) 118·000

[1] Lenhart was a member of the Philadelphia Club, USA, which won the team event. [2] Two competitions in 1906, one of five events and one of six. 1896 Event not held

FLOOR EXERCISES

	Gold	Silver	Bronze
1932	István Pelle (HUN) 9·60	Georges Miez (SUI) 9·47	Mario Lertora (ITA) 9·23
1936	Georges Miez (SUI) 18·666	Josef Walter (SUI) 18·5	Konrad Frey (GER) 18·466
			Eugen Mack (SUI) 18·466
1948	Ferenc Pataki (HUN) 38·7	János Mogyorósi-Klencs (HUN) 38·4	Zdenek Ružička (TCH) 38·1
1952	William Thoresson (SWE) 19·25	Tadao Uesako (JPN) 19·15	—
		Jerzy Jokiel (POL) 19·15	
1956	Valentin Muratov (URS) 19·20	Nobuyuki Aihara (JPN) 19·10	—
		William Thoresson (SWE) 19·10	
		Viktor Chukarin (URS) 19·10	
1960	Nobuyuki Aihara (JPN) 19·450	Yuriy Titov (URS) 19·325	Franco Menichelli (ITA) 19·275
1964	Franco Menichelli (ITA) 19·45	Viktor Lisitsky (URS) 19·35	—
		Yukio Endo (JPN) 19·35	
1968	Sawao Kato (JPN) 19·475	Akinori Nakayama (JPN) 19·400	Takeshi Kato (JPN) 19·275
1972	Nikolai Andrianov (URS) 19·175	Akinori Nakayama (JPN) 19·125	Shigeru Kasamatsu (JPN) 19·025
1976	Nikolai Andrianov (URS) 19·450	Vladimir Marchenko (URS) 19·425	Peter Kormann (USA) 19·300
1980	Roland Brückner (GDR) 19·750	Nikolai Andrianov (URS) 19·725	Aleksandr Ditiatin (URS) 19·700

1896–1928 Event not held

PARALLEL BARS

	Gold	Silver	Bronze
1896	Alfred Flatow (GER) d.n.a.	Jules Zutter (SUI)	Hermann Weingärtner (GER)
1904	George Eyser (USA) 44	Anton Heida (USA) 43	John Duha (USA) 40
1924	August Güttinger (SUI) 21·63	Robert Pražák (TCH) 21·61	Giorgio Zampori (ITA) 21·45
1928	Ladislav Vácha (TCH) 18·83	Josip Primožič (YUG) 18·50	Hermann Hänggi (SUI) 18·08
1932	Romeo Neri (ITA) 18·97	István Pelle (HUN) 18·60	Heikki Savolainen (FIN) 18·27
1936	Konrad Frey (GER) 19·067	Michael Reusch (SUI) 19·034	Alfred Schwarzmann (GER) 18·967
1948	Michael Reusch (SUI) 39·5	Veikkö Huhtanen (FIN) 39·3	Christian Kipfer (SUI) 39·1
			Josef Stalder (SUI) 39·1
1952	Hans Eugster (SUI) 19·65	Viktor Chukarin (URS) 19·60	Josef Stalder (SUI) 19·50
1956	Viktor Chukarin (URS) 19·20	Masami Kubota (JPN) 19·15	Takashi Ono (JPN) 19·10
			Masao Takemoto (JPN) 19·10
1960	Boris Shakhlin (URS) 19·400	Giovanni Carminucci (ITA) 19·375	Takashi Ono (JPN) 19·350
1964	Yukio Endo (JPN) 19·675	Shuji Tsurumi (JPN) 19·450	Franco Menichelli (ITA) 19·350
1968	Akinori Nakayama (JPN) 19·475	Mikhail Voronin (URS) 19·425	Vladimir Klimenko (URS) 19·225
1972	Sawao Kato (JPN) 19·475	Shigeru Kasamatsu (JPN) 19·375	Eizo Kenmotsu (JPN) 19·250
1976	Sawao Kato (JPN) 19·675	Nikolai Andrianov (URS) 19·500	Mitsuo Tsukahara (JPN) 19·475
1980	Aleksandr Tkachev (URS) 19·775	Aleksandr Ditiatin (URS) 19·750	Roland Brückner (GDR) 19·650

1900, 1906–1920 Event not held

POMMEL HORSE

	Gold	Silver	Bronze
1896	Jules Zutter (SUI) d.n.a.	Hermann Weingärtner (GER)	—
1904	Anton Heida (USA) 42	George Eyser (USA) 33	William Merz (USA) 29
1924	Josef Wilhelm (SUI) 21.23	Jean Gutweiniger (SUI) 21·13	Antoine Rebetez (SUI) 20·73
1928	Hermann Hänggi (SUI) 19·75	Georges Miez (SUI) 19·25	Heikki Savolainen (FIN) 18·83

1932	István Pelle (HUN) 19·07	Omero Bonoli (ITA) 18·87	Frank Haubold (USA) 18·57
1936	Konrad Frey (GER) 19·333	Eugen Mack (SUI) 19·167	Albert Bachmann (SUI) 19·067
1948	Paavo Aaltonen (FIN) 38·7	Luigi Zanetti (ITA) 38·3	Guido Figone (ITA) 38·2
	Veikkö Huhtanen (FIN) 38·7		
	Heikki Savolainen (FIN) 38·7		
1952	Viktor Chukarin (URS) 19·50	Yevgeniy Korolkov (URS) 19·40	—
		Grant Shaginyan (URS) 19·40	
1956	Boris Shakhlin (URS) 19·25	Takashi Ono (JPN) 19·20	Viktor Chukarin (URS) 19·10
1960	Eugen Ekman (FIN) 19·375	—	Shuji Tsurumi (JPN) 19·150
	Boris Shakhlin (URS) 19·375		
1964	Miroslav Cerar (YUG) 19·525	Shuji Tsurumi (JPN) 19·325	Yuriy Tsapenko (URS) 19·200
1968	Miroslav Cerar (YUG) 19·325	Olli Laiho (FIN) 19·225	Mikhail Voronin (URS) 19·200
1972	Viktor Klimenko (URS) 19·125	Sawao Kato (JPN) 19·000	Eizo Kenmotsu (JPN) 18·950
1976	Zoltan Magyar (HUN) 19·700	Eizo Kenmotsu (JPN) 19·575	Nikolai Andrianov (URS) 19·525
1980	Zoltan Magyar (HUN) 19·925	Aleksandr Ditiatin (URS) 19·800	Michael Nikolay (GDR) 19·775

1900, 1906–1920 Event not held

RINGS

	Gold	Silver	Bronze
1896	Ioannis Mitropoulos (GRE) d.n.a.	Hermann Weingärtner (GER)	Petros Persakis (GRE)
1904	Herman Glass (USA) 45	William Merz (USA) 35	Emil Voight (USA) 32
1924	Franco Martino (ITA) 21·553	Robert Pražák (TCH) 21·483	Ladislav Vácha (TCH) 21·430
1928	Leon Škutelj (YUG) 19·25	Ladislav Vácha (TCH) 19·17	Emanuel Löffler (TCH) 18·83
1932	George Gulack (USA) 18·97	William Denton (USA) 18·60	Giovanni Lattuada (ITA) 18·50
1936	Alois Hudec (TCH) 19·433	Leon Škutelj (YUG) 18·867	Matthias Volz (GER) 18·667
1948	Kari Frei (SUI) 39·60	Michael Reusch (SUI) 39·10	Zdenek Ružička (TCH) 38·30
1952	Grant Shaginyan (URS) 19·75	Viktor Chukarin (URS) 19·55	Hans Eugster (SUI) 19·40
			Dimitriy Leonkin (URS) 19·40
1956	Albert Azaryan (URS) 19·35	Valentin Muratov (URS) 19·15	Masao Takemoto (JPN) 19·10
			Masami Kubota (JPN) 19·10
1960	Albert Azaryan (URS) 19·725	Boris Shakhlin (URS) 19·500	Velik Kapsazov (BUL) 19·425
			Takashi Ono (JPN) 19·425
1964	Takuji Hayata (JPN) 19·475	Franco Menichelli (ITA) 19·425	Boris Shakhlin (URS) 19·400
1968	Akinori Nakayama (JPN) 19·450	Mikhail Voronin (URS) 19·325	Sawao Kato (JPN) 19·225
1972	Akinori Nakayama (JPN) 19·350	Mikhail Voronin (URS) 19·275	Mitsuo Tsukahara (JPN) 19·225
1976	Nikolai Andrianov (URS) 19·650	Aleksandr Ditiatin (URS) 19·550	Danut Grecu (ROM) 19·500
1980	Aleksandr Ditiatin (URS) 19·875	Aleksandr Tkachev (URS) 19·725	Jiri Tabak (TCH) 19·600

1900, 1906–1920 Event not held

HORIZONTAL BAR

	Gold	Silver	Bronze
1896	Hermann Weingärtner (GER) d.n.a.	Alfred Flatow (GER)	—
1904	Anton Heida (USA) 40	—	George Eyser (USA) 39
	Edward Hennig (USA) 40		
1924	Leon Štukelj (YUG) 19·730	Jean Gutweniger (SUI) 19·236	André Higelin (FRA) 19·163
1928	Georges Miez (SUI) 19·17	Romeo Neri (ITA) 19·00	Eugen Mack (SUI) 18·92
1932	Dallas Bixler (USA) 18·33	Heikki Savolainen (FIN) 18·07	Einari Teräsvirta (FIN) 18·07[1]
1936	Aleksanteri Saarvala (FIN) 19·367	Konrad Frey (GER) 19·267	Alfred Schwarzmann (GER) 19·233
1948	Josef Stalder (SUI) 39·7	Walter Lehmann (SUI) 39·4	Veikkö Huhtanen (FIN) 39·2
1952	Jack Günthard (SUI) 19·55	Josef Stalder (SUI) 19·50	—
		Alfred Schwarzmann (GER) 19·50	
1956	Takashi Ono (JPN) 19·60	Yuriy Titov (URS) 19·40	Masao Takemoto (JPN) 19·30
1960	Takashi Ono (JPN) 19·60	Masao Takemoto (JPN) 19·525	Boris Shakhlin (URS) 19·475
1964	Boris Shakhlin (URS) 19·625	Yuriy Titov (URS) 19·55	Miroslav Cerar (YUG) 19·50
1968	Mikhail Voronin (URS) 19·550	—	Eizo Kenmotsu (JPN) 19·375
	Akinori Nakayama (JPN) 19·550		
1972	Mitsuo Tsukahara (JPN) 19·725	Sawao Kato (JPN) 19·525	Shigeru Kasamatsu (JPN) 19·450
1976	Mitsuo Tsukahara (JPN) 19·675	Eizo Kenmotsu (JPN) 19·500	Eberhard Gienger (GER) 19·475
1980	Stoyan Deltchev (BUL) 19·825	Aleksandr Ditiatin (URS) 19·750	Nikolai Andrianov (URS) 19·675

[1] Teräsvirta conceded second place to Savolainen.   1900, 1906–1920 Event not held

HORSE VAULT

	Gold	Silver	Bronze
1896	Karl Schumann (GER) d.n.a.	Jules Zutter (SUI)	—
1904	Anton Heida (USA) 36	—	William Merz (USA) 31
	George Eyser (USA) 36		
1924	Frank Kriz (USA) 9·98	Jan Koutny (TCH) 9·97	Bohumil Mořkovsky (TCH) 9·93
1928	Eugen Mack (SUI) 9·58	Emanuel Löffler (TCH) 9·50	Stane Derganc (YUG) 9·46
1932	Savino Guglielmetti (ITA) 18·03	Alfred Jochim (GER) 17·77	Edward Carmichael (USA) 17·53
1936	Alfred Schwarzmann (GER) 19·200	Eugen Mack (SUI) 18·967	Matthias Volz (GER) 18·467
1948	Paavo Aaltonen (FIN) 39·10	Olavi Rove (FIN) 39·00	János Mogyorósi-Klencs (HUN) 38·50
			Ferenc Pataki (HUN) 38·50
			Leos Sotornik (TCH) 38·50
1952	Viktor Chukarin (URS) 19·20	Masao Takemoto (JPN) 19·15	Tadao Uesako (JPN) 19·10
			Takashi Ono (JPN) 19·10
1956	Helmuth Bantz (GER) 18·85	—	Yuriy Titov (URS) 18·75
	Valentin Muratov (URS) 18·85		
1960	Takashi Ono (JPN) 19·350	—	Vladimir Portnoi (URS) 19·225
	Boris Shakhlin (URS) 19·350		
1964	Haruhiro Yamashita (JPN) 19·600	Viktor Lisitsky (URS) 19·325	Hannu Rantakari (FIN) 19·300
1968	Mikhail Voronin (URS) 19·000	Yukio Endo (JPN) 18·950	Sergey Diomidov (URS) 18·925
1972	Klaus Köste (GDR) 18·850	Viktor Klimenko (URS) 18·825	Nikolai Andrianov (URS) 18·800
1976	Nikolai Andrianov (URS) 19·450	Mitsuo Tsukahara (JPN) 19·375	Hiroshi Kajiyama (JPN) 19·275
1980	Nikolai Andrianov (URS) 19·825	Aleksandr Ditiatin (URS) 19·800	Roland Brückner (GDR) 19·775

1900, 1906–1920 Event not held

TEAM (Women)

	Gold	Silver	Bronze
1928	NETHERLANDS 316·75 pts	ITALY 289·00	GREAT BRITAIN 258·25
1936	GERMANY 506·50 pts	CZECHOSLOVAKIA 503·60	HUNGARY 499·00
1948	CZECHOSLOVAKIA 445·45 pts	HUNGARY 440·55	UNITED STATES 422·63
1952	USSR 527·03 pts	HUNGARY 520·96	CZECHOSLOVAKIA 503·32
1956	USSR 444·80 pts	HUNGARY 443·50	ROMANIA 438·20
1960	USSR 382·320 pts	CZECHOSLOVAKIA 373·323	ROMANIA 372·053
1964	USSR 380·890 pts	CZECHOSLOVAKIA 379·989	JAPAN 377·889
1968	USSR 382·85 pts	CZECHOSLOVAKIA 382·20	GDR 379·10
1972	USSR 380·50 pts	GDR 376·55	HUNGARY 368·25
1976	USSR 390·35 pts	ROMANIA 387·15	GDR 385·10
1980	USSR 394·90 pts	ROMANIA 393·50	GDR 392·55

1896–1924, 1932 Event not held

INDIVIDUAL COMBINED EXERCISES (Women)

	Gold	Silver	Bronze
1952	Maria Gorokhovskaya (URS) 76·78	Nina Bocharova (URS) 75·94	Margit Korondi (HUN) 75·82
1956	Larissa Latynina (URS) 74·933	Ágnes Keleti (HUN) 74·633	Sofia Muratova (URS) 74·466
1960	Larissa Latynina (URS) 77·031	Sofia Muratova (URS) 76·696	Polina Astakhova (URS) 76·164
1964	Vera Čáslavskà (TCH) 77·564	Larissa Latynina (URS) 76·998	Polina Astakhova (URS) 76·965
1968	Vera Čáslavská (TCH) 78·25	Zinaida Voronina (URS) 76·85	Natalya Kuchinskaya (URS) 76·75
1972	Ludmila Tourischeva (URS) 77·025	Karin Janz (GDR) 76·875	Tamara Lazakovitch (URS) 76·850
1976	Nadia Comaneci (ROM) 79·275	Nelli Kim (URS) 78·675	Ludmila Tourischeva (URS) 78·625
1980	Elena Davydova (URS) 79·150	Maxi Gnauck (GDR) 79·075	—
		Nadia Comaneci (ROM) 79·075	

1896–1948 Event not held

ASYMMETRICAL BARS

	Gold	Silver	Bronze
1952	Margit Korondi (HUN) 19·40	Maria Gorokhovskaya (URS) 19·26	Ágnes Keleti (HUN) 19·16
1956	Ágnes Keleti (HUN) 18·966	Larissa Latynina (URS) 18·833	Sofia Muratova (URS) 18·800
1960	Polina Astakhova (URS) 19·616	Larissa Latynina (URS) 19·416	Tamara Lyukhina (URS) 19·399

1964	Polina Astakhova (URS) 19·332	Katalin Makray (HUN) 19·216	Larissa Latynina (URS) 19·199
1968	Vera Čáslavska (TCH) 19·650	Karin Janz (GDR) 19·500	Zinaida Voronina (URS) 19·425
1972	Karin Janz (GDR) 19·675	Olga Korbut (URS) 19·450	—
		Erika Zuchold (GDR) 19·450	
1976	Nadia Comaneci (ROM) 20·000	Teodora Ungureanu (ROM) 19·800	Marta Egervari (HUN) 19·775
1980	Maxi Gnauck (GDR) 19·875	Emilia Eberle (ROM) 19·850	Steffi Kräker (GDR) 19·775
			Melita Rühn (ROM) 19·775
			Maria Filatova (URS) 19·775

1896–1948 Event not held

BALANCE BEAM

	Gold	Silver	Bronze
1952	Nina Bocharova (URS) 19·22	Maria Gorokhovskaya (URS) 19·13	Margit Korondi (HUN) 19·02
1956	Ágnes Keleti (HUN) 18·80	Eva Bosáková (TCH) 18·63	—
		Tamara Manina (URS) 18·63	
1960	Eva Bosakova (TCH) 19·283	Larissa Latynina (URS) 19·233	Sofia Muratova (URS) 19·232
1964	Vera Čáslavská (TCH) 19·449	Tamara Manina (URS) 19·399	Larissa Latynina (URS) 19·382
1968	Natalya Kuchinskaya (URS) 19·650	Vera Čáslavská (TCH) 19·575	Larissa Petrik (URS) 19·250
1972	Olga Korbut (URS) 19·575	Tamara Lazakovitch (URS) 19·375	Karin Janz (GDR) 18·975
1976	Nadia Comaneci (ROM) 19·950	Olga Korbut (URS) 19·725	Teodora Ungureanu (ROM) 19·700
1980	Nadia Comaneci (ROM) 19·800	Elena Davydova (URS) 19·750	Natalya Shaposhnikova (URS) 19·725

1896–1948 Event not held

FLOOR EXERCISES

	Gold	Silver	Bronze
1952	Ágnes Keleti (HUN) 19·36	Maria Gorokhovskaya (URS) 19·20	Margit Korondi (HUN) 19·00
1956	Larissa Latynina (URS) 18·733	—	Elena Leustean (ROM) 18·70
	Ágnes Keleti (HUN) 18·733		
1960	Larissa Latynina (URS) 19·583	Polina Astakhova (URS) 19·532	Tamara Lyukhina (URS) 19·449
1964	Larissa Latynina (URS) 19·599	Polina Astakhova (URS) 19·500	Anikó Jánosi (HUN) 19·300
1968	Larissa Petrik (URS) 19·675	—	Natalya Kuchinskaya (URS) 19·650
	Vera Čáslavská (TCH) 19·675		
1972	Olga Korbut (URS) 19·575	Ludmila Tourischeva (URS) 19·550	Tamara Lazakovitch (URS) 19·450
1976	Nelli Kim (URS) 19·850	Ludmila Tourischeva (URS) 19·825	Nadia Comaneci (ROM) 19·750
1980	Nelli Kim (URS) 19·875	—	Natalya Shaposhnikova (URS) 19·825
	Nadia Comaneci (ROM) 19·875		Maxi Gnauck (GDR) 19·825

1896–1948 Event not held

HORSE VAULT

	Gold	Silver	Bronze
1952	Yekaterina Kalinchuk (URS) 19·20	Maria Gorokhovskaya (URS) 19·19	Galina Minaitscheva (URS) 19·16
1956	Larissa Latynina (URS) 18·833	Tamara Manina (URS) 18·800	Ann-Sofi Colling (SWE) 18·733
			Olga Tass (HUN) 18·733
1960	Margarita Nikolayeva (URS) 19·316	Sofia Muratova (URS) 19·049	Larissa Latynina (URS) 19·016
1964	Vera Čáslavská (TCH) 19·483	Larissa Latynina (URS) 19·283	—
		Birgit Radochla (GER) 19·283	
1968	Vera Čáslavská (TCH) 19·775	Erika Zuchold (GDR) 19·625	Zinaida Voronina (URS) 19·500
1972	Karin Janz (GDR) 19·525	Erika Zuchold (GDR) 19·275	Ludmila Tourischeva (URS) 19·250
1976	Nelli Kim (URS) 19·800	Ludmila Tourischeva (URS) 19·650	—
		Carola Dombeck (GDR) 19·650	
1980	Natalya Shaposhnikova (URS) 19·725	Steffi Kräker (GDR) 19·675	Melita Rühn (ROM) 19·650

1896–1948 Event not held

DISCONTINUED EVENTS
PARALLEL BARS (Men's Teams)

	Gold	Silver	Bronze
1896	GERMANY	GREECE	GREECE

HORIZONTAL BARS (Men's Teams)

	Gold	Silver	Bronze
1896	GERMANY[1]	—	—

[1] Walk-over.

ROPE CLIMBING (Men)

	Gold	Silver	Bronze
1896	Nicolaos Andriakopoulos (GRE) 23·4 sec	Thomas Xenakis (GRE)	Fritz Hofmann (GER)
1904	George Eyser (USA) 7·0 sec	Charles Krause (USA) 7·8	Emil Voigt (USA) 9·8
1906	Georgios Aliprantis (GRE) 11·4 sec	Béla Erödy (HUN) 13·8	Konstantinos Kozanitas (GRE) 13·8
1924	Bedrich Supcik (TCH) 7·2 sec	Albert Séguin (FRA) 7·4	August Güttinger (SUI) 7·8
			Ladislav Vácha (CZE) 7·8
1932	Raymond Bass (USA) 6·7 sec	William Galbraith (USA) 6·8	Thomas Connelly (USA) 7·0

1900, 1908–1920, 1928 Event not held

CLUB SWINGING (Men)

	Gold	Silver	Bronze
1904	Edward Hennig (USA) 13 pts	Emil Voigt (USA) 9	Ralph Wilson (USA) 5
1932	George Roth (USA) 8·97 pts	Philip Erenberg (USA) 8·90	William Kuhlmeier (USA) 8·63

1896–1900, 1906–1928 Event not held

TUMBLING (Men)

	Gold	Silver	Bronze
1932	Rowland Wolfe (USA) 18·90 pts	Edward Gross (USA) 18·67	William Herrmann (USA) 18·37

1896–1928 Event not held

NINE EVENT COMPETITION

	Gold	Silver	Bronze
1904	Adolf Spinnler (SUI) 43·49 pts	Julius Lenhart (AUT) 43·00	Wilhelm Weber (GER) 41·60

1896–1900 Event not held

TRIATHLON
(Comprised 100 yards, long jump and shot put).

	Gold	Silver	Bronze
1904	Max Emmerich (USA) 35·70 pts	John Grieb (USA) 34·00	William Merz (USA) 33·90

1896–1900 Event not held

SEVEN EVENT COMPETITION

	Gold	Silver	Bronze
1904	Anton Heida (USA) 161 pts	George Eyser (USA) 152	William Merz (USA) 135

1896–1900 Event not held

SIDEHORSE VAULT

	Gold	Silver	Bronze
1924	Albert Séguin (FRA) 10·00 pts	Jean Gounot (FRA) 9·93	—
		Francois Gangloff (FRA) 9·93	

1896–1920 Event not held

SWEDISH SYSTEM (Men's Teams)

Gold	Silver	Bronze
1912 SWEDEN 937·46 pts	DENMARK 898·84	NORWAY 857·21
1920 SWEDEN 1364 pts	DENMARK 1325	BELGIUM 1094

1896–1908 Event not held

FREE SYSTEM (Men's Teams)

Gold	Silver	Bronze
1912 NORWAY 114·25 pts	FINLAND 109·25	DENMARK 106·25
1920 DENMARK	NORWAY	—[1]

[1] Only two teams competed.   1896–1908 Event not held

PORTABLE APPARATUS (Women's Teams)

Gold	Silver	Bronze
1952 SWEDEN 74·20 pts	USSR 73·00	HUNGARY 71·60
1956 HUNGARY 75·20 pts	SWEDEN 74·20	POLAND 74·00

1896–1948 Event not held

GYMNASTICS—MEDALS

	Gold	Silver	Bronze	Total		Gold	Silver	Bronze	Total
USSR	61	61	39	161	SWEDEN	5	2	1	8
JAPAN	24	24	24	72	GREECE	3	2	3	8
UNITED STATES	18	13	17	48	NORWAY	2	2	1	5
SWITZERLAND	15	19	13	47	DENMARK	1	3	1	5
CZECHOSLOVAKIA	12	13	10	35	BULGARIA	1	—	2	3
HUNGARY	11	10	14	35	GREAT BRITAIN	—	1	2	3
GERMANY (FRG)	12	8	10	30	AUSTRIA	1	1	—	2
ITALY	12	8	9	29	BELGIUM	—	1	1	2
GDR	5	10	12	27	POLAND	—	1	1	2
FINLAND	8	5	12	25	NETHERLANDS	1	—	—	1
ROMANIA	5	5	8	18					
FRANCE	4	7	7	18		206	198	191	595
YUGOSLAVIA	5	2	4	11					

HANDBALL

In 1936 handball was played as an outdoor eleven-a-side game. When it was reintroduced into the Games in 1972 it was as an indoor seven-a-side competition.

Only two players have gained medals in three Games. Radu Voina and Adrian Cosma of the Romanian team won a silver in 1976 and bronzes in 1972 and 1980. Six of the Soviet women's team won gold medals in both 1976 and 1980: Lubov Odinokova, Zinaida Turchina, Tatyana Kochergina, Ludmila Poradnik, Aldona Nenenene and Larisa Karlova.

The oldest gold medallist was Yuriy Klimov (URS) aged 36 yr 6 days when a member of the winning team in 1976. The oldest female gold medallist was Ludmila Poradnik (URS) aged 34 yr 200 days in 1980.

A member of the GDR winning team in 1980 was Hans-Georg Beyer, the brother of 1976 shot put champion Uwe (who also won a bronze in 1980). To complete a remarkable family trio their sister Gisela narrowly missed a bronze medal in the ladies discus at Moscow. Their countrywoman Roswitha Krause, a member of the handball bronze medal team in 1980, and of the silver medal team in 1976, had been a silver medallist in the 4 × 100 m freestyle swimming team in 1968.

HANDBALL (Men)

Gold	Silver	Bronze
1936[1] GERMANY	AUSTRIA	SWITZERLAND
1972 YUGOSLAVIA	CZECHOSLOVAKIA	ROMANIA
1976 USSR	ROMANIA	POLAND
1980 GDR	USSR	ROMANIA

[1] Field handball played outdoors. 1896–1932, 1948–1968 Event not held

HANDBALL (Women)

Gold	Silver	Bronze
1976 USSR	GDR	HUNGARY
1980 USSR	YUGOSLAVIA	GDR

1896–1972 Event not held

HANDBALL—MEDALS
Men

	Gold	Silver	Bronze	Total
ROMANIA	—	1	2	3
USSR	1	1	—	2
GERMANY (FRG)	1	—	—	1
GDR	1	—	—	1
YUGOSLAVIA	1	—	—	1
AUSTRIA	—	1	—	1
CZECHOSLOVAKIA	—	1	—	1
POLAND	—	—	1	1
SWITZERLAND	—	—	1	1
	4	4	4	12

HANDBALL—MEDALS
Women

	Gold	Silver	Bronze	Total
USSR	2	—	—	2
GDR	—	1	1	2
YUGOSLAVIA	—	1	—	1
HUNGARY	—	—	1	1
	2	2	2	6

Here they come again. Indian hockey captain, Dhyan Chand races for the American goal in 1932 with his brother Roop Singh on his left. Of India's 24 goals the brothers scored 19 between them.

HOCKEY

The first Olympic game of hockey was won by Scotland who defeated Germany 4–0 on 29 October 1908, with the first goal scored by Ian Laing only two minutes after the start. In those London Games four of the six teams competing represented England, Ireland, Scotland and Wales. The latter two tied for third place at the end of the tournament as the Scots had to return home before they could play a deciding match. The final itself on 31 October was the last event of the 1908 Games which had begun on 27 April.

Since 1928, Olympic hockey has been dominated by teams from the Indian sub-continent with India winning eight times and Pakistan twice. However, it should be noted that Great Britain, probably the strongest team in the world at that time, did not participate in the 1928, 1932 and 1936 tournaments. The long awaited meeting between them, the masters, and India, the

pupils, came in the 1948 final which India won 4–0.

Seven members of Indian teams have won a record three gold medals: Richard Allen 1928–36, Dhyan Chand 1928–36, Randhir Singh Gentle 1948–56, Leslie Claudius 1948–56, Balbir Singh 1948–56, Ranganandhan Francis 1948–56, and Udham Singh 1952, 1956 and 1964. Of these only Claudius and Udham Singh also won a silver each in 1960. The oldest gold medallist was Abdul Rashid (PAK) aged 38 yr 100 days as a member of the winning team in 1960. Stanley Shoveller (IND) was also over 38 years old in 1920, while Dharam Singh (IND) was reputed to have been 45 years old when he played in the 1964 winning team. The youngest gold medallist was Chinadorai Deshmutu (IND) in 1952 aged 19 yr 272 days, although Arlene Boxhall was under 19 as a member of the gold medal winning Zimbabwe women's team in 1980 but did not play in the tournament. The oldest female player was the Zimbabwe coach/player Anthea Stewart aged 35 yr 253 days.

The highest score ever achieved in an international hockey match occurred at Los Angeles in 1932 when India beat the United States 24–1. The highest score in an Olympic final was also in 1932 when India beat Japan 11–1. The greatest individual score in an Olympic match was when Roop Singh scored 12 of India's goals in that 1932 match versus the USA. The Indian goalkeepers did not concede a single goal during the 1928 tournament (five matches) and only a total of three during the 1932 (two matches) and 1936 (five matches) tournaments. During that time the Indian team scored a total of 102 goals.

The longest game in Olympic hockey lasted 2 hr 25 min (into the sixth period of extra time) when the Netherlands defeated Spain 1–0 in Mexico on 25 October 1968.

Men

	Gold	Silver	Bronze
1908[1]	ENGLAND	IRELAND	SCOTLAND[2] WALES[2]
1920	ENGLAND[3]	DENMARK	BELGIUM
1928	INDIA	NETHERLANDS	GERMANY
1932	INDIA	JAPAN	UNITED STATES
1936	INDIA	GERMANY	NETHERLANDS
1948	INDIA	GREAT BRITAIN	NETHERLANDS
1952	INDIA	NETHERLANDS	GREAT BRITAIN
1956	INDIA	PAKISTAN	GERMANY
1960	PAKISTAN	INDIA	SPAIN
1964	INDIA	PAKISTAN	AUSTRALIA
1968	PAKISTAN	AUSTRALIA	INDIA
1972	FRG	PAKISTAN	INDIA
1976	NEW ZEALAND	AUSTRALIA	PAKISTAN
1980	INDIA	SPAIN	USSR

[1] Great Britain had four teams entered.   [2] Tie for third place.   [3] Great Britain represented by England team.
1896–1906, 1912, 1924 Event not held

Women

	Gold	Silver	Bronze
1980	ZIMBABWE	CZECHOSLOVAKIA	USSR

1896–1976 Event not held

HOCKEY—MEDALS
Women

	Gold	Silver	Bronze	Total
ZIMBABWE	1	—	—	1
CZECHOSLOVAKIA	—	1	—	1
USSR	—	—	1	1
	1	1	1	3

HOCKEY—MEDALS
Men

	Gold	Silver	Bronze	Total
INDIA	8	1	2	11
GREAT BRITAIN	2	2	3	7
PAKISTAN	2	3	1	6
GERMANY (FRG)	1	1	2	4
NETHERLANDS	—	2	2	4

AUSTRALIA	—	2	1	3		BELGIUM	—	—	1	1
SPAIN	—	1	1	2		USSR	—	—	1	1
NEW ZEALAND	1	—	—	1		UNITED STATES	—	—	1	1
DENMARK	—	1	—	1						
JAPAN	—	1	—	1			14	14	15[1]	43

[1] Two bronze medals in 1908.

JUDO

Introduced in 1964 at the Tokyo Games and appropriately the first gold medal was won by Japan's Takehide Nakatani in the lightweight category. One of the greatest upsets to a nation's sporting pride occurred in Tokyo's Nippon Budokan Hall in 1964 when the giant Dutchman Anton Geesink (1·98 m *6 ft 6 in* tall) beat the Japanese favourite for the Open division title before 15 000 home supporters. Another Dutchman, Wilhelm Ruska, is the only man to win two gold medals, in the 1972 93 kg plus and the Open classes. The only man to win three medals is Angelo Parisi, who won a bronze medal in 1972 representing Great Britain, and then gold and silver medals in 1980 representing France. The winning of medals for two different countries is very rare in the Olympic Games, but not unique. Parisi was born in Italy, went to Britain as a child, became a citizen, then married a French girl in 1973 and later changed his nationality again. The oldest judo gold medallist was Wilhelm Ruska (HOL) when he won the 1972 open category aged 32 yr 11 days, and the youngest was Isao Okano (JPN), the winner of the 1964 middleweight class aged 20 yr 275 days.

There have been a number of very big men competing in Olympic judo but the biggest has been Jong Gil Pak (PRK) who stood 2·13 m *7 ft 0 in* tall and weighed 163 kg *25 stone 9 lb* in the 1976 competition.

The disqualification of the Mongolian silver medallist, Bakhaavaa Buidaa, in the lightweight category in 1972 was the first time that a judo competitor had ever been disqualified for failing a dope test in international competition. Hector Rodriguez (CUB), the 1976 lightweight gold medallist said that he took up the sport as a youngster in order to learn to defend himself against his six older brothers.

Willem Ruska (HOL) defeats Vitali Kuznetsov (URS) to win the Open class judo gold medal. He had previously also won the 93 kg category.

OPEN CATEGORY, NO WEIGHT LIMIT

	Gold	Silver	Bronze
1964	Antonius Geesink (HOL)	Akio Kaminaga (JPN)	Theodore Boronovskis (AUS) Klaus Glahn (GER)
1972	Wilhelm Ruska (HOL)	Vitaliy Kuznetsov (URS)	Jean-Claude Brondani (FRA) Angelo Parisi (GBR)
1976	Haruki Uemura (JPN)	Keith Remfry (GBR)	Shota Chochoshvili (URS) Jeaki Cho (KOR)
1980	Dietmar Lorenz (GDR)	Angelo Parisi (FRA)	András Ozsvar (HUN) Arthur Mapp (GBR)

1968 Event not held

Over 95 kg

Gold	Silver	Bronze
1980 Angelo Parisi (FRA)	Dimitar Zaprianov (BUL)	Vladimir Kocman (TCH)
		Radomir Kovacevic (YUG)

Up to 95 kg

Gold	Silver	Bronze
1980 Robert Van de Walle (BEL)	Tengiz Khubuluri (URS)	Dietmar Lorenz (GDR)
		Henk Numan (HOL)

Up to 86 kg

Gold	Silver	Bronze
1980 Jürg Röthlisberger (SUI)	Isaac Azcuy Oliva (CUB)	Detlef Ultsch (GDR)
		Aleksandr Yatskevich (URS)

Up to 78 kg

Gold	Silver	Bronze
1980 Shota Khabaleri (URS)	Juan Ferrer La Hera (CUB)	Harald Heinke (GDR)
		Bernard Tchoullouyan (FRA)

Up to 71 kg

Gold	Silver	Bronze
1980 Ezio Gamba (ITA)	Neil Adams (GBR)	Karl-Heinz Lehmann (GDR)
		Ravdan Davaadalai (MGL)

Up to 65 kg

Gold	Silver	Bronze
1980 Nikolai Solodukhin (URS)	Tsendying Damdin (MGL)	Ilian Nedkov (BUL)
		Janusz Pawlowski (POL)

Up to 60 kg

Gold	Silver	Bronze
1980 Thierry Rey (FRA)	Rafael Carbonell (CUB)	Tibor Kincses (HUN)
		Aramby Emizh (URS)

PREVIOUS WINNERS
(categories changed in 1980)

Over 93 kg

Gold	Silver	Bronze
1964 Isao Inokuma (JPN)	A H Douglas Rogers (CAN)	Parnaoz Chikviladze (URS)
		Anzor Kiknadze (URS)
1972 Wilhelm Ruska (HOL)	Klaus Glahn (FRG)	Givi Onashvili (URS)
		Motoki Nishimura (JPN)
1976 Sergey Novikov (URS)	Gunther Neureuther (FRG)	Sumio Endo (JPN)
		Allen Coage (USA)

1968 Event not held

80 kg to 93 kg

	Gold	Silver	Bronze
1972	Shota Chochoshvili (URS)	David Starbrook (GBR)	Chiaki Ishii (BRA)
			Paul Barth (FRG)
1976	Kazuhiro Ninomiya (JPN)	Ramaz Harshiladze (URS)	David Starbrook (GBR)
			Jürg Röthlisberger (SUI)

1964–1968 Event not held

70 kg to 80 kg

	Gold	Silver	Bronze
1964	Isao Okano (JPN)	Wolfgang Hofmann (GER)	James Bregman (USA)
			Eui Tae Kim (KOR)
1972	Shinobu Sekine (JPN)	Seung-Lip Oh (KOR)	Brian Jacks (GBR)
			Jean-Paul Coche (FRA)
1976	Isamu Sonoda (JPN)	Valeriy Dvoinikov (URS)	Slavko Obadov (YUG)
			Youngchul Park (KOR)

1968 Event not held

63 kg to 70 kg

	Gold	Silver	Bronze
1964	Takehide Nakatani (JPN)	Eric Haenni (SUI)	Oleg Stepanov (URS)
			Aron Bogulubov (URS)
1972	Toyokazu Nomura (JPN)	Anton Zajkowski (POL)	Dietmar Hötger (GDR)
			Anatoliy Novikov (URS)
1976	Vladimir Nevzorov (URS)	Koji Kuramoto (JPN)	Patrick Vial (FRA)
			Marian Talaj (POL)

1964–1968 Event not held

Up to 63 kg

	Gold	Silver	Bronze
1972	Takao Kawaguchi (JPN)	—[1]	Yong Ik Kim (PRK)
			Jean-Jacques Mounier (FRA)
1976	Hector Rodriguez (CUB)	Eunkyung Chang (KOR)	Felice Mariani (ITA)
			Jozsef Tuncsik (HUN)

[1] Bakhaavaa Buidaa (MGL) disqualified after positive drug test.   1964–8 Event not held

JUDO—MEDALS

	Gold	Silver	Bronze	Total		Gold	Silver	Bronze	Total
USSR	5	4	9	18	BULGARIA	—	1	1	2
JAPAN	9	2	2	13	MONGOLIA	—	1	1	2
FRANCE	2	1	5	8	UNITED STATES	—	—	2	2
GREAT BRITAIN	—	3	4	7	YUGOSLAVIA	—	—	2	2
GDR	1	—	5	6	BELGIUM	1	—	—	1
GERMANY (FRG)	—	3	2	5	CANADA	—	1	—	1
KOREA	—	2	3	5	AUSTRALIA	—	—	1	1
NETHERLANDS	3	—	1	4	BRAZIL	—	—	1	1
CUBA	1	3	—	4	CZECHOSLOVAKIA	—	—	1	1
SWITZERLAND	1	1	1	3	NORTH KOREA (PRK)	—	—	1	1
POLAND	—	1	2	3					
HUNGARY	—	—	3	3		24	23[1]	48	95
ITALY	1	—	1	2					

[1] 1972 silver medal withheld due to disqualification.

MODERN PENTATHLON

The five events constituting the modern pentathlon are: riding (over an 800 m course); fencing (with épeé); shooting (pistol at 25 m); swimming (300 m freestyle) and cross-country running (4000 m). The order above is the current one but it has differed over the years. Also the points system has altered; prior to 1956 competitors were given points according to their placings in each event, ie, one point for first place, two for second etc. Since 1956 points have been allocated according to an international scoring table. It is therefore difficult to compare performers under the two systems, but it is generally accepted that the margin of victory by Willie Grut (SWE) in 1948 was the greatest ever. In that competition Grut, who is now the Secretary-General of the sport's governing body (UIPMB), placed first in riding, fencing and swimming, fifth in shooting, and eighth in running.

The most gold medals have been won by András Balczó (HUN) with three in 1960 (team), 1968 (team) and 1972 (individual). Only Lars Hall (SWE) has won two individual gold medals, in 1952 and 1956. Pavel Lednev (URS) holds the record for most medals of all types with a total of

seven (two gold, two silver, three bronze) from 1968 to 1980.

The oldest gold medallist was Pavel Lednev (URS) a member of the winning team in 1980 aged 37 yr 121 days. The youngest was Aladá Kovácsi (HUN) in the 1952 gold medal team aged 19 yr 227 days.

Gustaf Dyrssen (SWE) who won the gold medal in 1920, and a silver in 1924, and Sven Thofelt (SWE) who won the gold medal in 1928, both won silver medals as members of the 1936 Swedish épée fencing team. Thofelt also won a bronze in the Swedish fencing team in 1948 while his son competed in the 1960 modern pentathlon. Dyrssen later became Sweden's IOC representative, and Thofelt is the president of the UIPMB.

In fifth place in the 1912 competition was George Patton (USA), later the famous General of the Second World War. The detailed results indicate that he was not very good at shooting. Three men have scored maximums of 200 hits in the shooting event; Charles Leonard (USA) 1936 Daniel Massala (ITA) 1976 and George Horvath (SWE) in 1980. The fastest time ever recorded in the 300 m swimming event was 3 min 10·856 sec by Ivar Sisniega (MEX) in 1980. The other three disciplines are either not measurable or comparable.

One of the biggest scandals in Olympic history occurred in the fencing segment of the 1976 competition when Boris Onischenko (URS) previous winner of a gold and two silver medals was disqualified for using an illegal weapon. I transpired that he had tampered with his épée so that it registered a hit even when contact with an opponent had not taken place. The incident has caused speculation about whether he had used the implement in the 1972 Games, where his fencing victory over Britain's Jim Fox (against whom he was fencing when the Montreal incident came to light) cost the Briton the individual bronze medal.

Twice individual champion in the modern pentathlon, Lars Hall (SWE) is seen here finishing the cross country running segment of the event.

Individual

	Gold	Silver	Bronze
1912	Gustaf Lilliehöök (SWE) 27	Gösta Asbrink (SWE) 28	Georg de Laval (SWE) 30
1920	Gustaf Orzyssen (SWE) 18	Erik de Laval (SWE) 23	Gösta Rüno (SWE) 27
1924	Bo Lindman (SWE) 18	Gustaf Orzyssen (SWE) 39·5	Bertil Uggla (SWE) 45
1928	Sven Thofelt (SWE) 47	Bo Lindman (SWE) 50	Helmuth Kahl (GER) 52
1932	Johan Gabriel Oxenstierna (SWE) 32	Bo Lindman (SWE) 35·5	Richard Mayo (USA) 38·5
1936	Gotthard Handrick (GER) 31·5	Charles Leonard (USA) 39·5	Silvano Abba (ITA) 45·5
1948	Willie Grut (SWE) 16	George Moore (USA) 47	Gösta Gärdin (SWE) 49
1952	Lars Hall (SWE) 32	Gábor Benedek (HUN) 39	István Szondi (HUN) 41
1956	Lars Hall (SWE) 4843	Olavi Nannonen (FIN) 4774·5	Väinö Korhonen (FIN) 4750
1960	Ferenc Németh (HUN) 5024	Imre Nagy (HUN) 4988	Robert Beck (USA) 4981
1964	Ferenc Török (HUN) 5116	Igor Novikov (URS) 5067	Albert Mokeyev (URS) 5039
1968	Björn Ferm (SWE) 4964	András Balczó (HUN) 4953	Pavel Lednev (URS) 4795
1972	András Balczó (HUN) 5412	Boris Onischenko (URS) 5335	Pavel Lednev (URS) 5328
1976	Janusz Pyciak-Peciak (POL) 5520	Pavel Lednev (URS) 5485	Jan Bartu (TCH) 5466
1980	Anatoliy Starostin (URS) 5568	Tamás Szombathelyi (HUN) 5502	Pavel Lednev (URS) 5382

1896–1908 Event not held

Team

	Gold	Silver	Bronze
1952	HUNGARY 116	SWEDEN 182	FINLAND 213
1956	USSR 13 690·5	UNITED STATES 13 482	FINLAND 13 185·5
1960	HUNGARY 14 863	USSR 14 309	UNITED STATES 14 192
1964	USSR 14 961	UNITED STATES 14 189	HUNGARY 14 173
1968	HUNGARY 14 325	USSR 14 248	FRANCE 13 289[1]
1972	USSR 15 968	HUNGARY 15 348	FINLAND 14 812
1976	GREAT BRITAIN 15 559	CZECHOSLOVAKIA 15 451	HUNGARY 15 395
1980	USSR 16 126	HUNGARY 15 912	SWEDEN 15 845

[1] Sweden finished third in 1968 but were disqualified when a doping test indicated that a member of the team had an excessive level of alcohol. 1896–1948 Event not held

MODERN PENTATHLON—MEDALS

	Gold	Silver	Bronze	Total		Gold	Silver	Bronze	Total
SWEDEN	9	6	5	20	GREAT BRITAIN	1	—	—	1
HUNGARY	6	6	3	15	POLAND	1	—	—	1
USSR	5	5	4	14	FRANCE	—	—	1	1
UNITED STATES	—	4	3	7	ITALY	—	—	1	1
FINLAND	—	1	4	5					
GERMANY (FRG)	1	—	1	2		23	23	23	69
CZECHOSLOVAKIA	—	1	1	2					

ROWING

Rowing for men was first held in the 1900 Games on the Seine over a 1750 m course. In 1904 the course measured 2 miles *3219 m*, in 1908 1½ miles *2414 m* and in 1948 1 mile 300 yards *1883 m*. The standard length is now 2000 m for men and 1000 m for women. Even in recent Games when the course has been on still water, as opposed to

Triple gold medallist John Kelly later saw his son win a bronze medal in rowing, and his film star daughter marry a prince.

flowing rivers, water and weather conditions vary too much to allow the establishment of an official Olympic record for the events. However, as a matter of interest the following table lists the fastest times achieved over the standard courses in Olympic regattas. (Most of them were achieved in preliminary rounds.)

The exciting finish of the eights in 1932. From the top, **Italy** second, **Great Britain** fourth, **Canada** third and the **United States** first.

MEN

Event	Time	Crew	Year	Av Speed (km/h)
Single Sculls	6:52·46	Sean Drea (IRL)	1976	17·45
Double Sculls	6:12·48	Norway	1976	19·32
Quadruple Sculls	5:47·83	USSR	1976	20·69
Coxless Pairs	6:33·02	GDR	1976	18·31
Coxed Pairs	7:01·10	Bulgaria	1976	17·09
Coxless Fours	5:53·65	GDR	1976	20·35
Coxed Fours	6:09·28	USSR	1976	19·49
Eights	5:32·17	GDR	1976	21·67[1]

[1] This is the fastest time ever recorded anywhere by an eight on still water. However, the New Zealand crew in 1976 achieved an average speed of 22·48 km/h for the first 500 m in a heat.

WOMEN

Event	Time	Crew	Year	Av Speed (km/h)
Single Sculls	3:40·69	Sandra Toma (ROM)	1980	16·31
Double Sculls	3:16·27	USSR	1980	18·34
Quadruple Sculls	3:08·49	GDR	1976	19·09
Coxless Pairs	3:30·49	GDR	1980	17·10
Coxed Fours	3:19·27	GDR	1980	18·06
Eights	3:00·19	USSR	1976	19·97[2]

[2] The Soviet crew achieved an average speed of 20·78 km/h over the second 250 m in a heat.

One of the first winning crews in the Games, the 1900 German four, contained three brothers, Oskar, Gustav and Carl Gossler, the latter as coxswain. This was the beginning of a tradition of sibling participation and success which reached a landmark at Moscow in 1980 when the Landvoigt twins (GDR) beat the Pimenov twins (URS) in the coxless pairs final. Fathers and sons have also had great success in the sport, but usually independently of each other. The most famous are probably the Beresfords (GBR), Julius with a silver in 1912, and Jack with five medals (see below) in the next five Games; the Costellos (USA), Paul winning three golds and son Bernard a silver in 1956; the Kellys (USA), John Sr winning three gold medals (see below) and John Jr a bronze in 1956; the Nickalls (GBR) with Guy Sr winning a gold in the 1908 eight and Guy Jr getting two silvers in the 1920 and 1928 crews. However, the Burnells (GBR), Charles (1908) and Richard (1948) are the only father and son in Olympic rowing to both win gold medals.

Five oarsmen have won a record three gold medals: John Kelly (USA) in the sculls (1920) and the double sculls (1920 and 1924); his cousin Paul Costello (USA) in the double sculls (1920, 1924 and 1928); Jack Beresford (GBR) in the sculls (1924), coxless fours (1932) and the double sculls (1936); Vyacheslav Ivanov (URS) in the sculls (1956, 1960 and 1964); Siegfried Brietzke (GDR) in the coxless pairs (1972) and coxless fours (1976 and 1980). Of the above only Beresford also won two silver medals, in the sculls (1920) and the eights (1928) making him the most successful Olympic rower of all time. Ivanov is the only man to win three individual medals. When he won his first title at Melbourne he excitedly threw his medal in the air and lost it in the waters of Lake Wendouree. It was never recovered and later the IOC gave him a replacement. Beresford is the only oarsman to win medals at five Olympic celebrations, 1920–1936.

The youngest gold medallist in Olympic history

was the unknown French boy who coxed the winning Dutch pair in 1900. Believed to have been between seven and ten years of age he was recruited at the last moment to replace Hermanus Brockmann, their cox in the heats, who was considered to be too heavy. Incidentally Brockmann coxed the Dutch fours to a silver medal and the eight to a bronze. A number of other coxswains have been extremely youthful, the youngest of those whose birthdates are known was another French boy, Noël Vandernotte. He was aged 12 yr 233 days when he won bronze medals as cox to the 1936 French pairs and fours, the latter including his father and uncle. At the other end of the scale is Robert Zimonyi who was cox to the winning United States eight in 1964 aged 46 yr 180 days and the oldest ever gold medallist in rowing. In 1948 he had been cox of the bronze medal pairs from his native Hungary. The oldest oarsman to win a gold medal was Guy Nickalls (GBR) as a member of the winning eight in 1908 aged 42 yr 170 days.

Men

Event	Time	Av Speed (km/h)	Crew	Year
Single Sculls	6:52·46	17·45	Sean Drea (IRL)	1976
Double Sculls	6:12·48	19·32	Norway	1976
Quadruple Sculls	5:47·83	20·69	USSR	1976
Coxless Pairs	6:33·02	18·31	GDR	1976
Coxed Pairs	7:01·10	17·09	Bulgaria	1976
Coxless Fours	5:53·65	20·35	GDR	1976
Coxed Fours	6:09·28	19·49	USSR	1976
Eights	5:32·17	21·67[1]	GDR	1976

[1] This is the fastest time ever recorded anywhere by an eight on still water. However, the New Zealand crew in 1976 achieved an average speed of 22·48 km/h for the first 500 m in a heat.

Women

Event	Time	Av Speed (km/h)	Crew	Year
Single Sculls	3:40·69	16·31	Sandra Toma (ROM)	1980
Double Sculls	3:16·27	18·34	USSR	1980
Quadruple Sculls	3:08·49	19·09	GDR	1976
Coxless Pairs	3:30·49	17·10	GDR	1980
Coxed Fours	3:19·27	18·06	GDR	1980
Eights	3:00·19	19·97[2]	USSR	1976

[2] The Soviet crew achieved an average speed of 20·78 km/h over the second 250 m in a heat.

ROWING (Men)

SINGLE SCULLS

	Gold	Silver	Bronze
1900	Henri Barrelet (FRA) 7:35·6	André Gaudin (FRA) 7:41·6	St. George Ashe (GBR) 8:15·6
1904	Frank Greer (USA) 10:08·5	James Juvenal (USA) 2 lengths	Constance Titus (USA) 1 length
1906	Gaston Delaplane (FRA) 5:53·4	Joseph Larran (FRA) 6:07·2	—
1908	Harry Blackstaffe (GBR) 9:26·0	Alexander McCulloch (GBR) 1 length	Bernhard von Gaza (GER) d.n.a. Károly Levitzky (HUN) d.n.a.
1912	William Kinnear (GBR) 7:47·6	Potydore Veirman (BEL) 1 length	Everard Butter (CAN) d.n.a. Mikhail Kusik (URS) d.n.a.
1920	John Kelly (USA) 7:35·0	Jack Beresford (GBR) 7:36·0	Clarence Hadfield d'Arcy (NZL) 7:48·0
1924	Jack Beresford (GBR) 7:49·2	William Garrett-Gilmore (USA) 7:54·0	Josef Schneider (SUI) 8:01·1
1928	Henry Pearce (AUS) 7:11·0	Kenneth Myers (USA) 7:20·8	David Collet (GBR) 7:19·8
1932	Henry Pearce (AUS) 7:44·4	William Miller (USA) 7:45·2	Guillermo Douglas (URU) 8:13·6
1936	Gustav Schäfer (GER) 8:21·5	Josef Hasenöhrl (AUT) 8:25·8	Daniel Barrow (USA) 8:28·0
1948	Mervyn Wood (AUS) 7:24·4	Eduardo Risso (URU) 7:38·2	Romolo Catasta (ITA) 7:51·4
1952	Yuriy Tyukalov (URS) 8:12·8	Mervyn Wood (AUS) 8:14·5	Teodor Kocerka (POL) 8:19·4
1956	Vyacheslav Ivanov (URS) 8:02·5	Stuart Mackenzie (AUS) 8:07·7	John Kelly (USA) 8:11·8
1960	Vyacheslav Ivanov (URS) 7:13·96	Achim Hill (GER) 7:20·21	Teodor Kocerka (POL) 7:21·26
1964	Vyacheslav Ivanov (URS) 8:22·51	Achim Hill (GER) 8:26·34	Gottfried Kottmann (SUI) 8:29·68
1968	Henri Jan Wienese (HOL) 7:47·80	Jochen Meissner (FRG) 7:52·00	Alberto Demiddi (ARG) 7:57·19
1972	Yuriy Malishev (URS) 7:10·12	Alberto Demiddi (ARG) 7:11·53	Wolfgang Gueldenpfennig (GDR) 7:14·45
1976	Pertti Karppinen (FIN) 7:29·03	Peter Kolbe (FRG) 7:31·67	Joachim Dreifke (GDR) 7:38·03
1980	Pertti Karppinen (FIN) 7:09·61	Vasiliy Yakusha (URS) 7:11·66	Peter Kersten (GDR) 7:14·88

1896 Event not held

Men

DOUBLE SCULLS

	Gold	Silver	Bronze
1904	UNITED STATES 10:03·2 John Mulcahy William Varley	UNITED STATES d.n.a. John Hoben James McLoughlin	UNITED STATES d.n.a. John Wells Joseph Ravanack
1920	UNITED STATES 7:09·0 John Kelly Paul Costello	ITALY 7:19·0 Erminio Dones Pietro Annoni	FRANCE 7:21·0 Alfred Plé Gaston Giran
1924	UNITED STATES 7:45·0 John Kelly Paul Costello	FRANCE 7:54·8 Jean-Pierre Stock Marc Detton	SWITZERLAND d.n.a. Rudolf Bosshard Heini Thoma
1928	UNITED STATES 6:41·4 Charles McIlvaine Paul Costello	CANADA 6:51·0 Jack Guest Joseph Wright	AUSTRIA 6:48·8 Viktor Flessl Leo Losert
1932	UNITED STATES 7:17·4 William Garrett-Gilmore Kenneth Myers	GERMANY 7:22·8 Gerhard Boetzelen Herbert Buhtz	CANADA 7:27·6 Nöel de Mille Charles Pratt
1936	GREAT BRITAIN 7:20·8 Leslie Southwood Jack Beresford	GERMANY 7:26·2 Joachim Pirsch Willy Kaidel	POLAND 7:36·2 Jerzy Ustupski Roger Verey
1948	GREAT BRITAIN 6:51·3 Herbert Bushnell Richard D Burnell	DENMARK 6:55·3 Aage Larsen Ebbe Parsner	URUGUAY 7:12·4 Juan Rodriguez William Jones
1952	ARGENTINA 7:32·2 Tranquilo Capozzo Eduardo Guerrero	USSR 7:38·3 Georgiy Zhilin Igor Emchuk	URUGUAY 7:43·7 Miguel Seijas Juan Rodriguez
1956	USSR 7:24·0 Aleksandr Berkutov Yuriy Tyukalov	UNITED STATES 7:32·2 Bernard Costello James Gardiner	AUSTRALIA 7:37·4 Murray Riley Mervyn Wood
1960	CZECHOSLOVAKIA 6:47·50 Václav Kozák Pavel Schmidt	USSR 6:50·49 Aleksandr Berkutov Yuriy Tyukalov	SWITZERLAND 6:50·59 Ernst Huerlimann Rolf Larcher
1964	USSR 7:10·66 Oleg Tyurin Boris Dubrovsky	UNITED STATES 7:13·16 Seymour Cromwell James Storm	CZECHOSLOVAKIA 7:14·23 Vladimir Andrs Pavel Hofman
1968	USSR 6:51·82 Anatoliy Sass Aleksandr Timoshinin	NETHERLANDS 6:52·80 Henricus Droog Leendert van Dis	UNITED STATES 6:54·21 John Nunn William Maher
1972	USSR 7:01·77 Aleksandr Timoshinin Gennadiy Korshikov	NORWAY 7:02·58 Frank Hansen Svein Thogersen	GDR 7:05·55 Joachim Boehmer Hans-Ulrich Schmied
1976	NORWAY 7:13·20 Frank Hansen Alf Hansen	GREAT BRITAIN 7:15·26 Chris Baillieu Michael Hart	GDR 7:17·45 Hans-Ulrich Schmied Jürgen Bertow
1980	GDR 6:24·33 Joachim Dreifke Klaus Kröppelien	YUGOSLAVIA 6:26·34 Zoran Pancic Milorad Stanulov	CZECHOSLOVAKIA 6:29·07 Zdenek Pecka Vaclav Vochoska

1896–1900, 1906–1912 Event not held

COXLESS QUADRUPLE SCULLS

	Gold	Silver	Bronze
1976	GDR 6:18·65	USSR 6:19·89	CZECHOSLOVAKIA 6:21·77
1980	GDR 5:49·81	USSR 5:51·47	BULGARIA 5:52·38

1896–1972 Event not held

COXLESS PAIRS

	Gold	Silver	Bronze
1908	GREAT BRITAIN 9:41·0 (Leander I) J R K Fenning Gordon Thomson	GREAT BRITAIN 2½ lengths (Leander II) George Fairbairn Philip Verdon	—
1924	NETHERLANDS 8:19·4 Wilhelm Rösingh Antonie Beijnen	FRANCE 8:21·6 Maurice Bouton George Piot	—
1928	GERMANY 7:06·4 Bruno Müller Kurt Moeschter	GREAT BRITAIN 7:08·8 Archibald Nisbet Terence O'Brien	UNITED STATES 7:20·4 John Schmitt Paul McDowell
1932	GREAT BRITAIN 8:00·0 Arthur Edwards Lewis Clive	NEW ZEALAND 8:02·4 Frederick Thompson Cyril Stiles	POLAND 8:08·2 Janusz Mikolajczyk Henryk Budzynski
1936	GERMANY 8:16·1 Hugo Strauss Willi Eichhorn	DENMARK 8:19·2 Harry Larsen Richard Olsen	ARGENTINA 8:23·0 Julio Curatella Horacio Podestá
1948	GREAT BRITAIN 7:21·1 John Wilson William Laurie	SWITZERLAND 7:23·9 Josef Kalt Hans Kalt	ITALY 7:31·5 Bruno Boni Felice Fanetti
1952	UNITED STATES 8:20·7 Charles Logg Thomas Price	BELGIUM 8:23·5 Michael Knuysen Robert Baetens	SWITZERLAND 8:32·7 Kurt Schmid Hans Kalt
1956	UNITED STATES 7:55·4 James Fifer Duvall Hecht	USSR 8:03·9 Igor Buldakov Viktor Ivanov	AUSTRIA 8:11·8 Josef Kloimstein Alfred Sageder
1960	USSR 7:02·01 Valentin Boreyko Oleg Golovanov	AUSTRIA 7:03·69 Josef Kloimstein Alfred Sageder	FINLAND 7:03·80 Veli Lehtelä Toimi Pitkänen
1964	CANADA 7:32·94 George Hungerford Roger Jackson	NETHERLANDS 7:33·40 Steven Blaisse Ernst Veenemans	GERMANY 7:38·63 Michael Schwan Wolfgang Hottenrott
1968	GDR 7:26·56 Jörg Lucke Hans-Jürgen Bothe	UNITED STATES 7:26·71 Lawrence Hough Philip Johnson	DENMARK 7:31·84 Peter Christiansen Ib Ivan Larsen
1972	GDR 6:53·16 Siegfried Brietzke Wolfgang Mager	SWITZERLAND 6:57·06 Heinrich Fischer Alfred Bachmann	NETHERLANDS 6:58·70 Roelof Luynenburg Rudolf Stokvis
1976	GDR 7:23·31 Jörg Landvoigt Bernd Landvoigt	UNITED STATES 7:26·73 Calvin Coffey Michael Staines	FRG 7:30·03 Peter Vanroye Thomas Strauss
1980	GDR 6:48·01 Jörg Landvoigt Bernd Landvoigt	USSR 6:50·50 Juriy Pimenov Nikolai Pimenov	GREAT BRITAIN 6:51·47 Charles Wiggin Malcolm Carmichael

1896–1906, 1912–1920 Event not held

COXED PAIRS

	Gold	Silver	Bronze
1900	NETHERLANDS 7:34·2	FRANCE I 7:34·4	FRANCE II 7:57·2
1906[1]	ITALY I 4:23·0	ITALY II 4:30·0	FRANCE d.n.a.
1906[2]	ITALY 7:32·4	BELGIUM 8:03·0	FRANCE 8:08·6
1920	ITALY 7:56·0	FRANCE 7:57·0	SWITZERLAND d.n.a.
1924	SWITZERLAND 8:39·0	ITALY 8:39·1	UNITED STATES 3 m
1928	SWITZERLAND 7:42·6	FRANCE 7:48·4	BELGIUM 7:59·4
1932	UNITED STATES 8:25·8	POLAND 8:31·2	FRANCE 8:41·2
1936	GERMANY 8:36·9	ITALY 8:49·7	FRANCE 8:54·0
1948	DENMARK 8:00·5	ITALY 8:12·2	HUNGARY 8:25·2

1952	FRANCE 8:28·6	GERMANY 8:32·1	DENMARK 8:34·9
1956	UNITED STATES 8:26·1	GERMANY 8:29·2	USSR 8:31·0
1960	GERMANY 7:29·14	USSR 7:30·17	UNITED STATES 7:34·58
1964	UNITED STATES 8:21·23	FRANCE 8:23·15	NETHERLANDS 8:23·42
1968	ITALY 8:04·81	NETHERLANDS 8:06·80	DENMARK 8:08·07
1972	GDR 7:17·25	CZECHOSLOVAKIA 7:19·57	ROMANIA 7:21·36
1976	GDR 7:58·99	USSR 8:01·82	CZECHOSLOVAKIA 8:03·28
1980	GDR 7:02·54	USSR 7:03·35	YUGOSLAVIA 7:04·92

[1] Over 1000 m.   [2] Over 1600 m.   1896, 1904, 1908–1912 Event not held

COXLESS FOURS

	Gold	Silver	Bronze
1904	UNITED STATES 9:53·8	UNITED STATES d.n.a.	—
1908	GREAT BRITAIN 8:34·0	GREAT BRITAIN 1½ lengths	—
1924	GREAT BRITAIN 7:08·6	CANADA 7:18·0	SWITZERLAND 2 lengths
1928	GREAT BRITAIN 6:36·0	UNITED STATES 6:37·0	ITALY 6:31·6
1932	GREAT BRITAIN 6:58·2	GERMANY 7:03·0	ITALY 7:04·0
1936	GERMANY 7:01·8	GREAT BRITAIN 7:06·5	SWITZERLAND 7:10·6
1948	ITALY 6:39·0	DENMARK 6:43·5	UNITED STATES 6:47·7
1952	YUGOSLAVIA 7:16·0	FRANCE 7:18·9	FINLAND 7:23·3
1956	CANADA 7:08·8	UNITED STATES 7:18·4	FRANCE 7:20·9
1960	UNITED STATES 6:26·26	ITALY 6:28·78	USSR 6:29·62
1964	DENMARK 6:59·30	GREAT BRITAIN 7:00·47	UNITED STATES 7:01·37
1968	GDR 6:39·18	HUNGARY 6:41·64	ITALY 6:44·01
1972	GDR 6:24·27	NEW ZEALAND 6:25·64	FRG 6:28·41
1976	GDR 6:37·42	NORWAY 6:41·22	USSR 6:42·52
1980	GDR 6:08·17	USSR 6:11·81	GREAT BRITAIN 6:16·58

1896–1900, 1906, 1912–1920 Event not held

COXED FOURS

	Gold	Silver	Bronze
1900[1]	GERMANY 5:59·0	NETHERLANDS 6:33·0	GERMANY 6:35·0
1900[1]	FRANCE 7:11·0	FRANCE 7:18·0	GERMANY 7:18·2
1906	ITALY 8:13·0	FRANCE d.n.a.	FRANCE d.n.a.
1912	GERMANY 6:59·4	GREAT BRITAIN 2 lengths	NORWAY d.n.a.
			DENMARK d.n.a.
1920	SWITZERLAND 6:54·0	UNITED STATES 6:58·0	NORWAY 7:02·0
1924	SWITZERLAND 7:18·4	FRANCE 7:21·6	UNITED STATES 1 length
1928	ITALY 6:47·8	SWITZERLAND 7:03·4	POLAND 7:12·8
1932	GERMANY 7:19·0	ITALY 7:19·2	POLAND 7:26·8
1936	GERMANY 7:16·2	SWITZERLAND 7:24·3	FRANCE 7:33·3
1948	UNITED STATES 6:50·3	SWITZERLAND 6:53·3	DENMARK 6:58·6
1952	CZECHOSLOVAKIA 7:33·4	SWITZERLAND 7:36·5	UNITED STATES 7:37·0
1956	ITALY 7:19·4	SWEDEN 7:22·4	FINLAND 7:30·9
1960	GERMANY 6:39·12	FRANCE 6:41·62	ITALY 6:43·72
1964	GERMANY 7:00·44	ITALY 7:02·84	NETHERLANDS 7:06·46
1968	NEW ZEALAND 6:45·62	GDR 6:48·20	SWITZERLAND 6:49·04
1972	FRG 6:31·85	GDR 6:33·30	CZECHOSLOVAKIA 6:35·64
1976	USSR 6:40·22	GDR 6:42·70	FRG 6:46·96
1980	GDR 6:14·51	USSR 6:19·05	POLAND 6:22·52

[1] Two separate finals were held in 1900.   1896, 1904, 1908 Event not held

EIGHTS

	Gold	Silver	Bronze
1900	UNITED STATES 6:09·8	BELGIUM 6:13·8	NETHERLANDS 6:23·0
1904	UNITED STATES 7:50·0	CANADA d.n.a.	—
1908	GREAT BRITAIN I 7:52·0	BELGIUM 2 lengths	GREAT BRITAIN II d.n.a.
1912	GREAT BRITAIN I 6:15·0	GREAT BRITAIN II 6:19·0	GERMANY d.n.a.
1920	UNITED STATES 6:02·6	GREAT BRITAIN 6:05·0	NORWAY 6:36·0

1924	UNITED STATES 6:33·4	CANADA 6:49·0	ITALY ¾ length
1928	UNITED STATES 6:03·2	GREAT BRITAIN 6:05·6	CANADA 6:03·8
1932	UNITED STATES 6:37·6	ITALY 6:37·8	CANADA 6:40·4
1936	UNITED STATES 6:25·4	ITALY 6:26·0	GERMANY 6:26·4
1948	UNITED STATES 5:56·7	GREAT BRITAIN 6:06·9	NORWAY 6:10·3
1952	UNITED STATES 6:25·9	USSR 6:31·2	AUSTRALIA 6:33·1
1956	UNITED STATES 6:35·2	CANADA 6:37·1	AUSTRALIA 6:39·2
1960	GERMANY 5:57·18	CANADA 6:01·52	CZECHOSLOVAKIA 6:04·84
1964	UNITED STATES 6:18·23	GERMANY 6:23·29	CZECHOSLOVAKIA 6:25·11
1968	FRG 6:07·00	AUSTRALIA 6:07·98	USSR 6:09·11
1972	NEW ZEALAND 6:08·94	UNITED STATES 6:11·61	GDR 6:11·67
1976	GDR 5:58·29	GREAT BRITAIN 6:00·82	NEW ZEALAND 6:03·51
1980	GDR 5:49·05	GREAT BRITAIN 5:51·92	USSR 5:52·66

1896, 1906 Event not held

DISCONTINUED EVENTS
NAVAL ROWING BOATS (2000 m)

	Gold	Silver	Bronze
1906	ITALY 10:45·0	GREECE d.n.a.	GREECE d.n.a.

16-MAN NAVAL ROWING BOATS (3000 m)

	Gold	Silver	Bronze
1906	GREECE 16:35·0	GREECE 17:09·6	ITALY d.n.a.

COXED FOURS (INRIGGERS)

	Gold	Silver	Bronze
1912	DENMARK 7:47·0	SWEDEN 1 length	NORWAY d.n.a.

ROWING (Women)
Women's rowing was introduced in 1976 over a course of 1000 metres.
SINGLE SCULLS

	Gold	Silver	Bronze
1976	Christine Scheiblich (GDR) 4:05·56	Joan Lind (USA) 4:06·21	Elena Antonova (URS) 4:10·24
1980	Sandra Toma (ROM) 3:40·69	Antonina Makhina (URS) 3:41·65	Martina Schröter (GDR) 3:43·54

DOUBLE SCULLS

	Gold	Silver	Bronze
1976	BULGARIA 3:44·36 Svetla Otzetova Zdravka Yordanova	GDR 3:47·86 Sabine Jahn Petra Boesler	USSR 3:49·93 Leonora Kaminskaite Genovate Ramoshkene
1980	USSR 3:16·27 Elena Khloptseva Larisa Popova	GDR 3:17·63 Cornelia Linse Heidi Westphal	ROMANIA 3:18·91 Olga Homeghi Valeria Rosca-Racila

COXLESS PAIRS

	Gold	Silver	Bronze
1976	BULGARIA 4:01·22 Siika Kelbetcheva Stoyanka Grouitcheva	GDR 4:01·64 Angelika Noack Sabine Dahne	FRG 4:02·35 Edith Eckbauer Thea Eingeder
1980	GDR 3:30·49 Ute Steindorf Cornelia Klier	POLAND 3:30·95 Malgorzata Divzewska Czeslawa Koscianska	BULGARIA 3:32·39 Siika Barboulova Stoyanka Kubatova

COXED QUADRUPLE SCULLS

	Gold	Silver	Bronze
1976	GDR 3:29·99	USSR 3:32·49	ROMANIA 3:32·76
1980	GDR 3:15·32	USSR 3:15·73	BULGARIA 3:16·10

COXED FOURS

	Gold	Silver	Bronze
1976	GDR 3:45·08	BULGARIA 3:48·24	USSR 3:49·38
1980	GDR 3:19·27	BULGARIA 3:20·75	USSR 3:20·92

EIGHTS

	Gold	Silver	Bronze
1976	GDR 3:33·32	USSR 3:36·17	UNITED STATES 3:38·68
1980	GDR 3:03·32	USSR 3:04·29	ROMANIA 3:05·63

ROWING—MEDALS
Men

	Gold	Silver	Bronze	Total
UNITED STATES	26	14	12	52
GERMANY (FRG)	15	10	9	34
GREAT BRITAIN	14	15	5	34
USSR	11	13	6	30
ITALY	9	10	8	27
GDR	17	3	6	26
FRANCE	4	13	9	26
SWITZERLAND	4	6	9	19
CANADA	2	6	5	13
NETHERLANDS	3	4	4	11
DENMARK	3	3	5	11
CZECHOSLOVAKIA	2	1	7	10
AUSTRALIA	3	3	3	9
NORWAY	1	2	5	8
POLAND	—	1	7	8
NEW ZEALAND	2	2	2	6
BELGIUM	—	5	1	6
FINLAND	2	—	3	5
GREECE	1	2	1	4
ARGENTINA	1	1	2	4
AUSTRIA	—	2	2	4
URUGUAY	—	1	3	4
YUGOSLAVIA	1	1	1	3
HUNGARY	—	1	2	3
SWEDEN	—	2	—	2
BULGARIA	—	—	1	1
ROMANIA	—	—	1	1
	121	121	119	361

ROWING—MEDALS
Women

	Gold	Silver	Bronze	Total
GDR	8	3	1	12
USSR	1	5	4	10
BULGARIA	2	2	2	6
ROMANIA	1	—	3	4
UNITED STATES	—	1	1	2
POLAND	—	1	—	1
GERMANY (FRG)	—	—	1	1
	12	12	12	36

Vyacheslav Ivanov (URS)
after his successful defence
of his single sculls title in
1960 on Lake Albano. Four
years later he won again.

SHOOTING

The Swedish running deer shooting team in 1912 with the remarkable Oscar Swahn (second from right). His son Alfred is on the left of the picture.

Baron de Coubertin was a pistol shot of note in his youth and this obviously led to the sport being included in the Athens Games. The first Olympic shooting champion was Pantelis Karasevdas (GRE) who won the free rifle event over 200 m on 9 April 1896. The number of different events has varied considerably, especially in the early celebrations, from 21 in 1920 to only two in 1932, while there were none at all in 1928 (nor any official competitions in 1904). Since 1952 there has been some standardization.

The most successful competitor was Carl Osburn (USA), a Commander in the US Navy, who won a record 11 medals (five gold, four silver, two bronze) between 1912 and 1924. Six other men have won five gold medals as follows:

	Gold	Silver	Bronze	Year(s)
Konrad Stäheli (SUI)	5	2	1	1900
Willis Lee (USA)	5	1	1	1920
Louis Richardet (SUI)	5	1	—	1900
Ole Lilloe-Olsen (NOR)	5	1	—	1920–4
Alfred Lane (USA)	5	—	1	1912–20
Morris Fisher (USA)	5	—	—	1920–4

The only man to win three individual gold medals was Gudbrand Skatteboe (NOR) in 1906.

Women first competed in Olympic shooting in 1968 when three countries, Poland, Peru and Mexico, entered one each. The representative of Mexico, Nuria Ortiz, was the first to compete and she finished 13th in the skeet event. The first woman to win a medal was Margaret Murdock (USA) in the 1976 small-bore rifle (three positions). Initially she was listed as the winner, but then it was discovered that an error had been made and she was equal with her team-mate, Lanny Bassham. Then on the count-back rule relating to the last ten shots she was placed second, much to the embarrassment of Bassham, who pulled her up to the top of the rostrum at the medal ceremony.

The oldest gold medallist in Olympic history was the remarkable Oscar Swahn (SWE) in the 1912 running deer team aged 64 yr 258 days. At Antwerp in 1920 he became the oldest medallist and, indeed, competitor at any sport ever when he was again a member of the Swedish running deer silver medal team. He qualified for the 1924 Games in his 77th year, but illness prevented him from competing. The youngest winner of a gold medal was George Généreux (CAN) who won the individual trap shooting in 1952 aged 17 yr 147 days. In those same Games Szilárd Kun (HUN) became the youngest medallist when 20 days younger by winning the silver in the rapid fire pistol.

The first brothers to win gold medals in the Olympic Games were marksmen; the Paine brothers in 1896 (see p 14). Also the first twins to do so were Wilhelm and Eric Carlberg of Sweden (see p 24).

Walter Winans (USA) who had won a gold medal in the running deer event in 1908, became the only man to win medals in both sport and artistic events at the same Games in 1912 when he won a silver at shooting and a gold at sculpture. Károly Tákacs (HUN) was a European champion pistol shot in the 1930s, shooting with his right hand. In 1938 while on army training a grenade blew up in his hand destroying his right arm. After the Second World War he won the rapid fire pistol event with his left hand at the 1948 and 1952 Games, one of only four shooters who have successfully defended an Olympic title. The winner of the rapid pistol gold medal in 1960 was William McMillan (USA) who in 1976 competed in his record sixth Games.

Gerald Ouellette (CAN) won the small bore rifle (prone) in 1956 with a world record maximum possible score of 600, but it was not accepted as such as the range was found to be 1½ m short of the regulation 50 m distance. When Ho Jun Li (PRK) won the same event in 1972 with only one point short of the maximum he was asked how he concentrated so well. He answered that he pretended that he was 'aiming at a capitalist'.

One of the strangest occurrences in Olympic shooting was in the 1976 trap shooting event, when 65 year old Paul Cerutti of Monaco was disqualified for using drugs even though he had finished 43rd out of 44 competitors.

OLYMPIC RECORDS—SHOOTING

Event	Points	Name & Country	Year
Small bore rifle (3 pos)	1173	Viktor Vlasov (URS)	1980
Small bore rifle (prone)	599	Ho Jun Li (PRK)	1972
	599	Karl-Heinz Smieszek (FRG)	1976
	599	Karoly Varga (HUN)	1980
	599	Hellfried Heilfort (GDR)	1980
Free pistol	581	Aleksandr Melentev (URS)	1980
Rapid fire pistol	597	Norbert Klaar (GDR)	1976
Running game	589	Igor Sokolov (URS)	1980
	589	Thomas Pfeffer (GDR)	1980
Trap	199	Angelo Scalzone (ITA)	1972
Skeet	198	Yevgeny Petrov (URS)	1968
	198	Romano Garagnáni (ITA)	1968
	198	Konrad Wirnhier (FRG)	1968
	198	Josef Panacek (TCH)	1976
	198	Eric Swinkels (HOL)	1976
	198	Luciano Giovannetti (ITA)	1980

FREE PISTOL (50 metres)

	Gold	Silver	Bronze
1896	Sumner Paine (USA) 442	Viggo Jensen (DEN) 285	Holger Nielsen (DEN) d.n.a.
1900	Karl Röderer (SUI) 503	Achille Paroche (FRA) 466	Konrad Stäheli (SUI) 453
1906	Georgios Orphanidis (GRE) 221	Jean Fouconnier (FRA) 219	Aristides Rangavis (GRE) 218
1912	Alfred Lane (USA) 499	Peter Dolfen (USA) 474	Charles Stewart (GBR) 470
1920	Karl Frederick (USA) 496	Afranio da Costa (BRA) 489	Alfred Lane (USA) 481
1936	Torsten Ullmann (SWE) 559	Erich Krempel (GER) 544	Charles des Jammonières (FRA) 540
1948	Edwin Vazquez Cam (PER) 545	Rudolf Schnyder (SUI) 539	Torsten Ullmann (SWE) 539
1952	Huelet Benner (USA) 553	Angel Léon de Gozalo (ESP) 550	Ambrus Balogh (HUN) 549
1956	Pentti Linnosvuo (FIN) 556	Makhmud Oumarov (URS) 556	Offutt Pinion (USA) 551
1960	Aleksey Gushchin (URS) 560	Makhmud Oumarov (URS) 552	Yoshihisa Yoshikawa (JPN) 552
1964	Väinö Markkanen (FIN) 560	Franklin Green (USA) 557	Yoshihisa Yoshikawa (JPN) 554
1968	Grigory Kossykh (URS) 562	Heinz Mertel (FRG) 562	Harald Vollmar (GDR) 560
1972	Ragnar Skanakar (SWE) 567	Dan Iuga (ROM) 562	Rudolf Dollinger (AUT) 560
1976	Uwe Potteck (GDR) 573	Harald Vollmar (GDR) 567	Rudolf Dollinger (AUT) 560
1980	Aleksandr Melentyev (URS) 581	Harald Vollmar (GDR) 568	Lubcho Diakov (URS) 565

1904, 1908, 1924–1932 Event not held

SMALL-BORE RIFLE—THREE POSITIONS
(Prone, Kneeling, Standing)

	Gold	Silver	Bronze
1952	Erling Kongshaug (NOR) 1164	Vilho Ylönen (FIN) 1164	Boris Andreyev (URS) 1163
1956	Anatoliy Bogdanov (URS) 1172	Otakar Hořinek (TCH) 1172	Nils Sundberg (SWE) 1167
1960	Viktor Shamburkin (URS) 1149	Marat Niyasov (URS) 1145	Klaus Zähringer (GER) 1139
1964	Lones Wigger (USA) 1164	Velitchko Khristov (BUL) 1152	László Hammerl (HUN) 1151
1968	Bernd Klingner (FRG) 1157	John Writer (USA) 1156	Vitaly Parkhimovich (URS) 1154
1972	John Writer (USA) 1166	Lanny Bassham (USA) 1157	Werner Lippoldt (GDR) 1153
1976	Lanny Bassham (USA) 1162	Margaret Murdock (USA) 1162	Werner Seibold (FRG) 1160
1980	Viktor Vlasov (URS) 1173	Bernd Hartstein (GDR) 1166	Sven Johansson (SWE) 1165

1896–1948 Event not held

Britain's running deer team of 1924. Left is Lt Colonel Allen Whitty, Britain's oldest ever gold medallist. Right is Lt Colonel Philip Neame, the only Olympian to win a Victoria Cross.

Willy Rögeberg (NOR) won the 1936 prone small bore competition with a perfect score of 30 shots in the bull.

RAPID-FIRE PISTOL

	Gold	Silver	Bronze
1896	Jean Phrangoudis (GRE) 344	Georgios Orphanidis (GRE) 249	Holger Nielsen (DEN) d.n.a.
1900	Maurice Larrouy (FRA) 58	Léon Moreaux (FRA) 57	Eugene Balme (FRA) 57
1906	Maurice Lecoq (FRA) 250	Léon Moreaux (FRA) 249	Aristides Rangavis (GRE) 245
1908	Paul van Asbroeck (BEL) 490	Réginald Storms (BEL) 487	James Gorman (USA) 485
1912	Alfred Lane (USA) 287	Paul Palén (SWE) 286	Johan von Holst (SWE) 283
1920	Guilherme Paraense (BRA) 274	Raymond Bracken (USA) 272	Fritz Zulauf (SUI) 269
1924	Paul Bailey (USA) 18	Vilhelm Carlberg (SWE) 18	Lennart Hannelius (FIN) 18
1932	Renzo Morigi (ITA) 36	Heinz Hax (GER) 36	Domenico Matteucci (ITA) 36
1936	Cornelius van Oyen (GER) 36	Heinz Hax (GER) 35	Torsten Ullmann (SWE) 34
1948	Károly Takács (HUN) 580	Carlos Diaz Sáenz Valiente (ARG) 571	Sven Lundqvist (SWE) 569
1952	Károly Takács (HUN) 579	Szilárd Kun (HUN) 578	Gheorghe Lichiardopol (ROM) 578
1956	Stefan Petrescu (ROM) 587	Evgeniy Shcherkasov (URS) 585	Gheorghe Lichiardopol (ROM) 581
1960	William McMillan (USA) 587	Pentti Linnosvuo (FIN) 587	Aleksandr Zabelin (URS) 587
1964	Pentti Linnosvuo (FIN) 592	Ion Tripsa (ROM) 591	Lubomir Nacovsky (TCH) 590
1968	Jozef Zapedzki (POL) 593	Marcel Rosca (ROM) 591	Renart Suleimanov (URS) 591
1972	Jozef Zapedzki (POL) 595	Ladislav Faita (TCH) 594	Victor Torshin (URS) 593
1976	Norbert Klaar (GDR) 597	Jurgen Wiefel (GDR) 596	Roberto Ferraris (ITA) 595
1980	Corneliu Ion (ROM) 596	Jürgen Wiefel (GDR) 596	Gerhard Petrisch (AUT) 596

1904, 1928 Event not held

SKEET SHOOTING

	Gold	Silver	Bronze
1968	Evgeny Petrov (URS) 198	Romano Garagnani (ITA) 198	Konrad Wirnhier (FRG) 198
1972	Konrad Wirnhier (FRG) 195	Evgeny Petrov (URS) 195	Michael Buchheim (GDR) 195
1976	Josef Panacek (TCH) 198	Eric Swinkels (HOL) 198	Wieslaw Gawlikowski (POL) 196
1980	Hans Kjeld Rasmussen (DEN) 196	Lars-Goran Carlsson (SWE) 196	Roberto Garcia (CUB) 196

1896–1964 Event not held

RUNNING GAME TARGET

	Gold	Silver	Bronze
1900	Louis Debray (FRA) 20	P Nivet (FRA) 20	Comte de Lambert (FRA) 19
1972	Lakov Zhelezniak (URS) 569	Hanspeter Bellingrodt (COL) 565	John Kynoch (GBR) 562
1976	Aleksandr Gazov (URS) 579	Aleksandr Kedyarov (URS) 576	Jerzy Greszkiewicz (POL) 571
1980	Igor Sokolov (URS) 589	Thomas Pfeffer (GDR) 589	Aleksandr Gasov (URS) 587

1896, 1904–1968 Event not held

FREE RIFLE

	Gold	Silver	Bronze
1896	Georgios Orphanidis (GRE) 1583	Jean Phrangoudis (GRE) 1312	Viggo Jensen (DEN) 1305
1906	Gudbrand Skatteboe (NOR) 977	Konrad Stäheli (SUI) 943	Jean Reich (SUI) 933
1908	Albert Helgerud (NOR) 909	Harry Simon (USA) 887	Ole Saether (NOR) 883
1912	Paul Colas (FRA) 987	Lars Madsen (DEN) 981	Niels Larsen (DEN) 962
1920	Morris Fisher (USA) 997	Niels Larsen (DEN) 985	Östen Östensen (NOR) 980

1924	Morris Fisher (USA) 95	Carl Osburn (USA) 95	Niels Larsen (DEN) 93
1948	Emil Grunig (SUI) 1120	Pauli Janhonen (FIN) 1114	Willy Rögeberg (NOR) 1112
1952	Anatoliy Bogdanov (URS) 1123	Robert Bürchler (SUI) 1120	Lev Vainschtein (URS) 1109
1956	Vasiliy Borissov (URS) 1138	Allan Erdman (URS) 1137	Vilho Ylönen (FIN) 1128
1960	Hubert Hammerer (AUT) 1129	Hans Spillmann (SUI) 1127	Vasiliy Borissov (URS) 1127
1964	Gary Anderson (USA) 1153	Shota Kveliashvili (URS) 1144	Martin Gunnarsson (USA) 1136
1968	Gary Anderson (USA) 1157	Vladimir Kornev (URS) 1151	Kurt Müller (SUI) 1148
1972	Lones Wigger (USA) 1155	Boris Melnik (URS) 1155	Lajos Papp (HUN) 1149

1900–1904, 1928–1936, 1976–1980 Event not held

OLYMPIC TRAP SHOOTING

	Gold	*Silver*	*Bronze*
1900	Roger de Barbarin (FRA) 17	René Guyot (FRA) 17	Justinien de Clary (FRA) 17
1906[1]	Gerald Merlin (GBR) 24	Ioannis Peridis (GRE) 23	Sidney Merlin (GBR) 21
1906[2]	Sidney Merlin (GBR) 15	Anastasios Metaxas (GRE) 13	Gerald Merlin (GBR) 12
1908	Walter Ewing (CAN) 72	George Beattie (CAN) 60	Alexander Maunder (GBR) 57
			Anastasios Metaxas (GRE) 57
1912	James Graham (USA) 96	Alfred Goeldel-Bronikowen (GER) 94	Harry Blau (URS) 91
1920	Mark Arie (USA) 95	Frank Troeh (USA) 93	Frank Wright (USA) 87
1924	Gyula Halasy (HUN) 98	Konrad Huber (FIN) 98	Frank Hughes (USA) 97
1952	George Généreux (CAN) 192	Knut Holmquist (SWE) 191	Hans Liljedahl (SWE) 191
1956	Galliano Rossini (ITA) 195	Adam Smelczynski (POL) 190	Alessandro Ciceri (ITA) 188
1960	Ion Dumitrescu (ROM) 192	Galliano Rossini (ITA) 191	Sergey Kalinin (URS) 190
1964	Ennio Mattarelli (ITA) 198	Pavel Senichev (URS) 194	William Morris (USA) 194
1968	Robert Braithwaite (GBR) 198	Thomas Garrigus (USA) 196	Kurt Czekalla (GDR) 196
1972	Angelo Scalzone (ITA) 199	Michel Carrega (FRA) 198	Silvano Basagni (ITA) 195
1976	Don Haldeman (USA) 190	Armando Marques (POR) 189	Ubaldesco Baldi (ITA) 189
1980	Luciano Giovanetti (ITA) 198	Rustam Yambulatov (URS) 196	Jörg Damme (GDR) 196

[1] Single shot.   [2] Double shot.   1896, 1904, 1928–1948 Event not held

SMALL-BORE RIFLE (Prone)[1]

	Gold	*Silver*	*Bronze*
1908	A A Carnell (GBR) 387	Harry Humby (GBR) 386	G Barnes (GBR) 385
1912	Frederick Hird (USA) 194	William Milne (GBR) 193	Harry Burt (GBR) 192
1920	Lawrence Nuesslein (USA) 391	Arthur Rothrock (USA) 386	Dennis Fenton (USA) 385
1924	Pierre Coquelin de Lisle (FRA) 398	Marcus Dinwiddie (USA) 396	Josias Hartmann (SUI) 394
1932	Bertil Rönnmark (SWE) 294	Gustavo Huet (MEX) 294	Zoltán Hradetsky-Soós (HUN) 293
1936	Willy Rögeberg (NOR) 300	Ralph Berzsenyi (HUN) 296	Wladyslaw Karás (POL) 296
1948	Arthur Cook (USA) 599	Walter Tomsen (USA) 599	Jonas Jonsson (SWE) 597
1952	Josif Sarbu (ROM) 400	Boris Andreyev (URS) 400	Arthur Jackson (USA) 399
1956	Gerald Ouellette (CAN) 600[2]	Vasiliy Borissov (URS) 599	Gilmour Boa (CAN) 598
1960	Peter Kohnke (GER) 590	James Hill (USA) 589	Enrico Pelliccione (VEN) 587
1964	László Hammerl (HUN) 597	Lones Wigger (USA) 597	Tommy Pool (USA) 596
1968	Jan Kurka (TCH) 598	László Hammerl (HUN) 598	Ian Ballinger (NZL) 597
1972	Ho Jun Li (PRK) 599	Victor Auer (USA) 598	Nicolae Rotaru (ROM) 595
1976	Karlheinz Smieszek (FRG) 599	Ulrich Lind (FRG) 597	Gennadiy Lushchikov (URS) 595
1980	Karoly Varga (HUN) 599	Hellfried Heilfort (GDR) 599	Petar Zapianov (BUL) 598

[1] In 1908 and 1912 any position allowed; in 1920 it was a standing position. [2] Range found to be marginally short—record not allowed. 1896–1906, 1928 Event not held

DISCONTINUED EVENTS
FREE RIFLE

	Gold	*Silver*	*Bronze*
1896[1]	Pantelis Karasevdas (GRE) 2320	P Pavlidis (GRE) 1978	Nicolaos Tricoupes (GRE) 1718
1906[2]	Marcel de Stadelhofen (SUI) 243	Konrad Stäheli (SUI) 238	Léon Moreaux (FRA) 234
1906[3]	Gudbrand Skatteboe (NOR)	—	—
1906[4]	Konrad Stäheli (SUI)		
1906[5]	Gudbrand Skatteboe (NOR)	—	—
1908[6]	Jerry Millner (GBR) 98	Kellogg Casey (USA) 93	Maurice Blood (GBR) 92

[1] Over 200 m.   [2] Any position (300 m).   [3] Prone (300 m).   [4] Kneeling (300 m).   [5] Standing (300 m).   [6] Over 1000 yards.   1900–1904 Event not held

FREE RIFLE (Team)

	Gold	Silver	Bronze
1906	SWITZERLAND 4596	NORWAY 4534	FRANCE 4511
1908	NORWAY 5055	SWEDEN 4711	FRANCE 4652
1912	SWEDEN 5655	NORWAY 5605	DENMARK 5529
1920	UNITED STATES 4876	NORWAY 4741	SWITZERLAND 4698
1924	UNITED STATES 676	FRANCE 646	HAITI 646

1896–1904 Event not held

MILITARY RIFLE

	Gold	Silver	Bronze
1900[1]	Emil Kellenberger (SUI) 930	Anders Nielsen (DEN) 921	Ole Östmo (NOR) 917
1900[2]	Lars Madsen (DEN) 305	Ole Östmo (NOR) 299	Charles du Verger (BEL) 298
1900[3]	Konrad Stäheli (SUI) 324	Emil Kellenberger (SUI) 314	—
		Anders Nielsen (DEN) 314	
1900[4]	Achille Paroche (FRA) 332	Anders Nielsen (DEN) 330	Ole Östmo (NOR) 329
1906[5]	Léon Moreaux (FRA) 187	Louis Richardet (SUI) 187	Jean Reich (SUI) 183
1906[6]	Louis Richardet (SUI) 238	Jean Reich (SUI) 234	Raoul de Boigne (FRA) 232
1912[1]	Sándor Prokopp (HUN) 97	Carl Osburn (USA) 96	Embret Skogen (NOR) 95
1912[7]	Paul Colas (FRA) 94	Carl Osburn (USA) 94	Joseph Jackson (USA) 93
1920[4]	Otto Olsen (NOR) 60	Léon Johnson (FRA) 59	Fritz Kuchen (SUI) 59
1920[2]	Carl Osburn (USA) 56	Lars Madsen (DEN) 55	Lawrence Nuesslein (USA) 54
1920[8]	Hugo Johansson (SWE) 58	Mauritz Eriksson (SWE) 56	Lloyd Spooner (USA) 56

1908 Event not held

MILITARY RIFLE (Team)

	Gold	Silver	Bronze
1900	SWITZERLAND 4399	NORWAY 4290	FRANCE 4278
1908	UNITED STATES 2531	GREAT BRITAIN 2497	CANADA 2439
1912	UNITED STATES 1687	GREAT BRITAIN 1602	SWEDEN 1570
1920[2]	DENMARK 266	UNITED STATES 255	SWEDEN 255
1920[4]	UNITED STATES 289	FRANCE 283	FINLAND 281
1920[8]	UNITED STATES 287	SOUTH AFRICA 287	SWEDEN 287
1920[9]	UNITED STATES 573	NORWAY 565	SWITZERLAND 563

[1] Three positions (300 m).   [2] Standing (300 m).   [3] Kneeling (300 m).   [4] Prone (300 m).   [5] Standing or kneeling (200 m).   [6] Standing or kneeling (300 m).
[7] Any position (600 m).   [8] Prone (600 m).   [9] Prone (300 m and 600 m).   1896, 1904 Event not held

SMALL BORE RIFLE

	Gold	Silver	Bronze
1908[1]	A F Fleming (GBR) 24	M K Matthews (GBR) 24	W B Marsden (GBR) 24
1908[2]	William Styles (GBR) 45	H I Hawkins (GBR) 45	E J Amoore (GBR) 45
1912[2]	Wilhelm Carlberg (SWE) 242	Johan von Holst (SWE) 233	Gustaf Ericsson (SWE) 231

[1] Moving target.   [2] Disappearing target.

SMALL BORE RIFLE (Team)

	Gold	Silver	Bronze
1908	GREAT BRITAIN 771	SWEDEN 737	FRANCE 710
1912[3]	SWEDEN 925	GREAT BRITAIN 917	UNITED STATES 881
1912[4]	GREAT BRITAIN 762	SWEDEN 748	UNITED STATES 744
1920	UNITED STATES 1899	SWEDEN 1873	NORWAY 1866

[3] Over 25 m.   [4] Over 50 m.

LIVE PIGEON SHOOTING

	Gold	Silver	Bronze
1900	Léon de Lunden (BEL) 21	Maurice Faure (FRA) 20	D MacIntosh (AUS) 18
			C Robinson (GBR) 18

CLAY PIGEONS (Team)

Gold	Silver	Bronze
1908 GREAT BRITAIN 407	CANADA 405	GREAT BRITAIN 372
1912 UNITED STATES 532	GREAT BRITAIN 511	GERMANY 510
1920 UNITED STATES 547	BELGIUM 503	SWEDEN 500
1924 UNITED STATES 363	CANADA 360	FINLAND 360

RUNNING DEER SHOOTING

Gold	Silver	Bronze
1908[1] Oscar Swahn (SWE) 25	Ted Ranken (GBR) 24	A E Rogers (GBR) 24
1908[2] Walter Winans (USA) 46	Ted Ranken (GBR) 46	Oscar Swahn (SWE) 38
1912[1] Alfred Swahn (SWE) 41	Ake Lundeberg (SWE) 41	Nestori Toivonen (FIN) 41
1912[2] Ake Lundeberg (SWE) 79	Edvard Benedicks (SWE) 74	Oscar Swahn (SWE) 72
1920[1] Otto Olsen (NOR) 43	Alfred Swahn (SWE) 41	Harald Natwig (NOR) 41
1920[2] Ole Lilloe-Olsen (NOR) 82	Fredrik Landelius (SWE) 77	Einar Liberg (NOR) 71
1924[1] John Boles (USA) 40	C W Mackworth-Praed (GBR) 39	Otto Olsen (NOR) 39
1924[2] Ole Lilloe-Olsen (NOR) 76	C W Mackworth-Praed (GBR) 72	Alfred Swahn (SWE) 72

[1] Single shot   [2] Double shot

RUNNING DEER SHOOTING (Team)

Gold	Silver	Bronze
1908 SWEDEN 86	GREAT BRITAIN 85	—
1912 SWEDEN 151	UNITED STATES 132	FINLAND 123
1920[1] NORWAY 178	FINLAND 159	UNITED STATES 158
1920[2] NORWAY 343	SWEDEN 336	FINLAND 284
1924[1] NORWAY 160	SWEDEN 154	UNITED STATES 158
1924[2] GREAT BRITAIN 263	NORWAY 262	SWEDEN 250

[1] Single shot.   [2] Double shot.

RUNNING DEER SHOOTING (Single & Double Shot)

Gold	Silver	Bronze
1952 John Larsen (NOR) 413	Per Olof Sköldberg (SWE) 409	Tauno Mäki (FIN) 407
1956 Vitaliy Romanenko (URS) 441	Per Olof Sköldberg (SWE) 432	Vladimir Sevrugin (URS) 429

MILITARY REVOLVER

Gold	Silver	Bronze
1896 John Paine (USA) 442	Sumner Paine (USA) 380	N. Morakis (GRE) 205
1906 Louis Richardet (SUI) 253	Alexandros Theophilakis (GRE) 250	Georgios Skotadis (GRE) 240
1906[1] Jean Fouconnier (FRA) 219	Raoul de Boigne (FRA) 219	Hermann Martin (FRA) 215

[1] Model 1873.   1900–1904 Event not held

TEAM EVENT

Gold	Silver	Bronze
1900 SWITZERLAND 2271	FRANCE 2203	NETHERLANDS 1876
1908 UNITED STATES 1914	BELGIUM 1863	GREAT BRITAIN 1817
1912[1] UNITED STATES 1916	SWEDEN 1849	GREAT BRITAIN 1804
1912[2] SWEDEN 1145	RUSSIA d.n.a.	GREAT BRITAIN d.n.a.
1920[1] UNITED STATES 2372	SWEDEN 2289	BRAZIL 2264
1920[2] UNITED STATES 1310	GREECE 1285	SWITZERLAND 1270

[1] Over 50 m.   [2] Over 30 m.   1904–1906 Event not held

DUELLING PISTOL

Gold	Silver	Bronze
1906[1] Léon Moreaux (FRA) 242	Cesare Liverziani (ITA) 233	Maurice Lecoq (FRA) 231
1906[2] Konstantinos Skarlatos (GRE) 133	Johann von Holst (SWE) 115	Wilhelm Carlberg (SWE) 115

[1] Over 20 m.   [2] Over 25 m.   1896–1904 Event not held

SHOOTING—MEDALS

	Gold	Silver	Bronze	Total		Gold	Silver	Bronze	Total
UNITED STATES	40	22	17	79	BRAZIL	1	1	1	3
SWEDEN	13	21	18	52	BULGARIA	—	1	1	2
USSR	13	15	13	41[1]	NETHERLANDS	—	1	1	2
GREAT BRITAIN	11	13	16	40	JAPAN	—	—	2	2
FRANCE	11	13	12	36	NORTH KOREA (PRK)	1	—	—	1
NORWAY	15	7	10	32	PERU	1	—	—	1
SWITZERLAND	11	8	10	29	ARGENTINA	—	1	—	1
GREECE	5	7	6	18	COLOMBIA	—	1	—	1
DENMARK	3	7	6	16	MEXICO	—	1	—	1
FINLAND	3	5	8	16	PORTUGAL	—	1	—	1
GERMANY (FRG)	5	6	4	15	SOUTH AFRICA	—	1	—	1
GDR	2	7	5	14	SPAIN	—	1	—	1
HUNGARY	6	3	4	13	AUSTRALIA	—	—	1	1
ITALY	5	3	5	13	CUBA	—	—	1	1
ROMANIA	4	3	3	10	HAITI	—	—	1	1
CANADA	3	3	2	8	NEW ZEALAND	—	—	1	1
BELGIUM	2	3	1	6	VENEZUELA	—	—	1	1
POLAND	2	1	3	6					
CZECHOSLOVAKIA	2	2	1	5		160	158	157	475
AUSTRIA	1	—	3	4					

[1] One silver and one bronze in 1912 for Russia.

SOCCER

There were unofficial matches at Athens in 1896 when after two Greek towns had played an eliminator, the winner, Smyrna, was defeated by a Danish side 15–0. Although also sometimes considered to be unofficial, the tournaments of 1900, 1904 and 1906 are usually counted in medal tables. Therefore soccer was the first team game to be included in the Olympic Games and the first goal was scored by Great Britain (represented by Upton Park FC) in their match against France (4–0) in 1900. The 1904 tournament only had three entries, one Canadian and two American teams, while the 1906 soccer was a repeat of 1896 with Denmark again defeating Smyrna. This latter team contained five Britons named Whittal, who, if they were brothers as seems likely, set some sort of Olympic record. With the founding of FIFA (Fédération Internationale de Football Association) in 1904 Olympic soccer came under their control and from 1908 the competition grew in stature. In 1920 the first non-European country, Egypt, (excepting the North Americans of 1904) entered and by 1924 there were 22 countries competing. That tournament and the next was won by Uruguay—but they never again took part in Olympic soccer. Two years after their Amsterdam victory Uruguay won the inaugural World Cup in 1930 with nine of their Olympic team playing. Only three other footballers, all Italian, have been in both Olympic (1936) and World Cup (1938) winning sides. Over the years there was considerable disillusionment with the interpretation of the term 'amateur' as applied to the Games, similar to the troubles in ice hockey. These arguments about pseudo-amateurs have been exacerbated with the entry of the Eastern European powers into the game after 1948. Great Britain, after three gold medals in the early days, did not enter in 1924 or 1928 due to disagreement between the Football Association and FIFA about broken time payments to amateurs. In 1952 qualifying rounds were introduced and in 1972 there was a record entry of 91 teams. For the 1984 tournament players who have taken part in the 1982 World Cup (qualifying or final rounds) will not be eligible. FIFA is also considering imposing an age limit of 23 years for players in Olympic tournaments after 1984.

The highest team score in the Games was the 17–1 defeat of France by Denmark in 1908. During that game the Danish centre-forward Sophus Nielsen scored ten goals, a record that was equalled by Gottfried Fuchs for Germany when they beat Russia 16–0 in 1912. The highest team score in a final since 1908 occurred when

Hungary (4) beat Belgium (1) in 1968. The most goals scored by an individual in one tournament is twelve by Ferenc Bene (HUN) in 1964. The most scored in Olympic soccer by an individual is thirteen by Sophus Nielsen (DEN) 1908–1912, and by Antal Dunai (HUN) 1968–1972.

Highest Scoring Individuals in Olympic Tournaments

1908	11	Sophus Nielsen (DEN)
1912	10	Gottfried Fuchs (GER)
1920	7	Herbert Karlsson (SWE)
1924	8	Pedro Patrone (URU)
1928	7	Domingo Tarasconi (ARG)
1936	7	Annibale Frossi (ITA)
1948	7	Gunnar Nordahl (SWE) & Karl Aage Hansen (DEN)
1952	7	Branko Zebec (YUG) & Rajko Mitic (YUG)
1956	4	Dimiter Milanov (BUL) & Neville d'Souza (IND)
1960	7	Milan Galic (YUG) & Borivoje Kostic (YUG)
1964	12	Ferenc Bene (HUN)
1968	7	Kunishige Kamamoto (JPN)
1972	9	Kazimierz Deyna (POL)
1976	6	Andrzej Szarmach (POL)
1980	5	Sergey Andreyev (URS)

There has only been one draw in an Olympic final. That was in 1928 between Uruguay and Argentina (1–1), and the replay was won by the defending champions Uruguay 2–1.

Hungary is the only country to win on three occasions, 1952, 1964 and 1968. Their team which won in Helsinki was virtually the same team that 16 months later inflicted the first home defeat on England's professionals at Wembley stadium.

The most successful player has been Dezsö Nowak (HUN) who added gold medals in 1964 and 1968 to the bronze he won in 1960. Of the nine other players to win two gold medals only Arthur Berry and Vivian Woodward (both GBR) in 1908–1912, were not Uruguayan. Two of the latter, Antonio and Santos Urdinarán became the first brothers to win soccer gold medals in 1924. This feat was surpassed by the three Swedish Nordahl brothers, Bertil, Knut and Gunnar, in 1948. In 1960 another trio, Hans, Flemming and Harald Nielsen (DEN) gained silver medals. In 1908 the Middleboe brothers, Nils and Kristian had also won silvers with the Danish team, which included Harald Bohr, the brother of the famous atomic physicist Niels. The youngest gold medallist was Pedro Petrone (URU) in 1924 just two days short of his 19th birthday. The oldest was Vivian Woodward (GBR), who had just helped his club Chelsea to get back into the British First Division, aged 33 yr 32 days in the 1912 final.

One of the most remarkable goals in international football involved the Swedish centre-forward Gunnar Nordahl in the 1948 semi-final against Denmark. Unexpectedly caught offside by a quick reversal of play Nordahl realized that his team were attacking again. With lightning presence of mind he leapt into the back of the Danish goal, taking himself off the field of play, and duly caught the goal scoring header from his teammate Henry Carlsson with the goalkeeper lying on the ground

The 1912 soccer champions. After winning its second successive gold medal Britain never again won a medal in the Olympic football competition.

5 metres away.

In the 1920 final between Belgium and Czechoslovakia the latter team walked off the field in protest against the referee before half-time when they were 2–0 down. The match was abandoned and the Czechs disqualified. The 1936 tournament resulted in many incidents not least the withdrawal of the Peruvian team when its win over Austria in the second round was ordered to be re-played. Austria went on to reach the final.

SOCCER

	Gold	Silver	Bronze
1900	Great Britain	France	Belgium
1904	Canada	United States	United States
1906	Denmark	Greece	Greece
1908	Great Britain	Denmark	Netherlands
1912	Great Britain	Denmark	Netherlands
1920	Belgium	Spain	Netherlands
1924	Uruguay	Switzerland	Sweden
1928	Uruguay	Argentina	Italy
1936	Italy	Austria	Norway
1948	Sweden	Yugoslavia	Denmark
1952	Hungary	Yugoslavia	Sweden
1956	USSR	Yugoslavia	Bulgaria
1960	Yugoslavia	Denmark	Hungary
1964	Hungary	Czechoslovakia	Germany
1968	Hungary	Bulgaria	Japan
1972	Poland	Hungary	GDR[1]
			USSR[1]
1976	GDR	Poland	USSR
1980	Czechoslovakia	GDR	USSR

[1] Tie declared after extra time played. 1896, 1932 Event not held

After many years in the doldrums Olympic soccer had a revival in 1980 when the 56 games of the tournament, played in Moscow, Leningrad, Minsk and Kiev, attracted nearly two million spectators, over a third of all spectators for the Games.

SOCCER—MEDALS

	Gold	Silver	Bronze	Total
HUNGARY	3	1	1	5
DENMARK	1	3	1	5
YUGOSLAVIA	1	3	—	4
USSR	1	—	3	4
GREAT BRITAIN	3	—	—	3
GDR	1	1	1	3
SWEDEN	1	—	2	3
NETHERLANDS	—	—	3	3
URUGUAY	2	—	—	2
CZECHOSLOVAKIA	1	1	—	2
POLAND	1	1	—	2
BELGIUM	1	—	1	2
ITALY	1	—	1	2
BULGARIA	—	1	1	2
GREECE	—	1	1	2
UNITED STATES	—	1	1	2
CANADA	1	—	—	1
ARGENTINA	—	1	—	1
AUSTRIA	—	1	—	1
FRANCE	—	1	—	1
SPAIN	—	1	—	1
SWITZERLAND	—	1	—	1
GERMANY	—	—	1	1
JAPAN	—	—	1	1
NORWAY	—	—	1	1
	18	18	19[1]	55

[1] Third place tie in 1972

SWIMMING

Swimming has been an integral part of the Olympics from 1896 when the swimming events were held in the Bay of Zea near Piraeus. Competitors used to warm water were taken aback by the cold of the open sea. The first champion was Alfred Hajos (HUN) who won the 100 m freestyle on 11 April. Hajos, who was really named Guttmann and later changed officially to his alias, twice played soccer for his national side, and in later life won an Olympic artistic silver medal in the architecture category in 1924. The first female champion (women's events were

The start of the 200 m breaststroke final in the giant pool in the centre of the White City stadium, London in 1908.

introduced in 1912) was Australia's Fanny Durack in the 100 m freestyle.

The first Olympic competitions in a pool were those of 1908 when one which was 100 m long was constructed inside the track at the White City Stadium, London. Before that competitions had been held in the open sea (1896, 1906), in the River Seine (1900) and in an artificial lake (1904). The first 50 m pool came in 1924, outdoors, with the first one indoors at London in 1948. In 1904 Emil Rausch (GER) was the last person to win an Olympic title (880 yards and 1 mile) using the side-stroke technique.

The most successful swimmer in Olympic history was Mark Spitz (USA) with nine gold medals plus a silver and a bronze in 1968 and 1972. His seven golds in one Games (1972) is unmatched in any sport. The most individual gold medals won is four by Charles Daniels (USA) 1904–1908, Roland Matthes (GDR) 1968–1972 and Spitz in 1972. The most gold medals won by a woman is four by Dawn Fraser (AUS) 1956–1964 and Kornelia Ender (GDR) all in 1976 (itself a record for one Games by a woman). Fraser is the only swimmer, male or female, to win the same event (100 m freestyle) on three successive occasions. Three women have won a record eight medals: Fraser and Ender, both with four silvers to add to their four golds; and Shirley Babashoff (USA) who won two gold and six silver medals in 1972 and 1976. Both Mark Spitz and Shirley Babashoff set an endurance record of sorts when in 1972 and 1976 respectively they each took part in 13 races over a period of 8 days.

The first man to defend successfully an Olympic swimming title was Charles Daniels (USA) in the 100 m freestyle in 1908. The first woman to do so was Martha Norelius (USA) in 1928 in the 400 m freestyle. She was born in Sweden and her father had won a gold medal as a member of the winning Swedish gymnastics team in 1912. She later married the 1928 Canadian silver medallist oarsman Joseph Wright.

The youngest swimmer to win an Olympic gold medal was Deborah 'Pokey' Watson (USA) in the 4 × 100 m freestyle relay in 1964 aged 14 yr 96 days. The youngest male was Kusuo Kitamura (JPN) who won the 1500 m in 1932 aged 14 yr 309 days. The youngest known medallist in any sport in the Olympic Games was Inge Sörensen (DEN) aged 12 yr 24 days when she won the bronze medal in the 200 m breaststroke in 1936. The youngest known competitor in the Summer Games was Liana Vicens of Puerto Rico when she competed in the 1968 Games aged 11 yr 328 days. The oldest gold medallist was Louis Handley (USA) aged 30 yr 206 days as a member of the winning 4 × 50 yards relay team in 1904. The oldest female champion was Ursula Happe (GER) aged 30 yr 41 days when winning the 200 m breaststroke in 1956. The oldest medallist was William Henry (GBR) a last minute replacement in the 4 × 250 m relay in 1906 aged 46 yr 301 days.

The closest win in Olympic swimming was that by Gunnar Larsson (SWE) over Tim McKee (USA) in 1972 in the 400 m individual medley. The margin was two-thousandths of a second (4:31·981 to 4:31·983) or about 3 millimetres (estimated to be the length grown by a fingernail in 3 weeks). In 1964 there was an even closer decision in the 100 m freestyle when Hans-Joachim Klein (GER) was awarded the bronze medal over Gary Ilman (USA) because the timing indicated that he was one-thousandth of a second ahead. These results led to a change in the

Australia's Fanny Durack was the first woman to win an Olympic swimming gold medal.

The first of America's swimming superstars, Charles Daniels, who won five gold, one silver and three bronze medals in three Games.

Britain's 4 × 100 m relay champions of 1912 in surprisingly revealing costumes. From the left, Bella Moore, Jennie Fletcher, the chaperone Clara Jarvis, Anne Speirs and Irene Steer.

The legendary Johnny Weissmuller (USA), winner of five gold medals, with Katsuo Takaishi (JAP) the 1928 bronze medallist.

The youngest male swimmer to win an Olympic gold medal, Kusuo Kitamura (JAP) winner of the 1500 m in 1932.

Start of the women's 100 m freestyle final in Berlin in 1936 with the eventual winner, Ria Mastenbroek, in lane five.

rules of international swimming so that timings and placings are now decided to hundredths only, and the above would now be given as a dead heats.

There was another close decision in the 100 m freestyle in 1960 when Lance Larson (USA) was timed (manually) at one-tenth faster than John Devitt (AUS), but the judges placed the Australian first—and that is how the result remained despite protests. In the 1912 100 m competition the three best American swimmers missed the semi-finals because they had been told that there would not be any. Following protests it was agreed that if they were timed, in a special race, at faster than the slowest qualifier from those semi-finals then they would go through to the final. The outstanding Hawaiian swimmer Duke Kahanamoku was so incensed that he broke the world record, and then won the final. In 1920 the final had to be re-swum after the Australian, William Herald, had complained that he was impeded by Norman Ross (USA). This was before lane dividers were used. Kahanamoku won the second final but in a time 1 second slower than he had won the first (but his time in

that of 60·4 was recognized as a world record). Kahanamoku was the first of a line of great Hawaiian swimmers, and one of the first Americans to use the crawl stroke. He was born into the Hawaiian Royal Family and was named 'Duke' after the Duke of Edinburgh, Queen Victoria's second son, who was visiting the Royal Palace at the time. He was one of the pioneers of surfing, made a number of movies in Hollywood, was elected Sheriff of Honolulu, and was the oldest man to win an individual swimming gold medal in 1920 when 5 days past his 30th birthday.

The movies have attracted a number of Olympians including Austrian-born Johnny Weissmuller (USA) who won five gold medals 1924–1928 and then became the most famous 'Tarzan', Aileen Riggin (USA) the 1920 diving champion and Eleanor Holm (USA) the 1932 backstroke champion both took their good looks into movies, while Holm's teammate Clarence 'Buster' Crabbe, the 1932 400 m freestyle champion became 'Flash Gordon' and 'Buck Rogers' in children's serials.

Gertrude Ederle (USA) and Greta Andersen (DEN), gold medallists in 1924 and 1948 respectively, both later set Channel swimming records.

Mexico's first ever swimming gold medallist, Felipe Munoz who won the 200 m breaststroke in 1968, was nicknamed 'Tibio' which means

Four swimming and diving champions from the 1932 Games, left to right, Micky Galitzen, Georgia Coleman, Buster Crabbe, and Helene Madison.

'lukewarm' in English. This was no reflection on his determination but was the result of his father coming from Aguascalientes ('hot water') and his mother from Rio Frio ('cold river').

One of the greatest examples of domination by one country occurred in the women's events of the 1980 Games (albeit affected by the boycott of Moscow by numerous countries). Out of 13 events the GDR won 11 of them and gained a total of 24 medals out of a possible 33 in the individual events. In 1932 Japanese swimmers gained first and second places in four of the five individual events for men, as well as winning the relay. The United States had a similar domination of the men's events in 1948.

DIVING

Diving was introduced into the Games in 1904 for men and 1912 for women. The most successful diver has been Austrian-born Klaus Dibiasi (ITA) with three gold and two silver medals from 1964 to 1976. He is also the only one to win the same event three times and to have gained medals in four celebrations of the Games. Pat McCormick (USA) holds the female record with four gold medals having gained the double in 1952 and 1956. Dorothy Poynton-Hill (USA) 1928–1936 and Paula Myers-Pope (USA) 1952–1960 have won medals in three separate Games. Juno Stover-Irwin (USA) competed in four Games 1948–1960 placing fifth, third, second and fourth respectively in the highboard event.

Pat McCormick (USA) won her second diving double in 1956 only 5 months after having become a mother.

Marjorie Gestring (USA), the youngest person to win an Olympic individual event.

The youngest gold medallist, and the youngest individual champion in the history of the Olympic Games at any sport, was Marjorie Gestring (USA) who won the 1936 springboard title aged 13 yr 268 days. The youngest male diver to win a gold medal was Albert Zürner (GER) aged 18 yr 170 days when taking the 1908 springboard title. The youngest medallist was Dorothy Poynton (USA) who won a silver in 1928 aged 13 yr 23 days, and the youngest male medallist was Nils Skoglund (SWE) aged 14 yr 10 days when winning the silver in the 1928 plain diving. The oldest gold medallist was Hjalmar Johansson (SWE) aged 34 yr 186 days for the plain diving in 1908, and he was also the oldest medallist four years later with a silver aged 38 yr 173 days.

Four divers, three women and a man, have won medals at swimming as well as their own sport. Aileen Riggin (USA) won diving medals in 1920 (gold) and 1924 (silver) and a bronze in the 100 m backstroke at Paris. Hjördis Töpel (SWE) won bronzes at diving and in the 4 × 100 m relay, also in 1924. Katherine Rawls (USA) won a silver in the 1936 springboard and a bronze in the 4 × 100 m relay. Georg Hoffmann (GER) won silvers in 1904 at diving and the 100 m backstroke.

The first Olympic diver to be awarded a maximum 10·00 for a dive was Canadian-born Pete Desjardins (USA) in the 1928 springboard competition. It seemed he had failed to gain his expected double when the Egyptian diver Farid Simaika scored more points in the highboard event, and was declared the winner, but the result was then reversed as Desjardins had gained more first placement marks from the judges.

The most successful husband and wife team in diving was Clarence and Elizabeth (née Becker) Pinkston (USA) who between them won three gold, two silver and two bronze medals from 1920 to 1928.

WATER POLO

The first Olympic competition in 1900 was won by the Osborne Swimming Club, Manchester representing Great Britain.

Dezsö Gyarmati (right) **and Gyorgy Karpati won six gold, one silver and two bronze medals between them as members of Hungary's water polo teams from 1948 to 1964.**

Five players have won three gold medals each: George Wilkinson (GBR) 1900, 1908 and 1912; Paul Radomilovic (GBR) and Charles Smith (GBR) 1908, 1912 and 1920; Dezsö Gyarmati (HUN) and György Kárpáti (HUN) 1952, 1956

and 1964. Of these Radomilovic, Welsh-born of a Greek father and Irish mother, also won another gold in the British 4 × 200 m relay team in 1908, and competed in a record six Olympic tournaments from 1906 to 1928. Gyarmati was the most successful water polo player, adding a silver in 1948 and a bronze in 1960, and is one of the few Olympians in any sport to win medals in five Games. He is also the head of a remarkable Olympic family as his wife Eva Szekely won a gold medal (1952) and a silver (1956) in the 200 m breaststroke, and their daughter Andrea won silver and bronze medals in the 1972 backstroke and butterfly events respectively. Andrea then added to the family total of medals by marrying Mihaly Hesz (HUN) the canoeist who won a gold (1968 K1) and a silver (1964 K1).

The oldest gold medallist was Charles Smith (GBR) aged 41 yr 217 days in the 1920 final, while the youngest was György Kárpáti (HUN) aged 17 yr 40 days in 1952. Two sets of brothers have won gold medals in the same team; Ferenc and Alajos Keserü (HUN) in 1932, and Tulio and Franco Pandolfini (ITA) in 1948.

In 1924 Johnny Weissmuller the great American swimmer who won three gold medals at his specialty also gained a bronze medal as a member of the US water polo team.

In 1920 Great Britain beat Belgium in the final but the victory ceremony was delayed for some days because the band refused to play the British anthem and officials would not raise the Union Jack.

OLYMPIC RECORDS—SWIMMING

Event	min/sec	Name & Country	Year
Men			
100 metres freestyle	49·99	James Montgomery (USA)	1976
200 metres freestyle	1:49·81	Sergey Kopliakov (URS)	1980
400 metres freestyle	3:51·31	Vladimir Salnikov (URS)	1980
1500 metres freestyle	14:58·27	Vladimir Salnikov (URS)	1980
4 × 100 metres freestyle relay	3:26·42	USA	1972
4 × 200 metres freestyle relay	7:23·22	USA	1976
100 metres breaststroke	1:03·11	John Hencken (USA)	1976
200 metres breaststroke	2:15·11	David Wilkie (GBR)	1976
100 metres butterfly	54·27	Mark Spitz (USA)	1972
200 metres butterfly	1:59·23	Michael Bruner (USA)	1976
100 metres backstroke	55·49	John Naber (USA)	1976
200 metres backstroke	1:59·19	John Naber (USA)	1976
200 metres medley	2:07·17	Gunnar Larsson (SWE)	1972
400 metres medley	4:22·89	Aleksandr Sidorenko (URS)	1980
4 × 100 metres medley relay	3:42·22	USA	1976

Women

100 metres freestyle	54·79	Barbara Krause (GDR)	1980
200 metres freestyle	1:58·33	Barbara Krause (GDR)	1980
400 metres freestyle	4:08·76	Ines Diers (GDR)	1980
800 metres freestyle	8:28·90	Michelle Ford (AUS)	1980
4 × 100 metres freestyle relay	3:42·71	GDR	1980
100 metres breaststroke	1:10·11	Ute Geweniger (GDR)	1980
200 metres breaststroke	2:29·54	Lina Kachushite (URS)	1980
100 metres butterfly	1:00·13	Kornelia Ender (GDR)	1976
200 metres butterfly	2:10·44	Ines Geissler (GDR)	1980
100 metres backstroke	1:00·86	Rica Reinisch (GDR)	1980
200 metres backstroke	2:11·77	Rica Reinisch (GDR)	1980
200 metres medley	2:23·07	Shane Gould (AUS)	1972
400 metres medley	4:36·29	Petra Schneider (GDR)	1980
4 × 100 metres medley relay	4:06·67	GDR	1980

100 METRES FREESTYLE

	Gold	Silver	Bronze
1896	Alfred Hajós (HUN) 1:22·2	Efstathios Choraphas (GRE) 1:23·0	Otto Herschmann (AUT) d.n.a.
1904[1]	Zóltán von Halmay (HUN) 1:02·8	Charles Daniels (USA) d.n.a.	Scott Leary (USA) d.n.a.
1906	Charles Daniels (USA) 1:13·4	Zóltán von Halmay (HUN) 1:14·2	Cecil Healy (AUS) d.n.a.
1908	Charles Daniels (USA) 1:05·6	Zóltán von Halmay (HUN) 1:06·2	Harald Julin (SWE) 1:08·0
1912	Duke Kahanamoku (USA) 1:03·4	Cecil Healy (AUS) 1:04·6	Kenneth Huszagh (USA) 1:05·6
1920	Duke Kahanamoku (USA) 1:01·4	Pua Kealoha (USA) 1:02·2	William Harris (USA) 1:03·0
1924	Johnny Weissmuller (USA) 59·0	Duke Kahanamoku (USA) 1:01·4	Sam Kahanamoku (USA) 1:01·8
1928	Johnny Weissmuller (USA) 58·6	István Bárány (HUN) 59·8	Katsuo Takaishi (JPN) 1:00·0
1932	Yasuji Miyazaki (JPN) 58·2	Tatsugo Kawaishi (JPN) 58·6	Albert Schwartz (USA) 58·8
1936	Ferenc Csik (HUN) 57·6	Masanori Yusa (JPN) 57·9	Shigeo Arai (JPN) 58·0
1948	Walter Ris (USA) 57·3	Alan Ford (USA) 57·8	Géza Kádas (HUN) 58·1
1952	Clarke Scholes (USA) 57·4	Hiroshi Suzuki (JPN) 57·4	Göran Larsson (SWE) 58·2
1956	Jon Henricks (AUS) 55·4	John Devitt (AUS) 55·8	Gary Chapman (AUS) 56·7
1960	John Devitt (AUS) 55·2	Lance Larson (USA) 55·2	Manuel dos Santos (BRA) 55·4
1964	Don Schollander (USA) 53·4	Bobbie McGregor (GBR) 53·5	Hans-Joachim Klein (GER) 54·0
1968	Mike Wenden (AUS) 52·2	Ken Walsh (USA) 52·8	Mark Spitz (USA) 53·0
1972	Mark Spitz (USA) 51·22	Jerry Heidenreich (USA) 51·65	Vladimir Bure (URS) 51·77
1976	Jim Montgomery (USA) 49·99	Jack Babashoff (USA) 50·81	Peter Nocke (FRG) 51·31
1980	Jörg Woithe (GDR) 50·40	Per Holmertz (SWE) 50·91	Per Johansson (SWE) 51·29

[1] 100 yards.   1900 Event not held

200 METRES FREESTYLE

	Gold	Silver	Bronze
1900	Frederick Lane (AUS) 2:25·2	Zóltán von Halmay (HUN) 2:31·4	Karl Ruberl (AUT) 2:32·0
1904[1]	Charles Daniels (USA) 2:44·2	Francis Gailey (USA) 2:46·0	Emil Rausch (GER) 2:56·0
1968	Mike Wenden (AUS) 1:55·2	Don Schollander (USA) 1:55·8	John Nelson (USA) 1:58·1
1972	Mark Spitz (USA) 1:52·78	Steven Genter (USA) 1:53·73	Werner Lampe (FRG) 1:53·99
1976	Bruce Furniss (USA) 1:50·29	John Naber (USA) 1:50·50	Jim Montgomery (USA) 1:50·58
1980	Sergey Kopliakov (URS) 1:49·81	Andrej Krylov (URS) 1:50·76	Graeme Brewer (AUS) 1:51·60

[1] 220 yards.   1896, 1906–1964 Event not held

400 METRES FREESTYLE

	Gold	Silver	Bronze
1896[1]	Paul Neumann (AUT) 8:12·6	Antonios Pepanos (GRE) 30 m	Efstathios Choraphas (GRE) d.n.a.
1904[2]	Charles Daniels (USA) 6:16·2	Francis Gailey (USA) 6:22·0	Otto Wahle (AUT) 6:39·0
1906	Otto Scheff (AUT) 6:23·8	Henry Taylor (GBR) 6:24·4	John Jarvis (GBR) 6:27·2
1908	Henry Taylor (GBR) 5:36·8	Frank Beaurepaire (AUS) 5:44·2	Otto Scheff (AUT) 5:46·0
1912	George Hodgson (CAN) 5:24·4	John Hatfield (GBR) 5:25·8	Harold Hardwick (AUS) 5:31·2
1920	Norman Ross (USA) 5:26·8	Ludy Langer (USA) 5:29·2	George Vernot (CAN) 5:29·8
1924	Johnny Weissmuller (USA) 5:04·2	Arne Borg (SWE) 5:05·6	Andrew Charlton (AUS) 5:06·6
1928	Alberto Zorilla (ARG) 5:01·6	Andrew Charlton (AUS) 5:03·6	Arne Borg (SWE) 5:04·6
1932	Buster Crabbe (USA) 4:48·4	Jean Taris (FRA) 4:48·5	Tautomu Oyokota (JPN) 4:52·3
1936	Jack Medica (USA) 4:44·5	Shumpei Uto (JPN) 4:45·6	Shozo Makino (JPN) 4:48·1

1948	William Smith (USA) 4:41·0	James McLane (USA) 4:43·4	John Marshall (AUS) 4:47·7
1952	Jean Boiteux (FRA) 4:30·7	Ford Konno (USA) 4:31·3	Per-Olof Ostrand (SWE) 4:35·2
1956	Murray Rose (AUS) 4:27·3	Tsuyoshi Yamanaka (JPN) 4:30·4	George Breen (USA) 4:32·5
1960	Murray Rose (AUS) 4:18·3	Tsuyoshi Yamanaka (JPN) 4:21·4	John Konrads (AUS) 4:21·8
1964	Don Schollander (USA) 4:12·2	Frank Wiegand (GER) 4:14·9	Allan Wood (AUS) 4:15·1
1968	Mike Burton (USA) 4:09·0	Ralph Hutton (CAN) 4:11·7	Alain Mosconi (FRA) 4:13·3
1972	Brad Cooper (AUS) 4:00·27	Steven Genter (USA) 4:01·94	Tom McBreen (USA) 4:02·64
1976	Brian Goodell (USA) 3:51·93	Tim Shaw (USA) 3:52·54	Vladimir Raskatov (URS) 3:55·76
1980	Vladimir Salnikov (URS) 3:51·31	Andrej Krylov (URS) 3:53·24	Ivar Stukolkin (URS) 3:53·95

[1] 500 m. [2] 440 yards. 1900 Event not held

100 METRES BACKSTROKE

	Gold	Silver	Bronze
1904[1]	Walter Brack (GER) 1:16·8	Georg Hoffmann (GER) 1:18·0	Georg Zacharias (GER) 1:19·6
1908	Arno Bieberstein (GER) 1:24·6	Ludvig Dam (DEN) 1:26·6	Herbert Haresnape (GBR) 1:27·0
1912	Harry Hebner (USA) 1:21·2	Otto Fahr (GER) 1:22·4	Paul Kellner (GER) 1:24·0
1920	Warren Kealoha (USA) 1:15·2	Ray Kegeris (USA) 1:16·2	Gérard Blitz (BEL) 1:19·0
1924	Warren Kealoha (USA) 1:13·2	Paul Wyatt (USA) 1:15·4	Károly Bartha (HUN) 1:17·8
1928	George Kojac (USA) 1:08·2	Walter Laufer (USA) 1:10·0	Paul Wyatt (USA) 1:12·0
1932	Masaji Kiyokawa (JPN) 1:08·6	Toshio Irie (JPN) 1:09·8	Kentaro Kawatsu (JPN) 1:10·0
1936	Adolf Kiefer (USA) 1:05·9	Albert Van de Weghe (USA) 1:07·7	Masaji Kiyokawa (JPN) 1:08·4
1948	Allen Stack (USA) 1:06·4	Robert Cowell (USA) 1:06·5	Georges Vallerey (FRA) 1:07·8
1952	Yoshinobu Oyakawa (USA) 1:05·4	Gilbert Bozon (FRA) 1:06·2	Jack Taylor (USA) 1:06·4
1956	David Thiele (AUS) 1:02·2	John Monckton (AUS) 1:03·2	Frank McKinney (USA) 1:04·5
1960	David Thiele (AUS) 1:01·9	Frank McKinney (USA) 1:02·1	Robert Bennett (USA) 1:02·3
1968	Roland Matthes (GDR) 58·7	Charles Hickcox (USA) 1:00·2	Ronnie Mills (USA) 1:00·5
1972	Roland Matthes (GDR) 56·58	Mike Stamm (USA) 57·70	John Murphy (USA) 58·35
1976	John Naber (USA) 55·49	Peter Rocca (USA) 56·34	Roland Matthes (GDR) 57·22
1980	Bengt Baron (SWE) 56·53	Viktor Kuznetsov (URS) 56·99	Vladimir Dolgov (URS) 57·63

[1] 100 yards. 1896–1900, 1906, 1964 Event not held

1500 METRES FREESTYLE

	Gold	Silver	Bronze
1896[1]	Alfred Hajós (HUN) 18:22·2	Jean Andreou (GRE) 21:03·4	Efstathios Choraphas (GRE) d.n.a.
1900[2]	John Jarvis (GBR) 13:40·2	Otto Wahle (AUT) 14:53·6	Zóltán von Halmay (HUN) 15:16·4
1904[3]	Emil Rausch (GER) 27:18·2	Géza Kiss (HUN) 28:28·2	Francis Gailey (USA) 28:54·0
1906[3]	Henry Taylor (GBR) 28:28·0	John Jarvis (GBR) 30:13·0	Otto Scheff (AUT) 30:59·0
1908	Henry Taylor (GBR) 22:48·4	Sydney Battersby (GBR) 22:51·2	Frank Beaurepaire (AUS) 22:56·2
1912	George Hodgson (CAN) 22:00·0	John Hatfield (GBR) 22:39·0	Harold Hardwick (AUS) 23:15·4
1920	Norman Ross (USA) 22:23·2	George Vernot (CAN) 22:36·4	Frank Beaurepaire (AUS) 23:04·0
1924	Andrew Charlton (AUS) 20:06·6	Arne Borg (SWE) 20:41·4	Frank Beaurepaire (AUS) 21:48·4
1928	Arne Borg (SWE) 19:51·8	Andrew Charlton (AUS) 20:02·6	Buster Crabbe (USA) 20:28·8
1932	Kusuo Kitamura (JPN) 19:12·4	Shozo Makino (JPN) 19:14·1	James Christy (USA) 19:39·5
1936	Noboru Terada (JPN) 19:13·7	Jack Medica (USA) 19:34·0	Shumpei Uto (JPN) 19:34·5
1948	James McLane (USA) 19:18·5	John Marshall (AUS) 19:31·3	György Mitró (HUN) 19:43·2
1952	Ford Konno (USA) 18:30·0	Shiro Hashizune (JPN) 18:41·4	Tetsuo Okamoto (JPN) 18:51·3
1956	Murray Rose (AUS) 17:58·9	Tsuyoshi Yamanaka (JPN) 18:00·3	George Breen (USA) 18:08·2
1960	John Konrads (AUS) 17:19·6	Murray Rose (AUS) 17:21·7	George Breen (USA) 17:30·6
1964	Bob Windle (AUS) 17:01·7	John Nelson (USA) 17:03·0	Allan Wood (AUS) 17:07·7
1968	Mike Burton (USA) 16:38·9	John Kinsella (USA) 16:57·3	Greg Brough (AUS) 17:04·7
1972	Mike Burton (USA) 15:52·58	Graham Windeatt (AUS) 15:58·48	Doug Northway (USA) 16:09·25
1976	Brian Goodell (USA) 15:02·40	Bobby Hackett (USA) 15:03·91	Steve Holland (AUS) 15:04·66
1980	Vladimir Salnikov (URS) 14:58·27	Aleksandr Chaev (URS) 15:14·30	Max Metzker (AUS) 15:14·49

[1] 1200 m. [2] 1000 m. [3] 1 mile.

200 METRES BACKSTROKE

	Gold	Silver	Bronze
1900	Ernst Hoppenberg (GER) 2:47·0	Karl Ruberl (AUT) 2:56·0	Johannes Drost (HOL) 3:01·0
1964	Jed Graef (USA) 2:10·3	Gary Dilley (USA) 2:10·5	Robert Bennett (USA) 2:13·1
1968	Roland Matthes (GDR) 2:09·6	Mitchell Ivey (USA) 2:10·6	Jack Horsley (USA) 2:10·9
1972	Roland Matthes (GDR) 2:02·82	Mike Stamm (USA) 2:04·09	Mitchell Ivey (USA) 2:04·33

1976	John Naber (USA) 1:59·19	Peter Rocca (USA) 2:00·55	Don Harrigan (USA) 2:01·35
1980	Sandor Wladar (HUN) 2:01·93	Zóltán Verraszto (HUN) 2:02·40	Mark Kerry (AUS) 2:03·14

1896, 1904–1960 Event not held

100 METRES BREASTSTROKE

	Gold	*Silver*	*Bronze*
1968	Don McKenzie (USA) 1:07·7	Vladimir Kossinsky (URS) 1:08·0	Nikolai Pankin (URS) 1:08·0
1972	Nobutaka Taguchi (JPN) 1:04·94	Tom Bruce (USA) 1:05·43	John Hencken (USA) 1:05·61
1976	John Hencken (USA) 1:03·11	David Wilkie (GBR) 1:03·43	Arvidas Iuozaytis (URS) 1:04·23
1980	Duncan Goodhew (GBR) 1:03·34	Arsen Miskarov (URS) 1:03·82	Peter Evans (AUS) 1:03·96

1896–1964 Event not held

200 METRES BREASTSTROKE

	Gold	*Silver*	*Bronze*
1908	Frederick Holman (GBR) 3:09·2	William Robinson (GBR) 3:12·8	Pontus Hansson (SWE) 3:14·6
1912	Walter Barthe (GER) 3:01·8	Wilhelm Lützow (GER) 3:05·2	Kurt Malisch (GER) 3:08·0
1920	Häken Malmroth (SWE) 3:04·4	Thor Henning (SWE) 3:09·2	Arvo Aaltonen (FIN) 3:12·2
1924	Robert Skelton (USA) 2:56·5	Joseph de Combe (BEL) 2:59·2	William Kirschbaum (USA) 3:01·0
1928	Yoshiyuki Tsuruta (JPN) 2:48·8	Erich Rademacher (GER) 2:50·6	Teofilo Yldefonzo (PHI) 2:56·4
1932	Yoshiyuki Tsuruta (JPN) 2:45·4	Reizo Koike (JPN) 2:46·4	Teofilo Yldefonzo (PHI) 2:47·1
1936	Tetsuo Hamuro (JPN) 2:42·5	Erwin Sietas (GER) 2:42·9	Reizo Koike (JPN) 2:44·2
1948	Joseph Verdeur[1] (USA) 2:39·3	Keith Carter (USA) 2:40·2	Robert Sohl (USA) 2:43·9
1952	John Davies[1] (AUS) 2:34·4	Bowen Stassforth (USA) 2:34·7	Herbert Klein (GER) 2:35·9
1956	Masaru Furukawa[2] (JPN) 2:34·7	Masahiro Yoshimura (JPN) 2:36·7	Charis Yunitschev (URS) 2:36·8
1960	William Mulliken (USA) 2:37·4	Yoshihiko Osaki (JPN) 2:38·0	Wieger Mensonides (HOL) 2:39·7
1964	Ian O'Brien (AUS) 2:27·8	Georgy Prokopenko (URS) 2:28·2	Chester Jastremski (USA) 2:29·6
1968	Felipe Munoz (MEX) 2:28·7	Vladimir Kossinsky (URS) 2:29·2	Brian Job (USA) 2:29·9
1972	John Hencken (USA) 2:21·55	David Wilkie (GBR) 2:23·67	Nobutaka Taguchi (JPN) 2:23·88
1976	David Wilkie (GBR) 2:15·11	John Hencken (USA) 2:17·26	Rick Colella (USA) 2:19·20
1980	Robertas Shulpa (URS) 2:15·85	Alban Vermes (HUN) 2:16·93	Arsen Miskarov (URS) 2:17·28

[1] Used then permissible butterfly stroke.   [2] Used then permissible underwater technique.   1896–1906 Event not held

100 METRES BUTTERFLY

	Gold	*Silver*	*Bronze*
1968	Doug Russell (USA) 55·9	Mark Spitz (USA) 56·4	Ross Wales (USA) 57·2
1972	Mark Spitz (USA) 54·27	Bruce Robertson (CAN) 55·56	Jerry Heidenreich (USA) 55·74
1976	Matt Vogel (USA) 54·35	Joe Bottom (USA) 54·50	Gary Hall (USA) 54·65
1980	Pär Arvidsson (SWE) 54·92	Roger Pyttel (GDR) 54·94	David Lopez (ESP) 55·13

1896–1964 Event not held

200 METRES BUTTERFLY

	Gold	*Silver*	*Bronze*
1956	William Yorzyk (USA) 2:19·3	Takashi Ishimoto (JPN) 2:23·8	György Tumpek (HUN) 2:23·9
1960	Mike Troy (USA) 2:12·8	Neville Hayes (AUS) 2:14·6	David Gillanders (USA) 2:15·3
1964	Kevin Berry (AUS) 2:06·6	Carl Robie (USA) 2:07·5	Fred Schmidt (USA) 2:09·3
1968	Carl Robie (USA) 2:08·7	Martyn Woodruff (GBR) 2:09·0	John Ferris (USA) 2:09·3
1972	Mark Spitz (USA) 2:00·70	Gary Hall (USA) 2:02·86	Robin Backhaus (USA) 2:03·23
1976	Mike Bruner (USA) 1:59·23	Steven Gregg (USA) 1:59·54	William Forrester (USA) 1:59·96
1980	Sergey Fesenko (URS) 1:59·76	Phil Hubble (GBR) 2:01·20	Roger Pyttel (GDR) 2:01·39

1896–1952 Event not held

200 METRES INDIVIDUAL MEDLEY

	Gold	*Silver*	*Bronze*
1968	Charles Hickcox (USA) 2:12·0	Greg Buckingham (USA) 2:13·0	John Ferris (USA) 2:13·3
1972	Gunnar Larsson (SWE) 2:07·17	Tim McKee (USA) 2:08·37	Steve Furniss (USA) 2:08·45

1896–1964, 1976–1980 Event not held

400 METRES INDIVIDUAL MEDLEY

	Gold	Silver	Bronze
1964	Richard Roth (USA) 4:45·4	Roy Saari (USA) 4:47·1	Gerhard Hetz (GER) 4:51·0
1968	Charles Hickcox (USA) 4:48·4	Gary Hall (USA) 4:48·7	Michael Holthaus (FRG) 4:51·4
1972	Gunnar Larsson (SWE) 4:31·98	Tim McKee (USA) 4:31·98	András Hargitay (HUN) 4:32·70
1976	Rod Strachan (USA) 4:23·68	Tim McKee (USA) 4:24·62	Andrei Smirnov (URS) 4:26·90
1980	Aleksandr Sidorenko (URS) 4:22·89	Sergey Fesenko (URS) 4:23·43	Zóltán Verraszto (HUN) 4:24·24

1896–1960 Event not held

4 × 100 METRES FREESTYLE RELAY

	Gold	Silver	Bronze
1964	UNITED STATES 3:33·2	GERMANY 3:37·2	AUSTRALIA 3:39·1
1968	UNITED STATES 3:31·7	USSR 3:34·2	AUSTRALIA 3:34·7
1972	UNITED STATES 3:26·42	USSR 3:29·72	GDR 3:32·42

1896–1960 Event not held   1976–1980 Event not held

4 × 100 METRES MEDLEY RELAY
(Order of strokes: backstroke, breaststroke, butterfly, freestyle)

	Gold	Silver	Bronze
1960	UNITED STATES 4:05·4	AUSTRALIA 4:12·0	JAPAN 4:12·2
1964	UNITED STATES 3:58·4	GERMANY 4:01·6	AUSTRALIA 4:02·3
1968	UNITED STATES 3:54·9	GDR 3:57·5	USSR 4:00·7
1972	UNITED STATES 3:48·16	GDR 3:52·12	CANADA 3:52·26
1976	UNITED STATES 3:42·22	CANADA 3:45·94	FRG 3:47·29
1980	AUSTRALIA 3:45·70	USSR 3:45·92	GREAT BRITAIN 3:47·71

1896–1956 Event not held

400 METRES FREESTYLE

	Gold	Silver	Bronze
1920[1]	Ethelda Bleibtrey (USA) 4:34·0	Margaret Woodbridge (USA) 4:42·8	Frances Schroth (USA) 4:52·0
1924	Martha Norelius (USA) 6:02·2	Helen Wainwright (USA) 6:03·8	Gertrude Ederle (USA) 6:04·8
1928	Martha Norelius (USA) 5:42·8	Marie Braun (HOL) 5:57·8	Josephine McKim (USA) 6:00·2
1932	Helene Madison (USA) 5:28·5	Lenore Kight (USA) 5:28·6	Jennie Maakal (SAF) 5:47·3
1936	Henrika Mastenbroek (HOL) 5:26·4	Ragnhild Hveger (DEN) 5:27·5	Lenore Kight-Wingard (USA) 5:29·0
1948	Ann Curtis (USA) 5:17·8	Karen Harup (DEN) 5:21·2	Cathy Gibson (GBR) 5:22·5
1952	Valéria Gyenge (HUN) 5:12·1	Eva Nowák (HUN) 5:13·7	Evelyn Kawamoto (USA) 5:14·6
1956	Lorraine Crapp (AUS) 4:54·6	Dawn Fraser (AUS) 5:02·5	Sylvia Ruuska (USA) 5:07·1
1960	Chris von Saltza (USA) 4:50·6	Jane Cederquist (SWE) 4:53·9	Catharina Lagerberg (HOL) 4:56·9
1964	Virginia Duenkel (USA) 4:43·3	Marilyn Ramenofsky (USA) 4:44·6	Terri Stickles (USA) 4:47·2
1968	Debbie Meyer (USA) 4:31·8	Linda Gustavson (USA) 4:35·5	Karen Moras (AUS) 4:37·0
1972	Shane Gould (AUS) 4:19·04	Novella Calligaris (ITA) 4:22·44	Gudrun Wegner (GDR) 4:23·11
1976	Petra Thuemer (GDR) 4:09·89	Shirley Babashoff (USA) 4:10·46	Shannon Smith (CAN) 4:14·60
1980	Ines Diers (GDR) 4:08·76	Petra Schneider (GDR) 4:09·16	Carmela Schmidt (GDR) 4:10·86

[1] 300 metres.   1896–1912 Event not held

4 × 200 METRES FREESTYLE RELAY

	Gold	Silver	Bronze
1906[1]	HUNGARY 16:52·4	GERMANY 17:16·2	GREAT BRITAIN n.t.a.
1908	GREAT BRITAIN 10:45·6	HUNGARY 10:59·0	UNITED STATES 11:02·8
1912	AUSTRALASIA[2] 10:11·6	UNITED STATES 10:20·2	GREAT BRITAIN 10:28·2
1920	UNITED STATES 10:04·4	AUSTRALIA 10:25·4	GREAT BRITAIN 10:37·2
1924	UNITED STATES 9:53·4	AUSTRALIA 10:02·2	SWEDEN 10:06·8
1928	UNITED STATES 9:36·2	JAPAN 9:41·4	CANADA 9:47·8
1932	JAPAN 8:58·4	UNITED STATES 9:10·5	HUNGARY 9:31·4
1936	JAPAN 8:51·5	UNITED STATES 9:03·0	HUNGARY 9:12·3
1948	UNITED STATES 8:46·0	HUNGARY 8:48·4	FRANCE 9:08·0
1952	UNITED STATES 8:31·1	JAPAN 8:33·5	FRANCE 8:45·9
1956	AUSTRALIA 8:23·6	UNITED STATES 8:31·5	USSR 8:34·7
1960	UNITED STATES 8:10·2	JAPAN 8:13·2	AUSTRALIA 8:13·8
1964	UNITED STATES 7:52·1	GERMANY 7:59·3	JAPAN 8:03·8

1968	UNITED STATES 7:52·3	AUSTRALIA 7:53·7	USSR 8:01·6
1972	UNITED STATES 7:35·78	FRG 7:41·69	USSR 7:45·76
1976	UNITED STATES 7:23·22	USSR 7:27·97	GREAT BRITAIN 7:32·11
1980	USSR 7:23·50	GDR 7:28·60	BRAZIL 7:29·30

[1] 4 × 250 metres.   [2] Composed of three Australians and a New Zealander.   1896–1904 Event not held

Women

100 METRES FREESTYLE

	Gold	Silver	Bronze
1912	Fanny Durack (AUS) 1:22·2	Wilhelmina Wylie (AUS) 1:25·4	Jennie Fletcher (GBR) 1:27·0
1920	Ethelda Bleibtrey (USA) 1:13·6	Irene Guest (USA) 1:17·0	Frances Schroth (USA) 1:17·2
1924	Ethel Lackie (USA) 1:12·4	Mariechen Wehselau (USA) 1:12·8	Gertrude Ederle (USA) 1:14·2
1928	Albina Osipowich (USA) 1:11·0	Eleanor Garatti (USA) 1:11·4	Joyce Cooper (GBR) 1:13·6
1932	Helene Madison (USA) 1:06·8	Willemijntje den Ouden (HOL) 1:07·8	Eleanor Garatti-Saville (USA) 1:08·2
1936	Henrika Mastenbroek (HOL) 1:05·9	Jeanette Campbell (ARG) 1:06·4	Gisela Arendt (GER) 1:06·6
1948	Greta Andersen (DEN) 1:06·3	Ann Curtis (USA) 1:06·5	Marie-Louise Vaessen (HOL) 1:07·6
1952	Katalin Szöke (HUN) 1:06·8	Johanna Termeulen (HOL) 1:07·0	Judit Temmes (HUN) 1:07·1
1956	Dawn Fraser (AUS) 1:02·0	Lorraine Crapp (AUS) 1:02·3	Faith Leech (AUS) 1:05·1
1960	Dawn Fraser (AUS) 1:01·2	Chris van Saltza (USA) 1:02·8	Natalie Steward (GBR) 1:03·1
1964	Dawn Fraser (AUS) 59·5	Sharon Stouder (USA) 59·9	Kathleeen Ellis (USA) 1:00·8
1968	Jan Henne (USA) 1:00·0	Susan Pedersen (USA) 1:00·3	Linda Gustavson (USA) 1:00·3
1972	Sandra Neilson (USA) 58·59	Shirley Babashoff (USA) 59·02	Shane Gould (AUS) 59·06
1976	Kornelia Ender (GDR) 55·65	Petra Priemer (GDR) 56·49	Enith Brigitha (HOL) 56·65
1980	Barbara Krause (GDR) 54·79	Caren Metschuck (GDR) 55·16	Ines Diers (GDR) 55·65

1896–1908 Event not held

200 METRES FREESTYLE

	Gold	Silver	Bronze
1968	Debbie Meyer (USA) 2:10·5	Jan Henne (USA) 2:11·0	Jane Barkman (USA) 2:11·2
1972	Shane Gould (AUS) 2:03·56	Shirley Babashoff (USA) 2:04·33	Keena Rothhammer (USA) 2:04·92
1976	Kornelia Ender (GDR) 1:59·26	Shirley Babashoff (USA) 2:01·22	Enith Brigitha (HOL) 2:01·40
1980	Barbara Krause (GDR) 1:58·33	Ines Diers (GDR) 1:59·64	Carmela Schmidt (GDR) 2:01·44

1896–1964 Event not held

800 METRES FREESTYLE

	Gold	Silver	Bronze
1968	Debbie Meyer (USA) 9:24·0	Pamela Kruse (USA) 9:35·7	Maria Ramirez (MEX) 9:38·5
1972	Keena Rothhammer (USA) 8:53·68	Shane Gould (AUS) 8:56·39	Novella Calligaris (ITA) 8:57·46
1976	Petra Thuemer (GDR) 8:37·14	Shirley Babashoff (USA) 8:37·59	Wendy Weinberg (USA) 8:42·60
1980	Michelle Ford (AUS) 8:28·90	Ines Diers (GDR) 8:32·55	Heike Dähne (GDR) 8:33·48

1896–1964 Event not held

100 METRES BACKSTROKE

	Gold	Silver	Bronze
1924	Sybil Bauer (USA) 1:23·2	Phyllis Harding (GBR) 1:27·4	Aileen Riggin (USA) 1:28·2
1928	Marie Braun (HOL) 1:22·0	Ellen King (GBR) 1:22·2	Joyce Cooper (GBR) 1:22·8
1932	Eleanor Holm (USA) 1:19·4	Philomena Mealing (AUS) 1:21·3	Elizabeth Davies (GBR) 1:22·5
1936	Dina Senff (HOL) 1:18·9	Hendrika Mastenbroek (HOL) 1:19·2	Alice Bridges (USA) 1:19·4
1948	Karen Harup (DEN) 1:14·4	Suzanne Zimmermann (USA) 1:16·0	Judy Davies (AUS) 1:16·7
1952	Joan Harrison (SAF) 1:14·3	Geertje Wielema (HOL) 1:14·5	Jean Stewart (NZL) 1:15·8
1956	Judy Grinham (GBR) 1:12·9	Carin Cone (USA) 1:12·9	Margaret Edwards (GBR) 1:13·1
1960	Lynn Burke (USA) 1:09·3	Natalie Steward (GBR) 1:10·8	Satoko Tanaka (JPN) 1:11·4
1964	Cathy Ferguson (USA) 1:07·7	Cristine Caron (FRA) 1:07·9	Virginia Duenkel (USA) 1:08·0
1968	Kaye Hall (USA) 1:06·2	Elaine Tanner (CAN) 1:06·7	Jane Swaggerty (USA) 1:08·1
1972	Melissa Belote (USA) 1:05·78	Andrea Gyarmati (HUN) 1:06·26	Susie Atwood (USA) 1:06·34
1976	Ulrike Richter (GDR) 1:01·83	Birgit Treiber (GDR) 1:03·41	Nancy Garapick (CAN) 1:03·71
1980	Rica Reinisch (GDR) 1:00·86	Ina Kleber (GDR) 1:02·07	Petra Riedel (GDR) 1:02·64

1896–1920 Event not held

200 METRES BACKSTROKE

	Gold	Silver	Bronze
1968	Lillian Watson (USA) 2:24·8	Elaine Tanner (CAN) 2:27·4	Kaye Hall (USA) 2:28·9
1972	Melissa Belote (USA) 2:19·19	Susie Atwood (USA) 2:20·38	Donna Marie Gurr (CAN) 2:23·22
1976	Ulrike Richter (GDR) 2:13·43	Birgit Treiber (GDR) 2:14·97	Nancy Garapick (CAN) 2:15·60
1980	Rica Reinisch (GDR) 2:11·77	Cornelia Pilot (GDR) 2:13·75	Birgit Treiber (GDR) 2:14·14

1896–1964 Event not held

100 METRES BREASTSTROKE

	Gold	Silver	Bronze
1968	Djurdjica Bjedov (YUG) 1:15·8	Galina Prozumenshchikova (URS) 1:15·9	Sharon Wichman (USA) 1:16·1
1972	Catherine Carr (USA) 1:13·58	Galina Stepanova (URS) 1:14·99	Beverley Whitfield (AUS) 1:15·73
1976	Hannelore Anke (GDR) 1:11·16	Lubov Rusanova (URS) 1:13·04	Marina Koshevaya (URS) 1:13·30
1980	Ute Geweniger (GDR) 1:10·22	Elvira Vasilkova (URS) 1:10·41	Susanne Nielsson (DEN) 1:11·16

1896–1964 Event not held

200 METRES BREASTSTROKE

	Gold	Silver	Bronze
1924	Lucy Morton (GBR) 3:33·2	Agnes Geraghty (USA) 3:34·0	Gladys Carson (GBR) 3:35·4
1928	Hilde Schrader (GER) 3:12·6	Mietje Baron (HOL) 3:15·2	Lotte Mühe (GER) 3:17·6
1932	Claire Dennis (AUS) 3:06·3	Hideko Maehata (JPN) 3:06·4	Else Jacobson (DEN) 3:07·1
1936	Hideko Maehata (JPN) 3:03·6	Martha Genenger (GER) 3:04·2	Inge Sörensen (DEN) 3:07·8
1948	Petronella van Vliet (HOL) 2:57·2	Beatrice Lyons (AUS) 2:57·7	Eva Novák (HUN) 3:00·2
1952	Eva Székely[1] (HUN) 2:51·7	Eva Novák (HUN) 2:54·4	Helen Gordon (GBR) 2:57·6
1956	Ursula Happe[2] (GER) 2:53·1	Eva Székely (HUN) 2:54·8	Eva-Maria ten Elsen (GER) 2:55·1
1960	Anita Lonsbrough (GBR) 2:49·5	Wiltrud Urselmann (GER) 2:50·0	Barbara Göbel (GER) 2:53·6
1964	Galina Prozumenshchikova (URS) 2:46·4	Claudia Kolb (USA) 2:47·6	Svetlana Babanina (URS) 2:48·6
1968	Sharon Wichman (USA) 2:44·4	Djurdjica Bjedov (YUG) 2:46·4	Galina Prozumenshchikova (URS) 2:47·0
1972	Beverley Whitfield (AUS) 2:41·71	Dana Schoenfield (USA) 2:42·05	Galina Stepanova (URS) 2:42·36
1976	Marina Koshevaya (URS) 2:33·35	Marina Yurchenia (URS) 2:36·08	Lubov Rusanova (URS) 2:36·22
1980	Lina Kachushite (URS) 2:29·54	Svetlana Varganova (URS) 2:29·61	Yulia Bogdanova (URS) 2:32·39

[1] Used then permitted butterfly stroke. [2] Used then permitted underwater technique. 1896–1920 Event not held

100 METRES BUTTERFLY

	Gold	Silver	Bronze
1956	Shelley Mann (USA) 1:11·0	Nancy Ramey (USA) 1:11·9	Mary Sears (USA) 1:14·4
1960	Carolyn Schuler (USA) 1:09·5	Marianne Heemskerk (HOL) 1:10·4	Janice Andrew (AUS) 1:12·2
1964	Sharon Stouder (USA) 1:04·7	Aagje Kok (HOL) 1:05·6	Kathleen Ellis (USA) 1:06·0
1968	Lynette McClements (AUS) 1:05·5	Ellie Daniel (USA) 1:05·8	Susan Shields (USA) 1:06·2
1972	Mayumi Aoki (JPN) 1:03·34	Roswitha Beier (GDR) 1:03·61	Andrea Gyarmati (HUN) 1:03·73
1976	Kornelia Ender (GDR) 1:00·13	Andrea Pollack (GDR) 1:00·98	Wendy Boglioli (USA) 1:01·17
1980	Caren Metschuck (GDR) 1:00·42	Andrea Pollack (GDR) 1:00·90	Christiane Knacke (GDR) 1:01·44

1896–1952 Event not held

200 METRES BUTTERFLY

	Gold	Silver	Bronze
1968	Aagje Kok (HOL) 2:24·7	Helga Lindner (GDR) 2:24·8	Ellie Daniel (USA) 2:25·9
1972	Karen Moe (USA) 2:15·57	Lynn Colella (USA) 2:16·34	Ellie Daniel (USA) 2:16·74
1976	Andrea Pollack (GDR) 2:11·41	Ulrike Tauber (GDR) 2:12·50	Rosemarie Gabriel (GDR) 2:12·86
1980	Ines Geissler (GDR) 2:10·44	Sybille Schönrock (GDR) 2:10·45	Michelle Ford (AUS) 2:11·66

1896–1964 Event not held

200 METRES INDIVIDUAL MEDLEY

	Gold	Silver	Bronze
1968	Claudia Kolb (USA) 2:24·7	Susan Pedersen (USA) 2:28·8	Jan Henne (USA) 2:31·4
1972	Shane Gould (AUS) 2:23·07	Kornelia Ender (GDR) 2:23·59	Lynn Vidali (USA) 2:24·06

1896–1964 Event not held   1976–1980 Event not held

400 METRES INDIVIDUAL MEDLEY

	Gold	Silver	Bronze
1964	Donna De Varona (USA) 5:18·7	Sharon Finneran (USA) 5:24·1	Martha Randall (USA) 5:24·2
1968	Claudia Kolb (USA) 5:08·5	Lynn Vidali (USA) 5:22·2	Sabine Steinbach (GDR) 5:25·3
1972	Gail Neall (AUS) 5:02·97	Leslie Cliff (CAN) 5:03·57	Novella Calligaris (ITA) 5:03·99
1976	Ulrike Tauber (GDR) 4:42·77	Cheryl Gibson (CAN) 4:48·10	Becky Smith (CAN) 4:50·48
1980	Petra Schneider (GDR) 4:36·29	Sharron Davies (GBR) 4:46·83	Agnieszka Czopek (POL) 4:48·17

1896–1960 Event not held

4 × 100 METRES FREESTYLE RELAY

	Gold	Silver	Bronze
1912	GREAT BRITAIN 5:52·8	GERMANY 6:04·6	AUSTRIA 6:17·0
1920	UNITED STATES 5:11·6	GREAT BRITAIN 5:40·8	SWEDEN 5:43·6
1924	UNITED STATES 4:58·8	GREAT BRITAIN 5:17·0	SWEDEN 5:35·6
1928	UNITED STATES 4:47·6	GREAT BRITAIN 5:02·8	SOUTH AFRICA 5:13·4
1932	UNITED STATES 4:38·0	NETHERLANDS 4:47·5	GREAT BRITAIN 4:52·4
1936	NETHERLANDS 4:36·0	GERMANY 4:36·8	UNITED STATES 4:40·2
1948	UNITED STATES 4:29·2	DENMARK 4:29·6	NETHERLANDS 4:31·6
1952	HUNGARY 4:24·4	NETHERLANDS 4:29·0	UNITED STATES 4:30·1
1956	AUSTRALIA 4:17·1	UNITED STATES 4:19·2	SOUTH AFRICA 4:15·7
1960	UNITED STATES 4:08·9	AUSTRALIA 4:11·3	GERMANY 4:19·7
1964	UNITED STATES 4:03·8	AUSTRALIA 4:06·9	NETHERLANDS 4:12·0
1968	UNITED STATES 4:02·5	GDR 4:05·7	CANADA 4:07·2
1972	UNITED STATES 3:55·19	GDR 3:55·55	FRG 3:57·93
1976	UNITED STATES 3:44·82	GDR 3:45·50	CANADA 3:48·81
1980	GDR 3:42·71	SWEDEN 3:48·93	NETHERLANDS 3:49·51

1896–1908 Event not held

4 × 100 METRES MEDLEY RELAY
(Order of strokes: backstroke, breaststroke, butterfly, freestyle)

	Gold	Silver	Bronze
1960	UNITED STATES 4:41·1	AUSTRALIA 4:45·9	GERMANY 4:47·6
1964	UNITED STATES 4:33·9	NETHERLANDS 4:37·0	USSR 4:39·2
1968	UNITED STATES 4:28·3	AUSTRALIA 4:30·0	FRG 4:36·4
1972	UNITED STATES 4:20·75	GDR 4:24·91	FRG 4:26·46
1976	GDR 4:07·95	UNITED STATES 4:14·55	CANADA 4:15·22
1980	GDR 4:06·67	GREAT BRITAIN 4:12·24	USSR 4:13·61

1896–1956 Event not held

DISCONTINUED EVENTS

50 YARDS FREESTYLE

	Gold	Silver	Bronze
1904[1]	Zoltán von Halmay (HUN) 28·0	Scott Leary (USA) 28·6	Charles Daniels (USA) n.t.a.

[1] Race reswum after judges disagreed on result of first race.

100 m FREESTYLE (Sailors)

	Gold	Silver	Bronze
1896	Ioannis Malokinis (GRE) 2:20·4	S Chasapis (GRE) n.t.a.	Dimitrios Drivas (GRE) n.t.a.

200 m OBSTACLE EVENT

	Gold	Silver	Bronze
1900	Frederick Lane (AUS) 2:38·4	Otto Wahle (AUT) 2:40·0	Peter Kemp (GBR) 2:47·4

400 m BREASTSTROKE

	Gold	Silver	Bronze
1904	Georg Zacharias (GER) 7:23·6	Walter Brack (GER) 20 m	Jamison Handy (USA) d.n.a.
1912	Walter Bathe (GER) 6:29·6	Thor Henning (SWE) 6:35·6	Percy Courtman (GBR) 6:36·4
1920	Hakan Malmroth (SWE) 6:31·8	Thor Henning (SWE) 6:45·2	Arvo Aaltonen (FIN) 6:48·0

880 YARDS FREESTYLE

	Gold	Silver	Bronze
1904	Emil Rausch (GER) 13:11·4	Francis Gailey (USA) 13:23·4	Géza Kiss (HUN) n.t.a.

4000 m FREESTYLE

	Gold	Silver	Bronze
1900	John Jarvis (GBR) 58:24·0	Zoltán von Halmay (HUN) 1:08:55·4	Louis Martin (FRA) 1:13:08·4

UNDERWATER SWIMMING

	Gold	Silver	Bronze
1900	Charles de Vendeville (FRA) 188·4	A Six (FRA) 185·4	Peder Lykkeberg (DEN) 147·0

PLUNGE FOR DISTANCE

	Gold	Silver	Bronze
1904	Paul Dickey (USA) 19·05 m	Edgar Adams (USA) 17·53 m	Leo Goodwin (USA) 17·37 m

200 m TEAM SWIMMING

	Gold	Silver	Bronze
1900	GERMANY 32 pts	FRANCE 51	FRANCE 61

4 × 50 YARDS RELAY

	Gold	Silver	Bronze
1904	UNITED STATES (New York AC) 2:04·6	UNITED STATES (Chicago AC) n.t.a.	UNITED STATES (Missouri AC) n.t.a.

PLAIN HIGH DIVING

	Gold	Silver	Bronze
1912	Erik Adlerz (SWE) 40·0	Hjalmar Johansson (SWE) 39·3	John Jansson (SWE) 39·1
1920	Arvid Wallmann (SWE) 183·5	Nils Skoglund (SWE) 183·0	John Jansson (SWE) 175·0
1924	Richmond Eve (AUS) 160·0	John Jansson (SWE) 157·0	Harold Clarke (GBR) 158·0[1]

[1] Placed third due to less placement marks.

Men

SPRINGBOARD DIVING

	Gold	Silver	Bronze
1908	Albert Zurner (GER) 85·5	Kurt Behrens (GER) 85·3	George Gaidzik (USA) 80·8 Gottlob Walz (GER) 80·8
1912	Paul Günther (GER) 79·23	Hans Luber (GER) 76·78	Kurt Behrens (GER) 73·73
1920	Louis Kuehn (USA) 675·4	Clarence Pinkston (USA) 655·3	Louis Balbach (USA) 649·5
1924	Albert White (USA) 696·4	Peter Desjardins (USA) 693·2	Clarence Pinkston (USA) 653
1928	Peter Desjardins (USA) 185·04	Michael Galitzen (USA) 174·06	Farid Simaika (EGY) 172·46
1932	Michael Galitzen (USA) 161·38	Harold Smith (USA) 158·54	Richard Degener (USA) 151·82
1936	Richard Degener (USA) 163·57	Marshall Wayne (USA) 159·56	Al Greene (USA) 146·29
1948	Bruce Harlan (USA) 163·64	Miller Anderson (USA) 157·29	Samuel Lee (USA) 145·52
1952	David Browning (USA) 205·29	Miller Anderson (USA) 199·84	Robert Clotworthy (USA) 184·92
1956	Robert Clotworthy (USA) 159·56	Donald Harper (USA) 156·23	Joaquin Capilla Pérez (MEX) 150·69
1960	Gary Tobian (USA) 170·00	Samuel Hall (USA) 167·08	Juan Botella (MEX) 162·30
1964	Kenneth Sitzberger (USA) 159·90	Francis Gorman (USA) 157·63	Larry Andreasen (USA) 143·77
1968	Bernard Wrightson (USA) 170·15	Klaus Dibiasi (ITA) 159·74	James Henry (USA) 158·09
1972	Vladimir Vasin (URS) 594·09	Franco Cagnotto (ITA) 591·63	Craig Lincoln (USA) 577·29
1976	Philip Boggs (USA) 619·05	Franco Cagnotto (ITA) 570·48	Aleksandr Kosenkov (URS) 567·24
1980	Aleksandr Portnov (URS) 905·025	Carlos Giron (MEX) 892·140	Franco Cagnotto (ITA) 871·500

1896–1906 Event not held

HIGHBOARD DIVING

	Gold	Silver	Bronze
1904[1]	George Sheldon (USA) 12·66	Georg Hoffmann (GER) 11·66	Frank Nehoe (USA) 11·33 Alfred Braunschweiger (GER) 11·33
1906	Gottlob Walz (GER) 156·00	Georg Hoffman (GER) 150·20	Otto Satzinger (AUT) 147·40
1908	Hjalmar Johansson (SWE) 83·75	Karl Malström (SWE) 78·73	Arvid Spångberg (SWE) 74·00
1912	Erik Adlerz (SWE) 73·94	Albert Zürner (GER) 72·60	Gustaf Blomgren (SWE) 69·56
1920	Clarence Pinkston (USA) 100·67	Erik Adlerz (SWE) 99·08	Haig Prieste (USA) 93·73
1924	Albert White (USA) 97·46	David Fall (USA) 97·30	Clarence Pinkston (USA) 94·60
1928	Peter Desjardins (USA) 98·74	Farid Simaika (EGY) 99·58	Michael Galitzen (USA) 92·34
1932	Harold Smith (USA) 124·80	Michael Galitzen (USA) 124·28	Frank Kurtz (USA) 121·98
1936	Marshall Wayne (USA) 113·58	Elbert Root (USA) 110·60	Hermann Stork (GER) 110·31
1948	Samuel Lee (USA) 130·05	Bruce Harlan (USA) 122·30	Joaquin Capilla Pérez (MEX) 113·52
1952	Samuel Lee (USA) 156·28	Joaquin Capilla Pérez (MEX) 145·21	Günther Haase (GER) 141·31
1956	Joaquin Capilla Pérez (MEX) 152·44	Gary Tobian (USA) 152·41	Richard Connor (USA) 149·79
1960	Robert Webster (USA) 165·56	Gary Tobian (USA) 165·25	Brian Phelps (GBR) 157·13
1964	Robert Webster (USA) 148·58	Klaus Dibiasi (ITA) 147·54	Thomas Gompf (USA) 146·57
1968	Klaus Dibiasi (ITA) 164·18	Alvaro Gaxiola (MEX) 154·49	Edwin Young (USA) 153·93
1972	Klaus Dibiasi (ITA) 504·12	Richard Rydze (USA) 480·75	Franco Cagnotto (ITA) 475·83
1976	Klaus Dibiasi (ITA) 600·51	Gregory Louganis (USA) 576·99	Vladimir Aleynik (URS) 548·61
1980	Falk Hoffmann (GDR) 835·650	Vladimir Heynik (URS) 819·705	David Ambartsumyan (URS) 817·440

[1] Combined springboard and highboard event.   1896–1900 Event not held

Women

SPRINGBOARD DIVING

	Gold	Silver	Bronze
1920	Aileen Riggin (USA) 539·9	Helen Wainwright (USA) 534·8	Thelma Payne (USA) 534·1
1924	Elizabeth Becker (USA) 474·5	Aileen Riggin (USA) 460·4	Caroline Fletcher (USA) 434·4
1928	Helen Meany (USA) 78·62	Dorothy Poynton (USA) 75·62	Georgia Coleman (USA) 73·38
1932	Georgia Coleman (USA) 87·52	Katherine Rawls (USA) 82·56	Jane Fauntz (USA) 82·12
1936	Marjorie Gestring (USA) 89·27	Katherine Rawls (USA) 88·35	Dorothy Poynton-Hill (USA) 82·36
1948	Victoria Draves (USA) 108·74	Zoe Ann Olsen (USA) 108·23	Patricia Elsener (USA) 101·30
1952	Patricia McCormick (USA) 147·30	Madeleine Moreau (FRA) 139·34	Zoe Ann Jensen (USA) 127·57
1956	Patricia McCormick (USA) 142·36	Jeanne Stunyo (USA) 125·89	Irene Macdonald (CAN) 121·40
1960	Ingrid Krämer (GER) 155·81	Paula Myers-Pope (USA) 141·24	Elizabeth Ferris (GBR) 139·09
1964	Ingrid Krämer-Engel (GER) 145·00	Jeanne Collier (USA) 138·36	Mary Willard (USA) 138·18
1968	Sue Gossick (USA) 150·77	Tamara Pogozheva (URS) 145·30	Keala O'Sullivan (USA) 145·23
1972	Micki King (USA) 450·03	Ulrika Knape (SWE) 434·19	Marina Janicke (GDR) 430·92

| 1976 | Jennifer Chandler (USA) 506·19 | Christa Kohler (GDR) 469·41 | Cynthia McIngvale (USA) 466·83 |
| 1980 | Irina Kalinina (URS) 725·910 | Martina Proeber (GDR) 698·895 | Karin Guthke (GDR) 685·245 |

1896–1912 Event not held

HIGHBOARD DIVING

	Gold	Silver	Bronze
1912	Greta Johansson (SWE) 39·9	Lisa Regnell (SWE) 36·0	Isabelle White (GBR) 34·0
1920	Stefani Fryland-Clausen (DEN) 34·6	Eileen Armstrong (GBR) 33·3	Eva Ollivier (SWE) 33·3
1924	Caroline Smith (USA) 10·5	Elizabeth Becker (USA) 11·0	Hjördis Töpel (SWE) 15·5
1928	Elizabeth Pinkston (USA) 31·6	Georgia Coleman (USA) 30·6	Lala Sjöqvist (SWE) 29·2
1932	Dorothy Poynton (USA) 40·26	Georgia Coleman (USA) 35·56	Marion Roper (USA) 35·22
1936	Dorothy Poynton-Hill (USA) 33·93	Velma Dunn (USA) 33·63	Käthe Köhler (GER) 33·43
1948	Victoria Draves (USA) 68·87	Patricia Elsener (USA) 66·28	Birte Christoffersen (DEN) 66·04
1952	Patricia McCormick (USA) 79·37	Paula Myers (USA) 71·63	Juno Irwin (USA) 70·49
1956	Patricia McCormick (USA) 84·85	Juno Irwin (USA) 81·64	Paula Myers (USA) 81·58
1960	Ingrid Krämer (GER) 91·28	Paula Myers-Pope (USA) 88·94	Ninel Krutova (URS) 86·99
1964	Lesley Bush (USA) 99·80	Ingrid Krämer-Engel (GER) 98·45	Galina Alekseyeva (URS) 97·60
1968	Milena Duchková (TCH) 109·59	Natalia Lobanova (URS) 105·14	Ann Peterson (USA) 101·11
1972	Ulrika Knape (SWE) 390·00	Milena Duchková (TCH) 370·92	Marina Janicke (GDR) 360·54
1976	Elena Vaytsekhovskaya (URS) 406·59	Ulrika Knape (SWE) 402·60	Deborah Wilson (USA) 401·07
1980	Martina Jäschke (GDR) 596·250	Servard Emirzyan (URS) 576·465	Liana Tsotadze (URS) 575·925

1896–1908 Event not held

DIVING—MEDALS

	MEN				WOMEN				TOTAL				Total Medals
	Gold	Silver	Bronze		Gold	Silver	Bronze		Gold	Silver	Bronze		
UNITED STATES......	22	18	18	....	19	17	15	....	41	35	33	....	109
SWEDEN.................	4	5	4	....	2	3	3	....	6	8	7	....	21
GERMANY (FRG).......	3	5	5	....	3	1	1	....	6	6	6	....	18
USSR.....................	2	1	3	....	2	3	3	....	4	4	6	....	14
ITALY.....................	3	4	2	....	—	—	—	....	3	4	2	....	9
GDR.......................	1	—	—	....	1	2	3	....	2	2	3	....	7
MEXICO..................	1	3	3	....	—	—	—	....	1	3	3	....	7
GREAT BRITAIN	—	—	2	....	—	1	2	....	—	1	4	....	5
CZECHOSLOVAKIA	—	—	—	....	1	1	—	....	1	1	—	....	2
DENMARK..............	—	—	—	....	1	—	1	....	1	—	1	....	2
EGYPT....................	—	1	1	....	—	—	—	....	—	1	1	....	2
AUSTRALIA	1	—	—	....	—	—	—	....	1	—	—	....	1
FRANCE..................	—	—	—	....	—	1	—	....	—	1	—	....	1
AUSTRIA.................	—	—	1	....	—	—	—	....	—	—	1	....	1
CANADA.................	—	—	—	....	—	—	1	....	—	—	1	....	1
	37	37	39*		29	29	29		66	66	68*		200

* Two bronze medals awarded in a 1904 and a 1908 event.

SWIMMING—MEDALS (excluding Diving)

	MEN				WOMEN				TOTAL				Total Medals
	Gold	Silver	Bronze		Gold	Silver	Bronze		Gold	Silver	Bronze		
UNITED STATES.....	77	58	47	......	48	33	33	......	125	91	80	......	296
AUSTRALIA	21	15	22	......	14	10	7	......	35	25	29	......	89
GDR.......................	5	4	3	......	22	20	10	......	27	24	13	......	64
GREAT BRITAIN	9	11	9	......	4	8	10	......	13	19	19	......	51
USSR.....................	7	13	13	......	3	6	8	......	10	19	21	......	50
GERMANY (FRG).....	9	12	11	......	2	4	9	......	11	16	20	......	47
JAPAN....................	11	17	11	......	2	1	1	......	13	18	12	......	43
HUNGARY...............	7	10	10	......	4	4	3	......	11	14	13	......	38
NETHERLANDS	—	—	2	......	7	11	7	......	7	11	9	......	27
SWEDEN................	7	6	7	......	—	2	2	......	7	8	9	......	24
CANADA.................	2	4	3	......	—	4	8	......	2	8	11	......	21

FRANCE...............	2	4	6	......	—	1	—	......	2	5	6	 13
DENMARK............	—	1	1	......	2	3	3	......	2	4	4	 10
AUSTRIA..............	2	2	5	......	—	—	1	......	2	2	6	 10
GREECE...............	1	4	3	......	—	—	—	......	1	4	3	 8
SOUTH AFRICA	—	—	—	......	1	—	3	......	1	—	3	 4
ITALY..................	—	—	—	......	—	1	2	......	—	1	2	 3
BRAZIL................	—	—	3	......	—	—	—	......	—	—	3	 3
ARGENTINA..........	1	—	—	......	—	1	—	......	1	1	—	 2
YUGOSLAVIA	—	—	—	......	1	1	—	......	1	1	—	 2
MEXICO...............	1	—	—	......	—	—	1	......	1	—	1	 2
NEW ZEALAND	1	—	—	......	—	—	1	......	1	—	1	 2
BELGIUM.............	—	1	1	......	—	—	—	......	—	1	1	 2
FINLAND..............	—	—	2	......	—	—	—	......	—	—	2	 2
PHILIPPINES.........	—	—	2	......	—	—	—	......	—	—	2	 2
POLAND	—	—	—	......	—	—	1	......	—	—	1	 1
SPAIN	—	—	1	......	—	—	—	......	—	—	1	 1
	163*	162	162		110	110	110		273*	272	272	817

* Extra medal due to double counting of Australia/New Zealand relay team of 1912.

WATER POLO—MEDALS

	Gold	Silver	Bronze	Total
HUNGARY	6	3	3	12
USSR	2	2	2	6
UNITED STATES	1	1	4	6
BELGIUM	—	4	2	6
YUGOSLAVIA	1	4	—	5
GREAT BRITAIN	4	—	—	4
ITALY	2	1	1	4
GERMANY (FRG)	1	2	—	3
FRANCE	1	—	2	3
SWEDEN	—	1	2	3
NETHERLANDS	—	—	2	2
	18	18	18	54

WATER POLO—MEDALS

	Gold	Silver	Bronze
1900[1]	Great Britain	Belgium	France
1904[1]	United States	United States	United States
1908	Great Britain	Belgium	Sweden
1912	Great Britain	Sweden	Belgium
1920	Great Britain	Sweden	Belgium
1924	France	Belgium	United States
1928	Germany	Hungary	France
1932	Hungary	Germany	United States
1936	Hungary	Germany	Belgium
1948	Italy	Hungary	Netherlands
1952	Hungary	Yugoslavia	Italy
1956	Hungary	Yugoslavia	USSR
1960	Italy	USSR	Hungary
1964	Hungary	Yugoslavia	USSR
1968	Yugoslavia	USSR	Hungary
1972	USSR	Hungary	United States
1976	Hungary	Italy	Netherlands
1980	USSR	Yugoslavia	Hungary

[1] Entries were from clubs and not international teams.

1896, 1906 Event not held

TRACK AND FIELD ATHLETICS

The track and field events have been the centrepiece of every Olympic Games since 1896. From 1920 until the International Amateur Athletics Federation inaugurated their first world title meeting in 1983 they were official world championships. The first champion in modern Olympic history was James Connolly (USA) who won the triple jump (then called the hop, step and jump) on 6 April 1896. He also won medals in the high and long jumps, and was later a novelist and war correspondent. The first winner of an Olympic event was Francis Lane (USA) who had won heat 1 of the 100 m in 12·2 sec earlier on the same day. Women's events were first introduced in 1928 and the first female gold medallist in track and field was Halina Konopacka (POL) winner of the discus. Again the first winner of an Olympic women's event was Anni Holdmann (GER) who took the first heat of the 100 m the day before.

Hannes Kolehmainen, the first of the Flying Finns, beating Jean Bouin (FRA) in the 5000 m at Stockholm, both smashing the previous world best time.

Above, The Finnish juggernaut in the 10 000 m in Berlin, from left, Volmari Iso-Hollo third, Arvo Askola second and Ilmari Salminen first, with little Kohei Murakoso (JAP) fourth desparately hanging on. Right, The oldest athlete to win an Olympic gold medal was 42 year old Pat McDonald (USA) in the 56 lb weight throw at Antwerp. Thirteen years later he won the American title for the last time.

The most gold medals won was ten by Ray Ewry (USA), a feat unsurpassed in Olympic competition at any sport, in the standing jumps from 1900 to 1908. The most medals won was 12 by the Finnish distance runner Paavo Nurmi who won nine gold and three silver medals from 1920 to 1928. He won them in a record seven different events, and his five gold medals in 1924 is a record for one celebration of the Games. However, the most individual wins at one Games is the four by Alvin Kraenzlein (USA) in 1900. Nurmi's team-mate Ville Ritola won a record six medals in 1924, comprising four gold and two silver, incurring eight races in 8 days. In 1912 the forerunner of all the 'Flying Finns', Hannes Kolehmainen, had won six races, including heats, within 9 days.

The most gold medals won by a woman was four by three athletes: Fanny Blankers-Koen (HOL) in 1948, which is also a record for just one Games as is the three individual gold medals included; Betty Cuthbert (AUS) in 1956 and 1964; and Bärbel Wöckel (née Eckert) (GDR) in 1976 and 1980. A record seven medals were won by Shirley de la Hunty (née Strickland) of Australia with three gold, one silver and three bronze from 1948 to 1956, and by Irena Szewinska (née Kirszenstein) (POL) with three gold, two silver and two bronze medals from 1964 to 1976. In fact recent study of photo-finish photographs indicates that Shirley de la Hunty also came third in the 200 m in 1948, but no move officially to change the result has been made. Szewinska is the only woman to win medals at three successive Games, and also in five different events.

A unique track and field achievement, equalling that of yachting's Paul Elvström (see p 211), was the four successive gold medals in the same event by Al Oerter (USA) in the discus from 1956 to 1968. Almost as worthy was the three gold and one silver won in the triple jump by Viktor Sanayev (URS) from 1968 to 1980. Mildred Didrikson (USA) achieved a unique triple in 1932 when she won medals in a run (80 m hurdles—gold), a jump (high jump—silver) and a throw (javelin—gold). Another unusual spread of medals was by Micheline Ostermeyer (FRA) in 1948 with golds in the shot and discus and a bronze in the high jump. Perhaps even more remarkable was the fact that she was a concert pianist. Two men have won medals in throws and jumps at the same Games. Robert Garrett (USA) won golds in the shot and discus, and silvers in the high and long jumps in 1896, and then bronze medals in the shot and standing triple jump in 1900. Martin Sheridan (USA) won the shot and discus in 1906 and also won silver medals in the stone throw, and the standing high and long jumps. In 1908 he won the two styles of discus and a bronze medal in the standing long jump.

Stanley Rowley won bronze medals in the 60 m,

100 m and 200 m in 1900 running for the Australasian team (he was Australian), and then was drafted into the British team for the 5000 m team race and won a gold medal, although he finished last. The American distance runner George Bonhag finished a disappointed fourth in his chosen event the 5 miles in 1906. He entered the 1500 m walking event—his first attempt at the discipline—and won the gold medal. The judging was exceptionally strict and many of the more favoured competitors in front of him were disqualified.

The oldest gold medallist was Patrick 'Babe' McDonald (USA) who won the 56-lb weight throw in 1920 aged 42 yr 26 days. The youngest gold medallist was Barbara Jones (USA) in the 1952 sprint relay aged 15 yr 123 days, while the youngest individual event winner was Ulrike Meyfarth (FRG) who won the high jump in 1972 aged exactly 1 year older. The youngest male champion was Robert Mathias (USA) who won the 1948 decathlon aged 17 yr 263 days and later (1966) became a United States Congressman. The oldest female gold medallist was Lia Manoliu (ROM) who won the 1968 discus aged 36 yr 176 days. She also is co-holder of another record, that of attendance at six Games (1952–1972) by a woman (see p 000). Two men, both walkers, competed in five Games. Abdon Pamich (ITA) in the 50 km event from 1956 to 1972 by a woman (see p 71). Two men, both Vladimir Golubnichiy (URS) in the 20 km from 1960 to 1976, winning in 1960 and 1968.

The oldest medallist was Tebbs Lloyd Johnson (GBR) aged 48 yr 115 days when he took third place in the 1952 50 km walk. The oldest woman to win a medal was Dana Zátopková (TCH) winning her 1960 javelin silver aged 37 yr 248 days. The youngest medallist was Carolina Gisolf (HOL) who won the silver in the 1928 high jump

23 days after her 15th birthday. The youngest male medallist was Ture Persson (SWE), 34 days younger than Mathias when he was a member of the 1912 silver medal sprint relay team.

The only person to win an Olympic athletics title by a walk-over was Wyndham Halswelle (GBR) in the famous incident (see p 21) in the 400 m of 1908.

The first brothers to win Olympic medals in track and field were Patrick and Con Leahy, Irishmen representing Great Britain. In 1900 Patrick was second in the high jump and third in the long jump. At Athens in 1906 Con won the high jump and added a bronze in the long jump, and then placed second in the 1908 high jump.

The first brothers to win medals in the same Games were Platt and Ben Adams (USA) who came first and second in the 1912 standing high jump. They were equalled by Matti and Akilles Järvinen (FIN) who won gold and silver medals in the javelin and decathlon respectively in 1932. Most successful were the Press sisters (URS), Tamara with three golds and one silver, and Irina with two golds, in 1960 and 1964. The only twins to win medals were Patrick and Pascal Barré in the French bronze medal sprint relay team in 1980. The most successful brother and sister combination were Godfrey and Audrey Brown (GBR) in 1936, when he won a gold (4 × 400 m relay) and a silver (400 m) and she won a silver (4 × 100 m relay).

Father and son gold medallists are represented by two families. Werner Järvinen (FIN) won the 1906 Greek style discus, his son Matti won the 1932 javelin and his other son, Akilles, won silver medals in the 1928 and 1932 decathlons. In 1948 Imre Nemeth (HUN) won the hammer title, and 28 years later his son Miklos won the javelin with a world record throw. The most suc-

Forrest Smithson (USA) wins the 1908 high hurdles holding a bible as a protest against Sunday competition.

The German girls drop the baton (arrowed) in the 1936 relay final at the last exchange, between Dollinger and Dörffeldt.

Close scrutiny soon after the start of the 10 000 m walk in 1912, with (from the left) Webb (GB), Gylche (DEN), Goulding (CAN) and St Louis (SAF).

In 1912 Ralph Rose (USA) lost the shot (best hand) title he had previously gained in St Louis and London, but won the two-handed event as consolation.

The 1936 American relay team, of Owens, Metcalfe, Draper and Wykoff, set a world record wich lasted for over 20 years.

cessful mother/daughter combination were Elizabeta Bagriantseva (URS) who won the silver medal in the 1952 discus, and her daughter Irina Nazarova who won a gold medal as a member of the Soviet 4 × 400 m relay team in 1980. One of the more poignant stories in the Olympics relates to Marie Dollinger who was one of the girls involved in dropping the baton in the 1936 sprint relay when the German team 'couldn't lose'. One wonders what thoughts were going through the head of her daughter Brunhilde Hendrix in the 1960 relay final—happily she won a silver medal.

A number of married couples won gold medals before they were married, but only one, Emil and Dana Zatopek (TCH) won them as man and wife. Even more remarkable is the fact that Dana won hers on the same afternoon as one of Emil's in 1952—both of them were also born on the same day.

Frank Wykoff (USA) was the only sprinter to win gold medals in three Olympics, as a member of the winning 4 × 100 m relay teams from 1928 to 1936.

The first Olympic athlete to be disqualified for contravening the drugs regulations was Panuta Rosani (POL) in the women's discus in 1976. Two athletes previously disqualified, but later reinstated—Ilona Slupianek (GDR) and Nadyezda Tkachenko (URS)—won titles in 1980. It should be noted that many distance runners around the beginning of the century were using drugs as stimulants, and the winner of the 1904 marathon, Thomas Hicks (USA) was allegedly given a small dose of strychnine by his handlers when he was wilting with a few miles to go to the finish.

The scrutiny or 'sex testing' of women in the Games was introduced in 1968, many years too late in the opinion of some authorities. They had in mind the case of Dora Ratjen (GER) who had placed fourth in the 1936 high jump and was later found to be a man posing as a woman. Less clear cut were the cases of Eva Klobukowska (POL) who won a gold medal in the relay in 1964 and a bronze in the 100 m and was the first to fail such a test in 1967, and Stella Walasiewicz (Walsh) also Polish-born who won gold and silver 100 m medals in 1932 and 1936 respectively, and was reported, after her death in 1980, to have 'primary male characteristics'.

A number of Olympic medallists from track and field have later made their mark in Hollywood films. In particular, they have come from the ranks of the decathletes—Jim Thorpe, Glenn Morris, Bob Mathias, Rafer Johnson, C K Yang, Floyd Simmons and Bruce Jenner. The 1928 silver medallist in the shot, Herman Brix (USA), changed his name to Bruce Bennett and had many serious roles after an initial 'Tarzan' appearance. Norman Pritchard (IND) a 1900 medallist made many silent films, while more

Left: **One of the greatest of all Olympians, Al Oerter (USA), winner of the discus on four consecutive occasions.** Above: **Betty Cuthbert (AUS-468) wins the 100 m at Melbourne from** (left to right) **Daniels (USA), Leone (ITA), Matthews (AUS), Armitage (GBR) and Stubnick (GER).**

Lee Evans takes the baton from his American teammate Lawrence James in their record-breaking relay in Mexico City.

recent additions to the Hollywood scene have been 1952 relay gold medallist Dean Smith (USA) and 1968 pole vault champion Bob Seagren (USA). The film industries of other countries have welcomed Tapio Rautavaara (FIN) the 1948 javelin champion, Giuseppe Tosi (ITA) the 1948 discus silver medallist, Giuseppe Gentile (ITA) 1968 triple jump bronze medallist, and Adhemar Ferreira da Silva (BRA) the 1952 and 1956 triple jump champion.

The shortest time that an athlete has held an Olympic record (and the world record) was 0·4 sec by Olga Rukavishnikova (URS) at Moscow in the women's pentathlon. That is the difference between her second place time of 2 min 4·8 sec in the final 800 m event of the five-event contest, and that of the third-placed Nadyezda Tkachenko (URS) whose overall points score exceeded her team-mate's by 146.

TUG OF WAR

This sport was part of the track and field pro-gramme from 1900 to 1920. The gold medal team in 1900 was composed of three Swedes and three Danes. The 1904 competition was between

various American clubs, while the 1908 tourna-ment was between British police clubs, with London City Police beating Liverpool Police and K Division, Metropolitan Police. Three men won a record two gold and one silver from 1908 to 1920; John Shepherd, Frederick Humphreys and Edwin Mills, all from Great Britain.

The oldest gold medallist was Frederick Humph-reys (GBR) aged 42 yr 203 days in 1920, while the youngest was Karl Staaf (SWE) aged 19 yr 101 days in 1900. Three gold medallists won medals in other sports; Heinrich Schneidereit and Heinrich Rondi of the winning German team in 1906 both won bronze medals in weightlifting at the same Games, and Edmond Barrett of the winning City Police team in 1908 also won a bronze in heavyweight freestyle wrestling.

TUG OF WAR

	Gold	Silver	Bronze
1900	Sweden/Denmark	United States	France
1904	United States	United States	United States
1906	Germany	Greece	Sweden
1908	Great Britain	Great Britain	Great Britain
1912	Sweden	Great Britain	—
1920	Great Britain	Netherlands	Belgium

OLDEST AND YOUNGEST MEDALLISTS BY EVENT

MEN		YOUNGEST		OLDEST	
	Medal	Years/Days	Name/Country/Date	Years/Days	Name/Country/Date
100 m	G	19–128	Reggie Walker (SAF) 1908	28–83	Allan Wells (GBR) 1980
	M	18–234	Donald Lippincott (USA) 1912	31–226	McDonald Bailey (GBR) 1952
200 m	G	20–47	Percy Williams (CAN) 1928	28–30	Pietro Mennea (ITA) 1980
	M	17–256	Dwayne Evans (USA) 1976	30–170	Barney Ewell (USA) 1948
400 m	G	21–98	Archie Williams (USA) 1936	30–323	Mike Larrabee (USA) 1964
	M	20–347	Lawrence James (USA) 1968	30–323	Mike Larrabee (USA) 1964
800 m	G	20–237	Ted Meredith (USA) 1912	31–147	Albert Hill (GBR) 1920
	M	20–237	Ted Meredith (USA) 1912	32–58	Arthur Wint (JAM) 1952

1500 m	G	21–96	Arnold Jackson (GBR) 1912	**31–149**	Albert Hill (GBR) 1920
	M	21–96	Arnold Jackson (GBR) 1912	**31–149**	Albert Hill (GBR) 1920
5000 m	G	20–321	Joseph Guillemot (FRA) 1920	**36–78**	Miruts Yifter (ETH) 1980
	M	20–321	Joseph Guillemot (FRA) 1920	**36–78**	Miruts Yifter (ETH) 1980
10 000 m	G	22–212	Hannes Kolehmainen (FIN) 1912	**36–73**	Miruts Yifter (ETH) 1980
	M	20–324	Joseph Guillemot (FRA) 1920	**36–73**	Miruts Yifter (ETH) 1980
Marathon	G	20–301	Juan Zabala (ARG) 1932	**36–130**	Mamo Wolde (ETH) 1968
	M	19–178	Ernst Fast (SWE) 1900	**40–90**	Mamo Wolde (ETH) 1972
3000 m	G	21–37	Amos Biwott (KEN) 1968	**32–211**	Kip Keino (KEN) 1972
Steeplechase	M	21–37	Amos Biwott (KEN) 1968	**32–211**	Kip Keino (KEN) 1972
110 m	G	20–304	Fred Kelly (USA) 1912	**29–16**	Harrison Dillard (USA) 1952
Hurdles	M	20–304	Fred Kelly (USA) 1912	**33–50**	Willie Davenport (USA) 1976
400 m	G	20–329	Ed Moses (USA) 1976	**29–207**	Roy Cochran (USA) 1948
Hurdles	M	18–325	Eddie Southern (USA) 1956	**33–133**	Leonard Tremeer (GBR) 1908
4 × 100 m	G	18–118	Johnny Jones (USA) 1976	**30–355**	Mel Pender (USA) 1968
	M	17–229	Ture Persson (SWE) 1912	**33–292**	Jocelyn Delecour (FRA) 1968
4 × 400 m	G	19–100	Edgar Ablowich (USA) 1932	**32–62**	Arthur Wint (JAM) 1952
	M	17–+	Pal Simon (HUN) 1908	**32–62**	Arthur Wint (JAM) 1952
20 km Walk	G	23–109	Maurizio Damilano (ITA) 1980	**33–110**	Peter Frenkel (GDR) 1972
	M	21–253	Noel Freeman (AUS) 1960	**37–71**	Peter Frenkel (GDR) 1976
50 km Walk	G	25–103	Norman Read (NZL) 1956	**38–128**	Thomas Green (GBR) 1932
	M	25–26	Antal Róka (HUN) 1952	**48–115**	Tebbs Lloyd Johnson (GBR) 1948
High Jump	G	19–214	Jacek Wszola (POL) 1976	**30–3**	Con Leahy (GBR) 1906
	M	18–140	Valeriy Brumel (URS) 1960	**32–85**	Con Leahy (GBR) 1908
Pole Vault	G	17–360	Lee Barnes (USA) 1924	**30–280**	Bob Richards (USA) 1956
	M	17–360	Lee Barnes (USA) 1924	**30–280**	Bob Richards (USA) 1956
Long Jump	G	19–17	Randy Williams (USA) 1972	**28–113**	Arnie Robinson (USA) 1976
	M	19–17	Randy Williams (USA) 1972	**31–192**	Peter O'Connor (GBR) 1906
Triple Jump	G	20–225	Gustaf Lindblom (SWE) 1912	**31–195**	Peter O'Connor (GBR) 1906
	M	20–38	Arnoldo Devonish (VEN) 1952	**34–296**	Viktor Saneyev (URS) 1980
Shot	G	20–175	Parry O'Brien (USA) 1952	**32–151**	Wladyslaw Komar (POL) 1972
	M	19–226	Randy Matson (USA) 1964	**37–59**	Denis Horgan (GBR) 1908
Discus	G	20–69	Al Oerter (USA) 1956	**35–240**	Ludvik Danek (TCH) 1972
	M	20–69	Al Oerter (USA) 1956	**36–52**	Werner Järvinen (FIN) 1906
Hammer	G	20–161	József Csermák (HUN) 1952	**35–187**	John Flanagan (USA) 1908
	M	19–187	Uwe Beyer (GER) 1964	**45–205**	Matt McGrath (USA) 1924
Javelin	G	20–34	Erik Lundkvist (SWE) 1928	**33–149**	Tapio Rautavaara (FIN) 1948
	M	20–34	Erik Lundkvist (SWE) 1928	**38–332**	József Varszegi (HUN) 1948
Decathlon	G	17–263	Bob Mathias (USA) 1948	**30–102**[1]	Helge Lövland (NOR) 1920
	M	17–263	Bob Mathias (USA) 1948	**30–102**	Helge Lövland (NOR) 1920

[1] Thomas Kiely (GBR) won the all-round title in 1904 aged 34 years 314 days.   G = Gold Medallist   M = Medallist

WOMEN		YOUNGEST		OLDEST	
	Medal	Years/Days	Name/Country/Date	Years/Days	Name/Country/Date
100 m	G	16–343	Elizabeth Robinson (USA) 1928	30–98	Fanny Blankers-Koen (HOL) 1948
	M	16–343	Elizabeth Robinson (USA) 1928	30–98	Fanny Blankers-Koen (HOL) 1948
200 m	G	18–254	Betty Cuthbert (AUS) 1956	30–102	Fanny Blankers-Koen (HOL) 1948
	M	17–116	Raelene Boyle (AUS) 1968	30–102	Fanny Blankers-Koen (HOL) 1948
400 m	G	19–340	Monika Zehrt (GDR) 1972	30–66	Irena Szewinska (POL) 1976
	M	18–152	Christina Brehmer (GDR) 1976	30–66	Irena Szewinska (POL) 1976
800 m	G	20–251	Madeline Manning (USA) 1968	26–242	Nadyezda Olizarenko (URS) 1980
	M	20–100	Inge Gentzel (SWE) 1928	29–39	Ursula Donath (GER) 1960
1500 m	G	24–226	Tatyana Kazankina (URS) 1976	29–47	Ludmila Bragina (URS) 1972
	M	22–256	Ulrike Klapezynski (GDR) 1976	33–24	Gunhild Hoffmeister (GDR) 1976
80/100 m	G	17–19	Maureen Caird (AUS) 1968	31–133	Shirley Strickland (AUS) 1956
Hurdles	M	17–19	Maureen Caird (AUS) 1968	34–95	Karin Balzer (GDR) 1972
4 × 100	G	15–123	Barbara Jones (USA) 1952	31–136	Shirley Strickland (AUS) 1956
	M	15–123	Barbara Jones (USA) 1952	32–313	Marga Petersen (GER) 1952
4 × 400	G	18–154	Christina Brehmer (GDR) 1976	28–78	Nina Zuskova (URS) 1980
	M	17–236	Mable Fergerson (USA) 1972	28–78	Nina Zuskova (URS) 1980
High Jump	G	16–123	Ulrike Meyfarth (FRG) 1972	27–308	Iolanda Balas (ROM) 1964
	M	15–23	Carolina Gisolf (HOL) 1928	29–191	Yordanka Blagoyeva (BUL) 1976

Long Jump	G	20–256	Tatyana Kolpakova (URS) 1980	29–67	Viorica Viscopoleanu (ROM) 1968
	M	17–332	Willye White (USA) 1956	30–365	Tatyana Talysheva (URS) 1968
Shot	G	21–186	Galina Zybina (URS) 1952	34–255	Ivanka Khristova (BUL) 1976
	M	21–186	Galina Zybina (URS) 1952	34–255	Ivanka Khristova (BUL) 1976
Discus	G	20–121	Evelin Schlaak (GDR) 1976	36–176	Lia Manoliu (ROM) 1968
	M	20–100	Ruth Osburn (USA) 1932	36–176	Lia Manoliu (ROM) 1968
Javelin	G	17–86	Mihaela Penes (ROM) 1964	33–190	Herma Bauma (AUT) 1948
	M	17–86	Mihaela Penes (ROM) 1964	37–348	Dana Zatopkova (TCH) 1960
Pentathlon	G	21–271	Siegrun Siegl (GDR) 1976	33–59	Mary Peters (GBR) 1972
	M	21–85	Burglinde Pollak (GDR) 1972	33–59	Mary Peters (GBR) 1972

G = Gold Medallist   M = Medallist

Men

OLYMPIC RECORDS—TRACK & FIELD ATHLETICS

Event	hr min:sec	Name & Country	Year
100 metres	9·95	Jim Hines (USA)	1968
200 metres	19·83	Tommie Smith (USA)	1968
400 metres	43·86	Lee Evans (USA)	1968
800 metres	1:43·50	Alberto Juantorena (CUB)	1976
1500 metres	3:34·91	Kipchoge Keino (KEN)	1968
5000 metres	13:20·34	Brendan Foster (GBR)	1976
10 000 metres	27:38·35	Lasse Viren (FIN)	1972
Marathon	2 h 09:55·0	Waldemar Cierpinski (GDR)	1976
20 km walk	1 h 23:36·0	Maurizio Damilano (ITA)	1980
50 km walk	3 h 49:24·0	Hartwig Gauder (GDR)	1980
110 metres hurdles	13·24	Rod Milburn (USA)	1972
400 metres hurdles	47·64	Ed Moses (USA)	1976
3000 metres steeplechase	8:08·02	Anders Garderud (SWE)	1976
4 × 100 metres relay	38·19	USA	1972
4 × 400 metres relay	2:56·16	USA	1968
	metres		
High jump	2·36	Gerd Wessig (GDR)	1980
Pole vault	5·78	Wladyslaw Kozakiewicz (POL)	1980
Long jump	8·90	Bob Beamon (USA)	1968
Triple jump	17·39	Viktor Saneyev (URS)	1968
Shot put	21·35	Vladimir Kiselyev (URS)	1980
Discus throw	68·28	Mac Wilkins (USA)	1976
Hammer throw	81·80	Yuriy Sedykh (URS)	1980
Javelin throw	94·58	Miklos Nemeth (HUN)	1976
	points		
Decathlon	8617	Bruce Jenner (USA)	1976

Women

Event	min:sec	Name & Country	Year
100 metres	11·01	Annegret Richter (FRG)	1976
200 metres	22·03	Barbel Wöckel (GDR)	1980
400 metres	48·88	Marita Koch (GDR)	1980
800 metres	1:53·43	Nadyezda Olizarenko (URS)	1980
1500 metres	3:56·56	Tatyana Kazankina (URS)	1980
3000 metres	Not previously held		
Marathon	Not previously held		
100 metres hurdles	12·56	Vera Komissova (URS)	1980
400 metres hurdles	Not previously held		
4 × 100 metres relay	41·60	GDR	1980
4 × 400 metres relay	3:19·23	GDR	1976
	metres		
High jump	1·97	Sara Simeoni (ITA)	1980
Long jump	7·06	Tatyana Kolpakova (URS)	1980
Shot put	22·41	Ilona Slupianek (GDR)	1980
Discus throw	69·96	Evelin Jahl (GDR)	1980
Javelin throw	68·40	Maria Colon (CUB)	1980
Heptathlon	Not previously held		

TRACK AND FIELD—MEDALS (including Tug-of-War)

	MEN				WOMEN				TOTAL				Total Medals
	Gold	Silver	Bronze		Gold	Silver	Bronze		Gold	Silver	Bronze		
UNITED STATES......	226	167	141	......	19	12	8	......	245	179	149	......	573
USSR......................	29	31	36	......	25	18	28	......	54	49	64	......	167
GREAT BRITAIN	40	48	37	......	3	16	7	......	43	64	44	......	151
GERMANY (FRG)......	9	26	29	......	10	19	12	......	19	45	41	......	105
FINLAND...............	44	31	27	......	—	1	—	......	44	32	27	......	103
SWEDEN	19	22	41	......	—	—	3	......	19	22	44	......	85
GDR......................	11	11	11	......	21	14	14	......	32	25	25	......	82
AUSTRALIA	6	8	11	......	9	7	10	......	15	15	21	......	51
FRANCE..................	6	19	17	......	3	1	2	......	9	20	19	......	48
POLAND	9	7	4	......	6	8	7	......	15	15	11	......	41
CANADA.................	9	9	13	......	2	3	5	......	11	12	18	......	41
HUNGARY...............	6	13	16	......	3	1	2	......	9	14	18	......	41
ITALY....................	10	6	14	......	2	3	2	......	12	9	16	......	37
GREECE	3	9	11	......	—	—	—	......	3	9	11	......	23
CZECHOSLOVAKIA	5	6	3	......	3	2	2	......	8	8	5	......	21
NEW ZEALAND	7	1	7	......	1	—	1	......	8	1	8	......	17
JAMAICA................	4	7	4	......	—	—	1	......	4	7	5	......	16
KENYA	5	6	4	......	—	—	—	......	5	6	4	......	15
JAPAN....................	4	4	6	......	—	1	—	......	4	5	6	......	15
SOUTH AFRICA	4	4	3	......	1	1	1	......	5	5	4	......	14
NETHERLANDS	—	2	5	......	4	2	1	......	4	4	6	......	14
ROMANIA	—	—	1	......	5	4	2	......	5	4	3	......	12
CUBA.....................	2	5	1	......	1	1	2	......	3	6	3	......	12
NORWAY	3	2	7	......	—	—	—	......	3	2	7	......	12
BELGIUM................	2	5	4	......	—	—	—	......	2	5	4	......	11
ETHIOPIA	5	1	4	......	—	—	—	......	5	1	4	......	10
BULGARIA	—	—	1	......	1	5	3	......	1	5	4	......	10
BRAZIL...................	2	1	4	......	—	—	—	......	2	1	4	......	7
SWITZERLAND	—	5	1	......	—	—	—	......	—	5	1	......	6
ARGENTINA............	2	2	—	......	—	1	—	......	2	3	—	......	5
AUSTRIA.................	—	—	—	......	1	1	3	......	1	1	3	......	5
TRINIDAD	1	1	3	......	—	—	—	......	1	1	3	......	5
IRELAND................	4	—	—	......	—	—	—	......	4	—	—	......	4
TUNISIA	1	2	1	......	—	—	—	......	1	2	1	......	4
DENMARK...............	1	1	1	......	—	—	1	......	1	1	2	......	4
MEXICO..................	1	1	—	......	—	—	—	......	1	1	—	......	2
CHILE....................	—	1	—	......	—	1	—	......	—	2	—	......	2
INDIA.....................	—	2	—	......	—	—	—	......	—	2	—	......	2
TANZANIA...............	—	2	—	......	—	—	—	......	—	2	—	......	2
YUGOSLAVIA	—	2	—	......	—	—	—	......	—	2	—	......	2
ESTONIA.................	—	1	1	......	—	—	—	......	—	1	1	......	2
LATVIA...................	—	1	1	......	—	—	—	......	—	1	1	......	2
TAIWAN	—	1	—	......	—	—	1	......	—	1	1	......	2
PANAMA.................	—	—	2	......	—	—	—	......	—	—	2	......	2
PHILIPPINES...........	—	—	2	......	—	—	—	......	—	—	2	......	2
LUXEMBOURG........	1	—	—	......	—	—	—	......	1	—	—	......	1
UGANDA.................	1	—	—	......	—	—	—	......	1	—	—	......	1
HAITI	—	1	—	......	—	—	—	......	—	1	—	......	1
ICELAND	—	1	—	......	—	—	—	......	—	1	—	......	1
MOROCCO..............	—	1	—	......	—	—	—	......	—	1	—	......	1
PORTUGAL	—	1	—	......	—	—	—	......	—	1	—	......	1
SPAIN	—	1	—	......	—	—	—	......	—	1	—	......	1
SRI LANKA (Ceylon) ..	—	1	—	......	—	—	—	......	—	1	—	......	1
TURKEY	—	—	1	......	—	—	—	......	—	—	1	......	1
VENEZUELA	—	—	1	......	—	—	—	......	—	—	1	......	1
	482	479	476		120	·122	118		602	601	594		1797

TRACK AND FIELD (Men)
(Prior to 1972 automatic timings to one-hundredths of a second are shown additionally, where known)
100 METRES

	Gold	*Silver*	*Bronze*
1896	Thomas Burke (USA) 12·0	Fritz Hofmann (GER) 12·2	Alajos Szokolyi (HUN) 12·6
1900	Frank Jarvis (USA) 11·0	Walter Tewksbury (USA) 11·1	Stanley Rowley (AUS) 11·2
1904	Archie Hahn (USA) 11·0	Nathaniel Cartmell (USA) 11·2	William Hogenson (USA) 11·2
1906	Archie Hahn (USA) 11·2	Fay Moulton (USA) 11·3	Nigel Barker (AUS) 11·3
1908	Reginald Walker (SAF) 10·8	James Rector (USA) 10·9	Robert Kerr (CAN) 11·0
1912	Ralph Craig (USA) 10·8	Alvah Meyer (USA) 10·9	Donald Lippincott (USA) 10·9
1920	Charles Paddock (USA) 10·8	Morris Kirksey (USA) 10·8	Harry Edward (GBR) 11·0
1924	Harold Abrahams (GBR) 10·6	Jackson Scholz (USA) 10·7	Arthur Porritt (NZL) 10·8
1928	Percy Williams (CAN) 10·8	Jack London (GBR) 10·9	Georg Lammers (GER) 10·9
1932	Eddie Tolan (USA) 10·3 (10·38)	Ralph Metcalfe (USA) 10·3 (10·38)	Arthur Jonath (GER) 10·4 (10·48)
1936	Jesse Owens (USA) 10·3	Ralph Metcalfe (USA) 10·4	Martinus Osendarp (HOL) 10·5
1948	Harrison Dillard (USA) 10·3	Norwood Ewell (USA) 10·4	Lloyd LaBeach (PAN) 10·4
1952	Lindy Remigino (USA) 10·4 (10·79)	Herb McKenley (JAM) 10·4 (10·79)	Emmanuel McD. Bailey (GBR) 10·4 (10·83)
1956	Bobby-Joe Morrow (USA) 10·5 (10·62)	Thane Baker (USA) 10·5 (10·77)	Hector Hogan (AUS) 10·6 (10·77)
1960	Armin Hary (GER) 10·2 (10·32)	David Sime (USA) 10·2 (10·35)	Peter Radford (GBR) 10·3 (10·42)
1964	Bob Hayes (USA) 10·0 (10·06)	Enrique Figuerola (CUB) 10·2 (10·20)	Harry Jerome (CAN) 10·2 (10·27)
1968	James Hines (USA) 9·9 (9·95)	Lennox Miller (JAM) 10·0 (10·04)	Charles Greene (USA) 10·0 (10·07)
1972	Valeriy Borzov (URS) 10·14	Robert Taylor (USA) 10·24	Lennox Miller (JAM) 10·33
1976	Hasely Crawford (TRI) 10·06	Don Quarrie (JAM) 10·08	Valeriy Borzov (URS) 10·14
1980	Allan Wells (GBR) 10·25	Silvio Leonard (CUB) 10·25	Petar Petrov (BUL) 10·39

200 METRES

	Gold	*Silver*	*Bronze*
1900	Walter Tewksbury (USA) 22·2	Norman Pritchard (IND) 22·8	Stanley Rowley (AUS) 22·9
1904[1]	Archie Hahn (USA) 21·6	Nathaniel Cartmell (USA) 21·9	William Hogenson (USA) d.n.a.
1908	Robert Kerr (CAN) 22·6	Robert Cloughen (USA) 22·6	Nathaniel Cartmell (USA) 22·7
1912	Ralph Craig (USA) 21·7	Donald Lippincott (USA) 21·8	Willie Applegarth (GBR) 22·0
1920	Allen Woodring (USA) 22·0	Charles Paddock (USA) 22·1	Harry Edward (GBR) 22·2
1924	Jackson Scholz (USA) 21·6	Charles Paddock (USA) 21·7	Eric Liddell (GBR) 21·9
1928	Percy Williams (CAN) 21·8	Walter Rangeley (GBR) 21·9	Helmut Kornig[2] (GER) 21·9
1932	Eddie Tolan (USA) 21·2 (21·12)	George Simpson (USA) 21·4	Ralph Metcalfe[3] (USA) 21·5
1936	Jesse Owens (USA) 20·7	Mack Robinson (USA) 21·1	Martinus Osendarp (HOL) 21·3
1948	Mel Patton (USA) 21·1	Norwood Ewell (USA) 21·1	Lloyd LaBeach (PAN) 21·2
1952	Andrew Stanfield (USA) 20·7 (20·81)	Thane Baker (USA) 20·8 (20·97)	James Gathers (USA) 20·8 (21·08)
1956	Bobby-Joe Morrow (USA) 20·6 (20·75)	Andrew Stanfield (USA) 20·7 (20·97)	Thane Baker (USA) 20·9 (21·04)
1960	Livio Berutti (ITA) 20·5 (20·62)	Lester Carney (USA) 20·6 (20·69)	Abdoulaye Seye (FRA) 20·7 (20·82)
1964	Henry Carr (USA) 20·3 (20·36)	Paul Drayton (USA) 20·5 (20·58)	Edwin Roberts (TRI) 20·6 (20·63)
1968	Tommie Smith (USA) 19·8 (19·83)	Peter Norman (AUS) 20·0 (20·06)	John Carlos (USA) 20·0 (20·10)
1972	Valeriy Borzov (URS) 20·00	Larry Black (USA) 20·19	Pietro Mennea (ITA) 20·30
1976	Don Quarrie (JAM) 20·23	Millard Hampton (USA) 20·29	Dwayne Evans (USA) 20·43
1980	Pietro Mennea (ITA) 20·19	Allan Wells (GBR) 20·21	Don Quarrie (JAM) 20·29

[1] Race over straight course. Hahn's three opponents were all given two yard handicaps for false starting.   [2] Awarded bronze medal when Scholz (USA) refused to re-run after tie.   [3] Metcalfe's lane was later found to be 1½ metres too long.   1896, 1906 Event not held

400 METRES

	Gold	*Silver*	*Bronze*
1896	Thomas Burke (USA) 54·2	Herbert Jamison (USA) 55·2	Fritz Hofmann (GER) 55·6
1900	Maxwell Long (USA) 49·4	William Holland (USA) 49·6	Ernst Schultz (DEN) 15 m
1904	Harry Hillman (USA) 49·2	Frank Waller (USA) 49·9	Herman Groman (USA) 50·0
1906	Paul Pilgrim (USA) 53·2	Wyndham Halswelle (GBR) 53·8	Nigel Barker (AUS) 54·1
1908[1]	Wyndham Halswelle (GBR) 50·0	—	—
1912	Charles Reidpath (USA) 48·2	Hanns Braun (GER) 48·3	Edward Lindberg (USA) 48·4
1920	Bevil Rudd (SAF) 49·6	Guy Butler (GBR) 49·9	Nils Engdahl (SWE) 50·0
1924	Eric Liddell (GBR) 47·6	Horatio Fitch (USA) 48·4	Guy Butler (GBR) 48·6
1928	Ray Barbuti (USA) 47·8	James Ball (CAN) 48·0	Joachim Büchner (GER) 48·2

1932	William Carr (USA) 46·2 (46·28)	Ben Eastman (USA) 46·4	Alexander Wilson (CAN) 47·4
1936	Archie Williams (USA) 46·5 (46·66)	Godfrey Brown (GBR) 46·7 (46·68)	James LuValle (USA) 46·8 (46·84)
1948	Arthur Wint (JAM) 46·2	Herb McKenley (JAM) 46·4	Mal Whitfield (USA) 46·6
1952	George Rhoden (JAM) 45·9 (46·09)	Herb McKenley (JAM) 45·9 (46·20)	Ollie Matson (USA) 46·8 (46·94)
1956	Charles Jenkins (USA) 46·7 (46·86)	Karl-Friedrich Haas (GER) 46·8 (47·12)	Voitto Hellsten (FIN) 47·0 (47·15)
			Ardalion Ignatyev (URS) 47·0 (47·15)
1960	Otis Davis (USA) 44·9 (45·07)	Carl Kaufmann (GER) 44·9 (45·08)	Mal Spence (SAF) 45·5 (45·60)
1964	Mike Larrabee (USA) 45·1 (45·15)	Wendell Mottley (TRI) 45·2 (45·24)	Andrzej Badenski (POL) 45·6 (45·63)
1968	Lee Evans (USA) 43·8 (43·86)	Lawrence James (USA) 43·9 (43·97)	Ron Freeman (USA) 44·4 (44·41)
1972	Vince Matthews (USA) 44·66	Wayne Collett (USA) 44·80	Julius Sang (KEN) 44·92
1976	Alberto Juantorena (CUB) 44·26	Fred Newhouse (USA) 44·40	Herman Frazier (USA) 44·95
1980	Viktor Markin (URS) 44·60	Rick Mitchell (AUS) 44·84	Frank Schaffer (GDR) 44·87

[1] Re-run ordered after John Carpenter (USA) disqualified in first final. Only Halswelle showed up and 'walked over' for the title.

800 METRES

	Gold	Silver	Bronze
1896	Edwin Flack (AUS) 2:11·0	Nåndor Dáni (HUN) 2:11·8	Dimitrios Golemis (GRE) 2:28·0
1900	Alfred Tysoe (GBR) 2:01·2	John Cregan (USA) 2:03·0	David Hall (USA) d.n.a.
1904	James Lightbody (USA) 1:56·0	Howard Valentine (USA) 1:56·3	Emil Breitkreutz (USA) 1:56·4
1906	Paul Pilgrim (USA) 2:01·5	James Lightbody (USA) 2:01·6	Wyndham Halswelle (GBR) 2:03·0
1908	Mel Sheppard (USA) 1:52·8	Emilio Lunghi (ITA) 1:54·2	Hanns Braun (GER) 1:55·2
1912	James Meredith (USA) 1:51·9	Mel Sheppard (USA) 1:52·0	Ira Davenport (USA) 1:52·0
1920	Albert Hill (GBR) 1:53·4	Earl Eby (USA) 1:53·6	Bevil Rudd (SAF) 1:54·0
1924	Douglas Lowe (GBR) 1:52·4	Paul Martin (SUI) 1:52·6	Schuyler Enck (USA) 1:53·0
1928	Douglas Lowe (GBR) 1:51·8	Erik Bylehn (SWE) 1:52·8	Hermann Engelhardt (GER) 1:53·2
1932	Thomas Hampson (GBR) 1:49·7	Alexander Wilson (CAN) 1:49·9	Phil Edwards (CAN) 1:51·5
1936	John Woodruff (USA) 1:52·9	Mario Lanzi (ITA) 1:53·3	Phil Edwards (CAN) 1:53·6
1948	Mal Whitfield (USA) 1:49·2	Arthur Wint (JAM) 1:49·5	Marcel Hansenne (FRA) 1:49·8
1952	Mal Whitfield (USA) 1:49·2	Arthur Wint (JAM) 1:49·4	Heinz Ulzheimer (GER) 1:49·7
1956	Tom Courtney (USA) 1:47·7	Derek Johnson (GBR) 1:47·8	Audun Boysen (NOR) 1:48·1
1960	Peter Snell (NZL) 1:46·3	Roger Moens (BEL) 1:46·5	George Kerr[1] (BWI) 1:47·1
1964	Peter Snell (NZL) 1:45·1	Bill Crothers (CAN) 1:45·6	Wilson Kiprugut (KEN) 1:45·9
1968	Ralph Doubell (AUS) 1:44·3	Wilson Kiprugut (KEN) 1:44·5	Tom Farrell (USA) 1:45·4
1972	Dave Wottle (USA) 1:45·9	Yevgeniy Arzhanov (URS) 1:45·9	Mike Boit (KEN) 1:46·0
1976	Alberto Juantorena (CUB) 1:43·5	Ivo Van Damme (BEL) 1:43·9	Richard Wohlhuter (USA) 1:44·1
1980	Steve Ovett (GBR) 1:45·4	Sebastian Coe (GBR) 1:45·9	Nikolai Kirov (URS) 1:46·0

[1] Kerr was a Jamaican in the combined British West Indies team.

1500 METRES

	Gold	Silver	Bronze
1896	Edwin Flack (AUS) 4:33·2	Arthur Blake (USA) 4:34·0	Albin Lermusiaux (FRA) 4:36·0
1900	Charles Bennett (GBR) 4:06·2	Henri Deloge (FRA) 4:06·6	John Bray (USA) 4:07·2
1904	James Lightbody (USA) 4:05·4	William Verner (USA) 4:06·8	Lacey Hearn (USA) d.n.a.
1906	James Lightbody (USA) 4:12·0	John McGough (GBR) 4:12·6	Kristian Hellström (SWE) 4:13·4
1908	Mel Sheppard (USA) 4:03·4	Harold Wilson (GBR) 4:03·6	Norman Hallows (GBR) 4:04·0
1912[1]	Arnold Jackson (GBR) 3:56·8	Abel Kiviat (USA) 3:56·9	Norman Taber (USA) 3:56·9
1920	Albert Hill (GBR) 4:01·8	Philip Baker[1] (GBR) 4:02·4	Lawrence Shields (USA) 4:03·1
1924	Paavo Nurmi (FIN) 3:53·6	Willy Schärer (SUI) 3:55·0	Henry Stallard (GBR) 3:55·6
1928	Harri Larva (FIN) 3:53·2	Jules Ladoumègue (FRA) 3:53·8	Eino Purje (FIN) 3:56·4
1932	Luigi Beccali (ITA) 3:51·2	John Cornes (GBR) 3:52·6	Phil Edwards (CAN) 3:52·8
1936	Jack Lovelock (NZL) 3:47·8	Glenn Cunningham (USA) 3:48·4	Luigi Beccali (ITA) 3:49·2
1948	Henry Eriksson (SWE) 3:49·8	Lennart Strand (SWE) 3:50·4	Willem Slijkhuis (HOL) 3:50·4
1952	Josef Barthel (LUX) 3:45·1	Bob McMillen (USA) 3:45·2	Werner Lueg (GER) 3:45·4
1956	Ron Delany (IRL) 3:41·2	Klaus Richtzenhain (GER) 3:42·0	John Landy (AUS) 3:42·0
1960	Herb Elliott (AUS) 3:35·6	Michel Jazy (FRA) 3:38·4	István Rózsavölgyi (HUN) 3:39·2
1964	Peter Snell (NZL) 3:38·1	Josef Odlozil (TCH) 3:39·6	John Davies (NZL) 3:39·6
1968	Kipchoge Keino (KEN) 3:34·9	Jim Ryun (USA) 3:37·8	Bodo Tümmler (FRG) 3:39·0
1972	Pekka Vasala (FIN) 3:36·3	Kipchoge Keino (KEN) 3:36·8	Rod Dixon (NZL) 3:37·5
1976	John Walker (NZL) 3:39·2	Ivo Van Damme (BEL) 3:39·3	Paul-Heinz Wellmann (FRG) 3:39·3
1980	Sebastian Coe (GBR) 3:38·4	Jürgen Straub (GDR) 3:38·8	Steve Ovett (GBR) 3:39·0

[1] Jackson later changed name to Strode-Jackson and Baker changed to Noel-Baker.

5000 METRES

	Gold	Silver	Bronze
1912	Hannes Kolehmainen (FIN) 14:36·6	Jean Bouin (FRA) 14·36·7	George Hutson (GBR) 15:07·6
1920	Joseph Guillemot (FRA) 14:55·6	Paavo Nurmi (FIN) 15:00·0	Erik Backman (SWE) 15:13·0
1924[1]	Paavo Nurmi (FIN) 14:31·2	Ville Ritola (FIN) 14:31·4	Edvin Wide (SWE) 15:01·8
1928	Ville Ritola (FIN) 14:38·0	Paavo Nurmi (FIN) 14:40·0	Edvin Wide (SWE) 14:41·2
1932	Lauri Lehtinen (FIN) 14:30·0	Ralph Hill (USA) 14:30·0	Lauri Virtanen (FIN) 14:44·0
1936	Gunnar Höckert (FIN) 14:22·2	Lauri Lehtinen (FIN) 14:25·8	Henry Jonsson[2] (SWE) 14:29·0
1948	Gaston Rieff (BEL) 14:17·6	Emil Zatopek (TCH) 14:17·8	Willem Slijkhuis (HOL) 14:26·8
1952	Emil Zatopek (TCH) 14:06·6	Alain Mimoun (FRA) 14:07·4	Herbert Schade (GER) 14:08·6
1956	Vladimir Kuts (URS) 13:39·6	Gordon Pirie (GBR) 13:50·6	Derek Ibbotson (GBR) 13:54·4
1960	Murray Halberg (NZL) 13:43·4	Hans Grodotzki (GER) 13:44·6	Kazimierz Zimny (POL) 13:44·8
1964	Bob Schul (USA) 13:48·8	Harald Norpoth (GER) 13:49·6	Bill Dellinger (USA) 13:49·8
1968	Mohamed Gammoudi (TUN) 14:05·0	Kipchoge Keino (KEN) 14:05·2	Naftali Temu (KEN) 14:06·4
1972	Lasse Viren (FIN) 13:26·4	Mohamed Gammoudi (TUN) 13:27·4	Ian Stewart (GBR) 13:27·6
1976	Lasse Viren (FIN) 13:24·8	Dick Quax (NZL) 13:25·2	Klaus-Peter Hildenbrand (FRG) 13:25·4
1980	Miruts Yifter (ETH) 13:21·0	Suleiman Nyambui (TAN) 13:21·6	Kaarlo Maaninka (FIN) 13:22·0

[1] Nurmi won 5000 m only 1½ hours after winning the 1500 m.   [2] Jonsson later changed name to Kälarne.   1896–1908 Event not held

10 000 METRES

	Gold	Silver	Bronze
1906[1]	Henry Hawtrey (GBR) 26:11·8	John Svanberg (SWE) 26:19·4	Edward Dahl (SWE) 26:26·2
1908[1]	Emil Voigt (GBR) 25:11·2	Edward Owen (GBR) 25:24·0	John Svanberg (SWE) 25:37·2
1912	Hannes Kolehmainen (FIN) 31:20·8	Louis Tewanima (USA) 32:06·6	Albin Stenroos (FIN) 32:21·8
1920	Paavo Nurmi (FIN) 31:45·8	Joseph Guillemot (FRA) 31:47·2	James Wilson (GBR) 31:50·8
1924	Ville Ritola (FIN) 30:23·2	Edvin Wide (SWE) 30:55·2	Eero Berg (FIN) 31:43·0
1928	Paavo Nurmi (FIN) 30:18·8	Ville Ritola (FIN) 30:19·4	Edvin Wide (SWE) 31:00·8
1932	Janusz Kusocinski (POL) 30:11·4	Volmari Iso-Hollo (FIN) 30:12·6	Lauri Virtanen (FIN) 30:35·0
1936	Ilmari Salminen (FIN) 30:15·4	Arvo Askola (FIN) 30:15·6	Volmari Iso-Hollo (FIN) 30:20·2
1948	Emil Zatopek (TCH) 29:59·6	Alain Mimoun (FRA) 30:47·4	Bertil Albertsson (SWE) 30:53·6
1952	Emil Zatopek (TCH) 29:17·0	Alain Mimoun (FRA) 29:32·8	Aleksandr Anufriyev (URS) 29:48·2
1956	Vladimir Kuts (URS) 28:45·6	József Kovács (HUN) 28:52·4	Allan Lawrence (AUS) 28:53·6
1960	Pyotr Bolotnikov (URS) 28:32·2	Hans Grodotzki (GER) 28:37·0	David Power (AUS) 28:38·2
1964	Billy Mills (USA) 28:24·4	Mohamed Gammoudi (TUN) 28:24·8	Ron Clarke (AUS) 28:25·8
1968	Naftali Temu (KEN) 29:27·4	Mamo Wolde (ETH) 29:28·0	Mohamed Gammoudi (TUN) 29:34·2
1972	Lasse Viren (FIN) 27:38·4	Emiel Puttemans (BEL) 27:39·6	Miruts Yifter (ETH) 27:41·0
1976	Lasse Viren (FIN) 27:40·4	Carlos Lopes (POR) 27:45·2	Brendan Foster (GBR) 27:54·9
1980	Miruts Yifter (ETH) 27:42·7	Kaarlo Maaninka (FIN) 27:44·3	Mohammed Kedir (ETH) 27:44·7

[1] 5 miles (8046 m).   1896–1904 Event not held

MARATHON

The length of the marathon was standardised at the 1908 distance of 26 miles 385 yards (42 195 metres) from 1924. Previously the distances had been:

1896 & 1904	40 000 m
1900	40 260 m
1906	41 860 m
1912	40 200 m
1920	42 750 m

	Gold	Silver	Bronze
1896	Spyridon Louis (GRE) 2 h 58:50	Charilaos Vasilakos (GRE) 3 h 06:03	Gyula Kellner (HUN) 3 h 09:35
1900	Michel Theato (FRA) 2 h 59:45	Emile Champion (FRA) 3 h 04:17	Ernst Fast (SWE) 3 h 37:14
1904	Thomas Hicks (USA) 3 h 28:35	Albert Corey[1] (FRA) 3 h 34:52	Arthur Newton (USA) 3:47:33
1906	William Sherring (CAN) 2 h 51:23·6	John Svanberg (SWE) 2 h 58:20·8	William Frank (USA) 3 h 00:46·8
1908[2]	John Hayes (USA) 2 h 55:18·4	Charles Hefferon (SAF) 2 h 56:06·0	Joseph Forshaw (USA) 2 h 57:10·4
1912	Kenneth McArthur (SAF) 2 h 36:54·8	Christian Gitsham (SAF) 2 h 37:52·0	Gaston Strobino (USA) 2 h 38:42·4
1920	Hannes Kolehmainen (FIN) 2 h 32:35·8	Jüri Lossman (EST) 2 h 32:48·6	Valerio Arri (ITA) 2 h 36:32·8
1924	Albin Stenroos (FIN) 2 h 41:22·6	Romeo Bertini (ITA) 2 h 47:19·6	Clarence DeMar (USA) 2 h 48:14·0
1928	Mohamed El Ouafi (FRA) 2 h 32:57	Miguel Plaza (CHI) 2 h 33:23	Martti Marttelin (FIN) 2 h 35:02

1932	Juan Carlos Zabala (ARG) 2 h 31:36	Sam Ferris (GBR) 2 h 31:55	Armas Toivonen (FIN) 2 h 32:12
1936	Kitei Son (JPN) 2 h 29:19·2	Ernest Harper (GBR) 2 h 31:23·2	Shoryu Nan (JPN) 2 h 31:42·0
1948	Delfo Cabrera (ARG) 2 h 34:51·6	Tom Richards (GBR) 2 h 35:07·6	Etienne Gailly (BEL) 2 h 35:33·6
1952	Emil Zatopek (TCH) 2 h 23:03·2	Reinaldo Gorno (ARG) 2 h 25:35·0	Gustaf Jansson (SWE) 2 h 26:07·0
1956	Alain Mimoun (FRA) 2 h 25:00	Franjo Mihalic (YUG) 2 h 26:32	Veikko Karvonen (FIN) 2 h 27:47
1960	Abebe Bikila (ETH) 2 h 15:16·2	Rhadi Ben Abdesselem (MAR) 2 h 15:41·6	Barry Magee (NZL) 2 h 17:18·2
1964	Abebe Bikila (ETH) 2 h 12:11·2	Basil Heatley (GBR) 2 h 16:19·2	Kokichi Tsuburaya (JPN) 2 h 16:22·8
1968	Mamo Wolde (ETH) 2 h 20:26·4	Kenji Kimihara (JPN) 2 h 23:31·0	Michael Ryan (NZL) 2 h 23:45·0
1972	Frank Shorter (USA) 2 h 12:19·8	Karel Lismont (BEL) 2 h 14:31·8	Mamo Wolde (ETH) 2 h 15:08·4
1976	Waldemar Cierpinski (GDR) 2 h 09:55·0	Frank Shorter (USA) 2 h 10:45·8	Karel Lismont (BEL) 2 h 11:12·6
1980	Waldemar Cierpinski (GDR) 2 h 11:03	Gerard Nijboer (HOL) 2 h 11:20	Satymkul Dzhumanazarov (URS) 2 h 11:35

¹ Usually shown as an American incorrectly. ² Dorando Pietri (ITA) finished first but was disqualified due to assistance by officials on last lap of the track.

3000 METRES STEEPLECHASE

	Gold	Silver	Bronze
1900[1]	George Orton (CAN) 7:34·4	Sidney Robinson (GBR) 7:38·0	Jacques Chastanié (FRA) d.n.a.
1900[2]	John Rimmer (GBR) 12:58·4	Charles Bennett (GBR) 12:58·6	Sidney Robinson (GBR) 12:58·8
1904[3]	James Lightbody (USA) 7:39·6	John Daly (GBR) 7:40·6	Arthur Newton (USA) 25 m
1908[4]	Arthur Russell (GBR) 10:47·8	Archie Robertson (GBR) 10:48·4	John Eisele (USA) 20 m
1920	Percy Hodge (GBR) 10:00·4	Patrick Flynn (USA) 100 m	Ernesto Ambrosini (ITA) 30 m
1924	Ville Ritola (FIN) 9:33·6	Elias Katz (FIN) 9:44·0	Paul Bontemps (FRA) 9:45·2
1928	Toivo Loukola (FIN) 9:21·8	Paavo Nurmi (FIN) 9:31·2	Ove Andersen (FIN) 9:35·6
1932[5]	Volmari Iso-Hollo (FIN) 10:33·4	Tom Evenson (GBR) 10:46·0	Joseph McCluskey (USA) 10:46·2
1936	Volmari Iso-Hollo (FIN) 9:03·8	Kaarlo Tuominen (FIN) 9:06·8	Alfred Dompert (GER) 9:07·2
1948	Tore Sjöstrand (SWE) 9:04·6	Erik Elmsäter (SWE) 9:08·2	Göte Hagström (SWE) 9:11·8
1952	Horace Ashenfelter (USA) 8:45·4	Vladimir Kazantsev (URS) 8:51·6	John Disley (GBR) 8:51·8
1956	Chris Brasher (GBR) 8:41·2	Sándor Rozsnyói (HUN) 8:43·6	Ernst Larsen (NOR) 8:44·0
1960	Zdzislaw Krzyszkowiak (POL) 8:34·2	Nikolai Sokolov (URS) 8:36·4	Semyon Rzhishchin (URS) 8:42·2
1964	Gaston Roelants (BEL) 8:30·8	Maurice Herriott (GBR) 8:32·4	Ivan Belyayev (URS) 8:33·8
1968	Amos Biwott (KEN) 8:51·0	Benjamin Kogo (KEN) 8:51·6	George Young (USA) 8:51·8
1972	Kipchoge Keino (KEN) 8:23·6	Benjamin Jipcho (KEN) 8:24·6	Tapio Kantanen (FIN) 8:24·8
1976	Anders Garderud (SWE) 8:08·0	Bronislaw Malinowski (POL) 8:09·1	Frank Baumgartl (GDR) 8:10·4
1980	Bronislaw Malinowski (POL) 8:09·7	Filbert Bayi (TAN) 8:12·5	Eshetu Tura (ETH) 8:13·6

¹ 2500 m. ² 4000 m. ³ 2590 m. ⁴ 3200 m. ⁵ 3460 m in final due to lap scoring error. Iso-Hollo clocked 9:14·6 in a heat. 1896, 1906, 1912 Event not held

110 METRES HURDLES

	Gold	Silver	Bronze
1896[1]	Thomas Curtis (USA) 17·6	Grantley Goulding (GBR) 18·0	—
1900	Alvin Kraenzlein (USA) 15·4	John McLean (USA) 15·5	Fred Moloney (USA) 15·6
1904	Frederick Schule (USA) 16·0	Thaddeus Shideler (USA) 16·3	Lesley Ashburner (USA) 16·4
1906	R G Levitt (USA) 16·2	A H Healey (GBR) 16·2	Vincent Duncker (SAF) 16·3
1908	Forrest Smithson (USA) 15·0	John Garrels (USA) 15·7	Arthur Shaw (USA) 15·8
1912	Frederick Kelly (USA) 15·1	James Wendell (USA) 15·2	Martin Hawkins (USA) 15·3
1920	Earl Thomson (CAN) 14·8	Harold Barron (USA) 15·1	Frederick Murray (USA) 15·2
1924	Daniel Kinsey (USA) 15·0	Sydney Atkinson (SAF) 15·0	Sten Pettersson (SWE) 15·4
1928	Sydney Atkinson (SAF) 14·8	Stephen Anderson (USA) 14·8	John Collier (USA) 15·0
1932	George Saling (USA) 14·6 (14·56)	Percy Beard (USA) 14·7	Don Finlay (GBR) 14·8
1936	Forrest Towns (USA) 14·2	Don Finlay (GBR) 14·4	Fred Pollard (USA) 14·4
1948	William Porter (USA) 13·9	Clyde Scott (USA) 14·1	Craig Dixon (USA) 14·1
1952	Harrison Dillard (USA) 13·7 (13·91)	Jack Davis (USA) 13·7 (14·00)	Art Barnard (USA) 14·1 (14·40)
1956	Lee Calhoun (USA) 13·5 (13·70)	Jack Davis (USA) 13·5 (13·73)	Joel Shankle (USA) 14·1 (14·25)
1960	Lee Calhoun (USA) 13·8 (13·98)	Willie May (USA) 13·8 (13·99)	Hayes Jones (USA) 14·0 (14·17)
1964	Hayes Jones (USA) 13·6 (13·67)	Blaine Lindgren (USA) 13·7 (13·74)	Anatoliy Mikhailov (URS) 13·7 (13·78)
1968	Willie Davenport (USA) 13·3 (13·33)	Ervin Hall (USA) 13·4 (13·42)	Eddy Ottoz (ITA) 13·4 (13·46)
1972	Rod Milburn (USA) 13·24	Guy Drut (FRA) 13·34	Tom Hill (USA) 13·48
1976	Guy Drut (FRA) 13·30	Alejandro Casanas (CUB) 13·33	Willie Davenport (USA) 13·38
1980	Thomas Munkelt (GDR) 13·39	Alejandro Casanas (CUB) 13·40	Aleksandr Puchkov (URS) 13·44

Only two finalists.

400 METRES HURDLES

	Gold	Silver	Bronze
1900	Walter Tewksbury (USA) 57·6	Henri Tauzin (FRA) 58·3	George Orton (CAN) d.n.a.
1904[1]	Harry Hillman (USA) 53·0	Frank Waller (USA) 53·2	George Poage (USA) 30 m
1908	Charles Bacon (USA) 55·0	Harry Hillman (USA) 55·3	Leonard Tremeer (GBR) 57·0
1920	Frank Loomis (USA) 54·0	John Norton (USA) 54·3	August Desch (USA) 54·5
1924	Morgan Taylor (USA) 52·6[2]	Erik Vilen (FIN) 53·8	Ivan Riley (USA) 54·2
1928	Lord Burghley (GBR) 53·4	Frank Cuhel (USA) 53·6	Morgan Taylor (USA) 53·6
1932	Bob Tisdall (IRL) 51·7[2] (51·67)	Glenn Hardin (USA) 51·9 (51·85)	Morgan Taylor (USA) 52·0 (51·96)
1936	Glenn Hardin (USA) 52·4	John Loaring (CAN) 52·7	Miguel White (PHI) 52·8
1948	Roy Cochran (USA) 51·1	Duncan White (SRI) 51·8	Rune Larsson (SWE) 52·2
1952	Charlie Moore (USA) 50·8 (51·06)	Yuriy Lituyev (URS) 51·3 (51·51)	John Holland (NZL) 52·2 (52·26)
1956	Glenn Davis (USA) 50·1 (50·29)	Eddie Southern (USA) 50·8 (50·93)	Josh Culbreath (USA) 51·6 (51·74)
1960	Glenn Davis (USA) 49·3 (49·51)	Cliff Cushman (USA) 49·6 (49·77)	Dick Howard (USA) 49·7 (49·90)
1964	Rex Cawley (USA) 49·6 (49·69)	John Cooper (GBR) 50·1 (50·19)	Salvadore Morale (ITA) 50·1
1968	David Hemery (GBR) 48·1 (48·12)	Gerhard Hennige (FRG) 49·0 (49·02)	John Sherwood (GBR) 49·0 (49·03)
1972	John Akii-Bua (UGA) 47·82	Ralph Mann (USA) 48·51	David Hemery (GBR) 48·52
1976	Edwin Moses (USA) 47·64	Mike Shine (USA) 48·69	Yevgeniy Gavrilenko (URS) 49·45
1980	Volker Beck (GDR) 48·70	Vasiliy Arkhipenko (URS) 48·86	Gary Oakes (GBR) 49·11

[1] Hurdles only 2 ft 6 in *76·2 cm* high instead of usual 3 ft *91·4 cm*.   [2] Record not allowed because hurdle knocked down.   1896, 1906, 1912 Event not held

4 × 100 METRES RELAY

	Gold	Silver	Bronze
1912[1]	GREAT BRITAIN 42·4	SWEDEN 42·6	—
1920	UNITED STATES 42·2	FRANCE 42·6	SWEDEN 42·9
1924	UNITED STATES 41·0	GREAT BRITAIN 41·2	NETHERLANDS 41·8
1928	UNITED STATES 41·0	GERMANY 41·2	GREAT BRITAIN 41·8
1932	UNITED STATES 40·0	GERMANY 40·9	ITALY 41·2
1936	UNITED STATES 39·8	ITALY 41·1	GERMANY 41·2
1948[2]	UNITED STATES 40·6	GREAT BRITAIN 41·3	ITALY 41·5
1952	UNITED STATES 40·1 (40·26)	USSR 40·3 (40·58)	HUNGARY 40·5 (40·83)
1956	UNITED STATES 39·5 (39·59)	USSR 39·8 (39·92)	GERMANY 40·3 (40·34)
1960	GERMANY 39·5 (39·66)	USSR 40·1 (40·23)	GREAT BRITAIN 40·2 (40·32)
1964	UNITED STATES 39·0 (39·06)	POLAND 39·3 (39·36)	FRANCE 39·3 (39·36)
1968	UNITED STATES 38·2 (38·23)	CUBA 38·3 (38·39)	FRANCE 38·4 (38·42)
1972	UNITED STATES 38·19	USSR 38·50	FRG 38·79
1976	UNITED STATES 38·33	GDR 38·66	USSR 38·78
1980	USSR 38·26	POLAND 38·33	FRANCE 38·53

[1] German team finished second but was disqualified.   [2] United States disqualified but later reinstated.   1896–1908 Event not held

4 × 400 METRES RELAY

	Gold	Silver	Bronze
1908[1]	UNITED STATES 3:29·4	GERMANY 3:32·4	HUNGARY 3:32·5
1912	UNITED STATES 3:16·6	FRANCE 3:20·7	GREAT BRITAIN 3:23·2
1920	GREAT BRITAIN 3:22·2	SOUTH AFRICA 3:24·2	FRANCE 3:24·8
1924	UNITED STATES 3:16·0	SWEDEN 3:17·0	GREAT BRITAIN 3:17·4
1928	UNITED STATES 3:14·2	GERMANY 3:14·8	CANADA 3:15·4
1932	UNITED STATES 3:08·2	GREAT BRITAIN 3:11·2	CANADA 3:12·8
1936	GREAT BRITAIN 3:09·0	UNITED STATES 3:11·0	GERMANY 3:11·8
1948	UNITED STATES 3:10·4	FRANCE 3:14·8	SWEDEN 3:16·3
1952	JAMAICA 3:03·9	UNITED STATES 3:04·0	GERMANY 3:06·6
1956	UNITED STATES 3:04·8	AUSTRALIA 3:06·2	GREAT BRITAIN 3:07·2
1960	UNITED STATES 3:02·2	GERMANY 3:02·7	BRITISH WEST INDIES[2] 3:04·0
1964	UNITED STATES 3:00·7 (3:00·71)	GREAT BRITAIN 3:01·6 (3:01·69)	TRINIDAD 3:01·7
1968	UNITED STATES 2:56·1 (2:56·16)	KENYA 2:59·6 (2:59·64)	FRG 3:00·5 (3:00·57)
1972	KENYA 2:59·83	GREAT BRITAIN 3:00·46	FRANCE 3:00·65
1976	UNITED STATES 2:58·65	POLAND 3:01·43	FRG 3:01·98
1980	USSR 3:01·08	GDR 3:01·26	ITALY 3:04·3

[1] Medley relay—200 m, 200 m, 400 m, 800 m.   [2] Three from Jamaica, one from Trinidad.   1896–1906 Event not held

20 000 METRES ROAD WALK

	Gold	Silver	Bronze
956	Leonid Spirin (URS) 1 h 31:27·4	Antonas Mikenas (URS) 1 h 32:03·0	Bruno Junk (URS) 1 h 32:12·0
960	Vladimir Golubnichiy (URS) 1 h 34:07·2	Noel Freeman (AUS) 1 h 34:16·4	Stan Vickers (GBR) 1 h 34:56·4.
964	Ken Matthews (GBR) 1 h 29:34·0.	Dieter Lindner (GER) 1 h 31:13·2	Vladimir Golubnichiy (URS) 1 h 31:59·4
968	Vladimir Golubnichiy (URS) 1 h 33:58·4	José Pedraza (MEX) 1 h 34:00·0	Nikolai Smaga (URS) 1 h 34:03·4.
972	Peter Frenkel (GDR) 1 h 26:42·4	Vladimir Golubnichiy (URS) 1 h 26:55·2	Hans Reimann (GDR) 1 h 27:16·6
976	Daniel Bautista (MEX) 1 h 24:40·6	Hans Reimann (GDR) 1 h 25:13·8	Peter Frenkel (GDR) 1 h 25:29·4
980	Maurizio Damilano (ITA) 1 h 23:35·5	Pyotr Pochenchuk (URS) 1 h 24:45·4	Roland Wieser (GDR) 1 h 25:58·2

896–1952 Event not held

50 000 METRES ROAD WALK

	Gold	Silver	Bronze
932	Thomas Green (GBR) 4 h 50:10	Janis Dalinsh (LAT) 4 h 47:20	Ugo Frigerio (ITA) 4 h 59:06
936	Harold Whitlock (GBR) 4 h 30:41·1	Arthur Schwab (SUI) 4 h 32:09·2	Adalberts Bubenko (LAT) 4 h 32:42·2
948	John Ljunggren (SWE) 4 h 41:52	Gaston Godel (SUI) 4 h 48:17	Tebbs Lloyd Johnson (GBR) 4 h 48:31
952	Giuseppe Dordoni (ITA) 4 h 28:07·8	Josef Dolezal (TCH) 4 h 30:17·8	Antal Róka (HUN) 4 h 31:27·2
956	Norman Read (NZL) 4 h 30:42·8	Yevgeniy Maskinkov (URS) 4 h 32:57·0	John Ljunggren (SWE) 4 h 35:02·0
960	Don Thompson (GBR) 4 h 25:30·0	John Ljunggren (SWE) 4 h 25:47·0	Abdon Pamich (ITA) 4 h 27:55·4
964	Abdon Pamich (ITA) 4 h 11:12·4	Paul Nihill (GBR) 4 h 11:31·2	Ingvar Pettersson (SWE) 4 h 14:17·4
968	Christoph Höhne (GDR) 4 h 20:13·6	Antal Kiss (HUN) 4 h 30:17·0	Larry Young (USA) 4 h 31:55·4
972	Bernd Kannenberg (FRG) 3 h 56:11·6	Venjamin Soldatenko (URS) 3 h 58:24·0	Larry Young (USA) 4 h 00:46·0
980	Hartwig Gauder (GDR) 3 h 49:24	Jorge Llopart (ESP) 3 h 51:25	Yevgeniy Ivchenko (URS) 3 h 56:32

896–1928, 1976 Event not held

HIGH JUMP

	Gold	Silver	Bronze
896	Ellery Clark (USA) 1·81 m	James Connolly (USA) 1·65 m Robert Garrett (USA) 1·65 m	—
900	Irving Baxter (USA) 1·90 m	Patrick Leahy (GBR) 1·78 m	Lajos Gönczy (HUN) 1·75 m
904	Samuel Jones (USA) 1·80 m	Garrett Serviss (USA) 1·77 m	Paul Weinstein (GER) 1·77 m
906	Con Leahy (GBR) 1·77 m	Lajos Gönczy (HUN) 1·75 m	Herbert Kerrigan (USA) 1·72 m Themistoklis Diakidis (GRE) 1·72 m
908	Harry Porter (USA) 1·905 m	Con Leahy (GBR) 1·88 m István Somodi (HUN) 1·88 m Georges André (FRA) 1·88 m	—
912	Alma Richards (USA) 1·93 m	Hans Liesche (GER) 1·91 m	George Horine (USA) 1·89 m
920	Richmond Landon (USA) 1·94 m	Harold Muller (USA) 1·90 m	Bo Ekelund (SWE) 1·90 m
924	Harold Osborn (USA) 1·98 m	Leroy Brown (USA) 1·95 m	Pierre Lewden (FRA) 1·92 m
928	Robert King (USA) 1·94 m	Ben Hedges (USA) 1·91 m	Claude Ménard (FRA) 1·91 m
932	Duncan McNaughton (CAN) 1·97 m	Robert Van Osdel (USA) 1·97 m	Simeon Toribio (PHI) 1·97 m
936	Cornelius Johnson (USA) 2·03 m	David Albritton (USA) 2·00 m	Delos Thurber (USA) 2·00 m
948	John Winter (AUS) 1·98 m	Björn Paulsen (NOR) 1·95 m	George Stanich (USA) 1·95 m
952	Walt Davis (USA) 2·04 m	Ken Wiesner (USA) 2·01 m	Jose Telles da Conceicao (BRA) 1·98 m
956	Charlie Dumas (USA) 2·12 m	Chilla Porter (AUS) 2·10 m	Igor Kashkarov (URS) 2·08 m
960	Robert Shavlakadze (URS) 2·16 m	Valeriy Brumel (URS) 2·16 m	John Thomas (USA) 2·14 m
964	Valeriy Brumel (URS) 2·18 m	John Thomas (USA) 2·18 m	John Rambo (USA) 2·16 m
968	Dick Fosbury (USA) 2·24 m	Ed Caruthers (USA) 2·22 m	Valentin Gavrilov (URS) 2·20 m
972	Yuriy Tarmak (URS) 2·23 m	Stefan Junge (GDR) 2·21 m	Dwight Stones (USA) 2·21 m
976	Jacek Wszola (POL) 2·25 m	Greg Joy (CAN) 2·23 m	Dwight Stones (USA) 2·21 m
980	Gerd Wessig (GDR) 2·36 m	Jacek Wszola (POL) 2·31 m	Jörg Freimuth (GDR) 2·31 m

POLE VAULT

	Gold	Silver	Bronze
896	William Hoyt (USA) 3·30 m	Albert Tyler (USA) 3·25 m	Evangelos Damaskos (GRE) 2·85 m
900	Irving Baxter (USA) 3·30 m	M B Colkett (USA) 3·25 m	Carl-Albert Andersen (NOR) 3·20 m
904	Charles Dvorak (USA) 3·50 m	LeRoy Samse (USA) 3·43 m	Louis Wilkins (USA) 3·43 m
906	Fernand Gonder (FRA) 3·40 m	Bruno Söderström (SWE) 3·40 m	Ernest Glover (USA) 3·35 m

1908	Edward Cooke (USA) 3·70 m	—	Edward Archibald (CAN) 3·58 m
	Alfred Gilbert (USA) 3·70 m		Charles Jacobs (USA) 3·58 m
			Bruno Söderström (SWE) 3·58 m
1912	Harry Babcock (USA) 3·95 m	Frank Nelson (USA) 3·85 m	—
		Marcus Wright (USA) 3·85 m	
1920	Frank Foss (USA) 4·09 m	Henry Petersen (DEN) 3·70 m	Edwin Meyers (USA) 3·60 m
1924	Lee Barnes (USA) 3·95 m	Glenn Graham (USA) 3·95 m	James Brooker (USA) 3·90 m
1928	Sabin Carr (USA) 4·20 m	William Droegemuller (USA) 4·10 m	Charles McGinnis (USA) 3·95 m
1932	William Miller (USA) 4·31 m	Shuhei Nishida (JPN) 4·26 m	George Jefferson (USA) 4·19 m
1936	Earle Meadows (USA) 4·35 m	Shuhei Nishida (JPN) 4·25 m	Sueo Oe (JPN) 4·25 m
1948	Guinn Smith (USA) 4·30 m	Erkki Kataja (FIN) 4·20 m	Bob Richards (USA) 4·20 m
1952	Bob Richards (USA) 4·55 m	Don Laz (USA) 4·50 m	Ragnar Lundberg (SWE) 4·40 m
1956	Bob Richards (USA) 4·56 m	Bob Gutowski (USA) 4·53 m	Georgios Roubanis (GRE) 4·50 m
1960	Don Bragg (USA) 4·70 m	Ron Morris (USA) 4·60 m	Eeles Landström (FIN) 4·55 m
1964	Fred Hansen (USA) 5·10 m	Wolfgang Reinhardt (GER) 5·05 m	Klaus Lehnertz (GER) 5·00 m
1968	Bob Seagren (USA) 5·40 m	Claus Schiprowski (FRG) 5·40 m	Wolfgang Nordwig (GDR) 5·40 m
1972	Wolfgang Nordwig (GDR) 5·50 m	Bob Seagren (USA) 5·40 m	Jan Johnson (USA) 5·35 m
1976	Tadeusz Slusarski (POL) 5·50 m	Antti Kalliomaki (FIN) 5·50 m	David Roberts (USA) 5·50 m
1980	Wladislaw Kozakiewicz (POL) 5·78 m	Tadeusz Slusarski (POL) 5·65 m	—
		Konstantin Volkov (URS) 5·65 m	

LONG JUMP

	Gold	Silver	Bronze
1896	Ellery Clark (USA) 6·35 m	Robert Garrett (USA) 6·18 m	James Connolly (USA) 6·11 m
1900	Alvin Kraenzlein (USA) 7·18 m	Myer Prinstein (USA) 7·17 m	Patrick Leahy (GBR) 6·95 m
1904	Myer Prinstein (USA) 7·34 m	Daniel Frank (USA) 6·89 m	Robert Stangland (USA) 6·88 m
1906	Myer Prinstein (USA) 7·20 m	Peter O'Connor (GBR) 7·02 m	Hugo Friend (USA) 6·96 m
1908	Francis Irons (USA) 7·48 m	Daniel Kelly (USA) 7·09 m	Calvin Bricker (CAN) 7·08 m
1912	Albert Gutterson (USA) 7·60 m	Calvin Bricker (CAN) 7·21 m	Georg Aberg (SWE) 7·18 m
1920	William Pettersson (SWE) 7·15 m	Carl Johnson (USA) 7·09 m	Erik Abrahamsson (SWE) 7·08 m
1924	William DeHart Hubbard (USA) 7·44 m	Ed Gourdin (USA) 7·27 m	Sverre Hansen (NOR) 7·26 m
1928	Edward Hamm (USA) 7·73 m	Silvio Cator (HAI) 7·58 m	Alfred Bates (USA) 7·40 m
1932	Ed Gordon (USA) 7·63 m	Lambert Redd (USA) 7·60 m	Chuhei Nambu (JPN) 7·44 m
1936	Jesse Owens (USA) 8·06 m	Luz Long (GER) 7·87 m	Naoto Tajima (JPN) 7·74 m
1948	Willie Steele (USA) 7·82 m	Thomas Bruce (AUS) 7·55 m	Herbert Douglas (USA) 7·54 m
1952	Jerome Biffle (USA) 7·57 m	Meredith Gourdine (USA) 7·53 m	Odön Földessy (HUN) 7·30 m
1956	Greg Bell (USA) 7·83 m	John Bennett (USA) 7·68 m	Jorma Valkama (FIN) 7·48 m
1960	Ralph Boston (USA) 8·12 m	Irvin Roberson (USA) 8·11 m	Igor Ter-Ovanesyan (URS) 8·04
1964	Lynn Davies (GBR) 8·07 m	Ralph Boston (USA) 8·03 m	Igor Ter-Ovanesyan (URS) 7·99 m
1968	Bob Beamon (USA) 8·90 m	Klaus Beer (GDR) 8·19 m	Ralph Boston (USA) 8·16 m
1972	Randy Williams (USA) 8·24 m	Hans Baumgartner (FRG) 8·18 m	Arnie Robinson (USA) 8·03 m
1976	Arnie Robinson (USA) 8·35 m	Randy Williams (USA) 8·11 m	Frank Wartenberg (GDR) 8·02 m
1980	Lutz Dombrowski (GDR) 8·54 m	Frank Paschek (GDR) 8·21 m	Valeriy Podluzhny (URS) 8·18 m

TRIPLE JUMP
(Formerly known as the Hop, step and jump)

	Gold	Silver	Bronze
1896[1]	James Connolly (USA) 13·71 m	Alexander Tuffere (FRA) 12·70 m	Ioannis Persakis (GRE) 12·52 m
1900	Myer Prinstein (USA) 14·47	James Connolly (USA) 13·97 m	Lewis Sheldon (USA) 13·64 m
1904	Myer Prinstein (USA) 14·35 m	Frederick Englehardt (USA) 13·90 m	Robert Stangland (USA) 13·36 m
1906	Peter O'Connor (GBR) 14·07 m	Con Leahy (GBR) 13·98 m	Thomas Cronan (USA) 13·70 m
1908	Tim Ahearne (GBR) 14·91 m	Garfield McDonald (CAN) 14·76 m	Edvard Larsen (NOR) 14·39 m
1912	Gustaf Lindblom (SWE) 14·76 m	Georg Aberg (SWE) 14·51 m	Erik Almlöf (SWE) 14·17 m
1920	Vilho Tuulos (FIN) 14·50 m	Folke Jansson (SWE) 14·48 m	Erik Almlöf (SWE) 14·27 m
1924	Anthony Winter (AUS) 15·52 m	Luis Brunetto (ARG) 15·42 m	Vilho Tuulos (FIN) 15·37 m
1928	Mikio Oda (JPN) 15·21 m	Levi Casey (USA) 15·17 m	Vilho Tuulos (FIN) 15·11 m
1932	Chuhei Nambu (JPN) 15·72 m	Erik Svensson (SWE) 15·32 m	Kenkichi Oshima (JPN) 15·12 m
1936	Naoto Tajima (JPN) 16·00 m	Masao Harada (JPN) 15·66 m	John Metcalfe (AUS) 15·50 m
1948	Arne Ahman (SWE) 15·40 m	George Avery (AUS) 15·36 m	Ruhi Sarialp (TUR) 15·02 m
1952	Adhemar Ferreira da Silva (BRA) 16·22 m	Leonid Shcherbakov (URS) 15·98 m	Arnoldo Devonish (VEN) 15·52 m
1956	Adhemar Ferreira da Silva (BRA) 16·35 m	Vilhjalmur Einarsson (ISL) 16·26 m	Vitold Kreyer (URS) 16·02 m

⸍60	Jozef Schmidt (POL) 16·81 m	Vladimir Goryayev (URS) 16·63 m	Vitold Kreyer (URS) 16·43 m
⸍64	Jozef Schmidt (POL) 16·85 m	Oleg Fedoseyev (URS) 16·58 m	Viktor Kravchenko (URS) 16·57 m
⸍68	Viktor Saneyev (URS) 17·39 m	Nelson Prudencio (BRA) 17·27 m	Giuseppe Gentile (ITA) 17·22 m
⸍72	Viktor Saneyev (URS) 17·35 m	Jörg Drehmel (GDR) 17·31 m	Nelson Prudencio (BRA) 17·05 m
⸍76	Viktor Saneyev (URS) 17·29 m	James Butts (USA) 17·18 m	Joao de Oliveira (BRA) 16·90 m
⸍80	Jaak Uudmäe (URS) 17·35 m	Viktor Saneyev (URS) 17·24 m	Joao de Oliveira (BRA) 17·22 m

Winner took two hops with his right foot, contrary to present rules.

SHOT PUT

	Gold	Silver	Bronze
896[1]	Robert Garrett (USA) 11·22 m	Miltiades Gouskos (GRE) 11·15 m	Georgios Papasideris (GRE) 10·36 m
900[1]	Richard Sheldon (USA) 14·10 m	Josiah McCracken (USA) 12·85 m	Robert Garrett (USA) 12·37 m
904[1]	Ralph Rose (USA) 14·80 m	Wesley Coe (USA) 14·40 m	Leon Feuerbach (USA) 13·37 m
906	Martin Sheridan (USA) 12·32 m	Maihály Dávid (HUN) 11·83 m	Erik Lemming (SWE) 11·26 m
908	Ralph Rose (USA) 14·21 m	Dennis Horgan (GBR) 13·61 m	John Garrels (USA) 13·18 m
912	Patrick McDonald (USA) 15·34 m	Ralph Rose (USA) 15·25 m	Lawrence Whitney (USA) 14·15 m
920	Ville Pörhölä (FIN) 14·81 m	Elmer Niklander (FIN) 14·155 m	Harry Liversedge (USA) 14·15 m
924	Clarence Houser (USA) 14·99 m	Glenn Hartranft (USA) 14·98 m	Ralph Hills (USA) 14·64 m
928	John Kuck (USA) 15·87 m	Herman Brix (USA) 15·75 m	Emil Hirschfeld (GER) 15·72 m
932	Leo Sexton (USA) 16·00 m	Harlow Rothert (USA) 15·67 m	Frantisek Douda (TCH) 15·60 m
936	Hans Woellke (GER) 16·20 m	Sulo Bärlund (FIN) 16·12 m	Gerhard Stöck (GER) 15·66 m
948	Wilbur Thompson (USA) 17·12 m	Jim Delaney (USA) 16·68 m	Jim Fuchs (USA) 16·42 m
952	Parry O'Brien (USA) 17·41 m	Darrow Hooper (USA) 17·39 m	Jim Fuchs (USA) 17·06 m
956	Parry O'Brien (USA) 18·57 m	Bill Nieder (USA) 18·18 m	Jiri Skobla (TCH) 17·65 m
960	Bill Nieder (USA) 19·68 m	Parry O'Brien (USA) 19·11 m	Dallas Long (USA) 19·01 m
964	Dallas Long (USA) 20·33 m	Randy Matson (USA) 20·20 m	Vilmos Varju (HUN) 19·39 m
968	Randy Matson (USA) 20·54 m	George Woods (USA) 20·12 m	Eduard Grishchin (URS) 20·09 m
972	Wladyslaw Komar (POL) 21·18 m	George Woods (USA) 21·17 m	Hartmut Briesenick (GDR) 21·14 m
976	Udo Beyer (GDR) 21·05 m	Yevgeniy Mironov (URS) 21·03 m	Aleksandr Baryshnikov (URS) 21·00 m
980	Vladimir Kiselyev (URS) 21·35 m	Aleksandr Baryshnikov (URS) 21·08 m	Udo Beyer (GDR) 21·06 m

From a 7 ft 2·13 m square

DISCUS

	Gold	Silver	Bronze
896	Robert Garrett (USA) 29·15 m	Panagotis Paraskevopoulos (GRE) 28·95 m	Sotirios Versis (GRE) 28·78 m
900	Rudolf Bauer (HUN) 36·04 m	Frantisek Janda-Suk (BOH) 35·25 m	Richard Sheldon (USA) 34·60 m
904[1]	Martin Sheridan (USA) 39·28 m	Ralph Rose (USA) 39·28 m	Nicolaos Georgantas (GRE) 37·68 m
906	Martin Sheridan (USA) 41·46 m	Nicolaos Georgantas (GRE) 38·06 m	Werner Järvinen (FIN) 36·82 m
908	Martin Sheridan (USA) 40·89 m	Merritt Giffin (USA) 40·70 m	Marquis Horr (USA) 39·44 m
912	Armas Taipale (FIN) 45·21 m	Richard Byrd (USA) 42·32 m	James Duncan (USA) 42·28 m
920	Elmer Niklander (FIN) 44·68 m	Armas Taipale (FIN) 44·19 m	Augustus Pope (USA) 42·13 m
924	Clarence Houser (USA) 46·15 m	Vilho Niittymaa (FIN) 44·95 m	Thomas Lieb (USA) 44·83 m
928	Clarence Houser (USA) 47·32 m	Antero Kivi (FIN) 47·23 m	James Corson (USA) 47·10 m
932	John Anderson (USA) 49·49 m	Henri Laborde (USA) 48·47 m	Paul Winter (FRA) 47·85 m
936	Ken Carpenter (USA) 50·48 m	Gordon Dunn (USA) 49·36 m	Giorgio Oberweger (ITA) 49·23 m
948	Adolfo Consolini (ITA) 52·78 m	Giuseppe Tosi (ITA) 51·78 m	Fortune Gordien (USA) 50·77 m
952	Sim Iness (USA) 55·03 m	Adolfo Consolini (ITA) 53·78 m	James Dillion (USA) 53·28 m
956	Al Oerter (USA) 56·36 m	Fortune Gordien (USA) 54·81 m	Des Koch (USA) 54·40 m
960	Al Oerter (USA) 59·18 m	Rink Babka (USA) 58·02 m	Dick Cochran (USA) 57·16 m
964	Al Oerter (USA) 61·00 m	Ludvik Danek (TCH) 60·52 m	Dave Weill (USA) 59·49 m
968	Al Oerter (USA) 64·78 m	Lothar Milde (GDR) 63·08 m	Ludvik Danek (TCH) 62·92 m
972	Ludvik Danek (TCH) 64·40 m	Jay Silvester (USA) 63·50 m	Ricky Bruch (SWE) 63·40 m
976	Mac Wilkins (USA) 67·50 m	Wolfgang Schmidt (GDR) 66·22 m	John Powell (USA) 65·70 m
980	Viktor Rashchupkin (URS) 66·64 m	Imrich Bugár (TCH) 66·38 m	Luis Delis (CUB) 66·32 m

First place decided by a throw-off.

HAMMER

	Gold	Silver	Bronze
900[1]	John Flanagan (USA) 49·73 m	Truxton Hare (USA) 49·13 m	Josiah McCracken (USA) 42·46 m
904	John Flanagan (USA) 51·23 m	John DeWitt (USA) 50·26 m	Ralph Rose (USA) 45·73 m
908	John Flanagan (USA) 51·92 m	Matt McGrath (USA) 51·18 m	Con Walsh (CAN) 48·50 m
912	Matt McGrath (USA) 54·74 m	Duncan Gillis (CAN) 48·39 m	Clarence Childs (USA) 48·17 m

1920	Patrick Ryan (USA) 52·87 m	Carl Lind (SWE) 48·43 m	Basil Bennett (USA) 48·25 m
1924	Fred Tootell (USA) 53·29 m	Matt McGrath (USA) 50·84 m	Malcolm Nokes (GBR) 48·87 m
1928	Patrick O'Callaghan (IRL) 51·39 m	Ossian Skiöld (SWE) 51·29 m	Edmund Black (USA) 49·03 m
1932	Patrick O'Callaghan (IRL) 53·92 m	Ville Pörhölä (FIN) 52·27 m	Peter Zaremba (USA) 50·33 m
1936	Karl Hein (GER) 56·49 m	Erwin Blask (GER) 55·04 m	Fred Warngard (SWE) 54·83
1948	Imre Németh (HUN) 56·07 m	Ivan Gubijan (YUG) 54·27 m	Bob Bennett (USA) 53·73 m
1952	József Csermák (HUN) 60·34 m	Karl Storch (GER) 58·86 m	Imre Németh (HUN) 57·74 m
1956	Harold Connolly (USA) 63·19 m	Mikhail Krivonosov (URS) 63·03 m	Anatoliy Samotsvetov (URS) 62·56 m
1960	Vasiliy Rudenkov (URS) 67·10 m	Gyula Zsivótzky (HUN) 65·79 m	Tadeusz Rut (POL) 65·64 m
1964	Romuald Klim (URS) 69·74 m	Gyula Zsivótzky (HUN) 69·09 m	Uwe Beyer (GER) 68·09 m
1968	Gyula Zsivótzky (HUN) 73·36 m	Romuald Klim (URS) 73·28 m	Lázár Lovász (HUN) 69·78 m
1972	Anatoliy Bondarchuk (URS) 75·50 m	Jochen Sachse (GDR) 74·96 m	Vasiliy Khmelevski (URS) 74·04 m
1976	Yuriy Sedykh (URS) 77·52 m	Aleksey Spiridinov (URS) 76·08 m	Anatoliy Bondarchuk (URS) 75·48 m
1980	Yuriy Sedykh (URS) 81·80 m	Sergey Litvinov (URS) 80·64 m	Yuriy Tamm (URS) 78·96 m

[1] From a 9 ft 2·74 m circle.   1896, 1906 Event not held

JAVELIN

	Gold	*Silver*	*Bronze*
1906	Erik Lemming (SWE) 53·90 m	Knut Lindberg (SWE) 45·17 m	Bruno Söderström (SWE) 44·92 m
1908	Erik Lemming (SWE) 54·82 m	Arne Halse (NOR) 50·57 m	Otto Nilsson (SWE) 47·09 m
1912	Erik Lemming (SWE) 60·64 m	Juho Saaristo (FIN) 58·66 m	Mór Kóczán (HUN) 55·50 m
1920	Jonni Myyrä (FIN) 65·78 m	Urho Peltonen (FIN) 63·50 m	Pekka Johansson (FIN) 63·09 m
1924	Jonni Myyrä (FIN) 62·96 m	Gunnar Lindström (SWE) 60·92 m	Eugene Oberst (USA) 58·35 m
1928	Erik Lundkvist (SWE) 66·60 m	Béla Szepes (HUN) 65·26 m	Olav Sunde (NOR) 63·97 m
1932	Matti Järvinen (FIN) 72·71 m	Matti Sippala (FIN) 69·79 m	Eino Penttila (FIN) 68·69 m
1936	Gerhard Stöck (GER) 71·84 m	Yrjö Nikkanen (FIN) 70·77 m	Kalervo Toivonen (FIN) 70·72 m
1948	Tapio Rautavaara (FIN) 69·77 m	Steve Seymour (USA) 67·56 m	József Várszegi (HUN) 67·03 m
1952	Cyrus Young (USA) 73·78 m	Bill Miller (USA) 72·46 m	Toivo Hyytiainen (FIN) 71·89 m
1956	Egil Danielsen (NOR) 85·71 m	Janusz Sidlo (POL) 79·98	Viktor Tsibulenko (URS) 79·50 m
1960	Viktor Tsibulenko (URS) 84·64 m	Walter Krüger (GER) 79·36 m	Gergely Kulcsár (HUN) 78·57 m
1964	Pauli Nevala (FIN) 82·66 m	Gergely Kulcsár (HUN) 82·32 m	Janis Lusis (URS) 80·57 m
1968	Janis Lusis (URS) 90·10 m	Jorma Kinnunen (FIN) 88·58 m	Gergely Kulcsár (HUN) 87·06 m
1972	Klaus Wolfermann (FRG) 90·48 m	Janis Lusis (URS) 90·46 m	Bill Schmidt (USA) 84·42 m
1976	Miklos Németh (HUN) 94·58 m	Hannu Siitonen (FIN) 87·92 m	Gheorghe Megelea (ROM) 87·16 m
1980	Dainis Kula (URS) 91·20 m	Aleksandr Makarov (URS) 89·64 m	Wolfgang Hanisch (GDR) 86·72 m

1896–1904 Event not held

DECATHLON[1, 2]

	Gold	*Silver*	*Bronze*
1904[3]	Thomas Kiely (GBR) 6036 pts	Adam Gunn (USA) 5907	Truxton Hare (USA) 5813
1912[4]	Hugo Wieslander (SWE) 6162 pts	Charles Lomberg (SWE) 5943	Gösta Holmer (SWE) 5956
1920	Helge Lövland (NOR) 5970 pts	Brutus Hamilton (USA) 5912	Bertil Ohlsson (SWE) 5825
1924	Harold Osborn (USA) 6668 pts	Emerson Norton (USA) 6360	Aleksandr Klumberg (EST) 6260
1928	Paavo Yrjölä (FIN) 6774 pts	Akilles Järvinen (FIN) 6815	Ken Doherty (USA) 6593
1932	Jim Bausch (USA) 6986 pts	Akilles Järvinen (FIN) 7038	Wolrad Eberle (GER) 6830
1936	Glenn Morris (USA) 7421 pts	Robert Clark (USA) 7226	Jack Parker (USA) 6918
1948	Bob Mathias (USA) 6826 pts	Ignace Heinrich (FRA) 6740	Floyd Simmons (USA) 6711
1952	Bob Mathias (USA) 7731 pts	Milt Campbell (USA) 7132	Floyd Simmons (USA) 7069
1956	Milt Campbell (USA) 7708 pts	Rafer Johnson (USA) 7568	Vasiliy Kuznetsov (URS) 7461
1960	Rafer Johnson (USA) 8001 pts	Chuan-Kwang Yang (TAI) 7930	Vasiliy Kuznetsov (URS) 7624
1964	Willi Holdorf (GER) 7887 pts	Rein Aun (URS) 7842	Hans-Joachim Walde (GER) 7809
1968	Bill Toomey (USA) 8193 pts	Hans-Joachim Walde (FRG) 8111	Kurt Bendlin (FRG) 8064
1972	Nikolai Avilov (URS) 8454 pts	Leonid Litvinenko (URS) 8035	Ryszard Katus (POL) 7984
1976	Bruce Jenner (USA) 8617 pts	Guido Kratschmer (FRG) 8411	Nikolai Avilov (URS) 8369
1980	Daley Thompson (GBR) 8495 pts	Yuriy Kutsenko (URS) 8331	Sergey Zhelanov (URS) 8135

[1] The decathlon consists of 100 m, long jump, shot put, high jump, 400 m, 110 m hurdles discus, pole vault, javelin and 1500 m. The competition occupies two days, but in 1912 it occupied three days.   [2] The scores given above have all been calculated on the current 1962 tables. The 1912 scores were based on the then Olympic records the 1920–1932 scores on the Olympic records after the 1912 Games; the 1936 and 1948 scores on the 1934 tables; and the 1952–1960 scores on the 1952 tables. Note that i 1912, 1928 and 1932 the original medal order would have been different had the 1962 tables then been in use.   [3] Consisted of 100 yd, 1 mile, 120 yd hurdles, 880 y walk, high jump, long jump, pole vault, shot put, hammer and 56-lb weight.   [4] Jim Thorpe (USA) finished first with 6845 pts but was later disqualified for a breach c the then amateur rules. He was reinstated posthumously by the IOC in 1982, but only as joint first.   1896–1900, 1906–1908 Event not held

Women

100 METRES

Gold	Silver	Bronze
1928	Elizabeth Robinson (USA) 12·2	Fanny Rosenfeld (CAN) 12·3	Ethel Smith (CAN) 12·3
1932	Stanislawa Walasiewicz (POL) 11·9	Hilda Strike (CAN) 11·9	Wilhelmina von Bremen (USA) 12·0
1936	Helen Stephens (USA) 11·5	Stanislawa Walasiewicz (POL) 11·7	Kathe Krauss (GER) 11·9
1948	Fanny Blankers-Koen (HOL) 11·9	Dorothy Manley (GBR) 12·2	Shirley Strickland (AUS) 12·2
1952	Marjorie Jackson (AUS) 11·5 (11·65)	Daphne Hasenjager (SAF) 11·8 (12·04)	Shirley Strickland (AUS) 11·9 (12·10)
1956	Betty Cuthbert (AUS) 11·5 (11·82)	Christa Stubnick (GER) 11·7 (11·92)	Marlene Matthews (AUS) 11·7 (11·94)
1960	Wilma Rudolph (USA) 11·0 (11·18)	Dorothy Hyman (GBR) 11·3 (11·43)	Giuseppina Leone (ITA) 11·3 (11·48)
1964	Wyomia Tyus (USA) 11·4 (11·49)	Edith Maguire (USA) 11·6 (11·62)	Ewa Klobukowska (POL) 11·6 (11·64)
1968	Wyomia Tyus (USA) 11·0 (11·07)	Barbara Ferrell (USA) 11·1 (11·15)	Irena Szewinska (POL) 11·1 (11·19)
1972	Renate Stecher (GDR) 11·07	Raelene Boyle (AUS) 11·23	Silvia Chivas (CUB) 11·24
1976	Annegret Richter (FRG) 11·08	Renate Stecher (GDR) 11·13	Inge Helten (FRG) 11·17
1980	Ludmila Kondratyeva (URS) 11·06	Marlies Göhr (GDR) 11·07	Ingrid Auerswald (GDR) 11·14

200 METRES

Gold	Silver	Bronze
1948	Fanny Blankers-Koen (HOL) 24·4	Audrey Williamson (GBR) 25·1	Audrey Patterson[1] (USA) 25·2
1952	Marjorie Jackson (AUS) 23·7 (23·89)	Bertha Brouwer (HOL) 24·2 (24·25)	Nadyezda Khnykina (URS) 24·2 (24·37)
1956	Betty Cuthbert (AUS) 23·4 (23·55)	Christa Stubnick (GER) 23·7 (23·89)	Marlene Matthews (AUS) 23·8 (24·10)
1960	Wilma Rudolph (USA) 24·0 (24·13)	Jutta Heine (GER) 24·4 (24·58)	Dorothy Hyman (GBR) 24·7 (24·82)
1964	Edith Maguire (USA) 23·0 (23·05)	Irena Kirszenstein (POL) 23·1 (23·13)	Marilyn Black (AUS) 23·1 (23·18)
1968	Irena Szewinska (POL) 22·5 (22·58)	Raelene Boyle (AUS) 22·7 (22·73)	Jennifer Lamy (AUS) 22·8 (22·88)
1972	Renate Stecher (GDR) 22·40	Raelene Boyle (AUS) 22·45	Irena Szewinska (POL) 22·74
1976	Bärbel Eckert (GDR) 22·37	Annegret Richter (FRG) 22·39	Renate Stecher (GDR) 22·47
1980	Bärbel Wöckel (GDR) 22·03	Natalya Bochina (URS) 22·19	Merlene Ottey (JAM) 22·20

[1] A recently discovered photo-finish picture indicates that Shirley Strickland (AUS) was third.   1928–1936 Event not held

400 METRES

Gold	Silver	Bronze
1964	Betty Cuthbert (AUS) 52·0 (52·01)	Ann Packer (GBR) 52·2 (52·20)	Judith Amoore (AUS) 53·4
1968	Colette Besson (FRA) 52·0 (52·03)	Lillian Board (GBR) 52·1 (52·12)	Natalya Pechenkina (URS) 52·2 (52·25)
1972	Monika Zehrt (GDR) 51·08	Rita Wilden (FRG) 51·21	Kathy Hammond (USA) 51·64
1976	Irena Szewinska (POL) 49·29	Christina Brehmer (GDR) 50·51	Ellen Streidt (GDR) 50·55
1980	Marita Koch (GDR) 48·88	Jarmila Kratochvilova (TCH) 49·46	Christina Lathan (GDR) 49·66

1928–1960 Event not held

800 METRES

Gold	Silver	Bronze
1928	Lina Radke (GER) 2:16·8	Kinuye Hitomi (JPN) 2:17·6	Inga Gentzel (SWE) 2:17·8
1960	Ludmila Shevtsova (URS) 2:04·3	Brenda Jones (AUS) 2:04·4	Ursula Donath (GER) 2:05·6
1964	Ann Packer (GBR) 2:01·1	Maryvonne Dupureur (FRA) 2:01·9	Marise Chamberlain (NZL) 2:02·8
1968	Madeline Manning (USA) 2:00·9	Ilona Silai (ROM) 2:02·5	Maria Gommers (HOL) 2:02·6
1972	Hildegard Falck (FRG) 1:58·6	Niole Sabaite (URS) 1:58·7	Gunhild Hoffmeister (GDR) 1:59·2
1976	Tatyana Kazankina (URS) 1:54·9	Nikolina Shtereva (BUL) 1:55·4	Elfi Zinn (GDR) 1:55·6
1980	Nadyezda Olizarenko (URS) 1:53·5	Olga Mineyeva (URS) 1:54·9	Tatyana Providokhina (URS) 1:55·5

1932–1956 Event not held

1500 METRES

Gold	Silver	Bronze
1972	Ludmila Bragina (URS) 4:01·4	Gunhild Hoffmeister (GDR) 4:02·8	Paola Cacchi-Pigni (ITA) 4:02·9
1976	Tatyana Kazankina (URS) 4:05·5	Gunhild Hoffmeister (GDR) 4:06·0	Ulrike Klapezynski (GDR) 4:06·1
1980	Tatyana Kazankina (URS) 3:56·6	Christiane Wartenberg (GDR) 3:57·8	Nadyezda Olizarenko (URS) 3:59·6

1928–1968 Event not held

100 METRES HURDLES
(Over 80 m hurdles 1932–1968)

	Gold	Silver	Bronze
1932	Mildred Didrikson (USA) 11·7	Evelyne Hall (USA) 11·7	Marjorie Clark (SAF) 11·8
1936	Trebisonda Valla (ITA) 11·7 (11·73)	Anny Steuer (GER) 11·7 (11·81)	Elizabeth Taylor (CAN) 11·7 (11·81)
1948	Fanny Blankers-Koen (HOL) 11·2	Maureen Gardner (GBR) 11·2	Shirley Strickland (AUS) 11·4
1952	Shirley de la Hunty (AUS) 10·9 (11·03)	Maria Golubnichaya (URS) 11·1 (11·24)	Maria Sander (GER) 11·1 (11·38)
1956	Shirley de la Hunty (AUS) 10·7 (10·96)	Gisela Köhler (GER) 10·9 (11·12)	Norma Thrower (AUS) 11·0 (11·25)
1960	Irina Press (URS) 10·8 (10·94)	Carol Quinton (GBR) 10·9 (10·99)	Gisela Birkemeyer (GER) 11·0 (11·13)
1964	Karin Balzer (GER) 10·5 (10·54)	Tereza Ciepla (POL) 10·5 (10·55)	Pam Kilborn (AUS) 10·5 (10·56)
1968	Maureen Caird (AUS) 10·3 (10·39)	Pam Kilborn (AUS) 10·4 (10·46)	Chi Cheng (TAI) 10·4 (10·51)
1972	Annelie Ehrhardt (GDR) 12·59	Valeria Bufanu (ROM) 12·84	Karin Balzer (GDR) 12·90
1976	Johanna Schaller (GDR) 12·77	Tatyana Anisimova (URS) 12·78	Natalya Lebedeva (URS) 12·80
1980	Vera Komisova (URS) 12·56	Johanna Klier (GDR) 12·63	Lucyna Langer (POL) 12·65

1896–1928 Event not held

4 × 100 METRES RELAY

	Gold	Silver	Bronze
1928	CANADA 48·4	UNITED STATES 48·8	GERMANY 49·2
1932	UNITED STATES 47·0	CANADA 47·0	GREAT BRITAIN 47·6
1936	UNITED STATES 46·9	GREAT BRITAIN 47·6	CANADA 47·8
1948	NETHERLANDS 47·5	AUSTRALIA 47·6	CANADA 47·8
1952	UNITED STATES 45·9 (46·14)	GERMANY 45·9 (46·18)	GREAT BRITAIN 46·2 (46·41)
1956	AUSTRALIA 44·5 (44·65)	GREAT BRITAIN 44·7 (44·70)	UNITED STATES 44·9 (45·04)
1960	UNITED STATES 44·5 (44·72)	GERMANY 44·8 (45·00)	POLAND 45·0 (45·19)
1964	POLAND 43·6 (43·69)	UNITED STATES 43·9 (43·92)	GREAT BRITAIN 44·0 (44·09)
1968	UNITED STATES 42·8 (42·87)	CUBA 43·3 (43·35)	USSR 43·4 (43·41)
1972	FRG 42·81	GDR 42·95	CUBA 43·36
1976	GDR 42·55	FRG 42·59	USSR 43·09
1980	GDR 41·60	USSR 42·10	GREAT BRITAIN 42·43

4 × 400 METRES RELAY

	Gold	Silver	Bronze
1972	GDR 3:22·95	UNITED STATES 3:25·15	FRG 3:26·51
1976	GDR 3:19·23	UNITED STATES 3:22·81	USSR 3:24·24
1980	USSR 3:20·12	GDR 3:20·35	GREAT BRITAIN 3:27·5

1928–1968 Event not held

HIGH JUMP

	Gold	Silver	Bronze
1928	Ethel Catherwood (CAN) 1·59 m	Carolina Gisolf (HOL) 1·56 m	Mildred Wiley (USA) 1·56 m
1932	Jean Shiley (USA) 1·65 m	Mildred Didrikson (USA) 1·65 m	Eva Dawes (CAN) 1·60 m
1936	Ibolya Csák (HUN) 1·60 m	Dorothy Odam (GBR) 1·60 m	Elfriede Kaun (GER) 1·60 m
1948	Alice Coachman (USA) 1·68 m	Dorothy Tyler (GBR) 1·68 m	Micheline Ostermeyer (FRA) 1·61 m
1952	Esther Brand (SAF) 1·67 m	Sheila Lerwill (GBR) 1·65 m	Aleksandra Chudina (URS) 1·63 m
1956	Mildred McDaniel (USA) 1·76 m	Thelma Hopkins (GBR) 1·67 m Maria Pisaryeva (URS) 1·67 m	—
1960	Iolanda Balas (ROM) 1·85 m	Jaroslawa Jozwiakowska (POL) 1·71 m Dorothy Shirley (GBR) 1·71 m	—
1964	Iolanda Balas (ROM) 1·90 m	Michelle Brown (AUS) 1·80 m	Taisia Chenchik (URS) 1·78 m
1968	Miloslava Rezkova (TCH) 1·82 m	Antonina Okorokova (URS) 1·80 m	Valentina Kozyr (URS) 1·80 m
1972	Ulrike Meyfarth (FRG) 1·92 m	Yordanka Blagoyeva (BUL) 1·88 m	Ilona Gusenbauer (AUT) 1·88 m
1976	Rosemarie Ackermann (GDR) 1·93 m	Sara Simeoni (ITA) 1·91 m	Yordanka Blagoyeva (BUL) 1·91 m
1980	Sara Simeoni (ITA) 1·97 m	Urszula Kielan (POL) 1·94 m	Jutta Kirst (GDR) 1·94 m

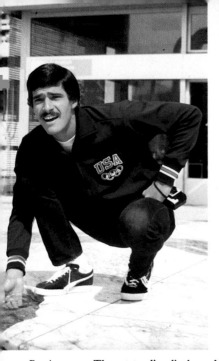

Previous page: **The outstanding displays which formed the centrepiece of the opening ceremony for the 1980 Games in Moscow will remain unforgettable by those who witnessed them.** Above left: **Mark Spitz (USA) set a record unlikely to be beaten when he won seven swimming gold medals in 1972.** Above right: **Although Olga Korbut (URS) was considered number two in the Soviet team to Ludmila Tourischeva, she was ranked number one by the spectators at Munich in 1972.** Below: **One of the few women in Olympic history to excel in two entirely different sports: Roswitha Krause (GDR) won a silver medal in the 4 × 100 m freestyle relay in 1968, then silver and bronze for handball in 1976 and 1980.**

Above: **Alberto Juantorena (CUB)** created a stir in 1976 when he won both the 400 m and 800 m finals. This double had not been achieved since 1906. Also in the picture, from the left, are Fred Newhouse (USA), Herman Frazier (USA), and, on the inside, Jan Werner (Pol).

Right: **John Curry** practising at Innsbruck in 1976 prior to winning the men's figure skating title. His gold medal was Britain's first skating medal for 24 years.

Right: **If the modern pentathlon is the event of the top all-round sportsman, then András Balczó (Hun) has a special place in Olympic annals. He has won three gold medals plus two silvers in the sport.**

Below: **The Landvoigt twins, Bernd and Jörg, in 1980 after successfully defending the pairs title they had originally won at Montreal. Their teammates won ten of the other thirteen rowing events in Moscow.**

Above left: **No skier has gained more gold medals at one Games than Nikolai Zimyatov (No 41) who won the 30 km and 50 km Nordic skiing events and was a member of the Soviet 4 × 10 km team at Lake Placid. The Finnish skier Juha Mieto (No 38) was runner-up in the 50 km.**

Above: **No man, and only one woman, has won more Olympic medals than Nikolai Andrianov, the Soviet gymnast. His record total of 15 comprises seven gold, five silver and three bronze medals. He has particularly excelled in the floor exercises, as here in 1976.**

Left: **Barbara Krause (centre) won the 100 m and 200 m freestyle titles in Moscow, as well as a third gold medal in the 4 × 100 m freestyle relay. The other 200 m medallists, her GDR teammates Ines Diers and Carmela Schmidt, won two gold, two silver and three bronze medals.**

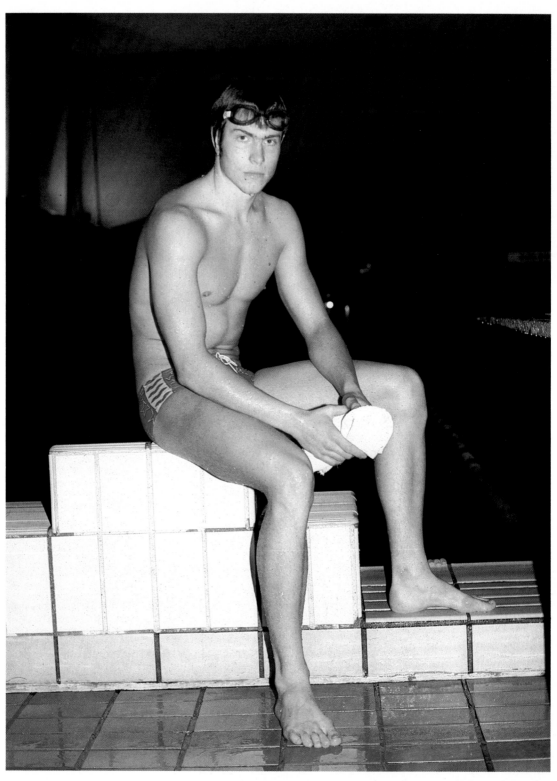

Vladimir Salnikov's 1500 m freestyle victory in Moscow, when he became the only man ever to swim the distance in under 15 minutes, was one of the great performances in Olympic history.

Above: **The victory of the United States team over Finland in 1980 gave them the Olympic ice hockey title for only the second time in history. Not surprisingly, wild scenes of rejoicing followed, as they had after an earlier win over the favoured Soviet team. Below: The only man to win the same boxing title on three occasions, Teofilo Stevenson of Cuba, here taking the measure of one of the few Africans to compete at the Montreal Games, Mamadou Drame of Senegal.**

Competitors in the shooting phase of the biathlon, a severe test of stamina and skill which has witnessed, in the last few Winter Games, the sportsmen of the USSR and GDR taking over from those representing the Nordic countries.

The symbol and mascot of the 1980 Olympic Games—Misha the bear—delineated by the cards of the well-drilled display team in the Lenin stadium.

LONG JUMP

	Gold	Silver	Bronze
1948	Olga Gyarmati (HUN) 5·69 m	Noemi Simonetto de Portela (ARG) 5·60 m	Ann-Britt Leyman (SWE) 5·57 m
1952	Yvette Williams (NZL) 6·24 m	Aleksandra Chudina (URS) 6·14 m	Shirley Cawley (GBR) 5·92 m
1956	Elzbieta Krzesinska (POL) 6·35 m	Willye White (USA) 6·09 m	Nadyezda Dvalishvili (URS) 6·07 m
1960	Vera Krepkina (URS) 6·37 m	Elzbieta Krzesinska (POL) 6·27 m	Hildrun Claus (GER) 6·21 m
1964	Mary Rand (GBR) 6·76 m	Irena Kirszenstein (POL) 6·60 m	Tatyana Schelkanova (URS) 6·42 m
1968	Viorica Viscopoleanu (ROM) 6·82 m	Sheila Sherwood (GBR) 6·68 m	Tatyana Talysheva (URS) 6·66 m
1972	Heidemarie Rosendahl (FRG) 6·78 m	Diana Yorgova (BUL) 6·77 m	Eva Suranova (TCH) 6·67 m
1976	Angela Voigt (GDR) 6·72 m	Kathy McMillan (USA) 6·66 m	Lidia Alfeyeva (URS) 6·60 m
1980	Tatyana Kolpakova (URS) 7·06 m	Brigitte Wujak (GDR) 7·04 m	Tatyana Skatchko (URS) 7·01 m

1928–1938 Event not held

SHOT PUT

	Gold	Silver	Bronze
1948	Micheline Ostermeyer (FRA) 13·75 m	Amelia Piccinini (ITA) 13·09 m	Ina Schäffer (AUT) 13·08 m
1952	Galina Zybina (URS) 15·28 m	Marianne Werner (GER) 14·57 m	Klavdia Tochenova (URS) 14·50 m
1956	Tamara Tyshkevich (URS) 16·59 m	Galina Zybina (URS) 16·53 m	Marianne Werner (GER) 15·61 m
1960	Tamara Press (URS) 17·32 m	Johanna Lüttge (GER) 16·61 m	Earlene Brown (USA) 16·42 m
1964	Tamara Press (URS) 18·14 m	Renate Garisch (GDR) 17·61 m	Galina Zybina (URS) 16·42 m
1968	Margitta Gummel (GDR) 19·61 m	Marita Lange (GDR) 18·78 m	Nadyezda Chizhova (URS) 18·19 m
1972	Nadyezda Chizhova (URS) 21·03 m	Margitta Gummel (GDR) 20·22 m	Ivanka Khristova (BUL) 19·35 m
1976	Ivanka Khristova (BUL) 21·16 m	Nadyezda Chizhova (URS) 20·96 m	Helena Fibingerova (TCH) 20·67 m
1980	Ilona Slupianek (GDR) 22·41 m	Svetlana Krachevskaya (URS) 21·42 m	Margitta Pufe (GDR) 21·20 m

1928–1936 Event not held

DISCUS

	Gold	Silver	Bronze
1928	Helena Konopacka (POL) 39·62 m	Lillian Copeland (USA) 37·08 m	Ruth Svedberg (SWE) 35·92 m
1932	Lillian Copeland (USA) 40·58 m	Ruth Osburn (USA) 40·11 m	Jadwiga Wajsówna (POL) 38·73 m
1936	Gisela Mauermayer (GER) 47·63 m	Jadwiga Wajsówna (POL) 46·22 m	Paula Mollenhauer (GER) 39·80 m
1948	Micheline Ostermeyer (FRA) 41·92 m	Edera Gentile (ITA) 41·17 m	Jacqueline Mazeas (FRA) 40·47 m
1952	Nina Romashkova (URS) 51·42	Elizaveta Bagriantseva (URS) 47·08 m	Nina Dumbadze (URS) 46·29 m
1956	Olga Fikotova (TCH) 53·69 m	Irina Beglyakova (URS) 52·54 m	Nina Ponomaryeva (URS) 52·02 m
1960	Nina Ponomaryeva (URS) 55·10 m	Tamara Press (URS) 52·59 m	Lia Manoliu (ROM) 52·36 m
1964	Tamara Press (URS) 57·27 m	Ingrid Lotz (GER) 57·21 m	Lia Manoliu (ROM) 56·97 m
1968	Lia Manoliu (ROM) 58·28 m	Liesel Westermann (FRG) 57·76 m	Jolán Kleiber (HUN) 54·90 m
1972	Faina Melnik (URS) 66·62	Argentina Menis (ROM) 65·06 m	Vasilka Stoyeva (BUL) 64·34 m
1976	Evelin Schlaak (GDR) 69·00 m	Maria Vergova (BUL) 67·30 m	Gabriele Hinzmann (GDR) 66·84 m
1980	Evelin Jahl (GDR) 69·96 m	Maria Petkova (BUL) 67·90 m	Tatyana Lesovaya (URS) 67·40 m

JAVELIN

	Gold	Silver	Bronze
1932	Mildred Didrikson (USA) 43·68 m	Ellen Braumüller (GER) 43·49 m	Tilly Fleischer (GER) 43·40 m
1936	Tilly Fleischer (GER) 45·18 m	Luise Krüger (GER) 43·29 m	Marja Kwasniewska (POL) 41·80 m
1948	Herma Bauma (AUT) 45·57 m	Kaisa Parviainen (FIN) 43·79 m	Lily Carlstedt (DEN) 42·08 m
1952	Dana Zatopková (TCH) 50·47 m	Aleksandra Chudina (URS) 50·01 m	Yelena Gorchakova (URS) 49·76 m
1956	Ines Jaunzeme (URS) 53·86 m	Marlene Ahrens (CHI) 50·38 m	Nadyezda Konyayeva (URS) 50·28 m
1960	Elvira Ozolina (URS) 55·98 m	Dana Zatopková (TCH) 53·78 m	Birute Kalediene (URS) 53·45 m
1964	Mihaela Penes (ROM) 60·54 m	Märta Rudas (HUN) 58·27 m	Yelena Gorchakova (URS) 57·06 m
1968	Angela Németh (HUN) 60·36 m	Mihaela Penes (ROM) 59·92 m	Eva Janko (AUT) 58·04 m
1972	Ruth Fuchs (GDR) 63·88 m	Jacqueline Todten (GDR) 62·54 m	Kathy Schmidt (USA) 59·94 m
1976	Ruth Fuchs (GDR) 65·94 m	Marion Becker (FRG) 64·70 m	Kathy Schmidt (USA) 63·96 m
1980	Maria Colon (CUB) 68·40 m	Saida Gunba (URS) 67·76 m	Ute Hommola (GDR) 66·56 m

1928 Event not held

PENTATHLON[1]

	Gold	Silver	Bronze
1964	Irina Press (URS) 5246 pts	Mary Rand (GBR) 5035	Galina Bystrova (URS) 4956
1968	Ingrid Becker (FRG) 5098 pts	Liese Prokop (AUT) 4966	Annamaria Tóth (HUN) 4959
1972[2]	Mary Peters (GBR) 4801 pts	Heidemarie Rosendahl (FRG) 4791	Burglinde Pollak (GDR) 4768
1976[3]	Siegrun Siegl (GDR) 4745 pts	Christine Laser (GDR) 4745	Burglinde Pollak (GDR) 4740
1980	Nadyezda Tkachenko (URS) 5083 pts	Olga Rukavishnikova (URS) 4937	Olga Kuragina (URS) 4875

[1] The pentathlon consisted of 100 m hurdles, shot put, high jump, long jump and 200 m from 1964 to 1976. In 1980 the 200 m was replaced by 800 m.
[2] New scoring tables were introduced in May 1971.   [3] Siegl finished ahead of Laser in three events.   1928–1960 Event not held

---

Women who have won medals under both their maiden and married names:

Becker—Mickler (FRG)	Odam—Tyler (GBR)
Brehmer—Lathan (GDR)	Richter—Górecka (POL)
Eckert—Wöckel (GDR)	Romashkova—Ponomaryeva (URS)
Foulds—Paul (GBR)	Schaller—Klier (GDR)
Khnykina—Dvalishvili (URS)	Schlaak—Jahl (GDR)
Kirszenstein—Szewinska (POL)	Vergova—Petkova (BUL)
Köhler—Birkemeyer (GDR)	Wieczorek—Ciepla (POL)
Manning—Jackson (USA)	Zharkova—Maslakova (URS)

DISCONTINUED EVENTS

60 METRES

	Gold	Silver	Bronze
1900	Alvin Kraenzlein (USA) 7·0	Walter Tewksbury (USA) 7·1	Stanley Rowley (AUS) 7·2
1904	Archie Hahn (USA) 7·0	William Hogenson (USA) 7·2	Fay Moulton (USA) 7·2

3000 METRES TEAM RACE

	Gold	Silver	Bronze
1912	UNITED STATES 9 pts	SWEDEN 13	GREAT BRITAIN 23
1920	UNITED STATES 10 pts	GREAT BRITAIN 20	SWEDEN 24
1924	FINLAND 8 pts	GREAT BRITAIN 14	UNITED STATES 25

3 MILES TEAM RACE

	Gold	Silver	Bronze
1908	GREAT BRITAIN 6 pts	UNITED STATES 19	FRANCE 32

5000 METRES TEAM RACE

	Gold	Silver	Bronze
1900	GREAT BRITAIN 26 pts	FRANCE 29	—

INDIVIDUAL CROSS-COUNTRY

	Gold	Silver	Bronze
1912[1]	Hannes Kolehmainen (FIN) 45:11·6	Hjalmar Andersson (SWE) 45:44·8	John Eke (SWE) 46:37·6
1920[2]	Paavo Nurmi (FIN) 27:15·0	Erick Backman (SWE) 27:17·6	Heikki Liimatainen (FIN) 27:37·4
1924[3]	Paavo Nurmi (FIN) 32:54·8	Ville Ritola (FIN) 34:19·4	Earl Johnson (USA) 35:21·0

[1] 12 000 metres   [2] 8000 metres   [3] 10 000 metres

TEAM CROSS-COUNTRY

Gold	*Silver*	*Bronze*
1904 UNITED STATES (New York AC)	UNITED STATES (Chicago AA)	—
1912 SWEDEN 10 pts	FINLAND 11	GREAT BRITAIN 49
1920 FINLAND 10 pts	GREAT BRITAIN 21	SWEDEN 23
1924 FINLAND 11 pts	UNITED STATES 14	FRANCE 20

200 METRES HURDLES

Gold	*Silver*	*Bronze*
1900 Alvin Kraenzlein (USA) 25·4	Norman Pritchard (IND) 26·6	Walter Tewksbury (USA) n.t.a.
1904 Harry Hillman (USA) 24·6	Frank Castleman (USA) 24·9	George Poage (USA) n.t.a.

PENTATHLON

Gold	*Silver*	*Bronze*
1906[1] Hjalmar Mellander (SWE) 24 pts	Istvan Mudin (HUN) 25	Erik Lemming 29
1912[2,3] Ferdinand Bie (NOR) 16 pts	James Donahue (USA) 24	Frank Lukeman (CAN) 24
1920[2] Eero Lehtonen (FIN) 14 pts	Everett Bradley (USA) 24	Hugo Lahtinen (FIN) 26
1924[2] Eero Lehtonen (FIN) 14 pts	Elemér Somfay (HUN) 16	Robert LeGendre (USA) 18

[1] Consisted of standing long jump, discus (Greek style), javelin, one-lap race (192 m), Greco-Roman wrestling.   [2] Consisted of long lump, javelin, 200 m, discus, 1500 m.   [3] Jim Thorpe (USA) finished first with 7 points but was subsequently disqualified. He was reinstated posthumously in 1982, but as joint first.

STANDING HIGH JUMP

Gold	*Silver*	*Bronze*
1900 Ray Ewry (USA) 1·655 m	Irving Baxter (USA) 1·525 m	Lewis Sheldon (USA) 1·50 m
1904 Ray Ewry (USA) 1·50 m	James Stadler (USA) 1·45 m	Lawson Robertson (USA) 1·45 m
1906 Ray Ewry (USA) 1·565 m	Martin Sheridan (USA) 1·40 m	—
	Léon Dupont (BEL) 1·40 m	
	Lawson Robertson (USA) 1·40 m	
1908 Ray Ewry (USA) 1·575 m	Konstantin Tsiklitiras (GRE) 1·55 m	—
	John Biller (USA) 1·55 m	
1912 Platt Adams (USA) 1·63 m	Benjamin Adams (USA) 1·60 m	Konstantin Tsiklitiras (GRE) 1·55 m

STANDING LONG JUMP

Gold	*Silver*	*Bronze*
1900 Ray Ewry (USA) 3·21 m	Irving Baxter (USA) 3·135 m	Emile Torcheboeuf (FRA) 3·03 m
1904 Ray Ewry (USA) 3·476 m	Charles King (USA) 3·28 m	John Biller (USA) 3·26 m
1906 Ray Ewry (USA) 3·30 m	Martin Sheridan (USA) 3·095 m	Lawson Robertson (USA) 3·05 m
1908 Ray Ewry (USA) 3·335 m	Konstantin Tsiklitiras (GRE) 3·23 m	Martin Sheridan (USA) 3·225 m
1912 Konstantin Tsiklitiras (GRE) 3·37 m	Platt Adams (USA) 3·36 m	Benjamin Adams (USA) 3·28 m

STANDING TRIPLE JUMP

Gold	*Silver*	*Bronze*
1900 Ray Ewry (USA) 10·58 m	Irving Baxter (USA) 9·95 m	Robert Garrett (USA) 9·50 m
1904 Ray Ewry (USA) 10·55 m	Charles King (USA) 10·16 m	James Stadler (USA) 9·53 m

56-POUND (25·4 kg) WEIGHT THROW

Gold	*Silver*	*Bronze*
1904 Etienne Desmarteau (CAN) 10·465 m	John Flanagan (USA) 10·16 m	James Mitchel (USA) 10·135 m
1920 Patrick McDonald (USA) 11·265 m	Patrick Ryan (USA) 10·965 m	Carl Lind (SWE) 10·25 m

STONE (6·40 kg) PUT

	Gold	Silver	Bronze
1906	Nicolaos Georgantas (GRE) 19·925 m	Martin Sheridan (USA) 19·035 m	Michel Dorizas (GRE) 18·585 m

DISCUS (Greek Style)

	Gold	Silver	Bronze
1906	Werner Järvinen (FIN) 35·17 m	Nicolaos Georgantas (GRE) 32·80 m	Istvan Mudin (HUN) 31·91 m
1908	Martin Sheridan (USA) 38·00 m	Marquis Horr (USA) 37·325 m	Werner Järvinen (FIN) 36·48 m

JAVELIN (Free Style)

	Gold	Silver	Bronze
1908	Erik Lemming (SWE) 54·445 m	Michel Dorizas (GRE) 51·36 m	Arne Halse (NOR) 49·73 m

SHOT (Both Hands)[1]

	Gold	Silver	Bronze
1912	Ralph Rose (USA) 27·70 m	Patrick McDonald (USA) 27·53 m	Elmer Niklander (FIN) 27·14 m

[1] Aggregate of throws with right and left hands.

DISCUS (Both Hands)[1]

	Gold	Silver	Bronze
1912	Armas Taipale (FIN) 82·86 m	Elmer Niklander (FIN) 77·96 m	Emil Magnusson (SWE) 77·37 m

[1] Aggregate of throws with right and left hands.

JAVELIN (Both Hands)[1]

	Gold	Silver	Bronze
1912	Julius Saaristo (FIN) 109·42 m	Väinö Siikaniemi (FIN) 101·13 m	Urho Peltonen (FIN) 100·24 m

[1] Aggregate of throws with right and left hands.

1500 METRES WALK

	Gold	Silver	Bronze
1906	George Bonhag (USA) 7:12·6	Donald Linden (CAN) 7:19·8	Konstantin Spetsiotis (GRE) 7:22·0

3000 METRES WALK

	Gold	Silver	Bronze
1906	György Sztantics (HUN) 15:13·2	Hermann Müller (GER) 15:20·0	Georgios Saridakis (GRE) 15:33·0
1920	Ugo Frigerio (ITA) 13:14·2	George Parker (AUS) n.t.a.	Richard Remer (USA) n.t.a.

3500 METRES WALK

	Gold	Silver	Bronze
1908	George Larner (GBR) 14:55·0	Ernest Webb (GBR) 15:07·4	Harry Kerr (NZL) 15:43·4

10 000 METRES WALK

	Gold	Silver	Bronze
1912	George Goulding (CAN) 46:28·4	Ernest Webb (GBR) 46:50·4	Fernando Altimani (ITA) 47:37·6
1920	Ugo Frigerio (ITA) 48:06·2	Joseph Pearman (USA) n.t.a.	Charles Gunn (GBR) n.t.a.
1924	Ugo Frigerio (ITA) 47:49·0	Gordon Goodwin (GBR) 200 m	Cecil McMaster (SAF) 300 m
1948	John Mikaelsson (SWE) 45:13·2	Ingemar Johansson (SWE) 45:43·8	Fritz Schwab (SUI) 46:00·2
1952	John Mikaelsson (SWE) 45:02·8	Fritz Schwab (SUI) 45:41·0	Bruno Junk (URS) 45:41·2

1928–1936 Event not held

10 MILES WALK

Gold	Silver	Bronze
1908 George Larner (GBR) 1:15:57·4	Ernest Webb (GBR) 1:17:31·0	Edward Spencer (GBR) 1:21:20·2

VOLLEYBALL

Introduced into the Games in 1964 for both men and women, volleyball has been dominated by Soviet teams. Their men's teams played 39 matches losing only four from 1964 to 1980, and the women's team played 28 matches, losing only two in the same period.

The most successful player was Inna Ryskal (URS) with two gold and two silver medals from 1964 to 1976. The best by a male player was two golds and one silver by Yuriy Poyarkov (URS) from 1964 to 1972.

The oldest gold medallist was Ludmila Buldakova (URS) aged 34 yr 105 days in 1972, while the oldest male winner of a gold medal was Edward Skorek (POL) aged 33 yr 47 days in 1976. The youngest was Ludmila Borozna (URS) in 1972 aged 18 yr 249 days and the youngest male champion was Oleg Antropov (URS) aged 20 yr 357 days in 1968. The oldest medallist was Bohumil Golián (TCH) who was aged 37 yr 215 days when he won a bronze in 1968.

VOLLEYBALL (Men)

Gold	Silver	Bronze
1964 USSR	CZECHOSLOVAKIA	JAPAN
1968 USSR	JAPAN	CZECHOSLOVAKIA
1972 JAPAN	GDR	USSR
1976 POLAND	USSR	CUBA
1980 USSR	BULGARIA	ROMANIA

1896–1960 Event not held

VOLLEYBALL (Women)

Gold	Silver	Bronze
1964 JAPAN	USSR	POLAND
1968 USSR	JAPAN	POLAND
1972 USSR	JAPAN	NORTH KOREA
1976 JAPAN	USSR	SOUTH KOREA
1980 USSR	GDR	BULGARIA

1896–1960 Event not held

VOLLEYBALL—MEDALS
Men

	Gold	Silver	Bronze	Total
USSR	3	1	1	5
JAPAN	1	1	1	3
CZECHOSLOVAKIA	—	1	1	2
POLAND	1	—	—	1
BULGARIA	—	1	—	1
GDR	—	1	—	1
CUBA	—	—	1	1
ROMANIA	—	—	1	1
	5	5	5	15

VOLLEYBALL—MEDALS
Women

	Gold	Silver	Bronze	Total
USSR	3	2	—	5
JAPAN	2	2	—	4
POLAND	—	—	2	2
GDR	—	1	—	1
BULGARIA	—	—	1	1
NORTH KOREA	—	—	1	1
SOUTH KOREA	—	—	1	1
	5	5	5	15

WEIGHTLIFTING

Two events were included in the 1896 Games, consisting of one-arm and two-arm lifts. The first Olympic weightlifting champion was Viggo Jensen (DEN) who won the two-arm competition from Launceston Eliot (GBR). Although both lifted the same weight the Dane was awarded the first place because Eliot had moved one of his feet. There was an amusing incident at one point when an attendant was having great trouble moving one of the weights. Prince George of Greece, one of the members of the organizing committee and an immensely big and strong man, bent down and easily lifted it aside. The sport was not included in the Games of 1900, 1908 or 1912. In 1920 the contests were decided on the aggregate of a one-hand snatch, a one-hand jerk and a two-hands jerk. In 1924 an additional two lifts were included, two-hands press and snatch. From 1928 to 1972 the result depended on the aggregate of three two-handed lifts; the press, snatch and clean and jerk. In 1976 the press was eliminated, owing to difficulty in judging it correctly, and the total now is that of the snatch and the clean and jerk. The forerunner of the International Weightlifting Federation was formed in 1920 at the suggestion of the IOC which had realized that the sport needed to be controlled with competitions conducted under generally accepted conditions.

Of the ten men who have won two gold medals only Tommy Kono (USA) and Norair Nurikyan (BUL) have won them in different categories.

Josef Steinbach (AUT), who won the one-hand lift in 1906, but here came second in the two-hand event to Dimitrios Tofalos (GRE-700).

In addition to his two Olympic heavyweight titles John Davis (USA) also won a record eight world weightlifting championships.

Kono won the 67·5 kg in 1952 and moved up to win the 82·5 kg in 1956. More unusually Nurikyan won the 60 kg in 1972 and moved down to the 56 kg in 1976. In addition to their gold medals three of the ten also won another medal: Kono 1952–1960; Louis Hostin (FRA) 1928–1936; Yoshinobu Miyake (JPN) 1960–1968; Arkadiy Vorobyev (URS) 1952–1960. The most medals won by a weightlifter is four by Norbert Schemansky (USA) with one gold, one silver and two bronze medals from 1948 to 1964.

The oldest gold medallist was Rudolf Plukfelder (URS) who won the 82·5 kg class in 1964 aged 36 yr 40 days. The youngest was Aleksey Vakhonin (URS) winner of the 56 kg class in 1964 aged 19 yr 207 days. The oldest man to win a medal was Norbert Schemansky (USA) with a bronze in 1964 aged 40 yr 141 days. The youngest man to win a medal was Mintcho Pachov (BUL) aged 18 yr 259 days when he won the 67·5 kg bronze in 1980. The oldest known competitor was 56 year old Teunist Jonck (SAF) in 1952, while the youngest known was 13 year old M Djemal (TUR) in 1924. The smallest champion was Joseph de Pietro (USA), winner of the 56 kg class in 1948, who stood 1·42 m *4 ft 8 in* tall.

Weightlifting

The only brothers to win medals in the same event in a single Games were Yoshinobu and Yoshiyuki Miyake (JPN) who won gold and bronze medals respectively in the 60 kg class of 1968. Peter and James George (USA) won one gold, three silvers and one bronze between them from 1948 to 1960 for a family record.

The gold medal won by Sultan Rakhmanov (URS), the last one of the 1980 Games competitions, was the 100th weightlifting gold medal since the sport was introduced into the Olympics.

The silver medallist in the 82·5 kg class in 1948, Harold Sakata (USA), later became a film actor, his best known portrayal being that of 'Oddjob' in the James Bond film *Goldfinger*.

Disqualification due to use of drugs has affected

Daniel Nunez (CUB) snatches 125 kg on his way to the gold medal and a new world record in the bantamweight division at Moscow in 1980.

this sport more than most. In 1976, a month after the competitions, a gold medallist (Zbigniev Kaczmarek of Poland) and a silver medallist (Blagoi Blagoyev of Bulgaria) were disqualified as well as unplaced competitors from Bulgaria, Sweden and the United States.

OLYMPIC RECORDS[1]—WEIGHTLIFTING

Event	Lift	Kg	Name and Country	Year
52 kg	Total	245	Kanybek Osmonoliev (URS)	1980
		245	Bong Chol Ho (PRK)	1980
		245	Gyong Si Han (PRK)	1980
		245	Bela Olah (HUN)	1980
	Snatch	110	Bong Chol Ho (PRK)	1980
		110	Gyong Si Han (PRK)	1980
		110	Bela Oláh (HUN)	1980
	Jerk	137·5	Kanybek Osmonoliev (URS)	1980
56 kg	Total	275	Daniel Nunez (CUB)	1980
	Snatch	125	Daniel Nunez (CUB)	1980
	Jerk	157·5	Yurik Sarkisian (URS)	1980
60 kg	Total	290	Viktor Mazin (URS)	1980
	Snatch	130	Viktor Mazin (URS)	1980
	Jerk	160	Nikolai Kolesnikov (URS)	1976
		160	Viktor Mazin (URS)	1980
		160	Stefan Dimitrov (BUL)	1980
67·5 kg	Total	342·5	Yanko Rusev (BUL)	1980
	Snatch	147·5	Yanko Rusev (BUL)	1980
		147·5	Daniel Senet (FRA)	1980
	Jerk	195	Yanko Rusev (BUL)	1980
75 kg	Total	360	Asen Zlatev (BUL)	1980
	Snatch	160	Asen Zlatev (BUL)	1980
	Jerk	200	Asen Zlatev (BUL)	1980
		200	Aleksandr Pervy (URS)	1980
82·5 kg	Total	400	Yurik Vardanyan (URS)	1980
	Snatch	177·5	Yurik Vardanyan (URS)	1980
	Jerk	222·5	Yurik Vardanyan (URS)	1980
90 kg	Total	382·5	David Rigert (URS)	1976
	Snatch	170	David Rigert (URS)	1976
		170	Peter Baczako (HUN)	1980
		170	Rumen Alexandrov (BUL)	1980
	Jerk	212·5	David Rigert (URS)	1976
100 kg	Total	395	Ota Zaremba (TCH)	1980
	Snatch	180	Ota Zaremba (TCH)	1980
	Jerk	217·5	Michael Hennig (GDR)	1980
110 kg	Total	422·5	Leonid Taranenko (URS)	1980
	Snatch	185	Valentin Christov (BUL)	1980
	Jerk	240	Leonid Taranenko (URS)	1980

110 kg+	Total	440	Vasiliy Alexeyev (URS)	1976
		440	Sultan Rakhmanov (URS)	1980
	Snatch	195	Sultan Rakhmanov (URS)	1980
	Jerk	255	Vasiliy Alexeyev (URS)	1976

[1] All competitors who have achieved the record mark are listed although officially the record, when tied by other lifters, goes to the one with the lightest bodyweight.

FLYWEIGHT
(Up to 52 kg)

	Gold	Silver	Bronze
1972	Zygmunt Smalcerz (POL) 337·5 kg	Lajos Szuecs (HUN) 330 kg	Sandor Holczreiter (HUN) 327·5 kg
1976	Aleksandr Voronin (URS) 242·5 kg	Gyorgy Koszegi (HUN) 237·5 kg	Mohammad Nassiri (IRN) 235 kg
1980	Kanybek Osmonoliev (URS) 245 kg	Bong Chol Ho (PRK) 245 kg	Gyong Si Han (PRK) 245 kg

1896–1968 Event not held

BANTAMWEIGHT
(Up to 56 kg)

	Gold	Silver	Bronze
1948	Joseph de Pietro (USA) 307·5 kg	Julian Creus (GBR) 297·5 kg	Richard Tom (USA) 295 kg
1952	Ivan Udodov (URS) 315 kg	Mahmoud Namdjou (IRN) 307·5 kg	Ali Mirzai (IRN) 300 kg
1956	Charles Vinci (USA) 342·5 kg	Vladimir Stogov (URS) 337·5 kg	Mahmoud Namdjou (IRN) 332·5 kg
1960	Charles Vinci (USA) 345 kg	Yoshinobu Miyake (JPN) 337·5 kg	Esmail Khan (IRN) 330 kg
1964	Aleksey Vakhonin (URS) 357·5 kg	Imre Földi (HUN) 355 kg	Shiro Ichinoseki (JPN) 347·5 kg
1968	Mohammad Nassiri (IRN) 367·5 kg	Imre Földi (HUN) 367·5 kg	Henryk Trebicki (POL) 357·5 kg
1972	Imre Földi (HUN) 377·5 kg	Mohammad Nassiri (IRN) 370 kg	Gennadiy Chetin (URS) 367·5 kg
1976	Norair Nurikyan (BUL) 262·5 kg	Grzegorz Cziura (POL) 252·5 kg	Kenkichi Ando (JPN) 250 kg
1980	Daniel Nunez (CUB) 275 kg	Yurik Sarkisian (URS) 270 kg	Tadeusz Dembonczyk (POL) 265 kg

1896–1936 Event not held

FEATHERWEIGHT
(Up to 60 kg)

	Gold	Silver	Bronze
1920	Frans de Haes (BEL) 220 kg	Alfred Schmidt (EST) 212·5 kg	Eugène Ryther (SUI) 210 kg
1924[1]	Pierino Gabetti (ITA) 402·5 kg	Andreas Stadler (AUT) 385 kg	Arthur Reinmann (SUI) 382·5 kg
1928	Franz Andrysek (AUT) 287·5 kg	Pierino Gabetti (ITA) 282·5 kg	Hans Wölpert (GER) 282·5 kg
1932	Raymond Suvigny (FRA) 287·5 kg	Hans Wölpert (GER) 282·5 kg	Anthony Terlazzo (USA) 280 kg
1936	Anthony Terlazzo (USA) 312·5 kg	Saleh Mohammed Soliman (EGY) 305 kg	Ibrahim Shams (EGY) 300 kg
1948	Mahmoud Fayad (EGY) 332·5 kg	Rodney Wilkes (TRI) 317·5 kg	Jaffar Salmassi (IRN) 312·5 kg
1952	Rafael Chimishkyan (URS) 337·5 kg	Nikolai Saksonov (URS) 332·5 kg	Rodney Wilkes (TRI) 322·5 kg
1956	Isaac Berger (USA) 352·5 kg	Yevgeniy Minayev (URS) 342·5 kg	Marian Zielinski (POL) 335 kg
1960	Yevgeniy Minayev (URS) 372·5 kg	Isaac Berger (USA) 362·5 kg	Sebastiano Mannironi (ITA) 352·5 kg
1964	Yoshinobu Miyake (JPN) 397·5 kg	Isaac Berger (USA) 382·5 kg	Mieczyslaw Nowak (POL) 377·5 kg
1968	Yoshinobu Miyake (JPN) 392·5 kg	Dito Shanidze (URS) 387·5 kg	Yoshiyuki Miyake (JPN) 385 kg
1972	Norair Nurikyan (BUL) 402·5 kg	Dito Shanidze (URS) 400 kg	Janos Benedek (HUN) 390 kg
1976	Nikolai Kolesnikov (URS) 285 kg	Georgi Todorov (BUL) 280 kg	Kuzumasa Hirai (JPN) 275 kg
1980	Viktor Mazin (URS) 290 kg	Stefan Dimitrov (BUL) 287·5 kg	Marek Seweryn (POL) 282·5 kg

[1] Aggregate of five lifts.   1896–1912 Event not held

LIGHTWEIGHT
(Up to 67·5 kg)

	Gold	Silver	Bronze
1920	Alfred Neuland (EST) 257·5 kg	Louis Williquet (BEL) 240 kg	Florimond Rooms (BEL) 230 kg
1924[1]	Edmond Decottignies (FRA) 440 kg	Anton Zwerina (AUT) 427·5 kg	Bohumil Durdis (TCH) 425 kg
1928[2]	Kurt Helbig (GER) 322·5 kg Hans Haas (AUT) 322·5 kg	—	Fernand Arnout (FRA) 302·5 kg
1932	René Duverger (FRA) 325 kg	Hans Haas (AUT) 307·5 kg	Gastone Pierini (ITA) 302·5 kg
1936[2]	Anwar Mohammed Mesbah (EGY) 342·5 kg Robert Fein (AUT) 342·5 kg	—	Karl Jansen (GER) 327·5 kg
1948	Ibrahim Shams (EGY) 360 kg	Attia Hamouda (EGY) 360 kg	James Halliday (GBR) 340 kg
1952	Tommy Kono (USA) 362·5 kg	Yevgeniy Lopatin (URS) 350 kg	Verne Barberis (AUS) 350 kg
1956	Igor Rybak (URS) 380 kg	Ravil Khabutdinov (URS) 372·5 kg	Chang-Hee Kim (KOR) 370 kg
1960	Viktor Bushuyev (URS) 397·5 kg	Howe-Liang Tan (SIN) 380 kg	Abdul Wahid Aziz (IRQ) 380 kg

1964	Waldemar Baszanowski (POL) 432·5 kg	Vladimir Kaplunov (URS) 432·5 kg	Marian Zielinski (POL) 420 kg
1968	Waldemar Baszanowski (POL) 437·5 kg	Parviz Jalayer (IRN) 422·5 kg	Marian Zielinski (POL) 420 kg
1972	Mukharbi Kirzhinov (URS) 460 kg	Mladen Koutchev (BUL) 450 kg	Zbigniev Kaczmarek (POL) 437·5 kg
1976[3]	Pyotr Korol (URS) 305 kg	Daniel Senet (FRA) 300 kg	Kazimierz Czarnecki (POL) 295 kg
1980	Yanko Rusev (BUL) 342·5 kg	Joachim Kunz (GDR) 335 kg	Mintcho Pachov (BUL) 325 kg

[1] Aggregate of five lifts.   [2] Tie-breaker rule relating to bodyweight not yet introduced.   [3] Zbigniev Kaczmarek (POL) finished in first place with 307·5 kg but was subsequently disqualified.   1896–1912 Event not held

MIDDLEWEIGHT
(Up to 75 kg)

	Gold	Silver	Bronze
1920	Henri Gance (FRA) 245 kg	Pietro Bianchi[1] (ITA) 237·5 kg	Albert Pettersson (SWE) 237·5 kg
1924[2]	Carlo Galimberti (ITA) 492·5 kg	Alfred Neuland (EST) 455 kg	Jaan Kikas (EST) 450 kg
1928	Roger Francois (FRA) 335 kg	Carlo Galimberti (ITA) 332·5 kg	August Scheffer (HOL) 327·5 kg
1932	Rudolf Ismayr (GER) 345 kg	Carlo Galimberti (ITA) 340 kg	Karl Hipfinger (AUT) 337·5 kg
1936	Khadr El Thouni (EGY) 387·5 kg	Rudolf Ismayr (GER) 352·5 kg	Adolf Wagner (GER) 352·5 kg
1948	Frank Spellman (USA) 390 kg	Peter George (USA) 382·5 kg	Sung-Jip Kim (KOR) 380 kg
1952	Peter George (USA) 400 kg	Gerard Gratton (CAN) 390 kg	Sung-Jip Kim (KOR) 382·5 kg
1956	Fyodor Bogdanovski (URS) 420 kg	Peter George (USA) 412·5 kg	Ermanno Pignatti (ITA) 382·5 kg
1960	Aleksandr Kurinov (URS) 437·5 kg	Tommy Kono (USA) 427·5 kg	Gyözö Veres (HUN) 405 kg
1964	Hans Zdrazila (TCH) 445 kg	Viktor Kurentsov (URS) 440 kg	Masashi Ouchi (JPN) 437·5 kg
1968	Viktor Kurentsov (URS) 475 kg	Masashi Ouchi (JPN) 455 kg	Károly Bakos (HUN) 440 kg
1972	Yordan Bikov (BUL) 485 kg	Mohamed Trabulsi (LIB) 472·5 kg	Anselmo Silvino (ITA) 470 kg
1976	Yordan Mitkov (BUL) 335 kg	Vartan Militosyan (URS) 330 kg	Peter Wenzel (GDR) 327·5 kg
1980	Asen Zlatev (BUL) 360 kg	Aleksandr Pervy (URS) 357·5 kg	Nedeltcho Kolev (BUL) 345 kg

[1] Bianchi and Pettersson drew lots for the silver medal.   [2] Aggregate of five lifts.   1896–1912 Event not held

LIGHT-HEAVYWEIGHT
(Up to 82·5 kg)

	Gold	Silver	Bronze
1920	Ernest Cadine (FRA) 290 kg	Fritz Hünenberger (SUI) 275 kg	Erik Pettersson (SWE) 272·5 kg
1924[1]	Charles Rigoulot (FRA) 502·5 kg	Fritz Hünenberger (SUI) 490 kg	Leopold Friedrich (AUT) 490 kg
1928	Said Nosseir (EGY) 355 kg	Louis Hostin (FRA) 352·5 kg	Johannes Verheijen (HOL) 337·5 kg
1932	Louis Hostin (FRA) 372·5 kg	Svend Olsen (DEN) 360 kg	Henry Duey (USA) 330 kg
1936	Louis Hostin (FRA) 372·5 kg	Eugen Deutsch (GER) 365 kg	Ibrahim Wasif (EGY) 360 kg
1948	Stanley Stanczyk (USA) 417·5 kg	Harold Sakata (USA) 380 kg	Gösta Magnusson (SWE) 375 kg
1952	Trofim Lomakin (URS) 417·5 kg	Stanley Stanczyk (USA) 415 kg	Arkadiy Vorobyev (URS) 407·5 kg
1956	Tommy Kono (USA) 447·5 kg	Vassiliy Stepanov (URS) 427·5 kg	James George (USA) 417·5 kg
1960	Ireneusz Palinski (POL) 442·5 kg	James George (USA) 430 kg	Jan Bochenek (POL) 420 kg
1964	Rudolf Plukfelder (URS) 475 kg	Géza Toth (HUN) 467·5 kg	Gyözö Veres (HUN) 467·5 kg
1968	Boris Selitsky (URS) 485 kg	Vladimir Belyayev (URS) 485 kg	Norbert Ozimek (POL) 472·5 kg
1972	Leif Jenssen (NOR) 507·5 kg	Norbert Ozimek (POL) 497·5 kg	György Horvath (HUN) 495 kg
1976[2]	Valeriy Shary (URS) 365 kg	Trendachil Stoichev (BUL) 360 kg	Peter Baczako (HUN) 345 kg
1980	Yurik Vardanyan (URS) 400 kg	Blagoi Blagoyev (BUL) 372·5 kg	Dusan Poliacik (TCH) 367·5 kg

[1] Aggregate of five lifts.   [2] Blagoi Blagoyev (BUL) finished in second place with 362·5 kg but was subsequently disqualified.   1896–1912 Event not held

MIDDLE-HEAVYWEIGHT
(Up to 90 kg)

	Gold	Silver	Bronze
1952	Norbert Schemansky (USA) 445 kg	Grigoriy Nowak (URS) 410 kg	Lennox Kilgour (TRI) 402·5 kg
1956	Arkadiy Vorobyev (URS) 462·5 kg	David Sheppard (USA) 442·5 kg	Jean Debuf (FRA) 425 kg
1960	Arkadiy Vorobyev (URS) 472·5 kg	Trofim Lomakin (URS) 457·5 kg	Louis Martin (GBR) 445 kg
1964	Vladimir Golovanov (URS) 487·5 kg	Louis Martin (GBR) 475 kg	Ireneusz Palinski (POL) 467·5 kg
1968	Kaarlo Kangasniemi (FIN) 517·5 kg	Jan Talts (URS) 507·5 kg	Marek Golab (POL) 495 kg
1972	Andon Nikolov (BUL) 525 kg	Atanas Chopov (BUL) 517·5 kg	Hans Bettembourg (SWE) 512·5 kg
1976	David Rigert (URS) 382·5 kg	Lee James (USA) 362·5 kg	Atanas Chopov (BUL) 360 kg
1980	Peter Baczako (HUN) 377·5 kg	Rumen Alexandrov (BUL) 375 kg	Frank Mantek (GDR) 375 kg

1896–1948 Event not held

UP TO 100 KG

Gold	Silver	Bronze
1980 Ota Zaremba (TCH) 395 kg	Igor Nikitin (URS) 392·5 kg	Alberto Blanco (CUB) 385 kg

HEAVYWEIGHT

(From 1920 to 1948 class was over 82·5 kg. From 1952 to 1968 class was over 90 kg. Since 1972 weight limit has been up to 110 kg)

Gold	Silver	Bronze
1896[1] Launceston Eliot (GBR) 71 kg	Viggo Jensen (DEN) 57·2 kg	Alexandros Nikolopoulos (GRE) 57·2 kg
1896[2] Viggo Jensen (DEN) 111·5 kg	Launceston Eliot (GBR) 111·5 kg	Sotirios Versis (GRE) 100 kg
1904[3] Oscar Osthoff (USA) 48 pts	Frederick Winters (USA) 45 pts	Frank Kungler (USA) 10 pts
1904[2] Perikles Kakousis (GRE) 111·58 kg	Oscar Osthoff (USA) 84·36 kg	Frank Kungler (USA) 79·83 kg
1906[1] Josef Steinbach (AUT) 76·55 kg	Tullio Camilotti (ITA) 73·75 kg	Heinrich Schneidereit (GER) 70·75 kg
1906[2] Dimitrios Tofalos (GRE) 142·5 kg	Josef Steinbach (AUT) 136·5 kg	Alexandre Maspoli (FRA) 129·5 kg
		Heinrich Rondl (GER) 129·5 kg
		Heinrich Schneidereit (GER) 129·5 kg
1920 Filippo Bottino (ITA) 270 kg	Joseph Alzin (LUX) 255 kg	Louis Bernot (FRA) 250 kg
1924[4] Giuseppe Tonani (ITA) 517·5 kg	Franz Aigner (AUT) 515 kg	Harald Tammer (EST) 497·5 kg
1928 Josef Strassberger (GER) 372·5 kg	Arnold Luhaäär (EST) 360 kg	Jaroslav Skobla (TCH) 357·5 kg
1932 Jaroslav Skobla (TCH) 380 kg	Václav Psenicka (TCH) 377·5 kg	Josef Strassberger (GER) 377·5 kg
1936 Josef Manger (AUT) 410 kg	Václav Psenicka (TCH) 402·5 kg	Arnold Luhaäär (EST) 400 kg
1948 John Davis (USA) 452·5 kg	Norbert Schemansky (USA) 425 kg	Abraham Charité (HOL) 412·5 kg
1952 John Davis (USA) 460 kg	James Bradford (USA) 437·5 kg	Humberto Selvetti (ARG) 432·5 kg
1956 Paul Anderson (USA) 500 kg	Humberto Selvetti (ARG) 500 kg	Alberto Pigaiani (ITA) 452·5 kg
1960 Yuriy Vlasov (URS) 537·5 kg	James Bradford (USA) 512·5 kg	Norbert Schemansky (USA) 500 kg
1964 Leonid Zhabotinsky (URS) 572·5 kg	Yuriy Vlasov (URS) 570 kg	Norbert Schemansky (USA) 537·5 kg
1968 Leonid Zhabotinsky (URS) 572·5 kg	Serge Reding (BEL) 555 kg	Joseph Dube (USA) 555 kg
1972 Jan Talts (URS) 580 kg	Alexandre Kraitchev (BUL) 562·5 kg	Stefan Grützner (GDR) 555 kg
1976[5] Yuriy Zaitsev (URS) 385 kg	Krastio Semerdiev (BUL) 385 kg	Tadeusz Rutkowski (POL) 377·5 kg
1980 Leonid Taranenko (URS) 422·5 kg	Valentin Christov (BUL) 405 kg	György Szalai (HUN) 390 kg

[1] One-hand lift.   [2] Two-hand lift.   [3] Dumbell lift.   [4] Aggregate of five lifts.   [5] Valentin Christov (BUL) finished in first place with 400 kg but was subsequently disqualified.   1900, 1908–1912 Event not held

SUPER-HEAVYWEIGHT
(Over 110 kg)

Gold	Silver	Bronze
1972 Vasiliy Alexeyev (URS) 640 kg	Rudolf Mang (GDR) 610 kg	Gerd Bonk (GDR) 572·5 kg
1976 Vasiliy Alexeyev (URS) 440 kg	Gerd Bonk (GDR) 405 kg	Helmut Losch (GDR) 387·5 kg
1980 Sultan Rakhmanov (URS) 440 kg	Jürgen Heuser (GDR) 410 kg	Tadeusz Rutkowski (POL) 407·5 kg

1896–1968 Event not held

WEIGHTLIFTING—MEDALS

	Gold	Silver	Bronze	Total		Gold	Silver	Bronze	Total
USSR	33	19	2	54	GREAT BRITAIN	1	3	2	6
UNITED STATES	15	15	9	39	GREECE	2	—	2	4
POLAND	4	2	15	21	BELGIUM	1	2	1	4
BULGARIA	7	10	3	20	SWITZERLAND	—	2	2	4
FRANCE	9	2	4	15	SWEDEN	—	—	4	4
HUNGARY	2	5	8	15	DENMARK	1	2	—	3
ITALY	4	5	5	14	TRINIDAD	—	1	2	3
GERMANY (FRG)	3	3	7	13	KOREA	—	—	3	3
AUSTRIA	5	5	2	12	NETHERLANDS	—	—	3	3
EGYPT	5	2	2	9	CUBA	1	—	1	2
JAPAN	2	2	5	9	ARGENTINA	—	1	1	2
IRAN	1	3	5	9	NORTH KOREA (PRK)	—	1	1	2
GDR	—	4	5	9	FINLAND	1	—	—	1
CZECHOSLOVAKIA	3	2	3	8	NORWAY	1	—	—	1
ESTONIA	1	3	3	7	CANADA	—	1	—	1

	Gold	Silver	Bronze	Total
LEBANON	—	1	—	1
LUXEMBOURG	—	1	—	1
SINGAPORE	—	1	—	1
AUSTRALIA	—	—	1	1
IRAQ	—	—	1	1
	102[1]	98	102[1]	302

[1] Two gold medals in 1928 and 1936 lightweight class, and two extra bronze medals in 1906 heavyweight class.

Ivar Johansson (SWE) was the first man to win two wrestling titles at the same Games. He won the freestyle middleweight and Greco-Roman welterweight events in 1932.

WRESTLING

Wrestling was the most popular sport in the Ancient Olympic Games with victors recorded from 708 BC. The most famous of those early wrestlers was Milon of Kroton who won the boy's title and then the men's crown for the next five Games, until he was finally beaten in his seventh Games in 512 BC.

Wrestling in the Greco-Roman style was included in the 1896 Games and freestyle in 1904. There was no bodyweight limit in the Athens contest and it was won surprisingly by Carl Schuhmann (GER), who had already won three gold medals in gymnastics. On his way to victory Schuhmann, who was only 1·63 m *5 ft 4 in* tall, beat the Games weightlifting champion Launceston Eliot (GBR), and the final against Georgios Tsitas (GRE) took place over two days. Until a limit was set in 1924 bouts often lasted for remarkable lengths of time. The most extreme, and a record for any international contest, was that between Martin Klein, an Estonian representing Russia, and Alfred 'Alpo' Asikáinen (FIN) in the 1912 Greco-Roman middleweight class which lasted for 11 hours 40 minutes. Klein won. In the 1912 Greco-Roman light-heavyweight final Anders Ahlgren (SWE) and Ivar Böhling (FIN) were declared equal second after 9 hours of wrestling without a decision. No gold medal was awarded.

Three men have won three gold medals: Carl Westergren (SWE) in 1920, 1924 and 1932; Ivar Johansson (SWE) in 1932 (two) and 1936; Aleksandr Medved (URS) 1964, 1968 and 1972. Johansson and Kristjan Palusalu (FIN) are the only men to win titles in both styles at the same

Games. The Swede won the Greco-Roman welterweight and the freestyle middleweight in 1932, and Palusalu won the two heavyweight titles in 1936. Wilfried Dietrich (GER/FRG) won the most medals with five (one gold, two silver, two bronze) at both styles between 1956 and 1968, but Imre Polyák (HUN) has the best record at one style with one gold and three silvers all in Greco-Roman events from 1952 to 1964. Dietrich and George Mackenzie (GBR) competed at five Games, 1956–1972 and 1908–1928 respectively, but Mackenzie had a span of 20 years.

The most successful brothers have been Kustaa and Hermanni Pihlajamäki (FIN) with three gold, one silver and one bronze between 1924 and 1936. The more recent pair of Ben and John Peterson (USA) won two gold and two silver medals in 1972 and 1976. The only twins to win gold medals were Anatoliy and Sergey Beloglazov (URS) in the 1980 freestyle competitions. The only father and son to become champions were Kaarlo (1928 freestyle) and Rauno (1956 Greco-Roman) Mäkinen (FIN). In 1968 56 year old Alexis Nihon and his son, Alexis Junior, were both in the same team, that of Bahamas, but the father did not actually compete.

The oldest gold medallist was Anatoliy Roschin (URS) who won the 1972 Greco-Roman super-heavyweight title aged 40 yr 184 days. The youngest was Suren Nalbandyan (URS) in the 1976 Greco-Roman lightweight class aged 20 yr 51 days. The heaviest wrestler and the heaviest competitor at any sport in Olympic history was the 1972 freestyle super-heavyweight bronze medallist Chris Taylor (USA) who weighed between 182 kg *401 lb* and 190 kg *419 lb*.

In 1948 the Turkish government was so overwhelmed by the success of their wrestling team who had won six golds, four silvers and one bronze, that they awarded them with gifts, including money—thereby making them ineligible to compete in the Games ever again.

In 1920 Nat Pendleton, then a lieutenant in the US Navy, lost the gold medal on a disputed decision. He later went to Hollywood and made many movies, usually in the role of a comic 'heavy'.

Osamu Watanabe (JPN) won the 1964 freestyle featherweight title with his 186th successive victory in the sport.

The 1912 Greco-Roman middleweight match between the Finn Alfred Asikainen (left) and Martin Klein, an Estonian competing for Russia, which lasted for a record 11 hr 40 min.

A team-mate of Pendleton's in 1920 was Edward Wilkie, the brother of Wendell Wilkie, the defeated Republican candidate for the US Presidency in 1940.

WRESTLING

The contemporary descriptions of some bodyweight classes have varied during the history of the Games. Current descriptions are used in the lists below.

FREE-STYLE—LIGHT FLYWEIGHT
(Weight up to *48 kg*)

	Gold	Silver	Bronze
1904	Robert Curry (USA)	John Heim (USA)	Gustav Thiefenthaler (USA)
1972	Roman Dmitriev (URS)	Ognian Nikolov (BUL)	Ebrahim Javadpour (IRN)
1976	Khassan Issaev (BUL)	Roman Dmitriev (URS)	Akira Kudo (JPN)
1980	Claudio Pollio (ITA)	Se Hong Jang (PRK)	Sergey Kornilayev (URS)

1896–1900, 1906–1968 Event not held

FREE-STYLE—FLYWEIGHT
Note: 1904 weight up to 115 lb, *52·16 kg*. From 1948 weight up to *52 kg*.

	Gold	Silver	Bronze
1904	George Mehnert (USA)	Gustave Bauer (USA)	William Nelson (USA)
1948	Lennart Viitala (FIN)	Halit Balamir (TUR)	Thure Johansson (SWE)
1952	Hasan Gemici (TUR)	Yushu Kitano (JPN)	Mahmoud Mollaghassemi (IRN)
1956	Mirian Tsalkalamanidze (URS)	Mohamad-Ali Khojastehpour (IRN)	Hüseyin Akbas (TUR)
1960	Ahmet Bilek (TUR)	Masayuki Matsubara (JPN)	Mohamad Saifpour Saidabadi (IRN)
1964	Yoshikatsu Yoshida (JPN)	Chang-sun Chang (KOR)	Said Aliaakbar Haydari (IRN)
1968	Shigeo Nakata (JPN)	Richard Sanders (USA)	Surenjav Sukhbaatar (MGL)
1972	Kiyomi Kato (JPN)	Arsen Alakhverdiev (URS)	Hyong Kim Gwong (PRK)
1976	Yuji Takada (JPN)	Aleksandr Ivanov (URS)	Hae-Sup Jeon (KOR)
1980	Anatoliy Beloglazov (URS)	Wladyslaw Stecyk (POL)	Nermedin Selimov (BUL)

1896–1900, 1906–1936 Event not held

FREE-STYLE—BANTAMWEIGHT
Note: The weight limit for this event has been: 1904, 125 lb *56·70 kg*; 1908, 119 lb *54 kg*; 1924–1936, *56 kg* and from 1948, *57 kg*.

	Gold	Silver	Bronze
1904	Isidor Niflot (USA)	August Wester (USA)	Z B Strebler (USA)
1908	George Mehnert (USA)	William Press (GBR)	Aubert Côté (CAN)
1924	Kustaa Pihlajamäki (FIN)	Kaarlo Mäkinen (FIN)	Bryant Hines (USA)
1928	Kaarlo Mäkinen (FIN)	Edmond Spapen (BEL)	James Trifunov (CAN)
1932	Robert Pearce (USA)	Ödön Zombori (HUN)	Aatos Jaskari (FIN)
1936	Ödön Zombori (HUN)	Ross Flood (USA)	Johannes Herbert (GER)
1948	Nasuk Akar (TUR)	Gerald Leeman (USA)	Charles Kouyos (FRA)

1952	Shohachi Ishii (JPN)	Rashid Mamedbekov (URS)	Kha-Shaba Jadav (IND)
1956	Mustafa Dagistanli (TUR)	Mohamad Yaghoubi (IRN)	Mikhail Chakhov (URS)
1960	Terrence McCann (USA)	Nejdet Zalev (BUL)	Tadeusz Trojanowski (POL)
1964	Yojiro Uetake (JPN)	Hüseyin Akbas (TUR)	Aidyn Ibragimov (URS)
1968	Yojiro Uetake (JPN)	Donald Behm (USA)	Abutaleb Gorgori (IRN)
1972	Hideaki Yanagide (JPN)	Richard Sanders (USA)	László Klinga (HUN)
1976	Vladimir Yumin (URS)	Hans-Dieter Brüchert (GDR)	Masao Arai (JPN)
1980	Sergey Beloglazov (URS)	Ho Pyong Li (PRK)	Dugarsuren Ouinbold (MGL)

1896–1900, 1906, 1912–1920 Event not held

FREE-STYLE—FEATHERWEIGHT

Note: The weight limit for this event has been: 1904, 135 lb *61·24 kg*; 1908, 133 lb *60·30 kg*; 1920, *60 kg*; 1924–1936, *61 kg*; 1948–1960, and 1972, *62 kg*; 1964–1968, *63 kg*.

	Gold	*Silver*	*Bronze*
1904	Benjamin Bradshaw (USA)	Theodore McLear (USA)	Charles Clapper (USA)
1908	George Dole (USA)	James Slim (GBR)	William McKie (GBR)
1920	Charles Ackerly (USA)	Samuel Gerson (USA)	P. W. Bernard (GBR)
1924	Robin Reed (USA)	Chester Newton (USA)	Katsutoshi Naito (JPN)
1928	Allie Morrison (USA)	Kustaa Pihlajamäki (FIN)	Hans Minder (SUI)
1932	Hermanni Pihlajamäki (FIN)	Edgar Nemir (USA)	Einar Karlsson (SWE)
1936	Kustaa Pihlajamäki (FIN)	Francis Millard (USA)	Gösta Jönsson (SWE)
1948	Gazanfer Bilge (TUR)	Ivar Sjölin (SWE)	Adolf Müller (SUI)
1952	Bayram Sit (TUR)	Nasser Guivehtchi (IRN)	Josiah Henson (USA)
1956	Shozo Sasahara (JPN)	Joseph Mewis (BEL)	Erkki Penttilä (FIN)
1960	Mustafa Dagistanli (TUR)	Stantcho Ivanov (BUL)	Vladimir Rubashvili (URS)
1964	Osamu Watanabe (JPN)	Stantcho Ivanov (BUL)	Nodar Khokhashvili (URS)
1968	Masaaki Kaneko (JPN)	Enyu Todorov (BUL)	Shamseddin Seyed-Abbassi (IRN)
1972	Zagalav Abdulbekov (URS)	Vehbi Akdag (TUR)	Ivan Krastev (BUL)
1976	Jung-Mo Yang (KOR)	Zeveg Oidov (MGL)	Gene Davis (USA)
1980	Magomedgasan Abushev (URS)	Mikho Doukov (BUL)	Georges Hadjiioannidis (GRE)

1896–1900, 1906, 1912 Event not held

FREE-STYLE—LIGHTWEIGHT

Note: The weight limit for this event has been: 1904, 145 lb *65·77 kg*; 1908, 146¾ lb *66·60 kg*; 1920 *67·5 kg*; 1924 to 1936, *66 kg*; 1948 to 1960, *67 kg*; 1964 and 1968, *70 kg* and from 1972, *68 kg*.

	Gold	*Silver*	*Bronze*
1904	Otto Roehm (USA)	Rudolph Tesing (USA)	Albert Zirkel (USA)
1908	George de Relwyskow (GBR)	William Wood (GBR)	Albert Gingell (GBR)
1920	Kalle Anttila (FIN)	Gottfrid Svensson (SWE)	Peter Wright (GBR)
1924	Russell Vis (USA)	Volmart Wickström (FIN)	Arvo Haavisto (FIN)
1928	Osvald Käpp (EST)	Charles Pacôme (FRA)	Eino Leino (FIN)
1932	Charles Pacôme (FRA)	Károly Kárpáti (HUN)	Gustaf Klarén (SWE)
1936	Károly Kárpáti (HUN)	Wolfgang Ehrl (GER)	Hermanni Pihlajamäki (FIN)
1948	Celál Atik (TUR)	Gösta Frandfors (SWE)	Hermann Baumann (SUI)
1952	Olle Anderberg (SWE)	Thomas Evans (USA)	Djahanbakte Tovfighe (IRN)
1956	Emamali Habibi (IRN)	Shigeru Kasahara (JPN)	Alimberg Bestayev (URS)
1960	Shelby Wilson (USA)	Viktor Sinyavskiy (URS)	Enyu Dimov (BUL)
1964	Enyu Valtschev[1] (BUL)	Klaus-Jürgen Rost (GER)	Iwao Horiuchi (JPN)
1968	Abdollah Movahed Ardabili (IRN)	Enyu Valtschev[1] (BUL)	Sereeter Danzandarjaa (MGL)
1972	Dan Gable (USA)	Kikuo Wada (JPN)	Ruslan Ashuraliev (URS)
1976	Pavel Pinigin (URS)	Lloyd Keaser (USA)	Yasaburo Sagawara (JPN)
1980	Saipulla Absaidov (URS)	Ivan Yankov (BUL)	Saban Sejdi (YUG)

[1] Valtschev competed as Dimov in 1960.

1896–1900, 1906, 1912 Event not held

FREE-STYLE—WELTERWEIGHT

Note: The weight limit for this event has been: 1904, 158 lb *71·67 kg*; 1924 to 1936, *72 kg*; 1948 to 1960, *73 kg*; from 1972, *74 kg*.

	Gold	*Silver*	*Bronze*
1904	Charles Erickson (USA)	William Beckmann (USA)	Jerry Winholtz (USA)

1924	Hermann Gehri (SUI)	Eino Leino (FIN)	Otto Müller (SUI)
1928	Arvo Haavisto (FIN)	Lloyd Appleton (USA)	Maurice Letchford (CAN)
1932	Jack van Bebber (USA)	Daniel MacDonald (CAN)	Eino Leino (FIN)
1936	Frank Lewis (USA)	Ture Andersson (SWE)	Joseph Schleimer (CAN)
1948	Yasar Dogu (TUR)	Richard Garrard (AUS)	Leland Merrill (USA)
1952	William Smith (USA)	Per Berlin (SWE)	Abdullah Modjtabavi (IRN)
1956	Mitsuo Ikeda (JPN)	Ibrahim Zengin (TUR)	Vakhtang Balavadze (URS)
1960	Douglas Blubaugh (USA)	Ismail Ogan (TUR)	Mohammed Bashir (PAK)
1964	Ismail Ogan (TUR)	Guliko Sagaradze (URS)	Mohamad-Ali Sanatkaran (IRN)
1968	Mahmut Atalay (TUR)	Daniel Robin (FRA)	Dagvasuren Purev (MGL)
1972	Wayne Wells (USA)	Jan Karlsson (SWE)	Adolf Seger (FRG)
1976	Jiichiro Date (JPN)	Mansour Barzegar (IRN)	Stanley Dziedzic (USA)
1980	Valentin Raitchev (BUL)	Jamtsying Davaajav (MGL)	Dan Karabin (TCH)

1896–1900, 1906–1920 Event not held

FREESTYLE—MIDDLEWEIGHT

Note: The weight limit for this event has been: 1908, 161 lb *73 kg*; 1920, 165¼ lb *75 kg*; 1924 to 1960, *79 kg*; 1964 and 1968, *87 kg*; from 1972, *82 kg*.

	Gold	*Silver*	*Bronze*
1908	Stanley Bacon (GBR)	George de Relwyskow (GBR)	Frederick Beck (GBR)
1920	Eino Leino (FIN)	Väinö Penttala (FIN)	Charles Johnson (USA)
1924	Fritz Hagmann (SUI)	Pierre Ollivier (BEL)	Vilho Pekkala (FIN)
1928	Ernst Kyburz (SUI)	Donald Stockton (CAN)	Samuel Rabin (GBR)
1932	Ivar Johansson (SWE)	Kyösti Luukko (FIN)	József Tunyogi (HUN)
1936	Emile Poilvé (FRA)	Richard Voliva (USA)	Ahmet Kireiççi (TUR)
1948	Glen Brand (USA)	Adil Candemir (TUR)	Erik Lindén (SWE)
1952	David Tsimakuridze (URS)	Gholamheza Takhti (IRN)	György Gurics (HUN)
1956	Nikola Stantschev (BUL)	Daniel Hodge (USA)	Georgiy Skhirtladze (URS)
1960	Hasan Güngör (TUR)	Georgiy Skhirtladze (URS)	Hans Antonsson (SWE)
1964	Prodan Gardschev (BUL)	Hasan Güngör (TUR)	Daniel Brand (USA)
1968	Boris Gurevitch (URS)	Munkbat Jigjid (MGL)	Prodan Gardschev (BUL)
1972	Levan Tediashvili (URS)	Jóhn Peterson (USA)	Vasile Jorga (ROM)
1976	John Peterson (USA)	Viktor Novoshilev (URS)	Adolf Seger (FRG)
1980	Ismail Abilov (BUL)	Magomedhan Aratsilov (URS)	Istvan Kovacs (HUN)

1896–1906, 1912 Event not held

FREE-STYLE—LIGHT-HEAVYWEIGHT

Note: The weight limit for this event has been: 1920, *82·5 kg*; 1924 to 1960, *87 kg*; 1964 and 1968, *97 kg*; from 1972, *90 kg*.

	Gold	*Silver*	*Bronze*
1920	Anders Larsson (SWE)	Charles Courant (SUI)	Walter Maurer (USA)
1924	John Spellman (USA)	Rudolf Svensson (SWE)	Charles Courant (SUI)
1928	Thure Sjöstedt (SWE)	Anton Bögli (SUI)	Henri Lefèbre (FRA)
1932	Peter Mehringer (USA)	Thure Sjöstedt (SWE)	Eddie Scarf (AUS)
1936	Knut Fridell (SWE)	August Neo (EST)	Erich Siebert (GER)
1948	Henry Wittenberg (USA)	Fritz Stöckli (SUI)	Bengt Fahlkvist (SWE)
1952	Wiking Palm (SWE)	Henry Wittenberg (USA)	Adil Atan (TUR)
1956	Gholam Reza Tahkti (IRN)	Boris Kulayev (URS)	Peter Blair (USA)
1960	Ismet Atli (TUR)	Gholam Reza Tahkti (IRN)	Anatoliy Albul (URS)
1964	Aleksandr Medved (URS)	Ahmet Ayik (TUR)	Said Mustafafov (BUL)
1968	Ahmet Ayik (TUR)	Shota Lomidze (URS)	József Csatári (HUN)
1972	Ben Peterson (USA)	Gennadiy Strakhov (URS)	Karoly Bajko (HUN)
1976	Levan Tediashvili (URS)	Ben Peterson (USA)	Stelica Morcov (ROM)
1980	Sanasar Oganesyan (URS)	Uwe Neupert (GDR)	Aleksandr Cichon (POL)

1896–1912 Event not held

FREE-STYLE—HEAVYWEIGHT

Note: The weight limit for this event has been: 1904, over 158 lb *71,6 kg*; 1908, over *73 kg*; 1920, over *82,5 kg*; 1924 to 1960, over *87 kg*; 1964 and 1968, over *97 kg*; from 1972, up to *100 kg*.

	Gold	*Silver*	*Bronze*
1904	Bernhuff Hansen (USA)	Frank Kungler (USA)	Fred Warmbold (USA)
1908	George O'Kelly (GBR)	Jacob Gundersen (NOR)	Edmond Barrett (GBR)[1]

1920	Robert Roth (SUI)	Nathan Pendleton (USA)	Ernst Nilsson (SWE)
			Frederick Meyer (USA)
1924	Harry Steele (USA)	Henry Wernli (SUI)	Andrew McDonald (GBR)
1928	Johan Richthoff (SWE)	Aukusti Sihovla (FIN)	Edmond Dame (FRA)
1932	Johan Richthoff (SWE)	John Riley (USA)	Nikolaus Hirschl (AUT)
1936	Kristjan Palusalu (EST)	Josef Klapuch (TCH)	Hjalmar Nyström (FIN)
1948	Gyula Bóbis (HUN)	Bertil Antonsson (SWE)	Joseph Armstrong (AUS)
1952	Arsen Mekokishvili (URS)	Bertil Antonsson (SWE)	Kenneth Richmond (GBR)
1956	Hamit Kaplan (TUR)	Hussein Mekhmedov (BUL)	Taisto Kangasniemi (FIN)
1960	Wilfried Dietrich (GER)	Hamit Kaplan (TUR)	Savkus Dzarassov (URS)
1964	Aleksandr Ivanitsky (URS)	Liutvi Djiber (BUL)	Hamit Kaplan (TUR)
1968	Aleksandr Medved (URS)	Osman Duraliev (BUL)	Wilfried Dietrich (FRG)
1972	Ivan Yarygin (URS)	Khorloo Baianmunkh (MGL)	József Csatári (HUN)
1976	Ivan Yarygin (URS)	Russell Hellickson (USA)	Dimo Kostov (BUL)
1980	Ilya Mate (YUG)	Slavtcho Tchervenkov (BUL)	Julius Strnisko (TCH)

[1] Tie for third place   1896–1900, 1906, 1912 Event not held

FREE-STYLE—SUPER-HEAVYWEIGHT
(Weight over *100 kg*)

	Gold	*Silver*	*Bronze*
1972	Aleksandr Medved (URS)	Osman Duraliev (BUL)	Chris Taylor (USA)
1976	Soslan Andiev (URS)	Jozsef Balla (HUN)	Ladislau Simon (ROM)
1980	Soslan Andiev (URS)	Jozsef Balla (HUN)	Adam Sandurski (POL)

1896–1968 Event not held

GRECO-ROMAN—LIGHT-FLYWEIGHT
(Weight up to *48 kg*)

	Gold	*Silver*	*Bronze*
1972	Gheorghe Berceanu (ROM)	Rahim Ahabadi (IRN)	Stefan Anghelov (BUL)
1976	Aleksey Shumakov (URS)	Gheorghe Berceanu (ROM)	Stefan Anghelov (BUL)
1980	Zaksylik Ushkempirov (URS)	Constantin Alexandru (ROM)	Ferenc Seres (HUN)

1896–1968 Event not held

GRECO-ROMAN—FLYWEIGHT
(Weight up to *52 kg*)

	Gold	*Silver*	*Bronze*
1948	Pietro Lombardi (ITA)	Kenan Olcay (TUR)	Reino Kangasmäki (FIN)
1952	Boris Gurevich (URS)	Ignazio Fabra (ITA)	Leo Honkala (FIN)
1956	Nikolai Solovyov (URS)	Ignazio Fabra (ITA)	Durum Ali Egribas (TUR)
1960	Dumitru Pirvulescu (ROM)	Osman Sayed (UAR)	Mohamad Paziraye (IRN)
1964	Tsutomu Hanahara (JPN)	Angel Kerezov (BUL)	Dumitru Pirvulescu (ROM)
1968	Petar Kirov (BUL)	Vladimir Bakulin (URS)	Miroslav Zeman (TCH)
1972	Petar Kirov (BUL)	Koichiro Hirayama (JPN)	Giuseppe Bognanni (ITA)
1976	Vitaliy Konstantinov (URS)	Nicu Ginga (ROM)	Koichiro Hirayama (JPN)
1980	Vakhtang Blagidze (URS)	Lajos Racz (HUN)	Mladen Mladenov (BUL)

1896–1936 Event not held

GRECO-ROMAN—BANTAMWEIGHT
Note: The weight limit for this event has been: 1924 to 1928, *58 kg*; 1932 to 1936, *56 kg*; since 1948, *57 kg*.

	Gold	*Silver*	*Bronze*
1924	Eduard Pütsep (EST)	Anselm Ahlfors (FIN)	Väinö Ikonen (FIN)
1928	Kurt Leucht (GER)	Jindrich Maudr (TCH)	Giovanni Gozzi (ITA)
1932	Jakob Brendel (GER)	Marcello Nizzola (ITA)	Louis François (FRA)
1936	Márton Lörincz (HUN)	Egon Svensson (SWE)	Jakob Brendel (GER)
1948	Kurt Pettersén (SWE)	Aly Mahmoud Hassan (EGY)	Habil Kaya (TUR)
1952	Imre Hódos (HUN)	Zakaria Chihab (LIB)	Artem Teryan (URS)
1956	Konstantin Vyrupayev (URS)	Evdin Veseterby (SWE)	Francisc Horvat (ROM)
1960	Oleg Karavayev (URS)	Ion Cernea (ROM)	Petrov Dinko (BUL)
1964	Masamitsu Ichiguchi (JPN)	Vladlen Trostiansky (URS)	Ion Cernea (ROM)
1968	János Varga (HUN)	Ion Baciu (ROM)	Ivan Kochergin (URS)

1972	Rustem Kazakov (URS)	Hans-Jürgen Veil (FRG)	Risto Björlin (FIN)
1976	Pertti Ukkola (FIN)	Ivan Frgic (YUG)	Farhat Mustafin (URS)
1980	Shamil Serikov (URS)	Jozef Lipien (POL)	Benni Ljungbeck (SWE)

1896–1920 Event not held

GRECO-ROMAN—FEATHERWEIGHT

Note: The weight limit for this event has been: 1912 to 1920, *60 kg*; 1924 to 1928, 1948 to 1960 and since 1972, *62 kg*; 1932 to 1936, *61 kg*; 1964 to 1968, *63 kg*.

	Gold	Silver	Bronze
1912	Kaarlo Koskelo (FIN)	Georg Gerstacker (GER)	Otto Lasanen (FIN)
1920	Oskari Friman (FIN)	Hekki Kähkönen (FIN)	Fridtjof Svensson (SWE)
1924	Kalle Antila (FIN)	Aleksanteri Toivola (FIN)	Erik Malmberg (SWE)
1928	Voldemar Väli (EST)	Erik Malmberg (SWE)	Giacomo Quaglia (ITA)
1932	Giovanni Gozzi (ITA)	Wolfgang Ehrl (GER)	Lauri Koskela (FIN)
1936	Yasar Erkan (TUR)	Aarne Reini (FIN)	Einar Karlsson (SWE)
1948	Mehmet Oktav (TUR)	Olle Anderberg (SWE)	Ferenc Tóth (HUN)
1952	Yakov Punkin (URS)	Imre Polyák (HUN)	Abdel Rashed (EGY)
1956	Rauno Mäkinen (FIN)	Imre Polyák (HUN)	Roman Dzneladze (URS)
1960	Müzahir Sille (TUR)	Imre Polyák (HUN)	Konstantin Vyrupayev (URS)
1964	Imre Polyák (HUN)	Roman Rurua (URS)	Branko Martinovič (YUG)
1968	Roman Rurua (URS)	Hideo Fujimoto (JPN)	Simeon Popescu (ROM)
1972	Gheorghi Markov (BUL)	Heinz-Helmut Wehling (GDR)	Kazimierz Lipien (POL)
1976	Kazimierz Lipien (POL)	Nelson Davidian (URS)	Laszlo Reczi (HUN)
1980	Stilianos Migiakis (URS)	Istvan Toth (HUN)	Boris Kramorenko (URS)

1896–1908 Event not held

GRECO-ROMAN—LIGHTWEIGHT

Note: The weight limit for this event has been: 1906, *75 kg*; 1908 *66·6 kg*; 1912 to 1928, *67·5 kg*; 1932 to 1936, *66 kg*; 1948 to 1960, *67 kg*; 1964 to 1968, *70 kg*; since 1972, *68 kg*.

	Gold	Silver	Bronze
1906	Rudolf Watzl (AUT)	Karl Karlsen (DEN)	Ferenc Holuban (HUN)
1908	Enrico Porro (ITA)	Nikolay Orlov (URS)	Avid Lindén-Linko (FIN)
1912	Eemil Wäre (FIN)	Gustaf Malmström (SWE)	Edvin Matiasson (SWE)
1920	Eemil Wäre (FIN)	Taavi Tamminen (FIN)	Fritjof Andersen (NOR)
1924	Oskari Friman (FIN)	Lajos Keresztes (HUN)	Kalle Westerlund (FIN)
1928	Lajos Keresztes (HUN)	Eduard Sperling (GER)	Eduard Westerlund (FIN)
1932	Erik Malmberg (SWE)	Abraham Kurland (DEN)	Eduard Sperling (GER)
1936	Lauri Koskela (FIN)	Josef Herda (TCH)	Voldemar Väli (EST)
1948	Gustaf Freij (SWE)	Aage Eriksen (NOR)	Károly Ferencz (HUN)
1952	Shazam Safin (URS)	Gustaf Freij (SWE)	Mikuláš Athanasov (TCH)
1956	Kyösti Lehtonen (FIN)	Riza Dogan (TUR)	Gyul Tóth (HUN)
1960	Avtandil Koridze (URS)	Branislav Martinovic (YUG)	Gustaf Freij (SWE)
1964	Kazim Ayvaz (TUR)	Valeriu Bularca (ROM)	David Gvantseladze (URS)
1968	Munji Mumemura (JPN)	Stevan Horvat (YUG)	Petros Galaktopoulos (GRE)
1972	Shamil Khisamutdinov (URS)	Stoyan Apostolov (BUL)	Gian Matteo Ranzi (ITA)
1976	Suren Nalbandyan (URS)	Stefan Rusu (ROM)	Heinz-Helmut Wehling (GDR)
1980	Stefan Rusu (ROM)	Andrzej Supron (POL)	Lars-Erik Skiold (SWE)

1896–1904 Event not held

GRECO-ROMAN—WELTERWEIGHT

Note: the weight limit for this event has been: 1932 to 1936, *72 kg*; 1948 to 1960, *73 kg*; 1964 to 1968, *78 kg*; since 1972, *74 kg*.

	Gold	Silver	Bronze
1932	Ivar Johansson (SWE)	Väinö Kajander (FIN)	Ercole Gallegatti (ITA)
1936	Rudolf Svedberg (SWE)	Fritz Schäfer (GER)	Eino Virtanen (FIN)
1948	Gösta Andersson (SWE)	Miklós Szilvási (HUN)	Henrik Hansen (DEN)
1952	Miklós Szilvási (HUN)	Gösta Andersson (SWE)	Khalil Taha (LIB)
1956	Mithat Bayrak (TUR)	Vladimir Maneyev (URS)	Per Berlin (SWE)
1960	Mithat Bayrak (TUR)	Günther Maritschnigg (GER)	René Schiermeyer (FRA)
1964	Anatoliy Kolesov (URS)	Cyril Todorov (BUL)	Bertil Nyström (SWE)
1968	Rudolf Vesper (GDR)	Daniel Robin (FRA)	Károly Bajkó (HUN)
1972	Vitezslav Macha (TCH)	Petros Galaktopoulos (GRE)	Jan Karlsson (SWE)

1976	Anatoliy Bykov (URS)	Vitezslav Macha (TCH)	Karlheinz Helbing (FRG)
1980	Ferenc Kocsis (HUN)	Anatoliy Bykov (URS)	Mikko Huhtala (FIN)

1896–1928 Event not held

GRECO-ROMAN—MIDDLEWEIGHT

Note: The weight limit for this event has been: 1906, *85 kg*; 1908, *73 kg*; 1912 to 1928, *75 kg*; 1932 to 1960, *79 kg*; 1964 to 1968, *87 kg*; since 1972, *82 kg*.

	Gold	*Silver*	*Bronze*
1906	Verner Weckman (FIN)	Rudolf Lindmayer (AUT)	Robert Bebrens (DEN)
1908	Frithiof Märtensson (SWE)	Mauritz Andersson (SWE)	Anders Andersen (DEN)
1912	Claes Johansson (SWE)	Martin Klein (URS)	Alfred Asikainen (FIN)
1920	Carl Westergren (SWE)	Artur Lindfors (FIN)	Matti Perttila (FIN)
1924	Eduard Westerlund (FIN)	Artur Lindfors (FIN)	Roman Steinberg (EST)
1928	Väinö Kokkinen (FIN)	László Papp (HUN)	Albert Kusnetz (EST)
1932	Väinö Kokkinen (FIN)	Jean Földeák (GER)	Axel Cadier (SWE)
1936	Ivar Johansson (SWE)	Ludwig Schweikert (GER)	József Palotás (HUN)
1948	Axel Grönberg (SWE)	Muhlis Tayfur (TUR)	Ercole Gallegatti (ITA)
1952	Axel Grönberg (SWE)	Kalervo Rauhala (FIN)	Nikolai Belov (URS)
1956	Givi Kartoziya (URS)	Dimiter Dobrev (BUL)	Rune Jansson (SWE)
1960	Dimiter Dobrev (BUL)	Lothar Metz (GER)	Ion Taranu (ROM)
1964	Branislav Simič (YUG)	Jiri Kormanik (TCH)	Lothar Metz (GER)
1968	Lothar Metz (GDR)	Valentin Olenik (URS)	Branislav Simič (YUG)
1972	Csaba Hegedus (HUN)	Anatoliy Nazarenko (URS)	Milan Nenadic (YUG)
1976	Momir Petkovic (YUG)	Vladimir Cheboksarov (URS)	Ivan Kolev (BUL)
1980	Gennadiy Korban (URS)	Jan Polgowicz (POL)	Pavel Pavlov (BUL)

1896–1904 Event not held

GRECO-ROMAN—LIGHT-HEAVYWEIGHT

Note: The weight limit in this event has been: 1908, *93 kg*; 1912 to 1928, *82·5 kg*; 1932 to 1960, *87 kg*; 1964 to 1968, *97 kg*; since 1972, *90 kg*.

	Gold	*Silver*	*Bronze*
1908	Verner Weckman (FIN)	Yrjö Saarela (FIN)	Carl Jensen (DEN)
1912	—[1]	Anders Ahlgren (SWE)	Béla Varga (HUN)
		Ivar Böhling (FIN)	
1920	Claes Johansson (SWE)	Edil Rosenqvist (FIN)	Johannes Eriksen (DEN)
1924	Carl Westergren (SWE)	Rudolf Svensson (SWE)	Onni Pellinen (FIN)
1928	Ibrahim Moustafa (EGY)	Adolf Rieger (GER)	Onni Pellinen (FIN)
1932	Rudolf Svensson (SWE)	Onni Pellinen (FIN)	Mario Gruppioni (ITA)
1936	Axel Cadier (SWE)	Edwins Bietags (LIT)	August Néo (EST)
1948	Karl-Erik Nilsson (SWE)	Kaelpo Gröndahl (FIN)	Ibrahim Orabi (EGY)
1952	Kaelpo Gröndahl (FIN)	Shalva Shikhladze (URS)	Karl-Erik Nilsson (SWE)
1956	Valentin Nikolayev (URS)	Petko Sirakov (BUL)	Karl-Erik Nilsson (SWE)
1960	Tevfik Kis (TUR)	Krali Bimbalov (BUL)	Givi Kartoziya (URS)
1964	Boyan Radev (BUL)	Per Svensson (SWE)	Heinz Kiehl (GER)
1968	Boyan Radev (BUL)	Nikolai Yakovenko (URS)	Nicolae Martinescu (ROM)
1972	Valeriy Rezantsev (URS)	Josip Corak (YUG)	Czeslaw Kwiecinski (POL)
1976	Valeriy Rezantsev (URS)	Stoyan Ivanov (BUL)	Czeslaw Kwiecinski (POL)
1980	Norbert Nottny (HUN)	Igor Kanygin (URS)	Petre Disu (ROM)

[1] Ahlgren and Böhling declared equal second after 9 hours of wrestling.   1896–1906 Event not held

GRECO-ROMAN—HEAVYWEIGHT

Note: The weight limit for this event has been: 1896, open: 1906, over *85 kg*; 1908, over *93 kg*; 1912 to 1928, over *82·5 kg*; 1932 to 1960, over *81 kg*; 1964 to 1968, over *91 kg*; since 1972, up to *100 kg*.

	Gold	*Silver*	*Bronze*
1896	Carl Schuhmann (GER)	Georgios Tsitas (GRE)	Stephanos Christopoulos (GRE)
1906	Sören Jensen (DEN)	Henri Baur (AUT)	Marcel Dubois (BEL)
1908	Richard Weisz (HUN)	Aleksandr Petrov (URS)	Sören Jensen (DEN)
1912	Yrjö Saarela (FIN)	Johan Olin (FIN)	Sören Jensen (DEN)
1920	Adolf Lindfors (FIN)	Poul Hansen (DEN)	Martti Nieminen (FIN)
1924	Henri Deglane (FRA)	Edil Rosenqvist (FIN)	Raymund Badó (HUN)

1928 Rudolf Svensson (SWE)	Hjalmar Nyström (FIN)	Georg Gehring (GER)
1932 Carl Westergren (SWE)	Josef Urban (TCH)	Nikolaus Hirschl (AUT)
1936 Kristjan Palusalu (EST)	John Nyman (SWE)	Kurt Hornfischer (GER)
1948 Ahmet Kireçci (TUR)	Tor Nilsson (SWE)	Guido Fantoni (ITA)
1952 Johannes Kotkas (URS)	Josef Ružička (TCH)	Tauno Kovanen (FIN)
1956 Anatoliy Parfenov (URS)	Wilfried Dietrich (GER)	Adelmo Bulgarelli (ITA)
1960 Ivan Bogdan (URS)	Wilfried Dietrich (GER)	Bohumil Kubat (TCH)
1964 István Kozma (HUN)	Anatoliy Roschin (URS)	Wilfried Dietrich (GER)
1968 István Kozma (HUN)	Anatoliy Roschin (URS)	Petr Kment (TCH)
1972 Nicolae Martinescu (ROM)	Nikolai Yakovenko (URS)	Ferenc Kiss (HUN)
1976 Nikolai Bolboshin (URS)	Kamen Goranov (BUL)	Andrzej Skrzylewski (POL)
1980 Gheorghi Raikov (BUL)	Roman Bierla (POL)	Vasile Andrei (ROM)

1900–1904 Event not held

GRECO-ROMAN—SUPER-HEAVYWEIGHT
(Weight over *100 kg*)

Gold	*Silver*	*Bronze*
1972 Anatoliy Roschin (URS)	Alexandre Tomov (BUL)	Victor Dolipschi (ROM)
1976 Aleksandr Kolchinsky (URS)	Alexandre Tomov (BUL)	Roman Codreanu (ROM)
1980 Aleksandr Kolchinsky (URS)	Alexandre Tomov (BUL)	Hassan Bchara (LIB)

1896–1968 Event not held

WRESTLING—MEDALS

	FREESTYLE				*GRECO-ROMAN*				
	Gold	*Silver*	*Bronze*	*Total*	*Gold*	*Silver*	*Bronze*	*Total*	*Grand Total*
USSR	23	12	12	46	10	18	9	57	103
FINLAND	8	7	9	24	18	17	17	52	76
UNITED STATES	29	27	18	74	—	—	—	—	74
SWEDEN	8	10	8	26	19	13	14	46	72
BULGARIA	6	13	6	25	7	11	6	24	49
HUNGARY	3	4	7	14	12	8	11	31	45
TURKEY	15	9	4	28	8	3	2	13	41
GERMANY (FRG)	1	2	5	8	3	12	8	23	31
JAPAN	13	4	5	22	3	2	1	6	28
ROMANIA	—	—	3	3	4	7	10	21	24
IRAN	3	6	9	18	—	1	1	2	20
ITALY	1	—	—	1	3	3	9	15	16
GREAT BRITAIN	3	4	9	16	—	—	—	—	16
CZECHOSLOVAKIA	—	1	2	3	1	6	4	11	14
SWITZERLAND	4	4	5	13	—	—	—	—	13
POLAND	—	1	3	4	1	4	4	9	13
YUGOSLAVIA	1	—	1	2	2	4	3	9	11
FRANCE	2	2	3	7	1	1	2	4	11
DENMARK	—	—	—	—	1	3	7	11	11
ESTONIA	2	1	—	3	3	—	4	7	10
MONGOLIA	—	4	4	8	—	—	—	—	8
GDR	—	2	—	2	2	1	1	4	6
GREECE	—	—	1	1	1	2	2	5	6
CANADA	—	2	4	6	—	—	—	—	6
AUSTRIA	—	—	1	1	1	2	1	4	5
EGYPT (UAR)	—	—	—	—	1	2	2	5	5
BELGIUM	—	3	—	3	—	—	1	1	4
KOREA	1	1	1	3	—	—	—	—	3
NORWAY	—	1	—	1	—	1	1	2	3
PRK	—	2	1	3	—	—	—	—	3
AUSTRALIA	—	1	2	3	—	—	—	—	3
LEBANON	—	—	—	—	—	1	2	3	3
LITHUANIA	—	—	—	—	—	1	—	1	1
INDIA	—	—	1	1	—	—	—	—	1
PAKISTAN	—	—	1	1	—	—	—	—	1
	123	123	124[1]	370	121[2]	123	122	366	736

[1] Tie for third place in 1920.   [2] Two silver medals and no gold awarded in 1912.

YACHTING

The first Olympic regatta should have been held in 1896 in the Bay of Salamis but it was cancelled because of bad weather. Since 1900 the classes were changed regularly until very recently when some measure of standardization was imposed. The current classes are as follows:

		Intro-duced	Crew
FINN	Centreboard dinghy	1952	One
470	Centreboard dinghy	1976	Two
TORNADO	Catamaran	1976	Two
STAR	Keel boat	1932	Two
FLYING DUTCHMAN	Centreboard dinghy	1960	Two
SOLING	Keel boat	1972	Three

In each class there are seven races over a pre-scribed course in which the fastest time wins. Yachts count their best six results.

In 1984 a board sailing competition may also be held, but the final decision had not been made at the time of writing. The only event which has been a permanent fixture is the Olympic Monotype, ie one-man dinghy, albeit represented by different types of boat prior to 1952 (now the Finn). In 1922 the IOC decided that it would be a compulsory event in future while other events would retain elective status, to be decided by the host Organizing Committee.

The most successful yachtsman was Paul Elvström (DEN) who won four successive gold medals in the Olympic Monotype class from 1948 to 1960—he was the first man to achieve such a run in any sport. He competed again in the 1968 Star class and finished in fourth place. The only man to win gold medals in solo and multiple crew classes was Valentin Mankin (URS) with the 1968 Finn title and wins in the 1972 Tempest and 1980 Star categories. Frances Clytie Rivett-Carnac (GBR) was the first woman to win a gold medal, in the 7 m class in 1908 with her husband, and the first woman to win in an event not restricted to women or mixed pairs in any sport.

The oldest gold medallist was Thomas Glen-Coats (GBR) in 1908 in the 12 m class aged 62 yr 175 days, while the oldest singlehanded champion was Jacques-Baptiste Lebrun (FRA) in 1932 aged 41 yr 327 days. The youngest yachting gold medallist was Franciscus Hin (HOL) who won the 1920 12-foot dinghy class with his elder brother Johannes aged 14 yr 163 days. The oldest to win a medal was Louis Noverraz (SUI) in the 5·5 m category in 1968 aged 66 yr 154 days.

Some of the most outstanding family achievements in Olympic history have occurred in yachting. In 1912 four Norwegian brothers, Henrik, Jan, Ole, and Kristen Östervold won gold medals in the 12 m (1907 Rating) class, and also in the nine-man crew were another pair of brothers, Rasmus and Halvor Birkeland. The full crew of the winning 5·5 m in 1968 were the Swedish brothers Ulf, Jörgen and Peter Sundelin, and the winning 6 m in 1912 was crewed by Amédée, Gaston and Jacques Thubé (FRA). The only twins to win gold medals were Sumner and Edgar White (USA) in the 5·5 m class in 1952. The first father and son to win gold medals together were Emile and Florimod Cornellie (BEL) in the 6 m (1907 Rating) in 1920. Other such pairings include August Ringvold Senior and Junior (NOR) in the 8 m in 1924, and Hilary and Paul Smart (USA) in the Star in 1948. The latter beat another father/son crew from Cuba for the gold medal. However, the greatest Olympic yachting family must surely be the Norwegians Lunde; Eugen won a gold in the 6 m class of 1924, his son Peder and daughter-in-law Vibeke along with Vibeke's brother won a silver medal in the 5·5 m in 1952, and grandson Peder Jr won a gold medal in the 1960 Flying Dutchman competition.

Only two full crews have retained an Olympic title, as opposed to individuals. Thor Thorvaldsen, Sigvie Lie and Haakon Barfod of Norway won the Dragon class in 1948 and 1952, while Poul Jensen, Valdemar Bandolowski and Erik Hansen of Denmark won the Soling in 1976 and 1980.

Rodney Pattisson and Iain Macdonald-Smith (GBR) scored the lowest number of penalty points (three) ever achieved in Olympic yachting when they won the 1968 Flying Dutchman competition with five wins, a second place and a disqualification in their seven starts (only six to count). Their boat *Superdocious* is now in the National Maritime Museum, Greenwich. The only yacht to win two gold medals in the same Games was *Scotia* crewed by Lorne Currie and John Gretton for Great Britain in the ½–1 ton and open classes in 1900. The United States yacht *Llanoria* won the 6 m class in 1948 and 1952, skippered both times by Herman Whiton.

In 1948 Magnus Konow (NOR) equalled the longest span of Olympic competition (see p 22) when he took part in the 6 m event 40 years after his début in the 8 m class in 1908. He won two golds and a silver in 1912, 1920 and 1936, the only other Games he attended. Durward Knowles competed in a record number of seven Games from 1948 when he competed for Great Britain. He represented the Bahamas in the next six celebrations and his record, all in the Star event, was as follows: 1948 – 4th, 1952 – 5th, 1956 – 3rd, 1960 – 6th, 1964 – 1st, 1968 – 5th, 1972 – 13th.

The greatest number of boats in an Olympic regatta was the 152 at Kiel in 1972, consisting of 35 Finns, 29 Flying Dutchmans, 23 Dragons, 21 Tempests, and 18 Stars. The 1960 regatta had a total of 138 boats in only five categories. The greatest entry in just one class was 36 in the 1968 Finn competition.

OLYMPIC YACHTING VENUES

1900	River Seine at Meulan (10–20 tonners at Le Havre)
1908	Cowes, Isle of Wight, and the Clyde
1912	Nyhäshamn
1920	Ostend
1924	River Seine at Meulan (6 m & 8 m at Le Havre)
1928	Zuider-Zee

1932	San Pedro Bay
1936	Kiel
1948	Torbay, Devon
1952	Harmaja
1956	Port Phillip Bay
1960	Bay of Naples
1964	Sagami Bay
1968	Acapulco Bay
1972	Kiel
1976	Kingston, Lake Ontario
1980	Tallinn

YACHTING—MEDALS

	Gold	Silver	Bronze	Total
GREAT BRITAIN	14	8	7	29
SWEDEN	9	10	9	28
UNITED STATES	11	7	9	27
NORWAY	14	10	1	25
FRANCE	7	6	8	21
DENMARK	7	8	2	17
GERMANY (FRG)	5	4	6	15
USSR	4	4	3	11
NETHERLANDS	3	4	4	11
FINLAND	1	1	6	8
AUSTRALIA	3	1	3	7
BELGIUM	2	3	2	7
ITALY	2	1	4	7
GDR	1	2	2	5
BRAZIL	2	—	2	4
GREECE	1	1	1	3
SPAIN	1	1	1	3
AUSTRIA	—	3	—	3
PORTUGAL	—	2	1	3
SWITZERLAND	—	2	1	3
CANADA	—	1	2	3
NEW ZEALAND	2	—	—	2
BAHAMAS	1	—	1	2
ARGENTINA	—	2	—	2
CUBA	—	1	—	1
IRELAND	—	1	—	1
ESTONIA	—	—	1	1
HUNGARY	—	—	1	1
	90	83[1]	77[1]	250

[1] A number of events in the early Games had no silver and/or bronze medallists.

It may be worth noting that three of the above (Austria, Hungary and Switzerland) do not have direct access to the sea.

YACHTING RESULTS

An attempt has been made to bring some method of comparison to the results of Olympic yachting, made particularly difficult because of the wide variety of classes and types of boat used over the years. Where boats have been superseded by those of a similar type, eg Dragon by Soling, they have been listed in the same table. Purists will no doubt be unhappy but the general reader will find it easier to follow.

OLYMPIC MONOTYPE

	Gold	Silver	Bronze
1920[1]	NETHERLANDS Franciscus Hin Johannes Hin	NETHERLANDS Arnoud van der Biesen Petrus Beikers	—
1920[2]	GREAT BRITAIN F A Richards T Hedberg	—	—
1924[3]	Léon Huybrechts (BEL)	Henrik Robert (NOR)	Hans Dittmar (FIN)
1928[4]	Sven Thorell (SWE)	Henrik Robert (NOR)	Bertil Broman (FIN)
1932[5]	Jacques Lebrun (FRA)	Adriaan Maas (HOL)	Santiago Cansino (ESP)
1936[6]	Daniel Kagchelland (HOL)	Werner Krogmann (GER)	Peter Scott (GBR)
1948[7]	Paul Elvström (DEN)	Ralph Evans (USA)	Jacobus de Jong (HOL)
1952[8]	Paul Elvström (DEN)	Charles Currey (GBR)	Rickard Sarby (SWE)
1956	Paul Elvström (DEN)	André Nelis (BEL)	John Marvin (USA)
1960	Paul Elvström (DEN)	Aleksandr Chuchelov (URS)	André Nelis (BEL)
1964	Willi Kuhweide (GER)	Peter Barrett (USA)	Henning Wind (DEN)
1968	Valentin Mankin (URS)	Hubert Raudaschl (AUT)	Fabio Albarelli (ITA)
1972	Serge Maury (FRA)	Ilias Hatzipavlis (GRE)	Viktor Potapov (URS)
1976	Jochen Schümann (GDR)	Andrei Balashov (URS)	John Bertrand (AUS)
1980	Esko Rechardt (FIN)	Wolfgang Mayrhofer (AUT)	Andrei Balashov (URS)

[1] 12-foot dinghy (note two-handed), no bronze medal.   [2] 18-foot dinghy (note two-handed), no silver and bronze medals.   [3] Meulan class, 12-foot dinghy.
[4] International 12-foot class.   [5] Snowbird class.   [6] International Olympia class.   [7] Firefly class.   [8] Since 1952 Finn class.   1896–1912 Event not held

INTERNATIONAL 470

	Gold	Silver	Bronze
1976	FRG Frank Hübner Harro Bode	SPAIN Antonio Gorostigui Pedro Millet	AUSTRALIA Ian Brown Ian Ruff
1980	BRAZIL Marcos Soares Eduardo Penido	GDR Jörn Borowski Egbert Swensson	FINLAND Jouko Lindgren Georg Tallberg

1896–1972 Event not held

INTERNATIONAL TORNADO

	Gold	Silver	Bronze
1976	GREAT BRITAIN Reg White John Osborn	UNITED STATES David McFaull Michael Rothwell	FRG Jörg Spengler Jörg Schmall
1980	BRAZIL Alexandre Welter Lars Björkström	DENMARK Peter Due Per Kjergard	SWEDEN Göran Marström Jörgen Ragnarsson

1896–1972 Event not held

INTERNATIONAL STAR

	Gold	Silver	Bronze
1932	UNITED STATES Gilbert Gray Andrew Libano Jr	GREAT BRITAIN Colin Ratsey Peter Jaffe	SWEDEN Gunnar Asther Daniel Sunden-Cullberg
1936	GERMANY Peter Bischoff Hans-Joachim Weise	SWEDEN Arved Laurin Uno Wallentin	NETHERLANDS Adriaan Maas Willem de Vries Lentsch
1948	UNITED STATES Hilary Smart Paul Smart	CUBA Carlos de Cardenas Carlos de Cardenas Jr	NETHERLANDS Adriaan Maas Edward Stutterheim
1952	ITALY Agostino Straulino Nicolo Rode	UNITED STATES John Reid John Price	PORTUGAL Francisco de Andrade Joaquim Fiuza

1956	**UNITED STATES**	ITALY	BAHAMAS
	Herbert Williams	Agostino Straulino	Durward Knowles
	Lawrence Low	Nicolo Rode	Sloan Farrington
1960	**USSR**	PORTUGAL	UNITED STATES
	Timir Pinegin	Mario Quina	William Parks
	Fedor Shutkov	José Quina	Robert Halperin
1964	**BAHAMAS**	UNITED STATES	SWEDEN
	Durward Knowles	Richard Stearns	Pelle Pettersson
	Cecil Cooke	Lyn Williams	Holger Sundström
1968	**UNITED STATES**	NORWAY	ITALY
	Lowell North	Peder Lunde	Franco Cavallo
	Peter Barrett	Per Olav Wiken	Camillo Gargano
1972	**AUSTRALIA**	SWEDEN	FRG
	David Forbes	Pelle Pettersson	Willi Kuhweide
	John Anderson	Stellan Westerdahl	Karsten Meyer
1980	**USSR**	AUSTRIA	ITALY
	Valentin Mankin	Hubert Raudaschl	Giorgio Gorla
	Aleksandr Muzychenko	Karl Ferstl	Alfio Peraboni

1896–1928, 1976 Event not held

FLYING DUTCHMAN

	Gold	*Silver*	*Bronze*
1956[1]	NEW ZEALAND	AUSTRALIA	GREAT BRITAIN
	Peter Mander	Roland Tasker	Jasper Blackall
	John Cropp	John Scott	Terence Smith
1960	NORWAY	DENMARK	GERMANY
	Peder Lunde Jr	Hans Fogh	Rolf Mulka
	Björn Bergvall	Ole Erik Petersen	Ingo von Bredow
1964	NEW ZEALAND	GREAT BRITAIN	UNITED STATES
	Helmer Pedersen	Keith Musto	Harry Melges Jr
	Earle Wells	Arthur Morgan	William Bentsen
1968	GREAT BRITAIN	FRG	BRAZIL
	Rodney Pattisson	Ullrich Libor	Reinaldo Conrad
	Iain Macdonald-Smith	Peter Naumann	Burkhard Cordes
1972	GREAT BRITAIN	FRANCE	FRG
	Rodney Pattisson	Yves Pajot	Ullrich Libor
	Christopher Davies	Marc Pajot	Peter Naumann
1976	FRG	GREAT BRITAIN	BRAZIL
	Jörg Diesch	Rodney Pattisson	Reinaldo Conrad
	Eckart Diesch	Julian Brooke Houghton	Peter Ficker
1980	SPAIN	IRELAND	HUNGARY
	Alejandro Abascal	David Wilkins	Szabolcs Detre
	Miguel Noguer	James Wilkinson	Zsolt Detre

[1] Sharpie class.　　1896–1952 Event not held

INTERNATIONAL SOLING

	Gold	*Silver*	*Bronze*
1972	UNITED STATES	SWEDEN	CANADA
1976	DENMARK	UNITED STATES	GDR
1980	DENMARK	USSR	GREECE

1896–1968 Event not held

DISCONTINUED EVENTS

SWALLOW

	Gold	*Silver*	*Bronze*
1948	GREAT BRITAIN	PORTUGAL	UNITED STATES
	Stewart Morris	Duarte De Almeida Bello	Lockwood Pirie
	David Bond	Fernando Coelho Bello	Owen Torry

INTERNATIONAL TEMPEST

	Gold	Silver	Bronze
1972	USSR	GREAT BRITAIN	UNITED STATES
	Valentin Mankin	Alan Warren	Glen Foster
	Vitaliy Dyrdyra	David Hunt	Peter Dean
1976	SWEDEN	USSR	UNITED STATES
	John Albrechtson	Valentin Mankin	Dennis Conner
	Ingvar Hansson	Wladislaw Akimenko	Conn Findlay

DRAGON

	Gold	Silver	Bronze
1948	NORWAY	SWEDEN	DENMARK
1952	NORWAY	SWEDEN	GERMANY
1956	SWEDEN	DENMARK	GREAT BRITAIN
1960	GREECE	ARGENTINA	ITALY
1964	DENMARK	GERMANY	UNITED STATES
1968	UNITED STATES	DENMARK	GDR
1972	AUSTRALIA	GDR	UNITED STATES

30 SQUARE METRES

	Gold	Silver	Bronze
1920	SWEDEN	—[1]	—[1]

[1] No silver or bronze medals.

40 SQUARE METRES

	Gold	Silver	Bronze
1920	SWEDEN	SWEDEN	—[1]

[1] No bronze medal.

5·5 METRES

	Gold	Silver	Bronze
1952	UNITED STATES	NORWAY	SWEDEN
1956	SWEDEN	GREAT BRITAIN	AUSTRALIA
1960	UNITED STATES	DENMARK	SWITZERLAND
1964	AUSTRALIA	SWEDEN	UNITED STATES
1968	SWEDEN	SWITZERLAND	GREAT BRITAIN

6 METRES

	Gold	Silver	Bronze
1908	GREAT BRITAIN	BELGIUM	FRANCE
1912	FRANCE	DENMARK	SWEDEN
1920	NORWAY	BELGIUM	—[1]
1924	NORWAY	DENMARK	NETHERLANDS
1928	NORWAY	DENMARK	ESTONIA
1932	SWEDEN	UNITED STATES	CANADA
1936	GREAT BRITAIN	NORWAY	SWEDEN
1948	UNITED STATES	ARGENTINA	SWEDEN
1952	UNITED STATES	NORWAY	FINLAND

[1] No bronze medal.

6 METRES (1907 Rating)

	Gold	Silver	Bronze
1920	BELGIUM	NORWAY	NORWAY

6·5 METRES

	Gold	Silver	Bronze
1920	NETHERLANDS	FRANCE	—[1]

[1] No bronze medal.

7 METRES

	Gold	Silver	Bronze
1908	GREAT BRITAIN	—[1]	—[1]
1920	GREAT BRITAIN	—[1]	—[1]

[1] No silver or bronze medals.   1912 Event not held

8 METRES

	Gold	Silver	Bronze
1908	GREAT BRITAIN	SWEDEN	GREAT BRITAIN
1912	NORWAY	SWEDEN	FINLAND
1920	NORWAY	NORWAY	BELGIUM
1924	NORWAY	GREAT BRITAIN	FRANCE
1928	FRANCE	NETHERLANDS	SWEDEN
1932	UNITED STATES	CANADA	—[1]
1936	ITALY	NORWAY	GERMANY

[1] No bronze medal.

8 METRES (1907 Rating)

	Gold	Silver	Bronze
1920	NORWAY	NORWAY	—[1]

[1] No bronze medal.

10 METRES

	Gold	Silver	Bronze
1912	SWEDEN	FINLAND	RUSSIA

10 METRES (1907 Rating)

	Gold	Silver	Bronze
1920	NORWAY	—[1]	—[1]

[1] No silver or bronze medals.

12 METRES

	Gold	Silver	Bronze
1908	GREAT BRITAIN	GREAT BRITAIN	—[1]
1912	NORWAY	SWEDEN	FINLAND

[1] No bronze medal.

12 METRES (1907 Rating)

	Gold	Silver	Bronze
1920	NORWAY	—[1]	—[1]

[1] No silver or bronze medals.

12 METRES (1919 Rating)

	Gold	Silver	Bronze
1920	NORWAY	—[1]	—[1]

[1] No silver or bronze medals.

½ TON CLASS

	Gold	Silver	Bronze
1900	FRANCE	FRANCE	FRANCE

½–1 TON CLASS

	Gold	Silver	Bronze
1900	GREAT BRITAIN	FRANCE	FRANCE

1–2 TON CLASS

	Gold	Silver	Bronze
1900	GERMANY	SWITZERLAND	FRANCE

2–3 TON CLASS

	Gold	Silver	Bronze
1900	GREAT BRITAIN	FRANCE	FRANCE

3–10 TON CLASS

	Gold	Silver	Bronze
1900	FRANCE	NETHERLANDS	GREAT BRITAIN[1] FRANCE

[1] Tie for third place.

10–20 TON CLASS

	Gold	Silver	Bronze
1900	FRANCE	FRANCE	GREAT BRITAIN

OPEN CLASS

	Gold	Silver	Bronze
1900	GREAT BRITAIN	GERMANY	FRANCE

DISCONTINUED SPORTS

In the early celebrations of the Olympic Games there were a number of sports included, often of a purely local interest to the host country. The last of these to remain on the programme was Polo which had its final outing in 1936. Below are listed all the medallists in these sports. (The various demonstration sports are dealt with elsewhere.)

CRICKET

On the only occasion that cricket was included in the Games, in 1900, Great Britain was represented by the Devon Wanderers CC, captained by C B Beachcroft. They beat a French team, which included mainly Britons living in France, in a 12-a-side match scoring 117 and 145 for five declared against the French score of 73 and 26.

CROQUET

The sport was only included in the 1900 Games when all competitors were French. Only gold medals were awarded in the singles (simple à la boule), won by Aumoitte, and the doubles, won by Aumoitte and Johin. In the singles (simple à deux boules) the medals went to Waydelick, Vignerot and Sautereau respectively.

GOLF

George Lyon (CAN) was aged 46 yr 59 days when he won the title in 1904. He won a total of eight Canadian amateur championships and also excelled at cricket, baseball, football, tennis, rowing and curling. Chandler Egan (USA) won a team gold and an individual silver in 1904. He won the United States Amateur Championship in 1904 and 1905.

JEU DE PAUME

The sport has been held once, in 1908, but it was a demonstration event twenty years later. The medals in 1908 were won by Jay Gould (USA), Eustace Miles (GBR) and Neville Lytton (GBR).

LACROSSE

Two Olympic tournaments were held in 1904 and 1908. Both were won by Canada, with the silver medals going to the United States and Great Britain respectively. Only two teams competed each time. The highest score reached in the tournaments was when Canada defeated Great Britain 14–10 in 1908. Demonstrations of the sport were held in 1928, 1932 and 1948.

MOTORBOATING

The only time that motorboating events were held in the Games was in 1908 when in each of the three classes contested only one boat finished and only the gold medal was awarded. The Open class was won by France, and the 60-foot and 8 metre classes went to Great Britain.

POLO

The only gold medallists to win another medal were Sir John Wodehouse (GBR), the third Earl of Kimberley, with a gold in 1920 and a silver in 1908, and Frederick Barrett (GBR) with a gold in 1920 and a bronze in 1924. The oldest man to win a gold medal was Manuel Andrada (ARG) in 1936 aged 46 yr 211 days, while the youngest was his team-mate Roberto Cavanagh aged 21 yr 269 days. The biggest winning margin was 16–2 by Argentina *v* Spain and Great Britain *v* France both in 1924, and by Mexico *v* Hungary in 1936.

	Gold	Silver	Bronze
1900	Great Britain	Great Britain	France
1908	Great Britain	Great Britain	Great Britain
1920	Great Britain	Spain	United States
1924	Argentina	United States	Great Britain
1936	Argentina	Great Britain	Mexico

ROQUE

The sport was only held in 1904 with all competitors from the United States. The medals were awarded to Charles Jacobus, S O Streeter and Charles Brown respectively.

RACKETS

Singles

	Gold	Silver	Bronze
1908	Evan Noel (GBR)	Henry Leaf (GBR)	John Jacob Astor (GBR)

Doubles

	Gold	Silver	Bronze
1908	Great Britain Vane Pennel John Jacob Astor	Great Britain Edward Bury Cecil Browning	Great Britain Evan Noel Henry Leaf

RUGBY UNION

A total of only six countries (Australia, France, Germany, Great Britain, Romania and the United States) competed in the four tournaments held. The 1908 title was won by Australia while the Wallabies were on their first tour of Britain. The team they beat in the final was the team from Cornwall, the English County Champions. Five American players won two gold medals in 1920 and 1924; Charles Doe, John O'Neil, Colby Slater, John Patrick and Rudolph Scholz. In addition Daniel Carroll, who had been on the winning Australian team in 1908, won his second gold medal in the 1920 United States team. Carroll was only 16 yr 149 days in the 1908 tournament making him the youngest ever player in the sport to play for his country—although 'purists' have never considered the Olympic matches to be 'full' internationals. In 1920 Morris Kirksey who had won a gold medal in the 4 × 100 m relay and a silver in the 100 m sprint, also won another gold as a member of the United States rugby team. The highest score was when France beat Romania 61–3 in 1924. It always comes as a shock to enthusiasts to realize that the United States is the reigning Olympic champion at rugby. After their Paris victory they played in Britain and were beaten by the Harlequins and Blackheath club teams. Probably one of the reasons for the game being in the Olympics in the first place is that Baron de Coubertin was a keen follower of the game having refereed France's first international match, against New Zealand, in 1906.

Discontinued Sports

	Gold	Silver	Bronze
1900	France	Germany	Great Britain
1908	Australia	Great Britain	—
1920	United States	France	—
1924	United States	France	Romania

TENNIS

The first gold medallist was Irish-born John Pius Boland (GBR) in the 1896 singles. The winner of the ladies singles in 1900, Charlotte Cooper (GBR) became the first woman to win an Olympic title at any sport. Over the years a number of medal winning pairs in the doubles competitions were composed of players from two countries. The most successful player was Max Decugis (FRA) who won a total of six medals comprising four golds, one silver and one bronze between 1900 and 1920. Kitty McKane (GBR) won a record total by a woman with five (one gold, two silver and two bronze medals) in 1920 and 1924. The oldest gold medallist was George Hillyard (GBR) in the 1908 men's doubles aged 44 yr 160 days. The oldest female was Winifred McNair (GBR) aged 43 yr 14 days when winning the women's doubles in 1920. She was also the oldest British woman to win a gold medal in any sport. The youngest gold medallist was Helen Wills (USA) who won the 1924 singles aged 18 yr 288 days, while the youngest male was Fritz Traun (GER) who won the men's doubles with Boland in 1896 aged 20 yr 13 days. The husband and wife team of Max and Marie Decugis (FRA) won the mixed doubles in 1906, while the famous brothers Reggie and Laurie Doherty (GBR) added the 1900 Olympic title to the eight Wimbledon doubles championships they won. Many of the greatest names in tennis played in the Olympics and there were 19 gold medal winners

The final of the 1912 mixed doubles in Stockholm, with Dora Köring and Heinrich Schomburgk (GER), far side, beating Sigrid Fick and Gunnar Setterwall (SWE).

who also won Wimbledon championships. One of the most remarkable of these was the Swiss-born Norris Williams (USA), who survived the sinking of the *Titanic* in 1912 swimming in icy water for over an hour, won the Croix de Guerre in World War I, a Wimbledon title in 1920, an Olympic gold medal in 1924, and lived to the decent age of 77 years. A demonstration of tennis was held in 1968 and there are strong moves to have tennis back in the Olympic Games in 1988.

Men's Singles

	Gold	Silver	Bronze
1900	Charles Sands (USA)	Walter Rutherford (GBR)	D D Robertson (GBR)
1904	George Lyon (CAN)	Chandler Egan (USA)	Bert McKinnie (USA) F C Newton (USA)

Men's Team

	Gold	Silver	Bronze
1904	UNITED STATES	UNITED STATES	—

Women's Singles

	Gold	Silver	Bronze
1900	Margaret Abbott (USA)	Polly Whittier (USA)	Huger Pratt (USA)

MEN'S SINGLES

	Gold	Silver	Bronze
1896	John Boland (GBR)	Demis Kasdaglis (GRE)	—
1900[1]	Hugh Doherty (GBR)	Harold Mahony (GBR)	Reginald Doherty (GBR) A B Norris (GBR)
1904	Beals Wright (USA)	Robert LeRoy (USA)	—
1906	Max Decugis (FRA)	Maurice Germot (FRA)	Zdenek Zemla (BOH)
1908	Josiah Ritchie (GBR)	Otto Froitzheim (GER)	Wilberforce Eves (GBR)
1908[2]	Wentworth Gore (GBR)	George Caridia (GBR)	Josiah Ritchie (GBR)
1912	Charles Winslow (SAF)	Harold Kitson (SAF)	Oscar Kreuzer (GER)
1912[2]	André Gobert (FRA)	Charles Dixon (GBR)	Anthony Wilding (NZL)
1920	Louis Raymond (SAF)	Ichiya Kumagae (JPN)	Charles Winslow (GBR)
1924	Vincent Richards (USA)	Henri Cochet (FRA)	Umberto De Morpurgo (ITA)

[1] Two bronze medals in 1900.   [2] Indoor tournaments.

MEN'S DOUBLES

	Gold	*Silver*	*Bronze*
1896	GREAT BRITAIN/GERMANY	GREECE	—
	John Boland	Demis Kasdaglis	
	Fritz Traun	Demetrios Petrokokkinos	
1900[1]	GREAT BRITAIN	USA/FRANCE	FRANCE
	Reginald Doherty	Spalding de Garmendia	A Prevost
	Hugh Doherty	Max Decugis	G de la Chapelle
			GREAT BRITAIN
			Harold Mahony
			A B Norris
1904	UNITED STATES	UNITED STATES	—
	Edgar Leonard	Alonzo Bell	
	Beals Wright	Robert LeRoy	
1906	FRANCE	GREECE	BOHEMIA
	Max Decugis	Zenophon Kasdaglis	Zdenek Zemla
	Maurice Germot	Ioannis Ballis	Ladislav Zemla
1908	GREAT BRITAIN	GREAT BRITAIN	GREAT BRITAIN
	George Hillyard	Josiah Ritchie	Charles Cazalet
	Reginald Doherty	James Parke	Charles Dixon
1908[2]	GREAT BRITAIN	GREAT BRITAIN	SWEDEN
	Wentworth Gore	George Simond	Gunnar Setterwall
	Herbert Barrett	George Caridia	Wollmar Boström
1912	SOUTH AFRICA	AUSTRIA	FRANCE
	Charles Winslow	Felix Pipes	Albert Canet
	Harold Kitson	Arthur Zborzil	Marc de Marangue
1912[2]	FRANCE	SWEDEN	GREAT BRITAIN
	André Gobert	Gunnar Setterwall	Charles Dixon
	Maurice Germot	Carl Kempe	Arthur Beamish
1920	GREAT BRITAIN	JAPAN	FRANCE
	Noel Turnbull	Ichiya Kumagae	Max Decugis
	Max Woosnam	Selichiro Kashio	Pierre Albarran
1924	UNITED STATES	FRANCE	FRANCE
	Vincent Richards	Jacques Brugnon	Jean Borotra
	Frank Hunter	Henri Cochet	René Lacoste

[1] Two bronze medals in 1900.   [2] Indoor tournaments.

WOMEN'S SINGLES

	Gold	*Silver*	*Bronze*
1900[1]	Charlotte Cooper (GBR)	Hélène Prévost (FRA)	Marion Jones (USA)
			Hedwiga Rosenbaumova (BOH)
1906	Esmeé Simiriotou (GRE)	Sophia Marinou (GRE)	Euphrosine Paspati (GRE)
1908	Dorothea Chambers (GBR)	Dorothy Boothby (GBR)	Joan Winch (GBR)
1908[2]	Gwen Eastlake-Smith (GBR)	Angela Greene (GBR)	Märtha Adlerstråhle (SWE)
1912	Marguerite Broquedis (FRA)	Dora Köring (GER)	Molla Bjurstedt (NOR)
1912[2]	Ethel Hannam (GBR)	Thora Castenschiold (DEN)	Mabel Parton (GBR)
1920	Suzanne Lenglen (FRA)	Dorothy Holman (GBR)	Kitty McKane (GBR)
1924	Helen Wills (USA)	Julie Vlasto (FRA)	Kitty McKane (GBR)

[1] Two bronze medals.   [2] Indoor tournaments.

WOMEN'S DOUBLES

	Gold	*Silver*	*Bronze*
1920	GREAT BRITAIN	GREAT BRITAIN	FRANCE
	Winifried McNair	Geraldine Beamish	Suzanne Lenglen
	Kitty McKane	Dorothy Holman	Elisabeth d'Ayen
1924	UNITED STATES	GREAT BRITAIN	GREAT BRITAIN
	Hazel Wightman	Edith Covell	Dorothy Shepherd-Barron
	Helen Wills	Kitty McKane	Evelyn Colyer

MIXED DOUBLES

	Gold	Silver	Bronze
1900[1]	GREAT BRITAIN	FRANCE/GBR	BOHEMIA/GBR
	Charlotte Cooper	Hélène Prévost	Hedwiga Rosenbaumova
	Reginald Doherty	Harold Mahony	A A Warden
			UNITED STATES/GBR
			Marion Jones
			Hugh Doherty
1906	FRANCE	GREECE	GREECE
	Marie Decugis	Sophia Marinou	Aspasia Matsa
	Max Decugis	Georgios Simiriotis	Xenophon Kasdaglis
1912	GERMANY	SWEDEN	FRANCE
	Dora Köring	Sigrid Fick	Marguerite Broquedis
	Heinrich Schomburgk	Gunnar Setterwall	Albert Canet
1912[2]	GREAT BRITAIN	GREAT BRITAIN	SWEDEN
	Ethel Hannam	Helen Aitchison	Sigrid Fick
	Charles Dixon	Herbert Barrett	Gunnar Setterwall
1920	FRANCE	GREAT BRITAIN	CZECHOSLOVAKIA
	Suzanne Lenglen	Kitty McKane	Milada Skrbkova
	Max Decugis	Max Woosnam	Ladislav Zemla
1924	UNITED STATES	UNITED STATES	NETHERLANDS
	Hazel Wightman	Marion Jessup	Cornelia Bouman
	Norris Williams	Vincent Richards	Hendrik Timmer

[1] Two bronze medals.   [2] Indoor tournament.

DEMONSTRATION SPORTS

Since 1904 there have been demonstrations of various sports held as part of the Games but not as official competitions eligible for medals. Some of them had been or later became one of the recognized sports of the Games, and these have been mentioned under the sections dealing with those sports. Other than those there have been the following:

AMERICAN FOOTBALL

In 1932 two teams representing the East and West of America played an exhibition game which the West won 7–6.

AUSTRALIAN RULES FOOTBALL

Two amateur Australian teams played an exhibition game which resulted in a 250–135 score.

BADMINTON

In 1972 twenty-five competitors from eleven countries provided a competition of the highest quality, highlighted by the victory of Rudy Hartano (INA) in the men's singles.

BANDY

A tournament of bandy, the most popular Scandinavian winter game, was included in the 1952 Winter Games at Oslo. None of the three teams was an outright winner and the placings were decided on goal average, Sweden winning from Norway and Finland.

BASEBALL

There have been four occasions on which American baseball has been exhibited, plus a demonstration of Finnish baseball in 1952. In 1912 a United States team, containing many of the athletes who had won medals in track and field events, beat a Swedish team 13–3. In 1936 a 'World's Amateurs' team beat an American 'Olympics' team before 100 000 people in the Berlin Olympic stadium. At Melbourne in 1956 an American Services team beat an Australian team 11–5 before an estimated crowd of 114 000, the largest number of spectators who have ever watched a single baseball game. In 1964 a United States team finished ahead of two Japanese teams after a two-game tournament.

BUDO

Exhibitions of Japanese archery, wrestling and fencing were given at Tokyo in 1964.

CURLING

A three-country tournament held in 1924 at Chamonix was won by Great Britain from Sweden and France. In 1932 at Lake Placid there were four Canadian Provincial teams and four American club teams. The Canadians took the first four places with the title won by Manitoba. In 1936 at Garmisch-Partenkirchen eight teams from Austria (3), Germany (3) and Czechoslovakia (2) took part in a specialized version of the game, German curling. The Austrian number one team, from the Tyrol, won the tournament. The Austrians demonstrated the game again in 1964 at Innsbruck.

DOG SLED RACING

A race for twelve dog sled teams, seven dogs to a sled, was held at Lake Placid in 1932. There were two races of approximately 25 miles *40 km* each with the aggregate times added together. The event was won easily by Emile St Goddard (CAN) who finished first in both races and finished with a combined time of 4 hr 23 min 12·5 sec, nearly 8 minutes ahead of the second man, Lennard Seppala (USA).

GLIDING

Fourteen countries participated in a gliding exhibition in 1936 but the main demonstrations were by German gliders.

MILITARY PATROL

This appeared in four Winter Games, and is considered to be the forerunner of the official biathlon contests which were introduced in 1960. The 'martial' character of the military patrol event created opposition in official Olympic circles but it proved to be very popular.

The contest in 1924 (won by Switzerland) had six national teams; that of 1928 (won by Norway) had nine; there were also nine in 1936 (won by Italy); and the 1948 competition (won again by Switzerland) had eight entries.

PELOTA BASQUE

The sport was demonstrated in 1924 by teams from Spain and France, and again in 1968 when the same countries were joined by players from Mexico, Argentina and Uruguay in a much more comprehensive display.

WATER SKIING

Demonstrations were held at Kiel in 1972 with 36 competitors from 20 countries, including many of the best skiers in the world. Events were won by Roby Zucchi (ITA), Ricky McCormick (USA), Liz Allan-Shetter (USA), Willy Stähle (HOL) and Sylvie Maurial (FRA).

WINTER PENTATHLON

Held in 1948 the winter pentathlon comprised a 10 km cross-country skiing race, a pistol shooting competition, fencing, downhill skiing, and horse riding over a distance of about 3500 m. The event was won by Gustaf Lindh of Sweden with team-mates taking the next two places. In second place was Willie Grut who later in the year won the modern pentathlon by a record margin at the Summer Games. Also in the winter competition, in sixth place, was Derek Allhusen (GBR) who 20 years later in his 55th year won a gold medal in the equestrian three-day event at Mexico City.

Separate Alpine skiing events were first introduced into the Games in 1948, but this type of skiing had been included in 1936 as an Alpine combination event consisting of an aggregate of points scored in a downhill and in a slalom race. Toni Sailer (AUT) in 1956 and Jean-Claude Killy (FRA) in 1968 both won a record three gold medals. Five girls won two gold medals each but German-born Hanni Wenzel (LIE) won a silver and bronze to make her the only Alpine skier, male or female, to win four medals. The only Alpine skiers to win gold medals in two Games were Trude Jochum-Beiser (AUT) with the combination in 1948 and the downhill in 1952, and Marielle Goitschel (FRA) with the giant slalom in 1964 and the slalom in 1968.

The oldest gold medallist was Zeno Colo (ITA) who won the 1952 downhill race aged 31 yr 231 days. The youngest was Marie-Therese Nadig (SUI) who was aged 17 yr 334 days when she won the 1972 downhill event. The youngest male was Toni Sailer (AUT) aged 20 yr 73 days when winning the giant slalom in 1956, and the oldest female champion was Ossi Reichert (GER) who won the 1956 giant slalom aged 30 yr 33 days. The oldest medallist was Heinrich Messner (AUT), who won the bronze medal in the 1972 downhill aged 32 yr 159 days, and the youngest was Gertrud 'Traudl' Hecher (AUT) aged 16 yr 145 days with a bronze in the 1960 downhill race. The youngest male medallist was Alfred Matt (AUT) who gained a bronze in the 1968 slalom aged 19 yr 281 days, and the oldest female medallist was Dorothea Hochleitner (AUT) aged 30 yr 201 days when she won the 1956 giant slalom bronze medal.

The highest average speed achieved in an Olympic downhill race was 102·828 km/h *63·894 mph* by Franz Klammer (AUT) when he won the 1976 title on the Patscherkofel course at Innsbruck. The greatest margin of victory in downhill was 4·7 sec by Madeleine Berthod

The 1936 Olympic winner of the Alpine combination Christel Cranz (GER) won a record total of twelve world championships.

(FRA) in 1956, while the best by a male skier was 4·1 sec by Henri Oreiller (FRA) in 1948. The smallest margin was 0·08 sec in the men's downhill in 1968, and the smallest in the women's race was 0·32 sec in 1972.

The greatest margin in slalom was 11·3 sec by Christel Cranz (GER) in the combination event in 1936, when the margin in the men's equivalent was 5·9 sec by Franz Pfnür (GER). Since then Toni Sailer (AUT) won the 1956 title by 4·0 sec and Anne Heggtveit (CAN) the women's race in 1960 by 3·3 sec. The smallest margin in slalom was 0·02 sec in the 1972 women's race, and there was a 0·09 sec difference in the 1968 men's race.

In the giant slalom the biggest margin was 6·2 sec by Toni Sailer in 1956, while that for women was 2·64 sec by Nancy Greene in 1968. The smallest margin was 0·1 sec (before electric timing) by Yvonne Rüegg (SUI) in the 1960 women's race, and 0·12 sec by Kathy Kreiner (CAN) in 1976. The record for the men's race was 0·20 sec by Heini Hemmi (SUI) in 1976.

Left: **Franz Klammer (AUT)** achieved the fastest average speed for an Olympic skiing event when he won the 1976 downhill.

Right: **After two silver medals in the 1972 Games, Annemarie Moser-Pröll (AUT)** finally won a gold in the 1980 down hill race.

ALPINE SKIING (Men)

GIANT SLALOM

	Gold	Silver	Bronze
1952	Stein Eriksen (NOR) 2:25·0	Christian Pravda (AUT) 2:26·9	Toni Spiss (AUT) 2:28·8
1956	Anton Sailer (AUT) 3:00·1	Andreas Molterer (AUT) 3:06·3	Walter Schuster (AUT) 3:07·2
1960	Roger Staub (SUI) 1:48·3	Josef Stiegler (AUT) 1:48·7	Ernst Hinterseer (AUT) 1:49·1
1964	Francois Boulieu (FRA) 1:46·71	Karl Schranz (AUT) 1:47·09	Josef Stiegler (AUT) 1:48·05
1968	Jean-Claude Killy (FRA) 3:29·28	Willy Favre (SUI) 3:31·50	Heinrich Messner (AUT) 3:31·83
1972	Gustavo Thoeni (ITA) 3:09·62	Edmund Bruggmann (SUI) 3:10·75	Werner Mattle (SUI) 3:10·99
1976	Heini Hemmi (SUI) 3:26·97	Ernst Good (SUI) 3:27·17	Ingemar Stenmark (SWE) 3:27·41
1980	Ingemar Stenmark (SWE) 2:40·74	Andreas Wenzel (LIE) 2:41·49	Hans Enn (AUT) 2:42·51

1908–1948 Event not held

SLALOM

	Gold	Silver	Bronze
1948	Edi Reinalter (SUI) 2:10·3	James Couttet (FRA) 2:10·8	Henri Oreiller (FRA) 2:12·8
1952	Othmar Schneider (AUT) 2:00·0	Stein Eriksen (NOR) 2:01·2	Guttorm Berge (NOR) 2:01·7
1956	Anton Sailer (AUT) 3:14·7	Chiharu Igaya (JPN) 3:18·7	Stig Sollander (SWE) 3:20·2
1960	Ernst Hinterseer (AUT) 2:08·9	Matthias Leitner (AUT) 2:10·3	Charles Bozon (FRA) 2:10·4
1964	Josef Stiegler (AUT) 2:21·13	William Kidd (USA) 2:21·27	James Huega (USA) 2:21·52
1968	Jean-Claude Killy (FRA) 1:39·73	Herbert Huber (AUT) 1:39·82	Alfred Matt (AUT) 1:40·09
1972	Francisco Fernandez Ochoa (ESP) 1:49·27	Gustavo Thoeni (ITA) 1:50·28	Rolando Thoeni (ITA) 1:50·30
1976	Piero Gros (ITA) 2:03·29	Gustavo Thoeni (ITA) 2:03·73	Willy Frommelt (LIE) 2:04·28
1980	Ingemar Stenmark (SWE) 1:44·26	Phil Mahre (USA) 1:44·76	Jacques Lüthy (SUI) 1:45·06

1908–1936 Event not held

DOWNHILL

	Gold	Silver	Bronze
1948	Henri Oreiller (FRA) 2:55·0	Franz Gabl (AUT) 2:59·1	Karl Molitor (SUI) 3:00·3 Rolf Olinger (SUI) 3:00·3
1952	Zeno Colo (ITA) 2:30·8	Othmar Schneider (AUT) 2:32·0	Christian Pravda (AUT) 2:32·4
1956	Anton Sailer (AUT) 2:52·2	Raymond Fellay (SUI) 2:55·7	Andreas Molterer (AUT) 2:56·2
1960	Jean Vuarnet (FRA) 2:06·0	Hans-Peter Lanig (GER) 2:06·5	Guy Perillat (FRA) 2:06·9
1964	Egon Zimmermann (AUT) 2:18·16	Leo Lacroix (FRA) 2:18·90	Wolfgang Bartels (GER) 2:19·48
1968	Jean-Claude Killy (FRA) 1:59·85	Guy Périllat (FRA) 1:59·93	Jean-Daniel Dätwyler (SUI) 2:00·32
1972	Bernhard Russi (SUI) 1:51·43	Roland Collombin (SUI) 1:52·07	Heinrich Messner (AUT) 1:52·40
1976	Franz Klammer (AUT) 1:45·73	Bernhard Russi (SUI) 1:46·06	Herbert Plank (ITA) 1:46·59
1980	Leonhard Stock (AUT) 1:45·50	Peter Wirnsberger (AUT) 1:46·12	Steve Podborski (CAN) 1:46·62

1908–1936 Event not held

ALPINE COMBINATION (Downhill and Slalom)

	Gold	Silver	Bronze
1936	Franz Pfnür (GER) 99·25 pts	Gustav Lantschner 96·26 pts	Emile Allais (FRA) 94·69 pts
1948	Henri Oreiller (FRA) 3·27 pts	Karl Molitor (SUI) 6·44 pts	James Couttet (FRA) 6·95 pts

ALPINE SKIING (Women)

GIANT SLALOM

	Gold	Silver	Bronze
1952	Andrea Mead-Lawrence (USA) 2:06·8	Dagmar Rom (AUT) 2:09·0	Annemarie Buchner (GER) 2:10·0
1956	Ossi Reichert (GER) 1:56·5	Josefine Frandl (AUT) 1:57·8	Dorothea Hochleitner (AUT) 1:58·2
1960	Yvonne Rüegg (SUI) 1:39·9	Penelope Pitou (USA) 1:40·0	Giuliana Chenal-Minuzzo (ITA) 1:40·2

1964	Marielle Goitschel (FRA) 1:52·24	Christine Goitschel (FRA) 1:53·11	Jean Saubert (USA) 1:53·11
1968	Nancy Greene (CAN) 1:51·97	Annie Famose (FRA) 1:54·61	Fernande Bochatay (SUI) 1:54·74
1972	Marie-Therese Nadig (SUI) 1:29·90	Annemarie Pröll (AUT) 1:30·75	Wiltrud Drexel (AUT) 1:32·35
1976	Kathy Kreiner (CAN) 1:29·13	Rosi Mittermaier (FRG) 1:29·25	Danielle Debernard (FRA) 1:29·95
1980	Hanni Wenzel (LIE) 2:41·66	Irene Epple (FRG) 2:42·12	Perrine Pelen (FRA) 2:42·41

1908–1948 Event not held

SLALOM

	Gold	Silver	Bronze
1948	Gretchen Fraser (USA) 1:57·2	Antoinette Meyer (SUI) 1:57·7	Erika Mahringer (AUT) 1:58·0
1952	Andrea Mead-Lawrence (USA) 2:10·6	Ossi Reichert (GER) 2:11·4	Annemarie Buchner (GER) 2:13·3
1956	Renée Colliard (SUI) 1:52·3	Regina Schöpf (AUT) 1:55·4	Jevginija Sidorova (URS) 1:56·7
1960	Anne Heggtveit (CAN) 1:49·6	Betsy Snite (USA) 1:52·9	Barbi Henneberger (GER) 1:56·6
1964	Christine Goitschel (FRA) 1:29·86	Marielle Goitschel (FRA) 1:30·77	Jean Saubert (USA) 1:31·36
1968	Marielle Goitschel (FRA) 1:25·86	Nancy Greene (CAN) 1:26·15	Annie Famose (FRA) 1:27·89
1972	Barbara Cochran (USA) 1:31·24	Danielle Debernard (FRA) 1:31·26	Florence Steurer (FRA) 1:32·69
1976	Rosi Mittermaier (FRG) 1:30·54	Claudia Giordani (ITA) 1:30·87	Hanni Wenzel (LIE) 1:32·20
1980	Hanni Wenzel (LIE) 1:25·09	Christa Kinshofer (FRG) 1:26·50	Erika Hess (SUI) 1:27·89

1908–1936 Event not held

DOWNHILL

	Gold	Silver	Bronze
1948	Hedy Schlunegger (SUI) 2:28·3	Trude Beiser (AUT) 2:29·1	Resi Hammerer (AUT) 2:30·2
1952	Trude Jochum-Beiser (AUT) 1:47·1	Annemarie Buchner (GER) 1:48·0	Giuliana Minuzzo (ITA) 1:49·0
1956	Madeleine Berthod (SUI) 1:40·7	Frieda Dänzer (SUI) 1:45·4	Lucile Wheeler (CAN) 1:45·9
1960	Heidi Biebl (GER) 1:37·6	Penelope Pitou (USA) 1:38·6	Traudl Hecher (AUT) 1:38·9
1964	Christl Haas (AUT) 1:55·39	Edith Zimmerman (AUT) 1:56·42	Traudl Hecher (AUT) 1:56·66
1968	Olga Pall (AUT) 1:40·87	Isabelle Mir (FRA) 1:41·33	Christl Haas (AUT) 1:41·41
1972	Marie-Thérèse Nadig (SUI) 1:36·68	Annemarie Pröll (AUT) 1:37·00	Susan Corrock (USA) 1:37·68
1976	Rosi Mittermaier (FRG) 1:46·16	Brigitte Totschnig (AUT) 1:46·68	Cindy Nelson (USA) 1:47·50
1980	Annemarie Moser-Pröll (AUT) 1:37·52	Hanni Wenzel (LIE) 1:38·22	Marie-Therèse Nadig (SUI) 1:38·36

1908–1936 Event not held

ALPINE COMBINATION (Downhill and Slalom)

	Gold	Silver	Bronze
1936	Christel Cranz (GER) 97·06 pts	Käthe Grasegger (GER) 95·26 pts	Laila Schou Nilsen (NOR) 93·48 pts
1948	Trude Beiser (AUT) 6·58 pts	Gretchen Fraser (USA) 6·95 pts	Erika Mahringer (AUT) 7·04 pts

ALPINE SKIING—MEDALS

Men	Gold	Silver	Bronze	Total
AUSTRIA	9	9	10	28
SWITZERLAND	4	7	5	16
FRANCE	7	3	5	15
ITALY	3	2	2	7
SWEDEN	2	—	2	4
GERMANY (FRG)	1	2	1	4
NORWAY	1	1	1	3
UNITED STATES	—	2	1	3
LIECHTENSTEIN	—	1	1	2
SPAIN	1	—	—	1
JAPAN	—	1	—	1
CANADA	—	—	1	1
	28	28	29	85

Women	Gold	Silver	Bronze	Total
AUSTRIA	5	8	8	21
GERMANY (FRG)	5	6	3	14
UNITED STATES	4	4	4	12
FRANCE	3	5	4	12
SWITZERLAND	6	2	3	11
CANADA	3	1	1	5
LIECHTENSTEIN	2	1	1	4
ITALY	—	1	2	3
NORWAY	—	—	1	1
USSR	—	—	1	1
	28	28	28	84

Men & Women	Gold	Silver	Bronze	Total
AUSTRIA	14	17	18	49
SWITZERLAND	10	9	8	27
FRANCE	10	8	9	27
GERMANY (FRG)	6	8	4	18
UNITED STATES	4	6	5	15
ITALY	3	3	4	10
CANADA	3	1	2	6
LIECHTENSTEIN	2	2	2	6
SWEDEN	2	—	2	4

NORWAY	1	1	2	4
SPAIN	1	—	—	1
JAPAN	—	1	—	1
USSR	—	—	1	1
	56	56	57	169

BOBSLEDDING

A bob competition for 4-man sleds was first held in 1924. The rules at the time allowed for either four or five men per team in the competitions of 1924 and 1928. The 2-man event was introduced in 1932. Both competitions have been held ever since then except for 1960 when the Squaw Valley Organizing Committee refused to build a run, stating that the high cost was not acceptable for the small number of entries expected.

In 1952 a situation arose which led to changes in the rules governing the overall weight of teams and bobs. The Germans combined their heaviest men from their two vehicles into one 4-man sled in which they averaged over 118 kg per man. Their resulting victory gave rise to complaints about the unfair advantage such excessive weight conferred on a team. The new rules stipulate that the maximum weight of the bobs, with crews, must not exceed 375 kg (2-man) and 630 kg (4-man), but that extra weights may be added to the vehicles within those limits.

The most gold medals won by an individual is three by Bernhard Germeshausen (GDR) and Meinhard Nehmer (GDR) both of them in the 1976 and 1980 4-man events and the 1976 2-man

Above: **Tony Nash and Robin Dixon** in 1964 with the only bobsledding gold medals ever won by British sportsmen.

Right: **After many years of trying Eugenio Monti (ITA)** finally won a gold medal, in fact two of them, in the 1968 bobsledding.

competition. The most medals won is six (two gold, two silver and two bronze) by Eugenio Monti (ITA) from 1956 to 1968.

The oldest gold medallist was Giacomo Conti (ITA) in the winning 2-man bob in 1956 aged 47 yr 218 days, which also makes him the oldest gold medallist in Winter Games history. The youngest gold medallist was William Fiske (USA) who piloted the winning 5-man bob in 1928 aged 16 yr 260 days, which also makes him the youngest male Winter Games champion ever. Additionally Conti was the oldest medallist while the youngest was Thomas Doe Jr (USA) in the silver medal 5-man bob in 1928 aged 15 yr 127 days, making him the youngest male Winter Games medallist in history. The tallest gold medallist was Edy Hubacher (SUI) in the 1972 4-man bob standing 2·01 m *6 ft 7 in.* Hubacher had competed in the shot put at the 1968 Summer Games.

In recent years there has been a move towards using top class track and field athletes, particularly hurdlers and decathletes, in the teams of various countries. Recent gold medallists in this

In 1936 Ivan Brown and Alan Washbond successfully defended the 2-man bobsled title which the USA had won in 1932.

category include Nehmer, Germeshausen, Hans-Jürgen Gerhardt and Bogdan Musiol of GDR, and Hubacher and Erich Schärer of Switzerland.

The first brothers to win gold medals were Alfred and Heinrich Schläppi (SUI) in the 4-man bob in 1924. The inaugural 2-man title was won by the Stevens brothers, Hubert and Curtis, of the United States.

The closest finish in Olympic bobsledding occurred in the 1968 2-man event when Italy I and FRG I had identical aggregate times after the four runs. The title went to Italy, driven by the 40-year-old Monti, as they had the fastest single run.

The winning Great Britain 2-man team in 1964 owed its victory to Eugenio Monti, as it was he who lent them an axle to replace the broken British one prior to their last run. The Canadian winners of the 4-man title in 1964 were nicknamed the 'Intellectual Sled'. They comprised an aircraft engineer, a plastic surgeon, a geologist and a teacher.

2-MAN BOB

	Gold	Silver	Bronze
1932	UNITED STATES I 8:14·14 Hubert Stevens Curtis Stevens	SWITZERLAND II 8:16·28 Reto Capadrutt Oscar Geier	UNITED STATES II 8:29·15 John Heaton Robert Minton
1936	UNITED STATES I 5:29·29 Ivan Brown Alan Washbond	SWITZERLAND II 5:30·64 Fritz Feierabend Joseph Beerli	UNITED STATES II 5:33·96 Gilbert Colgate Richard Lawrence
1948	SWITZERLAND II 5:29·2 Felix Endrich Friedrich Waller	SWITZERLAND I 5:30·4 Fritz Feierabend Paul Eberhard	UNITED STATES II 5:35·3 Frederick Fortune Schwyler Carron
1952	GERMANY I 5:24·54 Andreas Ostler Lorenz Nieberl	UNITED STATES I 5:26·89 Stanley Benham Patrick Martin	SWITZERLAND I 5:27·71 Fritz Feierabend Stephan Waser
1956	ITALY I 5:30·14 Lamberto Dall Costa Giacomo Conti	ITALY II 5:31·45 Eugenio Monti Renzo Alvera	SWITZERLAND I 5:37·46 Max Angst Harry Warburton
1964	GREAT BRITAIN I 4:21·90 Tony Nash Robin Dixon	ITALY II 4:22·02 Sergio Zardini Romano Bonagura	ITALY I 4:22·63 Eugenio Monti Sergio Siorpaes
1968	ITALY I 4:41·54 Eugenio Monti Luciano de Paolis	FRG I 4:41·54 Horst Floth Pepi Bader	ROMANIA I 4:44·46 Ion Panturu Nicolae Neagoe
1972	FRG II 4:47·07 Wolfgang Zimmerer Peter Utzschneider	FRG I 4:58·84 Horst Floth Pepi Bader	SWITZERLAND I 4:59·33 Jean Wicki Edy Hubacher
1976	GDR II 3:44·42 Meinhard Nehmer Bernhard Germeshausen	FRG I 3:44·99 Wolfgang Zimmerer Manfred Schumann	SWITZERLAND I 3:45·70 Erich Schärer Josef Benz
1980	SWITZERLAND II 4:09·36 Erich Schärer Josef Benz	GDR II 4:10·93 Bernhard Germeshausen Hans-Jürgen Gerhardt	GDR I 4:11·08 Meinhard Nehmer Bogdan Musiol

1908–1928 Event not held   1960 Event not held

4-MAN BOB

	Gold	Silver	Bronze
1924	SWITZERLAND I 5:45·54	GREAT BRITAIN II 4:48·83	BELGIUM I 6:02·29
1928[1]	UNITED STATES II 3:20·5	UNITED STATES I 3:21·0	GERMANY II 3:21·9
1932	UNITED STATES I 7:53·68	UNITED STATES II 7:55·70	GERMANY I 8:00·04
1936	SWITZERLAND II 5:19·85	SWITZERLAND I 5:22·73	GREAT BRITAIN I 5:23·41
1948	UNITED STATES II 5:20·1	BELGIUM 5:21·3	UNITED STATES I 5:21·5
1952	GERMANY 5:07·84	UNITED STATES I 5:10·48	SWITZERLAND I 5:11·70
1956	SWITZERLAND I 5:10·44	ITALY II 5:12·10	UNITED STATES I 5:12·39
1964	CANADA I 4:14·46	AUSTRIA I 4:15·48	ITALY II 4:15·60
1968[2]	ITALY I 2:17·39	AUSTRIA I 2:17·48	SWITZERLAND I 2:18·04
1972	SWITZERLAND I 4:43·07	ITALY I 4:43·83	FRG I 4:43·92
1976	GDR I 3:40·43	SWITZERLAND II 3:40·89	FRG I 3:41·37

1980   GDR I 3:59·92   SWITZERLAND I 4:00·87   GDR II 4:00·97

[1] Five-man team in 1928; aggregate of two runs.   [2] Aggregate of two runs.   1908–1920, 1960 Event not held

BOBSLEDDING—MEDALS

	Gold	Silver	Bronze	Total
SWITZERLAND	6	6	6	18
UNITED STATES	5	4	5	14
GERMANY (FRG)	3	3	4	10
ITALY	3	4	2	9
GDR	3	1	2	6
GREAT BRITAIN	1	1	1	3
AUSTRIA	—	2	—	2
BELGIUM	—	1	1	2
CANADA	1	—	—	1
ROMANIA	—	—	1	1
	22	22	22	66

FIGURE SKATING

The first Olympic title at a Winter Games event was won by Ulrich Salchow (SWE) in 1908 at the Prince's Rink, London. Salchow, who won a total of ten world championships, gave his name to one of the most popular jumps. In the 1908 Games there was also a special figures event, won by a Russian (Czarist variety), Nikolai Panin, who had been too ill to take part in the main event. Panin, whose real name was Kolomenkin but preferred his alias, appeared 4 years later in Stockholm as a member of the Russian fourth placed pistol shooting team. The first women's title went to Madge Syers (GBR), who 6 years previously had entered the world championships, ostensibly only for men, and had placed second to Salchow.

The most gold medals won by a figure skater is three by Gillis Grafström (SWE) 1920-1928, Sonja Henie (NOR) 1928–1936, and Irina Rodnina (URS) in the pairs event 1972–1980. Of these only Grafström also won a silver medal, in 1932, making him the only skater to win medals

in four Games. No skater has doubled completely successfully in singles and pairs at the Games. The best have been Ernst Baier (GER) with a pairs gold and a singles silver in 1936, and Madge Syers (GBR) with a singles gold and a pairs bronze in 1908.

The oldest gold medallist was Walter Jakobsson (FIN) who won the pairs title with his German-born wife Ludowika in 1920 aged 38 yr 80 days. Ludowika was the oldest female winner aged 35 yr 276 days. The youngest was Maxi Herber (GER) who was 15 yr 128 days when she won the pairs in 1936 with Ernst Baier whom she later married. The youngest male champion was Richard Button (USA) aged 18 yr 202 days when he won the 1948 singles title. Sonja Henie was 50 days short of her 16th birthday when she won her first title in 1928, after some last minute coaching by Britain's Alex Adams. She had been eighth and last in 1924 when still under 12 years of age. However, the youngest ever competitor in the Winter Games was her rival of 1936 Cecilia Colledge (GBR) who had been 11 yr 78 days in the 1932 Games. Only an unofficial competitor in 1920, a French boy in rowing (see page 16) has been a younger Olympian. The youngest medallist was Scott Allen (USA) 2 days short of his 15th birthday when winning the 1964 bronze medal in the singles, and the youngest female was Marina Tcherkasova (URS) just 3 days over her 15th birthday in the 1980 silver winning pair. The oldest medallist was Martin Stixrud (NOR) with a singles bronze in 1920 aged 44 yr 78 days.

Sonja Henie won ten world, six European and

Left: **The first Russian to win an Olympic gold medal, Nikolai Panin, who won the special figures event in 1908.** Below: **Maxi Herber and Ernst Baier (GER) the 1936 pairs champions.**

Figure Skating

three Olympic titles before turning professional and making an estimated $47 million in ice shows and films. The film world has attracted a number of other Olympic skaters, including Gladys Jepson-Turner (GBR) better known as 'Belita' and Vera Hruba-Ralston (TCH).

Sonja Henie is also usually credited with introducing jumps into the women's event but in 1920 Theresa Weld (USA), the bronze medallist, included a salchow in her programme which brought her a reprimand from the judges and a threat that she would be penalized if she continued with such 'unfeminine behaviour'.

Karl Schäfer (AUT) won the men's figure skating title in 1932 and then repeated in 1936

The winning of the 1972 title by Trixie Schuba (HOL), primarily on the basis of her excellent set figures (she was only seventh in free skating) led to a change in marking, whereby greater emphasis was given to free skating. Previously marks had been divided 50–50 between the two sections.

The Olympic pairs competition has often been the centre of attention but not always only because of the quality of performance. In 1972, although Irina Rodnina and Aleksey Ulanov (URS) won the pairs title it was the latter's dalliance with Ludmila Smirnova, silver medallist with Andrei Suraikin, which caught the interest. The result was a break-up of the top Soviet pair.

Rodnina then teamed up with Aleksandr Zaitsev while Ulanov and Smirnova got married. In the world championships the Rodnina/Zaitsev partnership beat the other pair for the title and getting married in 1975 went on to win two Olympic championships, the second less than a year after the birth of a son.

After the 1964 Games the silver medal pair of Marika Kilius and Hansjürgen Bäumler (GER) had to return their medals as it was revealed that they had signed professional contracts before the Games had begun. Marika had also made a record which was being advertised at the time of the competitions.

FIGURE SKATING (Men)

	Gold	Silver	Bronze
1908[1]	Nikolai Panin (URS) 219 pts	Arthur Cumming (GBR) 164	George Hall-Say (GBR) 104
1908	Ulrich Salchow (SWE) 1886·5 pts	Richard Johansson (SWE) 1826·0	Per Thorén (SWE) 1787·0
1920	Gillis Gräfström (SWE) 2838·5 pts	Andreas Krogh (NOR) 2634	Martin Stixrud (NOR) 2561·5
1924	Gillis Gräfström (SWE) 2575·25 pts	Willy Böckl (AUT) 2518·75	Georges Gautschi (SUI) 2233·5
1928	Gillis Gräfström (SWE) 2698·25 pts	Willy Böckl (AUT) 2682·50	Robert v. Zeebroeck (BEL) 2578·75
1932	Karl Schäfer (AUT) 2602·0 pts	Gillis Gräfström (SWE) 2514·5	Montgomery Wilson (CAN) 2448·3
1936	Karl Schäfer (AUT) 2959·0 pts	Ernst Baier (GER) 2805·3	Felix Kaspar (AUT) 2801·0
1948	Richard Button (USA) 1720·6 pts	Hans Gerschwiler (SUI) 1630·1	Edi Rada (AUT) 1603·2
1952	Richard Button (USA) 1730·3 pts	Helmut Seibt (AUT) 1621·3	James Grogan (USA) 1627·4
1956	Hayes Alan Jenkins (USA) 1497·95 pts	Ronald Robertson (USA) 1492·15	David Jenkins (USA) 1465·41
1960	David Jenkins (USA) 1440·2 pts	Karol Divin (TCH) 1414·3	Donald Jackson (CAN) 1401·0
1964	Manfred Schnelldorfer (GER) 1916·9 pts	Alain Calmat (FRA) 1876·5	Scott Allen (USA) 1873·6
1968	Wolfgang Schwarz (AUT) 1894·1 pts	Tim Woods (USA) 1891·6	Patrick Péra (FRA) 1864·5
1972	Ondrej Nepela (TCH) 2739·1 pts	Sergey Tchetveroukhin (URS) 2672·4	Patrick Péra (FRA) 2653·1
1976	John Curry (GBR) 192·74 pts	Vladimir Kovalev (URS) 187·64	Toller Cranston (CAN) 187·38
1980	Robin Cousins (GBR) 189·48 pts	Jan Hoffmann (GDR) 189·72	Charles Tickner (USA) 187·06

[1] Special Figures competition.   1912 Event not held

FIGURE SKATING (Women)

	Gold	Silver	Bronze
1908	Madge Syers (GBR) 1262·5 pts	Elsa Rendschmidt (GER) 1055·0	Dorothy Greenhough-Smith (GBR) 960·5
1920	Magda Julin-Mauroy (SWE) 913·5 pts	Svea Norén (SWE) 887·75	Theresa Weld (USA) 898·0

1924	Herma Planck-Szabo (AUT) 2094·25 pts	Beatrix Loughran (USA) 1959·0	Ethel Muckelt (GBR) 1750·50
1928	Sonja Henie (NOR) 2452·25 pts	Fritzi Burger (AUT) 2248·50	Beatrix Loughran (USA) 2254·50
1932	Sonja Henie (NOR) 2302·5 pts	Fritzi Burger (AUT) 2167·1	Maribel Vinson (USA) 2158·5
1936	Sonja Henie (NOR) 2971·4 pts	Cecilia Colledge (GBR) 2926·8	Vivi-Anne Hultén (SWE) 2763·2
1948	Barbara Scott (CAN) 1467·7 pts	Eva Pawlik (AUT) 1418·3	Jeanette Altwegg (GBR) 1405·5
1952	Jeanette Altwegg (GBR) 1455·8 pts	Tenley Albright (USA) 1432·2	Jacqueline du Bief (FRA) 1422·0
1956	Tenley Albright (USA) 1866·39 pts	Carol Heiss (USA) 1848·24	Ingrid Wendl (AUT) 1753·91
1960	Carol Heiss (USA) 1490·1 pts	Sjoukje Dijkstra (HOL) 1424·8	Barbara Roles (USA) 1414·8
1964	Sjoukje Dijkstra (HOL) 2018·5 pts	Regine Heitzer (AUT) 1945·5	Petra Burka (CAN) 1940·0
1968	Peggy Fleming (USA) 1970·5 pts	Gabrielle Seyfer (GDR) 1882·3	Hana Maskova (TCH) 1828·8
1972	Beatrix Schuba (AUT) 2751·5 pts	Karen Magnussen (CAN) 2673·2	Janet Lynn (USA) 2663·1
1976	Dorothy Hamill (USA) 193·80 pts	Dianne De Leeuw (HOL) 190·24	Christine Errath (GDR) 188·16
1980	Anett Pötzsch (GDR) 189·00 pts	Linda Fratianne (USA) 188·30	Dagmar Lurz (FRG) 183·04

1912 Event not held

PAIRS

	Gold	*Silver*	*Bronze*
1908	Anna Hübler Heinrich Burger (GER) 56·0 pts	Phyllis Johnson James Johnson (GBR) 51·5	Madge Syers Edgar Syers (GBR) 48·0
1920	Ludovika Jakobsson Walter Jakobsson (FIN) 80·75 pts	Alexia Bryn Yngvar Bryn (NOR) 72·75	Phyllis Johnson Basil Williams (GBR) 66·25
1924	Helene Engelmann Alfred Berger (AUT) 74·50 pts	Ludovika Jakobsson Walter Jakobsson (FIN) 71·75	Andrée Joly Pierre Brunet (FRA) 69·25
1928	Andrée Joly Pierre Brunet (FRA) 100·50 pts	Lilly Scholz Otto Kaiser (AUT) 99·25	Melitta Brunner Ludwig Wrede (AUT) 93·25
1932	Andrée Brunet Pierre Brunet (FRA) 76·7 pts	Beatrix Loughran Sherwin Badger (USA) 77·5	Emilia Rotter László Szollás (HUN) 76·4
1936	Maxi Herber Ernst Baier (GER) 103·3 pts	Ilse Pausin Erik Pausin (AUT) 102·7	Emilia Rotter László Szollás (HUN) 97·6
1948	Micheline Lannoy Pierre Baugniet (BEL) 123·5 pts	Andrea Kékessy Ede Király (HUN) 122·2	Suzanne Morrow Wallace Diestelmeyer (CAN) 121·0
1952	Ria Falk Paul Falk (GER) 102·6 pts	Karol Estelle Kennedy Michael Kennedy (USA) 100·6	Marianna Nagy László Nagy (HUN) 97·4
1956	Elisabeth Schwarz Kurt Oppelt (AUT) 101·8 pts	Frances Dafoe Norris Bowden (CAN) 101·9	Marianna Nagy László Nagy (HUN) 99·3
1960	Barbara Wagner Robert Paul (CAN) 80·4 pts	Marika Kilius Hansjürgen Bäumler (GER) 76·8	Nancy Ludington Ronald Ludington (USA) 76·2
1964[1]	Ludmila Belousova Oleg Protopopov (URS) 104·4 pts	Debbie Wilkes Guy Revell (CAN) 98·5	Vivian Joseph Ronald Joseph (USA) 98·2
1968	Ludmila Belousova Oleg Protopopov (URS) 315·2 pts	Tatyana Zhuk Aleksandr Gorelik (URS) 312·3	Margot Glockshuber Wolfgang Danne (FRG) 304·4
1972	Irina Rodnina Aleksey Ulanov (URS) 420·4 pts	Ludmila Smirnova Andrei Suraikin (URS) 419·4	Manuela Gross Uwe Kagelmann (GDR) 411·8
1976	Irina Rodnina Aleksandr Zaitsev (URS) 140·54 pts	Romy Kermer Rolf Oesterreich (GDR) 136·35	Manuela Grosse Uwe Kagelmann (GDR) 134·57
1980	Irina Rodnina Aleksandr Zaitsev (URS) 147·26 pts	Marina Tcherkasova Sergey Shakrai (URS) 143·80	Manuela Mager Uwe Bewersdorff (GDR) 140·52

[1] Marika Kilius and Hansjürgen Bäumler (GER) finished second but were subsequently disqualified.   1912 Event not held

ICE DANCE

	Gold	Silver	Bronze
1976	Ludmila Pakhomova	Irina Moiseyeva	Colleen O'Connor
	Aleksandr Gorshkov	Andrei Minenkov	James Millns
	(URS) 209·92 pts	(URS) 204·88	(USA) 202·64
1980	Natalya Linichuk	Krisztina Regöczy	Irina Moiseyeva
	Gennadiy Karponosov	András Sallay	Andrei Minenkov
	(URS) 205·48 pts	(HUN) 204·52	(URS) 201·86

1908–1972 Event not held

FIGURE SKATING—MEDALS

	Gold	Silver	Bronze	Total
UNITED STATES	8	8	12	28
AUSTRIA	7	9	4	20
USSR	8	6	1	15
GREAT BRITAIN	4	3	6	13
SWEDEN	5	3	2	10
CANADA	2	3	5	10
GERMANY (FRG)	4	3	2	9
GDR	1	3	4	8
FRANCE	2	1	4	7
NORWAY	3	2	1	6
HUNGARY	—	2	4	6
NETHERLANDS	1	2	—	3
CZECHOSLOVAKIA	1	1	1	3
FINLAND	1	1	—	2
BELGIUM	1	—	1	2
SWITZERLAND	—	1	1	2
	48	48	48	144

British skaters, Cecilia Colledge and Mollie Phillips, at Garmisch-Partenkirchen in 1936. Four years previously the former had become the youngest competitor to appear in the winter Games.

ICE HOCKEY

The game was introduced in 1920 as part of the Summer Olympics at Antwerp. The tournament was won by Canada, the first of a run of six victories only interrupted by Great Britain in 1936. The Canadians were always represented by a club side, not a national one; the first Olympic champions were the Winnipeg Falcons. Since 1948 the tournament has been decided on a championship format and not, as previously, on a knock-out basis. Thus there is not an Olympic final game as such, medals having been decided often prior to the last match. Seventeen medals are awarded to the medal winning team so that it is quite possible for a player to receive a gold medal even though he has not played in a single match. The game has been at the centre of some of the bitterest arguments about amateur/professional status, and in 1972 Canada withdrew from Olympic ice hockey in protest against the alleged 'professionalism' of the Eastern European teams in particular. Happily they returned in 1980. In 1948 there was a strange situation when two teams turned up at St Moritz to represent the United States (see p 51). There was a record entry of 16 teams in the 1964 tournament.

Four Soviet players have won a record three gold medals; Vitaliy Davidov, Anatoliy Firssov, Viktor Kuzkin and Aleksandr Ragulin, all in the winning teams of 1964, 1968 and 1972. The

ICE HOCKEY

	Gold	Silver	Bronze
1920	CANADA	UNITED STATES	CZECHOSLOVAKIA
1924	CANADA	UNITED STATES	GREAT BRITAIN
1928	CANADA	SWEDEN	SWITZERLAND
1932	CANADA	UNITED STATES	GERMANY
1936	GREAT BRITAIN	CANADA	UNITED STATES
1948	CANADA	CZECHOSLOVAKIA	SWITZERLAND
1952	CANADA	UNITED STATES	SWEDEN
1956	USSR	UNITED STATES	CANADA
1960	UNITED STATES	CANADA	USSR
1964	USSR	SWEDEN	CZECHOSLOVAKIA
1968	USSR	CZECHOSLOVAKIA	CANADA
1972	USSR	UNITED STATES	CZECHOSLOVAKIA
1976	USSR	CZECHOSLOVAKIA	FRG[1]
1980	UNITED STATES	USSR	SWEDEN

[1] Three-way tie for bronze with the United States and Finland decided on goal average.

longest span over which medals have been won is 20 years by Richard 'Bibi' Torriani (SUI) who won his first bronze in 1928 and his second in 1948, having also played in 1936.

The oldest gold medallist was George Abel (CAN) in 1952 on the day after his 36th birthday. The youngest was Mike Ramsey, a member of the winning United States team in 1980 aged 19 yr 83 days. The youngest medallist was Richard Torriani (SUI) aged 16 yr 141 days in 1932, while the oldest medallist was Erich Romer (GER) in 1932 aged 37 yr 256 days.

The first brothers to win gold medals were the Plaxtons (CAN), Herbert, Hugh and Roger, along with Frank and Joseph Sullivan, in 1928. When the United States won its first gold medal in 1960 much was owed to the efforts of two sets of brothers, Bill and Roger Christian, and Bill and Bob Cleary. The only twins to win gold medals were Boris and Yevgeniy Maiorov (URS) in 1964.

ICE HOCKEY—MEDALS

	Gold	Silver	Bronze	Total
CANADA	6	2	2	10
UNITED STATES	2	6	1	9
USSR	5	1	1	7
CZECHOSLOVAKIA	—	3	3	6
SWEDEN	—	2	2	4
GREAT BRITAIN	1	—	1	2
GERMANY (FRG)	—	—	2	2
SWITZERLAND	—	—	2	2
	14	14	14	42

When the Czechs won the silver medal in 1948 a member of the team was Jaroslav Drobny, who later won the 1954 Wimbledon tennis singles title.

The highest score and aggregate in Olympic ice hockey was the 33–0 defeat of Switzerland by Canada in 1924. In that tournament the Canadians totalled 110 goals in five matches and only had three scored against them.

NORDIC SKIING

CROSS-COUNTRY SKIING

This was the first form of skiing introduced in the Olympics. The most successful competitor was Sixten Jernberg (SWE) with four gold, three silver and two bronze medals, for a record total of nine medals from 1956 to 1964. He also gained

a fourth and two fifth placings having competed in 12 events in all. The best by a woman is four gold, two silver and two bronze medals, a record total of eight, by Galina Kulakova (URS) from 1968 to 1980. Only Jernberg won individual titles in three successive Games.

Nordic Skiing

Distance runners, not surprisingly, have had great successes in cross-country skiing. Hallgeir Brenden (NOR) was twice a national champion in the 3000 m steeplechase in 1953–54, as was his countryman Olle Ellefsäter in 1960 and 1962. Another Norwegian, Martin Stokken, set 17 national records on the track and gained fourth place in the 1948 Olympic 10 000 m race, as well as his silver medal in the 1952 Nordic relay.

The oldest gold medallist was Veikko Hakulinen (FIN) aged 35 yr 52 days in the 1960 relay, and the youngest was Eero Mäntyranta (FIN) also in that relay aged 22 yr 97 days. The oldest male medallist was Olaf Ökern (NOR) in the 1948 relay aged 36 yr 235 days, and the youngest male medallist was Ivar Formo (NOR) in the 1972 relay aged 20 yr 234 days. The oldest female gold medallist was Galina Kulakova (URS) in the 1976 relay aged 33 yr 289 days, and the youngest was Carola Anding (GDR) in the 1980 relay aged 19 yr 54 days. Kulakova was also the oldest medallist, male or female, aged 37 yr 289 days in the 1980 relay race which also had Anding as the youngest medallist.

Stanislaw Marusarz (POL) competed over a period of 20 years from 1932 to 1952.

NORDIC COMBINATION

This event was the 'blue riband' of Nordic skiing in the early Games. The all-round title, consisting of a cross-country race and a jump, was won on three successive occasions by Ulrich Wehling (GDR) 1972–1980, the only man to win a Winter Games individual title three times. The oldest

The proud possessor of nine Olympic medals Sixten Jernberg (SWE) here enter the snow stadium at Cortina in 1956 to win the 50 km race.

medallist was Simon Slattvik (NOR) who won in 1952 aged 34 yr 209 days, and the youngest was Wehling aged 19 yr 212 days in 1972.

Up until 1952 the cross-country section was held first, but at Oslo the jumping was made the first event.

BIATHLON

The combination of skiing and shooting was introduced in 1960. Aleksandr Tikhonov (URS) set a Winter Games record by winning a gold medal in the 4×7.5 km relay on four successive occasions 1968–1980. He also won an individual silver medal in 1968. The only man to successfully defend an individual title was Magnar Solberg (NOR) in 1972 when he was also the oldest gold medallist aged 35 yr 5 days. The youngest gold medal winner was Tikhonov in 1968 aged 21 yr 44 days. They are also the oldest and youngest medallists.

Left: Norway's Oddbjörn Hagen won a gold and two silver medals in the Nordic skiing events in 1936.

Right: Sulo Nurmela taps Klaes Karppinen at the first take-over in the 4×10 km relay in 1936. The Finnish team won this inaugural Olympic race.

SKI JUMPING

Introduced in 1924. The most successful jumper was Birger Ruud (NOR) with two gold and a silver medal from 1932 to 1948. He was also the only man to win two titles. He also came fourth in the alpine combination event of 1936, winning the downhill racing segment. His brother Sigmund won a silver medal in the jump in 1928. The longest jump achieved in Olympic jumping was 117 m by Jouko Törmänen (FIN) in 1980 on the 90 m hill. The first representative of a non-Nordic country to win a gold medal was Helmut Recknagel (GER) in 1960.

The oldest gold medallist was Yukio Kasaya (JPN) in 1972 aged 35 yr 173 days, while the youngest was Wojciech Fortuna (POL) also in 1972 aged 19 yr 189 days. The oldest medallist was Birger Ruud in 1948 aged 36 yr 168 days, and the youngest medallist was Toni Innauer (AUT) aged 17 yr 320 days in 1976.

Sepp Bradl (AUT) competed over a period of 20 years from 1936 to 1956 when he placed 12th. In 1936, at Planica in Yugoslavia, he had become the first to jump over 100 m, but failed to reproduce that form at Garmisch.

NORDIC SKIING (Men)

15 000 METRES

	Gold	Silver	Bronze
1924[1]	Thorleif Haug (NOR) 1 h 14:31·0	Johan Gröttumsbraaten (NOR) 1 h 15:51·0	Tipani Niku (FIN) 1 h 26:26·0
1928[2]	Johan Gröttumsbraaten (NOR) 1 h 37:01·0	Ole Hegge (NOR) 1 h 39:01·0	Reidar Ödegaard (NOR) 1 h 40:11·0
1932[3]	Sven Utterström (SWE) 1 h 23:07·0	Axel Wikström (SWE) 1 h 25:07·0	Veli Saarinen (FIN) 1 h 25:24·0
1936[1]	Erik-August Larsson (SWE) 1 h 14:38·0	Oddbjörn Hagen (NOR) 1 h 15:33·0	Pekka Niemi (FIN) 1 h 16:59·0
1948[1]	Martin Lundström (SWE) 1 h 13:50·0	Nils Östensson (SWE) 1 h 14:22·0	Gunnar Eriksson (SWE) 1 h 16:06·0
1952[1]	Hallgeir Brenden (NOR) 1 h 1:34·0	Tapio Mäkelä (FIN) 1 h 2:09·0	Paavo Lonkila (FIN) 1 h 2:20·0
1956	Hallgeir Brenden (NOR) 49:39·0	Sixten Jernberg (SWE) 50:14·0	Pavel Koltschin (URS) 50:17·0
1960	Haakon Brusveen (NOR) 51:55·5	Sixten Jernberg (SWE) 51:58·6	Veikko Hakulinen (FIN) 52:03·0
1964	Eero Mäntyranta (FIN) 50:54·1	Harald Grönningen (NOR) 51:34·8	Sixten Jernberg (SWE) 51:42·2
1968	Harald Grönningen (NOR) 47:54·2	Eero Mäntyranta (FIN) 47:56·1	Gunnar Larsson (SWE) 48:33·7
1972	Sven-Ake Lundback (SWE) 45:28·24	Fedor Simaschov (URS) 46:00·84	Ivar Formo (NOR) 46:02·86
1976	Nikolai Bajukov (URS) 43:58·47	Yevgenly Beliayev (URS) 44:01·10	Arto Koivisto (FIN) 44:19·25
1980	Thomas Wassberg (SWE) 41:57·63	Juha Mieto (FIN) 41:57·64	Ove Aunli (NOR) 42:28·62

[1] The distance was 18 km.   [2] The distance was 19·7 km.   [3] The distance was 18·2 km.   1908–1920 Event not held

30 000 METRES

	Gold	Silver	Bronze
1956	Veikko Hakulinen (FIN) 1 h 44:06·0	Sixten Jernberg (SWE) 1 h 44:30·0	Pavel Koltschin (URS) 1 h 45:45·0
1960	Sixten Jernberg (SWE) 1 h 51:03·9	Rolf Rämgård (SWE) 1 h 51:61·9	Nikolai Anikin (URS) 1 h 52:28·2
1964	Eero Mäntyranta (FIN) 1 h 30:50·7	Harald Grönningen (NOR) 1 h 32:02·3	Igor Voronchikin (URS) 1 h 32:15·8
1968	Franco Nones (ITA) 1 h 35:39·2	Odd Martinsen (NOR) 1 h 36:28·9	Eero Mäntyranta (FIN) 1 h 36:55·3
1972	Vyacheslav Vedenine (URS) 1 h 36:31·2	Paal Tyldum (NOR) 1 h 37:25·3	Johs Harviken (NOR) 1 h 37:32·4
1976	Sergey Savelyev (URS) 1 h 30:29·38	William Koch (USA) 1 h 30:57·84	Ivan Garanin (URS) 1 h 31:09·29
1980	Nikolai Simyatov (URS) 1 h 27:02·80	Vasiliy Rochev (URS) 1 h 27:34·22	Ivan Lebanov (URS) 1 h 28:03·87

1908–1952 Event not held

50 000 METRES

	Gold	Silver	Bronze
1924	Thorleif Haug (NOR) 3 h 44:32·0	Thoralf Strömstad (NOR) 3 h 46:23·0	Johan Gröttumsbraaten (NOR) 3 h 47:46·0
1928	Per Erik Hedlund (SWE) 4 h 52:03·0	Gustaf Jonsson (SWE) 5 h 05:30·0	Volger Andersson (SWE) 5 h 05:46·0
1932	Veli Saarinen (FIN) 4 h 28:00·0	Väinö Likkanen (FIN) 4 h 28:20·0	Arne Rustadstuen (NOR) 4 h 31:53·0
1936	Elis Wiklund (SWE) 3 h 30:11·0	Axel Wikström (SWE) 3 h 33:20·0	Nils-Joel Englund (SWE) 3 h 34:10·0

1948	Nils Karlsson (SWE) 3 h 47:48·0	Harald Eriksson (SWE) 3 h 52:20·0	Benjamin Vanninen (FIN) 3 h 57:28·0
1952	Veikko Hakulinen (FIN) 3 h 33:33·0	Eero Kolehmainen (FIN) 3 h 38:11·0	Magnar Estenstad (NOR) 3 h 38:28·0
1956	Sixten Jernberg (SWE) 2 h 50:27·0	Veikko Hakulinen (FIN) 2 h 51:45·0	Fedor Terentyev (URS) 2 h 53:32·0
1960	Kalevi Hämäläinen (FIN) 2 h 59:06·3	Veikko Hakulinen (FIN) 2 h 59:26·7	Rolf Rämgård (SWE) 3 h 02:46·7
1964	Sixten Jernberg (SWE) 2 h 43:52·6	Assar Rönnlund (SWE) 2 h 44:58·2	Arto Tiainen (FIN) 2 h 45:30·4
1968	Olle Ellefsaeter (NOR) 2 h 28:45·8	Vyacheslav Vedenine (URS) 2 h 29:02·5	Josef Haas (SUI) 2 h 29:14·8
1972	Paal Tyldrum (NOR) 2 h 43:14·75	Magne Myrmo (NOR) 2 h 43:29·45	Vyacheslav Vedenine (URS) 2 h 44:00·19
1976	Ivar Formo (NOR) 2 h 37:30·50	Gert-Dietmar Klause (GDR) 2 h 38:13·21	Benny Södergren (SWE) 2 h 39:39·21
1980	Nikolai Simyatov (URS) 2 h 27:24·60	Juha Mieto (FIN) 2 h 30:20·52	Aleksandr Savyalov (URS) 2 h 30:51·52

1908–1920 Event not held

4 x 10 000 METRES RELAY

	Gold	Silver	Bronze
1936	FINLAND 2 h 41:33·0	NORWAY 2 h 41:39·0	SWEDEN 2 h 43:03·0
1948	SWEDEN 2 h 32:08·0	FINLAND 2 h 41:06·0	NORWAY 2 h 44:33·0
1952	FINLAND 2 h 20:16·0	NORWAY 2 h 23:13·0	SWEDEN 2 h 24:13·0
1956	USSR 2 h 15:30·0	FINLAND 2 h 16:31·0	SWEDEN 2 h 17:42·0
1960	FINLAND 2 h 18:45·6	NORWAY 2 h 18:46·4	USSR 2 h 21:21·6
1964	SWEDEN 2 h 18:34·6	FINLAND 2 h 18:42·4	USSR 2 h 18:46·9
1968	NORWAY 2 h 08:33·5	SWEDEN 2 h 10:13·2	FINLAND 2 h 10:56·7
1972	USSR 2 h 04:47·94	NORWAY 2 h 04:57·6	SWITZERLAND 2 h 07:00·06
1976	FINLAND 2 h 07:59·72	NORWAY 2 h 09:58·36	USSR 2 h 10:51·46
1980	USSR 1 h 57:03·46	NORWAY 1 h 58:45·77	FINLAND 2 h 00:00·18

1908–1932 Event not held

SKI JUMPING

70 METRE HILL

	Gold	Silver	Bronze
1924[1]	Jacob Tullin Thams (NOR) 18 960 pts	Narve Bonna (NOR) 18 689	Anders Haugen (USA) 17 916
1928	Alf Andersen (NOR) 19 208 pts	Sigmund Ruud (NOR) 18 542	Rudolf Burkert (TCH) 17 937
1932	Birger Ruud (NOR) 228·1 pts	Hans Beck (NOR) 227·0	Kaare Wahlberg (NOR) 219·5
1936	Birger Ruud (NOR) 232·0 pts	Sven Eriksson (SWE) 230·5	Reidar Andersen (NOR) 228·9
1948	Petter Hugsted (NOR) 228·1 pts	Birger Ruud (NOR) 226·6	Thorleif Schjeldrup (NOR) 225·1
1952	Arnfinn Bergmann (NOR) 226·0 pts	Torbjörn Falkangar (NOR) 221·5	Karl Holmström (SWE) 219·5
1956	Antti Hyvärinen (FIN) 227·0 pts	Aulis Kallakorpi (FIN) 225·0	Harry Glass (GER) 224·5
1960	Helmut Recknagel (GER) 227·2 pts	Niilo Halonen (FIN) 222·6	Otto Leodolter (AUT) 219·4
1964	Veikko Kankkonen (FIN) 229·9 pts	Toralf Engan (NOR) 226·3	Torgeir Brandtzaeg (NOR) 222·9
1968	Jiri Raska (TCH) 216·5 pts	Reinhold Bachler (AUT) 214·2	Baldur Preiml (AUT) 212·6
1972	Yukio Kasaya (JPN) 244·2 pts	Akitsugu Konno (JPN) 234·8	Seiji Aochi (JPN) 229·5
1976	Hans-Georg Aschenbach (GDR) 252·0 pts	Jochen Danneberg (GDR) 246·2	Karl Schnabl (AUT) 242·0
1980	Toni Innauer (AUT) 226·3 pts	Manfred Deckert (GDR) 249·2 Hirokazu Yagi (JPN) 249·2	—

[1] Originally Thorleif Haug (NOR) placed third due to incorrect calculations at time. Error discovered and corrected in 1974.   1908–1920 Event not held

90 METRE HILL

	Gold	Silver	Bronze
1964	Toralf Engan (NOR) 230·7 pts	Veikko Kankkonen (FIN) 228·9	Torgeir Brandtzaeg (NOR) 227·2
1968	Vladimir Belousov (URS) 231·3 pts	Jiri Raska (TCH) 229·4	Lars Grini (NOR) 214·3
1972	Wojciech Fortuna (POL) 219·9 pts	Walter Steiner (SUI) 219·8	Rainer Schmidt (GDR) 219·3
1976	Karl Schnabl (AUT) 234·8 pts	Toni Innauer (AUT) 232·9	Henry Glass (GDR) 221·7
1980	Jouko Törmänen (FIN) 271·0 pts	Hubert Neuper (AUT) 262·4	Jari Puikkonen (FIN) 248·5

1908–1960 Event not held

NORDIC COMBINED (15 000 METRES and JUMPING)

	Gold	Silver	Bronze
1924[1]	Thorleif Haug (NOR)	Thoralf Strömstad (NOR)	Johan Gröttumsbraaten (NOR)
1928[1]	Johan Gröttumsbraaten (NOR)	Hans Vinjarengen (NOR)	John Snersrud (NOR)
1932	Johan Gröttumsbraaten (NOR) 446·0 pts	Ole Stenen (NOR) 436·05	Hans Vinjarengen (NOR) 434·60
1936	Oddbjörn Hagen (NOR) 430·30 pts	Olaf Hoffsbakken (NOR) 419·80	Sverre Brodahl (NOR) 408·10
1948	Heikki Hasu (FIN) 448·80 pts	Martti Huhtala (FIN) 433·65	Sven Israelsson (SWE) 433·40
1952	Simon Slåttvik (NOR) 451·621 pts	Heikki Hasu (FIN) 447·50	Sverre Stenersen (NOR) 436·335
1956	Sverre Stenersen (NOR) 455·0 pts	Bengt Eriksson (SWE) 473·4	Franciszek Gron-Gasienica (POL) 436·8
1960	Georg Thoma (GER) 457·952 pts	Tormod Knutsen (NOR) 453·000	Nikolai Gusakow (URS) 452·000
1964	Tormod Knutsen (NOR) 469·28 pts	Nikolai Kiselyev (URS) 453·04	Georg Thoma (GER) 452·88
1968	Frantz Keller (FRG) 449·04 pts	Alois Kälin (SUI) 447·94	Andreas Kunz (GDR) 444·10
1972	Ulrich Wehling (GDR) 413·34 pts	Rauno Miettinen (FIN) 405·55	Karl-Heinz Luck (GDR) 398·80
1976	Ulrich Wehling (GDR) 423·39 pts	Urban Hettich (FRG) 418·90	Konrad Winkler (GDR) 417·47
1980	Ulrich Wehling (GDR) 432·20 pts	Jouko Karjalainen (FIN) 429·50	Konrad Winkler (GDR) 425·32

[1] In 1924 and 1928, the scoring was decided upon a different basis from that used from 1932 onwards.   [2] From 1924–1952 distance was 18 km.

1908–1920 Event not held

BIATHLON

10 000 METRES

	Gold	Silver	Bronze
1980	Frank Ullrich (GDR) 32:10·69	Vladimir Alikin (URS) 32:53·10	Anatoliy Alyabiev (URS) 33:09·16

1908–1976 Event not held

20 000 METRES

	Gold	Silver	Bronze
1960	Klas Lestander (SWE) 1 h 33:21·6	Antti Tyrväinen (FIN) 1 h 33:57·7	Aleksandr Privalov (URS) 1 h 34:54·2
1964	Vladimir Melyanin (URS) 1 h 20:26·8	Aleksandr Privalov (URS) 1 h 23:42·5	Olav Jordet (NOR) 1 h 24:38·8
1968	Magnar Solberg (NOR) 1 h 13:45·9	Aleksandr Tikhonov (URS) 1 h 14:40·4	Vladimir Gundartsev (URS) 1 h 18:27·4
1972	Magnar Solberg (NOR) 1 h 15:55·5	Hans-Jürg Knauthe (GDR) 1 h 16:07·6	Lars Arvidsson (SWE) 1 h 16:27·03
1976	Nikolai Kruglov (URS) 1 h 14:12·26	Heikki Ikola (FIN) 1 h 15:54·10	Aleksandr Elizarov (URS) 1 h 16:05·57
1980	Anatoliy Alyabiev (URS) 1 h 08:16·31	Frank Ullrich (GDR) 1 h 08:27·79	Eberhard Rösch (GDR) 1 h 11:11·73

1908–1956 Event not held

BIATHLON RELAY (4 × 7 500 METRES)

	Gold	Silver	Bronze
1968	USSR 2 h 13:02·4	NORWAY 2 h 14:50·2	SWEDEN 2 h 17:26·3
1972	USSR 1 h 51:44·92	FINLAND 1 h 54:37·22	GDR 1 h 54:57·67
1976	USSR 1 h 57:55·64	FINLAND 2 h 01:45·58	GDR 2 h 04:08·61
1980	USSR 1 h 34:03·27	GDR 1 h 34:56·99	FRG 1 h 37:30·26

1908–1964 Event not held

NORDIC SKIING (Women)

5000 METRES

	Gold	Silver	Bronze
1964	Klaudia Boyarskikh (URS) 17:50·5	Mirja Lehtonen (FIN) 17:52·9	Alevtina Koltschina (URS) 18:08·4
1968	Toini Gustafsson (SWE) 16:45·2	Galina Kulakova (URS) 16:48·4	Alevtina Koltschina (URS) 16:51·6
1972	Galina Kulakova (URS) 17:00·50	Marjatta Kajosmaa (FIN) 17:05·50	Helena Sikolova (TCH) 17:07·32
1976	Helena Takalo (FIN) 15:48·69	Raisa Smetanina (URS) 15:49·73	Nina Baldycheva[1] (URS) 16:12·82
1980	Raisa Smetanina (URS) 15:06·92	Hilkka Riihivuori (FIN) 15:11·96	Kvetslava Jeriova (TCH) 15:23·44

[1] Galina Kulakova (URS) finished third but was disqualified.   1908–1960 Event not held

10 000 METRES

	Gold	Silver	Bronze
1952	Lydia Wideman (FIN) 41:40·0	Mirja Hietamies (FIN) 42:39·0	Siiri Rantanen (FIN) 42:50·0
1956	Lubov Kozyryeva (URS) 38:11·0	Radya Yeroschina (URS) 38:16·0	Sonja Edström (SWE) 38:23·0
1960	Maria Gusakova (URS) 39:46·6	Lubov Baranova-Kozyryeva (URS) 40:04·2	Radya Yeroschina (URS) 40:06·0
1964	Klaudia Boyarskikh (URS) 40:24·3	Yevdokia Mekshilo (URS) 40:26·6	Maria Gusakova (URS) 40:46·6
1968	Toini Gustafsson (SWE) 36:46·5	Berit Mördre (NOR) 37:54·6	Inger Aufles (NOR) 37:59·9
1972	Galina Kulakova (URS) 34:17·8	Alevtina Olunina (URS) 34:54·1	Marjatta Kajosmaa (FIN) 34:56·5
1976	Raisa Smetanina (URS) 30:13·41	Helena Takalo (FIN) 30:14·28	Galina Kulakova (URS) 30:38·61
1980	Barbara Petzold (GDR) 30:31·54	Hilkka Riihivuori (FIN) 30:35·05	Helena Takalo (FIN) 30:45·25

1908–1948 Event not held

4[1] × 5000 METRES RELAY

	Gold	Silver	Bronze
1956	FINLAND 1 h 09:01·0	USSR 1 h 09:28·0	SWEDEN 1 h 09:48·0
1960	SWEDEN 1 h 04:21·4	USSR 1 h 05:02·6	FINLAND 1 h 06:27·5
1964	USSR 59:20·2	SWEDEN 1 h 01·27·0	FINLAND 1 h 02:45·1
1968	NORWAY 57:30·0	SWEDEN 57:51·0	USSR 58:13·6
1972	USSR 48:46·15	FINLAND 49:19·37	NORWAY 49:51·49
1976	USSR 1 h 07:49·75	FINLAND 1 h 08:36·57	GDR 1 h 09:57·95
1980	GDR 1 h 02:11·10	USSR 1 h 03:18·30	NORWAY 1 h 04:13·50

[1] Over three stages prior to 1976.   1908–1952 Event not held

NORDIC SKIING—MEDALS

Men	Gold	Silver	Bronze	Total
NORWAY	27	27	20	74
FINLAND	14	22	12	48
USSR	16	8	17	41
SWEDEN	14	13	14	41
GDR	5	6	9	20
AUSTRIA	2	3	3	8
GERMANY (FRG)	3	1	3	7
JAPAN	1	2	1	4
SWITZERLAND	—	2	2	4
CZECHOSLOVAKIA	1	1	1	3
POLAND	1	—	1	2
UNITED STATES	—	1	1	2
ITALY	1	—	—	1
	85	86	84	255

Women	Gold	Silver	Bronze	Total
USSR	11	9	7	27
FINLAND	3	8	5	16
SWEDEN	3	2	2	7
NORWAY	1	1	3	5
GDR	2	—	1	3
CZECHOSLOVAKIA	—	—	2	2
	20	20	20	60

SPEED SKATING

The sport was introduced into the Olympics in 1924 with four races and an all-round title for men. Although there were demonstrations of women's speed skating at Lake Placid in 1932 the first official events for them were not held until 1960. There have been two major controversies in the sport at the Games, one in 1928 and the other in 1932. At St Moritz in 1928 the 10 000 m event was cancelled by the Norwegian referee because of bad weather. What caused the ill feeling, particularly in the American camp, was that at the time of the cancellation Irving Jaffee (USA) was the surprise leader and as all the best skaters had competed the medal pos-

238

itions appeared assured. Despite vigorous protests by all nationalities no medals were awarded. The other controversy was at Lake Placid in 1932 (see p 43) when the 'mass start' system was used; for the only time in Olympic competition, which undoubtedly gave the Americans and Canadians a tremendous advantage as the Europeans were completely unfamiliar with the tactics involved.

Lydia Skoblikova (URS) holds the record of six gold medals in speed skating in 1960 (two) and 1964 (four). This is also a record for any sport in the Winter Games for either a male or female competitor. The most gold medals won by a man is five by Clas Thunberg (FIN) in 1924 and 1928, and by Eric Heiden (USA) with all five in 1980. It should be noted that there have only been five events for men since 1976. The most medals won by a single competitor is seven by Thunberg, who added a silver and a bronze to his golds, and by Ivar Ballangrud (NOR) who won four gold, two silver and a bronze medal between 1928 and 1936.

Lydia Skoblikova (URS) won her four gold medals on successive days in the 1964 Games, while the best such achievement by a male skater was by Hjalmar Andersen (NOR) who won three on successive days in 1952. Heiden's five titles were won over a period of 9 days.

Clas Thunberg (FIN), Yevgeniy Grischin (URS), Erhard Keller (FRG) and Lydia Skoblikova (URS) have all successfully defended a title, but the only skater to regain one after having lost it was Ivar Ballangrud (NOR) in the 5000 m in 1928 and 1936.

Speed skaters Ivan Ballangrud (above) and Charles Mathiesen (both Norway).

The oldest gold medallist was Clas Thunberg (FIN) aged 35 yr 315 days when he won the 1500 m in 1928. The youngest was Anne Henning (USA) winning the 500 m in 1952 aged 16 yr 157 days. The youngest male was Jonny Nilsson (SWE) who won the 10 000 m in 1964 aged 20 yr 264 days. The oldest female gold medallist was Christina Baas-Kaiser (HOL) aged 33 yr 268 days when she took the 3000 m title in 1972.

Frank Stack (CAN) competed over a period of 20 years from 1932 to 1952 winning a bronze medal in 1932. Cornelius 'Kees' Broekman (HOL) competed at four Games from 1948 to 1960, winning two silvers in 1952, and starting in a total of thirteen events.

Many skaters have found a happy affinity between speed skating and cycle racing, including Yevgeniy Grischin (URS) and Eric Heiden (USA). The most successful has been Sheila Young (USA) who won the 1976 Olympic 500 m title and later that same year won the world amateur sprint cycle championship.

OLYMPIC RECORDS—SPEED SKATING

Event	min/sec	Name/Country	Year
Men			
500 metres	38·03	Eric Heiden (USA)	1980
1000 metres	1 15·18	Eric Heiden (USA)	1980
1500 metres	1 55·44	Eric Heiden (USA)	1980
5000 metres	7 02·29	Eric Heiden (USA)	1980
10 000 metres	14 28·13	Eric Heiden (USA)	1980
Women			
500 metres	41·78	Karin Enke (GDR)	1980
1000 metres	1 24·10	Natalya Petruseva (URS)	1980
1500 metres	2 10·95	Annie Borckink (HOL)	1980
3000 metres	4 32·13	Bjorg-Eva Jenssen (NOR)	1980

SPEED SKATING (Men)

500 METRES

	Gold	Silver	Bronze
1924	Charles Jewtraw (USA) 44·0	Oskar Olsen (NOR) 44·2	Roald Larsen (NOR) 44·8
			Clas Thunberg (FIN) 44·8
1928	Clas Thunberg (FIN) 43·4	—	John Farrell (USA) 43·6
	Bernt Evensen (NOR) 43·4		Roald Larsen (NOR) 43·6
			Jaako Friman (FIN) 43·6
1932	John Shea (USA) 43·4	Bernt Evensen (NOR) 5 m	Alexander Hurd (CAN) 8 m
1936	Ivar Ballangrud (NOR) 43·4	Georg Krog (NOR) 43·5	Leo Freisinger (USA) 44·0
1948	Finn Helgesen (NOR) 43·1	Kenneth Bartholomew (USA) 43·2	—
		Thomas Byberg (NOR) 43·2	
		Robert Fitzgerald (USA) 43·2	
1952	Kenneth Henry (USA) 43·2	Donald McDermott (USA) 43·9	Arne Johansen (NOR) 44·0
			Gordon Audley (CAN) 44·0
1956	Yevgeniy Grischin (URS) 40·2	Rafael Gratsch (URS) 40·8	Alv Gjestvang (NOR) 41·0
1960	Yevgeniy Grischin (URS) 40·2	William Disney (USA) 40·3	Rafael Gratsch (URS) 40·4
1964	Richard McDermott (USA) 40·1	Yevgeniy Grischin (URS) 40·6	—
		Vladimir Orlov (URS) 40·6	
		Alv Gjestvang (NOR) 40·6	
1968	Erhard Keller (FRG) 40·3	Richard McDermott (USA) 40·5	—
		Magne Thomassen (NOR) 40·5	
1972	Erhard Keller (FRG) 39·44	Hasse Borjes (SWE) 39·69	Valeriy Muratov (URS) 39·80
1976	Yevgeniy Kulikov (URS) 39·17	Valeriy Muratov (URS) 39·25	Daniel Immerfall (USA) 39·54
1980	Eric Heiden (USA) 38·03	Yevgeniy Kulikov (URS) 38·37	Lieuwe de Boer (HOL) 38·48

1908–1920 Event not held

1000 METRES

	Gold	Silver	Bronze
1976	Peter Mueller (USA) 1:19·32	Jorn Didriksen (NOR) 1:20·45	Valeriy Muratov (URS) 1:20·57
1980	Eric Heiden (USA) 1:15·18	Gaetan Boucher (CAN) 1:16·68	Frode Rönning (NOR) 1:16·91

1908–1972 Event not held

1500 METRES

	Gold	Silver	Bronze
1924	Clas Thunberg (FIN) 2:20·8	Roald Larsen (NOR) 2:22·0	Sigurd Moen (NOR) 2:25·6
1928	Clas Thunberg (FIN) 2:21·1	Bernt Evensen (NOR) 2:21·9	Ivar Ballangrud (NOR) 2:22·6
1932	John Shea (USA) 2:57·5	Alexander Hurd (CAN) 5 m	William Logan (CAN) 6 m
1936	Charles Mathiesen (NOR) 2:19·2	Ivar Ballangrud (NOR) 2:20·2	Birger Wasenius (FIN) 2:20·9
1948	Sverre Farstad (NOR) 2:17·6	Ake Seyffarth (SWE) 2:18·1	Odd Lundberg (NOR) 2:18·9
1952	Hjalmar Andersen (NOR) 2:20·4	Willem van der Voort (HOL) 2:20·6	Roald Aas (NOR) 2:21·6
1956	Yevgeniy Grischin (URS) 2:08·6	—	Toivo Salonen (FIN) 2:09·4
	Yuriy Michailov (URS) 2:08·6		
1960	Roald Aas (NOR) 2:10·4	—	Boris Stenin (URS) 2:11·5
	Yevgeniy Grischin (URS) 2:10·4		
1964	Ants Antson (URS) 2:10·3	Cornelis Verkerk (HOL) 2:10·6	Villy Haugen (NOR) 2:11·25
1968	Cornelis Verkerk (HOL) 2:03·4	Ard Schenk (HOL) 2:05·0	—
		Ivar Eriksen (NOR) 2:05·0	
1972	Ard Schenk (HOL) 2:02·96	Roar Gronvold (NOR) 2:04·26	Goran Clässon (SWE) 2:05·89
1976	Jan Egil Storholt (NOR) 1:59·38	Yuriy Kondakov (URS) 1:59·97	Hans Van Helden (HOL) 2:00·87
1980	Eric Heiden (USA) 1:55·44	Kai Stenshjemmet (NOR) 1:56·81	Jerje Andersen (NOR) 1:56·92

1908–1920 Event not held

5000 METRES

	Gold	Silver	Bronze
1924	Clas Thunberg (FIN) 8:39·0	Julius Skutnabb (FIN) 8:48·4	Roald Larsen (NOR) 8:50·2
1928	Ivar Ballangrud (NOR) 8:50·5	Julius Skutnabb (FIN) 8:59·1	Bernt Evensen (NOR) 9:01·1
1932	Irving Jaffee (USA) 9:40·8	Edward Murphy (USA) 2 m	William Logan (CAN) 4 m
1936	Ivar Ballangrud (NOR) 8:19·6	Birger Wasenius (FIN) 8:23·3	Antero Ojala (FIN) 8:30·1

1948	Reidar Liaklev (NOR) 8:29·4	Odd Lundberg (NOR) 8:32·7	Göthe Hedlund (SWE) 8:34·8
1952	Hjalmar Andersen (NOR) 8:10·6	Kees Broekman (HOL) 8:21·6	Sverre Haugli (NOR) 8:22·4
1956	Boris Schilkov (URS) 7:48·7	Sigvard Ericsson (SWE) 7:56·7	Oleg Gontscharenko (URS) 7:57·5
1960	Viktor Kositschkin (URS) 7:51·3	Knut Johannesen (NOR) 8:00·8	Jan Pesman (HOL) 8:05·1
1964	Knut Johannesen (NOR) 7:38·4	Per Moe (NOR) 7:38·6	Anton Maier (NOR) 7:42·0
1968	Anton Maier (NOR) 7:22·4	Cornelis Verkerk (HOL) 7:23·2	Petrus Nottet (HOL) 7:25·5
1972	Ard Schenk (HOL) 7:23·6	Roar Gronvold (NOR) 7:28·18	Sten Stensen (NOR) 7:33·39
1976	Sten Stensen (NOR) 7:24·48	Piet Kleine (HOL) 7:26·47	Hans Van Helden (HOL) 7:26·54
1980	Eric Heiden (USA) 7:02·29	Kai Stenshjemmet (NOR) 7:03·28	Tom Oxholm (NOR) 7:05·59

1908–1920 Event not held

10 000 METRES

	Gold	Silver	Bronze
1924	Julius Skutnabb (FIN) 18:04·8	Clas Thunberg (FIN) 18:07·8	Roald Larsen (NOR) 18:12·2
1932	Irving Jaffee (USA) 19:13·6	Ivar Ballangrud (NOR) 5 m	Frank Stack (CAN) 6 m
1936	Ivar Ballangrud (NOR) 17:24·3	Birger Wasenius (FIN) 17:28·2	Max Stiepl (AUT) 17·30·0
1948	Ake Seyffarth (SWE) 17:26·3	Lauri Parkkinen (FIN) 17:36·0	Pentti Lammio (FIN) 17:42·7
1952	Hjalmar Andersen (NOR) 16:45·8	Kees Broekman (HOL) 17:10·6	Carl-Erik Asplund (SWE) 17:16·6
1956	Sigvard Ericsson (SWE) 16:35·9	Knut Johannesen (NOR) 16:36·9	Oleg Gontscharenko (URS) 16:42·3
1960	Knut Johannesen (NOR) 15:46·6	Viktor Kositschkin (URS) 15:49·2	Kjell Bäckman (SWE) 16:14·2
1964	Jonny Nilsson (SWE) 15:50·1	Anton Maier (NOR) 16:06·0	Knut Johannesen (NOR) 16:06·3
1968	Johnny Höglin (SWE) 15:23·6	Anton Maier (NOR) 15:23·9	Örjan Sandler (SWE) 15:31·8
1972	Ard Schenk (HOL) 15:01·35	Cornelis Verkerk (HOL) 15:04·70	Sten Stensen (NOR) 15:07·08
1976	Piet Kleine (HOL) 14:50·59	Sten Stensen (NOR) 14:53·30	Hans Van Helden (HOL) 15:02·02
1980	Eric Heiden (USA) 14:28·13	Piet Kleine (HOL) 14:36·03	Tom Oxholm (NOR) 14:36·60

1908–1920 Event not held   1928 Event abandoned

SPEED SKATING (Women)

500 METRES

	Gold	Silver	Bronze
1960	Helga Haase (GER) 45·9	Natalya Dontschenko (URS) 46·0	Jeanne Ashworth (USA) 46·1
1964	Lydia Skoblikova (URS) 45·0	Irina Yegorova (URS) 45·4	Tatyana Sidorova (URS) 45·5
1968	Ludmila Titova (URS) 46·1	Mary Meyers (USA) 46·3	—
		Dianne Holum (USA) 46·3	
		Jennifer Fish (USA) 46·3	
1972	Anne Henning (USA) 43·33	Vera Krasnova (URS) 44·01	Ludmila Titova (URS) 44·45
1976	Sheila Young (USA) 42·76	Catherine Priestner (CAN) 43·12	Tatyana Averina (URS) 43·17
1980	Karin Enke (GDR) 41·78	Leah Poulos-Mueller (USA) 42·26	Natalya Petruseva (URS) 42·42

1000 METRES

	Gold	Silver	Bronze
1960	Klara Guseva (URS) 1:34·1	Helga Haase (GER) 1:34·3	Tamara Rylova (URS) 1:34·8
1964	Lydia Skoblikova (URS) 1:33·2	Irina Yegorova (URS) 1:34·3	Kaija Mustonen (FIN) 1:34·8
1968	Carolina Geijssen (HOL) 1:32·6	Ludmila Titova (URS) 1:32·9	Dianne Holum (USA) 1:33·4
1972	Monika Pflug (FRG) 1:31·40	Atje Keulen-Deelstra (HOL) 1:31·61	Anne Henning (USA) 1:31·62
1976	Tatyana Averina (URS) 1:28·43	Leah Poulos (USA) 1:28·57	Sheila Young (USA) 1:29·14
1980	Natalya Petruseva (URS) 1:24·10	Leah Poulos-Mueller (USA) 1:25·41	Sylvia Albrecht (GDR) 1:26·46

1500 METRES

	Gold	Silver	Bronze
1960	Lydia Skoblikova (URS) 2:25·2	Elvira Seroczynska (POL) 2:25·7	Helena Pilejeyk (POL) 2:27·1
1964	Lydia Skoblikova (URS) 2:22·6	Kaija Mustonen (FIN) 2:25·5	Berta Kolokoltseva (URS) 2:27·1
1968	Kaija Mustonen (FIN) 2:22·4	Carolina Geijssen (HOL) 2:22·7	Christina Kaiser (HOL) 2:24·5
1972	Dianne Holum (USA) 2:20·85	Christina Baas-Kaiser (HOL) 2:21·05	Atje Keulen-Deelstra (HOL) 2:22·05
1976	Galina Stepanskaya (URS) 2:16·58	Sheila Young (USA) 2:17·06	Tatyana Averina (URS) 2:17·96
1980	Annie Borckink (HOL) 2:10·95	Ria Visser (HOL) 2:12·35	Sabine Becker (GDR) 2:12·38

3000 METRES

	Gold	Silver	Bronze
1960	Lydia Skoblikova (URS) 5:14·3	Valentina Stenina (URS) 5:16·9	Eevi Huttunen (FIN) 5·21·0
1964	Lydia Skoblikova (URS) 5:14·9	Valentina Stenina (URS) 5:18·5	—
		Pil-Hwa Han (PRK) 5:18·5	
1968	Johanna Schut (HOL) 4:56·2	Kaija Mustonen (FIN) 5:01·0	Christina Kaiser (HOL) 5:01·3
1972	Christina Baas-Kaiser (HOL) 4:52·14	Dianne Holum (USA) 4:58·67	Atje Keulen-Deelstra (HOL) 4:59·91
1976	Tatyana Averina (URS) 4:45·19	Andrea Mitscherlich (GDR) 4:45·23	Lisbeth Korsmo (NOR) 4:45·24
1980	Björg Eva Jensen (NOR) 4:32·13	Sabine Becker (GDR) 4:32·79	Beth Heiden (USA) 4:33·77

DISCONTINUED EVENT

ALL-ROUND CHAMPIONSHIP
(Aggregate of placings in 500 m, 1500 m, 5 km and 10 km)

	Gold	Silver	Bronze
1924	Clas Thunberg (FIN) 5·5 pts	Roald Larsen (NOR) 9·5 pts	Julius Skutnabb (FIN) 11 pts

SPEED SKATING—MEDALS

Men	Gold	Silver	Bronze	Total
NORWAY	18	24	21	63
UNITED STATES	13	6	3	22
USSR	9	7	6	22
NETHERLANDS	5	9	6	20
FINLAND	6	6	7	19
SWEDEN	4	3	5	12
CANADA	—	2	5	7
GERMANY (FRG)	2	—	—	2
AUSTRIA	—	—	1	1
	57	57	54	168

Women	Gold	Silver	Bronze	Total
USSR	12	7	7	26
UNITED STATES	3	8	5	16
NETHERLANDS	4	4	4	12
FINLAND	1	2	2	5
GDR	1	2	2	5
GERMANY (FRG)	2	1		3
NORWAY	1	—	1	2
POLAND	—	1	1	2
CANADA	—	1	—	1
NORTH KOREA (PRK)	—	1	—	1
	24	27	22	73

Total (Men and Women)	Gold	Silver	Bronze	Total
NORWAY	19	24	22	65
USSR	21	14	13	48
UNITED STATES	16	14	8	38
NETHERLANDS	9	13	10	32
FINLAND	7	8	9	24
SWEDEN	4	3	5	12
CANADA	—	3	5	8
GERMANY (FRG)	4	1	—	5
GDR	1	2	2	5
POLAND	—	1	1	2
NORTH KOREA (PRK)	—	1	—	1
AUSTRIA	—	—	1	1
	81	84	76	241

TOBOGGANING-LUGEING

In 1928 and 1948 there were one-man skeleton sled races held on the famous Cresta Run at St Moritz. In those events the contestants laid face down. Luge racing, in which contestants sit up or lie back, was introduced in 1960 and has been held ever since.

The most successful luger was Thomas Köhler (GDR) with two gold medals (1964 singles and 1968 2-man) and a silver in the 1968 singles event. Hans Rinn (GDR) won the 2-man event twice (with Norbert Hahn) in 1976 and 1980, and won a bronze medal in the 1976 singles competition. The most successful woman was Margit Schumann (GDR) with a gold medal in 1976 to add to her bronze from 1972.

The oldest gold medallist was Wolfgang Scheidel (GDR) aged 28 yr 335 days when winning the singles in 1972. The youngest was Manfred Stengl (AUT) in the 2-man in 1964 aged 17 yr 310 days. The youngest female winner was Ortrun Enderlein (GER) aged 20 yr 65 days in 1964, and the oldest was Vera Sosulya (URS) in 1980 aged 24 yr 35 days.

The Heaton brothers (USA) deserve mention for their exploits in both skeleton events and bob-sledding. Jennison won a gold in the 1928 skeleton and a silver in the 5-man bob the same year. John came second to his brother in 1928,

won a bronze medal in the 2-man bob in 1932 and then returned in 1948 in his 40th year to win another skeleton silver medal.

In 1968 a scandal shook the Games when the first, second and fourth placed entries from the GDR in the women's event were all disqualified for illegally heating the runners of their sleds. The leading girl was Ortrun Enderlein who would have been the only female luger to retain the title.

TOBOGGANING—SKELETON SLED

	Gold	Silver	Bronze
1928[1]	Jennison Heaton (USA) 3:01·8	John Heaton (USA) 3:02·8	Earl of Northesk (GBR) 3:05·1
1948[2]	Nino Bibbia (ITA) 5:23·2	John Heaton (USA) 5:24·6	John Crammond (GBR) 5:25·1

[1] Aggregate of three runs.   [2] Aggregate of six runs.

LUGEING—SINGLE SEATER Men

	Gold	Silver	Bronze
1964	Thomas Köhler (GER) 3:26·77	Klaus Bonsack (GER) 3:27·04	Hans Plenk (GER) 3:30·15
1968	Manfred Schmid (AUT) 2:52·48	Thomas Köhler (GDR) 2:52·66	Klaus Bonsack (GDR) 2:55·33
1972	Wolfgang Scheidel (GDR) 3:27·58	Harald Ehrig (GDR) 3:28·39	Wolfram Fiedler (GDR) 3:28·73
1976	Detlef Günther (GDR) 3:27·688	Josef Fendt (FRG) 3: 28·196	Hans Rinn (GDR) 3:28·574
1980	Bernhard Glass (GDR) 2:54·796	Paul Hildgartner (ITA) 2:55·372	Anton Winkler (FRG) 2:56·545

1908–1960 Event not held

2-MAN

	Gold	Silver	Bronze
1964	AUSTRIA 1:41·62 Josef Feistmantl Manfred Stengl	AUSTRIA 1:41·91 Reinhold Senn Helmut Thaler	ITALY 1:42·87 Walter Aussendorfer Sigisfredo Mair
1968	GDR 1:35·85 Thomas Köhler Klaus Bonsack	AUSTRIA 1:36·34 Manfred Schmid Ewald Walch	FRG 1:37·29 Wolfgang Winkler Fritz Nachmann
1972	ITALY 1:28·35 Paul Hildgartner Walter Plaikner GDR 1:28·35 Horst Hörnlein Reinhard Bredow	—	GDR 1:29·16 Klaus Bonsack Wolfram Fiedler
1976	GDR 1:25·604 Hans Rinn Norbert Hahn	FRG 1:25·889 Hans Brandner Balthasar Schwarm	AUSTRIA 1:25·919 Rudolf Schmid Franz Schachner
1980	GDR 1:19·331 Hans Rinn Norbert Hahn	ITALY 1:19·606 Peter Gschitzer Karl Brunner	AUSTRIA 1:19·795 Georg Fluckinger Karl Schrott

1908–1960 Event not held

SINGLE SEATER Women

	Gold	Silver	Bronze
1964	Ortrun Enderlein (GER) 3:24·67	Ilse Geisler (GER) 3:27·42	Helene Thurrier (AUT) 3:29·06
1968	Erica Lechner (ITA) 2:28·66	Christa Schmuck (FRG) 2:29·37	Angelika Dünhaupt (FRG) 2:29·56
1972	Anna-Maria Müller (GDR) 2:59·18	Ute Rührold (GDR) 2:59·49	Margit Schumann (GDR) 2:59·54
1976	Margit Schumann (GDR) 2:50·621	Ute Rührold (GDR) 2:50·846	Elisabeth Demleitner (FRG) 2:51·056
1980	Vera Sosulya (URS) 2:36·537	Melitta Sollmann (GDR) 2:37·657	Ingrida Amantova (URS) 2:37·817

1908–1960 Event not held

LUGEING (and SKELETON SLED)—MEDALS

	Gold	Silver	Bronze	Total
GDR	9	5	4	18
GERMANY (FRG)	2	5	6	13
AUSTRIA	2	2	3	7
ITALY	3	2	1	6
UNITED STATES	1	2	—	3
USSR	1	—	1	2
GREAT BRITAIN	—	—	2	2
	18[1]	16	17	51

[1] Two gold medals in 1972 2-man event.

Inaugurating a fine Olympic tradition, Constantine Kondyllis of Greece carries the Olympic flame on the first leg of the 1936 relay, through the ruins of Olympia.

THE OLYMPIC OATH

At the opening ceremony a representative of the host country, usually a veteran of previous Games, mounts the rostrum, holds a corner of his national flag and, with the flag bearers of all the other countries drawn up around him in a semicircle, pronounces the oath: 'In the name of all competitors, I promise that we will take part in these Olympic Games, respecting and abiding by the rules which govern them, in the true spirit of sportsmanship, for the glory of sport and the honour of our teams.'

The following have taken the Olympic oath:

1920	Victor Boin	*Water Polo/Fencer*
1924	Georges André	*Athlete*
1928	Harry Denis	*Footballer*
1932	George Calnan	*Fencer*
1936	Rudolf Ismayr	*Weightlifter*
1948	Donald Finlay	*Athlete*
1952	Heikki Savolainen	*Gymnast*
1956	John Landy	*Athlete*
1960	Adolfo Consolini	*Athlete*
1964	Takashi Ono	*Gymnast*
1968	Pablo Garrido	*Athlete*
1972	Heidi Schüller	*Athlete*
1976	Pierre St Jean	*Weightlifter*
1980	Nikolai Andrianov	*Gymnast*

THE OLYMPIC FLAME

The Olympic flame was introduced to the modern Games at Amsterdam in 1928, and since then has always burned throughout the duration of a Games. It symbolises the endeavour for per-fection and struggle for victory. The torch relay from Olympia to the Games venue was first staged in 1936 (and for the Winter Games in 1964). The torch first travelled by air when the Games were held in Melbourne in 1956.

The following have lit the Olympic flame:

1936 Fritz Schilgen
1948 John Mark
1952 Paavo Nurmi
          (Hannes Kolehmainen—on tower)
1956 Ronald Clarke
1960 Giancarlo Peris
1964 Yoshinori Sakai
1968 Enriqueta Basilio
1972 Günter Zahn
1976 Stéphane Préfontaine
          & Sandra Henderson
1980 Sergei Belov

MERIT AWARDS

Olympic merit awards were made in 1924, 1932 and 1936 for alpinism and for aeronautics in 1936. The 1924 award went to Brigadier Charles Granville Bruce who led the 1922 Mount Everest Expedition. That for 1932 went to Franz and Toni Schmid (GER) for the first ascent of the North side of the Matterhorn in 1931. Unfortu-nately Toni Schmid was killed in May 1932 in a climbing accident. Hettie and Günter Dyhren-furth (SUI) won the 1936 climbing award for their expeditions to the Himalayas in 1930 and 1934, while the aeronautics award went to Hermann Schreiber (SUI) for a gliding flight over the Alps.

STAMPS

The first Olympic stamps were issued on 6 April 1896 by Greece to publicize and raise funds for the first Games of the modern era. The set consis-ted of 12 stamps, designed by Professor Gillieron and engraved by Edouard Mouchon, and

produced by the French Government Printing Office, Paris for the Greek Post Office. Among the designs were ancient boxers, the Olympic stadium, and Myron's statue of 'The Discus Thrower'. As Greece still used the Julian calendar at the time, indeed until 1923, the can-celling postmark was therefore dated 25 March. Although as many as 4 million copies of some of the smaller denominations were printed, only 23 760 of one of the designs appeared, thus fixing the possible number of sets at that figure. The smaller denominations were used for many years after the Games ended.

Though there was a special postmark for the 1900 Paris Exposition there was nothing issued to commemorate the Olympic Games of that year. Similarly a set of stamps was issued in con-nection with the 1904 World's Fair but nothing related to the Games. It was left to the Greeks again to issue a set of 14 stamps to commemorate the Intercalated Games of 1906. In addition a set of vignettes had been issued to advertise the Games abroad, interestingly marked with the date of the opening ceremony in the Gregorian calendar. Three special cancellation postmarks were used, that from the temporary post office at the stadium being very rare. For the 1908 Games no stamps were issued but a set of vignettes were used to publicize the Games and the Franco-British Exhibition. In 1912 again vignettes were used to publicize the Games, not only by Sweden, the hosts, but also by a number of other countries as a method of raising money to send their teams. These included Austria and Luxem-bourg. Vignettes were also issued by Germany and other countries in connection with the can-celled 1916 Games.

Three stamps, depicting an ancient runner, a charioteer, and Myron's discus thrower, were produced for the 1920 Games in Antwerp, and since then there has always been a special commemorative issue of stamps by every host country. France issued four in connection with the 1924 Olympics in Paris and after the Games Uruguay, the winner of the gold medal in soccer, produced a set of three stamps to immortalize its victory. In the French set the first ever depiction of a known Olympic champion was included with the use of a representation of Milon of Croton (see p 203).

The first issue of Olympic stamps to use representations of modern sportsmen was the set of eight issued for the 1928 Games at Amsterdam. Again after the Games, Uruguay who had successfully defended its soccer title, issued commemorative stamps. The Games at Lake Placid was the occasion for the issue of the first stamp depicting the Winter Games. Two more stamps were issued by the United States to commemorate the Los Angeles Olympics also in 1932. Prior to the 1936 Winter Games the German post office issued three stamps depicting a speed skater, a ski jumper and a 4-man bob team. For the 1936 Games at Berlin a set of eight stamps was brought out. These were also made available in miniature sheets. The Games of 1940 and 1944 were cancelled due to the Second World War but Finland had already used a postmark publicizing the former.

Four stamps were issued for the 1948 Winter Games by the host country Switzerland, and another four, plus a commemorative air mail envelope, were produced by Britain in connection with the London Games. By this time many countries were issuing stamps with an Olympic theme to commemorate the Games and, more likely, to raise funds for their participation. Norway, the hosts, produced three stamps for the 1952 Winter Games and Finland, the venue of the Summer Games, issued four. For the next Winter Games at Cortina, Italy issued a set of four, and Australia produced six for the Melbourne celebration. The US Post Office issued only one stamp to commemorate the 1960 Winter Games, but Italy set a new standard with 14 stamps. This was excelled by Japan who, starting in 1961, issued 25 stamps and seven miniature sheets related to the 1964 Games in Tokyo, after Austria had produced seven to commemorate that year's Winter Games. The contribution of the French Post Office to celebrate the Winter Games of 1968 was six, and then

Mexico set a then record of 39 stamps and 16 miniature sheets for the Games at Mexico City. The Sapporo meeting of 1972 produced five stamps and one miniature sheet, while for the Munich Olympics 24 stamps and three miniature sheets were issued. In 1976 eight stamps were issued by Austria relating to the Winter celebration at Innsbruck, and Canada issued the third largest total ever with 34 in connection with the Montreal Games. For the 1980 Winter Games four stamps were issued by the United States. All previous records were smashed by the issues produced by the Soviet Union in connection with the Games at Moscow. Starting with three stamps in 1976 to publicize their Olympics, they issued eight sets, comprising 41 stamps, on the various sports and another eight sets, comprising 30 stamps, depicting venues and cities hosting various sports on the programme; a total of 74 stamps.

In 1956 the Dominican Republic became the first country to issue stamps depicting modern Olympic champions with a set which included representations of Al Oerter, Shirley Strickland and Ron Delaney. However, the German set of 1936 included a depiction of a javelin thrower which was based on Gerhard Stöck, who later won the Berlin javelin title. This facet of Olympic stamps had become widespread, particularly in the issues emanating from Eastern Europe. Over 100 countries are known to have issued stamps relating to the Games, and such issues have become a very important publicity ploy for the Olympic movement.

Countries issuing stamps commemorating the various Games

Year	Number of Countries	Year	Number of Countries
1896	1	1956	23
1920	1	1960	51
1924	5	1964	94
1928	3	1968	114
1932	1	1972	112
1936	1	1976	109
1948	11	1980	122*
1952	12		

* This includes the set issued by the United States but withdrawn almost immediately because of the boycott of the 1980 Games. Incidentally these were the only stamps ever withdrawn from circulation by the US Post Office.

DOUBLES ACROSS SPORT

The only man to win gold medals in both summer and winter editions of the Olympic Games, Edward Eagan (USA) is seen after his 4-man bob team had won at Lake Placid in 1932.

There have been a number of multi-talented sportsmen who have won Olympic medals in different sports. The only one to win gold medals in both Summer and Winter Games was Eddie Eagan (USA) who won the 1920 light-heavyweight boxing title and was a member of the 1932 winning 4-man bob team. The only person to get near that was Jacob Tullin-Thams (NOR) who won the ski jumping in 1924. Four years later in defence of his title he was nearly killed when he jumped a phenomenal 73 m on a hill not designed for such distances (the next best jump was 64 m). By 1936 he was back again but this time in yachting where he won a silver in the 8 m class. Pierre Musy (SUI) won a gold medal in the 4-man bob team in 1936 and then was a member of the fourth-placed team in the 1948 equestrian three-day event. Martin Stokken (NOR) who placed fourth in the 10 km track race behind Emil Zatopek in 1948 later won a

silver medal in the Nordic skiing relay team in 1952. In 1948 the Swede Erik Elmsäter competed at both Winter and Summer Games with distinction coming ninth in the Nordic combination at St Moritz and winning a silver medal in the 3000 m steeplechase in London.

In the Summer Games the earliest double gold medal winner at two sports was Carl Schuhmann (GER) who won three gymnastics gold medals and the wrestling in 1896. A team-mate Fritz Hofmann won two gold medals at gymnastics and a silver in the 100 m track race. Another gymnast, Daniel Norling (SWE) won gold medals in 1908 and 1912, then switched sports and won a third gold in the show jumping team in 1920. In those Antwerp Games Morris Kirksey (USA) won gold medals in the 4 × 100 m relay and as a member of the American Rugby team. The man who took the oath at the opening ceremony in 1920, Victor Boin (BEL), had won silver (1908) and bronze (1912) medals at water polo, and then won a silver in the épée team at Antwerp. Examples of women excelling in two Olympic sports are rare but the most outstanding must be Roswitha Krause (GDR) who won a silver medal in the 1968 4 × 100 m freestyle relay and then won silver and bronze medals respectively in the 1976 and 1980 handball tournaments.

In recent years a number of top class track and field athletes have been incorporated into the bobsled teams of a number of countries. Edy Hubacher (SUI) who won a gold medal as a member of the winning 1972 4-man bob had competed in the 1968 shot put event (finishing 15th). Manfred Schumann (FRG) who won a silver and a bronze in the bob events of 1976 had competed in the 1972 heats of the 110 m hurdles. The 1968 Olympic champion in the 110 m hurdles, Willie Davenport (USA), whose achievements in that event were outstanding (see p 82), attempted in his fifth Games to emulate Eddie Eagan. However, the United States 4-man bob of which he was a member, only finished in 12th place.

One of the more unusual doubles was that of Fernand de Montigny (BEL) who won one gold, two silver and two bronze medals at fencing and another bronze as a member of the third placed hockey team in 1920.

ARTISTIC COMPETITIONS

In May 1906 a conference called by Baron de Coubertin proposed that contests in the five artistic areas of architecture, sculpture, painting, music and literature be held, and medals awarded, in conjunction with the Olympic Games. The first such events were included in the 1912 Games and in every celebration to 1948. The entries had to be related to, or inspired by, sport. The three medals were not always awarded because of the lack of entries, or sometimes because of their poor quality.

In 1912 the prize for literature was given to an entry *Ode to Sport*, ostensibly written by Georg Hohrod and Martin Eschbach of Germany. In fact it was later revealed that it was written by Baron de Coubertin who had used the two names as a pseudonym so that the prize would be awarded for the work's quality and not because it had been submitted by him.

A number of sportsmen won awards in these competitions as well as at their sports. The first to do so was Walter Winans (USA) who had won a gold at shooting in 1908 and took the sculpture prize in 1912. By also winning a silver in the 1912 shooting competitions he became the only person to win sporting and artistic medals at the same Games. Another sporting gold medallist was Alfred Hajos (HUN) the 1896 swimming champion who won a silver in the 1924 architecture category with a plan for a stadium.

The only man to win two gold medals was Jean Jacoby (LUX) in 1924, one for a painting and another for a drawing. Werner March (GER) won a gold and a silver, in two different sections of the architecture competition, for his 1936 Olympic stadium. In this respect he had been preceded in 1928 by Jan Wils (HOL) the architect of the Amsterdam stadium. The first woman to win a medal was Madame Brossin de Polanska (FRA) with a silver for painting in 1920.

One of the best known medallists was the Irish poet and wit, Oliver St John Gogarty who won a bronze medal in 1924 for an 'Ode to the Tailteann Games'.

A graphic piece of sculpture by Mahonri Young (USA) entitled 'The Knockdown', which won a gold medal in the artistic section of the 1932 Games.

MEDAL WINNERS IN THE OFFICIAL OLYMPIC ART COMPETITIONS 1912–48

	Gold	Silver	Bronze	Total
GERMANY	7	7	9	23
ITALY	5	7	2	14
FRANCE	5	4	5	14
UNITED STATES	4	5	—	9
GREAT BRITAIN	3	5	1	9
AUSTRIA	3	3	3	9
DENMARK	—	5	4	9
POLAND	3	2	3	8
BELGIUM	2	1	5	8
SWITZERLAND	2	4	1	7
NETHERLANDS	2	1	3	6
FINLAND	3	1	1	5
SWEDEN	2	—	2	4
HUNGARY	1	2	1	4
LUXEMBOURG	2	1	—	3
CZECHOSLOVAKIA	—	1	2	3
IRELAND	—	1	2	3
CANADA	—	1	1	2
SOUTH AFRICA	—	1	1	2
JAPAN	—	—	2	2
GREECE	1	—	—	1
NORWAY	—	1	—	1
MONACO	—	—	1	1
	45	53	49	147

TABLE OF SUPERLATIVES

Most gold medals (men)	10	Ray Ewry (USA) 1900–8
Most gold medals (women)	9	Larissa Latynina (URS) 1956–64
Most medals (men)	15	Nikolai Andrianov (URS) 1972–80
Most medals (women)	18	Larissa Latynina (URS) 1956–64
Oldest gold medallist (men)	64 yr 258 days	Oscar Swahn (SWE) 1912
Oldest gold medallist (women)	45 yr 13 days	Liselott Linsenhoff (FRG) 1972
Oldest medallist (men)	72 yr 280 days	Oscar Swahn (SWE) 1920
Oldest medallist (women)	45 yr 71 days	Ilona Elek (HUN) 1952
Youngest gold medallist (men)	7–10 yr	Unknown French boy 1900
Youngest gold medallist (women)	13 yr 267 days	Marjorie Gestring (USA) 1936
Youngest medallist (men)	7–10 yr	Unknown French boy 1900
Youngest medallist (women)	12 yr 24 days	Inge Sörensen (DEN) 1936
Most gold medals in one Games (women)	4	Seven women
Most medals in one Games (women)	7	Maria Gorochowskaya (URS) 1952
Oldest competitor (men)	72 yr 280 days	Oscar Swahn (SWE) 1920
Oldest competitor (women)	70 yr 5 days	Lorna Johnstone (GBR) 1972
Youngest competitor (men)	7–10 yr	Unknown French boy 1920
Youngest competitor (women)	11 yr 78 days	Cecilia Colledge (GBR) 1932
Most Games attended (men)	8	Raimondo d'Inzeo (ITA) 1948–76
Most Games attended (women)	6	Janice York-Romary (USA) 1948–68
	6	Lia Manoliu (ROM) 1952–72
Longest span (men)	40 yr	Ivan Osiier (DEN) 1908–48
	40 yr	Magnus Konow (NOR) 1908–48
Longest span (women)	24 yr	Ellen Müller-Preis (AUT) 1932–56

INDEX